"A work that is both enjoyable and utilitarian; something not always achieved in works of this kind. From the earliest settlers to the recent reforms in Kentucky government and education, topics are arranged to both inform and enlighten the reader about the nature of the Commonwealth's history."

—*Southern Historian*

"The people of Kentucky (and all persons interested in the Bluegrass state) now have a 'new history' that incorporates the findings of the last generation of historical research and writing."

—*Register of the Kentucky Historical Society*

A New History of Kentucky

A NEW HISTORY OF
KENTUCKY

Second Edition

JAMES C. KLOTTER
and
CRAIG THOMPSON FRIEND

 UNIVERSITY PRESS OF KENTUCKY

Publication of this volume was made possible in part by financial assistance from the Thomas D. Clark Foundation and the Snowy Owl Foundation, Inc.

Scholarly publisher for the Commonwealth,
serving Bellarmine University, Berea College, Centre College of Kentucky, Eastern Kentucky University, The Filson Historical Society, Georgetown College, Kentucky Historical Society, Kentucky State University, Morehead State University, Murray State University, Northern Kentucky University, Transylvania University, University of Kentucky, University of Louisville, and Western Kentucky University.

Editorial and Sales Offices: The University Press of Kentucky
663 South Limestone Street, Lexington, Kentucky 40508-4008
www.kentuckypress.com

Cataloging-in-Publication data available from the Library of Congress

ISBN 978-0-8131-7630-7 (hardcover : alk. paper)
ISBN 978-0-8131-7651-2 (pdf)
ISBN 978-0-8131-7650-5 (epub)

This book is printed on acid-free paper meeting the requirements of the American National Standard for Permanence in Paper for Printed Library Materials.

Manufactured in the United States of America

Member of the Association of University Presses

To Thomas D. Clark

and

Lowell H. Harrison

Contents

Illustrations and Tables

Maps

Figures

Tables

Preface

Kentucky has a rich history. What Kentucky *is* results from what the state *has been*. For citizens in the Commonwealth of Kentucky, an awareness of the lives of the people of the past and of the actions they took, therefore, is crucial to knowing the influences that even yet affect the state. By comprehending the actions of people of different times and backgrounds, modern citizens can better know those around them. Looking through the lens of history offers clearer images and, ultimately, better understanding of Kentuckians within the state, region, nation, and world.

The goal of this book is to present that history in a clear and comprehensive fashion so that readers can discover the historical influences that shaped how Kentuckians have lived and continue to live. Some readers come to this history for the stories, some for reference, some for understanding. All readers of a history of the commonwealth must appreciate that the state has been many things to many people at different times throughout its history. It was the First West, the initial state west of the mountains. It was a border state between the North and South, represented by a star in the flags of both the Confederate States and the United States. It was a place whose residents came to think of themselves as "southern"—with a few exceptions—and its cultural and social development is often categorized as having more in common with states to the south and southeast rather than those to the north and northeast. In reality, Kentucky blends many parts of the American experience, and studying its history helps us to understand the heritage of the United States.

Undertaking this task is a challenge. Such an account not only should be readable but also should cover all the relevant historical milestones. It also must consider internal interactions and external relationships. The resulting story is one of change and complexity, of continuity and the commonplace. There are many stories to be told, each one important. Our history of the state covers all parts of the commonwealth and all of its people—not just the great and near-great but also the often voiceless and forgotten. It is their story, too. Our narrative is broad-based. It focuses not only on the more traditional government-and-politics approach but also on the environment and conservation, economic history (agriculture, business, transportation, labor), social structures and life, gender, race and ethnicity, education, religion, social reforms, literature and the arts, agrarianism and urbanization, and the mind and spirit of Kentucky. Groups whose histories have been underrepresented in previous works, particularly women, Native Americans, and African Americans, receive greater recognition.

Similarly, we have attempted to provide a more regional coverage. The Bluegrass has often received a generous share of historical attention. Major resource collections and the state's chief newspapers draw attention to the Bluegrass so that other regions have often not had their pasts told carefully. That regional bias is hard to overcome, but our narrative strives to provide a more balanced state history.

To tell the state's story, each author has taken a portion of that past in which he has specialized and written on it. Craig Thompson Friend prepared the section covering the period to 1865 (chapters 1–9), and James C. Klotter wrote the material addressing the state's history since 1865 (chapters 10–21). Both depended heavily on those who have written interpretative accounts before, and the acknowledgments section herein only recognizes a few of those to whom a great debt is owed. Most importantly, both authors are in debt to Lowell H. Harrison, who collaborated with James Klotter on the first edition of this book. Readers familiar with the earlier text will note a significant difference between Harrison's interpretation of early Kentucky and Friend's interpretation. Historians, like all professionals, evolve in their understanding as new methods are imagined and new sources discovered. Still, careful readers will also recognize Harrison's continued influence on this text. The authors have also used the words of historical actors, their contemporary expressions, and primary sources whether in letters, diaries, newspapers, interviews, or other forms. Readers who wish to learn more about some aspect of the state's past should return to those primary sources to understand the forces at work in each era. Much of the state's history remains unwritten, and many people and events await historical interpretation as future writers revise history.

This, then, is the story of how one state's people over the ages loved and hated, how they failed and triumphed, how they acted and reacted, how they lived and died. It is an account of both noble and ignoble actions, of heroes and fools, of courage and cowardice. It is Kentucky's history.

1

A Place Called Kentucke

Creating the Hunting Grounds

The origins and meaning of *Kentucky* are unknown. The name may come from the Wyandottes, who referred to the region as "the land of tomorrow," or from a Haudenosaunee (Iroquois) word for "place of meadows." In the late eighteenth century, white colonists, surveyors, and observers wrote of the region as "Caintucke" or "Kentucke," which one might imagine had a long e (ē) as the final syllable. Settlers in the backcountry, the westernmost reaches of the British colonies along the eastern foothills of the Appalachian Mountains, often dropped the final syllable. They simply called the region "Caintuck" or "Kentuck." They most certainly did not end it with a "y"—that is an American invention. There is one constant, however: since the earliest human presence in what became Kentucky, people have understood the region as hunting grounds. This is the mythical foundation of the "Dark and Bloody Ground," a place where hunters from different cultural origins confronted each other over the abundance of large game, but that is a late chapter of a story that reaches far back into prehistory.

Between 22,000 and 17,000 BCE, glaciers encompassed much of the Northern Hemisphere and froze enough of the earth's waters to cause sea levels to drop. Shallow seas, like the Bering Strait between North America and Asia, emptied and exposed land across which ancient peoples slowly migrated. Were these Paleo-Americans the first humans in the Western Hemisphere? Until the late twentieth century, most archaeologists and historians thought so. Recent archaeological evidence from Chile, however, makes it clear that humans were in southern South America by 10,500 BCE, near-

ly one thousand years earlier than previously thought. The evidence does not align with what we know about Paleo-American migrations: nomadic peoples hardly could have spread over such a great distance in just a few centuries. Although the Bering land bridge was the primary route by which most ancient peoples entered the Americas, this new evidence suggests that at least one other migration occurred at an earlier time, as long ago as thirty thousand years, and probably via sea vessels.

The ancient Asians who crossed the Bering land bridge became physically isolated in the northwestern corner of North America, trapped by what archaeologists call the Wisconsin Glaciation, two great ice sheets that covered most of Canada. They stretched southward over what is now New England, the Great Lakes, and the Midwest as far south as the Ohio River, and to the Pacific Northwest. The two ice sheets converged on the eastern ridges of the Rocky Mountains and may have been separated by an ice-free corridor that allowed animals and humans to migrate slowly southward. By 15,500 BCE, the climate began to moderate. As glaciers slowly retreated and melted, the oceans gradually filled and submerged the land bridge. As the climate warmed over the next seven thousand years, more routes opened to Paleo-American migrations southward and eventually eastward across the American continents.

Around 10,500 BCE, small groups of Paleo-Americans followed woolly mammoths, giant sloths, and mastodons along the southern edges of the ice sheet into the region south of the Ohio River. The region's abundant salt licks drew mammals to the region. Warm saline waters bubbled up there, providing salt for the animals' diets. Early white settlers labeled

1

the marshy land that surrounded the licks "jelly ground." Large mammals occasionally became trapped and died in the marshes. When British colonist Nicholas Cresswell traveled through northern Kentucky in 1775, he came across a place which he called Elephant Bone Lick (later known as Big Bone Lick) for the large bones, tusk fragments, and teeth that he found. For decades, Europeans and Americans debated whether elephants had indeed lived in North America, while Native Americans argued that remains were from sacred white bison.

Not all mammoth and mastodons whose skeletons Cresswell found at Big Bone Lick had been trapped in the marshes. When early white explorers like Frenchman Charles LeMoyne in 1739 and British colonists Robert Smith in 1744, John Findley in 1752, and Robert McAfee in 1773 came upon Big Bone Lick, they thought they had found a natural preserve of ancient animal remains. Native American lore corroborated their beliefs. For example, a Delaware told McAfee that the "big bones just as he saw them now, had been there ever since his remembrance, as well as that of his oldest people." Yet, beginning with Paleo-Americans, the peoples who hunted Kentucky learned to recognize where animals congregated, and licks had become killing fields. Over millennia as humans hunted mammals at the licks, bones accumulated and, preserved by the minerals of the licks, gave credence to the myth of Kentucky as natural hunting grounds. In fact, humans shaped the circumstances that created it.

Paleo-Americans initiated this process with their heavy reliance on hunting. Clovis points—sharpened stone points that were bound to a bone or ivory shafts to be used as spears—provide the earliest evidence of human life in Kentucky. Paleo-Americans followed the large mammals and lived in small, short-term camps that included caves and rock shelters. As the climate continued to temper, the great coniferous forests of evergreens—needle- and cone-producing spruces, pines, and firs found adjacent to glaciers—began to disappear. Mammoth, mastodon, moose, and elk populations that had sustained Paleo-American diets gradually became extinct or followed the

Clovis point from Webster County dated to the early Paleoindian era, roughly around 11,000 BCE. (Kentucky Archaeological Survey, Lexington, KY)

glaciers as they receded northward. Mixed deciduous forests of flowering and nut-bearing trees like oak, beech, maple, chestnut, elm, walnut, and sweet gum combined with berry-producing shrubs and herbal plants to replace the older landscapes. People began to forage for berries and nuts and to hunt smaller animals such as fish, birds, reptiles, and small- to medium-sized mammals. Because smaller game animals were not herd animals and were less migratory, Paleo-Americans became less mobile. They settled into their environments. Thus, the Archaic culture evolved.

As native communities took root in Kentucky between 7000 and 1000 BCE, they formed less-migratory societies that combined hunting, fishing, and gathering. Archaeologists classify this as the Archaic period in North America. Although they did not actively cultivate nut and berry plants, Archaic peoples began burning underbrush to replenish soils that could sustain the growth of such plants. They also domesticated dogs: at the Indian Knoll site in Ohio County, Kentucky, archaeologists discovered twenty-three dog burials, some in isolated graves, others with humans both adults and children. Standing medium height, about fourteen to eighteen inches tall at the shoulder, dogs had long hair, looked similar to wolves, and probably helped with hunts. Archaeologists also have found the oldest evidence of atlatl usage in Kentucky, dating to the Archaic era. Atlatls consisted of a handle and hook made of wood, bone, or antler onto which Archaic peoples fitted a counterweight to sling a wooden spear with a stone spear point. Atlatls extended range and accuracy, making the weapon more useful than just a spear by itself. Archaic peoples created other specialized tools like grooved axes for clearing out plants and grinding stones for crushing nuts and seeds. They also participated in extensive trade networks. Archaeological digs in burial sites have revealed copper from the Great Lakes region as well as shells from the southeastern Atlantic coast. The presence of such mortuary items suggests that some individuals received social distinction in Archaic culture.

Roughly between 1000 BCE and 1000 CE, the stability created by secure food sources and immersion in trade gave rise to the Woodland culture. Native peoples continued many of the cultural patterns found among their Archaic ancestors, but they also cultivated indigenous plants, settled in more nuclear villages, constructed earthworks, and created more elaborate burial rituals. Although hunting remained the primary source of food, Woodland peoples began to purposefully cultivate nut- and seed-bearing plants like sunflowers. Pottery made from clay and fine sand provided a way to preserve nuts and seeds, as well as grasses and other vegetation. By 1000 CE, pottery had become a defining characteristic of Woodland Kentucky. Yet in more rugged areas, along the Upper Green River, for example, pottery would have been difficult to transport. In such regions, Woodland peoples commonly continued to use baskets.

Despite occurring irregularly throughout Kentucky, the development of bow-and-arrow technology also defined Woodland culture. Projectile points began to take the form that we typically associate with arrowheads, mak-ing it easier to hunt larger mammals like bison and elk for food and skins. Paleo-Americans and Archaic peoples had prepared animal hides using chipped-stone scrapers. Woodland peoples shifted to bone beamers made from the front-leg bone of a deer to scrape hides. Bone beamers not only made tanning easier but evidenced a new stage of animal usage among native peoples in which they fully used meat, skins, fatty tissues, sinew, and bones. To entice game into their hunting grounds, Woodland peoples used "burning out" techniques to create meadows and canebrakes where larger mammals would graze. The weight of the herds of bison, deer, and elk compacted soils, which made it difficult for underbrush and small trees to grow and which enlarged the meadows into expansive barrens. Through trade networks extending well into Central America, maize and beans arrived in western Kentucky around 800 CE. These crops gave some Woodland Kentuckians a more reliable and sustained agriculture as well. Stable food sources—both plant cultivation and hunting—allowed for more long-term villages in which Woodland culture flourished. Nevertheless, most Woodland peoples moved from settlement site to settlement site in a larger region. They followed herds of animals, and several years sometimes passed before they returned to a previous village location.

Around 450 BCE, Woodland peoples in the Ohio River valley introduced new cultural practices that archaeologists label the Adena tradition. Burial mounds in which males and females were interred are the most significant cultural markers of the Adena because they suggest development of increasingly complex ideas about the afterlife. The culture, in fact, got its name from a large burial mound located on the early nineteenth-century Adena estate, located in Chillicothe, Ohio, and owned by Thomas Worthington. The burial mounds of the Ohio River valley excited and confused Europeans and Americans in the late 1700s and early 1800s just as the bones at Big Bone Lick had. They considered the mounds too sophisticated to have been built by the indigenous peoples who lived nearby. The Woodland peoples often entombed ritual goods like cop-

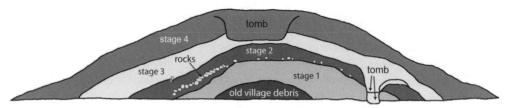

Crosscut profile of the Adena-era Robbins Mound in Boone County, used as a burial site for more than one hundred individuals. (Kentucky Archaeological Survey, Lexington, KY)

per bracelets and mica-head ornaments, accumulated through the trade networks first established in the Archaic era, alongside village leaders. Mortuary processing camps that were often adjacent to the mounds signified another cultural change: the segregation of ritual sites from domestic habitations. Although centered north of the Ohio River, Adena culture spread across northern and eastern Kentucky (from the Salt and Kentucky Rivers eastward into the Big Sandy region). The Adena cultural tradition evolved into the more-ritualistic and influential Hopewell tradition that emerged across the midsection of North America. Although Hopewell cultural forms and effects were most evident in southeastern Ohio, south of the Ohio River, very few Hopewell patterns manifested in Kentucky. Some archaeologists suggest that they did not appear here because Kentucky had become peripheral to regional native life—a hinterland of Adena-Hopewell culture. Still, much of Kentucky remained occupied by Woodland peoples who hunted and farmed. Some crafted pottery, made arrowheads and advanced tools, and lived in increasingly complicated and hierarchical societies.

Roughly between 1000 and 1600, two distinct cultures evolved from the Woodland era: the Mississippian culture along the length of the Mississippi River, and the Fort Ancient culture along the Ohio River basin. The cultivation of maize became the foundation for each. Along the entire length of the Mississippi River, sustained maize production led to greater centralization of peoples into larger and permanent fortified towns, higher mounds with ritual plazas topped by temples, and village populations that sometimes exceeded one thousand residents. These larger towns sat on broad floodplains where residents took advantage of greater agricultural output to support high population densities. Stretching away from the Mississippi River valley, along the Tennessee, Salt, Green, and Cumberland Rivers, were smaller villages and hamlets. Along the Upper Cumberland and Upper Green Rivers, floodplains narrowed, and people lived on smaller farmsteads and in hunting camps and rock shelters.

Similar to their Woodland ancestors, the Mississippians continued to rely on hunting. Even as they promoted maize-based diets and cultivated hickory nuts, marsh elder, and persimmons, hunting remained a primary characteristic of their culture. Nevertheless, life became more permanent, encouraging development of centralized political chiefdoms and religious institutions. Large Mississippian temples arose at Cahokia in modern-day Missouri, Aztalan in modern-day Wisconsin, and Moundville in modern-day Alabama. Their existence attests to the extent of Mississippian culture. At such temples, community elites used information and goods obtained through trade to legitimize their social positions. One such Mississippian settlement was at Wickliffe Mounds in modern Ballard County, Kentucky. First occupied around 1100, the village sat on bluffs overlooking the Mississippi River, with houses and a central plaza surrounded by earthworks. One mound served as a cemetery. It includes as many as nine hundred interments. Around another mound archaeologists have found higher numbers of cooking vessels, evidence of better cuts of meats, new tools like hoes, and trade goods like Burlington chert—a fine-grained quartz rock from the upper Mississippi River valley that was particularly good for making arrowheads. Although many of the tools the Mississippian peoples used were similar to those of their Woodland ancestors, they created more-elaborate pottery. Instead of sand, they mixed crushed mussel shell into the clay, creating smoother and thinner pottery vessels. Before fire-hardening the vessels, potters incised into their creations artistic symbols that appeared repeatedly but whose meanings have remained undecipherable. The new pottery technologies, known to archaeologists as Ramey Incised pottery from Cahokia, suggest the rise of more elite chieftains who dominated local life and distant trade. Yet, Mississippian culture at Wickliffe Mounds and elsewhere was not stable. Most villages existed for only 50 to 150 years before populations either moved or power shifted to a different chieftain, who established a new village center.

Along the Ohio River valley, the introduction of maize contributed to the rise of the Fort Ancient culture. Their towns were most vibrant in summer, when they farmed adjacent fields of maize, squash, beans, gourds, sunflowers, and tobacco. They practiced swidden agriculture, a system in which a tract of land was cultivated until its fertility depleted and the community relocated to new farmlands. Evidence also exists that they kept, although did not domesticate, turkeys. In contrast to their Adena ancestors, the Fort Ancients reduced consumption of nuts and grasses, but they remained reliant on hunting, which occupied them in winter. Bison and deer remained in the region, drawn by the abundant plant life that had been cultivated through centuries of Woodland-era burnings.

In contrast to Mississippian life, Fort Ancient life was less sedentary. Fort Ancient communities, therefore, established fewer and less-elaborate ritualistic centers. Entire family groups of twenty to thirty people migrated in search of bison herds in the winters, and when they exhausted lands from overfarming, villages uprooted to find new farmlands in spring and summer. Even in a village of forty or fifty people, households appeared scattered. These groups located ritual areas far from domestic habitations. Burials took place away from settlements and without social distinction. The

patterns of life—kinship as the organizing principle, related but semi-autonomous households, non-segregated burials—suggest some notion of egalitarianism.

By 1200, however, the Fort Ancients began to demonstrate more social organization and stratification. Fort Ancient villages became larger as multiple family groups joined together under "Big Men," who had demonstrated hunting prowess, natural leadership skills, and access to exchange networks. Some villages housed up to 500 residents, taking the shape of circles or arcs with distinct activity zones surrounding a central plaza: mortuary areas (sometimes a low mound) near the plaza, then domestic habitations, and finally storage and trash areas. One such Fort Ancient site was at Fox Farm in Mason County, Kentucky. Located on a ridgetop overlooking the Licking River, the village contained at least 5 low mounds, 2 fire basins, and 208 burials. Even though they employed mounds as burial sites, the mounds were never as large as those of Mississippian villages. Fort Ancients relied heavily on maize and beans as well as deer, elk, and bear. Nuts had nearly disappeared from their diets. The presence of engraved shell gorgets—crescent-shaped ornaments worn around the neck—and copper artifacts demonstrates villagers' participation in broader exchange networks that may have introduced incised pottery from Mississippian culture as well. Even though they were somewhat remote from the Mississippians, the Fort Ancients at Fox Farm increasingly interacted with and borrowed from the inhabitants of western Kentucky. The central role of the plaza suggests the importance of group ceremonies and rituals to the strengthening of community ties. The erection of low burial mounds reveals a recognition of individual status. Ornamenting graves with limestone, pottery, stone and bone tools, copper, and marine shell beads evidences their immersion in Mississippian trade networks. And increased size of villages points to more complex political organizations.

Both Fort Ancients and Mississippians inherited the hunting grounds of Kentucky. The former used central and northern Kentucky as winter hunting grounds, and the latter hunt-

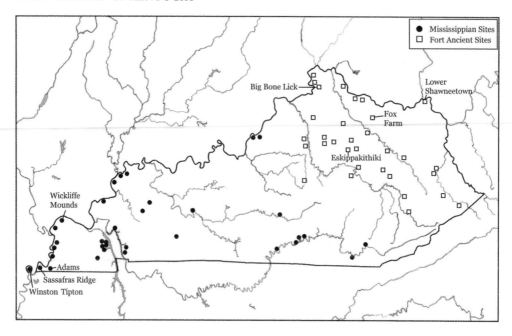

Notable Mississippian and Fort Ancient archaeological sites, from figures 6.1 and 7.1 in David Pollack, ed., *The Archaeology of Kentucky: An Update*, 2 vols. (Frankfort: Kentucky Heritage Council, 2008), 2: 610, 740. (Courtesy of Craig Friend)

ed western Kentucky and eastward along the Green and Barren Rivers. But the region was not just hunting grounds: it was a homeland. Archaeologists, at sites like Adams, Sassafras Ridge, and Winston Tipton, have uncovered proof that Mississippian villages persisted in western Kentucky as late as the 1600s. Fort Ancients continued to use central and northern Kentucky, but for reasons not yet understood, they abandoned settlements in the central region and moved their villages closer to the Ohio River. Only a few smaller villages like Eskippakithiki in Clark County remained as seasonal hunting camps. Later, in the mid-1730s, a more substantial settlement of eight hundred to one thousand Shawnee residents repopulated Eskippakithiki. They protected it with a stockade and farmed over thirty-five hundred acres surrounding the village. In 1752, British trader John Findley commented on the impressive settlement, but by then, Eskippakithiki's days were numbered. The Shawnees, descendants of the Fort Ancients, were consolidating populations and relocating villages close to the Ohio River following patterns

of their ancestors. As European explorers and American colonists wandered into Kentucky in the mid-eighteenth century, they encountered abandoned settlements like Eskippakithiki. They interpreted this to mean that the land was empty and theirs for the taking. Native Kentuckians, however, retained communities in more remote areas, such as the eastern mountains and the far-western floodplains, long after native settlements in more accessible areas disappeared.

From Prehistory to History

Mississippian and Fort Ancient cultures developed within a temperate climate that since the eleventh century had averaged a few degrees above the temperatures of previous centuries. By about 1350, however, a Little Ice Age enveloped North America as well as Europe. Average temperatures fell, disrupting agricultural cycles and creating food shortages. Heavily invested in maize production, Mississippians could no longer produce enough to sustain their large towns. The decline in agriculture weakened people's faith in their leaders, and populations began to splinter. They abandoned villages for smaller settlements. By 1700, Mississippian peoples, many now identifying themselves as Creeks, Chickasaws, Choctaws, Yuchis, and dozens of other nations, had migrated southeastward, where they joined with smaller groups to form confederacies. Beyond the archaeological evidence of this cultural transformation, the Chickasaws' oral tradition relates that, before contact with white explorers, they and the Choctaws migrated from west of the Mississippi River. In fact, the Chickasaws remained on the eastern banks of the Mississippi River, including western Kentucky, and claimed the region as their ancestral homelands.

Climate change did not affect the Fort Ancients so detrimentally because they had retained a more-balanced economy of agriculture and hunting. They continued long-distance hunting and shifting-field agriculture. Still, the Fort Ancients did reorganize when they abandoned smaller villages that they had inhabited and consolidated into larger settlements closer to the Ohio River valley. Shawnee oral tradition links them to the Fort Ancients, and they claimed the Fort Ancient homelands as their own. The Shawnees did not form confederacies as the Chickasaws had, but they did welcome other indigenous groups into the new villages. To oversee village life, the Shawnees developed a political structure: a clan system in which each division acted as an autonomous unit. The clans were patrilineal (an individual traced his or her family line through the father and always belonged to the father's clan) and exogamous (an individual could not marry within the clan but had to marry a person from a different clan). Similar to Fort Ancient Big Man traditions, each clan selected leaders who demonstrated superior skills: a civil chief who worked to foster good relations for his kin group in communal and international affairs, and a war chief who defended his clan against threats. Each clan also had a peace woman and a war woman who oversaw agricultural work and advised the chiefs. In the larger settlements, these clan leaders met in a new type of communal building—the council house—where they collectively decided on village issues.

From the arrival of Paleo-Americans circa 10,500 BCE until native populations' reactions to the Little Ice Age in the fifteenth and sixteenth centuries, prehistoric peoples migrated, settled, hunted, and farmed Kentucky's hunting grounds. Archaeological evidence provides the only means to understand them and their lives because none of these native peoples had written languages with which to record their histories. Without a written language, individual names from prehistory went unrecorded. We only know prehistoric peoples as groups like the Mississippians or through their roles as Big Men or peace women. Sometimes, oral traditions offer a glimpse into prehistoric individual lives, but myth and rumor plague oral history. It has to be used cautiously. So, at what point did prehistoric peoples become historic peoples? They clearly began to appear in the written historic narrative in European accounts, but they also may have become historic peoples a little bit before they came into contact with whites. Native Kentuckians keenly felt the impact of early European exploration through trade and disease.

Two hundred and fifty years before British colonists attempted to hunt and settle in Kentucky, Christopher Columbus's crew in 1492 and successive Spanish voyages brought germs that spread across the Caribbean Sea into Florida and farther inland, following the trade routes that had connected prehistoric peoples over millennia. Ironically, by the 1500s and 1600s, the trade that brought highly sought-after mortuary items—copper and shell ornaments for grave decorations—also swept smallpox, bubonic plague, typhus, mumps, influenza, yellow fever, measles, diphtheria, and other communicable diseases across the Mississippi and Ohio river valleys. Between 1540 and 1680, the Shawnees buried brass and copper ornaments with their dead that native peoples living along the Gulf of Mexico fashioned from recycled kettles given to them by Spanish explorers and then traded as ritual goods along traditional exchange routes. So, when smallpox epidemics began to ravage Shawnee populations around the mid-to-late 1600s, the disease most likely originated in Spanish trade to the south. Still, by the mid-1600s, the Shawnees also may have contracted disease from the French, who were in the Great Lakes region, or the British, who had found their way into the Appalachian Mountains and the Cherokee villages.

Regardless of the source, the Shawnees lost approximately 40 percent of their population, which was low compared to many other native nations. Many ethnographers estimate that epidemics sparked by Spanish contact killed 75 percent of the southeastern Indian populations, including 90 percent of Creek populations. Importantly, epidemics struck native peoples around Kentucky while many were still reacting to the Little Ice Age. Patterns of migration, confederacy building, and amalgamation that helped indigenous nations adapt to climate change also served them in surviving epidemics. When Europeans explored the North American continent, they met native peoples who had formed confederacies to protect themselves against other native populations, and others who, faced with the erasure of their cultures, joined with other native groups in order to survive. Although disease spread through trade, it also brought information to native peoples: all had knowledge of the white explorers and settlers who had arrived far to the east, who wanted land and resources, who had enticing trade goods, and whose appearance coincided with widespread misery and death.

British traders from South Carolina who had found their way into the Cherokee villages offered iron kettles and pots, pewter plates, teacups, glass mirrors, flannel breeches, silk handkerchiefs, candlesticks, eyeglasses, guns, and alcohol. In return for their fine goods, traders expected the Cherokees to provide them with fur and deerskins, easily acquired in the Kentucky hunting grounds. French, Spanish, and British traders repeated this pattern within native villages, financing expeditions to find and identify potential native trading partners, including the Shawnee villages that lined the Ohio River. In 1671, Virginia colonist Abraham Wood sent Thomas Batts and Robert Fal-

lam into the Blue Ridge Mountains and beyond. The two men wandered the Tug Fork of the Big Sandy River, marking trees and laying claim to the region for England, Governor William Berkeley of Virginia, Wood, and themselves. But Wood was not particularly interested in land: he wanted furs, and the Carolina traders monopolized the trade with the Cherokees. So, in 1673, Wood hired James Needham and an indentured servant, Gabriel Arthur, to find routes through western Virginia to a Cherokee village that would negotiate with Wood. A guide attacked Needham and Arthur after they had arranged a trade agreement with one village. Needham died, but Arthur escaped. He fled back to the Cherokee village and eventually became an adopted member of the community. For a year, he joined in war campaigns against the Shawnees, which took him along the Big Sandy River to the lower Shawnee Town at the mouth of the Scioto River in modern Greenup County. In the summer of 1674, he returned to Virginia, probably the first European to have wandered Kentucky.

The Cherokee attack on lower Shawnee Town was most likely among the last conflicts between those two nations in the seventeenth century. Recent wars with the Eries and the Neutral confederacy to the north and Cherokees to the south weakened the Shawnees. At the same time, the Haudenosaunees were forcing the Shawnees out of the Ohio Valley. By 1656, the Haudenosaunees were a powerful native confederation in modern-day New York. They had conquered and assimilated most of their neighbors, although they remained at war with the Susquehannocks in Pennsylvania. One group of Haudenosaunees in particular, the Senecas, were determined to have the Kentucky hunting grounds so that they could create their own trade agreements with Europeans. They waged war against Miamis, Kickapoos, and other smaller nations of the Ohio River valley, pushing them west of Lake Michigan. The Shawnees, however, were allied to the Susquehannocks and held firm in their villages with Susquehannock help. In 1658, the Cayugas and Onondagas joined their Seneca kin in escalating war. They forced the Susquehannocks to dedicate resources to protect their own villages, which left the Shawnees exposed. Three years later, a smallpox epidemic ravaged the Susquehannocks. The epidemic destroyed their ability to stave off the Haudenosaunees.

Unable to protect themselves, the Shawnees began to flee their Ohio River towns and abandoned Kentucky. Two clans migrated across the hunting grounds into eastern Tennessee, adjacent to the Cherokees. Although relations had not been friendly between them, the Shawnees and Cherokees had a common enemy in the Haudenosaunees. Another clan settled south of the Cherokees in northern Georgia. A third clan moved westward into the Illinois country, but the Senecas persisted in warring against them and native groups who harbored them. The final clan traveled eastward, joining their Susquehannock allies in southern Pennsylvania. This Shawnee diaspora led to further conflict with native populations who either resented the intrusion onto their lands or suddenly found themselves under Haudenosaunee attack for aiding the Shawnees. By the 1710s, each clan discovered that it had outlived its welcome. The Haudenosaunees successfully persuaded native peoples in Illinois to abandon the Shawnees, who then fled to Georgia. In 1715, the Yamassee War dislocated Shawnees in Tennessee and Georgia and forced them to join their kin in Pennsylvania.

By 1720, then, the Shawnees had become refugees, and Kentucky sat largely depopulated. It only had a handful of Chickasaw encampments in its far western reaches. Yet, although the Shawnees had been pushed from the region, they would return to Kentucky and come to dominate it by the mid-eighteenth century. Much of their later success was born in these years as refugees. While the splintering of the Shawnees weakened their cultural unity, it strengthened their commercial relations. Before they left the Ohio River valley, some Shawnee towns had strong economic relations with a French trader named Martin Chartier, who operated a trading post in the Piqua clan village, married a Shawnee woman, and joined the Shawnees in their migration. He set up new shops in Pennsylvania. Even as the Shawnees

in Pennsylvania developed new relations with British traders out of Philadelphia, they continued to look to the French as potential trade partners. In 1728, new French officials courted the Shawnees. Many Shawnees began trading with French traders at Detroit even as they maintained a vibrant trade with the Pennsylvanians. In the early 1740s, the Senecas persuaded the Haudenosaunees to undermine French influence by repopulating the Ohio River valley with Shawnees bound to the Haudenosaunee economy. These Shawnees created a series of villages that would provide supplies to Haudenosaunee warring parties, extend Haudenosaunee influence, and connect the Ohio River valley to the Haudenosaunees. So certain were the Haudenosaunees of their hegemony that, in 1744 at the Treaty of Lancaster, Chief Tachanoontia boasted that "all the world knows we conquered the several nations living on the Susquehannah, Cohongowntown, and on the back of the great mountains of Virginia . . . as to what lies beyond the mountains, we conquered the nations residing there, and that land, if the Virginians ever get a good right to it, it must be by us."

The Shawnees did not wait for Haudenosaunee approval. They were already on the move. People took flight during a malaria epidemic that swept through southern Pennsylvania in 1744. Thousands of Shawnees pushed into the western Pennsylvania mountains. Seven years later, French Canadians hoped to bring the Shawnees into their sphere of influence and persuaded the Wyandottes in the Ohio country to invite the Shawnees westward. This invitation initiated a flood of second-generation migrants who, as they crossed the Allegheny Mountains, returned to a region that their parents and grandparents had known as homeland. The French and Wyandottes encouraged the Shawnees to settle closer to Detroit, where the French could have economic and diplomatic access to them. The Shawnees, however, interpreted the opportunity as one to reclaim ancestral homelands, and they settled along the Miami and Scioto Rivers, far from French influence and with easy access to the hunting grounds. They numbered no more than four thousand by 1750, their population diminished by disease, wars, and the trials of diaspora.

Both French and British traders followed the migrating Shawnees. As early as 1736, a small group of Shawnees had reconstructed Eskippakithiki, and nine years later, French trader Peter Chartier (Martin Chartier's son) and Pennsylvanian George Croghan had established competing trading posts there. By 1749, lower Shawnee Town reemerged at the confluence of the Scioto and Ohio Rivers: over one hundred houses sat on the north side of the Ohio River overlooking the floodplains and agricultural fields, while forty houses scattered on the south side of the Ohio. By 1750, dozens of other villages arose along the Scioto River, among them the central clan towns of Chillicothe, Piqua, Kispoki, Wakatomica, and Maquachake. Far to the west, an old abandoned village was revitalized as Shawneetown. All these settlements contained European trading posts intended to tie native residents to either French or British economies. The flight westward created new problems, however. The Haudenosaunees resented Chartier's presence in Kentucky and pressured him and his Shawnee clients to leave Eskippakithiki. Hoping to take control of Kentucky's fur trade, Chartier led his followers unsuccessfully against the Chickasaws in western Kentucky, then fled northward. They lived in Shawneetown until 1761.

The new Shawnee villages along the Ohio and Scioto Rivers filled with native peoples from many nations, including Seneca warriors who represented Haudenosaunee influence and power. One Canadian denounced the villages as a "sort of republic," but the great cultural differences among their residents required clan leaders to weigh many perspectives when considering issues like war. Lenni Lenapes and Miamis were matrilineal; the Shawnees were patrilineal. Some Shawnees, Miamis, and Wyandottes preferred trade with the French at posts in Vincennes and Detroit. Mingos, Lenni Lenapes, and other Shawnees looked eastward to the British for trade opportunities and goods.

As the Shawnees repopulated the Ohio River valley, they attempted to control northern and central Kentucky, and because Haudenosaunees invested in the Shawnees' success, other native groups faced negative repercussions if they tried to hunt there. In particular, the Cherokees and Catawbas to the southeast resented the Shawnees' monopoly. In the sixteenth century, after a defeat at the hands of the Haudenosaunees and Lenni Lenapes in the north, the Catawbas had moved southward into the southern Appalachian foothills. Creeks, Yuchis, Choctaws, and Cherokees, an indigenous nation of two hundred large villages that called the southern Appalachians their ancestral home, already crowded the region. The Catawbas found a natural ally in the Cherokees, who had a long-standing animosity against the Haudenosaunees.

Two Women in the French and Indian War

From their earliest expeditions along the Mississippi and Ohio Rivers, the French were keenly interested in Kentucky's potential for their fur trade. In 1669, René-Robert Cavelier, the Sieur de la Salle, crossed overland from Canada to the Ohio River. He then traveled as far as the Falls of the Ohio, near present-day Louisville, and claimed the region for New France. Although the instability of the region's native populations between the 1660s and 1740s discouraged French efforts to establish strong trade relations, they remained in the Great Lakes region. They tempted the Shawnees and other indigenous nations away from the British sphere of influence. In 1729, military engineer Gaspard-Joseph Chaussegros de Léry surveyed France's claims in North America, including much of the Ohio and Mississippi River valleys. Ten years later, Charles Le Moyne III, the Baron de Longuiel and governor of Montréal, led an expedition down the Ohio River. Montréal's governor intended to help his counterpart in French Louisiana, Jean-Baptiste Le Moyne de Bienville, attack the Chickasaws. French success in North America depended upon clear and unquestioned control of the Mississippi River as well as the

Great Lakes. In the Illinois territory, French villages—Kaskaskia, Vincennes, Cahokia, Peoria, Ste. Genevieve—arose connecting the Great Lakes region with the Mississippi River. These communities created a great crescent of French influence that trapped the British on the eastern side of the Appalachians. In 1749, de Bienville departed Montréal with a military expedition that traveled down the Allegheny and Ohio Rivers. Members of the expedition buried lead plates inscribed with France's claim to the region. Along the way, the French troops demanded that the Shawnees, who were re-populating villages, reject the British traders living among them. Three years later, to prove French intent to dominate the regional economy, the new governor of Canada, Michel-Ange Duquesne de Menneville, sent more than two thousand French troops to carve a road from Lake Erie to the headwaters of the Ohio River, where they were to construct a fort. By doing so, the French hoped to intercept British traders' access to the main route to the Shawnee villages.

The British, too, showed great interest in Kentucky. Following the Treaty of Lancaster, during which Tachanoontia had bragged of Haudenosaunee dominance over the Shawnees, British officials began awarding western lands to speculators. Between 1745 and 1754, they doled out over 2.5 million acres through the newly formed Ohio Company. The company commissioned Christopher Gist to survey the Ohio River valley and produce notes on trails, river routes, and soil qualities. Often with the assistance of insiders in the British government, land companies like the Ohio Company sought profit for their stockholders, including members of the Fairfax and Washington families in Virginia. Other Virginians, including members of the Jefferson and Randolph families, denounced the Ohio Company and invested in the Loyal Company. These families appealed to Parliament for their own lands to sell. They also hired Thomas Walker to survey tracts for them. In 1750, Walker set out on his four-month expedition. The party passed into Kentucky through Cave Gap, and Walker named a nearby river for the Duke of

Cumberland, a name that stuck to the gap as well. As his party traveled through the Appalachian Mountains north of Cumberland Gap, they came across trees marked with crosses and other figures, indicating to Walker that he was only the latest white man to wander the region. They built a small cabin near present-day Barbourville and planted corn—a common ritual for claiming a tract of land. Later in 1750, Gist began his expedition for the Ohio Company. His travels were far more extensive. They took him through lower Shawnee Town to Big Bone Lick, across the Bluegrass region, and up the Kentucky River into the Appalachians. But both Gist's and Walker's reports to their respective companies were unenthusiastic. Gist reported that increasing numbers of native peoples allied with the French. This increase in French influence would make British encroachments on the hunting grounds difficult.

Gist was right. From New York to the Carolinas, tensions between French-backed native peoples and British colonists increased in the early 1750s. While not fully in the French sphere of influence, the Shawnees still worked with the French to keep British colonists out of the Ohio River valley. The Cherokees, in contrast, tried to stake out a neutral position, even though they were attached to the British in trade. In 1752, Cherokees traveled to lower Shawnee Town to negotiate hunting rights in Kentucky. Pressured by Carolina traders, they hoped to make allies out of their old enemies, but the Shawnees and Haudenosaunees did not welcome them and denied access to the hunting grounds. A year later, a Haudenosaunee war party on its way to attack the Cherokees bumped into a caravan of British traders near Eskippakithiki. When they attempted to take a Cherokee servant hostage, battle erupted and the Haudenosaunees took the British colonists captive.

Virginia governor Robert Dinwiddie blamed the French for backing the Haudenosaunee offensive. He sent Joshua Fry and a very small contingent to warn the French not to construct a fort at the confluence of the Allegheny and Monongahela Rivers in western Pennsylvania. Fry died before arriving at the headwaters of the Ohio River. The Virginians were no match for the five hundred French troops that were constructing Fort Duquesne. In April 1754, the French defeated the Virginians under the command of Fry's second-in-command, George Washington, but allowed them safe passage home in return for two British officers left behind as captives. Over two thousand British troops under General William Braddock were stationed in Maryland, and the British hoped that a quick, retaliatory strike against the smaller contingent of French troops and their native allies would end French presence in the region. The British were wrong: Braddock was overconfident, and at the Battle of Monongahela in early July 1755, he was killed and his troops sent into retreat. The French and Indian War (1754–1763) had begun.

The French and Indian War was the North American theater of the larger Seven Years' War. Great Britain and France precipitated the conflict, but it involved most of the great European powers. Fighting erupted globally: in Europe, the Caribbean, western Africa, India, the Philippines, and South America. Fighting spread across the eastern half of North America as the far-reaching influences of the two European powers pulled Virginia colonists and Shawnee trade partners into the conflict. Governor Dinwiddie appointed George Washington colonel of the Virginia regiment and charged him with securing the colony's backcountry settlements. The task was overwhelming. Colonists refused to serve in the regiment when they felt the need to protect their individual homesteads. As the Shawnees attacked British colonists along the eastern foothills of the Appalachians, a cloud of defeatism swept across western Virginia.

One of the colonizing families that found itself embroiled in the conflict was the Drapers. The family laid claim to Draper's Meadow in western Virginia in 1748. Since that time, family members had hosted Shawnee war parties headed southward to fight the Catawbas. The Drapers' daughter, Mary, would play a significant role in the way that the war played out in North America. She had married William Ingles in 1750, and they had two sons. Soon after Braddock's army fled western Pennsylvania

in defeat, the Shawnees came for the Drapers and Ingles. They took Mary Draper Ingles captive, along with her sons and sister-in-law, Bettie Draper. The Shawnees killed other colonists and burned their cabins and crops. The warring party then traveled for twenty-nine days through the Appalachian Mountains before reaching lower Shawnee Town. Ingles's anguish is unfathomable: she did not know of her husband's fate, gave birth on the third evening of the journey, was separated from Bettie Draper as the party reached its destination, and faced adoption into a nation of people with whom she could only minimally communicate.

While captivity terrified white women, many found opportunity living among the Shawnees. In the British colonies, white women lived as dependents within their husbands' patriarchal spheres. They were confined to the domestic realm and had authority solely over lesser dependents like children and enslaved laborers. Men were the warriors and negotiators, producers and consumers, and they exerted patriarchal authority over their wives and daughters. Shawnee traditions, however, accommodated more balanced gender relations: recall the presence of both male and female war and peace chiefs. Also, with matrilineal and patrilineal cultures represented in the Shawnee settlements, the multinational villages exhibited greater gender balance. Shawnee women served as negotiators, producers, consumers, and occasionally warriors alongside men. Not surprisingly, then, over the eighteenth century, many captive white women elected to stay with the Shawnees rather than return to white society. Initially, Ingles seemed resigned to her situation: two French traders persuaded her to sew clothes for them in exchange for supplies for her baby. The shirts became symbols of prestige and elevated Ingles's status, leading Shawnee war chief Captain Wildcat to adopt her into his household. Ingles interpreted and rejected his action as sexual overtures. Her refusal angered Wildcat. He took her sons and left for his clan village at Kispoki.

In the fall, the Shawnees divided into their seasonal hunting parties. Ingles accompanied one party to Big Bone Lick to gather salt to preserve venison and bison meat, but she actually intended to escape. Along with an older German woman, she slipped into the Kentucky wilderness, leaving her infant behind. Although this decision may seem particularly harsh, the circumstances presented only difficult options. Ingles had to choose between leaving the child in a nurturing community or carrying the infant through a rugged wilderness. She probably felt that she acted in her child's best interests. On their sixth day, the women arrived at a smaller village along the Ohio River that, for the most part, had been abandoned for the fall excursions. They took corn to survive the journey ahead, but unfamiliar with the terrain, they struggled for nearly two months in the wilderness. The corn did not last, and while nuts were not difficult to find in the fall, more substantial food was scarce. The German woman slipped into insanity and, in one moment of delusion, attempted to kill Ingles. Somewhere near the headwaters of the Kanawha River, Ingles abandoned the old woman and headed southward along an old trail until rescuers found her. In time, they located the German woman as well.

News of Mary Draper Ingles's ordeal inspired Governor Dinwiddie to attack the Shawnees. With the Cherokees' assurance that they would aid Virginia in a campaign against the Shawnees, he formed the Sandy Creek expedition. Nearly 250 colonists, under the leadership of Major Andrew Lewis, joined 100 Cherokees on a mission against lower Shawnee Town. The expedition set out early in 1756, but torrential rains, icy rivers, and an undersupply of food doomed it. Disgusted by the incompetence of the colonial effort, the Cherokees withdrew their offer of support.

Mary Draper Ingles likely interacted with Nonhelema when she first arrived in lower Shawnee Town. Born into the Chillicothe clan, Nonhelema spent her early youth in Pennsylvania, when the Shawnees had lived under the careful watch of the Haudenosaunees. Her father, Okowellos, and her mother, Katee—a metís (of mixed Native American and European ancestry)—traveled to the Georgia country in 1725. Nonhelema and her brother Hokolewskwa accompanied them, but the family

returned to Pennsylvania within five years. In 1734, Nonhelema married her first husband, a chief with whom she later had two daughters. By 1750, she was herself a war chief. Four years later when her husband died, Nonhelema wedded Moluntha, a cousin from her mother's Maquachake clan, and had two more daughters and a son. She migrated with the Maquachakes into the Ohio country, where she rejoined Hokolewskwa. He had relocated during the earlier Shawnee resettlement and became known among the British as Cornstalk. Nonhelema's migrations demonstrate the Shawnee practice of patrilocality (in residence with the husband's clan). She took her father's clan identity and migrated first with her father's group and then with her husband.

Nonhelema became a wife and an overseer of domestic productions. Female chiefs sustained women's primary responsibilities as producers and nurturers. Nonhelema assumed leadership over domestic affairs, directed the planting and harvest of the fields, and organized feasts. As a chief and leader of Shawnee women, she exerted tremendous influence living in her own village separate from Moluntha. Some women like Nonhelema also served as warriors. Although they sought foremost to prevent the unnecessary spillage of blood, if war was inevitable, they joined the battle. This draws a sharp contrast with white women like Mary Draper Ingles, who were never expected to fight, much less serve as military leaders.

As the French and Indian War escalated, Nonhelema counseled her fellow chiefs on the wisdom of joining the battles between the French and British. Not until the war ended, the French had lost, and their allies like the Shawnees felt abandoned and desperate, however, did Nonhelema take to the battlefield. At the Treaty of Paris in 1763, the French gave up their claims in North America. They handed Canada and the Ohio River valley over to the British and gave the Mississippi River valley and its port at New Orleans to the Spanish. They also ceased their trade operations among the Native Americans. Furious that he had been abandoned by the French, Ottawa chief Pontiac struck against the British, and Nonhelema joined a warring party of Lenni Lenapes, Mingos, Shawnees, and Hurons who targeted Fort Pitt (formerly Fort Duquesne), clashing with British troops at the Battle of Bushy Run in 1763. Though the British eventually won Pontiac's Rebellion (1763–1765), several Shawnees made their reputations, including Nonhelema, who became respected among whites as the "Grenadier Squaw."*

For women, the years of the French and Indian War were transformative. Mary Draper Ingles was fortunate: she returned to a grateful husband, bore four more children, and lived another sixty years. But her life after captivity evidences a woman and family desperate to reverse the effects of tragedy. Her brother persisted in trying to find his wife Bettie. At a gathering with Cherokees that occurred five years after Ingles's return, he discovered that Bettie had been sent to live among them. He ransomed her and returned her to the Virginia settlements. In 1768, the Ingles family found and ransomed one of the sons, Thomas. They also discovered that George had died in captivity. After thirteen years in Kispoki, Thomas had become fully acculturated and spoke only Shawnee. The Ingles paid Thomas Walker to reeducate Thomas so as to reintegrate him into colonial society. A decade later, Thomas Ingles waged war against the Shawnees as a member of the Virginia militia. He also eventually lost his wife and two children to a Native American attack.

The French and Indian War affected Nonhelema as well. By the 1770s, she abandoned her warrior status. She spent most of the decade as a peace chief. In 1778, she even warned the Americans of an impending attack on Fort Randolph. Tensions increased among the Shawnees as American colonists attempted to settle Kentucky. Divisions and villages splintered between those who wanted to fight the threat and those who sought peace and accommodation. Nonhelema, Moluntha, and other residents of the Maquachake village were among those who chose peace with the Americans, but they could not dissuade most

Shawnees from waging war against American settlements in Kentucky. As violence increased in the Ohio River valley in the 1770s, the Shawnees abandoned Chillicothe, Nonhelema's Town, Maquachake, and other villages along the Scioto River, and migrated northwestward to establish new villages. Hoping to preserve her way of life, Nonhelema petitioned the Confederation Congress in 1785 for a two-thousand-acre grant in Ohio. She sought compensation for her warning about the attack on Fort Randolph, her subsequent activities to bring peace to the Ohio country, and her loss of livestock. Congress responded by allocating to her "one suit or dress of Cloaths including a blanket per annum, and one ration of provisions each day during her life." The following year, Benjamin Logan's American army raided the Shawnee villages. In the new Maquachake village, they found Moluntha flying an American flag as evidence of his friendship. He surrendered peacefully, but an enraged Kentuckian took up a hatchet and hacked him to death. The Kentuckians abducted Nonhelema and her daughters and returned to Kentucky. Shawnee oral tradition relates that they cut off the fingers on Nonhelema's right hand, disabling the great "Grenadier Squaw," and then she disappeared from history.

The Long Hunters

In March 1775, Cherokee leader Dragging Canoe agreed to a treaty that transferred part of the Cherokees' Kentucky claims to American colonist Richard Henderson. Upon signing the Treaty of Sycamore Shoals, Dragging Canoe reportedly warned that a dark cloud hung over the hunting grounds, which he labeled "the Bloody Ground." What did Dragging Canoe mean? Henderson and other American colonists thought that Dragging Canoe called Kentucky "the Bloody Ground" because native peoples like the Cherokees and Shawnees were fighting over who controlled it. This interpretation turned Kentucky into a no-man's-land in their minds. Choosing to believe that no one

---

* This term is racially offensive today and should be used thoughtfully in historically appropriate contexts.

owned or controlled the hunting grounds justified the colonists' own desires to claim Kentucky for themselves.

Early white colonists made accurate assessments regarding multiple native nation claims over Kentucky and about the rivalry between them for control of the region. While dozens of native groups hunted Kentucky, four nations either had villages in or considered the region as part of their homelands: the Chickasaws, the Yuchis, the Cherokees, and the Shawnees. The Haudenosaunees also claimed sovereignty over the hunting grounds and kept a wary eye on its use. Each of these native nations sought access to the hunting grounds to enlarge trade relations with Europeans, who wanted bison, deer, and beaver skins.

British colonists also desired access to Kentucky, but at the end of the French and Indian War in 1763, the victorious King George III restricted colonists from wandering westward. By royal proclamation, he drew a boundary line along the ridge of the Appalachian Mountains past which they could not go. Yet the British could not enforce that restriction, and hunters from western Virginia, North Carolina, and Pennsylvania breached the Proclamation Line. Because their hunting trips were often months long, the men who encroached upon Kentucky became known among historians as Long Hunters. They typically sneaked into Kentucky through a gap in the Appalachian Mountains. The Cumberland Gap was one of the more accessible and most famous routes. These hunters characteristically separated into parties of three to four hunters and scattered across an area to hunt and gather as many skins as they could transport back through the mountains. Hunters from Virginia and South Carolina slipped into Kentucky through the Cumberland Gap in 1766 and traveled northward, where they bumped into James Harrod and Michael Stoner, hunters from Pennsylvania who came down the Ohio River. The following year, James Findley of North Carolina returned from his hunting trip with tales of the grandeur and abundance of Kentucky's game. Those who hunted Shawnee lands in central and northern Kentucky took their skins back

eastward. Others, like Benjamin Cutbird's party who traveled westward through Cherokee, Yuchi, and Chickasaw territories in 1766, carried their hunting bounty to New Orleans, where they persuaded Spanish officials to let them sell the skins. Hancock Taylor mimicked Cutbird's accomplishments in 1769. James Knox likewise led hunts into the lands south of the Green River in 1770 and 1771.

The most famous Long Hunter, of course, was Daniel Boone. Boone's family migrated from Pennsylvania to Yadkin County, North Carolina, in the early 1750s. In 1755, he was a wagon driver delivering supplies to General Braddock's ill-fated British troops when he first heard of Kentucky from James Findley, who had been trading with the Shawnees. Findley's descriptions of the hunting grounds' beauty and abundance stuck with Boone, and when Findley knocked on Boone's door fourteen years later, the two decided to make a long hunt. Along with Boone's brother-in-law John Stuart and several others, they headed westward. On the eastern side of Cumberland Gap, they came across Joseph Martin and a crew of men clearing land and building cabins. The Findley party traveled northward through the gap and eventually set up a base camp near abandoned Eskippakithiki. Over six months, they broke into smaller parties to hunt between the Red and Kentucky Rivers.

Other Long Hunters were present, as well as Shawnee and Cherokee hunting parties. One group of Long Hunters lost its supplies and shoes to a party of Cherokees shortly after passing through Cumberland Gap, pressing them to return homeward. A group of Shawnees, led by a metís Cherokee named Will Emery, came across Boone and Stuart and forced the colonists to lead them to the base camp. The two made noise to warn the others, who successfully fled, but Emery's party still confiscated supplies and the large piles of skins that the colonists had accumulated. Leaving Boone and Stuart with a few provisions to survive the trip home, Emery warned them: "Now, brothers, go home and stay there. Don't come here anymore, for this is the Indians' hunting ground, and all the animal skins and furs are

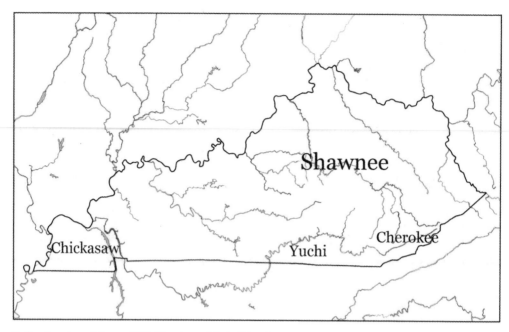

Native American claims, c. 1750. (Courtesy of Craig Friend)

ours. And if you are so foolish as to venture here again, you may be sure the wasps and yellow jackets will sting you severely." Boone and Stuart tracked Emery's party, waited for them to fall asleep, and retrieved their horses. By sunrise, the Shawnees had caught up to Boone and Stuart, retaken the horses, and captured the two North Carolinians. Seven days later, as the party approached lower Shawnee Town, Boone and Stuart escaped.

The two men made their way back to the base camp only to find that their companions had given up hope. Still, Alexander Neeley and Daniel's brother Squire recently had arrived with additional horses and supplies. The Boone brothers, Stuart, and Neeley remained in Kentucky as the others returned to North Carolina. In early 1770, Stuart disappeared. This discouraged Neeley, who departed for home. A few months later, Squire Boone took the cache of skins back east, planning to return in the fall. In the meantime, Daniel stayed in Kentucky alone. He amused himself by reading *Gulliver's Travels,* exploring the hunting grounds, and singing. When Caspar Mansker's hunting party wandered into the Green River region, they

were startled one day to hear a strange sound. They discovered Boone, lying on the ground, bellowing at the top of his lungs. Boone traveled northward across the Kentucky River into the Great Meadow of the Bluegrass region, then beyond the Licking River to the banks of the Ohio. He followed herds of bison along an impressively worn trail known as the Old Buffalo Trace. This trail directed him to the Lower Blue Licks, where he found hundreds of bison meandering around the salt licks. He went southward again, following the Kentucky River, where he stood on bluffs overlooking the wilderness. The adventures of Daniel Boone in these solitary interludes made him an expert on Kentucky's geography and fauna. He also became well aware of its dangers.

After meeting Boone, Mansker and his fellow Long Hunters were hunting along the Kentucky River when a party of Cherokees overtook them. One of the Virginians recognized the Cherokee leader Captain Dick and so flattered the old man that he directed the Long Hunters to the rich hunting lands along another river to the south, which the party subsequently named for their Cherokee friend. Still,

Portrait of Daniel Boone, by Chester Harding, 1820. (The Filson Historical Society, Louisville, KY)

Captain Dick also sternly counseled the Long Hunters to "kill it and go home." Some of the party took his warning seriously, taking their skins southward to the Spanish markets in Natchez. Others returned to Virginia. Once a party of forty Long Hunters, only twelve remained when, one day, Will Emery and his Shawnee companions came upon the camp, capturing two men and taking the supplies and skins. When the others returned to camp, they discovered their friends, horses, and profits gone. Probably quite insightful as to what they regretted most, one of the frustrated hunters carved "2300 deer skins lost. Ruination by God" on a tree. Similarly, Daniel and Squire Boone lost all of their profits in a moment. Squire had rejoined Daniel in the fall, and the brothers spent another six months hunting. When they started home in early 1771, a party of Cherokees intercepted them and confiscated their horses and cargo. Daniel had spent two years in Kentucky and had nothing to show for it.

How was Boone able to survive capture by first the Shawnees and then the Cherokees?

Time and again, Native Americans ordered Long Hunters to leave Kentucky, minus their bison and deer skins, but unharmed. If encroaching hunters had crossed less friendly Native Americans determined to eliminate white colonial settlements, they most likely would have perished. Emery and his fellow hunters, however, were willing to share the hunting grounds. Approaching Boone and his party as fellow hunters, they cautioned them only to kill what was needed for food and not for profit.

The Long Hunters continued the exploitation of Kentucky that French and British traders had undertaken a century earlier. Neither traders nor hunters were interested in settling Kentucky. They just wanted to gain profit from its natural resources. European traders had used Shawnees, Cherokees, and others to do the hunting for them. Long Hunters were willing to do the work themselves but were greedy. They took skins and showed little interest in the consequences of overhunting. Even though Shawnee and Cherokee hunters likewise dealt with the temptation of overhunting Kentucky to profit in the European markets, most Native Americans were disturbed when they came across fields of decaying bison and deer carcasses that had been left behind after Long Hunters skinned the animals. As deer and bison populations migrated and diminished, the Long Hunters had to travel farther into the hunting grounds. In doing so, they risked even greater chance of bumping into Shawnee and Cherokee hunters who were infuriated by the squandered meats. Even Shawnees who were resigned to the shared hunting grounds could not justify the wastefulness.

Such episodes reveal growing strains within Native American nations, particularly among the Shawnees, about how to deal with British colonists who trespassed into Kentucky. The Maquachake clan, led by Nonhelema's brother Hokolewskwa, was determined to live in peace, while somehow sustaining Shawnee control over the hunting grounds. But events worked against Hokolewskwa. At the Treaty of Fort Stanwix in 1768, the Haudenosaunees surrendered their claim to sovereignty over the Ohio

River valley. With this treaty, they betrayed the Shawnees and led British colonists to assume that the region was available for settlement. John Murray, the fourth Earl of Dunmore and the new governor of Virginia, pushed Shawnee chiefs to sign over lands along the upper Ohio River, which angered more Shawnee warriors who resented the loss of hunting grounds. As Long Hunters escalated their raids on Kentucky, Hokolewskwa and other peace chiefs found it increasingly difficult to withstand fellow Shawnees' calls for war.

The Fallacies of Kentucky Frontier History

American scholars have been *doing* history since about the 1870s, making the profession less than two centuries old. Frederick Jackson Turner, one of the first professional historians, has cast a very long shadow over the way that we think about early Kentucky. In trying to explain the development of the United States, Turner argued that "the existence of an area of free land, its continuous recession, and the advance of American settlement westward, explain American development." Each time European and American settlers moved westward, they engaged the environment's "primitive conditions," which Turner defined as "the meeting point between savagery and civilization." Having read the stories of Kentucky related by its early white settlers, Turner adopted their point of view: by labeling Native Americans as uncivilized, whites justified taking lands as an act of civilization ordained by providential destiny (or as Americans labeled it in the 1840s, "Manifest Destiny"). In Turner's writings, Native Americans ceased to exist and the land simply became wilderness—free land.

There are many flaws in Turner's thesis. He accepted only one definition of civilization, that of European progress. Before contact with European peoples, Native Americans had elaborate and advanced forms of civilization: agricultural and hunting systems that sustained villages with large populations; extensive economic, communication, and social networks; socioeconomically distinctive ritual sites and habitation neighborhoods; complex leadership structures; and a productive and healthy relationship to the environment that served their needs. For many white captives who decided to remain with their captors, Native American civilization proved superior and preferable to European civilization.

Turner was also wrong about the frontier as a line between savagery and civilization. No historical map shows it. Plenty of maps show Europeans' and Americans' claims to the lands, and when Native Americans appear at all, they are allies of one side or the other. Such boundaries were critical to establishing claims to sovereignty, political administration, and military power, and this is what Turner equated with civilization. Native nations, however, drew boundaries between themselves and other native peoples to define their sovereignties in North America long before any Europeans did. When the Shawnees returned to the Ohio River valley in the 1740s, they entered a region that native peoples not only claimed but used. Only their previous trade relations and a common distrust of the British and their American colonists minimized the challenge to territorial sovereignty that the Shawnees posed. When white settlers began to crest the Appalachian Mountains, they were just the latest migratory group to enter Kentucky, following a pattern established centuries, even millennia, before. Their arrival merely complicated an already diverse and complicated region.

Turner was interested in the political relationships between Native American and European nations, but we may learn more about the character of early Kentucky by considering social relations between peoples. When we look beyond the narratives of nations to the stories of individuals, we see humans mingling, working, disagreeing, and figuring out how to live with each other. Despite their suspicions of each other, Native Americans and Europeans wanted to exchange goods, and their trade networks stretched across the North American continent. European traders offered beads, ribbons, blankets, clothes, copper kettles, and weapons—knives, axes, guns, ammunitions. Recall how Mary Draper Ingles became a valuable individual at lower Shawnee Town simply because she made quality shirts. In return, Europeans expected bison, deer, and beaver skins from Kentucky. Native American men, who had formerly hunted seasonally to provide for their families and communities, began to hunt year-round for the market, putting greater pressure on the hunting grounds. As animal populations declined or migrated, hunters wandered farther from home and risked intruding on territory claimed by another nation. Since European traders expected to trade with other men, Native American men increasingly assumed roles as economic negotiators, roles that had traditionally been held by women, weakening the leadership roles of Nonhelema and other war and peace women. Such gradual transformations in gender roles, the purposes for hunting, and territorial boundaries already had taken place among native peoples closer to British traders on the east coast, Spanish traders along the Gulf of Mexico, and French traders in Canada. By the 1750s and 1760s, these pressures transformed Native American cultures around Kentucky.

European cravings for skins and Native American desires for manufactured goods forced all to find ways to behave and interact, creating a "middle ground" between cultures. Native Americans and British colonists found inventive ways to interact, giving rise to a world that was neither European nor Native American. As British colonists wandered into Kentucky, they developed relationships with indigenous peoples. Sometimes these relationships developed through simple interactions based on economic exchange. George Croghan and other Pennsylvania traders interacted with Native Americans in this way. At other times, they clashed over resources. Native peoples confronted Long Hunters regarding the way they took advantage of the ready availability of game for their own profit. Finally, powerful and emotional associations sometimes arose that made them feel like kin. Thomas Ingles began his experience as a captive and became fully integrated into the Native American culture.

Social interactions often led to interracial relationships, resulting in metís children like Nonhelema's mother, Katee. If Mary Draper Ingles had accepted Captain Wildcat's offer, she may have had metís children as well. Such children became cultural brokers as they grew up, "in-betweens" who often fulfilled roles as translators, negotiators, traders, and in some cases, social and military leaders like the Cherokee Will Emery. In Kentucky's middle ground, diverse peoples mingled in systems of exchange, social interaction, and interpersonal relationships. Sometimes peaceful, sometimes violent, and sometimes through the intercession of the British government, by the mid-1760s, the peoples living around Kentucky—Shawnees, Chickasaws, Choctaws, Yuchis, Creeks, Cherokees, Catawbas, Carolinians, Virginians, Pennsylvanians, and other British colonists—were finding ways to coexist. Only one thing could truly destroy this middle ground: the intention of one group to change the rules and use Kentucky for more than hunting.

2

The Invasion of Kentucky

Lord Dunmore's War

In 1775, Hokolewskwa lamented, "We are often inclined to believe that there is no resting place for us and that your Intentions were to deprive us entirely of our whole Country." He had good reason to think poorly of the Virginians with whom he met. Despite the Proclamation Line of 1763, Long Hunters from Virginia and other British colonies had encroached on the Kentucky hunting grounds for over a decade. The Treaty of Fort Stanwix in 1768 had stretched the Proclamation Line farther west, at least on paper. In that same year, Cherokees conceded some territory along the southern Appalachians in the Treaty of Hard Labor. Both treaties seemed to signify that native territorial boundaries were negotiable, particularly in light of the ever-growing colonial populations pushing against the Proclamation Line.

Until France gave up its claims at the end of the French and Indian War, Great Britain lusted to have Kentucky as part of its empire in order to extract its resources. In the seventeenth and eighteenth centuries, France and Great Britain practiced mercantilism, an economic system in which the government regulated the economy in order to increase its wealth and power, often at the expense of rival nations. Mercantilism made colonies essential because they provided raw goods—gold, silver, furs, and staple crops like sugar, indigo, and tobacco—to the nation, with little investment by the government. In the seventeenth century, French and British traders established exchange relations with native peoples of the Ohio River valley, taking the first steps to bind the region to their respective nations economically by setting up trading posts. These trad-

ers relied on the labor of indigenous peoples to provide skins. This was extractive colonialism, a system in which empires removed wealth from indigenous peoples and lands. Citizens of the empire may have worked for a time as soldiers, traders, planters, or colonial officials in extractive colonies, but they had not imagined it as their homeland. To oversee economic development under extractive capitalism, the European powers established colonial governments. For example, the Virginia General Assembly sanctioned the western expeditions that Abraham Wood funded beginning in 1669. Lord Dinwiddie intended expeditions against French encroachment in the Ohio River valley to protect British economic interests. Mercantilism demanded that any economic and imperial competitors be eliminated, and the French and the British had fought three previous wars in North America toward that end: King William's War (1688–1697), Queen Anne's War (1702–1713), and King George's War (1744–1748). When the British won the French and Indian War, they finally succeeded in eliminating the main threat to their extraction of North America's raw goods. Even with the Proclamation Line of 1763, they did little to restrict colonial Long Hunters because the skin trade contributed to the empire's larger economic needs.

In the 1770s, however, another form of colonialism in Kentucky replaced extractive colonialism. The wars of the 1770s and 1780s—Lord Dunmore's War (1774–1775), the American Revolutionary War (1775–1783), and the Cherokee-American War (1776–1794)—were fought in part to facilitate colonial expansion. Whereas natural and human resources are the motivation behind extractive colonialism, land provides the primary motivation for settler colonialism, a system in which settlers move onto native lands in order to create a new homeland. Great Britain tried to regulate settlement and profit from the land by chartering stock companies that allowed private investors to take the economic risk, and the government guaranteed each company's monopoly over a tract of land. The Ohio Company, established in 1747, and the Loyal Company, established in 1749, were such stock companies, organized to sell lands in the colonial backcountries. To realize the most profit, the British government gave incentives to both companies. Originally granted 200,000 acres, the Ohio Company determined to quickly settle one hundred families on its grant within seven years. If successful, the government would provide an additional 300,000 acres. The Loyal Company initially received a much larger grant of 800,000 acres. But in the explosive 1750s, as tensions between Native Americans and British colonists increased, both companies met with limited success.

With the elimination of the French challenge in 1763, British and colonial land companies found new opportunities. The British government accepted land companies' negotiations as legitimate as treaty-making by its own agents. Backed by the Virginia House of Burgesses, representatives of the Loyal Company and the smaller Greenbrier Company persuaded the Cherokees at the Treaty of Lochaber in 1770 to accept the Kentucky River as the northern boundary of their hunting grounds. The treaty seemingly opened the lands between the Kentucky and Ohio Rivers to sale and settlement. By 1773, over 200,000 acres had been sold, most to speculators who planned to profit from reselling the land. No colonists had yet settled in Kentucky, however, because of the Proclamation Line of 1763. This boundary declared illegal any private purchases of land from Native Americans and ordered anyone beyond the line to withdraw east of the Appalachian Mountains. The British wanted time to push Native Americans out of the region to avoid violence when white settlers moved into Kentucky.

Virginia colonists were livid. They claimed their colony's 1609 charter placed western lands under their control. To establish their authority, they organized Kentucky as Fincastle County, Virginia's westernmost territory. With the Shawnees' defeat at the Battle of Bushy Run in 1763, Native American resistance in the upper Ohio River valley subsided. Travel down river became more viable, inspiring Virginia authorities to begin the process of doling out four-hundred-acre tracts of land to its French and Indian War veterans. The land companies, however, had not waited. The Ohio Company had floundered in its effort to profit from western land sales. It, therefore, appealed to the Crown to double its western claims. Without the influence of Governor Robert Dinwiddie, who no longer served in Virginia, the company failed to gain support in Parliament. In 1771, the Loyal Company offered an investment opportunity to the new governor, John Murray, the Fourth Earl of Dunmore, gaining his backing. Not to be outdone, a group of Pennsylvania investors, including Benjamin Franklin and George Croghan, successfully formed the Grand Ohio Company in 1772 and claimed thirty million acres along the Ohio River valley. This territory included the lands north of the Kentucky River that the Cherokees had abdicated at the Treaty of Lochaber. The British military contested the Grand Ohio Company because its actions threatened to spark war with Native Americans. For the next two years, the land company's efforts to sell lands stalled as a result.

In the meantime, Dunmore sent Thomas Bullitt to survey Fincastle County on behalf of the Loyal Company. At the mouth of the Kanawha River, they met another group of surveyors, led by James, Robert, and George McAfee. By the time it reached lower Shawnee Town, Bullitt's party numbered over forty men. Bullitt headed a small contingent northward to Chillicothe, where they conferred with Hokolewskwa. The Shawnee chief rejected both the Treaty of Fort Stanwix and the Treaty of Lochaber, claiming neither the Haudenosaunees nor the Cherokees had the right to sell the Ohio River valley to British colonists. Bullitt guaranteed that Governor Dunmore would pay the Shawnees for the lands south

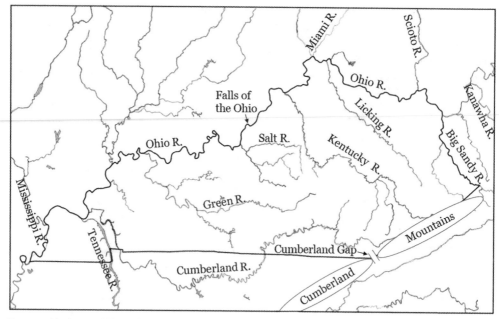

Topographical map of Kentucky. (Courtesy of Craig Friend)

of the Ohio River and that the Virginians would honor Shawnees' hunting rights. In return, Hokolewskwa promised to try to restrain Shawnees' anger over the new white presence in Kentucky.

Bullitt's party moved south of the Ohio River and began surveying along Salt Lick Run (near present-day Vanceburg) and Big Bone Creek. As they concluded their work, they split into smaller groups: the McAfees, Hancock Taylor, and others laid out smaller claims along the Kentucky River near the future site of Frankfort. Bullitt led a group to the Falls of the Ohio, and James Harrod went southward and explored the lands that became the future site of Harrodstown. By the end of the summer of 1773, the surveying party had completed its work and returned to Virginia to register the surveys. William Preston, the official colonial surveyor for Fincastle County, rejected the surveys, claiming that the lands surveyed by the Loyal Company were the same lands that the colony of Virginia had intended to distribute to its French and Indian War veterans. The Loyal Company had a powerful ally in Governor Dunmore, however, who interceded and declared the surveys valid. Only veterans'

claims that preceded Bullitt's registrations were recognized as legitimate.

In the meantime, Daniel Boone wanted to obtain good lands in Kentucky. In summer 1773, he led his family and a settlement party northward into Virginia, where they joined another group of settlers under the leadership of William Russell. By early October, the party approached Cumberland Gap and split into three camps for the night. Boone's camp was closest to the gap. Several miles behind, eight men followed Russell's group with additional supplies. At daybreak, around twenty Delawares attacked the middle camp, killing all but one of the men. The Delawares wounded and tortured James Boone and Henry Russell, sons of the expedition's leaders, until the young men pleaded for death. The Delawares left their corpses alongside the road as a warning. The attack jolted the rest of the settlement party. Those who survived abandoned the quest to settle in Kentucky.

Boone and Russell's settlement effort and Bullitt's surveying claims worried William Preston, who quickly sent forth a new surveying party under John Floyd to produce what became known as the Fincastle surveys. While charged to measure tracts for military warrants, Floyd also privately agreed to survey claims for George Washington, Patrick Henry, and other interested citizens. In May 1774, Preston's men arrived at the Falls of the Ohio, where they surveyed the private tracts. The tools of surveying were a compass atop a tripod and a four-pole (sixty-foot) chain. One man set up the compass, peering through its sights as another walked ahead, cutting through vegetation and establishing a sightline to the next point. The compass was then moved to the new point, and the process begun anew. Two chainmen followed, laying the chain in the sight path and measuring out the tract. While their directions were fairly accurate, at times the party's measurements were off significantly. The parameters of Floyd's own claim were particularly incorrect. Registered at 400 poles square, his claim really measured 485 poles square. Floyd also surveyed enlarged plots for his friends.

James Harrod, too, busily established his claims in Fincastle County. In early 1774, he led a private surveying party of thirty-one men down the Ohio River and then up the Kentucky River. They traveled overland a couple miles and, in June 1774, began laying out Harrodstown. The men drew up a compact whereby a cabin was built for each person. Each cabin was numbered, and upon completion of construction, a lottery determined ownership. Other groups led by Michael Cresap, Ebenezer Zane, and George Rogers Clark also sought out good lands, although they remained in the eastern parts of Fincastle County.

The Shawnees and their allies were unhappy with the rush to survey Kentucky. Despite Hokolewskwa's assurances to maintain peace, angry Shawnees began attacking white surveyors in the hunting grounds and white families along the colonial backcountries. Governor Dunmore sent Daniel Boone and Michael Stoner into Kentucky to warn the surveyors. Harrod and his men abandoned their construction of Harrodstown. The Cresap and Clark parties fled to Wheeling for protection. Fearful of an alliance between Cherokees and Shawnees, Dunmore and his western agent William Preston sent orders to Cresap to deflate the natives' offensive. Cresap defeated one Shawnee war party at Pipe Creek and then massacred a party of Mingos at Yellow Creek, which was a grave error. The Mingos, Iroquoian peoples who had migrated westward when the Haudenosaunees sought to repopulate the Ohio River valley, had been colonial allies under Chief Tachnedorus (known among the British as John Logan). Cresap's ambush pushed the Mingos into alliance with Shawnees intent on eliminating the colonists. Tachnedorus immediately led raids into the Pennsylvania settlements.

Dunmore responded by planning a military invasion of the Ohio River valley in the summer of 1774. A thousand Virginia militiamen came down the river from the newly renamed Fort Dunmore. Andrew Lewis led another militia of thirteen hundred men through the Kanawha River valley in western Virginia. Soldiers who manned the expedition became important names in the colonization of Kentucky: Isaac Shelby, William Russell, William Fleming, Samuel McDowell, William Preston, James Harrod, William Christian, and George Rogers Clark. If successful, Lord Dunmore's War would secure the Ohio River valley and Kentucky for Virginia, making the Loyal Company's land claims legitimate, thus eliminating competition from Pennsylvania's Grand Ohio Company. Preston declared that "the Opportunity we have so long wished for, is now before us."

In early October 1774, Lewis's troops arrived at Point Pleasant at the mouth of the Kanawha River, where they came upon a large contingent of Shawnees. With little option but to defend the Shawnee homeland, Hokolewskwa had no choice but to lead warriors against Virginia colonists. Between three and eleven hundred Shawnees (the colonists who fought against them usually suggested the larger number) engaged the Virginians at the Battle of Point Pleasant. Although they killed nearly two hundred Virginians, the Shawnees could not match the colonists' numerical advantage. The victory gave Virginia's negotiators the upper hand at the Treaty of Camp Charlotte, in which the Shawnees acceded to the terms of the Treaty of Fort Stanwix and relinquished their claim to Kentucky. They also promised to return captives, enslaved laborers, horses, and goods. In return, the Virginians vowed to remain south of the Ohio River.

The invasion of Kentucky began years earlier with Long Hunters and land surveyors, but Lord Dunmore's War opened up a route down the Ohio River by which colonial settlers could travel. The war exposed deep divisions within Native American populations: in the Shawnees' multinational villages, residents could not agree on how to deal with the colonial invasion, making it difficult for them to respond to white migration. Tachnedorus and the Mingos continued to harass white settlers. Hokolewskwa tried to regain a more neutral stance, but thousands of Shawnees resented the loss at Point Pleasant and the Virginians' eagerness to settle the hunting grounds. As whites threatened their homelands and hunting grounds, they saw their opportunities diminish. This was true particularly among younger warriors. Many Shawnees were unwilling to abide by their leaders' wishes to maintain some sort of peace. Upon returning to their villages along the Scioto River following the Treaty of Camp Charlotte, the Shawnees began uprooting their homes. They relocated farther west along the Miami River, hoping to create greater distance between themselves and the white invasion.

Planting Kentucky

When, in 1609, King James I expanded Virginia's original charter of 1606, he defined the colony's boundaries as two hundred miles north and south of modern Hampton Roads, inland "from Sea to Sea, West and Northwest." Such a broad description was open to a lot of interpretation, and Virginia claimed much of the West as a result. The British used the 1763 Treaty of Paris that ended the French and Indian War to curtail Virginia's grandiose claims. The French handed over Canada, and although the British would have liked the lands on the western side of the Mississippi River as well, the French gave that territory to the Spanish. The British could tolerate this as long as the French no lon-

ger held any part of North America. Then, the British drew the Proclamation Line. Virginia watched as its claims to the West diminished. The Treaty of Camp Charlotte, then, played a significant role in defining Virginia's western ambitions. The treaty stretched the colony as far west as the Tennessee River. Despite assuring the Shawnees that whites would stay south of the Ohio River, colonial leaders did not give up their desire to acquire the north side as well.

Hundreds of aspiring western settlers, who flooded into Kentucky over the next two decades, therefore, became the winners of Lord Dunmore's War. Virginia tried to organize settler colonialism through early surveys of Kentucky like those performed by the Loyal Company and in the Fincastle claims. Within a year of the Treaty of Camp Charlotte, the Ohio Company sent Hancock Lee westward to locate a two-hundred-acre tract along the south fork of the Licking River and the north fork of Elkhorn Creek. There his party laid out Leestown, near the future site of Frankfort. Expedition members then surveyed numerous tracts for themselves. Upon Lee's return to Virginia, the Loyal Company blocked him from registering the deeds for the Ohio Company. Competition between the land companies paralyzed much of their work. This rivalry left open the possibility that individuals could preempt official surveys by locating lands and settling there. Building a cabin and planting corn on these parcels became a legally accepted custom that preempted claims of other surveys. Such cabin rights entitled the claimant not only to four hundred acres but also a claim to an additional thousand acres of adjacent property. The claimant was expected to deliver a warrant to the colonial land office to secure the land. Many failed to do so. Preemption was a system that brought money into Virginia's treasury but resulted in overlapping or "shingled" land rights by multiple settlers. It led to years of boundary disputes and occasional violence. It also created a large demand for lawyers, who were needed to unravel the confused land claims.

Among the first in Kentucky following Lord Dunmore's War were Harrod and his fellow Pennsylvanians who, in early 1775, re-

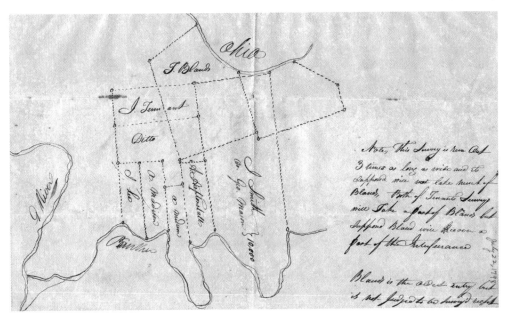

Shingled land claims in Jefferson County, 1798. (Special Collections Research Center, University of Chicago Library)

turned to the settlement they had begun building to find much of it destroyed. They began to construct a fort on high ground surrounded by twenty-by-thirty-foot cabins with adjacent gardening plots. Soon, however, they discovered other surveyors in the region, including the McAfee brothers, who claimed that Harrod had infringed on the surveys they had made in 1773. Although most of their claims lay north of Harrod's tract, there was some overlap, and they contested his rights. Because he built cabins and planted corn, Harrod had an advantage in this early dispute.

Preemption represented just one method by which to claim land in Kentucky. Chartered land companies offered another way. They, however, depended upon the favor of colonial governments and governors. In 1774, North Carolinian Richard Henderson created the Louisa Company (later known as the Transylvania Company). Ignoring the Proclamation Line as well as colonial Virginia and North Carolina laws that prohibited individuals from negotiating directly with Native Americans, Henderson made overtures to the Cherokees to purchase a vast tract from them. After

promising preliminary negotiations, in March 1775, they agreed to meet at Sycamore Shoals in what is now eastern Tennessee. Henderson hired Daniel Boone, the foremost authority on Kentucky and someone Henderson knew well. Boone previously had been in debt to him, and Henderson had issued a warrant for his arrest in 1770 for nonpayment. By 1775, however, Boone was Henderson's right-hand man in aiding with negotiations and determining boundaries. Once the treaty was signed, Boone would construct a road into Kentucky and select a site for the company's initial settlement. In return, he would receive two thousand acres of prime land. Soon after Boone departed for Sycamore Shoals, an annoyed creditor came to his North Carolina home seeking payment on a loan. The sheriff wrote on the back of the warrant "Gone to Kentucky." Debt often plagued Boone and other men like him. Many who left for Kentucky did so to escape financial problems.

Over one thousand Cherokees accompanied their leaders to Sycamore Shoals for the negotiations. Each side employed numerous in-betweens to translate. Henderson and eight associates offered two thousand pounds sterling for lands between the Kentucky and Cumberland Rivers, previously protected by the Treaty of Lochaber. Little Carpenter, Dragging Canoe, and Oconostota represented the Cherokees, but they struggled to reach a consensus as to whether they should sell Henderson lands or even if they had the right to sell those lands. In the end, the Cherokees accepted Henderson's offer. They granted him a large but somewhat vaguely defined tract and a passageway through the Cumberland Gap. Oconostota warned Henderson: "We have given you a fine land, but I believe you will have much trouble in settling it."

Even before the treaty was signed, Boone left to begin clearing the Wilderness Road. He led a party of thirty-five, including his daughter Susanna, a couple of enslaved laborers, and several supply wagons. Making this trek must have been difficult for Boone: two years earlier, he had lost his son James along this same old trail to the gap. The way was narrow. The party advanced slowly as it tried to widen the passage to accommodate wagons. From the gap northward, Boone and his expedition hacked through thick forest and heavy canebrakes just to open a trail that packhorses could travel.

Although the Cherokees agreed to Henderson's designs, the Shawnees, Delawares, and other Native Americans of the Ohio River valley met Boone's road-clearing party in Kentucky with displeasure. In late March, two attacks left three colonists dead and another one dying. Boone considered it urgent to build a fort for protection and wrote Henderson, who was making plans to follow Boone into Kentucky. "Your company is desired greatly, for the people are very uneasy," Boone pleaded, "but are willing to stay and venture their lives with you, and now is the time to flusterate the intention of the Indians, and keep the country whilst we are still in it. If we give way to them now, it will ever be the case." When the letter reached Henderson, he had reached the gap. He had several wagons loaded with food, ammunition, seed corn, and garden seed that could move no further, and his men worked to transfer the goods to packhorses in order to navigate the rest of the trip. Upon word of the attacks, several of Henderson's party turned back to North Carolina. He pushed the rest of the party onward, but they met several members of Boone's expedition fleeing the danger. When he finally arrived in late April, Henderson was relieved to find a fort and a calm camp. In appreciation for Boone's ability to keep the venture from falling apart, Henderson increased his pay to five thousand prime acres, and the little community was named Boonesborough.

Henderson, however, wanted a more substantial settlement. As larger defensive structures, forts housed a community of settlers rather than a single family. The original fort at Boonesborough was a rather small structure situated on the Kentucky River floodplain. Henderson picked a different site for a new fort, a meadow where there was less danger of flooding, and he planned to build a larger rectangular structure with two-story blockhouses at each corner. When constructed well, blockhouses could withstand arrows and rifles. Henderson designated the blockhouses as homes for the company's investors. For the rest of Boonesborough's residents, the long sides of the fort contained eight houses, and the short sides held five houses. The outer walls formed the stockade. It was a fairly typical fort plan: Harrodstown similarly arose around Fort Harrod, a rectangular structure with two-story blockhouses at the corners connected by solid rows of log cabins. Early settlers constructed such fortifications of thick logs. They often chinked the cracks with clay to seal the holes.

Yet Henderson's men showed little interest in building the fort at Boonesborough. Since the attacks of late March, the Native Americans had left the settlers alone. Because threats from Native Americans seemed to diminish, colonists attempted to use the time to clear lands, build cabins, and plant crops on their own tracts. Frustrated, Henderson wrote that "the Indians should do us a favor of annoying us, and regularly scalping a man every week." The colonists also spent far too much time hunting. When Boone's party initially arrived, the region teemed with bison, but within a month, their wasteful hunting decimated the herds. In late April, William Calk worried that "This day

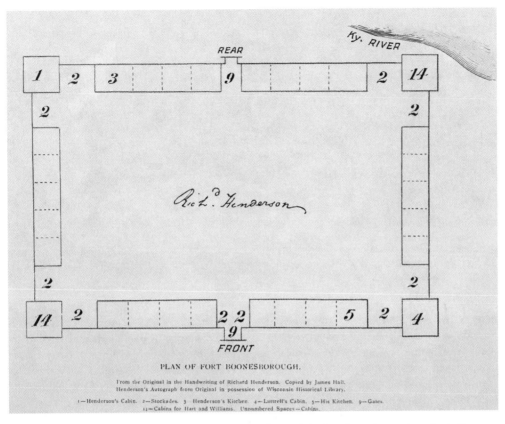

REAR

FRONT

PLAN OF FORT BOONESBOROUGH.

From the Original in the Handwriting of Richard Henderson. Copied by James Hall.
Henderson's Autograph from Original in possession of Wisconsin Historical Library.

1—Henderson's Cabin. 2—Stockades. 3—Henderson's Kitchen. 4—Luttrell's Cabin. 5—His Kitchen. 9—Gates.
14—Cabins for Hart and Williams. Unnumbered Spaces—Cabins.

"Plan of Fort Boonesborough." (George W. Ranck, *Boonesborough; its founding, pioneer struggles, Indian experiences, Transylvania days, and revolutionary annals* [Louisville: John P. Morton & Co., 1901], 35)

we Begin to live with out Bread." Food became scarce. Hunters had to travel farther to find bison and deer, exposing themselves to assault. The small gardens would not produce until months later, and food supplies were low.

As the Transylvania settlers struggled, another party of colonists arrived in Kentucky. John Floyd, deputy surveyor for Fincastle County, led thirty men through Cumberland Gap and northward along the Wilderness Road before veering westward. Among his party was Virginian Benjamin Logan. Some twenty miles from Harrodstown, they established St. Asaph. Henderson cautioned them by encouraging the new arrivals to "settle somewhere in a compact body for mutual Defense." But as in Boonesborough, many did little to shore up defenses. They preferred instead to pursue their individual interests. Logan took the lead in pushing for the construction of Fort Logan, a smaller

version of the typical fortification model with blockhouses at three corners separated by three cabins along one of the longer walls and four along the other.

Henderson had no one to blame but himself for the colonists' lackadaisical attitude toward security. They had, after all, traveled to Kentucky for land. A trader or blacksmith occasionally set up shop inside a fort, but most settlers used them as a base from which to establish a family farm, and as a retreat to which to escape when threat arose. The Transylvania Company dictated that only pioneers who raised a crop of corn in 1775 would be eligible for five-hundred-acre tracts at twenty shillings per hundred acres. It was late spring already when most of the colonists arrived. Ambitious men quickly had to clear and plant the fields to meet Henderson's rules. Disappointed, dozens of colonists abandoned Transylvania because

"Meeting of the Transylvania House of Delegates at Boonesborough, May 1775." (George Washington Ranck, *Boonesborough; its founding, pioneer struggles, Indian experiences, Transylvania days, and revolutionary annals* [Louisville: John P. Morton & Co., 1901], 30)

they failed to establish those fields of corn (and therefore their land claims). The population fell from eighty on the day that Henderson arrived to only twenty by September.

Concerned about the sustainability of his Transylvania venture, Henderson organized a colony-wide meeting in May. He invited representatives from each settlement: Daniel and Squire Boone and Richard Callaway from Boonesborough; James Harrod from Harrodstown; and John Floyd from St. Asaph. The group convened under a large elm near the unfinished walls of Boonesborough. Here Henderson attempted to impose his vision of colonial government over the settlers of Transylvania. He proposed a lower representative house, an upper house of twelve larger property owners, and a council composed of the company's largest investors. The proposal gave unrestricted authority to the council to alter terms of land sales, but in all other regards it was quite liberal. It called for electing the lower house annually and guaranteeing freedom of religion. Judges had to answer to the colonists for malfeasance in office. Additionally, Henderson appointed Boone to consider solutions to overhunting and to raise awareness about the need to preserve game. Only William Preston and the Virginia colony he represented potentially stood in the way of the fulfillment of

Henderson's colonial plans. After all, Transylvania sat on lands that Virginia claimed as its own. Henderson bribed Floyd, who worked for Preston, to keep the Virginia officials at bay by assuring them that Transylvania would not interfere with Fincastle County's official claims.

After the May 1775 meeting in Boonesborough, Henderson feared that his leadership of Transylvania colony would erode. He did not convene another meeting in the fall as promised, and the company doubled the price of land while setting aside the best tracts around the Falls of the Ohio for its proprietors. James Harrod, James McAfee, and Benjamin Logan rejected the company's authority over their land claims. Lord Dunmore denounced Henderson's enterprise, and after the Revolutionary War erupted, the new states of North Carolina and Virginia overruled Henderson's claim to western lands. Henderson then appealed to the First Continental Congress but was unsuccessful.

Additionally, George Rogers Clark took the lead in binding Kentucky's future to Virginia and not Transylvania. Having migrated from Virginia the previous year, Clark called an assembly at Harrodstown in June 1776. This assembly elected him and John Gabriel Jones to deliver a petition to the Virginia legislature that requested the creation of Kentucky as a separate county. The petition suggested Virginia would be foolish to wage war against the British while allowing "such a respectable body of prime riflemen to remain in a state of neutrality." Before Clark and Jones arrived in Williamsburg, Virginia's General Assembly resolved that "no purchase of Lands within the chartered limits of *Virginia* shall be made, under any pretense whatever, from any *Indian* tribe or nation, without the approbation of the *Virginia* Legislature." Clark and Jones arrived too late to meet the full assembly, but Clark appealed to the Executive Council to donate five hundred pounds of gunpowder to their "Friends in Distress" in Kentucky. Clark declared that "if a country was not worth protecting, it was not worth claiming." The donation of gunpowder, then, signaled Virginia's claim to Kentucky. Finally, on the last day of 1776, Montgomery, Washington, and Kentucky counties formed from the old Fincastle County. With the exception of the lands west of the Tennessee River, the boundaries of Kentucky roughly had taken shape. Two years later, Virginia specifically voided Henderson's Transylvania claim.

By the time Clark approached the Virginia legislature, its citizens' attentions were no longer focused on the western county. In May 1775, some of the colony's most influential men held a convention that expressed sympathy for Massachusetts's rebellion against Great Britain. In June, George Washington accepted the post as military commander of a new continental army. Governor Dunmore feared for his safety and his authority over the colony. He recalled his military from the western outposts, which left the Virginia backcountry exposed. In November, Dunmore offered freedom to enslaved African Americans and contracted servants who would join his military. With weakened western defenses that might encourage Native American attacks and an enlarging and increasingly African American army congregating in Norfolk, white Virginians (and white Americans generally) found the emerging rebellion against George III to be more racialized than they had expected. These conditions inspired Thomas Jefferson months later to write in the Declaration of Independence that King

George "has excited domestic insurrections against us, and has endeavoured to bring on the inhabitants of our frontiers, the merciless Indian Savages." In late 1775 and afterward, men (and eventually women and children) who crossed into Kentucky carried with them the anxieties and anger of this racialized fear.

Keeping the Family Together

When Boonesborough began to lose colonists in 1775, many left not only because they were hungry but also lonely. Only one settler, William Mays, had brought his wife to Kentucky, Boone's fourteen-year-old daughter Susanna. In June, even Daniel Boone and Richard Callaway departed Boonesborough under the pretense of retrieving salt and other supplies. But neither stopped south of the gap to get the supplies: Boone journeyed back to North Carolina to gather his family and other potential settlers, and Callaway did the same in Virginia. The arrival of families transformed the purposes and character of settler colonialism.

The return trip to Boonesborough was difficult. The party started out in mid-June. Rebecca Boone was in the ninth month of pregnancy. In late July, before the group breached the Cumberland Gap, she delivered a son who died shortly thereafter. The difficulty of her delivery delayed the migration for several weeks. The rest of the party refused to continue without Daniel Boone. Not until September did the migrants reach Boonesborough. Later that month, Callaway followed with several dozen settlers, including his family and two others. Squire Boone arrived soon thereafter. Yet more families accompanied him.

Women and children required a more defensive posturing. Men, who had spent more effort extracting fur supplies than actually settling the region, had to commit to colonizing Kentucky. Susannah Johnson recalled that, when her father decided to move from South Carolina to Kentucky, her mother consented so that "her children, when arrived at maturity, might seek homes in new counties, and for the sake of keeping the family together." Visions of a new home, a fertile garden, and the perpet-

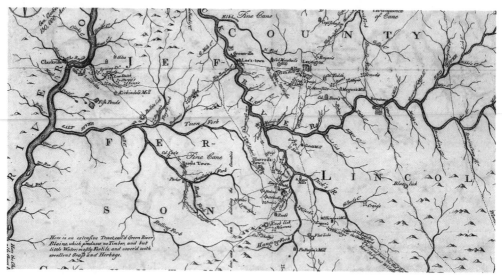

Bluegrass section of John Filson's 1784 "Map of Kentucke." (The Filson Historical Society, Louisville, KY)

uation of family drew white women to Kentucky. In making that decision, Mrs. Johnson and other white women joined their husbands and fathers in transforming Kentucky from an extractive colony to a settler colony. Intent on being good wives and daughters, white women who migrated westward worked and harvested the fields, sheared sheep, milked cows, killed and plucked chickens, prepared food, spun and dyed thread and yarn, wove cloth, made clothes. They birthed, nursed, reared, and educated children as part of their civic duties. In other words, women forfeited their own interests to their husbands' and fathers' pursuits.

To defend their families, white men built a network of small, defensible residential stations interspersed among larger defensible forts with connecting paths. John Filson's 1784 map illustrates the stations and forts, as well as the trails that connected them. As the most immediate defensive structures, stations were ubiquitous across the landscape: there were at least 187 in the Bluegrass region alone. A station normally consisted of a fortified single-family cabin that could accommodate two or three nearby families during attack. Many stations had a stockade and a second floor that overhung the first, designed to thwart Native Americans' attempts to climb onto the roof. Even as they

retained the name of a station, some became corner blockhouses for larger fort structures, supplemented by additional houses and longer stockades. The name given a station left little doubt as to which man controlled it—the Bryan brothers, Isaac Ruddle, Squire Boone, John Strode, James Estill, Joseph Martin, John Glover, James Skaggs, and so on.

Life in the forts was difficult. Settler families faced food shortages, uncleanliness, and disease. Upon visiting Boonesborough in 1778, Daniel Trabue remarked that "it was hard times—no bred, no salt, no vegetables, no fruit of any kind, no Ardent sperrets, indeed nothing but meet." Another visitor in the same year found "a poor distressed ½ naked, ½ starved people, daily surrounded by the savages, which made it so difficult, the hunters were afraid to go out to get Buffalo Meat." More than difficult, life was terrifying.

Moreover, few forts had immediate access to water. With little understanding of germs, early Americans feared living in immediate proximity to water sources which could become miasmatic—polluted with bad air—and, therefore, ridden with disease. In 1780, William Fleming visited the fort in Harrodstown and found "that the whole dirt and filth of the Fort, putrified flesh, dead dogs, horse, cow, hog excrements and human odour all wash into the spring which with the Ashes and sweepings of filthy Cabbins, the dirtiness of the people, steeping skins to dress and washing every sort of dirty rags and cloths in the spring perfectly poisons the water." Even if clean, springs or creeks were usually beyond the fort walls. Residents had no choice but to expose themselves to danger to retrieve water. Clever colonists, like those at Logan's Fort at St. Asaph, built a cabin over the springs and connected it to the fort via a ditch covered with logs and dirt. They had access to the spring even during attack. Most settlers never expected forts to become permanent residences, so access to water seemed only a temporary problem.

Women were complicit in the settler colonialism that threatened Native American control of the hunting grounds. Because they often were alone or unarmed, women became the primary targets when Native Americans attacked. Women were often easier to integrate into native communities when taken captive. Moreover, women and children held more value in diplomatic negotiations. Native Americans did not hesitate as well to scalp and kill women to terrorize other colonial settlers. On occasion, women became victims through white men's decisions. One group of migrants, after a Shawnee attack, forced the women to "wear big coats . . . and made them ride with sticks on their shoulders." During the 1782 siege of Bryan's Station, the men induced the women to wander out to the spring and retrieve water, despite their pleading that "*they* were not bullet-proof, and that the Indians made no distinction between male and female scalps!" In neither case could the women protect themselves. They depended on men to safeguard them.

As whites arrived in Kentucky in the 1770s and 1780s, they faced a peculiar paradox: white families required greater protection but white women also risked their lives by participating actively in that defense. Beyond dressing as men, some women fought like men. Esther Whitley impressed white and Native American men alike as among the best shooters in Kentucky. She told one group of visiting Cherokees that she had learned "in order to kill them should occasion ever make it necessary." She was not alone: "Hugh Luper's, Samuel Daviess', General Logan's, Whitley's wives, kept rifles, and were mighty hard to beat, 100 yards." When one group of settlers migrating down the Ohio River suspected a threat, the "women who were armed, as most of them were with pistols, took positions with their husbands." After John Merrill was shot during an Indian attack, his wife took an axe to four Indians as they tried to breach the cabin door, killing two and wounding two others. Then, as more came down the chimney, she stoked the fire, and when they fell, she chopped them up. When Shawnees attacked a cabin near St. Asaph, Hannah Woods took up an axe and severed the arm of an Indian attempting to push open the door. She then assisted her mother in "finishing" him with a "Broad Ax & Bar of Iron."

Still, the pretense remained that as dependents reliant on the protection of white men, white women were not supposed to be soldiers. They were to be spectators of men's heroic actions and served as arbiters of manhood. As Nathaniel Hart recalled, "The women could read the character of a man with invariable certainty. If he lacked courage, they seemed to be able to discover it, at a glance." Particularly, "if a man was found to be a coward, he stood a poor chance to get his washing, or mending, or anything done." Because white women supposedly depended on men for protection, the bolstering of manly heroism and the ridicule of cowardice figured in such narratives as their best weapons against Native Americans.

Most white families confined themselves to the limited geography of forts, stations, and their immediate environs. They called it being forted, the psychological consequences of which were summed up by Daniel Trabue: "They was a coruagus people but yet I will say they all looked very wild. You might frequently see the women a walking around the fort looking and peeping about seeming that they did not know what they was about but would try to incourage one another and hopt for the best." Forts and stations were the only safe spaces available to colonists, and that safe-

"Station at Lexington." (Z. F. Smith, *The History of Kentucky* [Louisville: Courier-Journal Printing, 1886], 149)

ty could easily be destroyed by a foolish action. When Rachel McCutchens wandered beyond the fort walls with her son, Shawnees captured her and killed the boy.

Colonists often considered white women who survived captivity, however brief it may have been, as damaged. They targeted many of them with ostracism. Devalued as wives and mothers, they were often ignored and occasionally just left to roam about. A description of McCutchens provides a pertinent example: she "was crazy after she returned" and "went about with a rake, turning over the leaves in the fence corners, looking for her son." When they rescued Mrs. McClure in 1785, colonists presumed her to be psychologically scarred from having cooked for her captors beside a rack on which hung "six scalps stretched in hoops"— four of which had belonged to her children. The circumstances of her captivity and escape affected Mary Draper Ingles so that "she appeared absorbed in a deep melancholy, and left the arrangement of household concerns & the reception of strangers to her lovely daughters." Hannah Sovereigns had been captive for six years, and when she came back to Kentucky, the community considered her ill-suited for marriage. In some cases, colonists expected recovered captives to have been sexually compro-

mised. After Jenny Wiley's return, rumors circulated that she gave birth to a dark-skinned, dark-complexioned daughter.

Native Americans also took Boone's daughter Jemima hostage. In July 1776, she and Betsy and Frances Callaway left the security of Boonesborough to canoe on the Kentucky River, where two Cherokees and three Shawnees grabbed them. Their screams alarmed the settlers, including the girls' fathers. They quickly formed a rescue party and took pursuit. Richard Callaway worried that the Indians would "violate his daughters," despite Daniel Boone's assurances that rape was not the way of the Native Americans. When they stopped for the first night, the Native Americans cut the girls' "clothes off to the knees, took off their shoes and stockings, and put on moccasins." The journey continued for another day and night. Not until the third day did the rescue party catch up and save the girls. Their return to Boonesborough was certainly upsetting to their families and other settlers: they *looked* like Native Americans. In fact, members of the rescue party misidentified and almost shot one of the Callaway girls during their recapture. The episode traumatized the girls. They formed strong emotional bonds with their rescuers. Within eighteen months, all three married men who were among those who liberated them. At fifteen years of age, Jemima wed Flanders Callaway, a cousin of the Callaway girls. She bore her first child two years later.

Unlike many white women whom Native Americans seized, however, Jemima Boone Callaway seemed to recover rather quickly and even expressed a quirky humor about it. A few years later, as she attempted to ford a river, Jemima fell from her horse. Upon being saved, she announced that "a ducking is very disagreeable this chilly day but much less so than capture by the Indians." Still, her brief captivity affected her significantly. Jemima pointed to that episode as a decisive bonding moment with Daniel. When he was captured and presumed dead in 1778, the rest of the family returned to North Carolina, but Jemima remained at Boonesborough waiting for him. Years later, when he decided to move to the Missouri frontier, she persuaded her husband to join the migration. Her father lived his later years with Jemima, and when he died in 1820, she perpetuated his myth until her own death nine years later. Daniel's relationship to Jemima was common. The loss of husbands or fathers upon whom white women and children depended for food and defense posed the most potent threat to their livelihood, and, therefore, bonds between them were often quite strong.

Loss of a husband or father could leave women in precarious situations. The trials of widowhood are apparent in the life of Ann Kennedy Wilson Pogue Lindsay McGinty, among the first women to arrive in Kentucky and credited with carrying the first spinning wheel westward. Ann Kennedy lost her first husband, John Wilson, and first child in 1761 to a Native American raid on the Virginia backcountry. In 1762, she married William Pogue, and fifteen years and five children later, the family joined Richard Callaway's migration to Boonesborough. She had two more children. By 1778, they had relocated to Harrodstown, where Shawnees killed Pogue the following year. For two years, Ann struggled as a widow until 1781, when she married Joseph Lindsey, a former member of the American Army of the West. He was killed a year later in the Battle of Blue Licks. For the next five years, she managed on her own. She experimented with grasses, nettles, and buffalo hair to spin a unique thread and cloth. She also operated a tavern out of her home. By 1787, she had accumulated sizeable wealth and decided to marry again. Her last husband, James McGinty, turned out to be quite abusive and violent. It quickly became evident that he married her solely for her wealth. Within a few years, she negotiated a separation from him. For the rest of her life, she remained single. As the head of her own household, she retained her independence. Her wealth finally allowed her a degree of control over her own existence that few women experienced. More typically, deaths of husbands left their widows exposed. Communities did not abandon such women, but they certainly became secondary considerations to men defending their own families and lives.

The forts filled with orphans as well. For many young people, Native Americans occupied a central role in their psyches and being forted was the only protection they knew. Betsy Callaway terrified her son with stories of her own capture and rescue. He feared "that the yard was full of Indians and I was afraid to go outdoors." Native Americans often targeted children because they were easy to overtake. Hannah Woods's daughter barely escaped. She ran into the cabin just ahead of her captors. When under attack, young people helped as they could. During the 1779 siege of Boonesborough, sixteen-year-old Jemima Boone ran among the men, carrying ammunition and loading their guns. As she entered a doorway, she felt a slap on her backside and soon realized she had been shot. The ball lodged in the folds of her petticoat, only superficially breaking the skin and falling out when she tugged at her clothes.

Still, parents could not hide the violence of life in Kentucky from their children. Eleven-year-old Keturah Leitch witnessed the horrors as she migrated into Kentucky: mangled bodies, a scalp with beautiful blonde ringlets hanging from a tree limb. For children, life in Kentucky was traumatic, and the horrors remained with them throughout their lives. Well into old age, William Niblick recalled how, as a child, "I stood at the little gate, having hold of my mother's apron, and heard the women crying; and directly I saw them bring in Wymore in a sheet that was all bloody, hanging on a pole." Similarly, Daniel Drake remembered how his mother put him and his younger siblings to bed with the admonition to "lie still and go to sleep, or the Shawnees will catch you."

Within this difficult environment, families tried to make life as normal as possible. Being forted provided companionship that families often missed when they moved to individual farms. On occasion, celebration punctuated fort life. In 1779, settlers gathered at the Falls of the Ohio to christen a new fort with a good supply of rum and sugar from the French towns to the northwest. Fifteen men and three women made the journey from Harrodstown. Donning their best clothes, they drank and danced jigs to the music of a French violinist. Such merriments were rare, however, because settlers could seldom let down their guard. Kentucky's evolution from an exploitative colony to a settler colony demanded much of the most vulnerable of its settlers—white women and children who had little option in making the trek westward.

Cornstalk, Blackfish, and Plukkemehnotee

During the six decades between the French and Indian War and the War of 1812, British and then American colonists witnessed a series of military conflicts that seemed to relate only minimally to each other—the French and Indian War, Pontiac's Rebellion, Lord Dunmore's War, the Revolutionary War, the Cherokee-American War, the Northwest Indian War (1785–1795), and the War of 1812 (1812–1815). These were formal wars in which British armies fought on behalf of the colonists before 1775, and American armies and militias fought on behalf of citizens after 1776. In Kentucky and elsewhere along the American backcountry, hundreds of unofficial conflicts also broke out that shattered times of "peace": sustained attacks between white colonists and native peoples. What Europeans and Americans identified as separate conflicts, the Shawnees, Cherokees, and other indigenous peoples in and around Kentucky understood as just one large struggle for their survival. As one Shawnee put it in 1781, "'tis now upwards of Twenty years since we have been alone engaged against the Virginians." This fight would continue for another thirty years!

Kentucky's hunting grounds were still Native American country in 1775. White settlers of the mid- to late eighteenth century portrayed Native Americans as largely nomadic and unsettled. They characterized Kentucky as largely empty by the 1770s. Shawnees, Cherokees, and other natives, however, most certainly viewed the white colonists as the nomadic invaders. By the 1770s, indigenous peoples throughout eastern North America complained to British authorities about the empire's failure to control its colonists. The British knew of the problem but could do little about it. Moreover, as the Revolutionary War erupted in 1775, many white colonists suspected Native Americans would join with the British against them, as Lord Dunmore's coalition of escaped slaves, British troops, and native allies seemed to forebode.

As long as American colonialism was exploitative, whites had regular contact with Native Americans on the middle ground through diplomacy and trade. Still, many Shawnees resented the colonists' use of the hunting grounds. Only chiefs like Cornstalk from the Maquachake division tempered the call to war from Chillicothe chief Blackfish and other Shawnees. As extractive colonialism evolved into settler colonialism, more Native Americans joined Blackfish in voicing their desire for war to repel the American invaders, and Cornstalk found it increasingly difficult to dissuade the Shawnee towns from striking against the white colonists. While the Maquachake division of Shawnees insisted on peaceful coexistence, the Chillicothes, Piquas, and Kispokis determined to resist the invaders. In August 1776, representatives from those divisions carried a nine-foot-long war belt to the Cherokees, hoping to inspire their old enemies to join them in warfare against the Virginia and North Carolina colonists.

White settler colonialism clearly bothered even the most neutral and accommodating of Shawnees, like Cornstalk. In November 1776, he traveled to Philadelphia to appeal to the Continental Congress:

> When God created this World he gave this Island to the red people & placed your younger Brethren the Shawnees here in the Center—Now we & they see your people seated on our Lands which all Nations esteem as their & our heart—all our lands are covered by white people & we are jealous that you still intend to make larger strides—We never sold you our Lands which you now possess on the Ohio between the Great Kenhawa & the Cherokee, & which you are settling without ever

asking our leave, or obtaining our consent—Foolish people have desired you to do so, & you have taken their advice.

Throughout the war, Cornstalk, Moluntha, and other Shawnee war and peace chiefs remained in contact with American negotiators. On occasion, they even thwarted their own warriors' attacks, as when Nonhelema warned the Americans of an impending siege on Fort Randolph. Cornstalk insistently cautioned American negotiators that it was not the Shawnees but rather the Mingos who incited younger warriors to violence. During Lord Dunmore's War, the Mingos under Tachnedorus had been particularly active along the Pennsylvania backcountry. Among the warriors was Plukkemehnotee (whom the Americans called Pluggy), a Mohawk who had migrated westward in the 1760s and settled among other relocated Haudenosaunees. By the Revolutionary War, Plukkemehnotee was a leading voice against American settler colonialism. He allied with the British, and Pluggy's Town along the Scioto River became a base from which Wyandottes, Chippewas, Ottawas, and renegade Shawnees staged attacks.

In December 1776, Plukkemehnotee led a war party against Harrodstown before ambushing a group of white men, which included John Todd and John Gabriel Jones, as they attempted to reach the hidden store of gunpowder that George Rogers Clark had secured from Virginia. The Shawnees killed most of the men and took captive the survivors. Plukkemehnotee then turned to McClelland's Station. In October 1775, John McClelland had built a station at Royal Spring (near modern Georgetown). Six months later, an attack on nearby Leestown alarmed the settlers around McClelland's Station. When Plukkemehnotee's warriors arrived in December 1776, the colonists were in full panic. They successfully defended the station, but John McClelland died, as did Plukkemehnotee, when a pursuing war party of colonists shot him. Afterward the surviving settlers abandoned McClelland's Station and moved to Harrodstown.

In 1776, Shawnee leaders traveled to De-troit to approach Henry Hamilton, lieutenant governor of the Quebec colony, for assistance in confronting American colonists. Hamilton, however, waited for advice from his superiors. By spring 1777, he received his orders: arm the Native Americans and escalate attacks in Kentucky. Hamilton contacted the British superintendent of Indian affairs south of the Ohio and directed him to coordinate the major southern and northwestern native nations against the American colonists. He encouraged the Shawnees and Haudenosaunees to set aside their centuries-old differences to join against white settlements. Detroit became the base for British-led raiding parties to lay siege against Kentucky. Fifteen war parties organized, each averaging nineteen Native Americans and two British officers.

In April, Blackfish led a force against Boonesborough. One of his warriors scalped a colonist found outside the stockade. As he waved the bloody scalp, Simon Kenton shot him, which sent the rest into retreat. When Daniel Boone, Michael Stoner, and a dozen others rushed out to pursue the war party, the Shawnees turned and confronted them. One shot Boone in the ankle. As a warrior approached to scalp him, Kenton shot him and then smashed the skull of another with his rifle butt before carrying Boone into the fort. "Simon, you have behaved like a man today," Boone attested. "Indeed you are a fine fellow." Frustrated, Shawnees laid siege to Logan's Fort at St. Asaph for thirteen days. In desperation, the colonists sent several women out of the fort to milk the cows, certain the Shawnees would not harm them. But Blackfish's forces killed or injured their armed escorts and sent the women scurrying back to safety. Under the cover of nightfall, Benjamin Logan sneaked out of the fort to retrieve one of the injured men, using a bale of wool to protect himself. The following months of 1777 were harrowing, leading the white colonists to label the year "the terrible sevens."

Other setbacks followed. When Barney Stanger tried to pasture his horse outside Boonesborough, Shawnees killed and scalped him. In midsummer, settlers found a scalped corpse with

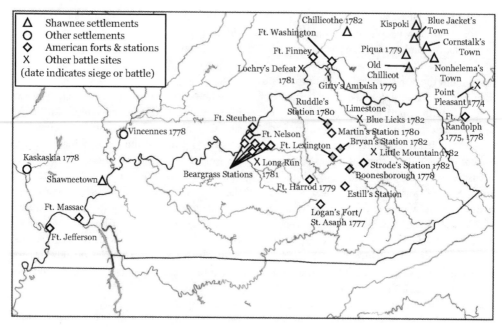

The American Revolutionary War in Kentucky and the Ohio River Valley. (Courtesy of Craig Friend)

an attached letter from Hamilton. He promised two hundred acres to any American willing to fight for the British. At Harrodstown, Shawnees attacked a group of colonists making maple sugar. A member of the search party, Hugh McGary, found the mutilated bodies, including that of his stepson. When the Shawnees and Mingos later turned on Harrodstown, McGary and other colonists rushed out of the fort to counterattack. As the war party retreated, McGary found a dead warrior wearing his stepson's shirt. Insane with rage, he hacked the body up and fed it to the dogs. In Virginia, John Bowman desperately raised a hundred militiamen to aid the Kentucky colonists. If they could resist the Native Americans and hold Kentucky, the militia would remain. If they could not retain control of Kentucky, the militia would escort the settlers to safety.

Trying to impose a civility on the violence that he had unleashed, Hamilton entreated his Native American allies not to "redden your axe with the blood of Women and Children or innocent men. I know that men, kill men and not children." Among the colonists, however, Hamilton became known as the "famous hair

buyer general." Although he did not actually pay per scalp, Hamilton did accept them without close scrutiny as to whether they were male or female, adult or child. He rewarded his allies handsomely for their service and success. By the end of 1777, he had received 72 prisoners and 129 scalps.

Cornstalk's failure to inspire neutrality aided Hamilton's cause. In October 1777, a Virginia militia detained Cornstalk and his son near Point Pleasant and brutally slaughtered them. The governors of Pennsylvania and Virginia sent urgent messages of regret to the Shawnees, but the damage was done. Cornstalk's voice as an advocate for neutrality and compromise had been silenced. Promoters of war, like Blackfish, therefore, rose to prominence among the Shawnees. By early 1778, most of the Shawnee villages were in full rebellion against American colonists. To distance themselves and make themselves less vulnerable to attack, the residents of the villages along the Scioto River, including those of Cornstalk's Town and Nonhelema's Town, relocated northwestward along the Miami River.

The Revolutionary War dislocated white

colonists as well, creating even more uncertainty and insecurity. In July 1776, John Floyd informed his supervisor William Preston about the near-desperate situation: "I think more than 300 men have left the country since I came out, and not one has arrived—except a few down the Ohio." Nearly one thousand colonists were in Kentucky in early 1776, but by the end of the year, only about two hundred colonists remained. Most of them crammed fearfully into the forts at Boonesborough, Harrodstown, and St. Asaph. They abandoned the region north of the Kentucky River in large numbers. Even two years later when the population had climbed to 280 colonists, only 121 were able-bodied riflemen. During the Revolutionary War, a Kentucky colonist was seven times more likely to be killed than were colonists in the thirteen eastern colonies. Men, women, children—all were complicit in the settler colonialism that Native Americans resented, and all became targets of retaliatory violence.

In early January 1778, Daniel Boone led several dozen men on a salt-making expedition to the Lower Blue Licks, where Blackfish's war party, 120 men strong, ambushed them. Boone negotiated with Blackfish. He guaranteed the men would return to Chillicothe without violence. He also assured Blackfish that, in the spring, he would negotiate the surrender of Boonesborough and lead the settlers to Chillicothe, where "all live with you as one people." Blackfish adopted Boone. He replaced a son who had been killed during the attempted kidnapping of Jemima Boone and the Callaway girls. When the captives arrived in Chillicothe, Boone ran the gauntlet. Nearly one hundred Shawnees flogged him. When they inflicted pain by making captives run the gauntlet, the Shawnees symbolically vented their grief over loss of sons and husbands. Afterward, the women of the village cleaned and cut Boone's hair Shawnee style. Finally, Blackfish renamed him Sheltowee, or Big Turtle, and adopted Boone into the nation. The other Americans were not as willing: nearly half were sent to Detroit for the British to ransom.

Residents of Boonesborough first heard that Boone and the others had been killed, and then that they had been captured. In the end, a few escapees returned to Boonesborough telling of Boone's apparent treason. Boone, however, was doing what was necessary to survive. Under guise of a hunting trip, he escaped Chillicothe and returned to Boonesborough. He covered 160 miles in four days. Except for Jemima and her husband, Boone's family had returned to North Carolina, believing him to be dead. Boone warned of the impending attack, but weeks passed and no Shawnees arrived. Already suspicious of Boone for supposedly surrendering Boonesborough to Blackfish, Callaway discouraged fellow colonists from trusting him. In late August, Boone led a small raiding party against a Shawnee town. On the return trip, they discovered that Blackfish was ahead of them. He led 350 Shawnees, Wyandottes, Lenni Lenapes, Mingos, Miamis, and some British military determined to recapture Boone and take all of Boonesborough captive. Boone and his raiders bypassed the war party and arrived at Boonesborough in early September.

The ten-day siege on Boonesborough was the longest against any Kentucky fort. Boone met with Blackfish, who expressed his sincerity in assimilating the colonists (even bringing forty horses to accommodate women and children on the return trip to Chillicothe). Blackfish also presented a letter from Hamilton guaranteeing pardon and safe conduct to Detroit for any not wishing to live among the Shawnees. When Boone returned to the fort with the offer, however, debate raged. Richard Callaway led the majority of settlers in rejecting Blackfish's offer. Boone played for more time as Callaway positioned shooters atop the fort walls, including several women disguised as men to create the illusion of a larger fighting force. Blackfish requested a parley during which leaders on both sides would meet, but it dissolved into violence. The Shawnees cut Boone on the back and shot his brother Squire in the shoulder. As the colonists ran back into the fort, the Native Americans attempted unsuccessfully to breach the gates. For days, Shawnees tried to uproot the colonists by setting fire to the cabins. But Squire Boone made squirt guns from old musket barrels so that defenders did not have to go onto the roofs to put out the fires. The Shawnees also began a tunnel under the fort walls. In response, the colonists dug a countertrench, and a heavy rain caused the tunnel to collapse. Maybe because Blackfish was intent on capturing the Americans rather than killing them, the siege ensued without great physical violence. The failure to tunnel into the fort ended the effort, and Shawnees abandoned the siege.

Callaway and Benjamin Logan soon filed charges of treason against Boone. At the trial at Logan's Fort, Kentucky militia officers deliberated whether Boone actually had betrayed his fellow colonists or Blackfish. Boone claimed that he had the salt makers surrender to prevent attack against Boonesborough, and, thereafter, he misled the British and the Shawnees. He believed his actions during the siege spoke for themselves. The court agreed. It dismissed the charges, and Boone was promoted to major.

The Rise of George Rogers Clark

In May 1778, George Rogers Clark organized an army to attack the British support network that promoted Shawnee aggressions—the forts at the former French villages of Kaskaskia and Vincennes in the Illinois country, and ultimately the fort at Detroit. "I knew our case was desperate," he recalled later, "but the more I reflected on my weakness, the more I was pleased with the enterprise." His small army accompanied several families to Corn Island, near the Falls of the Ohio, where they constructed a fort and drilled. When he revealed his plans to invade the Illinois country, most of the company deserted.

About 175 men accompanied Clark down the Ohio River to Fort Massac, an abandoned military ruin from the French and Indian War. The force marched to Kaskaskia and took it by surprise in early July. The French inhabitants accepted Clark's authority, and some joined his army in excursions against Prairie du Rocher, St. Philips, Cahokia, and Vincennes. As he conquered the British-controlled settlements, Clark established good relations with the Spanish commander at St. Louis, Fernando de Leyba, who provided supplies to the villagers. Clark was less generous with local Native Americans. He confronted them with a peace belt and a war belt. He cautioned them to choose wisely because "this is the last speech you may ever expect from the Big Knives; the next thing will be the tomahawk." Most either decided to support Clark or remain neutral as he took the war to Detroit.

In late January 1779, Clark received word that Henry Hamilton had a force to retake the

"Corn Island at the Falls of the Ohio." (Z. F. Smith, *The History of Kentucky* [Louisville: Courier-Journal Printing, 1892], opp. 160)

Illinois country and had already recaptured Vincennes. But winter was upon the Illinois country, and many of Hamilton's allies—Native American and French residents—had gone home, anticipating no more activity until the spring. Clark determined the time to strike was immediate. He planned a winter campaign: the men would march across the Illinois country to retake Vincennes, and a riverboat armed with artillery would wind its way across several rivers to lend support. Winter flooding made the march difficult. Troops grew exhausted and depressed. By late February, they arrived outside Vincennes. Clark demanded surrender. As Hamilton considered his situation, a British-allied Native American raiding party arrived. Greatly outnumbered by Clark's troops, the Native Americans quickly fell. Clark was merciless. He killed most and tomahawked four warriors. "He had just come from his Indian triumph all bloody and sweating," remembered Hamilton, "his hands and face still reeking from the human sacrifice in which he had acted as chief priest." Shaken by the display, outnumbered, and unable to count on Native American alliances, Hamilton surrendered. Clark sent him to Virginia for imprisonment. On his way, Hamilton arrived as a captive at Logan's Fort, where Jane Menifee took up a tomahawk that she found among his possessions. She threatened to scalp him with it in the same way it certainly had been used against women and children. "We were accosted by the females especially in pretty coarse terms," Hamilton recalled.

Emboldened by his success in the Illinois country and against Hamilton, Clark encouraged Kentucky colonists to take the war to the Shawnees. John Bowman, who had led the raids against Prairie du Rocher and Cahokia, recruited 160 men for a May 1779 attack on Chillicothe. Unlike the Maquachake villages, the Chillicothe and Piqua villages had been slow to move from the Scioto River valley. The Kentuckians surprised the Shawnees in those towns, burned houses, stole horses, and mortally wounded Blackfish. Shaken by the assault, the last of the Shawnee villages abandoned the Scioto River valley and joined those along the

Portrait of George Rogers Clark, by Matthew Harris Jouett, 1825. (The Filson Historical Society, Louisville, KY)

Miami River. Clark then turned his focus to the Chickasaws. He appealed to Virginia governor Thomas Jefferson to fund construction of a fort. Clark calculated that building such a fort would intimidate any Chickasaw aspirations regarding an eastern attack. By early 1780, Fort Jefferson stood at the confluence of the Ohio and Mississippi Rivers, with the small settlement of Clarksville beside it. By spring 1780, Clark traveled to all reaches of the western settlements as settlers begged him to defend them. He went to St. Louis to help the Spanish defend against a British force. He rushed back to Fort Jefferson, where he led a defense against one thousand Chickasaws. As the British organized an offensive to retake the West, Clark established the Falls of the Ohio as his base for protecting both Kentucky and Illinois. Militia leaders throughout Kentucky criticized his decision. They suggested his attention to Illinois, which drained Kentucky of manpower, left their settlements exposed.

In midsummer, Captain William Bird led a British force out of Detroit with some seven hundred Native American allies to raid the Kentucky settlements. Ruddle's Station fell in late June. Bird could not control his allies' anger, and the Shawnees killed a number of captives. Martin's Station fell a few days later. Holding nearly 350 captives and facing a food shortage, Bird retreated northward. More than half of the captives remained in the Shawnee villages. Only 150 arrived in Detroit. Clark planned a speedy retaliation and again recruited an army. But volunteers were slow to sign up. On his visit to Harrodstown, Clark found men lined up at the land office trying to register deeds. They were, however, unwilling to sign up for military service. He closed the land office and stationed guards at Cumberland Gap to stop any men who attempted to flee militia enrollment. By August, he had one thousand troops ready to invade the Shawnee villages. They found Chillicothe empty, and while some Shawnees resisted at Piqua, most successfully escaped. Clark's forces burned Piqua to the ground. Chief Wryneck appealed to the British at Detroit. "We see ourselves as weak and our arms feeble to the force of the Enemy," he said. With Clark occupied, the Chickasaws renewed their attack on Fort Jefferson. They successfully scared a majority of Clarksville's residents into fleeing the Mississippi River valley. Within the year, a flood wiped out what remained of Fort Jefferson and Clarksville. Those residents who lingered abandoned the colony.

Clark's offensive into the Shawnee villages in 1781 represented part of a larger American scheme to take Detroit and sever British relations with the Shawnees. New leadership emerged, however, that revitalized the Native American war effort. Thayendanegea, known among the Americans as Joseph Brant, was a Mohawk chief sent to Detroit to thwart Clark's plan to capture the British stronghold. In late August, Brant's party came across Archibald Lochry's Pennsylvania militia on its way to reinforce Clark. Suffering no losses, Brant's men killed or captured all of the Pennsylvanians. He, thus, effectively ended Clark's threat. A few weeks later, another war party attacked the Beargrass Stations. When the residents of Painted Stone Station attempted to find securi-

Monk. (Z. F. Smith, *The History of Kentucky* [Louisville: Courier-Journal Printing, 1892], 194)

ty at Linn Station, Brant's men ambushed and massacred them at Long Run.

Another member of the new leadership was Simon Girty, who as a young man had been taken captive from the Pennsylvania backcountry and fully assimilated into Seneca culture. Even after he returned to his colonial family and community, Girty remained sympathetic to Native American efforts to retain their lands and cultures. He served as Hamilton's interpreter and scout. Upon Hamilton's surrender, Girty worked to sustain Shawnee and Wyandotte war efforts. In mid-1779, he led an ambush against colonial forces in northern Kentucky, just across the Ohio River from Fort Washington. Throughout late 1781 and into 1782, Girty escalated attacks in the Ohio River valley. In March 1782, Wyandottes struck Estill's Station. They killed a fourteen-year-old girl and took a slave named Monk captive. As word spread of the attack, James Estill led twenty-five men in pursuit. When they caught up to the raiding party at Little Mountain (near modern Mount Sterling), a particularly vicious battle ensued. Monk yelled to the colonists about Native American numbers. Half of the settlers were killed, including Estill. Monk escaped and carried one of the wounded twenty-five miles to Estill's Station.

Little Mountain inspired the Native Americans who, at a council in June, determined to eliminate the Kentucky settlements while British help was still available. In August, Girty led some three hundred Shawnees, Wyandottes, Mingos, and Lenni Lenapes who joined a contingent of British rangers under the command of William Caldwell as it moved into central Kentucky. The party attacked Bryan's Station to little effect before retreating northward along the Old Buffalo Trace that stretched to the Ohio River. Behind them raged 182 Kentucky colonists determined to confront the larger force. The Americans finally caught up to them at Lower Blue Licks on August 19, when John Todd led the militias to the southern banks of the Licking River. Before them stood a hill where Daniel Boone suspected the Native Americans planned an ambush. He encouraged Todd to wait until Benjamin Logan's reinforcements arrived. But Hugh McGary, eager to engage the enemy, urged attack, mounted his horse, and forded the river. He yelled out, "Them that ain't cowards, follow me." Most of the men followed, as did their officers who hoped to restrain them. Boone recalled thinking, "We are all slaughtered men." Girty's and Caldwell's forces waited as the colonial militias advanced up the hill—Todd's troops in the center, Stephen Trigg's to the west, and Boone's to the east. When the colonists reached the crest of the hill, they were met with close-range fire. Todd and Trigg fell immediately, and their troops scattered. Boone's militia turned to run but found Girty's men upon them. They had no choice but to engage their opponents in hand-to-hand combat. Before he escaped down

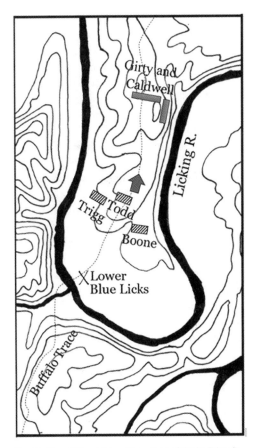

The Battle of Blue Licks. (Courtesy of Craig Friend)

the hill and across the river, Boone saw his son Israel shot and killed.

Seventy-seven colonists died at Blue Licks. The Native Americans burned the captives alive. Those who escaped gradually found their way back to Bryan's Station. When Logan's reinforcements arrived at the Lower Blue Licks four days later, they found bodies of former friends and neighbors arranged along the Buffalo Trace, intended to intimidate the colonists. Determined to save face, George Rogers Clark led eleven hundred men to the Shawnee villages along the Miami River. By the time he and his men arrived in November, the Native Americans had abandoned all the towns. They had relocated yet again into the Mad River region. Exasperated, the Kentuckians returned home. Once there, Clark received a letter from the governor in which he asked him to account for the many failures of 1781 and 1782, including the Battle of Blue Licks. Clark defended his decisions for months before traveling to Virginia to retire his commission and settle his accounts. In July 1783, Governor Benjamin Harrison accepted Clark's resignation and thanked him "for the very great and singular services you have rendered your country in wresting so great and valuable a territory out of the hands of the British enemy, repelling the attacks of their savage allies, and carrying on a successful war in the heart of their country." The war seemed over. The Battle of Blue Licks indeed was the last major confrontation of the American Revolutionary War (which had ended in the east with the Battle of Yorktown nearly a year earlier). Yet it took place merely at the midway point in the Shawnees' six-decade war against Kentucky's settler colonials.

Daniel Boone Was a Big Man

Daniel Boone was once described as "a sort of pony-built man," a bit undersized but strong like a horse. Through bravery, leadership, and marksmanship, Boone achieved wide renown as a Big Man, a status similar to that which Native Americans gave to men who proved heroic. Among white colonists, it also represented personal independence that came with land ownership. Among white colonists, Big Man status often eclipsed other claims to leadership like family lineage or wealth, but it also exacerbated the competition for resources and land that lay at the heart of the conflict between Native Americans and white colonists. Although Native American cultures had formal, often inherited, positions of leadership assumed by men like Hokolewskwa, they had long relied on a man's (or woman's) actions to determine who deserved to be a war chief. The first whites in Kentucky also had formal positions of leadership—militia commanders, governmental officials. Nevertheless, James Harrod, Benjamin Logan, Simon Kenton, and other Big Men proved more influential as leaders among their fellow colonists than men like Richard Henderson and John Floyd. The Revolutionary War created opportunities for Big Men to re-

inforce their status through military leadership and success. By taking advantage of these opportunities, George Rogers Clark, John Bowman, and other men of military stature added their names to the ranks of Big Men. Military failure, in contrast, could damage one's status, as when Boone faced trial for treason or when Hugh McGary foolishly charged into battle at Blue Licks. The centrality of Big Men on both sides of the conflict created an environment where violence and force dominated life. This environment contributed to and reinforced the idea of Kentucky as a "dark and bloody ground."

Before settler colonialism defined life in Kentucky, forts and stations were sites of masculine culture. The arrival of families transformed those spaces. Cabins continued to be crude and minimal. Furnishings often only included a wooden table, a bed that either had a feather tick for a mattress or was covered with buffalo skins, and a fireplace made of logs and chinked with mud. Archaeological remains from Boonesborough attest to the persistence of masculine culture: for example, hand-wrought nails, lead bullets and gunflints, and tobacco pipestems. The pipestems indicate the role of smoking as a leisure activity. The need to grow tobacco forced men to farm outside the security of defensive structures, as did the cultivation of corn for sustenance. But archaeologists have also uncovered the domestic material culture of family life: fragments of English-made tableware, red-clay earthenware cookware, a teapot, and decorated ceramics. Women carried such items with them into Kentucky to remind them of home and the comforts of a less-rugged way of life.

Despite the emerging domestic character of fort and station life, white settlements remained the scenes of Big Man culture. Hunting, surveying, contests of bravery and marksmanship, and other frolics allowed men to challenge each other for influence, but so too did land ownership and political maneuvering. Before the war, for example, three men positioned for authority in Boonesborough: Daniel Boone enjoyed the reputation of a Big Man; Richard Callaway, as a militia colonel, had garnered such respect previously in Virginia; and Richard Henderson, as the leader of the Transylvania colony, expected deference. Henderson's authority was short lived. It collapsed with the interference of colonial governments. The contest of masculinity between Callaway and Boone evolved differently. Callaway had resented Boone's command during the building of the Wilderness Road and Boone's wood craft—his knowledge of the landscape and the Native Americans—during the rescue of Jemima Boone and his daughters Betsy and Frances. During the siege of Boonesborough, Callaway aggressively took the lead in defending the fort and in charging Boone with treason. Boone's Big Man reputation helped him not only survive the trial but emerge with higher militia rank.

Simon Kenton, too, was a Big Man. Kenton fled from Virginia to Kentucky under the alias Simon Butler because he thought he had killed a rival in a fight over a girl. With Thomas Williams, he arrived in 1775 at Limestone Creek, where they cleared land and planted a field of corn. Standing an inch over six feet and weighing about 190 pounds, Kenton was strong yet swift and agile. In 1786, a Virginia magistrate told to collect a small debt refused because it was "Too dangerous to go where Kenton is." As a woodsman, Kenton rivaled Daniel Boone. Like Boone, Kenton survived running a Shawnee gauntlet. One tale relates how, during one of his travels, Boone sensed another person in the forests. For hours, each tried to outmaneuver the other. Finally, Boone stepped into a clearing and called, "That you, Simon?" Kenton stepped out and replied, "Howdy, Boone."

The violent landscape of Revolutionary War–era Kentucky also allowed Big Man status to extend to women. In conversation with an elder Cherokee chief, Cephas Washburn recalled a woman who "moulded bullets and loaded the rifles for her husband," as he held off the attacking Shawnees. His Cherokee acquaintance concluded, "*She* was a *man*, and worthy to sit at the council fire with the wisest chiefs." By participating in war, women could act like Big Men, but such actions did not

translate into leadership positions as they often did in Shawnee culture. Gender barriers were more rigid among white Americans.

Still, the increased violence of the Revolutionary War altered masculine culture in Kentucky. The conflict opened the way for more formal leadership that began to displace the Big Man ideal. Time and again, Native American attacks exposed the impotence of men to protect their families and themselves. Virginia stepped into the breach and organized its western claims under the authority of militia units and county structures. The state assembly created Kentucky County in 1776, establishing the administrative seat at Harrodstown. The county militia that the legislature authorized first mustered in March 1777. Virginia officials devised the militia chain of command with George Rogers Clark as brigadier general and John Bowman as colonel. John Todd, Benjamin Logan, Daniel Boone, and James Harrod served as regimental captains. Importantly, in assigning leadership positions, Virginia gave higher command to Clark and Bowman, who had held earlier militia leadership roles in the colony, but it designated regimental command to Big Men who could influence and encourage their fellow settlers. At the Battle of Blue Licks, where three of the regiments advanced under the leadership of their captains without waiting for Logan's regiment or directives from their superiors, that tactic proved disastrous.

Statutes required all free white men, ages eighteen to forty-five, to serve in the militia and muster seven times annually. Each man provided his own musket or rifle, a half-pound of powder, and one pound of lead ammunition. Some mustered with sticks because they were too poor to provide their own weapons. Others deemed essential to Virginia's economic and political interests were exempt: for example, blacksmiths, tobacco inspectors, legal clerks, elected officials, and seminary professors did not have to enlist. Alternately, an individual could perform other services like road service or mail delivery. Physical disability, in contrast, was not a reason to avoid service. James Dunlap was certain he would "be excused on a/c of having but one eye," but a regimental colonel informed him that such an impairment did not exempt him. The colonel told Dunlap that "as good a soldier as he ever had in his regiment was Joe Young, & he had but 1 eye." Still, there were ways around joining the militia: Dunlap eventually paid forty shillings for a substitute. Others, like Tice Brock, just refused to fight when called upon, hiding under a bed during the siege of Boonesborough. He pleaded, "I was not made for a fighter—I was not made for a fighter."

Militias were merely the smallest units of governmental organization that Virginia imposed on Kentucky County. Six months after the first militia muster, the first county court of quarter sessions sat in Harrodstown. The county court named a sheriff, surveyor, and ten justices of the peace—one for each of the major stations. In time, the court expanded its authority over the construction and maintenance of roads, support for the poor, licensure of taverns, regulation of grist mills, and admission of lawyers to the bar.

Despite the varied economic interests that kept the courts occupied, given the ways in which land had been distributed prior to 1779—war veterans' surveys, preemptions, shingled land claims, and absentee land claims—legal disputes were bound to clog up the courts. In 1776, Virginia had set Kentucky's eastern boundary. It began at the low-water mark on the Ohio River opposite the mouth of the Scioto River, traced along the Big Sandy to its junction with Tug Fork, and ran along Laurel Ridge of the Cumberland Mountains to a spot called "seven pines and two black oaks" at the Virginia–North Carolina line. Over the following four years, white men worked to establish their land claims by surveying and registering at the land office, which was located in Williamsburg, Virginia. The distance made it inconvenient, and many men just waited to make their claims. They farmed the lands without any legal authority to do so.

During and after the Revolutionary War, the American government replaced the British in treaty making and overseeing settler migrations into Kentucky. British companies like the Ohio Company and the Transylvania Company lost influence as the colonies broke away from Great Britain. When Virginia passed the Land Act of 1779, it ended the influence of the land companies and signaled the opening of Kentucky for settlement, although the region was deeply embroiled in war. Off limits were the lands south of the Green River. If colonists intruded there, they could potentially agitate the Chickasaws, who had refrained thus far from attacks. Still, Thomas Walker, the Loyal Company's original explorer and agent, surveyed the southern boundary of Kentucky County from "seven pines and two black oaks" west to the Tennessee River. He projected the extension of the line through Chickasaw territory to the Mississippi River. Known as the Walker Line, the survey actually strayed from the intended 36'30° parallel it should have followed, a problem addressed four decades later. Virginia formally recognized French and Indian War veterans' claims, which had been surveyed under John Floyd years earlier, and set aside lands at the Falls of the Ohio for the veterans of Clark's armies in the Illinois territory. Virginia also accepted pre-1779 preemptions that the poorest of settlers had made and sanctioned absentee claims of thousands of acres belonging to George Washington, Patrick Henry, William Preston, and other elite white Virginia men. The law then authorized the sale of remaining Kentucky lands through treasury warrants at forty pounds per one hundred acres "to create a sinking fund in aid of the annual taxes to discharge the public debt." There was no limit on the acreage that could be claimed. This opened the door for land speculators, who invested heavily in large tracts of land with the intention of reselling them at exaggerated prices.

To secure a tract of land, the law established a four-step process. First, a colonist had to obtain a land warrant. Military warrants were granted to veterans. Treasury warrants could be purchased. Individuals who helped bring larger groups of immigrants westward could apply for importation rights. Second, the warrant holder had to file with a county surveyor, listing the acreage and locating the boundaries. Third, the surveyor had to con-

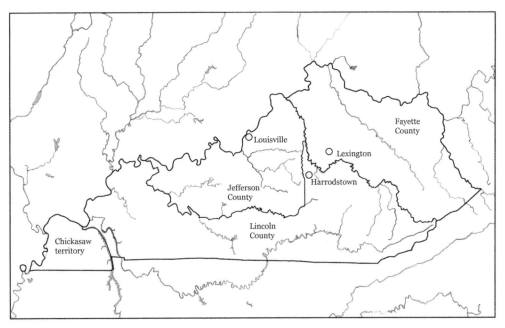

Jefferson, Fayette, and Lincoln Counties. (Courtesy of Craig Friend)

duct an actual survey, something that many were not qualified to do accurately. Fourth, the plat and field notes were to be registered with the land office. The land office then finally issued a land patent. To facilitate land claims, a land office opened in Harrodstown. To resolve disputed claims, Virginia set up a court of land commissioners. During its brief session at Logan's Station between October 1779 and April 1780, the court settled 1,328 claims covering more than 1.3 million acres.

Among the first speculators to take advantage of the 1779 law was John May, a Virginia merchant who, with the financial backing of his partner Samuel Beall, became Kentucky County's largest trader in preemption and settlement warrants. May excitedly wrote Beall in 1780 that, despite the law having gone into effect a year earlier, the continued war with the Shawnees had kept others from surveying and claiming much land. As thousands of settlers poured into Kentucky County in the later years of the Revolutionary War, May was at the vanguard of a new land rush: Some hoped to secure preemptions they had made and then abandoned under the threat of Na-

tive American attack. Some worked as land jobbers, hired to establish and record a claim on behalf of an absentee investor. Others entered the land rush as outliers. They preempted a tract of land by clearing and planting a field, building a cabin, and then selling the "improved" land to a newcomer at a profit. "Weak *Kentucke* is distracted with the clashing interests of Cabinning and surveying," complained one colonist. "How it may end Heaven Knows! I'm afraid to loose sight of my House lest some Invader takes possession." Reverend David Rice predicted, "I looked forward fifty or sixty years and saw the inhabitants engaged in very expensive and demoralizing litigations about their landed property."

The land rush forced Virginia to carve Kentucky County quickly into three counties to administer settlement and land claims: Jefferson County, Fayette County, and Lincoln County. By 1781, the land office approved over 3.5 million acres of land claims through 557 settlement certificates, 699 French and Indian War veterans' claims, 700 preemptions, and 2,847 treasury warrants. Most of these claims lay north of the Kentucky River in what was called the Great Meadow or the Bluegrass region. Only 9,400 acres were claimed in the Big Sandy River valley of Appalachia. Yet land distribution was not very democratic or equitable. Nearly 100,000 acres of the newly distributed lands belonged to only twenty-one investors. Anticipating more land sales and more money in the state coffers, Virginia opened the lands south of the Green River. Intending to distribute them to its Revolutionary War veterans, it merely created opportunity for investors to purchase and trade in veterans' warrants. Confusion reigned. Some surveyors and settlers purposefully created shingled claims to force land claims into courts, where it was easier to win land than actually secure it on the ground.

White Americans believed that land ownership led to independence. A man could establish a home, take care of his family, and subsist off the produce of the land, if only he owned it. Acquiring land in Kentucky, however, was deceptively difficult. Persistent war interfered with land claims. When the violence subsided, settlers and surveyors found themselves in competition with thousands of new claimants. In 1777, 280 people had bunkered in Boonesborough and Harrodstown. Within thirteen years, over 73,000 colonists knew Kentucky as home. Many, unsuccessful in securing land, fell into poverty and would be forced to rent land in order to pursue the ideal of independent farming. In reality, for large numbers of settlers the independence they sought would remain elusive.

3

Colonial Kentucky, 1774–1792

Landscapes of an American Colony

In the 1783 Treaty of Paris, the British acknowledged their thirteen former American colonies to be free, sovereign, and independent states. The treaty drew the boundary between the new United States and British Canada. The British abandoned claims to the Mississippi River valley, conceding it to the Spanish. The British were not foolish, however: they expected the United States to remain economically tied to its former mother country. The concession of Kentucky and other lands between the Appalachian Mountains and the Mississippi River would facilitate growth of the American nation and, therefore, create markets for British goods. They also expected Spain to keep the port at New Orleans open to the lucrative trade that American expansion promised. Suddenly, the United States had a western territory beyond the crest of the Appalachian Mountains, one that stretched to the Mississippi River. Much of it—the lands north of the Ohio River, which became known as the Old Northwest, and roughly the lands south of the Tennessee River, which became known as the Old Southwest—remained controlled and inhabited by Native Americans. Virginia's Jefferson, Fayette, and Lincoln Counties, and North Carolina's Tennessee settlements occupied the space between.

Kentucky and Tennessee became colonies for the new American nation, just as the thirteen states along the Atlantic coast had once been colonies for the British empire. They provided raw goods for extractive colonialism and land for settler colonialism. Neither trans-Appalachian region, however, could long sustain the exploitation of its resources: bison migrated westward to escape the hunters; beaver and deer populations were depleted in many places. Moreover, interesting resources existed elsewhere, as in the lead-mining regions of the upper Mississippi River valley and the indigo fields and naval stores of West Florida. But Kentucky in particular, as confused as its property distribution may have been, beckoned American settler colonialism. The soils were rich and promised large yields. The rivers were navigable and, despite the Falls of the Ohio, provided a transportation system by which goods could go to market in New Orleans and beyond. At least for a brief time, the Native American threat subsided with the conclusion of the American Revolutionary War and the loss of British support. And Kentucky's physical landscape was as appealing and diverse as any in the United States. It contains five distinct geological regions: the Cumberland Plateau, the Bluegrass, the Pennyrile, the Western Coalfield, and the Mississippi Embayment.

Whether they had traveled down the Ohio River or through the Cumberland Gap, colonists had passed through the Cumberland Plateau. The easternmost edge of the plateau is comprised of the Allegheny and Cumberland Mountains, both part of the larger Appalachian Mountain range. The Pottsville Escarpment, a ridge of limestone that, millions of years ago, folded and tilted as the earth formed so that rivers flowing westward drop between 700 and 1,800 feet over it, forms the western edge of the plateau. Along the escarpment are sheer cliffs, rock shelters, natural bridges, caves, deep gorges, and waterfalls. Cumberland Falls, among the many waterfalls of the region, boasts the only predictable lunar rainbow in the Americas. Moonlight strikes the river dramatically, creating a rainbow where it flows northward.

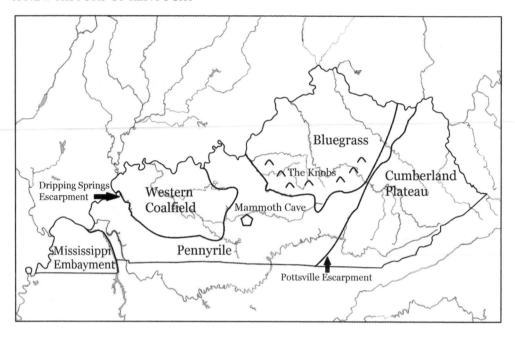

Kentucky's Physiological Regions. (Courtesy of Craig Friend)

Fort Ancient peoples had lived in and used the Cumberland Plateau. In particular, they had made pendants, arrowheads, gorgets, and beads from cannel coal, a soft form of bituminous coal also known as candle coal—so named because it lights easily, burns brightly, and leaves little ash. In 1742, along the banks of a tributary of the Kanawha River in the Alleghanies, John Howard and John Peter Salling "discovered" the resource. Eight years later, Thomas Walker noted coal north of the Cumberland Gap. Its visibility meant that it could be extracted through simple surface mining, as had been done in England since the 1500s. The abundance of firewood in Kentucky, however, made coal irrelevant to eighteenth-century settlers. Other natural resources brought better profit in the markets of the East: deer and beaver remained plentiful in the Cumberland Plateau, although transporting skins could be difficult. Land was also available, but it was rocky, uneven, and heavily wooded with white and red oaks, sugar maples, sycamore, ash, and pine. Still, in the 1760s, the land companies had sold thousands of acres in the Cumberland Plateau to wealthy, absentee investors. These

large investments made securing a land claim problematic for any potential settler.

Most colonists headed for the Bluegrass, the most renowned of Kentucky's regions and named for a European grass (*Poa pratensis*) that had arrived in the Americas earlier in the 1700s. It spread westward ahead of British settlers. The Bluegrass sits atop a limestone aquifer that is permeable and porous. Water flows easily beneath its topsoils. Consequently, the region contains many springs, sinkholes, and salt licks. Originally, colonists exploited the bison that congregated by the thousands in the Bluegrass. The saltiness of the licks and the fibers of the canebrakes drew them. After the bison populations declined, salt became another extractive resource that colonists harvested, as well as maple sugar. Very early, settlers realized the agricultural potential of the Bluegrass: the limestone made the land particularly rich with minerals. Forests and canebrakes existed in abundance, but they were not so thick that land clearing was difficult. The relative ease with which they could create open land contributed to the settlers' idea that the Bluegrass would make excellent farmlands and pas-

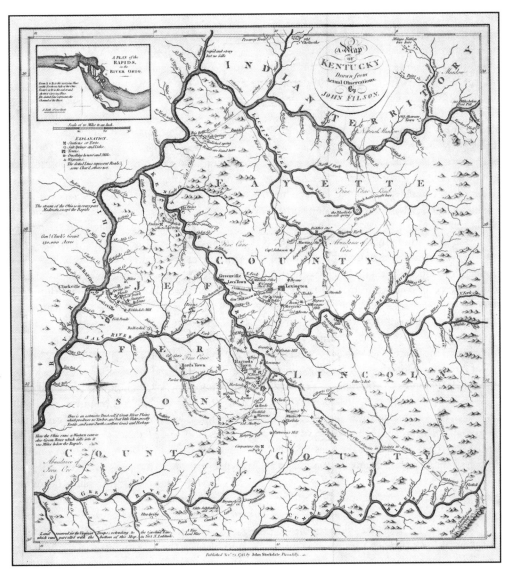

John Filson's 1784 "Map of Kentucke." (The Filson Historical Society, Louisville, KY)

turage. Transportation was easier in the Bluegrass as well. Its many rivers flow into the Ohio River, which bounds the region to the north and west, and its terrain's gently rolling hills made its roads more navigable than those in the Cumberland Plateau. When Virginia formed Jefferson, Fayette, and Lincoln Counties in 1780, it ranked the lands around Lexington—the "inner Bluegrass"—as "first-rate," which meant that taxes were higher for its settlers. Virginia officials made this ranking based

on tree species: cherry, white walnut, buckeye, elm, hackberry, ash, black jack oak, honey locust, coffee, and paw-paw. These varieties indicated the best soil fertilities, in contrast to those found in the Cumberland Plateau, which indicated second- and third-rate lands.

Among the Bluegrass's early settlers was John Filson, who took up surveying and land speculating in the early 1780s. In 1783, he moved to Lexington, where he wrote *The Discovery, Settlement and Present State of Kentucke*

49

and produced an accompanying map, published the following year. Filson had written the first "history" of Kentucky, although he was not interested as much in the past as in promoting future sales of lands and books. The watermark on Filson's map contained the words "Work & Be Rich," and he promoted that philosophy to Kentucky's colonists. Throughout his book, he described a land so fertile that a colonist need only perform his role as a good farmer and he would be rich! The map not only detailed stations and forts but also roads and rivers, which highlighted the potential for shipping agricultural productions to markets.

Along the southern rim of the Bluegrass are the Knobs, hundreds of isolated, steep, conical limestone rises that create a more rugged landscape in contrast to the rolling hills of the inner Bluegrass. Unlike hills that are usually part of a rolling landscape descending from higher mountains, knobs or monadnocks stand solitarily on the landscape, remnants of millennia of stream erosion that left hardened limestone shelves atop steep and loose shale slopes. The Knobs define the lands through which the Salt River, the Kentucky River, and their tributaries flow. There are monadnocks elsewhere in Kentucky. They often define the edge of a distinct geographic region. Many are found along the Green River. The Green River Knob, at 1,789 feet, stands as the highest point in Kentucky outside the Cumberland Plateau.

South of the Bluegrass lies another region named for a plant, an indigenous member of the mint family known as the pennyroyal (*Hedeoma pulegioides*)—or the more familiar colloquial pronunciation, the "pennyrile." Also known as the Mississippian Plateau, the Pennyrile region is underlain with a limestone aquifer that drains substantially more water from the surface than occurs in the similarly formed Bluegrass region. Consequently, the Pennyrile has fewer streams compared to the rest of Kentucky. To the east, the region is marked by the Pottsville Escarpment. To the west, a series of sandstone folds known as the Dripping Springs Escarpment separate the Pennyrile from the Western Coalfield region. The Pennyrile forks around the Western Coalfield, and these corridors directed early colonists westward into the Illinois territory.

By the 1780s, Americans were familiar with the Pennyrile's quality lands, some of which had been settled north of the Green River. Yet, the Pennyrile did not thrive with the higher-quality tree species that signaled first-rate lands. Oaks predominated—white, red, and blackjack—as well as sugar maples, hickories, elms, and persimmons. The farther south and west one moved through the Pennyrile, the more rugged the terrain. Thousands of sink holes, streamless valleys, springs, sinking streams, and caverns sit across the region. Mississippian peoples had lived in the caves and rock shelters of the Pennyrile. Over millennia, groundwater transformed miles of underground passages, often only inches wide, into large caverns more than one hundred feet wide. The most impressive is the Mammoth-Flint Ridge cave system: with over four hundred miles of surveyed passageways, it is the longest cave in the world. It also served as a sacred place for Woodland and Mississippian Kentuckians. Archaeologists have found cane torches, woven grass moccasins, gourd fragments, and wall drawings as well as burial sites. Mississippian peoples also mined the cave, as evidenced by the remains of an indigenous miner on whom a boulder fell when he dislodged its base.

To the west of the Pennyrile is the Western Coalfield, the southernmost part of a larger coal basin that stretches into Indiana and Illinois. Like the coal deposits of the Cumberland Plateau, the bituminous coal in the Western Coalfield lay close to the surface and was easy to extract once coal became a popular resource. Unlike the Pennyrile and the Bluegrass, sandstone predominates in the Western Coalfield, which is harder than limestone and slower to erode. The hills are steeper and the valleys deeper than in the other regions, making farming and transportation more challenging. Bald cypress swamps border some creeks. Red and white oaks, hickories, butternuts, bald cypress, poplar, sweetgum, and green ash populated the third-rate woodlands.

The Mississippi Embayment is the flattest of Kentucky's geological regions. It contains numerous lakes, ponds, and swamps. Hawthorn, water tupelo, water elm, water locust, Nuttal oaks, and water hickories comprised the embayment's woodlands, species that depend on moist soils. In the 1780s, the Mississippi Embayment remained under Chickasaw control. Still, as Thomas Walker's projection of Kentucky's southern boundary to the Mississippi River indicates, white Americans anticipated its acquisition. The Tennessee, Ohio, and Mississippi rivers framed the region that would eventually become more familiar as the Jackson Purchase, but that is a historical label and not a geographical one.

Lying beneath the embayment is the New Madrid fault, the most active earthquake zone in central North America. The tearing apart of the earth's crust, a phenomenon known as a rift, created the New Madrid, rather than the more characteristic sliding of two tectonic plates past each other that is more commonly found in other notable earthquake zones. About 750 million years ago, the continent began to split, but the rift failed. The New Madrid remains as an underground scar. As tectonic plates continue to drift, they reactivate the scarred rift. This drift makes the fault susceptible to earthquakes, despite its being far from places where tectonic plates collide. By examining sand blow deposits—cones of sand that are ejected during seismic activity—and carbon-14 dating, archaeologists and geologists have determined that the region experienced significant earthquakes in 2350 BCE and 300, 900, and 1450 CE. In 1699, a French missionary traveling the Mississippi River made the first historical record of a New Madrid earthquake experience.

In the early 1780s, few white colonists knew of the lands of the Mississippi Embayment, the Western Coalfields, or much of the western Pennyrile. The fertile lands of the Bluegrass and the upper Pennyrile attracted the most attention because they fit the narrative of the new United States—a narrative that men like John Filson promoted. They projected the image that farming would create profit and good citizenship. American leaders were eager to establish a nation founded on republican aspirations like land ownership, independent farming, market participation, and patriarchy. Such ideals inspired Thomas Jefferson when he wrote *Notes on the State of Virginia* in 1781, in which he surveyed the state's natural resources and economic opportunities. He contextualized them in a larger argument about a good society and good republican citizenship. He recorded the navigability of the Salt, Green, and Kentucky Rivers, listing how far one could take a boat up each waterway. He described the potential for iron mining in the Pennyrile, marble mining along the Kentucky River, and sulfur extractions at various salt licks. He praised Louisville as a well-situated port for both economic and military purposes. Combined with the benefits that Jefferson located throughout the rest of Virginia, Kentucky's geographical advantages seemed well suited to the establishment of a commonwealth that would advance the republican ideas that came out of the American Revolutionary War.

Whichever regions Americans traveled through or settled in, they embraced Kentucky as a new place, an American paradise of unbounded promise. When words failed Baptist minister Lewis Craig as he tried to describe the beauty of heaven during a sermon, he exclaimed that "it is a mere Kentucky of a place." A gentleman making a leisurely overland trip in 1792 reported passing 221 Kentucky-bound zealots during a day's ride of thirty miles: "They seemed absolutely infatuated by something like the old crusading spirit to the holy land." Another observer also noted the crusading spirit of the migrants. "Ask these Pilgrims what they expect when they git to Kentucke," he said. "The Answer is land. Have you any? No, but I expect I can get it. Have you anything to pay for land? No. Did you Ever see the Country? No, but Every Body says it is good land." Despite the dangers of the westward journey and the uncertainty of life in America's first West, men, women, and children poured westward chasing a myth.

The Great Migration

In 1777, during the height of Native American–white colonial violence, less than 300 colonists huddled in the forts. As the tide shifted

Table 3.1. Population of Kentucky, 1790–1860

Year	Whites	Enslaved Persons	Free Blacks	Totals
1790	61,133	12,430	114	73,677
1800	179,871	40,343	741	220,955
1810	324,237	80,561	1,711	406,509
1820	434,644	126,732	2,759	564,135
1830	517,787	165,213	4,917	687,917
1840	590,253	182,258	7,317	779,828
1850	761,413	210,981	10,011	982,405
1860	919,517	225,483	10,684	1,155,684

Source: US Census.

in favor of the settler colonials, populations again turned their sights westward, and Kentucky began to fill with inhabitants. By the end of the Revolutionary War in 1783, nearly 30,000 whites and a small number of blacks had crossed the Appalachians. Those numbers swelled to 61,133 whites and 11,994 blacks within seven years; 179,871 whites and 41,084 blacks by 1800; and 324,237 whites and 82,272 blacks in 1810. This great migration into Kentucky was part of a larger peopling of the continent by residents of the new American nation.

In the 1780s, however, Kentucky's colonization was disorganized and beyond the control of any government. Thousands of individuals claimed their piece of the future. Revolutionary War veterans migrated westward, filling much of the Bluegrass, but only 49 percent of them were Virginians with military warrants. Another 34 percent traveled from Maryland and Pennsylvania in nearly equal numbers. They also came in notable numbers from New Jersey and North Carolina. Although they arrived under the rule of Virginia's Land Law, they represented the more diverse populations of the eastern states.

Most migrants from central and southern Virginia, North Carolina, and farther south entered Kentucky through the Cumberland Gap following the Wilderness Road. As it squeezed through the gap, the road was little more than a footpath. It was not paved, heavy rains occasionally made it impassable, and wagons and furniture piled up on the southern side of the gap as settlers discovered they could take few of their belongings any farther. The narrowness

of the passage through the Cumberland Mountains also made it easy for Native American raiding parties and bands of white outlaws to ambush migrants. Many potential settlers waited just south of the gap at Martin's Station until large numbers congregated to provide mutual protection for the rest of the journey. Once into Kentucky, some continued northward toward Boonesborough, but most turned westward along Scagg's Trace to Crab Orchard and then onward to the series of stations, forts, and villages—Whitley's Station, Stanford (formerly St. Asaph), Danville, Harrodsburg (renamed from Harrodstown in 1785), Bardstown. These stations provided safe, midway destinations that made transportation through the southern Bluegrass more secure by the mid-1780s. From there, arriving settlers could continue westward to Louisville or turn northward toward Lexington and the Inner Bluegrass.

Migrants from northern Virginia, Maryland, Pennsylvania, and points north typically traveled down the Ohio River, as did wealthier Virginians who wished to transport furniture and other household items. The most popular mode of travel was the flatboat, a rectangular, flat-bottomed wooden vessel that usually measured at least twenty-five by fifty feet. Most had a cabin, a pen for livestock, and a long rear oar to provide steering. Migrants could purchase ready-made flatboats in Redstone on the Monongahela River south of Pittsburgh for about a dollar per foot. When they arrived at Limestone (now known as Maysville) or the Falls of the Ohio, they often dismantled the flatboats and used the lumber to construct their new homes. Other options included keelboats, ranging from forty to one hundred feet in length and seven to twenty feet in width. Keelboats had pointed ends and a beam or keel running the length of the hull that made the boat relatively easy to steer. Colonists with fewer goods often boarded canoes or dugouts, more narrow crafts that could reach thirty-five to fifty feet in length.

Like the Wilderness Road, Ohio River travel had its own perils. Since flatboats could haul heavy shipments, they moved slowly down the Ohio River. They became easy targets for angry Shawnees and notorious white outlaws like the Harpe Brothers and the bandits who hid out at Cave-in-Rock on the Illinois side of the Ohio River. The river too was inhospitable: sandbars or low water immobilized boats, occasionally for weeks; winter ice, fallen trees, and other hazards threatened to overturn vessels.

Upon arrival at one of Kentucky's river towns, migrants turned inland along roads that, like the Wilderness Road, were unimproved and difficult to traverse. One such road was the Old Buffalo Trace, known as the Limestone Road by the 1780s, which directed colonists to another series of forts, stations, and villages in the northern Bluegrass. Southward from Limestone on the banks of the Ohio, colonists passed through Washington, Mayslick, Blue Licks, Ellis's Station (later renamed Ellisville), Miller's Station (Millersburg), Martin's Station, Hopewell (renamed Paris during the French Revolution in the 1790s), and Bryan's Station before arriving in Lexington, where they resupplied for their final destinations. The road was terrible. It meandered from hill crests, where wagons could tip over, to creek valleys, which often flooded and thus delayed travel. To improve travel and facilitate economic development of their western colony, in 1785, the Virginia legislature assigned three days of annual road maintenance to all males who had reached at least sixteen years of age. Road overseers conscripted neighbors to clear and level paths with hoes and horse-drawn scrapers. Road maintenance became the second required civic activity (militia duty being the first), binding citizens to their communities and the larger nation.

It was also a fundamental part of Virginia's continued organization of its western colony. Virginia state government situated Fayette, Jefferson, and Lincoln Counties in a new judicial District of Kentucky so that residents would not have to make the long journey east of the Appalachians to resolve legal disputes. The District of Kentucky Supreme Court first met on March 3, 1783. John Floyd and Samuel McDowell presided. In 1785, a third justice—George Muter—joined the bench. Additionally, as the original three counties filled with colonists, Virginia began to divide them into smaller administrative units: Nelson was formed in 1784; Bourbon, Madison, and Mercer in 1785; and Woodford and Mason in 1788. Each had a county court and a quarter session court, court clerks and justices of the peace, and representation in the Virginia House of Representatives. Each county in the Kentucky District sent two delegates each session.

Kentucky's morass of land claims and its new civic structures attracted a new leadership. Those who joined this circle not only could read and write but also were trained in oratory, composition, and, most important, the law. Surveying had been shoddy, often performed by inexperienced, illiterate, or unscrupulous men. Many who surveyed never registered with Virginia's land office. Others based their surveys on reference points that were unreliable. Surveys identified a corner of a lot at "three oak trees" or "a sharp bend in the creek"—places that disappeared with the axe or were just too indefinite and, therefore, difficult to determine. One disgruntled colonist complained, "Who buys land there, buys a lawsuit." Daniel Boone and Simon Kenton eventually lost all of their land claims due to poor surveys, as did hundreds of others. The wave of migration that characterized the 1780s and 1790s shifted Kentucky leadership away from the Big Men of the 1770s, who were ill prepared to fight the legal battles necessary to secure land and independence. Boone, Kenton, James Harrod, George Rogers Clark, and others faded from prominence as new men like Samuel McDowell and George Muter arrived. Judges, attorneys, justices of the peace, clerks, legislators—the civic ranks filled with men from every eastern state.

They imagined Kentucky as a new homeland and themselves as leaders of the settler colonialism that would transform Kentucky into part of the American nation.

Many among the new leadership were religious leaders. Far from the prejudices of more settled eastern populations, Kentucky offered an ideal location to protect religious freedoms. In 1781, Lewis Craig led five hundred Separate Baptists through the Cumberland Gap, who settled at Craig's Station (in modern Fayette County). His brother Elijah followed the next year with another group. Unlike Regular Baptists, Separate Baptists had refused to abide by Virginia law that required them to be licensed to preach. As a result, they faced regular intimidation and discrimination. Elijah had been jailed for preaching in 1768. The Separate Baptists' departure for Kentucky, then, was an opportunity to be celebrated. A fellow preacher composed a hymn for the migration:

Let me sing of my best beloved,
Whose vineyard a great while most fruitful prov'd
But lately got blasted and now is earthbound.
Lord Jesus, do plead for Thy poor cumber'd ground.
Great sorrows of late have fill'd my poor heart
To think the dearest of friends soon must part;
A few left behind, while many will go
To settle the desert down the Ohio.

The "Travelling Church," as the group became known, established multiple congregations in the southern Bluegrass. Over the decade, approximately one-quarter of Virginia's Separate and Regular Baptists packed up and moved to Kentucky, eventually requiring the creation of two organizing bodies: the Elkhorn Association in 1785 for Regular Baptist churches, and the South Kentucky Association in 1787 for Separate Baptist churches.

Another large religious migration arrived in 1785. The League of Catholic Families abandoned St. Mary's County, Maryland, in large numbers for Kentucky. They settled in small groups in Nelson, Scott, and Breckinridge Counties. They brought tobacco farming, distilling, and a traditional dish known as Southern Maryland stuffed ham. In 1792, the first Catholic church west of the Appalachian Mountains arose at Rohan Knob, just south of Bardstown. By 1808, the Roman Catholic Church formed the Diocese of Bardstown to serve all Catholics in the western United States.

Other religious groups were not as successful as the Travelling Church or the St. Mary's Catholics in securing their faiths in Kentucky. In 1780, two groups of Dutch Reformists migrated into Kentucky. One group settled the Low Dutch Station along Beargrass Creek and the other at the Low Dutch Station just west of Boonesborough. By 1786, the separate settlements joined to purchase an 8,600-acre tract. Each family was to farm a 200-acre tract, although they held the land collectively through the Low Dutch Company. They committed to call a minister and build a church. They also agreed to maintain their language and other traditions: "that we will indeavouer to have our children Taught and instructed in the Low Dutch Tongue so that they may Read the word of God and understand the Gospel when Preached unto them." But intermittent attacks by Native Americans delayed, and eventually undermined, these efforts. By the turn of the nineteenth century, most of the Dutch colonists had acclimated to Kentucky. They spoke English and joined Presbyterian churches.

Economic opportunity inspired migration as well. Yet economic motives were not always distinct from other factors like religious freedom. In fact, the first verse of the Separate Baptist hymn is about a drought that struck parts of Virginia in 1781, forcing residents to seek better economic conditions elsewhere. Nonetheless, for many colonists seeking economic betterment, religion was a minor consideration. They came on John Filson's promise that they could "work & be rich."

Depleting soils in eastern states pushed many Americans westward. Families like the Drakes and Shotwells of New Jersey purchased land from land speculators before migrating. In 1786, they arrived in Mason County near Mayslick. Daniel Drake recalled his youth when the family "ceased to be Jerseymen, and became Virginians." As Regular Baptists, they found strange the Separate Baptists around them. They carried regional prejudices as well: the "Jersey emigrants, as a body, were superior. Next came the Virginians, and last and lowest, the Marylanders." Drake's derogatory comments generally related to those who were landless and struggling, but to Drake, the son of a small farmer living in a tight-knit community of like-minded persons, his neighbors' poverty reinforced biases from the East.

Poverty was a real problem. A 1781 act empowered county courts to survey lands for people who could not afford to hire surveyors. A family also could acquire four hundred acres for only twenty shillings per hundred acres, a price reduced to thirteen shillings in 1783. Thousands of poorer whites migrated over the next thirty years believing Kentucky to be the "best poor man's country." They had heard that, because Kentucky had never been farmed much, soils were rich with nutrients. Tremendous claims were made as to the size of corn harvests—sixty bushels an acre! Experiments with potential cash crops like tobacco, hemp, flax, and wheat promised profits as well. By 1792, however, the wealthiest 107 men owned one-third of Kentucky, and approximately two-thirds of white adult males could not secure land. In the Inner Bluegrass, over 80 percent of households were landless. Inequality was everywhere.

Still, they came. When he traveled westward in 1803, Methodist bishop Francis Asbury wrote of the "men, women, and children, almost naked, paddling bare-foot and bare-legged along, or laboring up the rocky hills, whilst those who are best off have only a horse for two or three children to ride at once." Unable to find land, the majority of white men became tenants to large landholders. They labored as hands or hirelings to pay rent while their wives and children created supplemental income as domestic help or through the home production of such things as sugar loaves, needlework, or soap. No longer could the desperate—poor mothers, abandoned wives, orphaned children, and vulnerable widows—be

hidden behind fort walls, and that abjection was conspicuous. "All were illiterate, but in various degrees—& all were poor, or in moderate circumstances," described one new colonist. Another noted of his new Kentucky neighbors that they were "indolent, ignorant people . . . destitute of every convenience of life."

Poverty existed in every county. Debt cases were the most common issues that came before local courts, which made the plights of poor families a community concern. After statehood in 1792, the Kentucky General Assembly required county courts to appoint overseers of the poor, who had the power to regulate private households. They provided cash and supplies to the poor, sent the feeble to recover under individual care, and placed orphaned children with new families. But they also stripped children from single mothers and contracted or indentured them as apprentices, domestic servants, or field workers. The overseers integrated the poor into existing households because they blamed poverty on the failure of white men to secure independence and, therefore, to fulfill their husbandly and fatherly roles. A 1795 vagrancy law not only targeted loitering and begging but also criminalized men who "quit their habitations" and left "wives or children without suitable means of subsistence." The law charged local sheriffs to administer lashings to such men.

It is difficult to exaggerate the impact of the mass migration across the Appalachian Mountains. In less than twenty years, Kentucky boomed from a population of several hundred colonists to over seventy-three thousand colonists. In addition, many expected Kentucky to provide a solution to the economic problems of the East. These pressures intensified the strain placed on governmental, social, economic, and political structures. Frustrations ran high. So many had traveled to Kentucky for land, yet for most, land was inaccessible.

Colonists and promoters had glowed about Kentucky's promise. In 1775, Anglican minister John Brown wondered, "What a Buzzel is this amongst People about Kentuck? To hear people speak of it one would think it was a new Paradise." Many Americans viewed Kentucky as a new Promised Land, not just because it offered economic opportunity but also because, after the Revolutionary War, it fit nicely the notion of providential destiny: that God had chosen the Americans for the grandest experiment in history—freedom—and had given them North America on which to create it. That ideal faded rather quickly in Kentucky as religious and ethnic differences, poverty, and other tensions began to manifest.

The land itself seemed to show strain. "Where the early stations were established, the wild herbage, consisting of Cane & pea vine is entirely eat out and the place of it supplied by weeds," complained David Meade. Trees were essential to everyday life—houses, barns, mills, furniture, rail fences, wagons and coaches, and fuel for heating, cooking, and salt manufacturing—and were cut down at alarming rates. As deforestation accelerated, boundary markers like "three oak trees" disappeared, creating an ever-growing morass of legal suits to protect property claims. Thousands of individual decisions to cut down a tree here or dig up limestone rocks there collectively transformed Kentucky's landscape. Erosion of topsoils became more common. Canebrakes disappeared as food for domestic livestock, which then turned their appetites to cornfields. This forced farmers to create pasturage for their herds and to protect farmlands with fences. From killing off the bison to clearing the land to fencing properties, thousands of small actions revised the natural environment, transforming Kentucky into a landscape that resembled those back east.

A Society with Slaves in a Slave Society

Colonists who secured land were advantaged in Kentucky, and most needed labor to work their lands. During the decades of extractive colonialism, British merchants and traders had relied on Native Americans to do much of the work for them. They traded manufactured goods for much-desired skins and furs. Settler colonialism, in contrast, pushed Native Americans from the land. Enslaved African Americans replaced their labor. One cheap labor source succeeded another. Enslaved peoples joined in the colonization of Kentucky, although never by choice and usually without hope of creating a sense of home for themselves.

Slavery as an economic and legal institution varied significantly within the new American nation. Many northern states functioned as "societies with slaves" in which the institution was not necessary to local economies. Some states had made slavery and the slave trade illegal. They had fewer large-scale farms, and enslaved African Americans often worked in domestic service, manufacturing, artisanal trades, or as dockhands. While men with political power in these societies with slaves may or may not have enslaved people, they did not rely on slavery to bolster their authority. In contrast, the southern states were "slave societies," where the institution was at the center of politics, local economies, and social identities. In these societies, slave ownership was necessary for the acquisition of power. Slaveholders constituted the ruling class, and relationships between slave owners and enslaved peoples shaped society and daily life.

In the 1780s, as thousands of colonists arrived in Kentucky from various states and regions in the East, they brought a variety of attitudes about slavery with them that made political agreement on the institution difficult. Despite the creation of some plantations, a plantation system never developed in Kentucky, and even some of the largest farms were worked without enslaved labor. Yet, because Kentucky was part of Virginia, its economy, politics, and race relations formed under the laws of the oldest and most traditional of the eastern slave societies. Kentucky, therefore, classified as a society with slaves embedded in a slave society.

Enslaved peoples arrived early in Kentucky. They accompanied the earliest white colonists and occasionally met similar fates at the hands of Native Americans—either captivity or death. In 1773, Shadrach was fortunate to survive the Native Americans who killed James Boone and another young man. In 1775, Sam died as he worked for Daniel Boone in clearing the Wilderness Road. Three years later, London shot at Shawnees throughout the night as they lay siege to Fort Boone, until the flash of his gun finally revealed his position to a Shawnee marks-man. In 1782, "Black Sam" was in the fields when he heard an attack on his owner's cabin. He noticed a Shawnee placing one of the fami-ly's babies in the grass, and he stealthily retrieved the child and raced to a nearby station to get help. Near Crab Orchard, an attack on Hannah Wood's cabin ended when one Native American breeched the cabin door. The family's enslaved laborer wrestled him to the floor and, lying un-derneath, held on while Hannah and her daugh-ter hacked the intruder to death with an ax.

The most famous enslaved African Ameri-can was Monk. His owner, James Estill, forced him along with his enslaved wife to migrate westward in the mid-1770s. At Boonesbor-ough, Monk farmed, tanned hides, and made gunpowder. He was credited with cultivating an apple orchard at Boonesborough. When Es-till established his own station in 1780, Monk, his wife, and a newborn son relocated. Two years later, Monk played the central role in the Battle of Little Mountain. Estill and fellow white settlers tried to recover Monk, who had been captured during a Wyandotte attack on Estill's Station. Estill and thirteen others were killed or badly injured. Monk escaped and car-ried an injured man back to the station, earn-ing his freedom from Estill's son in gratitude for his bravery. He may have been the first slave manumitted in Kentucky. He lived out the rest of his life as a Baptist minister.

Most African Americans lived with more difficulty. Enslaved labor met an immediate need in Kentucky: providing bodies to clear the land, plant and harvest foods, and cook for white colonists. There are many stories of cou-rageous enslaved peoples like Monk who sur-vived Native American attacks. A large majori-ty of them, however, would not have faced such life-threatening circumstances had it not been for their enslavement. In the 1780s, white col-onists like land speculator John May sent their enslaved laborers ahead to prepare lands and cabins. Thomas Hart confessed that it was eas-ier and safer to "send a parcel of poor slaves where I dare not go myself." John Bruce left two slaves behind to work his land claim while he gathered supplies back east: the man was

scalped and the woman taken captive. So too did Nathaniel and William Ewing leave slaves behind when they went to Virginia to register their claims. One of the enslaved men panicked and fled to a nearby station. He returned a few days later to find the others slaughtered.

With some modifications, over a century of Virginia slave laws set the patterns of Ken-tucky enslavement. By 1670, law declared that children born to enslaved women would en-ter into slavery. It also prescribed that owners who killed their enslaved laborers in the course of punishing them were to be acquitted of any crime. A slave code of 1705 denied enslaved persons the right to marry, forbade them from testifying in court, required written permis-sions for them to travel, and established harsh physical punishments for even the smallest of crimes (since enslaved people could seldom pay fines). Other colonies soon appropriated Virginia's code and later laws as well. They ad-opted measures of the 1723 law of the colony that made illegal any slave gathering, stripped free blacks of the right to vote, and denied all blacks—enslaved or free—the license to carry weapons. In 1750, Virginia defined the dif-ference between servants and slaves. This law explicitly identified the latter as property that could be inherited, bought, and sold, and other colonies again followed suit.

Slave laws that were passed before the American Revolutionary War dictated the for-mation of slavery in Virginia's western colony. But laws passed in the 1780s addressed new is-sues related to Kentucky's growth. A law passed in 1782 restricted slave owners from "hiring out" or renting their chattel to another per-son. In the same year, Virginia set terms for manumitting slaves based on their contribu-tion to the revolutionary effort. Monk received his freedom through this manumission law. In 1785, Virginia required migrants who relocat-ed to Kentucky to swear that they had no in-tention of selling slaves. Three years later, its general assembly strengthened the law. One settler described the consequences slave owners might face if they did not follow the require-ment: anyone who brought enslaved laborers into Kentucky and neglected "to take the Oath prescribed, by law his Negroes were entitled to freedom, and himself liable to heavy penalties."

In the 1780s, however, it did not appear that Virginia's slave laws would apply well to Kentucky's underdeveloped economic and social structures. The price of transportation to market worked against cash crops, and the Spanish interfered with shipments through New Orleans. Despite the influx of enslaved African Americans, there was just not enough agricultural demand to keep them busy. So, despite the law forbidding it, many colonists hired out their African American slaves to make sure that their investments in enslaved laborers would be profitable.

Despite the presence of a market for labor, white servants were not always the best choice. White laborers were not enslaved, so they had the freedom to work for whomever they wished and to leave whenever they wanted. If they contracted or indentured themselves, however, they often had to fulfill a specific term before leaving. White laborers acted more independently than employers liked. One landowner complained that, when he hired whites, they were apathetic "and expect at all times to be at the same table with their masters." They found that hiring an enslaved laborer to help with farm and domestic tasks on a seasonal basis presented a good solution to this problem. The *Kentucky Gazette* routinely ran ads that read similar to this one: "TO BE HIRED . . . a number of negroes consisting of men, women, boys and girls one of them a good carpenter— the property of Mrs. Annie Christian." Given

the variety of colonists' religious and regional backgrounds, many considered slavery an unethical institution, but even they hired a slave or two on occasion.

While beneficial to slave owners and those who employed enslaved persons, hiring out was against the law for a reason: African Americans could often negotiate some share of the profit and eventually purchase freedom. When John Craig joined his brothers in the "Travelling Church" migration of the mid-1780s, he brought Peter Durrett with him to Kentucky. Durrett had asked Craig to purchase him so he could join his wife, one of Craig's enslaved laborers, in the move westward. Craig hired out the couple in Lexington, where they saved sufficient money to purchase a house. Durrett began preaching to crowds of the town's enslaved population. He eventually established the African Baptist Church in 1790, the first black congregation in Kentucky and the third oldest in the United States. Still, Durrett and other enslaved persons who benefited from hiring out posed challenges to Kentucky's evolving social order. As in Virginia's slave society, Kentucky's social order had rules designed to create a laboring class that would be in perpetual servitude. A church for enslaved and free blacks tested laws, particularly those against assembly and education. Without good economic purposes, slavery in Kentucky became less about labor and more about class and race relations.

Although they had no real plan for how to use enslaved blacks in Kentucky, most white colonists brought them anyway because

Table 3.2. Distribution of Slavery, 1790

County	Free Persons	Enslaved Persons	Total Population	Percentage Enslaved
Bourbon	6,929	908	7,837	11.5
Fayette	14,658	3,752	18,410	20.3
Jefferson	3,862	902	4,765	18.9
Lincoln	5,454	1,094	6,548	16.7
Madison	5,035	737	5,772	12.7
Mason	2,500	229	2,729	8.3
Mercer	5,752	1,339	7,091	18.8
Nelson	10,067	1,248	11,315	11.0
Woodford	6,900	2,220	9,210	24.1
Totals	61,247	12,430	73,677	16.9

Source: US Census, 1790.

"The Coffle Gang." (J. Winston Coleman Jr. Collection on Slavery in Kentucky, University of Kentucky Special Collections and Research Center, Lexington, KY)

that was the tradition in the eastern states. As northern states began to dismantle slavery, arguments that the institution was counter to the ideals that had inspired the new nation rumbled throughout Virginia as well. But enslaved laborers were a monetary investment, and their critical role in Virginia's staple crop economy made them indispensable. In Kentucky, tradition, not economy, led to the establishment of slavery. Enslaved laborers, however, did come to serve an important economic role: they were a form of money. They symbolized the wealth, property, and inheritances that some men could leave to their children.

By 1790, slavery had become most entrenched in the wealthiest counties of the Inner Bluegrass. Enslaved laborers comprised over 19.4 percent of Fayette, Woodford, and Bourbon Counties. Although primarily rural, each of these counties had at least one village or town where enslaved African Americans were a sizeable portion of the community, especially at Lexington in Fayette County. Even outside the villages, enslaved African Americans were found everywhere. By 1790, 12,430 slaves resided in Kentucky, comprising over 16.9 percent of the population, and over 17 percent of

white families owned at least one slave. In other words, nearly one in five Kentuckians was black and enslaved. Very few whites lived without some contact with slavery.

Enslaved laborers were so ubiquitous that even the humblest of white colonists tried to purchase one or two. Among the Jersey colonists who settled in Mayslick, all except Isaac Drake became slaveholders (but even Drake, who opposed slavery on moral grounds, hired a slave on occasion). The desire for a little help and a little status stimulated the slave market, inspiring colonists to bring their enslaved laborers to Kentucky solely to sell them, contrary to Virginia laws. Isaac Drake's son remembered seeing along the Limestone Road "great wagons, laden with merchandise for the interior; the caravans of travelers, mounted on horseback; and the gangs of negroes on foot— all moving south." Often chained together in coffles, enslaved blacks were sold at market sites and through newspaper advertisements. By 1792, at least 10 percent of Inner Bluegrass slave owners had purchased slaves on the market during the previous five years. Prices rose higher in Kentucky than in Virginia, and enslaved laborers became liquid assets. A newly

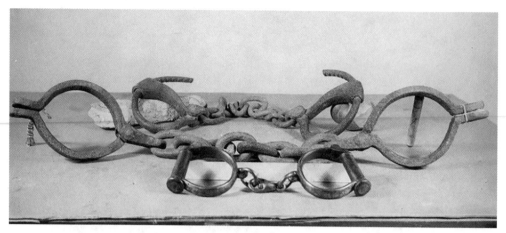

Slave handcuffs and chains. (J. Winston Coleman Jr. Collection on Slavery in Kentucky, University of Kentucky Special Collections and Research Center, Lexington, KY)

arrived colonist could expect to pay $350 to $450 for a female laborer and between $400 and $700 for a male laborer. Samuel McDowell encouraged a friend to bring "7 or 8 Negroes amongst whome would be Some young fellows of which I might have my Choice and I might depend that Some of them would be very valuable and likely."

Once enslaved laborers became a significant portion of the population, slavery also served to police race relations. As with other institutions, the state structured and administered slavery, but it also had the force of thousands of owners, slave traders and auctioneers, overseers, and slave patrollers behind it. Laws limited how harshly owners and overseers could treat their enslaved laborers, but enforcement was lax. James Rodgers, who owned lands near Bryan's Station, was widely known as "negro whipper John" for his abuse of enslaved African Americans. The slave patrol constituted the most effective form of control. In 1727, Virginia had established slave patrols as a way to preserve slavery and protect whites from black insurrection. When militias were not employed against Native Americans, their members formed slave patrols. They harassed African Americans who were "strolling about," broke up church meetings where slaves might learn to read, stormed black homes and terrorized families, and shot indiscriminately into

black gatherings. In 1795, antislavery Baptist preacher David Barrow complained that "If the Indians whip and cruelly treat the whites; it is no more than the whites serve the blacks."

Importantly, as more African Americans arrived as enslaved Kentuckians, white and black relationships formed, and a generation of cross-racial children cropped up in late-eighteenth-century Kentucky. According to Virginia law, children of enslaved black women and white men followed their mothers' status into enslavement. Their presence served as a reminder that, despite their white parentage, laws created for Virginia's slave society denied blacks and their children the freedoms that white Americans associated with the new western lands. Despite the handful of free persons of color in Kentucky by 1790, few whites viewed blacks as anything but laborers and possibly a threat to their security.

Patriarchy, Women, and Families

Historian David Hackett Fischer once wrote, "Whenever a culture exists for many generations in conditions of chronic insecurity, it develops an ethic that exalts war above work, force above reason, and men above women." In the 1770s, Kentucky's colonial population had been nearly all male and all white. Big Man culture evidenced the rule of force and violence. By 1790, however, 39 percent of Kentucky's colonists were white women, another 17 percent were enslaved, and 24 percent were white males under sixteen years of age. The percentages remained very similar for the next decade. In other words, only 20 percent of the population were free white adult males. Still, they dominated as patriarchs over Kentucky's political and social structures.

Patriarchy is a social system in which men hold power on account of their presumed political and moral authority. It was central to republicanism, the ideology of the era of the American Revolution. When the colonists broke free from Great Britain, they rejected the monarchical form of government that had not represented their interests. Thomas Jefferson, John Adams, and other political theorists encouraged a representative government modeled very much on the ancient republics of Greece and Rome. These ancient republics celebrated the virtuous citizen, someone willing to sacrifice his private interests for the sake of the community. A man could not be virtuous if he depended on others because he then would always be obligated to their demands and not to the best interest of the community. Nor could a man be virtuous if he were overly involved in pursuing profits. A man who was too consumed with making profits always would be seeking his own interests. Only through disinterested, virtuous, independent patriarchy could a republic of equal, active, and independent citizens exist. Such patriarchy gave men a moral authority over dependents—women, children, servants, and slaves.

In many ways, colonial Kentucky was an experiment in republican patriarchy. Promises of abundant land, fine soils, and good harvests drew thousands of white men, who all knew the challenge of producing for far-away markets. The mountains made trade with the East very problematic and expensive, and commerce down the Mississippi River was difficult. Local economies and subsistence farming would be the way of life, which made it easier to avoid the temptations of the market. Militias, slave patrols, and road clearing engaged citizens in civic service. Such citizenship would lead to

a government "of the people," and in return, government would reinforce the virtuous patriarchy to which independent men aspired. In order to inspire good republicanism, everyone else had to accept their roles as well: County courts could fine poor white men who did not act as good patriarchs in their households. These courts and overseers of the poor even could take away their children. Enslaved peoples who learned to read or assembled without permission became targets of the slave patrols.

White women, too, found their lives regulated and limited as patriarchal institutions formed in Kentucky. In the 1780s and early 1790s, most fulfilled their roles as good republican wives and mothers. They contributed to the work and production of households, reared children, and supported their husbands. Under Virginia law, married women were under coverture, which meant that they had little legal right to property or guardianship of their children. Such *femes covert* (covered women) relied on husbands as "wing, protection, and cover." When women had no husband, father, or other close male relative to assume that role, county courts often stepped in to protect and dictate their lives. For *femes covert,* their labor and status belonged to the men in their lives.

The majority of white women lived on farms where they helped their husbands raise a variety of vegetables for domestic consumption. They dabbled in corn, wheat, oats, flax, hemp, and tobacco for both domestic use and possibly sale in local markets. Alongside their husbands, and with the help of enslaved laborers, contracted servants, relatives, and neighbors, many women also harvested crops, shelled corn, slaughtered hogs and chickens, cleared and burned brush, cut firewood, tapped maple trees, and plowed the land. They made domestic productions by churning butter, smoking pork, molding candles, baking bread, making sugar loaves, distilling salt from brine water, and spinning cloth. Even when the demands of farming waned in the late fall and winters they gathered firewood, ground meal, and salted meats. Farming was time-consuming and exhausting for all members of the household.

White women in villages lived differently. Many tended vegetable gardens and raised chickens, pigs, and cows. Their domestic productions resembled those of farm women. But village women were also more likely to entertain guests as hostesses in taverns or inns or to assist merchant husbands in stocking shelves. Some taught French, needlework, or dance to the daughters of wealthier neighbors. Farm women occasionally enjoyed social outlets at corn huskings, barn raisings, weddings, and other frolics. Village women, in contrast, were expected to be social constantly: at markethouses and in stores, on court days when acquaintances from throughout a county would gather, at dances and churches, in passing on the streets, and increasingly even at slave auctions. As one colonist wrote a few weeks after arriving in Lexington in 1788, "Since I have been here I have been visited by the genteel people in the place and receiv'd several Invitations both in town & Country." Even sociability was a chore, however. A woman had to be educated properly, which is why schools existed to teach French and dance.

The chaos of colonialism, particularly widowhood and abandonment, transformed many white women into *femes sole*—single women who lacked the protection of male relatives. Although patriarchal laws and institutions still limited their lives, many became heads of their own households, and some accumulated substantial wealth, as we saw with Ann Kennedy Wilson Pogue Lindsay McGinty. Between 1787 and 1791 in Fayette County, thirty-one *femes sole* managed their own households, often with enslaved laborers or contracted servants. Considering the inequality in land ownership in the Inner Bluegrass, those thirty-one women represented a significant achievement of independence.

At Bullitt's Lick (in today's Bullitt County), Anne Christian became a wealthy and influential *feme sole* when she inherited the local salt manufactory upon her husband's death in 1786. In time, Christian hired Hannah Hinch as a business manager after Hinch's husband died. Christian's sister-in-law, Mary Daniel, supervised the laborers and operated a tavern. In Lexington, Rebecca Green filed for divorce in 1793, when her husband abandoned her, but the General Assembly did not grant her request

for five more years. Still, she acted as an independent woman. She transformed her Lexington home into a cape manufactory, where she and Mary, her seamstress, produced women's clothing. Green had a credit line at a local store. She sold her own productions and owned her property, including Mary. In Mercer County in the early 1790s, Barbara Bibbs left her husband and accumulated enough property that her husband tried to sue for it during their divorce. The court determined that she had earned it as a *feme sole* and had full right to it. In Fayette County, Sarah Garton and her husband Uriah agreed to end their marriage in 1788. Four years later, she advertised cider in the *Kentucky Gazette*. These women represented different statuses and levels of success as *femes sole,* but they all lived independently.

Whether *femes sole* or *femes covert,* most white women lived in kinship networks. Most Kentucky colonists had extended families with whom they often migrated and who provided guidance and support. Sometimes kin were more immediate relatives like siblings; sometimes they were more distant cousins; other times they were fictive kin, like church migrations filled with "brothers" and "sisters." In all cases, they guided and supported each nuclear family, the social unit at the heart of republicanism. Colonists migrated to Kentucky for land, but in most cases, it was land on which families would take up residence and remain. One migrant voiced his wish to have a house: "let it be in whatever part of the Globe was most agreeable, I care not where it is, so we could all be together." The house was eventually in Kentucky, where his mother, four siblings, nieces and nephews, two aunts and uncles, and numerous cousins joined him.

Migration to Kentucky severed eastern female kinship networks, which forced women to become dependent upon their husbands. Once they settled in Kentucky, white men could create new businesses or political relationships. Civic structures like militias and road maintenance crews facilitated their sociability. In contrast, life in Kentucky offered women few avenues for the creation of new social networks, and sisters, mothers, or other female kin seldom joined women who left with their husbands to move west. Most often these female relatives were obligated to remain with their own patriarchs back east. Women, therefore, often remained isolated, yearning for the connections they left behind. Rosanna Wallace recognized the "little prospect I have of ever seeing my dear mammy again in this world." Women like Mary Trigg, who lost husbands after they arrived, often felt as if they were "in a wilderness country far distant from every relation I have on earth." Letters became the way in which Kentucky women sustained kinship, knowing they had little chance of ever seeing their relatives again.

Many women threw themselves into taking care of husbands and children. Raising children to become good citizens became critical to appearing a good republican family. In the East, schools and homes worked in tandem to develop model citizens. A few private academies appeared in colonial Kentucky: a grammar school arose in 1785 near Danville and four years later moved to Lexington as Transylvania Seminary; in 1794, Kentucky Academy opened in Woodford County. Schools offered curricula heavy with Latin, Greek, and natural history—subjects that trained students in classical republican values. Most Kentucky colonists could not afford to send their sons to private academies, and without widespread access to schools, the burden of education fell upon mothers. Sons learned the demands of farming or business; daughters learned domestic skills. Teaching proper gender roles took precedence as the primary educational goal. Daniel Drake remembered how "it was quite too 'gaal-ish' for a boy to milk." There were correct gender roles that, if maintained, helped a young man or woman find a suitable mate and become a contributing citizen.

Many children often found themselves indentured because they were orphaned or lived with single mothers, or because their families were desperate for money. Overseers of the poor also sometimes determined that they would be better off in a different home. Indentured children moved to the homes of craftsmen and merchants. Boys received training for market-able skills, like weaving, masonry, tanning, or metalworking. Girls generally were bound to domestic service, although they occasionally would learn needlework, spinning, knitting, or other crafts. Typically, masters agreed to clothe, feed, and educate their servants in reading, writing, and, for boys, arithmetic. In addition, they set aside cash and a new suit of clothes to be provided the apprentice upon completion of the indenture. They also promised to treat the individual "with humanity."

Masters, however, did not always treat their indentured apprentices humanely. Physical punishment was common. Apprentices often ran away when they became unhappy with their situations. Masters placed ads in the *Kentucky Gazette* to recover them, with texts similar to the one that follows: "One cent reward— Ran away from subscriber on Monday last an indented apprentice by name John Nash. All persons are forbid to harbor him under penalties of the law. The above reward for the return of said boy to me, *but no thanks.*" Another placed in the newspaper stated: "One cent reward for Cecelia, aged 14 years. Persons are warned not to trust or employ her." The wording of these ads reveals that masters may have been ambivalent about taking back their runaway servants. Unlike runaway slaves, who were a substantial monetary investment, indentured apprentices often proved more trouble than they were worth. Some were indolent; others stole; and all of them required a final payment in cash and clothes, a gift that many masters were willing to forego.

The Road to Statehood

In 1776, George Rogers Clark considered statehood for Kentucky. After all, the colonies were in revolution against the mother country, and independence was in the air. Four years later, Kentucky and Illinois colonists petitioned the Continental Congress to create a new state along the Ohio River, but they were unsuccessful. Thomas Paine argued in *The Public Good* (1780) that the Proclamation Line of 1763 had effectively stripped Virginia of any claim to Kentucky. According to this reasoning, the trans-Appalachian West was actually a colony of the new nation and not of one particular state. After *The Public Good* was published, Kentucky colonists began to panic that their land titles might not be valid. The movement for statehood, therefore, accelerated.

After the war, Kentucky's colonists had legitimate complaints against Virginia. State officials seemed indifferent to the incessant violence between its colonists and Native Americans. The Virginia General Assembly passed a law that prevented offensive actions against Native Americans without its prior approval. State taxes were unfair: colonists paid the same rates as other Virginians but received fewer services. Even the postal service had not been extended to Kentucky. A 1782 tax charged five shillings per one hundred acres on treasury warrants that exceeded fourteen hundred acres. The tax hit large landowners and surveyors quite hard.

Unfavorable trade that siphoned money to the East hurt Kentucky economically and hindered its economic development. Neither Virginia nor the new national government, established by the Articles of Confederation in 1781, expressed concern about Spanish control over the Mississippi River that stymied trade in Kentucky. In September 1784, the Spanish closed the river and New Orleans to American use. The Confederation Congress tried to negotiate a treaty through John Jay, its secretary of foreign affairs. The Americans would concede usage of the Mississippi River for twenty-five to thirty years in return for commercial trade that would benefit merchants in the East. Even though the treaty was eventually blocked, Kentucky's colonists were furious. Some observers noted how the complaints from Kentucky echoed those of the Americans during the revolutionary war: high taxes, inaccessibility to courts, impediments to self-protection, unfavorable trade, and tyrannical government. The only difference, explained one Kentucky colonist, was that Kentucky did have representation in Virginia's General Assembly, in contrast to Americans' lack of representation in the British Parliament.

Not surprisingly, then, in 1784 when Benjamin Logan, colonel of the Lincoln County militia, called a meeting to discuss rumors of a Shawnee attack, the issues of separation and statehood arose. Some attendees wanted to strike against the Shawnees. One attendee suggested that Kentucky separate from Virginia so that residents could take matters into their own hands. In the end, there was no real threat, but the idea of independence had been raised. The men decided to reconvene in Danville in late December 1784 to discuss separation from Virginia. Each militia company was to send a delegate.

On the issue of separation, politically astute colonists fell into three, loosely associated factions: partisans, the "country party," and the "court party." Partisans generally were landless, and they wanted Kentucky to separate from Virginia so that the new state would break up the large landholdings and redistribute property more equitably. Ebenezer Brooks, Samuel Taylor, and John Campbell were among the leading partisans. They wished to replace the hierarchical structures inherited from Virginia with a more democratic government that would represent their interests. These men had been excluded from the new leadership that had arisen with the new arrivals of the 1780s. Their lack of education and status worked against them.

The country faction was comprised mostly of planters and surveyors, men with large landholdings and slaveholdings determined to maintain their properties. Thomas Marshall led the country party. In 1783, he had received appointment as Kentucky's surveyor general, and he had a vested interest in making sure land distribution served those who paid for it. His nephew Humphrey Marshall was the faction's most controversial member. He often infuriated his opponents and found himself embroiled in duels and fights. Robert Bullitt, Robert Breckinridge, John Edwards, and Joseph Crockett joined the Marshalls in pushing for separation on terms that would preserve the structures of social and political power that had migrated westward and that favored men with land.

Judges and lawyers dominated the court faction. Most had arrived too late to acquire large tracts of the best lands. As members of the new leadership of the 1780s, they were adept at delivering speeches, drafting documents, and persuading constituents. They also were interested in economic development, specifically in expanding markets for agricultural productions and creating opportunity for manufacturing. Some, like James Wilkinson, thought that Kentucky should not only separate from Virginia but also might want to leave the new American nation as well. Other court party leaders, like John Fowler, Benjamin Sebastian, Harry Innes, John Brown, Caleb Wallace, and Samuel McDowell, were less certain about leaving the nation, but they knew that if they were to elevate their own influence they would need to sever ties with Virginia.

Between 1784 and 1792, Kentucky colonists met ten times to discuss separation. Samuel McDowell, who presided over all except the first and ninth conventions, and Thomas Todd, who was the clerk for all but the first convention, provided some continuity. The Virginia Constitution of 1776 established an orderly procedure by which a territory could separate, but that procedure made quick separation difficult. When delegates at the first convention decided that they wanted representation according to population rather than county at the second convention, Virginia blocked that change to protect the interests of the wealthiest of its western migrants—specifically the country faction. Although the conventions wanted to represent the wishes of the "good people of Kentucky," the process was drawn out. After each convention, representatives had to return to their counties to learn the wishes of their constituents. Other circumstances also impeded speedy separation. In 1786, the fourth convention did not have a quorum because so many delegates were engaged in expeditions against the Shawnees. By the time they returned, Virginia had called for another convention. When Kentucky colonists appealed for statehood in 1788, the outgoing Confederation Congress told them they would have to wait until the new federal government that would be formed under the Constitution took its seat.

The slow road to statehood allowed colonists to discuss and debate the issues. The process cultivated a body of thoughtful and knowl-

edgeable leaders who would become Kentucky's future statesmen. In particular, the Danville Political Club, which organized in December 1786, became the center of political discussion. The club's membership, including Harry Innes, Christopher Greenup, Thomas Todd, George Muter, Peyton Short, Samuel McDowell, and Benjamin Sebastian, debated topics related to separation: the best structure for a general assembly, the use of the Mississippi River, and the essential elements of a constitution. They conducted a four-meeting analysis of the new federal constitution. They also engaged tangential topics like the feasibility of tobacco and intermarriage with Native Americans. Discussions were often heated. A visitor complained in 1787 that he was "very much disturbed by a Political Club which met in the next room where we slept and kept us awake until 12 or 1 o'clock." The club's discussions often served as practice for debates during the conventions.

The new Constitution of the United States, ratified in 1789, posed an additional challenge to Kentucky's move toward statehood. Five years into the statehood process, the national government changed from one that was a loose confederation of states to one that was more federal and centralized. When Virginia held its ratification convention for the new national constitution, Kentucky sent fourteen delegates. The proponents of the Constitution, led by James Madison and John Marshall, defended the document and pointed out that its amending processes allowed changes to be made. George Nicholas, Madison's friend and correspondent, assured the Kentucky delegates specifically that the new government would benefit them. He was preparing to move to Kentucky himself. On June 25, 1789, the convention ratified the Constitution by an eighty-nine to seventy-nine vote. Ten of the Kentucky colonists voted against it.

While most Kentucky colonists wanted to remain part of the new nation (and some even wanted to stay in Virginia), a few tested the idea of seceding from both Virginia and the United States. As members of the court faction, they believed their best opportunity to overcome the advantages of the landed gentry was to forge a relationship with the Spanish and situate themselves as leaders of the alliance.

James Wilkinson led this scheme. A Marylander, Wilkinson had a solid reputation during the American Revolutionary War, despite his occasional disagreements with superiors like George Washington. He moved to Kentucky in 1784, opened a store in Lexington, and speculated in land. He also created a following of loyal constituents through his friendliness, generosity of food and drink, and extravagant speaking and writing styles. But Wilkinson was not economically successful. In 1787, he traveled to New Orleans seeking relief. He convinced Louisiana governor Esteban Rodríguez Miró that he could deliver Kentucky into the Spanish orbit and, by directing immigration into the Mississippi River valley, prevent an American invasion of Spanish territory. In return, he wanted a trade monopoly, a royal pension, and rank and position in the Spanish military. Miró had to refer the requests to Spain but offered Wilkinson the rights to sell $37,000 worth of goods in New Orleans. Wilkinson provided the only outlet through which Kentucky colonists could get their goods to market. Profits soared as Wilkinson shipped Kentucky produce down river. Miró eventually had to ask him to curtail the shipments.

Wilkinson's success coincided with the seventh convention in November 1788. The delegates were furious because the Confederation Congress delayed consideration of their statehood petition for the new constitutional government. Some men demanded immediate secession from the United States. During debate, Wilkinson emphasized that neither the national government nor the state government had helped Kentucky colonists gain access to the Mississippi River. With Spain's newfound interest, he contended that they should draft a constitution, separate from Virginia, and organize a government. He argued that, if the United States were not interested in Kentucky's admission, then Kentucky colonists should look elsewhere. Wilkinson then turned to John Brown, Kentucky's former senator in the Virginia legislature and one of Wilkinson's faithful supporters. Through conversations with Spanish diplomat

Portrait of James Wilkinson, by John Wesley Jarvis, c. 1820–1825. (The Filson Historical Society, Louisville, KY)

Don Diego de Gardoqui, Brown had learned that Spain would *never* grant river rights to the United States. Wilkinson hoped this would push delegates to his position. But Brown's response was lukewarm: he had grown distrustful of his old associate's intentions. Wilkinson's appeal, therefore, persuaded no one.

The following year, Wilkinson returned to New Orleans to shore up his finances. He wrote up a list for Governor Miró that included a number of prominent Kentucky colonists who, Wilkinson believed, could be bought. Miró provided some expense money. Wilkinson, however, had missed the opportunity. By 1791 he left Kentucky to serve in the Legion of the United States, an army organized under Anthony Wayne to deal with Native Americans north of the Ohio River.

Historians do not agree on Wilkinson's goals or seriousness in the Spanish Conspiracy. Did he aspire to move an independent Kentucky into the Spanish empire, perhaps as a semi-independent province that he would govern? Or did he finesse a gullible Governor Miró into granting trade concessions solely to line his own pocket? Or did he have no goal at all, just reacting to the circumstances in order to get whatever he could?

Whatever his goals, Wilkinson did inspire movement toward statehood. His failure to persuade the seventh convention to declare independence provided incentive to the country faction to grab statehood as quickly as possible. In December 1789, Virginia passed the Enabling Act (the fourth one designed to help Kentucky separate from Virginia). Better known as the Virginia Compact, the law set forth the conditions of separation, calling for another convention in July 1790. If that convention accepted the terms of the compact, then a convention would be called to finalize a new state government. The contingency—the new United States Congress had to agree to all terms of the compact by November 1791. The details involved the release of Virginia from all obligations in regard to Kentucky, the retention of the boundaries that existed for the District of Kentucky, and the securing and validation of land grants. Kentucky would assume "a just proportion" of Virginia's lingering war debt and also pay the costs of Virginia's expeditions against Native Americans that had taken place since January 1785. Virginia would still hold rights to issue military warrants in Kentucky until May 1792. Use of the Ohio River was to be free and available to all citizens of the United States.

The ninth convention voted twenty-four to eighteen to accept the terms of the Virginia Compact and arranged for the final constitutional convention to meet in Danville in April 1792. On February 4, 1791, Congress passed the bill to admit Kentucky to the United States, and on June 1, 1792, Kentucky formally became the fifteenth state.

The Vanishing Indian

From the first white family's arrival at Boonesborough to the founding of a new state, the myth behind Kentucky's settler colonialism was that American colonists had occupied free or virgin land. It was a difficult claim to make. Burial mounds were visible throughout Ken-

tucky, attesting to the presence of native peoples sometime in the past. Archaeological evidence shows that Fort Ancients and Mississippians had built the mounds as burial sites. In the years of settler colonialism, however, American colonists (who did not understand the evolution of native peoples) saw them as ancient "monuments," certainly not created by the Shawnees, Cherokees, or Chickasaws, who seemingly lacked the technological skills to build such mounds. They reasoned that, if the mounds had been constructed by native peoples, they belonged to more "civilized" cultures than the more violent Native Americans whom Kentuckians now encountered. According to this scenario, Kentuckians warred with Native Americans who had conquered these more civilized groups, and their cultures, as a result, had disappeared. Benjamin Franklin declared that the mounds must have been built by Spanish explorers in the 1500s; others theorized that the Mound Builders were either the Lost Tribe of Israel or Welsh migrants who had arrived in North America centuries earlier. Interest in the ancient Mound Builders persisted because it justified American Indian policy and American settler colonialism. The more "uncivilized" that Native Americans were thought to be, the easier to advocate violence against them. Since the great Mound Builders no longer existed and contemporary native peoples had been pushed out or killed, Native Americans could make no claim on Kentucky. In other words, the Indians had vanished.

Interest in the Mound Builders also bound Kentucky to the development of an American identity. Americans, in the 1780s and 1790s, formed new ideas about who they were as a people, distinct from their European forebears. Thomas Jefferson argued with the French naturalist the Comte de Buffon about whether the North American continent could compare to the antiquity of Europe. When, in 1790, Kentucky colonist Harry Innes sent Jefferson a description of a burial mound near Lexington as well as a ten-inch statuette of a kneeling woman giving birth that had been unearthed, Jefferson seemed convinced of the technological skills of the ancients, although he was unsure if they had come from Mexico or Asia. The statu-

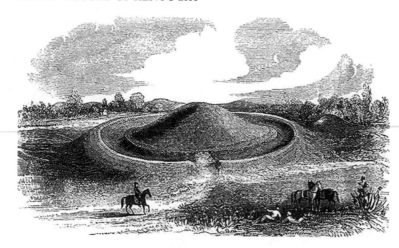

Earthworks and mound in Greenup County. (E. G. Squier and E. H. Davis, *Ancient Monuments of the Mississippi Valley* [New York: Bartlett and Welford, 1848], 82)

ette was "the best piece of workmanship I ever saw from their hands." The mounds and their contents became symbols of North America's notable antiquity. They allowed Jefferson to claim that the new United States rested on a continent as old and distinguished as Europe.

As president, Jefferson oversaw the purchase of the Louisiana Territory. He sent Meriwether Lewis, William Clark, and their Corps of Discovery in 1803 to explore and catalog the American landscape west of the Mississippi River. Among the items Jefferson directed them to collect were descriptions of ancient monuments. Clark, the younger brother of George Rogers Clark, had arrived outside Louisville with his family in 1785, coming of age at the estate at Mulberry Hill. Accompanying him on the migration from Virginia and on the westward expedition was Monk, one of Lewis's enslaved laborers, and nine other Kentucky colonists who composed one-third of the corps. As the expedition moved westward, reports sent back to the United States often arrived first in Louisville. These reports were printed in the city, and its residents were among the first to read about the exotic Native Americans of the West. Lewis and Clark's expedition reinforced the idea that Native Americans had vanished from the East—and from Kentucky. By 1803, Americans were convinced that no exotic, uncivilized peoples lived in Kentucky anymore.

The myth of Kentucky's vanished Indian culminated in 1815, when Ohioan Nahum

Ward purchased a mummy that Lexington merchant Charles Wilkins's enslaved laborers had unearthed at Wilkins's salt mines in Short Cave, Warren County, four years earlier. Wilkins had placed the mummy, later named Fawn Hoof, on display in Mammoth Cave, but Ward wanted to share her with other Americans. She was taken east to be exhibited. Eventually, she resided at the American Antiquarian Society in Worcester, Massachusetts, where she remained for much of the nineteenth century. Thousands of visitors viewed Fawn Hoof not only as a symbol of North America's antiquity but also of what must happen to all native populations if the United States were to spread across North America to fulfill its destiny.

Native peoples, however, were not gone from Kentucky. Most obvious were the Chickasaws just beyond the western reaches of the state, the Cherokees who still hunted in the southeasternmost corner, and the Western Confederacy of Shawnees, Miamis, Lenni Lenapes, Wyandottes, and other indigenous nations north of the Ohio who had joined together to resist American expansion. Their war against the Americans, begun in 1754, would continue into the 1810s. Even in the midst of war, both sides continued to interact. Some Native Americans sustained trade relations with white Kentuckians. They made trips to stores in Louisville or Lexington to barter for refined goods. Yet, American colonists were increasingly unwilling to interact with Native

GREAT NATURAL CURIOSITY.

TO be seen until Wednesday, the 4th Sept. at the Park Coffee House, next door to the Theatre, on its way from the Mammoth Cave in Kentucky, to Boston in Massachusetts,

A FEMALE MUMMY,
IN ENTIRE PRESERVATION.

She was recently discovered in a Saltpetre Cave. The proprietors of the Cave allowed that she was found 156 feet under ground ; at the time, she was dressed in a superb shroud of the bark of willow, and ornamented with beads, feathers, shells, having her instruments for working and music lying by her, as was also a very curious wooden bowl containing burnt bones, the relics of some of her friends, and the preserved skin of an immense Rattle Snake, and a variety of articles either for use or ornament ; all of which are preserved, and now presented to the view of the curious. She appears to have been about 5 feet 3 inches in height, and of the most delicate and elegant symmetry, the hair is still on her head, some of her teeth still remain and the nails of her fingers and toes are still perfect.

It is presumed that she (together with the articles found with her) is one of the greatest curiosities ever exhibited to the American world.— Great conjectures are formed as to the period of her existence : but we presume it is no exaggeration to say, that, in all probability, she is as ancient as the immense mounds of the western country, which have so much astonished the philosophic world.

With the above Curiosity there may also be seen A MAMMOTH'S TOOTH, and a STONE petrified from wood.

Admittance for Grown Persons Fifty Cents, Children half price.   Aug 30 4t*

Advertisement for viewing of Fawn Hoof in Boston. (*The Evening Post* [New York], August 30, 1816)

Americans. Animosities that already existed hardened. In 1807, Shawnee chief Kekewepellethe led a contingent to Russellville to harvest salt. Finding that private business protected access to the salt licks, he frustratingly vowed to "kill all the white people, and give the Indians all their country." For Kentucky colonists, the threat had no bite: it was that of a defeated and vanishing people.

Native Americans did not just live beyond Kentucky's boundaries. Some who had been captives like Nonhelema and her daughters became integrated into white colonial society. Others voluntarily married white or black partners and joined the American settlements. The

practice was common enough that the Danville Club discussed it in 1787. Decades of relationships between white colonists, native peoples, and enslaved and free blacks led to a generation of cross-racial children. Some white and black women who had been captured, for example, eventually became wives to native men, and through captivity exchanges, their children often found themselves in a foreign culture south of the Ohio River. They clung to their indigenous identities. Similarly, some whites who had been taken captive as children and raised as Native Americans continued to identify as indigenous even after reuniting with families in Kentucky. When his two sons returned to him in 1795 after fifteen years as captives, an old militia captain cried, "My cheldrin is Indians!" He tried to dress them in American clothing, which they rejected.

In the 1840s and 1850s, John Dabney Shane interviewed hundreds of Kentuckians who had participated in the state's settler colonialism in the 1770s, 1780s, and 1790s. White settlers whom he interviewed assumed that the violence of those decades had led to the expulsion of Native Americans. Upon considering all he was told, however, Shane concluded that native displacement resulted from something subtler: "It was not, in truth, our superiority in war, or warlike implements. It was the plough that overturned the Indians." For those Native Americans who remained in Kentucky, this was true. They ceased resembling traditional Shawnees and Cherokees, Chickasaws and Miamis. Instead, they acclimated to American settler colonial society and economy. They became farmers and villagers, craftsmen and apprentices, and slave owners and enslaved laborers. To ensure that they no longer identified as Native Americans, censuses in 1790 and 1800 listed many of them as "other free persons of color." The censuses simply categorized others who became trapped in enslavement as "slaves" with no other qualifications. They disappeared from our view in the historical records. Though they seemed to have vanished, they persisted.

4

Kentucky in the New Nation

The First Constitution of Kentucky, 1792

Although nine conventions to secure the opportunity for Kentucky to be a state were held in Danville between 1784 and 1790, the final one did not take place until April 1792. Writing and implementing a state constitution was not an easy task. The delegates to the tenth state convention arrived with dozens of ideas. Before the meeting convened, colonists who identified with the partisan faction organized committees in Bourbon, Fayette, Madison, Mason, and Mercer counties to write petitions and demand a more democratic government. The *Kentucky Gazette* published their petitions, which alarmed many Kentuckians who found the ideas too radical. Harry Innes complained that "the People of Kentucky are mere Fanatics in Politics. Constitutions are forming in every Neighborhood." He contended that this was not a good thing because the pretensions of the "peasantry" gave "a very serious alarm to every thinking man."

Still, the petitions inspired other colonists to voice their desires to the convention delegates. "A Medler" complained against the "great men" in the country party and encouraged the constitution to be formed by "those who live above poverty but below affluence." "Salamander" denounced the court party, writing that "the fewer Lawyers and Pick pockets there are in a country, the better the chance honest people have to keep their own." Publishing letters under pseudonyms was a way in which people engaged politically without facing retribution for their opinions. A very public activity, politics dominated conversations in inns and taverns. Debates about the issues often descended into brawls. Such a political atmosphere left many individuals exposed to the vengeance of more powerful men who could terminate rental agreements or deny credit in local stores. Pseudonyms, then, provided protection and opportunity. "The Medler" identified as a woman, and if true, then she would not have had access either to the ballot box or to the tavern discussions. She may have had some political conversations within her household, but her anonymous letter was her best opportunity to talk about politics publicly.

Despite the efforts of the county committees, the forty-five delegates who arrived in Danville to craft a constitution were nearly all well above poverty. Two-thirds of them owned at least five slaves, and nearly all had considerable investments in land, horses, cattle, and household goods. Although Kentucky attracted many lawyers during the 1780s and early 1790s, most were young and had yet to form the political connections, experience, and knowledge to situate them as great constitutional thinkers like John Adams and James Madison. Among them, only Madison's friend George Nicholas, who had been instrumental in helping Virginia ratify the federal constitution in 1789, immediately became prominent. Late that same year, he received appointment as the first United States attorney for the District of Kentucky. He moved to Danville and quickly became the district's leading legal and constitutional mind. At the tenth convention, he also became the "Father of the First Kentucky Constitution."

The constitutional delegates faced difficult decisions. How would power be balanced among a governor, legislature, and judiciary?

How would the state deal with the morass of land cases that clogged up the courts? Would Kentucky be a slave state? Who should be considered a citizen? Nicholas understood the constitutional challenge: the convention needed to appease the country faction, protect the interests of the court faction, and seem to be concerned for the partisans. "Government must be strong enough to compel confidence and respect in the people," he wrote, "or they will resort to expedients that will destroy it."

As the convention opened, citizenship was a hotly debated topic. Nicholas consulted with Madison, who believed that property ownership made good citizens. Kentucky's high levels of landlessness, however, forced Nicholas to reconsider: "If a man is poor treat him as a freeman, his ambition will make him rich." White universal manhood suffrage easily passed the convention, as did most of Nicholas's proposals: an indirectly elected senate and a powerful and independent governor to check and balance the popularly elected house of representatives, popularly elected sheriffs and other county officials, and an independent court of appeals to address land-title cases. Such proposals addressed the county committees' concern that "the people" be heard.

Constructing a government seemed to go well until the issue of slavery came to the floor. Reverend David Rice, a Presbyterian minister and staunch opponent of enslavement, attacked the institution as immoral, unjust, and harmful to the community. Six other delegates, ministers who shared his antislavery sympathies (two Presbyterians, three Baptists, and one Methodist), supported his argument. They did not think that slavery could be immediately ended, but Rice and his supporters did hope to initiate the gradual emancipation of enslaved Kentuckians. The people debated the issue in the *Kentucky Gazette*. "Phillip Philips" of Mercer County predicted the abolition of slavery, but he feared that educating black Kentuckians would inspire them to think they were equal to whites. "Brutus Senior" responded that enslaved African Americans had been forced into ignorance and desperation by enslavement, and, once freed, they would prove they really were equal to whites as credible members of society.

Nicholas led the defense of slavery. Citing the Bible and historical precedents, he argued that the institution was ancient and moral. Ending slavery would violate slave owners' property rights. Moreover, expecting the state to purchase and free slaves was beyond its financial abilities. Of course, individuals could free slaves as they wished, but mass emancipation might result in widespread miscegenation and racial debasement. On Rice's motion to delete the proslavery article of the new constitution, the vote was closer than expected: a sixteen to twenty-six defeat.

After the debates concluded in mid-April, twenty-two resolutions went to a committee charged with writing the constitution. This committee fully drafted the document within five days and submitted it to the entire convention. Samuel McDowell predicted, "We will have a tolerable good Constitution." The constitution outlined a new government with a bicameral (two-house) legislature. Representatives in the house were to be elected annually, and voting would be based on population rather than by county. A census was to be taken every four years to determine representation. A body of electors was to select senators to four-year terms. Each county had one senator, and the electors would choose additional senators from across the state. Given the youthfulness of Kentucky's population, the committee established low age limits for these officeholders: twenty-four years old for house members and twenty-seven years old for senators. A body of electors would also select a governor for a four-year term. The governor, in turn, would appoint the attorney general and the secretary of state, as well as dozens of local officials. The constitution ended voice voting. Citizens would vote by ballot. Because sheriffs oversaw elections and would see individuals' ballots, governors would not appoint them. This provision prevented the governor from taking advantage of such information to exert influence on elections. Instead, sheriffs were to be popularly elected, along with coroners. The state was to have a supreme court, known as the Kentucky Court of Appeals, and inferior courts when needed as determined by the general assembly.

Kentucky's 1792 constitution looked very much like the constitutions of the earlier states with one important exception that made Kentucky unique in the United States. It was the first state to guarantee universal white male suffrage regardless of property ownership while also endorsing slavery. Nicholas later claimed that those who supported slavery insisted on including measures that protected the importation of slaves and prohibited the general assembly from manumitting them only because the antislavery ministers had been so persistent. Without these constitutional protections, Nicholas suspected that slavery might have died out in Kentucky.

On April 19, 1792, the convention approved the constitution, and Kentucky became a commonwealth.* Two weeks later, citizens implemented it by voting for electors, representatives, sheriffs, and coroners. When the electors gathered in Lexington in mid-May, they selected Isaac Shelby as governor and eleven senators, one from each of the nine counties and two at large. At that point, Kentucky became a state.

Governor Shelby took his oath of office in early June. A veteran of the American Revolutionary War and an early settler of Lincoln County, Shelby attracted many partisans who saw him as a Big Man. By the 1790s, he owned a large estate at Traveler's Rest. His wife, Susannah Hart, was sister to Nathaniel Hart Jr., a large landowner and an emerging merchant. This relationship made Shelby appealing to court party and country party members as well. All factions found Shelby a man of integrity and fair judgment. When he presented his first governor's message to the Kentucky General Assembly, Shelby encouraged the assembly to embrace the political venture before them. Over the next month, the assembly met in Lexington and accomplished a great deal. It

Portrait of Isaac Shelby, by Matthew Harris Jouett, 1820. (Transylvania University Library, Lexington, KY)

made appointments and passed legislation to set up the new government. The legislators selected surveyors and tax commissioners, a state auditor, and militia leaders. They appointed George Nicholas attorney general, formed four counties, chartered multiple towns, and issued regulations on stray animals and inspecting tobacco. A joint session of the house and senate selected a state treasurer and appointed John Brown and John Edwards as Kentucky's first members of the United States Senate. The assembly also appointed Harry Innes, Benjamin Sebastian, and Caleb Wallace justices on the Kentucky Court of Appeals, and George Muter, Samuel McDowell, and Christopher Greenup became justices on the Kentucky Court of Oyer and Terminer, the high criminal court of the state. Of the six men who received judicial appointments, only Wallace had not been a member of the Danville Political Club.

With the exception of the Kentucky

*Kentuckians chose "commonwealth" rather than "state" because Virginia was a commonwealth. The Anglo-Saxon term "wela" means "sound and prosperous state," so a commonwealth is a government that provides stability and prosperity to all of its citizens.

Court of Appeals, which the 1792 constitution established, the assembly had to create a judicial system for the state. A remnant of colonial America, each county had a squire's court—an informal tribunal of a community's leading men who, although not lawyers, used common sense and their familiarity with neighbors to adjudicate misdemeanors, resolve neighborly disputes, and confirm the validity of marriages. The assembly made many of these men official justices of the peace, who could serve on county courts. Each county, depending upon its population, received between eight and sixteen justices of the peace. Three justices of the peace would constitute a county court, but all justices in a county could sit on an important case. They met monthly except for the three months during which the Kentucky Courts of Quarter Sessions—the courts that heard civil suits involving large sums of money—convened. The county courts served important administrative functions: validating wills and probate issues, determining guardianship and the indenturing of children, making decisions about residents of poor houses. Citizens had more contact with their county courts than state or national governments. They often came to the court with meager complaints.

County courts heard both criminal cases and civil cases. If a penalty exceeded forty shillings in a criminal case, a person could appeal the decision to the court of oyer and terminer, which met irregularly. In a civil case, a citizen could appeal a decision to the courts of quarter sessions when a county court's decision involved a fine of fifty shillings or five hundred pounds of tobacco or more. The courts of quarter sessions met regularly but only three times a year. The final appellate court was the court of appeals, although the constitution specified that it was to have original and final jurisdiction over land disputes.

Land claims and ownership remained a significant problem in Kentucky, and the court of appeals soon found itself at the center of Kentuckians' political outrage. In 1780, Virginia's land commission had settled a claim dispute between Alexander McConnell and Simon Kenton, but Kenton sued in the court of appeals to have the decision overturned. In *McConnell v. Kenton* (1794), the justices concluded in a two-to-one decision that the commission had overstepped its authority, calling into question all of the land claims that it had verified. Citizens flooded the assembly with petitions that demanded the two justices be removed from office. Lacking that power, the assembly censured the justices. Even though the court reversed its decision in the following session, the damage was done. In 1795, the assembly dismantled the judicial system. It abolished the court of oyer and terminer and redistributed jurisdiction over land cases from the court of appeals to six district courts.

As its final action, the first state assembly selected a location for the state capital. A Kentucky State Election Committee formed to solicit bids from interested communities. Andrew Holmes, a wealthy businessman who had purchased large tracts of land in Frankfort from James Wilkinson, proposed his lands for a permanent state capital. He offered seven years of rent-free use of a large house, lots on which to build, fifteen hundred pounds of nails, ten boxes of glass, other building materials, and three thousand dollars in specie. When the assembly opened its December session, members accepted the proposal and determined "to hold its next session in the house of Andrew Holmes, at Frankfort on the Kentucky River."

The Village West

In the 1770s and 1780s, traveling merchants, itinerant preachers, and circuit court justices had visited the stations and forts that speckled Kentucky's landscape. Neighbors gathered for such events on court day or market day. As the defensive roles of stations and forts waned in the 1780s, they transformed into villages, the largest of which by 1790 were Lexington, Washington, Bardstown, Louisville, and Danville. Soon after its founding in 1786, Frankfort quickly joined the list, second only to Lexington. They did not compose an "urban frontier," for none of the places preceded more rural settlement and none developed distinctly from the rural environs that surrounded

Kentucky's first statehouse in Frankfort, constructed in 1793–1794; burned in 1813. (Kentucky Historical Society Collections, Frankfort, KY)

them. Still, they were administratively separate from the counties, run by boards of trustees that the general assembly established whenever it chartered a town. As they became hubs of communal activity, such places filled with merchants, artisans, lawyers, and many poorer men who, having failed to secure land, found work in stores, warehouses, artisans' shops, liveries, construction, and on the docks.

Lexington was the new state's most important village. Although not situated on a navigable waterway, the town sat along the Old Buffalo Trace that connected it to the Ohio River at Maysville. Some long hunters had given it the name Lexington in 1775, when they heard news of a battle between British troops and Minutemen in Massachusetts. Still, another four years passed before Robert Patterson built a fort, and another three years before Virginia's legislature provided a board of trustees to set up the village. By 1790, Lexington counted 834 residents and grew into a town of 1,795 by the end of the eighteenth century.

Lexington had an advantage because large numbers of wealthy Virginians settled in the Inner Bluegrass in the 1780s and early 1790s. This wealthy, well-connected population made the village an economic and cultural hub, and its trustees, therefore, assumed that the state capital would be located there. They even had begun constructing a statehouse before Frankfort was chosen instead. Despite being passed over as the seat of state government, Lexington still became the center of refinement and com-

merce. In 1787, brothers Fielding and John Bradford began printing the *Kentucke Gazette* in Lexington, and James H. Stewart followed with the *Kentucky Herald* in 1793. Merchants from Philadelphia and Trenton like John W. Hunt, Andrew McCalla, and William Leavy migrated to Lexington in the 1790s to profit from the demand for goods. James Trotter and his sons, George and Samuel, created extensive commercial networks. They imported finished and refined products from the east and exported domestic productions. Merchants sold out of shops not only in Lexington but also in multiple stores across the state, and they also offered loans and provided insurance for customers who wished to ship goods.

At the northern end of the Old Buffalo Trace, Washington sat just a few miles south of the Ohio River. A post office arose in the village in 1789, the first west of the Appalachians, serving not only Kentucky but all of the territory north of the Ohio River as well. Just north of Washington, Limestone (renamed Maysville in 1799) had been the largest village in the region. "The dêpot of whatever goods pass from Baltimore and Philadelphia to Kentucky," the village sat along the Ohio River and ushered immigrants into the state. Merchants hiked up prices to take advantage of new residents. By the mid-1790s, Washington surpassed Limestone as the state's third largest village, and it became the county seat of Mason County in 1801. Once travelers left Maysville and passed through Washington on their way to Lexington in the center of the Bluegrass, the Old Buffalo Trace took them through Mayslick, Blue Licks, Millersburg, and Paris, as well.

Throughout Kentucky, roads like the trace connected dozens of little places into a constellation of village life. A network of villages cut across the southern Bluegrass: Stanford, Danville, Bardstown, and on to Louisville, with a tangent route through Harrodsburg. Some villages, like Danville, began to fade with the growth of Lexington. Following the constitutional conventions in Danville throughout the 1780s, the village lost political significance. Transylvania Academy, founded in 1783, moved to Lexington in 1789.

Bluegrass section of "A Map of Kentucky from Actual Survey," by Elihu Barker, 1795. (Library of Congress, Geography and Map Division)

Other villages, like Louisville, took more time to develop. Plans for a town at the Falls of the Ohio dated to 1773, when speculator John Connolly sent Thomas Bullitt to survey two thousand acres and lay out a village. Connolly and his partner, John Campbell, advertised town lots in 1774, as if the town already existed. In 1778, a few families gathered on Corn Island, where George Rogers Clark mustered his forces for his invasion of the Illinois territory. That winter, they moved to a stockade on the Kentucky shore. The following year, John Floyd built a house on Beargrass Creek,

amid other stations and dozens of squatters. Although chartered in 1780, Louisville grew more slowly than Lexington and Frankfort. Persistent threat of attack by Native Americans north of the Ohio River kept many settlers away. In April 1782, Floyd complained, "We are all obliged to live in our forts in this country, and notwithstanding all the caution we use, forty-seven . . . have been killed or taken prisoner by the savages, besides a number wounded, since January." Without guaranteed trade along the Mississippi River, the village's potential as a commercial port did not come

Table 4.1. Ethnic Distribution among White Kentuckians, 1790–1820

Ethnicity	As % of total white population 1790	As % of total white population 1820
English	51.6	56.6
Scots-Irish	24.8	18.2
Irish	9.0	8.2
Welsh	6.7	8.7
German	4.9	5.6
French	1.6	1.5
Dutch	1.2	1.0
Swedish	0.2	0.2

Source: Thomas L. Purvis, "The Ethnic Descent of Kentucky's Early Population: A Statistical Investigation of European and American Sources of Emigration, 1790–1820," *Register of the Kentucky Historical Society* 80 (1982): 263.

to fruition easily. By 1800, there were only 359 residents. The *Louisville Gazette* did not begin publication until 1807. Still, even if they were slow growing like Louisville, villages arose to complement the farmlands around them and provide the economic and governmental services that residents required.

Although most new Kentuckians came from eastern states, the villages of the West drew Europeans as well. Lexington actively recruited immigrants through the Lexington Emigrant Society. The Washington Emigration Society advertised the benefits of settling in Mason County. The St. Andrew's Society recruited immigrants from Scotland. When they arrived, European immigrants became the core of village economic life, providing much of the artisanal and domestic skills that drew rural folk to village markets. In town after town, Germans served as bakers, butchers, tanners, carpenters, and bricklayers. Arrivals from Great Britain occupied different crafts: watchmakers, weavers, and bluedyers—who dyed thread or wool before it went to a weaver to be turned into cloth. French settlers opened schools of dance and language, operated coffeehouses and confectionaries, and worked in metals.

As the villages grew into towns, trustees faced the challenges of food supply and sanitation. Before the 1790s, some merchants sold foodstuffs, but most people grew their own in small gardens. As village populations became denser, the amount of land available for private gardens decreased. Trustees constructed mar-

kethouses, where farmers sold produce to villagers. Over time, hoping to regulate the types and qualities of produce that were sold, trustees empowered a new population of grocers, who acted as intermediaries between farmers and consumers. Sanitation too became a problem, as villages transformed into towns. Boards of trustees charged residents with cleaning the streets in front of their homes, but most did not take on this responsibility. The majority of town dwellers, instead, merely threw trash out of windows. Roving herds of hogs roamed the streets feeding on this garbage. Villages were disgusting. The residue of hogs, horses, and humans kept streets smelly and unclean. Sometimes, during heavy rains, the waste seeped into wells and springs. Lexington sat along a small creek that regularly flooded, contaminating drinking water and leading to diseases like dysentery. Clean drinking water became such a challenge that entrepreneurs began bottling spring waters from Blue Licks and Olympia Springs to sell at village markets.

Having markets in which to buy and sell became critical, so merchants became the most powerful men in villages. In 1793, they had the loudest voices among those who demanded negotiations for a treaty between the United States and the Spanish to open New Orleans to Kentucky trade. The issue of Mississippi River rights dominated state politics during the 1790s. Many former partisans and country party men coalesced into Democratic-Republicans, led by George Nicholas by virtue of his

Portrait of George Nicholas, unknown artist, n.d. (The Filson Historical Society, Louisville, KY)

Portrait of John Breckinridge, unknown artist, n.d. (The Filson Historical Society, Louisville, KY)

work on the state constitution. Although not a pure political party, the Democratic-Republicans generally supported Thomas Jefferson in his fights with Alexander Hamilton over the shape of the new nation's government.

Virginian John Breckinridge arrived in Kentucky in 1793 and contested Nicholas's authority. Breckinridge was more conservative than Nicholas, distrusting the uneducated masses and their democratic impulses. He formed the Lexington Democratic-Republican Society. (Other chapters of the society arose in Georgetown and Paris.) He also wrote *Remonstrance of the Citizens West of the Mountains to the President and Congress of the United States*. In *Remonstrance*, he appealed to the federal government to acknowledge that navigation of the Mississippi River "is the NATURAL RIGHT of the inhabitants of the counties bordering on the waters." Kentuckians were reasonable "to expect that the present Federal Government would before this time have taken effectual measures."

Although John Breckinridge was more conservative than Nicholas, he was not so socially conservative as to become a Federalist, like his brother, Robert. Kentucky's Federal-

Humphrey Marshall. (Anderson Chenault Quisenberry, *The Life and Times of Hon. Humphrey Marshall* [Wincester, KY: Sun Publishing Co., 1892], frontispiece)

ists generally supported Alexander Hamilton's plans for broad economic growth. They, therefore, looked eastward for solutions to the state's economic problems, not westward down the Mississippi River. Led by the outspoken Humphrey Marshall, Federalists believed that the state constitution had empowered "the people" too much at the expense of a "natural" ruling class. This attitude made them targets of mob violence. On one occasion, a Frankfort mob carried Federalist William Murray to the Kentucky River to dunk him. Marshall, a noted atheist, appealed to the Baptists in the crowd: "Now allow me to say that according to Baptist rules it is irregular to administer baptism before the receiver gives his experience." The mob erupted in laughter and let him go.

Still, the Federalists had enough influence in Kentucky to challenge the Democratic-Republicans, but usually only when politics was out of the hands of "the people." In 1794, the Kentucky Senate selected a new US senator. In the first round of voting, Humphrey Marshall and John Breckinridge emerged with the highest votes. Marshall, who was in the Kentucky House, successfully outmaneuvered Breckinridge, winning the vote by twenty-eight to twenty-two.

Despite his political loss, Breckinridge remained wildly popular because he demanded the opening of the Mississippi River. When Breckinridge's proclamation arrived on President George Washington's desk, the president, more a Federalist than Democratic-Republican, worried, "The lopping off of Kentucky from the Union is dreadful to contemplate, even if it should not attach itself to some other power." Washington had reason to fear for the nation's future. A French diplomat, Citizen Edmond-Charles Genêt, actively courted Democratic-Republicans to help his nation in its war against Great Britain and Spain. He informed Jefferson, secretary of state for the United States, that "a little spontaneous eruption of the inhabitants of Kentucky" could inspire American reaction against Spanish control over the Mississippi River. In Kentucky, Genêt visited village after village, trying to garner support for his scheme. His rhetoric inspired George Rogers Clark. Embittered by what he considered to be a dismissive federal government, Clark offered to lead the military effort. Although sympathetic to the cause, Lex-ington's Democratic-Republican Society did not endorse the expedition against the Spanish in New Orleans. Still, John Breckinridge and other members committed private funds to the effort. The French Conspiracy was born.

Genêt was not a very capable diplomat, and President Washington pushed back against Kentuckians' interest in inciting war with Spain. When Washington appealed to Governor Shelby, however, he received little sympathy. Shelby supported citizens' rights to leave the state and bear arms. When Washington forbade any private expeditions against foreign powers, the conspiracy died, but demands for opening the Mississippi River did not. In 1794, as rebellion broke out in Pennsylvania over a federal whiskey tax, Lexington's Democratic-Republican Society threatened its own rebellion, unless the federal government resolved the Mississippi River issue. In March 1796, the Treaty of San Lorenzo (or Pinckney's Treaty) guaranteed freedom of navigation and rights to trade in New Orleans.

In Paris and Georgetown, the Democratic-Republican Societies also argued for opening the Mississippi, but they were far less aggressive than the Lexington chapter. Farmers dominated those chapters, and although Kentucky farmers needed markets for their goods, they did not have the financial influence found among Lexington's Democratic-Republicans. Lexington's merchants not only wielded political power on state and national levels but also served as financiers for many regional farmers, creating patron-client networks that further empowered them on local levels. As the opening of the Mississippi River transformed Louisville into a larger town, its merchants played the same roles. In the state's first half century, village merchants drove Kentucky's development.

Old Problems in a New State

In 1789, George Nicholas warned James Madison that Kentuckians had legitimate complaints. He informed him that, if the federal government could not help to redress those issues, like his western neighbors, he "shall be ready to join in any other Modes for obtaining our rights." Use of the Mississippi River and trade through New Orleans were only the most immediate problems. Others—threats of Native American attacks, questions over land distribution, and the shape of slavery—lingered from previous decades, and many Kentuckians hoped to resolve these issues permanently.

In autumn 1789, a party of Shawnees, Cherokees, and Wyandottes wandered through Kentucky's eastern mountains and came upon a pregnant Virginia "Jenny" Wiley, her four children, and her brother. Only Jenny Wiley, her unborn child, and a toddler survived. Like Mary Draper Ingles thirty years earlier, she found herself hiking through the forests on her way to lower Shawnee Town. Unlike Ingles, Wiley panicked. At one point, she bolted into the woods to escape. When she was caught, one of the Cherokees dashed her baby against a tree before scalping the child. As the party moved on, Wiley became increasingly weak, and when they reached the banks of the Ohio River, she gave birth in a rock shelter. Patiently, her captors set up camp for the winter. Three months later, they performed a ritual test on the baby, placing him in the cold waters of a nearby creek. If he cried, he would be scalped. He cried.

For a year, Wiley continued to live with the hunting party, serving as a domestic slave as they migrated from camp to camp. One evening, a party of Cherokees arrived with a young white man as their captive. They tortured him and burned him alive. They then bound Wiley's hands, tied her to a tree, and threatened to burn her as well. Since they did not light the fire, they were probably testing her. Still, she was sold to one of the Cherokees to become his wife. As she began her trip to the Cherokee Overhill Towns, Wiley escaped and navigated her way to Harmon's Station, at the junction of John's Creek and the Louisa Fork of the Big Sandy River. Months later, a war party that was tracking Wiley laid siege to Harmon's Station, frightening its residents to abandon the region soon after the siege ended.

Jenny Wiley's ordeal and the demise of Harmon's Station incited Kentuckians. They organized small raids across the Ohio River and struck anyone they thought looked like an enemy. Their retaliation was often ill placed. John Hardin led a raid that killed a dozen Piankashaws along the Wabash River. Secretary of War Henry Knox furiously wrote President Washington about such vigilante groups: "possessing an equal aversion to all bearing the name of Indians, they destroyed a number of peaceable Piankeshaws, who prided themselves in their attachment to the United States." Federal troops north of the Ohio River raised concerns that the Kentuckians would drag the nation into war. "This Kentuck affair will undo everything," wrote one officer. The Western Confederacy of Shawnees, Miamis, Lenni Lenapes, and Wyandottes found new allies as neutral nations came under attack. Native Americans escalated attacks on Kentucky settlements, and Kentuckians continued to invade native villages. Federal judge Harry Innes estimated that, between 1783 and 1790, Indians killed or captured fifteen hundred people and stole twenty thousand horses.

To end the violence, in April 1790, Kentucky's militia general, Charles Scott, led 200 militiamen to join General Joseph Harmar's federal troops on an excursion to track down raiding parties. Harmar again called militias to join his troops in October, this time to strike against the Shawnee villages of Kekionga and New Chillicothe. This mission proved to be a disaster for the Americans. Nearly 60 men died in the initial battle, and when a detachment attempted to recover the injured, another 180 were ambushed and killed. The victory empowered the Western Confederacy, which spurned any American efforts to negotiate.

President Washington set up a 5-man board of advisers in Kentucky. Scott, Harry Innes, John Brown, Benjamin Logan, and Isaac Shelby recommended an offensive attack against the Western Confederacy. Thomas Jefferson hoped that "we shall give them a *thorough* drubbing this summer, and then change our tomahawk into a golden chain of friendship." In May 1791, Scott led some 700 volunteers against the Miami village of Ouiatanon, where they killed over 70 people, burned the town, and destroyed the crops. Three months later, James Wilkinson invaded the upper Wabash River villages with over 500 troops. Hopeful that the two offenses proffered greater success, Secretary of War Knox ordered Arthur St. Clair, governor of Ohio Territory, to lead a larger offensive. St. Clair began his march in October 1791 with nearly 2,000 men, almost half of whom were Kentucky militias. The army blundered into an ambush: over 630 men died and another 270 were wounded. Abandoning their injured comrades to fate, the rest of the army fled back to Kentucky. Those who died on the battlefield had soil stuffed in their mouths. The Native Americans used the stage of battle to mock the Americans' land lust.

Emboldened by their victory, small parties from the Western Confederacy harassed Kentucky villages and farms. Militias routinely patrolled villages and roads on the lookout for them, including a forty-man regiment along the Wilderness Road. Occasionally, a skirmish erupted between Indians and militiamen. One of these skirmishes occurred near Rolling Fork of the Salt River in August 1792. Determined to assert federal military power, President Washington appointed "Mad" Anthony Wayne to find a solution. Wayne prepared for two years. When he began his excursion north of the Ohio River in 1794, he had some fifteen hundred mounted Kentucky riflemen alongside his one thousand regular troops. Charles Scott again commanded the Kentuckians. Their target was Fort Miami, a British fortification that had been built in defiance of the peace treaty of 1783. About thirteen hundred Native Americans hid among the timbers that had been felled to clear the land for the fort. The Americans proved victorious in less than an hour by using the regulars to attack with bayonets as the Kentuckians rode in on the flanks. Shocked by the attack, the British in the fort refused to provide refuge to their Indian allies. Within months, Britain signed Jay's Treaty, agreeing to withdraw its military from American soil. Betrayed by the British and their defeat at the Battle of Fallen Timbers, the Western Confederacy signed the Treaty of Greenville in 1795, which opened much of the Northwest Territory to American colonists.

Momentary resolution of the Indian problem just exacerbated the land problem. Many Kentuckians who failed to obtain land in Kentucky jumped at the opportunity that the Treaty of Greenville opened. In Kentucky, a new land rush began. No longer fearful of Indian attacks, people claimed squatters' rights to millions of acres and wanted their titles cleared cheaply. The Land Act of 1795 permitted individuals already claiming land—by virtue of having built a cabin and planted corn—to purchase two hundred acres at thirty dollars per hundred acres. It also opened the region south of the Green River to organized settlement. As thousands migrated south of the Green, the general assembly had to revise the land act to take advantage of the demand. The Land Act of 1797 raised prices to sixty dollars per one hundred acres for first-rate lands and forty dollars per one hundred acres of second-rate lands. (All lands south of the Green were categorized as second-rate.) The act extended the time in which payment could be made.

Not everyone who sought land needed the extra time. Between 1795 and 1797, on behalf of a Philadelphia land speculation firm, Elisha I. Hall recruited George Nicholas, John Breckinridge, and other notable Democratic-Republicans to help him secure four to six million acres of unclaimed land. He offered $260,000 (averaging roughly 5.5 cents per acre), but the Kentucky House rejected the deal.

To politicians from the Bluegrass, development of the lands south of the Green looked like a threat to their political dominance. Not only was the region populating quickly, but new counties were being created rapidly. This growth brought larger numbers of representatives into the general assembly. John Breckinridge derided the region as being "filled with nothing but hunters, horse-thieves & savages, . . . where wretchedness, poverty & sickness will always reign." He was wrong. The region south of the Green River looked dramatically more egalitarian than the rest of the state, where, by 1800, only 49.2 percent of households owned land. In contrast, nearly two-thirds of heads of households in in the southern counties owned land, and a large majority owned the maximum two hundred acres. Although many who purchased on credit lost their lands, others managed to make meager profits. Some tested cotton in their soils, although they could not yet afford the labor to produce it in large quantities.

By 1800, Kentucky had grown to forty-two counties. To address the emerging power of the southern counties, the general assembly (still dominated by the Bluegrass) restricted county representation: a new county gained a representative only as its parent county gave up a seat. The restrictions placed upon representation led to vicious legislative battles. Some counties lost significant political clout. Fayette County had nine seats in the house in 1793, but only four in 1800. Nelson County lost half of its representation over the same period. It had only three seats by 1800. Yet the populations of some of the counties that gained seats over the decade discovered that they did not have enough qualified men interested in political service.

The opening of lands south of the Green River and the introduction of cotton production enlivened the topic of slavery. Although only one-fourth of Kentucky households owned slaves by 1800, the state's slave population still grew proportionally faster than the white population. The 1792 constitution had not repealed an older Virginia law that prohibited whites from bringing slaves into Kentucky for economic purposes. Offenders were fined and often lost their slaves. Greater economic opportunity meant greater labor demands, however, and planters and aspiring slave owners called on the general assembly to eliminate the law. In 1794, the Kentucky general assembly altered, but did not repeal, the law. Importing slaves for commercial use remained illegal. However, it altered one significant provision. Owners who brought slaves in illegally were fined three hundred dollars, but their slaves no longer would be freed as they had been previously. The new law also permitted individuals to bring slaves into Kentucky for personal use, although the nature of that use went undefined. The revision also made manumission of slaves easier. It relieved owners of legal responsibility for a freed person should he or she fail to support him or herself.

Antislavery advocates had hoped to retain the old law. They believed that any compromise would make abolition impossible. In reaction to the revision, David Rice tried unsuccessfully to start an abolition society. Still, he did gain the support of the Transylvania Presbytery in pressing for slave education "to prepare them for the enjoyment of liberty, an event which they contemplate with the greatest pleasure, and which, they hope, will be accomplished as soon as the nature of things will admit."

Slavery, Marriage, and Keeping the Peace

When Isaac Shelby retired as governor in 1796, Kentucky's largest problems seemed solved. The Western Confederacy was reeling, the Mississippi River was open, land sales were orderly and profitable to the state, and the slave trade remained regulated. The 1796 gubernatorial election to replace Shelby, however, revealed another problem: the constitution was flawed. When the electors met in May, Benjamin Logan received twenty-one votes, James Garrard seventeen votes, Thomas Todd fourteen, and John Brown one. The constitution was unclear as to whether victory required a majority or plurality, so the electors decided to vote a second time on the top two candidates. Most of the Todd votes went to Garrard, a Baptist minister and planter who supported religious tolerance and opposed slavery. He had served in five of the statehood conventions and had helped to write the 1792 constitution. Logan's supporters challenged the final vote, but neither Attorney General John Breckinridge nor the state senate believed it had the constitutional authority to interfere. Garrard became governor.

The election of 1796 sparked years of debate over the problems with Kentucky's constitution. Again, commentary in the pages of the *Kentucky Gazette* questioned the undemocratic use of electors and appointment of officials, an unresponsive court system, life terms for judges, continued protection of slavery, and rules against clergy serving in the general assembly. Logan's gubernatorial loss also was a major issue. George Nicholas had insisted in 1792 that the constitution be reconsidered within a decade, and the constitutional convention had planned for referenda in 1797 and 1798 to gauge citizens' support for constitutional revision. Either a majority of voters or two-thirds of both houses in the general assembly could call a new convention. As the more democratic side of the assembly, the house called for a new constitution in 1793 and 1794, only to see the senate dash their efforts. In early 1797, the general assembly voted to place the referendum on the ballot for the May elections. When the citizens voted, the returns were confusing. Some 5,400 voters wanted a new constitution. Only 440 opposed the idea. But over 3,900 had voted on other items on the ballot and ignored the issue of the constitution. When it met in January 1798, the general assembly did not know what to make of the widespread indifference. No convention was called.

Debates continued to rage in the press and public meetings. John Breckinridge denounced efforts to revise the constitution, characterizing those who called for change as idlers who spent their time "sauntering in the street, hanging around billiard tables, scampering through race fields, and mid-night carousing." Representing a more aristocratic faction of the Democratic-Republicans, Breckinridge claimed that, if enslaved property could be taken, then land rights were not secure either. Among his opponents was a newcomer to Kentucky, Henry Clay. Clay had apprenticed under Breckinridge and George Nicholas, and he had joined their Democratic-Republican ranks. As a young lawyer, he developed a strong reputation for debt collection and resolving land disputes, often to the benefit of more common men. Demonstrating the wide disagreement among Democratic-Republicans about how to create good government, Clay wrote a series of letters under the pseudonym of "Scaevola," in which he argued for direct elections and the gradual abolition of slavery. Without the promise of constitutional revision, the general assembly sought to order the state as much as it could through the constitution in place.

In 1798, the general assembly passed two codes of laws to address the state's most pressing political issues. The first was slavery, which most people recognized as a potentially explosive issue. After the constitutional convention of 1792, slave sales increased in Kentucky because the institution had been embedded in the state's foundational document. In 1798, the general assembly rewrote all of the state's slave laws into a new code that detailed every aspect of the institution. The new laws restrcited slaves' legal access. They could not sue, and they could not witness against whites in court trials. Their mobility was curtailed: slaves had to carry passes signed by their owners, and they could not visit other plantations for more than four hours without their owners' expressed consent. The code prohibited slaves from selling or buying anything without their owners' knowledge. It also forbade slave owners from arming their enslaved laborers, unless they lived in far western Kentucky where the threat of Indian attack persisted. Even in those circumstances, a county justice had to give permission for a slave to have a gun.

The second pressing problem was marriage, to which most people had given little thought. Many people largely agreed that the state—first Virginia and now Kentucky—was too lax. The 1792 constitution did not impose explicit requirements for government or church sanctioning of the institution. Many Kentuckians declared themselves married informally and unofficially. Many others "divorced" by simply walking away from their spouses and families. For those who sought official divorces, their cases went before the general assembly, where lawmakers subtly tried to strengthen men's roles and strip women of any liberties they had gained during Kentucky's pre-state era, which included women's ability to divorce.

In 1798, the assembly passed a marriage code that, like the slave code, rewrote and consolidated into one document all of the laws about the institution of marriage. Kentuckians who wanted to marry now had to seek out a Christian minister to perform and sanction the ceremony. Marriage was to be a formal institution, one certified by licensed ministers on behalf of the state. The code also dictated husbands' rights to their wives' dowers—the money and property that a woman brought into marriage. Dowers could be used by husbands during marriage, but in cases of divorce or abandonment, wives retained rights to their dowers. Although it benefited women, the code actually intended to protect marriage dowries as investments of fathers of the bride. The code also restricted a woman's rights to own property, sign legal documents, enter into contracts, and even employ herself outside the household. If she did work elsewhere, she had to relinquish her wages to her husband.

The slave and marriage codes of 1798 were part of a larger process of ordering Kentucky. Until statehood, because Virginia's government was so far away, county courts had been the most important form of government in residents' lives. Local justices kept "the peace"—a term that expressed the ideal order for a community. They made decisions based on listening to their neighbors, many of whom had no political rights, like white women, but who could not be ignored if social order was to be maintained.

Statehood brought a state government, however, that acted in ways incongruent to county courts. Three years earlier, Harry Innes arrived as the new chief justice of the United States Court for the District of Kentucky, and he had initiated the process of introducing English common law, with its layers of precedence and codification. When the 1792 constitution created a Kentucky Court of Appeals, many cases that county justices had decided by consulting with neighbors and using plain sense became subject to appeal. So, a court case like *Kenton v. McConnell* was about more than just land. The case had begun in 1789, when Simon Kenton and the estate of Francis McConnell went to court in Danville over improvements to a pond. As an issue of local peace, the court resolved the case in McConnell's favor. Kenton, who had fallen on desperate times since his heydays with Daniel Boone and George Rogers Clark, appealed the decision.

The Kentucky Court of Appeals sustained the lower court's decision, which should have appeased most Kentuckians accustomed to the authority of local government. But McConnell's lawyer, George Nicholas, effectively employed the rhetoric and reason of English common law

and precedence. He convinced two of the three justices that, although there was no reason to overturn the Land Act of 1779 through which thousands of residents had acquired properties, theoretically those titles could be ruled invalid. When the justices ruled against Kenton, then, they also questioned the authority of the land commissioners who had implemented the Land Act of 1779. The decision sent Kentucky into a panic. If the state could negate land titles, all claims verified by the land commissioners would be susceptible. Petitions from county courts flooded the general assembly demanding the appellate justices be replaced with men who would decide cases "with as little formality and legal criticisms as possible."

Even though new state institutions like the general assembly and the court of appeals arose in the 1790s, they did not replace the local systems of government and social order. Yet, the two systems became increasingly distinct in purpose. County courts worked to maintain the peace. State institutions existed to define rights, specifically those of white, male citizens. The marriage and slave codes of 1798 were just part of a larger process through which state government defined white men's rights and strengthened patriarchy. At the time, the belief predominated that only through a disinterested, virtuous, independent patriarchy could a republic of equal, active, and independent citizens exist. Such patriarchy gave white men moral authority over dependents—women, children, servants, and slaves.

Many Kentuckians were unhappy with the state institutions that challenged more traditional patterns of life. When a referendum for a constitutional convention was held in the election of 1798, then, supporters of change achieved a clear victory: over 9,100 of 16,388 voters voted to hold a convention. They selected representatives to that convention in elections in May 1799.

The Kentucky Resolutions

When the general assembly gathered in fall 1798, a more urgent issue drew attention away from preparing for the convention vote. Two years earlier, the Federalists had succeeded in electing John Adams as president, but his vice president was Thomas Jefferson, leader of the Democratic-Republicans. In 1810, passage of the Twelfth Amendment would prevent such an awkward political and constitutional situation from reoccurring, but in the late 1790s, this circumstance caused political tensions to run high. In time, Jefferson and Adams's friendship crumbled.

Most Kentuckians supported the Democratic-Republicans and distrusted President Adams. He openly criticized the French, whom many Kentuckians and Americans viewed as the nation's most important allies. Federalists, like Adams, were suspicious of the French revolutionary mobs that provoked widespread social disorder during the 1790s. In their opinion, too many Americans admired the French revolutionaries and might try to effect the same type of revolution in the United States. Some Kentuckians, like Caleb Wallace, believed that the president wanted an opportunity to "send an army into this country to awe the people, and enable it to punish those, who by speaking, writing, or otherwise, should oppose such of its measures as were thought to be unconstitutional or rigorous."

When the Federalist-dominated Congress passed the Alien and Sedition Acts in 1798, Wallace's prophecy seemed accurate. The laws were designed to suppress critics of Federalist policies and politicians. The Naturalization Act increased from five to fourteen years the time required for naturalization of a foreigner, making it more difficult for French immigrants to come to the United States. The Alien Friends Act authorized the president to imprison or deport any foreigners considered a threat to the nation during peacetime. The Alien Enemies Act extended that power to wartime. The Sedition Act made it a crime to assemble and oppose the legal measures of the government or to publish false or malicious writings about the president or Congress. Those found guilty faced up to five thousand dollars in fines and five years' imprisonment.

As most Kentuckians were Democratic-Republicans, they reacted immediately. John Breckinridge encouraged meetings statewide to petition for repeal of the laws. In Clark County, residents penned a series of resolutions. One declared the laws "unconstitutional, impolitic, unjust and disgraceful to the American character." Another framed the Sedition Act as "the most abominable that was ever attempted to be imposed upon a nation of free men." Finally, the gathering resolved that "there is sufficient reason to believe, and we do believe, that our liberties are in danger; and we pledge ourselves to each other and to our country, that we will defend them against all unconstitutional attacks that are made upon them." In Lexington, George Nicholas described the laws as unconstitutional and called for them to be settled in the courts. Then Henry Clay arose and delivered an extemporaneous speech that thrilled the audience. He denounced the Federalists so emphatically that the crowd refused to let any Federalist speak and eventually hoisted Clay upon their shoulders and paraded away.

In the US House of Representatives, Federalist Roger Griswold of Connecticut physically attacked Democratic-Republican Matthew Lyon of Vermont for refusing to apologize when Lyon spit tobacco juice toward Griswold. Months later, when the House considered the Sedition Act, Lyon predicted he would be the first person arrested by the Federalists. As Kentuckians met to denounce the laws in summer 1798, Lyon published a letter in which he criticized President Adams and started his own magazine to counter Federalist propaganda. He was arrested, convicted, and sentenced to four months in prison. Even after serving his sentence, Lyon returned to Congress, where he continued to irritate the Federalists. When Adams lost the presidential election of 1800, Lyon wrote to the outgoing president telling him that he planned to move west "where I have fixed for myself an asylum from the persecutions of a party the most base, cruel, assuming, and faithless that ever disgraced the councils of any nation." He had already invested in and encouraged a mass migration of Vermonters, including his daughters and their families, to western Kentucky, where they founded Eddyville. Lyon followed in 1801 and became a

"Congressional Pugilists." (Collection of the US House of Representatives, Washington, DC)

leading Democratic-Republican. In 1803, his Kentucky neighbors sent him back to the US House of Representatives for the first of four terms.

In the meantime, Breckinridge traveled to Virginia to meet with Thomas Jefferson and James Madison. Along with George Nicholas, the men plotted to undermine the Alien and Sedition Acts through state legislation. The legislation they drafted decreed that a state legislature could not be charged with sedition. Madison wrote resolutions for the Virginia legislature. Jefferson's resolutions originally had been intended for North Carolina, but Democratic-Republicans actually lost some power in that state's elections in fall 1798. Kentucky's outrage was well known. Members of the general assembly demanded "resolutions praying for a repeal of every obnoxious and unconstitutional act." So, Breckinridge's visit to Virginia was well timed, and upon his return to Kentucky, he carried Jefferson's document with him.

Pledged to keep Jefferson's authorship secret, Breckinridge pushed the resolutions through the assembly with ease. Federalist William Murray insisted that a state legislature did not have the authority to question congressional actions; only the courts could de-

clare laws unconstitutional. Breckinridge responded with a speech in which he explained the compact theory of government: that the states possessed all the powers that had not been granted to the federal government and they could determine whether it had exceeded its just powers. "I hesitate not to declare it as my opinion that it is then the right and duty of the several states to nullify those acts," he said, "and to protect their citizens from their operations." On November 10, the house accepted the resolutions. Murray voted against all nine of the provisions. On at least five votes, his was the only negative one.

The Kentucky Resolutions stopped short of nullifying federal laws. Instead, they called for other states to join Kentucky's members of Congress in pressing for their repeal. But Federalists elsewhere mocked Kentuckians' efforts. "If these sagacious and learned citizens had assembled in any place where there had been a single magistrate of spirit and good sense," a Federalist newspaper declared, "he would have dispersed them by his constables and thereby spared his country the disgrace." Kentuckians "appear to be just civilized enough to be the tools of faction, and that's all." Other opponents were more serious in their condemnations. Vermont's legislature responded that "the people," not the states, had formed the government, and no state had the right to judge the actions of the national government. Making a case of nullification had never been Breckinridge's or Jefferson's intent, but the legacy of the Kentucky Resolutions would be a states' rights philosophy that justified state nullification of federal acts. Carried to an extreme, the doctrine would be used to justify secession if a state decided it could not protect its rights any other way.

Penal and Constitutional Reform

As Breckinridge led the fight against the Alien and Sedition Acts, his popularity rose. As early as 1793, Breckinridge had pushed for penal reform. Kentucky had appropriated Virginia's penal code, one rooted in the state's colonial British origins. The English system still imposed the death penalty for more than two hundred crimes, including stealing fish. Thomas Jefferson had tried, but failed, to reform Virginia's system. Breckinridge mustered the influence of the Lexington Democratic-Republican Society behind his efforts. The society petitioned the state legislature in 1796 to make punishment commensurate with the offense. As a member of the Kentucky House in 1798, he introduced legislation to create a more humane code.

Breckinridge put forth four objectives of penal reform: to rehabilitate offenders, to make reparations to victims, to repay the public for prosecutorial costs, and to make an example to deter future crime. He then proposed abolishing the death penalty for all crimes except murder. Imprisonment and hard labor should force criminals to reflect and repent. Pennsylvania had developed a rehabilitation program that trained prisoners in honest trades. "Let us remember that those unfortunate wretches are our fellow citizens," he reminded the legislature, "that to err is the lot of humanity, & that in punishing offenses, larger, very large allowances ought to be made for the frailties of Human nature."

The legislature approved a new penal code in 1798. It abolished the death penalty except for first-degree murder. The reform included construction of a thirty-inmate penitentiary in Frankfort. Prisoners worked as stonecutters, and at making nails, shoes, chairs, and tinware. Humphrey Marshall criticized the experiment. He complained that "these penitentiary convicts, are better accommodated, than the army of the revolution very frequently were, for months at a time." If their accommodations were better, it was only by a matter of degrees. The prisoners' rations consisted of bread or corn meal with two portions of meat each week.

Certainly, with his success in penal reform, Breckinridge believed he could effect constitutional reform as well. He acted along with George Nicholas, whose own popularity swelled during the fight over the Alien and Sedition Acts. Nicholas and Breckinridge planned to take advantage of their influence as the May 1799 elections for representatives to the constitutional convention approached. In Fayette County, Nicholas delivered a major address to a large public gathering at Bryan's Station. At such public meetings, the more conservative faction of Democratic-Republicans put forth slates of preferred candidates and resolutions for constitutional change. The tactic worked. Fayette County elected all six of the candidates Nicholas proposed.

The May 1799 elections were about change. Tensions that had grown between local and state governments during the 1790s and the more recent visible contest between state and federal governments frustrated Kentuckians. Of the fifty-eight delegates selected to revise the state constitution, only ten had served in the 1792 convention. Only three were ministers, compared to seven at the earlier meeting. The number of lawyers increased from two to nine. Although all the delegates were wealthy, only Patrick Brown of Hardin County was not a slaveholder (he had recently freed slaves and become an antislavery advocate). Twenty-eight of the men owned ten or more slaves. And George Nicholas would not be there. He had refused to run for a convention seat, although he worked exhaustedly to make sure that one would take place. He died suddenly on July 25, three days after the convention opened. Still, the convention was not without Nicholas's influence: he had worked with Breckinridge and

Caleb Wallace to draft a series of resolutions to guide revisions to the constitution.

As the convention approached in summer 1799, newspapers filled with complaints about what needed to be altered in the constitution. The senate was too aristocratic. The county governments were too invasive and possibly unconstitutional. Slavery had not been adequately addressed in 1792. Electors stood between "the people" and their government. Unlike in 1792, when most delegates fell into three camps, the political intrigues of the 1790s had divided the 1799 delegates into less discernible groups, and Humphrey Marshall noted "greater disparity between the extremes."

When George Nicholas spoke at Bryan's Station earlier in the year, he had presented his own ideas for constitutional revision: an independent judiciary, more democratic representation in the general assembly, and barriers to legislative emancipation of slaves. These became the foundation for the Bryan's Station party, a faction of men who wanted to protect property rights from too much democracy. Breckinridge and Wallace became the foremost spokesmen for the faction, while Samuel Taylor and John Bailey opposed the Bryan's Station party, consistently proving to be more democratic. Alexander Bullitt, Robert Johnson, and Philemon Thomas opposed the Bryan's Station crowd on separation of powers. They wished to empower the legislature more, not less. And then there was Green Clay, who delighted in outraging the convention with statements about the constitutionality of the Alien and Sedition Acts and asserting that a state constitution did not matter because the national government had accumulated all significant powers. States existed "to mind the poor & straighten the roads," he once declared. Breckinridge wrote in his journal, "give no answer to this man."

Although no one man dominated the convention, as Nicholas had in 1792, Breckinridge was armed with the Bryan's Station resolutions and was able to dictate the conversations to a large degree. He did not hide his fear of "the people" who would overturn society to gain a bit of an advantage for themselves. "Where is the difference whether I am robbed of my horse

by a highwayman, or of my slave by a set of people called a Convention?" he said. Slavery and land titles had to be protected. Debate over ending slavery was ferocious. Philemon Thomas had once vowed that he "would wade to his knees in blood before it should take place." There was not enough emancipationist sentiment among the delegates to end slavery, however. Instead, the convention defined citizenship to exclude free blacks, mulattos, and Indians. The 1792 constitution had not been that explicit. The convention also revised the state's bill of rights to read that "all free men, when they form a social compact, are equal," signaling a determination to draw racial lines clearly and definitively. By a vote of thirty-seven to fourteen, the convention even denied the legislature the power to prohibit importation of slaves. With those votes, George Nicholas's 1792 expectation that Kentucky might one day shed slavery died, ironically less than a week after he did.

Although more conservative delegates won the slavery debates, more democratic candidates found their own successes. Some of the governor's appointment power transferred to county courts, and the courts also gained an advisory role in the governor's selection of justices of the peace, sheriffs, and coroners. The convention replaced ballot voting, which many citizens distrusted, with voice voting. Of course, voice voting exposed a citizen to greater pressure when he announced his vote. The delegates also disposed of the elector system that selected the governor and state senators, replacing it with direct election of those officials. They also constituted the new position of lieutenant governor. More conservative delegates tried unsuccessfully to push through requirements for office holding, including property ownership and marriage status in order to sit in the Kentucky Senate.

If "the people" were to have full voice, however, representation had to be reconsidered. The Bluegrass counties, with their larger populations, dominated the state government throughout the 1790s, and its leaders were reluctant to sacrifice any power. Breckinridge wanted to retain representation based on population. Delegates from south of the Green

Resolutions and Proceedings in Committee of the Whole, on the 31st day of July 1799. (Library of Congress, Rare Book and Special Collections Division, Printed Ephemera Collection, Washington, DC)

RESOLUTIONS AND PROCEEDINGS
IN COMMITTEE OF THE WHOLE,
On the 31st day of July, 1799.

I. ARTICLE 5th, section 1st, The judicial power of this commonwealth, both as to matters of law and equity, ought to be vested in one Supreme Court, which ought to be stiled the Court of Appeals.

II. RESOLVED, that there shall be a County Court established within each county in this commonwealth.

River wanted county representation since their part of the state had seen the greatest growth in county development, although most were sparsely populated. The convention hammered out a compromise that allowed adjoining counties with insufficient populations to join together to elect representatives. The larger counties countered that their excess populations were not truly represented. Their objections led to a compromise late in the convention that provided additional representation to adjoining counties above the quota set by the assembly. Ironically, by trying to provide true representation by numbers, the new constitution reinforced the influence of the most populous counties in the Bluegrass.

The convention also reduced the governor's veto power. Originally, two-thirds of both legislative houses were required to override a veto. The new constitution allowed a majority of both legislative houses to negate the governor's actions. The delegates placed another limit on the governor, who became ineligible for reelection for seven years after the end of his term.

Then the convention turned to the judiciary. Certainly, frustrations lingered over *Kenton v. McConnell*. Alexander Bullitt wanted to empower the legislature to review judges' opinions and remove those who rendered questionable opinions. Others thought a less-centralized judiciary would weaken the Kentucky Court of Appeals. Two young lawyers—Felix Grundy and William Bledsoe—argued that justices in the quarter sessions courts were often ignorant

about the law and that the district court system had never fully been realized. They presented a plan for a circuit court system, but Breckinridge countered that only the legislature should have authority over the judicial structure. The proposal lost twenty-three to thirty, but the narrow vote inspired continued work on judicial reform that resulted in the creation of a circuit court system three years later.

The convention also decided on a system for future constitutional revision. Individual amendments would not be permitted, but within the first twenty days of a regular legislative session a majority of both houses could call for a referendum for a new constitutional convention. Then a majority of eligible voters had to approve the convention. One year later, the electorate would again have to approve a convention.

Although much of the revision to the constitution centered upon empowering democracy, the delegates did not feel obligated to set the new constitution before the public. The convention approved it, fifty-three to three, on August 1, 1799. Then the delegates signed it. Thomas Clay of Madison County created a stir when he scribbled "I protest against it" after his name. His statement was erased, and he was persuaded to confine his comment to the convention journal. Once signed by the delegates, the new government went into effect on June 1, 1800. It was more democratic and more decentralized, with some powers reverting to the counties, but it also protected the landed and chattel property of the state's wealthiest men.

5

The First Generation of Kentuckians

The Frontier Heritage

In the 1770s, 1780s, and well into the 1790s, residents of Kentucky did not see themselves or others as Kentuckians. They consistently spoke of Marylanders and Carolinians, Yankees and Virginians, Pennsylvanians and Georgians among them. By the mid-1790s, these settler colonials had supplanted Native Americans, but most had not been born in Kentucky, and they, therefore, did not view it as home.

Still, the settler colonials who had overtaken Kentucky and defended it during the American Revolutionary War had children, a generation that began to come of age contemporaneous with the creation of the state in the 1790s. The eldest among them, born in the late 1760s, participated in the settlement of Kentucky as children. Henry Clay and others joined them. As immigrant members of the same generation, they shared a similar understanding of their neighbors and themselves as a collective—a group with common interests as Americans. Jefferson's presidential election in 1800 proved a catalyzing moment for the first generation. This first generation of Kentuckians wanted to believe what the new president stated in his inaugural address about the unity of the United States. "We are all Republicans, we are all Federalists," Jefferson declared. They greatly outnumbered their parents' generation, and they saw the War of 1812 as an opportunity to prove their worthiness in inheriting their parents' revolutionary legacy. Building upon that legacy, they worked to create and sustain their state and nation, and they were willing to make concessions to do so. As Clay declared in 1850, "Life itself is but a compromise between death and life, the struggle continuing throughout our whole existence. . . . All legislation, all government, all society, is formed upon the principle of mutual concession, politeness, comity, courtesy; upon these, everything is based." But the idealism of this first generation did not pass to their children. The youngest members of the first generation would live long enough to see their children erode that sense of American unity in the animosities leading to civil war.

Most of the first generation of Kentuckians had heard of John Filson's *The Discovery, Settlement and Present State of Kentucke*. It had inspired many of their parents to make the journey westward in the 1780s. It also laid the foundation for the frontier myth—tales of Boone and Native Americans and virgin land—that would shape their imaginations. Gilbert Imlay's books also profoundly influenced the first generation of Kentuckians. Imlay had arrived in Kentucky in 1783. Nine years later, after returning to England, he published *Topographical Description of the Western Territory of North America*. His was a story of progress: Kentucky as the natural inheritor of the American experiment that began with the American Revolutionary War: "Such has been the progress of the settlement of this country, from dirty stations or forts, and smoky huts, that it has expanded into fertile fields, blushing orchards, pleasant gardens, luxuriant sugar groves, neat and commodious houses, rising villages, and trading towns. Ten years have produced a difference in the population and comforts of this county, which to be pourtrayed in just colours would appear marvelous." He followed his first book with *The Emigrants; or, The History of an Expatriated Family* (1783), considered to be the first Kentucky novel. Through

Table 5.1. The First Generation of Kentuckians: Demographics, 1790–1850

	Their Parents' Generation	Their Generation	Their Children's Generation
1790	15,000	17,000	
1800	49,000	58,000	72,000
1810	31,000	114,000	179,000
1820	n/a	121,000	154,000
1830		18,000	248,000
1840		10,000	132,000
1850		4,000	32,000

Source: Rough estimates based on censuses from *Historical Statistics of the United States: Colonial Times to 1970, Part 1* (Washington, DC: US Bureau of the Census, 1975), 28.

a series of fictional letters, Imlay's novel related the romantic adventures of an English family that migrated to Louisville.

Nostalgia for Kentucky's frontier past became increasingly important as the first generation aged. The frontier myth became central to the way Kentuckians imagined themselves. The mysteries and adventures of frontier life permeated the culture that they produced. It emerged in public displays like Charles Wilkins's 1816 exhibit of the unearthed native mummy named Fawn Hoof at Mammoth Cave and in public celebrations like the ceremony and funeral held in Maysville in 1824 for Puckshunubbe, a Choctaw chief and veteran of the wars of the 1780s and 1790s. It was pervasive in journalism like John Bradford's "Notes on Kentucky," a series of historical sketches published in the *Kentucky Gazette* in the mid-1820s; poetry like Daniel Bryan's "The Mountain Muse" (1826); and history like James Alexander McClung's *Sketches of Western Adventure* (1832). The frontier myth also invaded science texts like Constantine Rafinesque's *Ancient Annals of Kentucky* (1824). Nostalgia inspired the creation of the Kentucky Historical Society in 1836 to "collect and preserve authentic information and facts connected with the early history of the State." In 1838, John Dabney Shane began to collect oral histories from aging members of Kentucky's earliest colonists. The frontier even inspired women's cookbooks. Although she was of the next generation, Lettice Pierce Bryan, born in Lincoln County in 1805, published *The Kentucky Housewife* in 1839, which provided over thirteen hundred recipes for medical remedies, domestic productions, and food.

A large number of the food recipes evoked the frontier experience by including "Indian" in their names: Indian corn, baked Indian pudding, boiled Indian pudding, Indian pudding without eggs, Indian dumplings, Indian fritters, Indian muffins, Indian butter cakes, Indian flappers, Indian short cake, Indian hoe cakes, Indian water cakes, Indian mush, light Indian bread, and "a very good Indian bread."

Across the United States, Kentucky's place in the revolutionary past permeated American culture. Even though the stories were placed in other geographies, James Fenimore Cooper created a thinly disguised Daniel Boone as his protagonist in *The Pioneers* (1823) and *Last of the Mohicans* (1826). From the late 1810s through the 1820s, Noah M. Ludlow, one of the nation's more popular actors and a pioneer of American theater, portrayed a Boone character. In 1826, Kentucky's frontier narrative was etched permanently into the rotunda walls of the nation's new capitol as part of an emerging national mythology.

Yet that frontier past was also contentious in the Kentucky mind. In 1812, Humphrey Marshall published *The History of Kentucky*. As a Federalist, Marshall believed Kentucky had strayed politically from the promise of its frontier past. Of an older generation, Marshall saw himself as a guardian of patriarchal republican ideals. He believed that the younger generation appeared to have forgotten the sacrifices of their fathers, his fellow revolutionaries. He denounced Kentuckians of his own generation who betrayed those ideals, like Harry Innes, who had conspired with James Wilkinson in the late 1780s and seemingly again with Burr

Conflict of Daniel Boone and the Indians, bas-relief by Enrico Causici, 1826–1827. (Courtesy of the Architect of the Capitol, Washington, DC)

Marshall considered it demagoguery—Clay playing to Kentuckians' emotions and prejudices rather than appealing to their reason. The two men exchanged insults that led to a duel in early 1809. Clay lightly grazed Marshall's stomach with a bullet, and Marshall returned the favor in Clay's thigh. When Marshall wrote his *History*, then, he argued that historians should "single out the ambitious demagogue, who from time, to time, deluded the credulous people, under the mask of *patriotism,* and the name of REPUBLICAN."

Marshall was not widely popular, however, and for the rising generation of Kentuckians, he represented an old, deferential order that no longer had a place in a young, dynamic republic. For them, frontier heritage was only nostalgia. As they became political leaders, the new generation sought to shed the eighteenth-century past and push Kentucky's economy into the new century. The most famous effort to discard its vestiges was Clay's "American System," an economic plan that he promoted at the federal level. Clay included a tariff in his system to protect American productions, a national bank, and federal investments in internal improvements. Kentucky's governors from the first generation also pushed forward measures to modernize the state. Gabriel Slaughter advocated for reform of the penal system, internal improvements, a state library, and a comprehensive public school system funded through lotteries. The state legislature rejected Slaughter's efforts. The next governor, Joseph Desha, was a bit more successful. He persuaded the assembly to fund the Louisville and Portland Canal. His ideas for a turnpike from Maysville through Lexington to Louisville died, however, as did his advocacy to construct hard-surfaced roads. His successor, Thomas Metcalfe, pushed for protective tariffs, internal improvements, and investment in railroads. Even the lone Jacksonian Democrat among the first-generation governors, John Breathitt, supported public funding for the Lexington and Ohio Railroad. Another five governors, all Whigs, were also members of the first generation, and all similarly promoted economic and educational development.

in 1806. Marshall also denounced the ambitions of the younger generation, particularly Henry Clay. When, in 1808, Clay began wearing homespun clothing to protest British imports and encourage American manufacturing,

Table 5.2. Governors of the First Generation of Kentuckians

	Born	Years in Office	Political Party
Gabriel Slaughter	1767	1816–1820	Democratic-Republican
Joseph Desha	1768	1824–1828	Democratic-Republican
Thomas Metcalfe	1780	1828–1832	National Republican
John Breathitt	1786	1832–1834	Democrat
James Clark	1779	1836–1839	Whig
Charles A. Wickliffe	1788	1839–1840	Whig
Robert P. Letcher	1788	1840–1844	Whig
William Owsley	1782	1844–1848	Whig
John J. Crittenden	1787	1848–1850	Whig

Louisiana and the Burr Conspiracy

Most people who identified as Kentuckians thrilled at the presidential election of Thomas Jefferson in 1800. It had not been certain: Jefferson and Aaron Burr had tied in the presidential count, and the decision went to the House of Representatives. In the end, many of Jefferson's detractors decided him the better choice over the more erratic Burr. Kentuckians saw Jefferson as a relief from the administrations of George Washington and John Adams. Neither had made much effort to encourage western development. Although Washington had determined to crush the Western Confederacy of Native Americans who threatened American settler colonialism, in trade relations, the federal government had acted directly against western interests. So, Jefferson's presidency was welcomed. As Hubbard Taylor noted, "I cannot but express my heart felt joy to find so general a satisfaction pervade this country I live in, at the election of Mr. Jefferson." Democratic-Republicans in Kentucky swept the 1800 election. Governor James Garrard successfully ran for reelection as governor, and John Breckinridge became the state's newest federal senator.

Jefferson's dedication to western Americans was tested quickly. Since the 1795 Treaty of San Lorenzo, western Americans had increased their shipments down the Mississippi River and through New Orleans. In the autumn of 1802, however, Spanish intendant Don Juan Ventura Morales declared that Americans would no longer enjoy the right of deposit of goods at New Orleans. The treaty required him to designate an alternative port,

but he refused. Jefferson was unaware of a secret treaty—the Treaty of San Ildefonso—that Napoleon Bonaparte, as leader of the French revolutionary government, strongly pushed Spain to sign in 1800. In return for lands in Tuscany, Spain returned to France the Louisiana territory that it had acquired at the end of the American Revolutionary War. The return of the Louisiana territory laid the foundation for Napoleon's plan to reestablish a French empire in North America.

Jefferson had to act. Kentuckians were angry and vocal about their loss of exporting rights. Many citizens, including Governor Garrard, called for unilateral action. The state's militia prepared to send thirty thousand troops southward to invade New Orleans. Federalists, taking advantage of the growing frustrations with France, claimed unity with disgruntled westerners and demanded that Jefferson confront Napoleon. Senator Breckinridge proposed that the US Senate provide eighty thousand men and unlimited money for an invasion, leaving the call for action to the president. The Senate approved his resolution.

Hoping to undermine Napoleon's ambitions and resolve western Americans' economic challenge, Jefferson instructed his minister to France, Robert Livingston, to purchase New Orleans, Florida, or another port. He knew that "the day that France takes possession of New Orleans, we must marry ourselves to the British fleet and nation." Moreover, he had exhorted against this situation for over a decade. He sent James Monroe, who was popular among westerners, as a special envoy to assist Livingston. By the time Monroe arrived in

Paris, the French unexpectedly had offered to sell Louisiana to the United States for approximately fifteen million dollars. Neither Livingston nor Monroe had authority to accept the offer, but they feared that hesitation might give Napoleon opportunity to change his mind.

Jefferson gladly endorsed Livingston and Monroe's decision to purchase Louisiana. In August 1803, he warned Breckinridge, with whom he had collaborated on the Kentucky Resolutions in 1799, that "the constitution has made no provision for our holding foreign territory, still less for incorporating foreign nations into our Union." Nevertheless, he insisted that Congress "must ratify & pay for it, and throw themselves on their country for doing for them unauthorized what we know they would have done for themselves had they been in a situation to do it."

Jefferson did not worry, as did many other eastern politicians, that purchase of Louisiana would fracture the new republic. He had a vision for the American West:

> The future inhabitants of the Atlantic & Missipi States will be our sons. We leave them in distinct but bordering establishments. We think we see their happiness in their union, & we wish it. Events may prove it otherwise; and if they see their interest in separation, why should we take side with our Atlantic rather than our Missipi descendants? It is the elder and the younger son differing. . . . the best use we can make of the country for some time, will be to give establishments in it to the Indians on the East side of the Missipi, in exchange for their present country, and open land offices in the last & thus make this acquisition the means of filling up the Eastern side, instead of drawing off its population. When we shall be full on this side, we may lay off a range of States on the Western bank from the head to the mouth, & so, range after range, advancing compactly as we multiply.

Always more practical than concerned about constitutionalism, Breckinridge already

had begun mustering support for the purchase. "Far from believing that a republic ought to be confined within narrow limits," he argued in Senate debates, "I believe, on the contrary, that the more extensive its dominion the more safe and more durable it will be." Ignoring Jefferson's plea for a constitutional amendment, Breckinridge successfully pushed the purchase and a plan for governance of Louisiana.

As the election of 1804 approached, Breckinridge became a natural possible candidate to replace Aaron Burr as vice president. The Democratic-Republicans selected George Clinton of New York instead, concerned that a Jefferson-Breckinridge ticket would not appeal to northerners. An editorial circulated throughout American newspapers calling on electors to write in Breckinridge for vice president. The editorial forced the Kentuckian to publish his own response. He asked all Democratic-Republicans to be loyal to the ticket as it was composed. Even as the Louisiana Purchase bolstered Breckinridge's political fortunes, it became a thorn in Jefferson's side. His political opponents accused him of constitutional hypocrisy. After all, he had spent much of the previous decade insisting that Alexander Hamilton too loosely interpreted the Constitution when he implemented his economic programs.

And then there was Burr. Jefferson distrusted his vice president, and in his bid for reelection in 1804, he dropped Burr from the party's ticket. In July, Burr killed Alexander Hamilton in a duel and was indicted for murder in New Jersey. "In New York I am to be disfranchised, in New Jersey, hanged," Burr wrote. "Having substantial objections to both, I shall not . . . hazard either, but shall seek another country." Disgraced and no longer vice president, he arrived in Frankfort, Kentucky, in late May 1805.

What Burr had in mind remains debated, but Louisiana and Kentucky were both central to his plans. Burr, indeed, may not have been sure what he wanted. He apparently contacted Robert Murray, British minister to the United States, to see if England would assist with the West's secession from the United States. He visited Kentucky politicians John Brown and John Adair to explore whether Mexico could be captured if the United States were coaxed into a war with Spain. He visited Andrew Jackson in Tennessee and James Wilkinson at Fort Massac in Illinois territory. He garnered some financial support from Herman Blennerhassett, an Irish immigrant who wanted to establish a colony on an island in the Ohio River. Burr was not cautious. His activities drew attention. In early November 1805, the *Kentucky Gazette* warned about the man whose political career "was fraught with a degree of duplicity which can never be satisfactorily defended." In January 1806, Joseph Hamilton Daveiss, federal district attorney in Kentucky, wrote several letters to Jefferson warning of Burr's actions. Jefferson asked for more information but did nothing.

In July, a new Frankfort newspaper, *The Western World*, published a series of articles on Wilkinson's Spanish Conspiracy of the 1780s. The articles named conspirators, including Benjamin Sebastian, a justice on the state's court of appeals. Kentucky's House of Representatives found him guilty of accepting a two-thousand-dollar annual pension from Spain and demanded his resignation. Federal district judge Harry Innes successfully sued the newspaper for implicating him. The newspaper's editors continued with their series, however, and in their fourth issue, they charged that another conspiracy was underway, led by the notorious Aaron Burr. Jefferson sent John Graham, secretary of the Territory of Orleans, to investigate.

When Burr returned to Kentucky in fall 1806, Daveiss pounced. He appealed to the district court to demand that Burr answer charges that he was preparing an expedition against Mexico, which belonged to a friendly foreign power. Judge Innes delayed granting the request, a decision that would make him suspect among many observers. Finally, a court date was set. On November 11, Burr arrived with his attorneys, among them, Henry Clay. Daveiss could not produce a key witness, however, and Burr seized the opportunity to plead that all of his actions related to private business dealings. Innes rescheduled for December 2. Clay, concerned for his own reputation in defending a potential traitor, demanded a written denial from Burr. "My views have been ex-

plained to, and approved by several of the principal officers of the government," his client responded, "and I believe are well understood by the administration, and seen by it with complacency." Satisfied, Clay accompanied Burr to court, but Daveiss still did not have his witnesses lined up. The jury dismissed Daveiss's charges against John Adair as a coconspirator and then against Burr, having heard nothing that incriminated either man.

Yet, neither man was innocent. A letter that James Wilkins wrote to Jefferson exposed Burr's planned expedition. When Graham arrived in Ohio to investigate, he had local militias seize several boats. In late November, President Jefferson issued an order that any expedition be stopped. When Burr reached the mouth of the Cumberland River to join the expeditionary force, fewer than one hundred people awaited him. Many of them were women and children. Wilkinson had John Adair arrested in New Orleans along with other minor conspirators. Burr tried to escape, but authorities captured him and sent him to Virginia to be tried in federal circuit court. The resulting trial is well known in American history. Jefferson claimed executive privilege to withhold state secrets from the court, while John Marshall challenged the executive branch's authority. Burr escaped conviction but lived in exile in Europe thereafter.

Kentucky could not escape the fallout from Burr's activities. Many Americans questioned Kentuckians for supporting Burr's plans. Clay tried to distance himself from the episode by declaring that Burr had misled him. Citizens meeting in Lexington in January 1807 pleaded "that all charges & insinuations against the people of this State, of dissatisfaction to the Union or the Government of the United States, are gross misapprehensions and without foundation." When John Adair sued James Wilkinson for false arrest and won an apology and a $2500 award, Kentucky seemed to be redeemed as well.

The War of 1812

As the Burr affair subsided, foreign relations became problematic. Many Kentuckians had

Tecumseh. (Benson J. Lossing, *Pictorial Field Book of the War of 1812* [New York: Harper & Row, 1896], 283)

Tenskwatawa. (Benson J. Lossing, *Pictorial Field Book of the War of 1812* [New York: Harper & Row, 1896], 189)

relatives who had migrated across the Ohio River into the Northwest Territory. Land titles in Kentucky continued to be challenged in the courts, and the surveying and distribution of lands north of the Ohio were more systematic and less prone to legal confusion. Many others, therefore, purchased lands in the region. Some Kentuckians even looked beyond the Northwest Territory to Canada for future expansion.

Since the Treaty of Greenville, the Western Confederacy of Native Americans had compressed into a small area as American settler colonials pushed into the northwest. By 1808, a large number of Shawnees lived at Prophetstown, led by Chief Tecumseh and his brother, Tenskwatawa, the Shawnee Prophet. Tenskwatawa believed that a coming apocalypse would destroy the Americans and return the homeland to the Shawnees. His teaching attracted other native peoples who, in time, outnumbered the Shawnees, creating a new pan-national confederation. As Tenskwatawa inspired, Tecumseh recruited. With encouragement from the British in Canada, he convinced native peoples in the northwest and southwest of the neces-

sity for military response to the Americans. He denounced the Treaty of Fort Wayne in 1809 that seemingly secured another three million acres for American settlement. "Sell a country!? Why not sell the air, the great sea, as well as the earth? Didn't the Great Spirit make them all for the use of his children?" he asked, and then determined that "the only way to stop this evil is for the red man to unite in claiming a common and equal right in the land, as it was first, and should be now, for it was never divided."

Determined to stop white settlement in the Wabash River region, Tecumseh gathered a force of warriors at Prophetstown and then traveled southward to recruit Choctaws and Chickasaws for his war against the Americans. During his absence, William Henry Harrison, governor of the Territory of Indiana, confronted the confederation at Tippecanoe Creek. On November 7, 1811, the two armies collided. Fighting was fierce. Sixty-two Americans died, including Joseph Hamilton Daveiss, who had so actively pursued Burr as a traitor. Another 126 were wounded. The confederation faced more severe losses: about 200 died. A regiment of Kentucky riflemen outflanked the remaining Native Americans and forced them to retreat. The Americans burned Prophetstown.

The loss at Tippecanoe convinced Tecumseh that he needed British assistance to defeat the Americans, and the British were more than willing to help. British-American relations had been eroding for years. Since the mid-1790s, the British and French had been at war. The United States insisted on neutrality to protect its commercial interests. In his Farewell Address of 1796, George Washington laid out a policy of neutrality so that Americans might avoid trade regulations that the European great powers imposed on their enemy's allies. But neither France nor Britain would accept American neutrality. Each imposed trade restrictions, hoping to manipulate the Americans' desire for free trade against its enemy. President Jefferson and his Secretary of State, James Madison, worked to protect neutrality. Throughout this time, the United States maintained a small and unprepared military.

Few Kentuckians cared about the nuances of the nation's diplomatic situation. When the British stopped American ships, they often impressed sailors into service for the British Navy. In one such episode in June 1807, the British ship *Leopard* tried to stop the US frigate *Chesapeake,* eventually firing upon it in American waters. Kentuckians interpreted such actions as an assault on the nation's honor and demanded retaliation. In 1807, Jefferson tried to coerce the British and French with an embargo. As Jefferson's successor in the president's house, Madison signed the Non-Intercourse Act in 1809 and Macon's Bill No. 2 in 1810. All of these laws injured the American economy, and none resolved the diplomatic problem.

The congressional elections of 1810–1811 brought a cohort of War Hawks into the United States House of Representatives. Kentucky's Henry Clay, Joseph Desha, and Richard M. Johnson were among them. Kentuckians wanted war. Newspapers filled with editorials demanding vindication. Citizens congregated at mass meetings and sent petitions to Congress. Finally, Madison sent a war message to Congress. Federalists and some Democratic-Republicans argued and voted against war. Kentucky senator John Pope, for example, insisted that the United States declare war against France as well as Britain. Most congressmen had less concern with the French. By mid-June 1812, the United States was at war with Britain again.

Kentuckians fell into a frenzy of unrestrained nationalism. Nearly twenty-two hundred enlisted as United States Regulars, and another nine thousand joined volunteer units that fought in specific campaigns. In their minds, Kentuckians were still fighting an Indian war. The *Kentucky Gazette* proclaimed "the hour is at hand; we are not yet prepared to kiss the hand that wields the tomahawk and scalping knife against the heads of our old men, our women and infants." Yet, the Native Americans were just tools of Britain. British military leaders incited them "to murder the inhabitants of our defenseless frontier; furnishing them with arms and ammunition lately, to attack our forces." Kentuckians needed an old warrior to lead them in this new war. In 1812, they elected Isaac Shelby, former governor and veteran of the Indian wars, as governor and commander of the commonwealth's military operations. Before he took office, Shelby worked with Governor Charles Scott to increase the US War Department's request for two thousand men to thirty-four hundred. He also asked William Henry Harrison to lead them as a brevet major general in the Kentucky militia. Shelby, upon assuming office, approached the national government with a proposal to form a board of western men to direct the war in the West. The War Department rejected the suggestion but did give Harrison command over the entire army in the Northwest.

Early in the war, many Kentuckians proposed an invasion of Canada. Some argued that such an invasion could be used to win concessions from Britain, while others saw the war as an opportunity to grab territory. Efforts to take Canada failed, and when General William Hull surrendered Detroit in August 1812, the dream of Canada died. Harrison determined to retake Detroit. Shelby supported him with one thousand mounted volunteers, under the command of Major General Samuel Hopkins. The troops were to invade Illinois and Indiana territories, diverting attention from Harrison's larger force headed to Detroit. But so many of Hopkins's men deserted that the army had to return to Kentucky.

Harrison's army continued on toward Detroit, albeit slowly. Winter hit hard. When he heard rumors of British supplies at Frenchtown, General James Winchester directed his division of thirteen hundred Kentuckians toward the Raisin River. He sent half of the men to capture the weapons and ammunition. On January 18, 1813, Lieutenant Colonels James Allen and William Lewis captured the small village, but four days later, a force of Canadians and Native Americans overwhelmed the Kentuckians. Cannon fire battered the fortifications. Many of the troops panicked and ran. Allen was killed, and Winchester and Lewis were captured. Native Americans slaughtered some of the captive Kentuckians and many of the eighty wounded soldiers left on the battlefield. At least four hundred Kentuckians died. "Remember the Raisin" became Kentucky's battle cry for the rest of the war.

The war had not begun well for Kentucky. The general assembly issued a call for 3,000 more troops, but Kentuckians did not respond. Governor Shelby had no choice but to use a draft to fill the ranks. Shelby complained to Harrison and Madison that, until they had control of the situation in the Northwest, he could not assure Kentuckians' participation. Harrison's army dwindled to about 2,000 by spring 1813. Nearly half of them were at Fort Meigs on the Maumee River, which the British had under siege by May. General Green Clay had 1,200 troops with him to relieve the garrison. He sent Lieutenant Colonel William Dudley with 700 men to spike the British cannons. But Dudley's men attacked prematurely. The British killed Dudley, and 650 of the troops were killed or captured. Again, the Native Americans allied to the British had little mercy for the prisoners. Only the arrival of Tecumseh ended the bloodbath. Although Fort Meigs remained in American hands, morale in Kentucky collapsed upon hearing of Dudley's defeat.

In July, however, a small incident suggested a shift in the Kentuckians' and Americans' fortunes. The British again laid siege to Fort Meigs. Unsuccessful, they turned their sights on the smaller Fort Stephenson, an American supply base on the Sandusky River commanded by Major George Croghan and 160 US Regulars. The Americans held off the British, who retreated to Canada. Croghan emerged a hero in a war that was short of them.

Governor Shelby left Kentucky with thirty-five hundred riflemen in September and, by early October, had arrived to reinforce Harrison's army. The Americans had defeated the British Navy on Lake Erie, reducing the threat that American supply lines might be cut should they advance into Canada. Harrison had five thousand men, most Kentuckians, on the shore of Lake Erie to confront a British force at Detroit of one thousand joined by another three thousand soldiers of Tecumseh's confederation. Fearful of being cut off, the British abandoned Detroit and retreated up the River Thames, with some three thousand of the Americans in pursuit. On October 5, the pursuers, including Richard M. Johnson's mounted riflemen, caught up to their enemy. Johnson's regiment rode through and routed the British regulars before coming under heavy fire from Native Americans hiding in the swampy grounds along the Thames. The Kentuckians dismounted to engage on foot, some part of a "forlorn hope"—a band of soldiers who took the lead in a highly risky operation. Fifteen of the twenty men died immediately, among them the old settler colonial William Whitley. Johnson sustained five wounds during the fight. Not until Shelby sent reinforcements to root out the Native Americans did the tide of battle change. Tecumseh was killed, shattering his fellow warriors' spirit and ending the dream of confederation that inspired their war.

The months following the Battle of the Thames were among the brightest of the war for Kentuckians. Enthusiasm for the war ran high, and when President Madison accepted the British offer to negotiate, many Kentuckians argued that he should accelerate the war effort and take Canada. Fighting in the West subsided as the theater of war shifted to the East, where the British set the US Capitol ablaze and laid siege to Baltimore's Fort McHenry. Vol-

Company roster for Sixteenth Kentucky Militia. (Gregg Family Papers, The Filson Historical Society, Louisville, KY)

unteer recruits declined from 11,114 in 1812 to 4,156 in 1814. Governor Shelby refused to commit any more Kentuckians to the war until they received their pay from previous action.

But Kentuckians' participation in the War of 1812 was not finished. News of a British attack on New Orleans once again threatened Kentucky's use of the Mississippi River. When Louisiana's governor asked for help, Kentuckians quickly signed up. Three regiments formed, but there were insufficient supplies. Richard Taylor, quartermaster of the state militia, mortgaged his farm to raise six thousand dollars to finance the expedition. Despite Taylor's financial support, these soldiers were inadequately prepared. When the soldiers arrived in New

Orleans in January 1815, General Andrew Jackson remarked that they did not meet his usual expectations: "I have never seen a Kentuckian without a gun and a pack of cards and a bottle of whiskey in my life."

Nine thousand British troops attempted to break the five thousand American troops that defended New Orleans. General John Adair found weapons for about one thousand of the Kentuckians. They backed up the center of the American line that slaughtered two thousand of the British, including their commander General Sir Edward Pakenham. About five hundred Kentucky troops under Colonel John Davis reinforced Louisiana militiamen on the west banks of the Mississippi River. Only about half were armed, so when a large British army attacked, they were unable to hold off the assault. Still, the British were in such disarray that they did not follow upon their success. After the battle, Jackson understated Kentuckians' contribution to the main battle and blamed them for the debacle on the western banks. His comments insulted Kentuckians, and Adair demanded an apology. Some years later, Jackson conceded that he had insufficient information when he wrote his report, and a court-martial cleared Davis of poor conduct.

In early 1814, Henry Clay had joined four other diplomats to negotiate terms for a treaty to end the war. His fellow Americans seemed eager to accept British concessions, but Clay thought the British too assertive. They demanded a buffer state between the United States and Canada to be populated by their Native American allies, and they wanted navigation rights on the Mississippi River. Clay insisted they receive neither, and as the war turned in the Americans' favor in late 1814, the British acceded to those demands. The Treaty of Ghent effectively ended the war. The British signed it before the Battle of New Orleans, but news had not reached Louisiana in time. Although the treaty did little to resolve matters that strained relations between the United States and Britain, the war settled many issues that Kentuckians considered important. Tecumseh was dead, as was the confederation he hoped to create. Native peoples would no lon-

ger threaten Kentucky or stand in the way of settlement of the Northwest. Nearly 65 percent of qualified white men in Kentucky participated in the war. Some 25,705 served as regulars, volunteers, or militia. Of the 1,876 Americans killed in the war, approximately 1,200 were Kentuckians. The first generation of Kentuckians proved their patriotism.

Patriotism and Panic

In New Orleans, Noah Ludlow made his career by performing "The Hunters of Kentucky," a song written at the end of the war to celebrate the Battle of New Orleans. Its eight verses recounted Kentuckians' role in the fight. The second verse caught the flavor of the legend:

> We are a hardy, free-born race,
>   Each man to fear a stranger,
> Whate'er the fame, we join in chase
>   Despising toil and danger;
> And if a daring foe annoys,
>   Whate'er his strengths and forces,
> We'll show him that Kentucky boys
>   Are "alligator horses."
> Oh! Kentucky, the hunters of Kentucky!
> Oh! Kentucky, the hunters of Kentucky!

A wave of nationalism swept across the United States, and Kentucky seemed to be very much at the heart of it. The Federalist Party had doomed itself late in the war when it presented an ultimatum to Congress that called the United States to retreat from war or see New England leave the union. Most Kentuckians condemned the Hartford Convention, although much of the Federalists' argument had arisen from Kentucky's appeal to states' rights in 1799. With the Federalist Party in decline, the Democratic-Republican Party faced little challenge, and Americans found it easier to agree on political issues. The Tariff of 1816 and the Second Bank of the United States became law during James Madison's administration, which inspired Henry Clay to push forward his American System. James Monroe's administration confronted the world with more confidence, culminating in the Monroe Doctrine. In cas-

Hunters of Kentucky, or Half
HORSE AND HÂLF ALLIGATOR.

"Hunters of Kentucky, or Half Horse and Half Alligator" (Boston: William Rutler, n.d.). (Library of Congress, Rare Book and Special Collections Division, Printed Ephemera Collection, Washington, DC)

YE gentlemen and ladies fair,
Who grace this famous city,
Just listen if you've time to spare,
While I rehearse a ditty;
And for the opportunity
Conceive yourselves quite lucky,
For 'tis not often that you see
A hunter from Kentucky.
Oh Kentucky, the hunters of Kentucky!
Oh Kentucky, the hunters of Kentucky!

We are a hardy, free-born race,
Each man to fear a stranger;
Whate'er the game we join in chase,
Despoiling time and danger
And if a daring foe annoys,
Whate'er his strength and forces,
We'll show him that Kentucky boys
Are alligator horses.
　　　　Oh Kentucky, &c.

I s'pose you've read it in the prints,
How Packenham attempted
To make old Hickory Jackson wince,
But soon his scheme repented;
For we, with rifles ready cock'd,
Thought such occasion lucky,
And soon around the gen'ral flock'd
The hunters of Kentucky.
　　　　Oh Kentucky, &c.

You've heard, I s'pose how New-Orleans
Is fam'd for wealth and beauty,
There's girls of ev'ry hue it seems,
From snowy white to sooty.
So Packenham he made his brags,
If he in fight was lucky,
He'd have their girls and cotton bags,
In spite of old Kentucky.
5 6 5　　　Oh Kentucky, &c.

But Jackson he was wide awake,
And was not scar'd at trifles,
For well he knew what aim we take
With our Kentucky rifles.
So he led us down to Cypress swamp,
The ground was low and mucky,
There stood John Bull in martial pomp
And here was old Kentucky.
　　　　Oh Kentucky, &c.

A bank was rais'd to hide our breasts,
Not that we thought of dying,
But that we always like to rest,
Unless the game is flying.
Behind it stood our little force,
None wished it to be greater,
For ev'ry man was half a horse,
And half an alligator.
　　　　Oh Kentucky, &c.

They did not let our patience tire,
Before they show'd their faces;
We did not choose to waste our fire,
So snugly kept our places.
But when so near we saw them wink,
We thought it time to stop 'em,
And 'twould have done you good I think,
To see Kentuckians drop 'em.
　　　　Oh Kentucky, &c.

They found, at last, 'twas vain to fight,
Where *lead* was all the *booty*,
And so they wisely took to flight,
And left us all our *beauty*.
And now, if danger e'er annoys,
Remember what our trade is,
Just send for us Kentucky boys,
And we'll protect ye, ladies.
　　　　Oh Kentucky, &c.

Sold wholesale & retail by William Rutler, No. 1, Snow's Wharf, Boston.

es like *Fletcher v. Peck* (1810), *Martin v. Hunter's Lessee* (1816), and *McCulloch v. Maryland* (1819), John Marshall's Supreme Court expanded the power of the national government.

The nation enjoyed an economic boom after the war, and Kentuckians joined in the prosperity. Foodstuffs were needed in Europe. England suffered from poor crop yields and continental Europe struggled with the destruction of war. Thousands migrated to the new American southwest to establish cotton farms. This growth in cotton production increased demand for hemp, used to make bailing and rope for cotton shipments. Cotton bloomed south of the Green River; tobacco and hemp grew throughout the Bluegrass. State banks, like the Kentucky

Insurance Company founded in 1802 and the Bank of Kentucky in 1806, extended credit readily. The Second Bank of the United States opened branches in Lexington and Louisville. The general assembly chartered forty-six new banks in 1818 to meet the demand for investment funds. Most printed their own currency to circulate as money. Although many Kentuckians took loans to invest in land, slaves, improvements, seeds, and tools, the ease with which loans could be obtained led to widespread speculation as well. The many private banks became known as "wildcat banks" because a wildcat was someone who rashly speculated in as many profit-making schemes as he could.

Louisville benefited most from the postwar boom. Prior to the war, in 1811, the steamboat *New Orleans*, the first steamboat operating in the West, had docked in Louisville on its maiden voyage from Pittsburgh to New Orleans. It has always been easy to travel downriver: in 1807 alone, nearly 2,000 flatboats had arrived at Louisville. But traveling upriver was far more difficult and inhibited economic imports from New Orleans. The steamboat made upriver travel possible and profitable. As the war subsided, Louisville quickly became the commonwealth's major port, exporting flour, hemp rope and bailing for cotton, tobacco, bacon, lard, apples, and bourbon. By 1820, the town's population pushed above 4,000 residents. Only Lexington was larger with 5,200 citizens.

A wave of town making took place. Lots were advertised in new villages like Covington, Middletown, Simpsonville, Portland, and Newport. All were offered with promises. Isaac Watkins endorsed Simpsonville by hoping to "incorporate a company for the purpose of turnpiking the great state road, leading from Frankfort to Louisville." New towns along the Ohio River advertised as local ports that would complement the one emerging in Louisville. Promoters of Shippingsport, south of the Falls of the Ohio, proclaimed it "the natural and inevitable port of navigation with New Orleans, Saint Louis and all other places situated on the Mississippi, Missouri, and the tributary streams emptying therein." Morris Birkbeck, an Englishman who migrated to the Illinois

territory in 1817, remarked on all of the town-building: "Gain! Gain! Gain! is the beginning, the middle and the end, the *alpha* and *omega* of the founders of American towns."

The good times were short lived. As Europe recovered from the war, its economy grew. By 1817, demand for American agriculture declined by half. England began to increase imports of cotton from India to avoid higher-priced American cotton. Robert B. McAfee later recalled that "the Country was immensely in debt and the Price of all produce was lower than ever known in Kentucky, indeed very little of the Products could ever be sold at a price." In Hartford in Ohio County, only one store remained open. To protect itself from inflated bank notes, the Second Bank of the United States decided to no longer accept bank notes from state-chartered banks. When, in 1818, the United States Treasury demanded that the Second Bank of the United States transfer $2 million to pay off bonds on the Louisiana Purchase, it just did not have the specie, or hard coin money, on hand. It called in loans that had been made to state and private banks which, in turn, called in loans from farmers and speculators. Land values plummeted as banks foreclosed on properties and transferred the land titles to their creditor: the Second Bank of the United States.

The Panic of 1819 hit Kentucky early and deeply. The Bank of Kentucky's notes had circulated widely, and suddenly they were worthless. In Congress, Senator Richard M. Johnson fought to salvage Kentuckians' land ownership, claiming that it was not by their "own impudence" but by unforeseen economic forces that they had found themselves in debt. A relief law passed Congress that allowed debtors to retain a portion of their landed holdings, but such a large number of Kentuckians found themselves so deeply in debt that the law proved insufficient. In 1815, the state had passed a law to protect its bank notes, providing a twelve-month stay on any creditor who would not accept Bank of Kentucky notes. That law was all that stood between indebted citizens and poverty.

In June 1819, a group of Franklin County residents drew up a set of resolutions that be-

came widely known as the Frankfort Resolutions. The petitioners blamed banks for largely
causing the economic crisis by extending loans
too readily, thereby encouraging speculation and
extravagant spending. They concluded that the
banks should help to solve the crisis by allowing debtors to pay with paper money and should
print more to make that possible. The Frankfort Resolutions became rather controversial
throughout the nation, but in Kentucky, they
incited more political debate than the commonwealth had seen since the constitutional convention of 1799. In Bourbon, Scott, and Shelby Counties, citizens demanded a special session
of the general assembly to suspend specie payments. Harrison County residents asked banks
to issue new paper notes and to postpone calling
in debts independent of the state government.
But the *Kentucky Argus* and the *Kentucky Herald* both denounced the resolutions as "shielding
the extravagant debtor from his honest creditor."
They suspected that most small debtors had already paid off their debts; it was larger debtors and speculators who were attempting to escape their responsibilities. Additionally, printing
more paper notes would only lead to inflation,
which would only exacerbate the panic. Citizen
meetings in Washington, Mason, Nelson, and
Green Counties agreed and opposed any relief.
A special session was not called, but assembly
elections were scheduled for the fall.

Kentuckians sent pro-relief representatives
to Frankfort, and they immediately passed a
stay law to protect debtors. The law required
creditors to accept notes from the Bank of Kentucky or wait two years before calling in a debt.
Still, the bank notes continued to plummet in
value. Butchers in Lexington and tavern keep-
ers in Frankfort refused to accept paper notes
that they could not redeem at local banks.
Governor Gabriel Slaughter agreed to repeal
the 1818 law that had created forty-six banks,
and as their notes were rejected, they began to
close their doors. By mid-1820, only the Bank
of Kentucky remained in operation.

In August, John Adair became governor.
A pro-relief advocate, Adair supported the
charter of the state-owned Bank of the Commonwealth, under the directorship of John

J. Crittenden. With capital stock of two million dollars, the bank would be able to issue
three million dollars in banknotes. Supporters
hoped that such a measure would ease the burden of debts. The general assembly also modified the relief act to favor notes from the Bank
of the Commonwealth over those of the Bank
of Kentucky. The federal government, however, refused to accept the notes. Within a year,
their value had declined so much that Adair
concluded that the state government could do
very little to ameliorate financial downturns.
In 1821, the legislature authorized the burning
of over $1 million in bank notes to reduce the
supply and increase their value. Bank of Commonwealth notes went up in flames at public
bonfires in Frankfort. Although the Bank of
Kentucky was re-chartered in 1819 for another twenty-five years, the assembly angrily revoked its privileges in late 1822. The legislators
believed it had undermined the success of the
Bank of the Commonwealth.

The fight over whether state government
could or even should aid its citizens in economically difficult times pushed into Kentucky's
courts when Bourbon County Circuit Court
judge James Clark heard *Williams v. Blair* in
1822. Clark decided that the relief acts violated both state and federal constitutions. His decision infuriated the pro-relief forces in the general assembly, which narrowly failed to remove
him from the bench. That same year, *Lapsley v.
Brashear* received a similar ruling in the Fayette
County Circuit Court. Both cases were heard in
the Kentucky Court of Appeals in 1823. After
heated debates, Chief Justice John Boyle and Associate Justices William Owsley and Benjamin
Mills resolved that the stay law and all other efforts to alter contracts were unconstitutional.

Relief advocates, particularly in the general assembly, called for the justices' dismissal
from the court of appeals, but they could not
muster the two-thirds majority. The state divided sharply over the situation. Some feared civil
war. Anti-reliefer George Robertson noted that
"no popular controversy, waged without bloodshed, was ever more absorbing and acrimoni-
ous than that which raged, like a hurricane,
over Kentucky for about three years."

"Judge Breaking," political cartoon by Hannibal Scratchi, c. 1825. (Kentucky Historical Society Collections, Frankfort, KY)

Frustrated by the court decisions and their inability to replace the justices, the Relief Party made the gubernatorial election of 1824 a referendum on relief. Their candidate, Joseph Desha, won overwhelmingly. His supporters again pushed to oust the justices. Although the house of representatives voted to remove, the senate fell short. In late 1824, however, the senate did vote to replace the law that had established the court of appeals with a new four-justice court of appeals. When the bill went to the house, Governor Desha personally lobbied legislators to support it. When it passed, he appointed William T. Barry as the new chief justice and three other relief advocates as associate justices. But the Old Court refused to recognize the New Court. Its clerk disobeyed a legislative mandate that he turn over his records by January 1825. The New Court clerk broke into the Old Court clerk's office and took what he found.

Petitions, letters, and pamphlets flooded the state government. George Robertson wrote such a fiery and masterful argument on behalf of the Old Court that the Relief majority in the senate refused to print it in the *Senate Journal* for fear that it would "blow us sky-high." In Louisville, Albert G. Hodges and William Tanner coedited the *Louisville Morning Post*, although they disagreed on the court situation. Tanner filled two pages with pro–New Court materials, while Hodges praised the Old Court

in the other two pages. Unable to remain collaborators, they eventually flipped a coin to see who would buy out the other: Tanner won.

During the election of 1825, supporters of the Old Court took control of the Kentucky House of Representatives and immediately repealed the New Court law. The Kentucky Senate, however, split between Old Court and New Court partisans, failed to pass the repeal. Frustrated, the house passed a bill that would have required all judges on both courts, all legislators, the governor, and the lieutenant governor to resign. The state would just start all over. Of course, the senate did not agree, but it did provoke some movement among senators. In December 1826, both houses decided to restore the Old Court's authority and revoke the New Court. Governor Desha's veto was overridden, and in January 1827, the New Court dissolved. Still, the Old Court would be revised: Chief Justice John Boyle resigned to accept a federal judgeship, and the two associate justices resigned so that they could be officially reappointed by the senate. The senate, however, refused to confirm them and selected two new justices. In 1829, in *Hildreth's Heirs v. McIntire's Devisees,* the new justices of the Kentucky Court of Appeals declared all of the actions and decisions of the New Court void.

Kentucky's lingering economic problems

as well as the constitutional crisis that it had precipitated made the commonwealth less attractive to potential residents. Thousands of artisans, laborers, poorer farmers, and debtors fled Kentucky as the economy collapsed. That trend continued throughout the 1820s, as more people left the commonwealth than entered it. Kentucky's postwar reputation tarnished as eastern politicians mocked it during the Old Court–New Court struggle. The depression and the constitutional crisis together, however, changed the first generation of Kentuckians. They had always understood themselves as part of a larger collective of Americans. Now they understood more clearly the intimate relationship between the federal economy and the federal government.

The Fire Bell in the Night

In February 1819, as economic problems became more apparent throughout Kentucky and the United States, James Tallmadge of New York introduced a resolution in the US House of Representatives to stop the importation of slaves and to initiate gradual abolition of slavery in the Missouri territory. Missourians had applied for statehood, and the fight over whether it would enter a free or slave state shattered the myth that Americans lived in "an era of good feelings." From Monticello, Thomas Jefferson characterized the debate, "like a fire bell in the night, [that] awakened and filled me with terror." Politicians from the eleven slave states worried that Missouri's admission as a twelfth free state would upset the balance of power in the Senate. When Maine submitted its petition for statehood, the Senate quickly took the opportunity to forge a compromise. But factions in the House refused to accept aspects of it. Southern representatives rejected a proviso that would exclude slavery from all remaining territories in the Louisiana Purchase. Northern representatives held out hope that Missouri would still enter as a free state. Henry Clay, as Speaker of the House, designed a solution by dividing the bills and coaxing different contingents into voting in separate aspects of the compromise, including approval of the

36'30⁰ North latitude as the dividing line between slave and free territories.

In 1820, Henry Clay owned about thirty slaves on his Ashland plantation just east of Lexington. On the issue of slavery, he very much agreed with Thomas Jefferson that African Americans deserved freedom, but racism made it difficult to imagine how blacks and whites could coexist in the same society. He was also dedicated to the rule of law and operating within the rules. For Clay, then, emancipation was not a plausible end to slavery for it would trample on state's rights and destabilize the Union. Slavery was quickly becoming the most important political issue in the United States and in Kentucky.

Even among Kentucky's earliest settler colonials, there had been opposition to slavery. The 1792 constitutional convention had seen the most vocal denouncements of slavery. As Abraham Lincoln explained in 1859, however, "When the Kentuckians came to form the [state] Constitution, they had the embarrassing circumstance of slavery among them—they were not a free people to make the Constitution." Kentucky's future had been dictated to a large degree by Virginia's slave society. But in 1792 and again in 1799, Kentuckians themselves had chosen to retain slavery, but not all of them.

Presbyterian minister David Rice was among Kentucky's earliest antislavery proponents, publishing *Slavery Inconsistent with Justice and Good Policy* just months before the 1792 convention. Rice argued that "as creatures of God we are, with respect to liberty, all equal." He reasoned that slavery not only unfairly oppressed black Americans but also made whites less virtuous and promoted laziness. Slavery's persistence in Kentucky kept many Americans from migrating to the state, Rice claimed. Ending slavery would deprive slave owners of property, but the greater injustice was enslavement itself. Although Rice was ineffective at the constitutional convention, he had laid a foundation for future antislavery activism in Kentucky.

Many of the earliest churches openly opposed slavery, but they were always a minority. Presbyterians like Rice took the lead. In 1796, members of the Transylvania Presbytery rec-

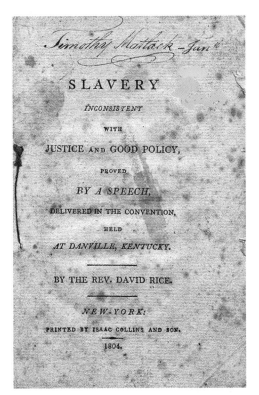

Rev. David Rice, *Slavery Inconsistent with Justice and Good Policy, Proved by a Speech Delivered at the Convention Held at Danville, Kentucky* (New York: Isaac Collin and Son, 1804). (Special Collections Research Center, University of Chicago Library)

ognized slavery as an evil: "yet they view the final remedy as alone belonging to the civil power; and also do not think that they have sufficient authority from the word of God to make it a term of church communion." In less centralized denominations, individual churches often took antislavery stances. In 1811, 300 congregants of twelve Baptist churches denounced slavery. They were a small minority of the 17,511 Baptists in the commonwealth. Still, Baptists who opposed slavery were passionate about it. Preacher David Barrow had moved to Kentucky in 1798 because Virginia had become so dependent upon slave labor that a common man like him could not succeed without owning slaves. His first years in Kentucky were difficult: the North District Baptist Association expelled him for his antislavery views. He formed the Licking-Locust Associa-

tion, Friends of Humanity as an alternative for Baptists who questioned slavery. In 1808, he formed the Kentucky Abolition Society, dedicated to ending the slave trade and slavery, educating African Americans, and advocating for better treatment of the enslaved. He wrote *Involuntary, Unmerited, Perpetual, Absolute, Hereditary Slavery, Examined; on the Principles of Nature, Reason, Justice, Policy, and Scripture* in which he argued that African Americans were not equal simply because they had been deprived the same opportunities for education that whites enjoyed. In thinking about the sexual abuse of female slaves, he asserted that "any woman who is good enough to make a man's concubine, etc. ought to serve him for a wife." By 1821, the Kentucky Abolition Society had a newspaper, the *Abolition Intelligencer and Missionary Magazine,* one of only two antislavery newspapers in the nation. Editor John Finley Crowe produced it in Shelbyville, but only twelve issues appeared in print.

By 1827, eight antislavery societies with about two hundred members operated in Kentucky. Yet, not all antislavery advocates agreed on the solution. Emancipationists believed slavery was immoral, but they also believed in the rule of law and the protection of slave owners' property rights. Because slavery was legal, they argued that compensating slave owners would be necessary if they were deprived of them. More important, a challenge to the institution of slavery threatened to disrupt the entire economy. After the Panic of 1819, few emancipationists were willing to make that case. Most embraced gradual emancipation, a very slow process of freeing slaves that would allow economies to adjust.

Other antislavery advocates were less patient. Abolitionists demanded the immediate, uncompensated freeing of all slaves. They argued that the institution was immoral and sinful and that no moral person could compromise with it. Humans had been kidnapped, stolen, abused: why should the state compensate criminals for their crimes? They denounced emancipationists who called for gradualism as needlessly delaying the inevitable.

Whether emancipationists or abolitionists, antislavery advocates in Kentucky generally agreed on one issue: they struggled to envision a society in which free whites and free blacks lived together. Colonization appealed to many as a solution. Once freed from enslavement, African Americans would settle elsewhere, separate from white America. In 1816–1817, the American Colonization Society for the Free People of Color organized in Washington, DC. Five years later, it began sending free African Americans to Liberia to establish a new American colony. Henry Clay was among its founders and its first president. In 1829, the Kentucky Colonization Society formed. By 1832, the commonwealth had thirty-one local auxiliaries, second only to Virginia and Ohio. Clay and Joseph R. Underwood of Bowling Green often spoke publicly on colonization. They praised the societies' goal of paying owners to free enslaved African Americans and helping them leave the United States.

Yet, colonization was not the answer. Abolitionists questioned whether purchasing slaves' freedom could ever end slavery; it seemed to just contribute to the profit-making of slave ownership. Many slave owners suspiciously viewed colonization as prelude to a much more devious plan to deprive them of their property rights. Many freed people distrusted colonization as well. They had no interest in leaving families and friends behind in the United States.

Still, some black Kentuckians chose to colonize Liberia. When Richard Bibb of Logan County freed fifty-one slaves, thirty-two of them offered to emigrate. In April 1833, they boarded the *Ajax* in New Orleans, along with fifty-nine others from Kentucky and fifty-one emancipated slaves from Tennessee. The voyage was harrowing. Twenty-nine died en route. The Kentucky Abolition Society had purchased a forty-square-mile site in Liberia. The society named it Kentucky in Africa, and Clay-Ashland became the colony's main town. The investment exhausted all of the society's funds, delaying any future trips for seven years. Black Kentuckians had mixed reactions to migrating to Liberia. In 1846, two colonists refused to leave the ship when they arrived. Some became discouraged and returned to the United States.

Others, like Nelson Sanders, celebrated: "We enjoy liberty & our lives in a degree which is impossible for the negro to enjoy in any other country." Among them was Alfred F. Russell, a former Fayette County slave, who was emancipated in 1833 with his mother and cousin. In Liberia, he served as a Methodist missionary and eventually owned a large coffee and sugar farm. In 1884, he became president of Liberia. So too did William David Coleman, only eleven years old when his mother and three other family members left Fayette County to find liberty and success in Liberia. As a trained carpenter, his skills were in demand in a growing colony, and he found educational opportunities that he could never have had if he had stayed in Kentucky. In 1896, Coleman too became president of Liberia.

Hoping to reduce the numbers of free blacks living in the state, in 1851, the general assembly required the emigration of all newly freed African Americans. Five years later, it appropriated five thousand dollars annually to resettle black Kentuckians. Still, colonization had lost much of its favor by the 1850s as white Americans became more radical on all sides of the slavery debate. The last notable group of Liberian colonists left Kentucky in 1857. Ultimately, colonization was a failure. Between 1829 and 1859, the Kentucky Colonization Society had relocated only 658 former slaves to Liberia, a minuscule number when considered against the number of Kentucky slaves: over 165,000 in 1830 and over 225,000 by 1860.

Four Biographies from a Generation

The opening of Louisiana territory, the Burr intrigues, the War of 1812 and the wave of postwar patriotism that integrated Kentucky into the national culture, the economic challenges of the Panic of 1819, the constitutional crisis that threatened the commonwealth in the 1820s, and the increasingly politicized issue of slavery—all of these events shaped the first generation of Kentuckians as they became political, social, religious, and economic leaders.

Henry Clay was the foremost representative of his generation. He arrived in Kentucky in 1797 with little wealth but great promise. As he admitted later in life, "I never studied half enough. I always relied too much upon the resources of my genius." His greatest resource was his oratory: he was a dramatic and effective speaker, which made him a successful lawyer. Nearly six feet tall, lanky, with an expressive face and a friendly personality, Clay loved to drink and gamble. Even his enemies (with the exception of Humphrey Marshall) appreciated him. John C. Calhoun once admitted, "I don't like Henry Clay. He is a bad man, an imposter, a creature of wicked schemes. I wouldn't speak to him, but, by God, I love the man."

Fortune smiled on Henry Clay. In 1799, he married Lucretia Hart, a woman who was as antisocial as he was social. But she had connections: the Hart family was extensive and had vast commercial relationships across the state and nation. During her husband's absences, Lucretia Clay was not particularly effective at managing the Ashland plantation, just east of Lexington, but she attended to the family—the eleven Clay children (two of whom died in infancy and another four in youth)—allowing Henry to concentrate on his politics. Again, good fortune smiled on him. When George Nicholas died in 1799, Kentuckians began to notice Clay. He served in the Kentucky House from 1803 to 1806, and then completed John Adair's term in the US Senate in 1806–1807. When John Breckinridge died in 1806, Clay had become the natural successor as the commonwealth's leading politician. He had little difficulty returning in January 1808 to the Kentucky House, where he became speaker and had his contentious arguments with Marshall. In 1810–1811, he again filled a vacant US Senate seat before leading the War Hawks to a landslide sweep of Congress in 1811. Clay's peers elected him Speaker of the House on his first day. He was only thirty-four years old.

Henry and Lucretia Clay moved to Washington, taking some of their slaves, including Charlotte "Lottie" Dupuy, with them. In 1829, Lottie filed a freedom suit against Clay. In the suit, she demanded emancipation for herself and her two children based on the argument that her mother had been emancipated, and

Portrait of Henry Clay, by Matthew Harris Jouett, c. 1818. (Transylvania University Library, Lexington, KY)

therefore, she should have followed her mother's status into freedom as well. Clay tried to send Dupuy back to Kentucky, but her lawyer successfully argued that to do so would condemn her family to "be held as slaves for life." Yet the court did send her husband and children back to Clay's Ashland plantation. During the eighteen months of the trial, Dupuy worked in Secretary of State Martin Van Buren's house. When the court finally decided that Lottie's mother had been emancipated *after* her birth, not affecting Dupuy's enslavement, she refused to leave Washington. Clay pondered, "How shall I now get her?" He ordered his agent to have her arrested and shipped to New Orleans, where she remained enslaved another decade before Clay eventually freed her and her son. Dupuy's case, however, was an important judicial milestone. Slaves had no legal standing. The court judges, therefore, had to regard Lottie as a free woman to recognize her right to sue. It was among the first steps in carving judicial space for slaves' claims to freedom, ultimately making the *Dred Scott* case possible.

Clay embodied the outlook of so many who belonged to the first generation of Kentuckians. He found himself trapped by debates over internal improvements, the American system, and slavery. (Ironically, the Dupuy trial coincided with Clay's colonization efforts, so his fight to hold so tightly onto a slave seemed questionable to many observers.) The political atmosphere became increasingly tense. Political arguments often appeared in newspapers and pamphlets. The tone of the writers could be easily misinterpreted. Political disputes became personal affronts, and animosity often escalated as sides argued back and forth in the press. When politicians debated face-to-face, then, the rhetoric of their opponents often already had angered them, and their arguments devolved into physical altercations. Clay's duel with Humphrey Marshall was only the first. Beginning with Andrew Jackson's invasion of West Florida in 1819, which Clay denounced as unconstitutional, he and the war hero developed a caustic relationship that often bordered on physical violence. When John Randolph, a long-time adversary, criticized Clay's actions as secretary of state in 1826, Clay challenged him to a duel. Both men missed on their first shot, although Clay grazed his opponent's coat. Randolph fired into the air on his second shot, signaling to Clay that he had no intention of dueling further. He merely stated, "You owe me a coat, Mr. Clay." Clay responded that he was glad the debt was not greater.

Henry Clay always considered Kentucky his home, but he also acted politically as a citizen of the larger nation. He famously declared, "I have heard something said about allegiance to the South: I know no South, no North, no East, no West, to which I owe any allegiance." Mary Austin Holley, too, was such a Kentuckian. Born in Connecticut in 1784, she married Horace Holley in January 1805. When Transylvania University hired her husband as president in 1818, Mary arrived in Lexington, Kentucky, and found a very different society than the one she left behind in Boston. Kentucky women seemed backward and ridiculously pretentious, wearing outdated fashions: "No Boston lady would ever be so conspicuous. 'How is Dr. Holley,' they would ask and would adjust their flounces, scarcely touching their backs to the parlor chair lest they form a wrinkle or disturb a hair."

Mary Austin Holley. (Mary Austin Hatcher, *Letters of an Early American Traveller: Mary Austin Holley, Her Life and Her Works, 1784–1846* [Dallas, TX: Southwest Press, 1933], frontispiece)

Dr. Holley transformed Transylvania University from a small college to a nationally recognized school. During his twelve-year tenure, Transylvania produced six hundred graduates, ten times more than it had over the previous two decades. He attracted eminent scholars like Constantine Rafinesque, a specialist in biology, natural history, and prehistoric cultures. When political squabbling in Transylvania University led to Horace's dismissal in 1827, Mary wrote a poem, "On Leaving Kentucky," which began:

> Farewell to the land in which broad rivers flow,
>> And vast prairies bloom as in Eden's young day!
> Farewell to the land in which lofty trees grow,
>> And the vine and the mistletoe's empire display.

They moved to New Orleans, where Mary seemed more satisfied with the culture. "All the fashion of the place was there and it seemed so gay . . . not like our Lexington concerts." Within months, the Holleys decided to vacation in New York. Aboard the *Louisiana,* both contracted yellow fever. Horace died and was buried at sea.

The opportunities for a widow were few. In 1829, she became governess to a Louisiana family. She dreamed of joining her brother, Henry, and cousin, Stephen F. Austin, in colonizing Texas, but she opposed the extension of slavery. "Pray be firm against slavery," she wrote Stephen. "I witness such cruelties as fill me with abhorrence *of myself* and my species." Upon visiting them in 1831, she wrote about her travels in *Texas: Observations, Historical, Geographical, and Descriptive . . .* (1833). She returned to Lexington in 1833 and stayed for two years, working on another book titled *Texas,* published in 1836 as the first history of the territory. She became an advocate for Texas independence and remained fascinated with the new American West. She made another three trips to Texas before returning to her governess position in Louisiana, where she died in 1846.

During her years in Kentucky, Mary Holley was positioned to be quite influential. She had a passion for music and patronized a local German music teacher, Wilhelm Iucho. She wrote poetry and literature. Married to the leader of Lexington's intellectual community, she drew attention from the commonwealth's most notable families. Yet, upon her death, she had left little impact on the state. Despite her intelligence, in the end, Mary was a wife. Her primary role was to be a republican wife and mother, supporting her husband and raising their children. Although his prominent position required her to serve as socialite and hostess, Mary came under suspicion by many Kentuckians for her shameful parties where "all kinds of tunes and songs are used for entertainment of the company."

Among the Holleys' many guests was Daniel Drake. Unlike Henry Clay and Mary Holley, Drake migrated to Kentucky as a child. He accompanied his parents from New Jersey in the late 1780s. The Drakes settled at Mayslick. He studied medicine in Cincinnati, receiving the college's first medical diploma. He attended medical school at the University of

Daniel Drake. (Henry Howe, *Historical Collections of Ohio,* 2 vols. [Cincinnati: C. J. Krehbiel & Co., 1907], 1: 821)

Pennsylvania before returning to Kentucky as a lecturer in *materia medica* for Transylvania University in 1816. The following year, he moved to Cincinnati. As Horace Holley transformed Transylvania University in the late 1810s, Daniel Drake organized the Medical College of Cincinnati and founded the *Western Journal of the Medical and Physical Sciences.* Like Holley, Drake could not avoid the politics of educational reform. Before the Medical College of Cincinnati opened its doors, he and a professor had a nasty fight that led to a duel challenge. The duel resulted in the dismissal of the other professor. The remaining faculty also voted to dismiss Drake as the college president, but public support reinstated him. Yet, Transylvania offered a position, and Drake left for Lexington. In fact, he spent much of his life moving back and forth between Lexington's, Cincinnati's, and Louisville's medical communities. Ten years later, when he returned to the

Medical College of Cincinnati, politics again forced him back to Transylvania.

Drake interpreted these fights over medical education as the consequences of a changing world, one in which professional preparation and standards proved increasingly important. In his *Practical Essays on Medical Education* (1832), Drake concluded that the "establishment of medical schools is a prolific source of discord in the profession." He willingly accepted such strife if it advanced the profession against a greater danger: "inferior men" who were quack practitioners peddling false remedies and dangerous surgeries.

Medical educational reform was only one of Drake's interests. He promoted the construction of poorhouses to accommodate paupers and the homeless, although he rather callously also considered using "these wretched people" as medical guinea pigs, doing "in sickness, what they did not perform in health—support themselves." He advocated for temperance in drinking, and cofounded the Physiological Temperance Society of Louisville in 1841. He condemned slavery and its westward extension, supporting the work of the American Colonization Society. He founded a school for the blind in Louisville in the mid-1840s. All of this work was accomplished through voluntary associations. Associations became the mechanism by which the first generation of Kentuckians and Americans promoted social reform. Antislavery and colonization societies, library associations, humane societies, Bible and missionary organizations, societies for the promotion of temperance, agriculture, literacy, manufacturing, relief for the poor, and so many other causes peppered the American landscape.

Despite the rage for reform, the first enslaved generation of Kentuckians did not benefit from it much. Born before 1800 in Virginia, Asa Taylor came to Boone County involuntarily, as John Taylor's slave. Soon after arrival, Asa joined the Bullittsburg Baptist Church, which his owner had organized in the mid-1790s. Although a minister, John Taylor was not an antislavery Baptist. Still, he taught Asa to read and regularly baptized new congregants, black and white. In 1800, John baptized Asa, following the standard Baptist practice of immersion in local creeks. Asa's sister, Letty, was a different story. She rejected all religion. Her disavowal of faith frustrated John Taylor and led Asa to claim she was "of the Devil." The confrontation shook Letty who, three weeks later, converted to Christianity and received baptism as well.

John Taylor apparently was grooming Asa and another slave, Christopher Wilson, for the ministry, anticipating that Asa might "be useful among his fellow Blacks as there is the greatest sphere of his action." Yet, only two years after Asa's baptism, John left Boone County for Gallatin County, and sold Asa to John Graves. Although Wilson was ordained in 1807, Asa Taylor never officially became a Baptist preacher. Baptists often allowed only formally recognized members of the congregation to preach. For eighteen years, Asa was silenced. Eventually, church elders conceded that Asa had a talent for preaching, but this talent did not make him any less a slave. Between 1819 and 1835, he was sold twice more, the final time to Ezra Ferris, a Baptist preacher and medical doctor in Lawrenceburg, Indiana. Ferris requested that Asa Taylor and his wife, Rachel, "be granted dismissal from the Bullitsburg Baptist congregation" and moved them to Lawrenceburg, where they became free. In the 1840 census, Ferris listed seven free whites and seven free blacks in his household.

The lives of Asa Taylor, Daniel Drake, Mary Holley, and Henry Clay demonstrate the themes of a generation. They reveal the divisiveness of slavery and the ways in which politics came to permeate even educational institutions. Mary Holley and Asa Taylor show the advantages that mobility offered women and African Americans. Together their lives evidence the strains that began to appear in Kentucky and throughout the United States as a nation once trapped east of the Mississippi River stretched yearningly toward the Pacific. These political milestones shaped the first generation of Kentuckians, but other factors also contributed to the development of a modern culture and society that separated Kentuckians further from their parents' revolutionary world.

6

The World They Made

Binding the Commonwealth Together

As did the rest of the United States, Kentucky experienced a market revolution in the nineteenth century that transformed it from a traditional agrarian economy to a capitalist, commercial society. The Panic of 1819 was the first strain of this economic evolution. It exposed how unprepared many Kentuckians were for new models of financing that fueled this great change. As the depression of the 1810s and early 1820s subsided, Kentuckians rebuilt their economy. They invested significantly in transportation infrastructure that would contribute to that transformation.

Barter had been a hallmark of agrarian Kentucky. In 1788, John Bradford offered subscriptions to his *Kentucky Gazette* for "Beef, Pork, Flour, Wheat, Rye, Barley, Oats, Indian Corn, Cotton, Wool, Hackled Flax or Hemp, Linen or Good Whiskey"—anything that he could then sell to a trader for cash. Still, there was a need for paper money that could easily be carried and exchanged. In 1780, John Sanders traded for furs and skins at the Falls of the Ohio. He issued paper receipts that circulated as local cash. After selling the cargo in New Orleans, he returned to Louisville with Spanish dollars that he used to redeem the receipts. James Wilkinson used the same model for purchasing tobacco to resell. When the wildcat banks arose in the late 1810s, they all printed bank notes. They flooded the economy with fairly worthless currency and contributed to inflated prices and the economic collapse. By 1822, the general assembly repealed the charters of the Bank of Kentucky and the Bank of the Commonwealth. Only the Bank of the United States continued to operate in the state. When Andrew Jackson won reelection in 1832, however, he targeted the Bank of the United States as an enemy of the people. Its charter was allowed to expire, Jackson had the government's deposits withdrawn, and its branches closed. To address the limited supply of currency that resulted, in 1834, the general assembly chartered the Louisville Bank of Kentucky. The Northern Bank of Kentucky also received a charter. It had branches in Richmond, Paris, Covington, Louisville, Barbourville, and Glasgow. Both began issuing their own paper currencies.

The towns in which the new branches arose were part of an evolving village West. With a surprising number of private academies, bookstores, printing houses, a subscription library, and Transylvania University, Lexington had earned the nickname Athens of the West. The wealth that sustained its cultural institutions came from the rich soils of the Bluegrass. During and immediately after the War of 1812, regional planters raised hemp. They fed the town's rope walks that converted hemp into rope and bagging. The commonwealth's wealthiest lived around Lexington or visited it regularly, often staying at the opulent Phoenix Hotel, which was constructed in the 1820s. Upon his visit to the town in 1818, James Flint wrote that "Lexington is still considered the capital of fashion in Kentucky. There are here many genteel families, a few of whom keep coaches. The town, on the whole, exhibits a well-dressed population." Although the depression of the late 1810s and early 1820s drained much of the vitality from Lexington's development, the town remained refined.

Yet Louisville was poised to surpass Lexington. The river port boomed from over 4,000

Bank note from the Northern Bank of Kentucky, 1856. (The National Numismatic Collection, National Museum of American History, Smithsonian Institution, Washington, DC)

residents in 1820 to 11,345 in 1830, making it the first city in the commonwealth. In the fat years before the Panic of 1819, entrepreneurs invested heavily in developing its manufacturing sector. Paul Skidmore began making steam engines in 1812. The Hope Distillery opened in 1815. So too did a six-story Merchant Manufacturing Mill that produced flour. Rising industrialists and businessmen, like Skidmore, established soap factories, rope walks, tobacco plants, commission houses, and other commercial ventures that took advantage of access to the Ohio-Mississippi River system. Exporters, commodity insurers, bankers, and lawyers found opportunity in Louisville's new economic landscape.

Still, shippers complained about the Falls of the Ohio. In an earlier era, when George Rogers Clark mustered men for his expedition against the Western Confederacy and when Lewis and Clark gathered for their excursion to explore the West, the rapids and small islands in the Ohio River had proved useful. In an age of steamboats and manufactures, they were just in the way. The need for unencumbered transportation drove development. At the falls, the river drops 24 feet over 2.5 miles. The rapids were so treacherous that flatboats and canoes had difficulty navigating them. Travelers down the Ohio River got as far as the Falls of the Ohio and then had to debark and transfer their goods or property to boats at the southern end of the falls before continuing on their way. Many, weary from the travel, decided to just settle in Louisville and its environs.

Eager to solve the problem, the Ohio Canal Company received a charter in 1804 to dig a canal on the Indiana side of the river. De-

spite the $50,000 that the commonwealth invested, political bickering and the outbreak of war ended the project. In 1818, Indiana chartered a company too, but it did not survive the Panic of 1819. In the mid-1820s, Charles Thruston pushed a bill through the general assembly to charter the Louisville and Portland Canal Company. Shares in the company sold throughout the state, among Philadelphia investors, and even to the US Congress. Although building it was a difficult project that ultimately required more funding than expected, the canal opened in 1830. It served Louisville well for about two decades. By the 1850s, however, steamboats had grown too large for the canal, and shippers found themselves again transferring cargo from ships at one end of the falls to ships at the other end.

Wealthier residents of Louisville sought to replicate Lexington's gentility. Refined shops cropped up along Main Street. Literary societies, theatrical performances, and dancing schools kept the social elite occupied. Yet, a large population of young, single men also formed in the city, working the factories and docks. Many were rivermen who enjoyed taverns, gambling, and brothels. A less respectable society emerged along Louisville's waterfront where bite-and-gouge fights regularly erupted. As early as 1806, Thomas Ashe described Louisville's inhabitants as "universally addicted to gambling and drinking. The billiards rooms are crowded from morning to night, and often all night through." Like the Hunters of Kentucky who became almost mythic in the American imagination following the War of 1812, Ohio and Mississippi rivermen became part of the nation's folklore in the person of Mike

The Phoenix Hotel along Lexington's Main Street, 1850. (J. Winston Coleman Jr. Collection on Slavery in Kentucky, University of Kentucky Special Collections and Research Center, Lexington, KY)

Fink. According to popular legend, he could drink a gallon of whiskey and still shoot the tail off a pig. Fink represented the resurrection of the Big Man ideal that had inspired so many settler colonials, except his "frontier" was the great rivers of the West. Davy Crockett supposedly labeled him "half horse, half alligator," an image that every riverman and hunter of Kentucky tried to appropriate. He could "out-run, out-jump, out-shoot, out-drink" and apparently out-brag any other man. Since Louisville's wealthier residents needed the rivermen to ply

their productions down the Ohio and Mississippi Rivers, they had to tolerate the baser entertainments that kept the Mike Finks who existed among them occupied.

Other towns grew as well. Paris, Georgetown, Harrodsburg, Shelbyville, Bardstown, Maysville, Hopkinsville, and Russellville each boasted over one thousand residents by 1820. Covington and Newport, located opposite Cincinnati along the Ohio River, benefited from the Ohio town's growth. Frankfort, along the Kentucky River, also profited from river

"Louisville's Main Street, 1846." (Richard H. Collins, *History of Kentucky*, 2 vols. [Covington: Collins & Co., 1874], 2: 360)

Chafin Tollhouse near Sharpsburg, KY, c. 1887. (Kentucky Historical Society Collections, Frankfort, KY)

trade, and sessions of the state legislature annually boosted the town's population and economy. All of these communities bloomed in the new economy of the late 1820s and 1830s, aided by banks and improved transportation.

A network of roads connected the constellation of towns and villages. Their condition in Kentucky had been a concern since the early 1790s, when the legislature funded the widening of the Wilderness Road. Travelers paid a toll at Cumberland Ford for use of the road, although post riders, women, and children were exempt. A traveler paid 9 pence for himself and each horse, mule, or mare he took with him along the road. Each head of cattle that moved eastward demanded 3 pence. Individuals riding carriages paid an additional 3 or 6 pence, depending on whether they rode on two or four wheels. Tolls were one way to pay for roads; lotteries were another. In 1810, the general assembly authorized a $5,000 lottery to improve the road between Maysville and Washington, which coursed up a steep hill. Between 1792 and the Civil War, the legislature authorized more than eighty lotteries, ranging from $500 to $100,000 in prizes. Schools and internal improvements received the bulk of lottery earnings, but libraries, a fire engine, a linen factory, and a bridge also benefited from the proceeds. Although many Kentuckians found lotteries immoral and tried to outlaw their use, the courts upheld lotteries as constitutional. By the early 1860s, Kentucky was one of only three states that still employed lotteries to fund public measures. In 1862, Englishman Edward Dicey wrote, "Kentucky is the first state in the Union where I saw lottery offices in every street, and where the old notices in the shop windows . . . caught my eye, requesting passersby to tempt fortune, and to win five thousand dollars at the risk of one."

The majority of lottery-funded projects were internal improvements. After the War of 1812, Henry Clay's promotion of commercial and industrial progress brought attention to the need for markets and improved transportation. The state chartered the Lexington and Louisville Turnpike Road Company and the Louisville and Maysville Turnpike Road Company in 1817. Each company was to invest private funds, and each received twenty years in which to recover its investment through tolls and to make profits for its shareholders. When a traveler paid the toll, the gatekeeper then turned or lifted the pike to allow him to pass. Toll booths would be situated five miles apart (although none could be within one mile of a town). To assist the turnpike companies, the general assembly increased toll rates. But it also extended the list of those exempt from tolls: people going to church, a militia muster, a funeral, or to the election polls. At the end of two decades, the state reserved the right to purchase toll roads that had been private/public ventures.

As Henry Clay actively advanced his American System, the rhetoric of internal improvements inspired greater investments. In 1830, Kentuckian Thomas Metcalfe, then in the US House of Representatives, proposed that the federal government fund improvements to the Old

Buffalo Trace between Maysville and Lexington, but President Jackson vetoed the bill. The general assembly chartered another company to undertake the work. This was just one of ninety-three turnpike road projects in which it invested between 1834 and 1842. Companies built roads from Glasgow to Bowling Green, from Bowling Green to Scottsville, and from Burlington to Covington. By 1837, the state had invested over $2.5 million in such companies, and private investment totaled about $2 million. Some 343 miles of stone-surfaced roads had been completed, and another 236 were under construction. Better roads increased stage and wagon travel as well as better movement of livestock. Goods more easily arrived at local markets and at ports for shipping down river.

River transportation became equally important, then. Early steamboats like the *New Orleans,* which arrived in Louisville in 1811, had deep hulls and two masts for sails. The design did not work well on the region's rivers. Flat-bottomed boats with paddle wheels worked much better, as did moving the machinery—an engine for each paddle wheel—from the hull to the first deck. By riding higher in the water, the steamboats could tread up rivers previously inaccessible to large-scale importing and exporting. But smaller rivers came with greater risk. Sandbars often snagged steamboats. Steamboat operators then had to wait for rain waters to raise the river, and by the time they could set off again, their cargoes sometimes already had spoiled. Sometimes a crew member waded in the shallow water ahead of the boat to feel out the channels. As steamboat technology advanced, their use expanded beyond just delivering goods. Companies began to offer entertainments: scenic cruises, minstrel shows, concerts, and parties. The shift to coal-burning engines meant hotter fires, more steam, and faster travel. Louisville benefited from the rise of the steamboats, not only as a port for steamboats but as a construction site. The *General Shelby* was the first, built in 1815. When the Louisville and Portland Canal opened in 1830, the steamboat market increased. By 1850, boats totaling 14,820 tons were registered with the city.

Bowling Green, too, profited from the steamboats. Located 30 miles up the Barren River from its juncture with the Green River, and another 145 miles from Henderson where the Green met the Ohio, Bowling Green did not seem a likely candidate for steamboat travel. James Rumsey Skiles promoted the opening of the Green River, preaching the need for locks and canals to provide adequate navigation. In early 1828, the *United States,* a small single-stacked steamboat, arrived at Bowling Green. The Green and Barren River Navigation Company formed in 1830 but accomplished little. After a brief term in the Kentucky House of Representatives, Skiles became a lobbyist and, in 1833, persuaded the general assembly to fund improvements to the Green River. He served as a commissioner, overseeing construction of locks and dams. He also built wharfs and warehouses in Bowling Green. In consultation with engineer Alonzo Livermore, he dreamed of opening the Green River another one hundred miles to Greensburg then of building a canal to the Cumberland River. Steam had made dreams possible, but they proved always more expensive than planned. By 1847, the cost of opening the Green River totaled $859,126, an average of nearly $5,000 per mile. Despite low toll rates, only a couple boats made regular trips between Bowling Green and the Ohio River. Passage through five locks cost 88 cents. Skiles lost most of his wealth in the enterprise and ruined his health.

Even as steamboats plied Kentucky's rivers, railroad entrepreneurs began to challenge for investment funds. The general assembly chartered eleven railroad companies between 1834 and 1842. Lexington, anxious to connect to the importing and exporting opportunities that steamboats created, received a charter in 1830 for a rail line to Louisville. Henry Clay led the effort, and by early 1834, it had reached Frankfort. On the earliest rail lines, the cars were drawn by horses. Any hills along a route made travel difficult. Upon making a descent, like the very steep hill into Frankfort, the teams were disconnected, and the conductor tried to control the cars using handbrakes. Passengers often debarked and rented a carriage

"The L&N bridge across the Green River near Munfordville, Ky." (*Harper's Weekly*, February 25, 1860)

to take them down the hill. Steam engines soon replaced horse-drawn cars. Some residents of Louisville, however, opposed extending the railroad to their town, fearing that it would benefit Lexington at Louisville's expense. They sued to defund the project. They took their case to the Kentucky Court of Appeals, but it rejected their request. By 1851, the Lexington-Louisville Railroad was complete.

Railroad investors' imaginations were limitless. One group of entrepreneurs pursued a plan to bind Louisville to Cincinnati by rail and then planned to build on to Charleston, South Carolina. The *Kentucky Gazette* predicted the idea would "strengthen the bonds of union between the South and the West, and . . . make Kentucky what the God of her creation designed—the finest portion of the inhabitable globe." The Panic of 1837 undermined the project. The Henderson and Nashville Company planned a railroad in 1852 but failed to garner much support. Citizens instead expressed more interest in the Mobile and Ohio Railroad that promised to connect Columbus, Kentucky, with the Gulf Coast. The completion of the Kentucky Central Railroad, which connected Lexington to Cincinnati, inspired commencement of construction on the Lexington and Big Sandy Railroad in 1853. However, the line ended at Mount Sterling. Railroads were expensive, and the technology changed between the 1830s and 1850s. Original plans, therefore, became obsolete, and early railroad entrepreneurs wasted some initial investment funds.

The most successful railroad of the era was the Louisville and Nashville (L&N), chartered in 1850. Towns and counties along the proposed route invested much of the $3.8 million needed to initiate the project. To force the railroad through Bowling Green, residents of Warren County raised $1 million and then secured a charter to build their own railroad to Nashville. The investors in the L&N quickly agreed to connect to Bowling Green to avoid the competition. Completed in 1859, the L&N cost $7,221,000. James Guthrie, former secretary of the US Treasury, became vice president of the railroad in 1857 and then president from 1860 to 1868. Albert Fink, a prominent railroad engineer, joined the L&N Railroad in 1857 and supervised construction of the more challenging stretches of the line. He designed the bridge that spanned the Green River near Munfordville, which received national attention as the second-longest iron bridge in the nation. He remained the chief engineer through the Civil War, during which the L&N served as a supply line for Union troops as they fought farther into the South.

Economic Innovations

The economic energy that fueled town growth and internal improvements filtered across the countryside. As rail lines and steamboats opened up markets to greater numbers of participants, more Kentuckians sought to make a profit. Access to good farmlands had motivated most Americans and Europeans who migrated to Kentucky in the late eighteenth century. The ideal of "work and be rich" had inspired many. It equated agricultural production with virtuous living. After the War of 1812, the first generation of Kentuckians interpreted "work and be rich" in a more capitalistic way. It was not enough to live virtuously. With better transportation, access to more markets, and wider availability of loans, one could aspire to make a lot of money.

Holders of family farms had always dabbled in growing diverse products: tobacco, hemp, bacon, hams, eggs, apples. Domestic productions, like cloth, butter, lard, sugar loaves, and whiskey, were also common. Some years, farm families had plenty that they sold or bartered for other goods or even luxuries, like imported silks and satins. Other years, productions were lean, as families struggled to grow enough to survive. Still, they went to local stores and purchased on store credit, filling ledger books with debt that they promised to pay back later.

From the early years of Kentucky's colonization, every story of economic success originated in the inequitable land distribution that advantaged some people over others. In the 1780s, Cornelius Hughes had received two thousand Kentucky acres for his service in the American Revolutionary War. As many of his smaller landed neighbors worked to grow enough to eat, he dedicated much of his lands to hemp production. His son, Jacob, inherited the estate, and transformed it into a large-scale agricultural enterprise by the 1850s. He converted the hemp farm into a livestock ranch. He sold three hundred cattle in the eastern markets and two hundred hogs in Cincinnati each year. In 1830, fifteen slaves worked the ranch and served the family. By the mid-1830s, Hughes made nearly $10,000 annually (approximately $278,000 in today's currency). In 1840, he acquired eight more slaves. By 1850, he had thirty slaves. His estate outside Lexing-

ton became known as Leafland. Hughes invested some of his profits in banking, establishing himself among the wealthiest of Kentuckians. The grand transformation to the national economy that took place in the early nineteenth century as well as the advantage that his father's initial land grant gave him made Hughes's story possible. Transforming a hemp farm to a livestock ranch and investing in enslaved labor to work it required access to land, loans, markets, and transportation.

So too the economic evolution also transformed the Green River. In the early 1800s, as Bluegrass planters dominated the political realm and demanded the state's attention to their economic needs, Kentucky south of the Green River quietly epitomized Thomas Jefferson's vision for an agrarian republic: thousands of settlers tilling their two-hundred-acre tracts and tapping into an emerging cotton market—and four of five households did so without slaves. That would not last. As rivers and roads opened distant markets up to farmers south of the Green, slaves came to comprise more than 10 percent of county populations. In some counties, they made up as much as 30 percent. Yet many did not work cotton farms. Despite the introduction of cotton south of the Green, only in westernmost Kentucky did the crop thrive, binding that region to the markets of St. Louis and Nashville.

Hemp, the state's most profitable crop before and during the War of 1812, was *the* money crop, and Lexington was the center of hemp production. In 1838, eighteen rope and bagging factories operated in the town, most peopled by enslaved workers. An acre of hemp could yield close to nine hundred pounds of fiber. Once prepared for market, fibers brought $70 to $112 a ton. As cotton became more popular in the lower South as a cash crop, demand for hemp increased to make bagging for cotton bales. To protect American hemp production, Congress required the US Navy to use only American-produced rope beginning in 1841.

Tobacco had been the state's oldest cash crop. Early settler colonials had grown it to use as money under Virginia's old laws. As early as 1787, tobacco warehouses began to appear throughout Kentucky to ensure the quality of tobacco crops. By 1859, Kentuckians produced over 108 million pounds annually, nearly a quarter of the nation's production. Tobacco farmers too benefited from improving markets and roads. Transported in hogsheads that weighed over one thousand pounds, tobacco was difficult to move to market. For decades, most tobacco was transported by wagon, but the weight of the loads could mire wagons in muddy roads or deep ruts. These problems often delayed delivery and reduced the value of the precious cargo. Road improvements and then the advent of the railroads promised more reliable transportation. The growth of Louisville offered a new market, as well. To meet the new demand, it became a center for the production of cigars, snuff, chewing tobacco, and pipe tobacco.

Like Jacob Hughes, many Kentuckians found herding a profitable enterprise. Although settler colonials had brought farm animals with them, later ranchers wanted herds of quality cattle, hogs, and sheep. When Matthew Patton arrived near Nicholasville in 1790, he advertised his bull Mars and fine cow Venus as "improved" cattle. When Henry Clay visited England in 1815, he purchased four Herefords to import to his Ashland estate. But the greatest investments in cattle took place in the 1830s and 1840s, as transportation to markets improved. Robert W. Scott, a former lawyer, converted lands in Franklin and Woodford Counties into his Locust Hill plantation. His Durham shorthorn cattle and herds of improved hogs and sheep sold well for breeding stock. Scott was a tireless proponent of scientific agriculture. Agricultural journals advocated the development of profitable farms, advising farmers and ranchers on crops and breeds. Scott lobbied the general assembly for support for scientific agriculture, including an agricultural college. Other men, too, took it upon themselves to advance the quality of Kentucky livestock. In 1839, Samuel Martin organized the Fayette County Importing Company to bring quality bulls and cows to the region for breeding. In 1853, the Northern Kentucky Importing Company sold twenty-five cattle from England at a profit of $36,080. Hoping to contribute to the improvement of herds statewide, Brutus Clay of Bourbon County sold his cattle only to Kentuckians who promised not to take the animals out of the state for at least a year. Bourbon County and the Bluegrass became widely known for the quality of cattle. Its livestock producers often publicly shamed other regions for their lack of innovation, as evidenced in a colloquialism of the era. When describing a thin woman, a Kentuckian sometimes responded that "she's as bony as the hips of a Green River cow."

In the late eighteenth century, horses were more common than cattle. One of the first laws passed at Boonesborough in 1782 had been to improve the breeding of horses. By 1800, 92 percent of taxpayers owned an average of 3.2 horses. Kentucky had 12 percent of the nation's horses in that year. Like cattle, however, the breeding of horses became increasingly important, as opportunities to make profit unfolded. At Cabell's Dale north of Lexington, John Breckinridge arranged for three years of stud services by Speculator, an English-bred horse. When Breckinridge died in 1806, at least 125 horses were stabled at Cabell's Dale, indicative of Kentuckians' growing passion. By the 1830s, the horse industry already had become substantial and was integral to the state's identity. "Horses are raised in great numbers, and of the noblest kinds," wrote Timothy Flint. "A handsome horse is the highest pride of a Kentuckian; and common farmers own from ten to fifty. Great numbers are carried over the mountains to the Atlantic states; and the principal supply of saddle and carriage horses in the lower country is drawn from Kentucky, or the other western states." As with cattle, importation of English stock became popular among horsemen. In 1797, Blaze was the first English-bred horse in Kentucky. That same year, the Kentucky Jockey Club formed in Lexington. The club sponsored four-mile heat races and established rules for horse racing that would define the sport.

The English had the *General Stud Book* (1791) to trace equine bloodlines. In Kentucky, such knowledge lay with men like Eli-

Races—Races—Races!

Over the GREEN LAWN COURSE, Smithland, Ky.

THE proprietor of the " Green Lawn Course,"
Smithland, Ky., would most respectfully notify
gentlemen of Alabama, Tennessee, Louisiana, Missouri, Arkansas, Illinois and Kentucky, together with
all others who may feel a disposition to visit us, and
who have studs of race horses whose metal they may
wish " to try," that the Races over the above mentioned Course will commence on *Monday, the 26th October,*
and will continue six days.

The Course has just been established in a beautiful
lawn, not more than a mile from the Rock Landing in
Smithland, and the public may rest assured that no
pains or expense will be spared to render all who may
visit us entirely satisfied with the fixtures on and about
the place, and the treatment they shall receive.

Advertisement for Green Lawn Course, Smithland, KY. (*The Times-Picayune* [New Orleans], September 11, 1846)

sha Warfield Jr., the professor of surgery and obstetrics at Transylvania University's medical school, one of the founders of the Lexington and Ohio Railroad, and a leader in thoroughbred horse breeding. In 1826, Warfield was a founder of the Kentucky Association, an organization dedicated to breeding and racing thoroughbreds. The association acquired sixty-five acres where it constructed a one-mile racetrack with grandstand and stables. In 1850 at The Meadows, his horse farm north of Lexington, Warfield's experiments in horse breeding produced Darley, later renamed Lexington. The horse won six of his seven races and became

one of the greatest breeding stallions. Lexington led the sire list for sixteen years and made Warfield a great deal of money. The profitability of horse breeding, racing, and studding inspired innovations like harness horses. James B. Clay, son of Henry Clay, purchased Mambrino Chief in New York in 1854 and brought the horse to Kentucky, where he became the most-celebrated trotter of the era.

Mules also became subjects of Kentuckians' attentions in the 1830s. Looking to Europe for finer stock, farmers imported jacks from Spain, Malta, and southern France. Within a few generations, Kentucky-bred jacks were two to three hands taller than European mules. As cotton production became widespread throughout the lower South, so too did the rearing of Kentucky mules. Many farmers dedicated their farms to breeding and raising mules because the sale prices were so high.

Scientific agriculture underlay the advances that Kentuckians enjoyed in cattle, horse, and mule raising. In 1816, Lewis Sanders organized the state's first livestock show, offering silver julep cups as prizes. Agricultural fairs, which rewarded farmers with premiums for successful breeding and notable produce, became popular throughout the commonwealth. In 1838, the Kentucky Agricultural Society formed to promote agricultural fairs. Domestic productions like preserved foods and cooked dishes soon joined farm produce on display ta-

Portrait of Lexington, by Edward Troye, 1868. (J. Winston Coleman Photographic Collection, Transylvania University Library, Lexington, KY)

119

bles, as did home-produced textiles. The larger fairs exhibited new inventions like mowers, reapers, and threshers.

By the 1850s, agriculture seemingly offered profit to anyone willing to invest money and energy in improvements. Over that decade, an additional 1,675,938 acres of farmland came into production in the state. This growth increased profits made from agriculture and herding from $155 million in 1850 to $291 million in 1860. Of the fifteen states with legalized slavery, Kentucky ranked first in production of rye, barley, horses, and mules; second in hemp, tobacco, corn, wheat, and sheep; third in hogs; and fourth in cattle.

Yet agriculture was just one economic sector in which Kentucky excelled. In 1832, Henry Clay crowed, "In Kentucky, almost every manufactory known to me, is in the hands of enterprising and self-made men, who have acquired whatever wealth they possess by patient and diligent labor." Alney McLean and his son William epitomized Clay's self-made men. They dug up coal on their Muhlenberg County farm and transported it by barge down the Green River to sell in Evansville and Owensboro. In 1820, the McLean drift bank became the state's first commercial mine, producing 328 tons of coal in its first year. Coal remained a meager extractive industry. Investors found it difficult to sell because wood was still plentiful for heat and cooking. In 1838, when geologist William Williams Mather submitted a report to the general assembly on the advantages of coal over wood, the market began to change. Ten bushels of coal cost $1.00; a cord of wood $2.50. The amounts produced comparable heat, but the coal weighed one-third as much and required one-quarter the labor. Industries like iron works and steam-powered mills began to use coal. Steamboats eventually consumed around two hundred bushels per day.

Similarly, oil was an early extractive industry that became profitable later in the century. As he drilled for saltwater along the South Fork of the Cumberland River in McCreary County, Martin Beatty struck oil, which ruined his well, overflowed into the river, and was accidentally set afire. A decade later, drilling on a farm near Burkesville, Beatty again hit an oil reserve, creating Kentucky's first gusher. Four days later, the geyser still erupted at least fifteen feet high. Kentuckians quickly discovered that the oil "burns well in a lamp and is said to paint and oil leather and I have no doubt it will be a good medicine for many complaints particularly the Rumatick plan. The whole atmostpheir is perfumed with it. It is a compleat Phenominon."

Salt and saltpeter extraction were among Kentucky's earliest industries. Salt works arose at Bullitt's Lick in the 1780s. Workers boiled down the saltwater to extract the salt and formed it into bricks to sell. Typically, a bushel of salt could be distilled from 100 gallons of water. At Henley Haddix Salt Lick in Perry County, laborers produced 10 bushels a day by 1838. In contrast, diggers scraped saltpeter from the floors of caves. They then refined the mineral and mixed it with charcoal and sulfur to make gunpowder. By 1800, more than 100,000 pounds of gunpowder had been made with productions from twenty-eight caves. Lexington had six powder mills by 1810. During the War of 1812 as demand and prices made the enterprise more profitable, Mammoth Cave became a major source of the mineral. Some seventy slaves dug in the cave, transported the dirt by oxcarts, poured water over the dirt to siphon the calcium nitrate, boiled off the excess water to reveal the saltpeter crystals, and then packed the product into barrels for shipment to the East.

The wave of nationalism that shaped America after the War of 1812 benefited Kentucky's nascent industries. Congress passed tariffs that encouraged and promoted economic development. In 1817, the Kentucky Society for the Encouragement of Domestic Manufactures organized in Lexington. The Panic of 1819, however, created many problems for investors and innovators: substantial losses of wealth in speculative schemes, loss of investment loans, and a scarcity of laborers. As whites fled Kentucky during the 1820s, skilled workers who remained could demand higher pay, forcing some capitalists to turn to enslaved laborers. Many of these slaves received training and became specialized in manufactures.

The manufacture of bourbon evidenced these trends. In the late eighteenth century, Americans distilled corn whiskey that could be sold locally or shipped in barrels to distant markets more cheaply than shipping the corn itself. In Kentucky, at least five hundred distilleries operated by the early 1790s. So many American farmers made and sold whiskey that the federal government, in 1791, believed it could pay off much of its lingering debt from the American Revolutionary War simply by taxing whiskey. Distillers in Pennsylvania incited a rebellion. Maryland and Kentucky farmers, too, complained loudly about their loss of profits. President Washington led several thousand federal troops into western Pennsylvania to squash the rebellion. Congress repealed the tax in 1802. As animosities with England increased during the early 1800s, Congress placed tariffs on rum to curb British profits, which contributed to increased whiskey consumption.

Elijah Craig, a Baptist preacher in Scott County, is often credited with the invention of bourbon by aging his distilled whiskey in charred oak barrels that provided the smooth taste that became associated with bourbon. More likely, several farmers created the recipe over time. It evolved so that, by the War of 1812, bourbon was one of Kentucky's more profitable exports. Any farmer could make it, including women. Catherine Spears Carpenter Frye of Casey County, who had nine children and outlived two husbands, partially supported her family by distilling bourbon. After her second husband died in 1806, she and her slave Joseph distilled. In 1818, she recorded her recipe:

> Put into the mash tub Six Bushells of Very hot Slop then put in one Bushel of Corn meal Ground pretty Course Stir well then Sprinkle a little meal over the mash let it Stand 5 Days that is 3 full Day betwixt the Day you mash and the Day you Cool off—on the fifth Day put in 3 gallon of Rye Meal and one gallon of Malt Work it Well into the mast and Stir for 3 quarters of an hour then fill the tub half full of Luke warm water. Stir it well and with a fine sieve or otherwise Break all the lumps fine then let stand for three hours then fill up the tub with luke warm water.

When the Panic of 1819 hit, many farmers found that bourbon production was one of the few ways in which they could continue to make money. Farmers with larger distilleries hired master distillers to oversee the work. They also relied on enslaved field hands to gather grains and on skilled slaves to make the barrels and assist with the distilling.

As with bourbon, by using tariffs to raise prices on British goods, Americans created greater demand for their own productions and stimulated investment and innovation. Iron production became more profitable in Kentucky with the Tariff of 1816, which raised rates on imports. Joseph Bruen's Iron Foundry and Machine Shop in Lexington, the Aetna Furnace in Hart County, the Bush Creek Iron Furnace near Greensburg, and Raccoon Furnace in Greenup County benefited from a booming economy after the War of 1812. Greenup County, in particular, became the center for iron production by 1837, making Kentucky third nationally. By the 1850s, Muhlenberg County had surpassed Greenup County, but the enterprise spread to all parts of the state. In Lyon County, William C. Kelly innovated in the manufacture of steel by blasting cold air through molten iron to distill the impurities. Although Englishman Henry Bessemer received a patent in 1856 for the process, the US Patent Office eventually acknowledged Kelly as the original inventor.

Profits from agriculture and herding, manufacturing and extracting gave Kentuckians more purchasing power. Merchants became partners to agricultural producers in the economic expansion, particularly for farmers who lived outside the villages and towns. Many became reluctant to accept goods for barter, preferring specie or store credit that promised cash later. The need for cash, then, drove many smaller farmers to engage in profit-making agriculture. Large- and small-scale farmers sought out merchants who could also provide access to export networks. Livestock proved easiest to get to market because they walked. Shipping tobacco and hemp was more difficult. As bulk crops began to flourish, farmers needed not only better roads and rivers but also intermediaries to arrange shipments. With extensive trade partners, merchants became natural importers and exporters.

Becoming a Slave Society

Early in Harriet Beecher Stowe's *Uncle Tom's Cabin* (1852) she wrote that "Perhaps the mildest form of the system of slavery is to be seen in the State of Kentucky." Scholars have been arguing about the nature of Kentucky enslavement ever since. For decades, Kentucky had operated as a society with slaves, but it was never really dependent upon slave labor. Yet the commonwealth certainly maintained the institution for social, economic, and cultural reasons. The nineteenth century's economic transformation, however, changed Kentucky's relationship to slavery and the slave trade. The state's slave population grew more slowly than that of most other slave states, but it did grow: from 40,343 in 1800 to 126,732 by 1820 to 182,258 in 1840 and 225,483 in 1860. The Nonimportation Act of 1833 slowed the growth of the enslaved population by making it illegal for migrants to bring slaves into the state to sell. Nevertheless, the number of slaves increased, particularly in the towns. Although hemp and tobacco never required a large number of workers, slaves toiled in hemp walks and tobacco manufactories, on the docks and in distilleries, shelving in local stores, ranching cattle, and raising horses. In contrast to most other slave states, in Kentucky the use of slave labor was more diverse and the numbers of enslaved peoples less concentrated.

By the 1830s, as hemp, bourbon, and cattle became the commonwealth's most profitable exports, slaves became its most conspicuous export. Visitors noted the coffles that walked along Kentucky's roads headed southward. Although hemp farms and horse ranches often comprised more than five hundred acres and required the use of slaves, most farms in Kentucky remained small. By 1860, two-thirds of the state's 83,689 farms consisted of fewer than one hundred acres, and most of those had fewer than fifty acres. A farmer may have had a slave or two, but the demand for enslaved labor remained low. So, white slave owners sold excess slaves "down the river," where cotton, sugar, and rice plantations had exploded across the Old Southwest. As Louisiana, Arkansas, Mississippi, Alabama, and west Georgia opened up to American colonization between 1803 and the 1830s, culminating in the removal of the Cherokees and other native southern nations, prices for slaves began to climb. These price increases tempted all Kentucky slaveholders. Some slave owners considered themselves more paternal toward their slaves. They acted as protective fathers more than greedy task masters and refused to participate in the trade, choosing to live more meagerly rather than part with people whom they considered members of their households.

Lexington was the heart of Kentucky's slave trade, although almost every town had an auction block. Broadsides and newspaper advertisements alerted residents about local sales. On the Cheapside auction block in Lexington, the state permitted county commissioners to sell slaves who had not been deeded in wills or listed in estate sales. Slave traders, like Silas Marshall, Lewis Robards, and William Pullman, bought up many of the enslaved and held them in slave jails until they could form a coffle to march southward. Robards was the state's largest slave dealer, although poor business management led to bankruptcy in the 1850s when his business was acquired by Bolton, Dickens, and Company, a multi-state slave trading company. In the 1830s, an average of 2,300 slaves left Kentucky annually for lower South slave auctions. The average dropped slightly to 2,000 annually in the 1840s, before climbing to 3,400 annually in the 1850s. Nearly 77,000 enslaved humans were forced from homes, families, and friends in Kentucky to work and die in the fields of the deep South. Slave labor had to show a return, and if that could not be achieved on the farm or in the factory, then it could be accomplished through sale. The sale of slaves, therefore, became more purposeful, embedding those who sold slaves in the new, profit-driven economy.

By the 1830s, a male slave aged eighteen to thirty-five drew $400 to $700 in Kentucky's slave market, and a female slave of the same age brought $350 to $450. These were substantial investments, which often cost more than two years of income. Most white Kentuckians could not afford to buy slaves. By 1850, only 28 percent of white households owned slaves, and they averaged 5.4 slaves. Most of these held smaller numbers—only 1 or 2 enslaved laborers. Only five households in the entire state had more than 100 slaves, including that of Robert Wickliffe. He owned 200 enslaved humans who worked his plantation.

The enslaved faced a life of endless toil and few rewards. Slaves lived in cramped quarters, often two to three families per room. Cooks lived in the kitchens. Household slaves might have lived inside the white family's house, so that they could be available at any time. Slaves in industrial settings lived in dormitories or camps, often packed in tight and unsanitary conditions. When a cholera epidemic swept through Kentucky in 1833, it struck urban slaves most harshly: in Lexington, four in Joshua Weir's rope walk died, another seven succumbed in Benjamin Gratz's rope walk, and nineteen died in James Brand's hemp bagging factory. Not only were conditions unhealthy, but food rations were minimal. Pork was the most common meat, but it was not eaten daily. Many slaves had their own vegetable gardens, kept chickens, and fished to supplement their diets. Special treats like oranges and candy were given at Christmas and other frolics. Stealing food was common, as Sophie Wood remembered: "we would slip in the house after the master and mistress wuz sleeping and cook to suit ourselves." Clothing too was minimal. Many wore "Kentucky jeans" (coarse cotton and linsey) or "negro cloth" (cotton and wool) imported from New England textile factories. Clothing was designed for wear, not comfort. On larger plantations and in the factories, slaves received distributions of clothing and shoes at most twice a year.

The greatest concentration of slaves was in Woodford County, where more than 52 percent of the population was enslaved. Of the state's 109 counties in 1860, 21 had slave populations of 30 percent or higher. Twenty-three counties had enslaved populations of less than 6 percent. The Bluegrass counties had the heaviest concentration, followed closely by Henderson and Oldham Counties along the Ohio River and Trigg, Christian, Todd, and Warren Counties. Johnson County's enslaved population was only 0.9 percent, and Jackson and Campbell Counties had 1 percent each. Still, although many white Kentuckians did not own slaves, they had regular contact with the institution of slavery. They knew local slaveholders, served on slave patrols to control black Kentuckians, hired out slaves to help with harvests, and bumped into enslaved peoples during daily routines.

Slavery was a brutal system. Despite antislavery advocates' efforts to humanize the enslaved, as when a Warren County judge ruled in 1838 that slaves were "human beings, with like passions, sympathies and affections with ourselves," slave owners had total control over their lives. Laws like the 1798 slave code empowered all white Kentuckians over black Kentuckians as well. Slaves often faced cruel punishments like brandings and ear croppings. Some had metal collars or weights attached to their necks or legs. Whippings were most common. Every town had a whipping post as well as stocks and gallows.

Sometimes, slaves retaliated. In Daviess County, for example, slaves struck back when several slaves strangled Jim Kizzie, their brutal overseer, to death. His violence was so notorious that the jury found only one of the slaves guilty. Still, to ward off any future attacks, most slaves in the community were forced to watch the execution. The courts occasionally drew attention and condemned the most heinous of treatment. In December 1811, Lilburne and Isham Lewis, of Livingston County, angrily killed a slave named George and dismembered his body. They attempted to burn his body, but an earthquake toppled the fireplace. The crime was discovered, and the Lewises put on trial for murder. The brothers agreed on a suicide pact,

NEGROES FOR SALE.

PERSONS wishing to purchase NEGROES can always be supplied with field hands, mechanics or house servants, by calling on

LEWIS C. ROBARDS,
Lexington, Ky.

a23 dtf

The institution of slavery as advertised in the *Louisville Daily Courier*, August 5, 1853.

WANTED

TO purchase (for my own use) eight or ten SLAVES. Highest cash prices will be paid.

J. H. HILLARD,
at Brannin & Summers

n18 dtf

The institution of slavery as advertised in the *Louisville Daily Courier*, July 27, 1859.

S. W. STONE,
Assignees of Cupp & Barnett.

au1 dtf

FOR SALE.

I HAVE at my jail, in Lexington, 35 or 40 LIKELY NEGROES. men, women, boys and girls, which I will sell for cash. Persons desiring to purchase, would do well to give me a call, as I will sell superior Negroes at fair prices.   j26 dtf   **L. C. ROBARDS.**

The institution of slavery as advertised in the *Louisville Daily Courier*, December 25, 1851.

RUNAWAY.

RUNAWAY from the undersigned, on Thursday, July 21st the negro Logan, or Edward, as he is sometimes called, aged 20 years, a mulatto, freckles on his face, bushy head, hight about 5 feet 10 inches, slender built, and rather likely in appearance. Had on when last seen, a soft hat, black frock coat, black pants, white shirt with plaits across he breast. I will give $25 reward if taken in the county, or $100 if caught out of the State and secured so I can get him.

M. OGLESBY,
Louisville Hotel.

jy25 d8

The institution of slavery as advertised in the *Louisville Daily Courier*, December 18, 1852.

but Isham cowered after Lilburne shot himself. Isham escaped jail and disappeared, rumored to have died at the Battle of New Orleans. Another Lewis family, Alpheus and Margaret of Bourbon County, notoriously beat and burned their slaves, including twelve-year-old Martha. Officials confiscated the slaves and sold them at auction, but they returned the profits to the slave owners, as required by law.

Although Kentucky slave laws were more lenient than in several other slave states, arguments contending that somehow slavery was milder in the commonwealth cannot be defended. While no laws existed that prohibited slaves from learning to read and write, few owners actually permitted slaves to become literate. Fewer still freed their slaves, despite no law to prohibit them from doing so. Whites distrusted blacks, particularly those they enslaved. *The Kentucky Housewife* instructed women to "Have established rules for domestics and slaves to be governed by, and fail not to give them such advice as is really necessary to promote their own welfare as well as your own. Examine frequently your cupboard and other household furniture, kitchen, smoke-house, and cellar, to see that every thing is in its proper place." Events like Nat Turner's rebellion, which occurred in Virginia in 1831, kept white Kentuckians on edge. Laws restricted slave mobility and assembly, even in religious meetings. At Christmas in 1856, rumors spread of slave insurrection, and several suspected participants were killed before it became evident that no such uprising had taken place.

Some slaves elected to run away rather than rebel. In 1825, a Maryland slave owner sent Josiah Henson, along with his other slaves, to Daviess County to avoid creditors. Henson traveled fairly widely through free and slave states on his owner's behalf. He, therefore, had ample opportunity to escape enslavement, but his family was in Kentucky. When he learned he might be sold down the river in September 1830, Henson found a friend to row him and his family across the Ohio River. Two children were so young that Henson and his wife carried them in knapsacks. Traveling only at night, they took two weeks to walk to Cincinnati be-

fore continuing on to Sandusky, then to Buffalo and Canada. He wrote a memoir, *The Life of Josiah Henson, formerly a Slave* (1849), that supposedly inspired Harriett Beecher Stowe to write *Uncle Tom's Cabin*.

The Refinement of Kentucky

Colonial America had been a closed, genteel, and hierarchical society. The economy benefited those who already owned land and wanted to "keep the peace." Power controlled wealth, and wealth empowered. Most settler colonials, many of whom had been excluded from that closed society, expressed excitement about Kentucky in the late eighteenth century because it offered opportunity that had been denied them east of the Appalachians. In the 1810s, Kentuckians' quest for opportunity led to wildcat banks and irresponsible investments that plunged the commonwealth into a depression, one that started earlier and lasted longer than it did throughout the rest of the nation. Yet, by the 1830s, agriculture, manufacturing, industry, and commerce had transformed the commonwealth. New opportunities threatened social order, and gentility seemed to fade, replaced by a crasser democratic culture. When the younger generation of state politicians refused to back pensions for veterans of the War of 1812, Governor Charles Scott denounced them, exposing a general disgust with their entire generation: "These men who were dirtying their little clothes when I was fighting for my country ought to have more grace, than to spit lies in my face, because I have purchased the privilege of their doing so." Grace, gratitude, gentility—the features of an earlier American culture disappeared as a more modern America and Kentucky emerged.

Like Charles Scott, Marquis Calmes clung to the genteel styles of his generation. A veteran of the Virginia militia during the Revolutionary War, he had arrived in Woodford County soon after the American Revolution with his wife, Priscilla Heale Calmes. In time, he commanded the first brigade of Kentucky riflemen during the War of 1812 and served as a county court justice for years. He owned Caneland plantation in Woodford County, worked by forty slaves in 1820, many of whom were trained in carpentry, blacksmithing, shoemaking, and brewing. Calmes insisted on wearing his hair in a queue, tied with a black ribbon under a broad cocked hat. He accented this look with a sweeping blue coat, velvet knee pants, and silver-buckled shoes. His gentility represented his status and wealth. An 1806 portrait of Priscilla depicts her wearing fine fabrics and holding a tea cup, as if to convince viewers that gentility existed west of the Appalachian Mountains.

Intent on displaying their status and wealth, the gentry built refined houses on landscaped estates to distinguish themselves from their more rustic neighbors. Kentuckians demanded opening the Mississippi River to trade in the 1790s not only because they needed to export farm productions but also because they desired the importation of refined goods. Margaretta Brown dishearteningly told her husband that "where none are *beaux,* 'tis vain to be a Belle." More Kentuckians were trying to be beaux. By the early 1800s, luxuries announced those who had been successful. "God must be prospering you if you can have a Silver Teapott & Shugar Dish," a relative wrote Thomas Davis. In 1802, François Michaux estimated that "seven-tenths of the manufactured articles in Kentucky . . . are imported from England," among which were jewelry, cutlery, drapery, fine earthenware, muslins, teas, and coffees. As Kentucky's economy expanded after the War of 1812, a consumer revolution made even the most expensive markers of gentility—portraits, porcelain tea services, elegant clothing—more widely available. The line that once divided Scott, Calmes, and other gentry from less wealthy Kentuckians faded, allowing for displays of respectability among a new middle class that arose out of the profit-making opportunities of the market and transportation revolutions.

Visitors and newcomers to Kentucky often commented on architecture as a measure of the state's gentility. When he arrived in the mid-1790s, David Meade described the "many (I will not say elegant) handsome brick hous-

Portrait of Priscilla Heale Calmes, by Jacob Frymire, c. 1810. (Chicago History Museum, ICHi-066133)

es—and some few of stone—framed houses likewise & many of logs." Meade soon learned that it was difficult to acquire the best building materials. William Whitley's Sportsman Hill was probably the first brick house in Kentucky. Other notable brick estates arose before statehood: Levi Todd's Ellerslie east of Lexington and William Croghan's Locust Grove near Louisville were among them. Meade discovered, however, that a brick mansion was a substantial investment. Although he was among the wealthiest of Kentuckians, he had to begin with a log house, to which he added a frame house and eventually a brick octagonal pavilion. Still, even with its mixed architecture, in the mid-1790s, Meade's Chaumière des Prairies was among the most formal of Bluegrass estates. The architecture of the 1790s might best be described as regional, a hodgepodge of national forms limited by the availability of materials. The first statehouse, built between 1793 and 1794, was "plain, but roomy and commodious," but it was not architecturally noteworthy.

Many of the early estates, like John Brown's Liberty Hall in Frankfort, were Georgian in

Kentucky's Second Capitol, designed by Matthew Kennedy, burned in 1824. (Lewis and Richard Collins, *Historical Sketches of Kentucky,* 2 vols. [Covington: 1878], 2: 246)

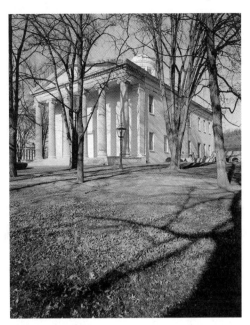

Old Statehouse, 1827. (The Library of Congress, Prints and Photographs Division, Washington, DC)

style. Not surprisingly, then, as more Kentuckians found profits in the evolving economy, they built homes that mimicked what they considered to be the most genteel of their neighbors: Henry Clay's Ashland (1814), John Wesley Hunt's Hopemont (1814), and John McCalla's Mount Hope (1819) in Lexington; Beriah Magoffin's Clay Hill (1812) in Harrodsburg; John Rowan's Federal Hill (1818) and Charles Wickliffe's Wickland (1825) near Bardstown; Henry Massie's Ridgeway (1816) near Louisville; and James B. January's house (before 1820), later known as Coolavin, in Louisville. Occasionally, a resident sought out an architect, but most hired a local carpenter, who consulted builders' handbooks for designs and specifications.

A competing architectural style was the Classic Revival, which drew from Roman and Renaissance forms. It dominated public architecture. When the first statehouse burned in 1813, architect Matthew Kennedy designed a classical-style second state capitol with a portico and colossal columns that was completed three years later. It too burned down, in 1824. Political bickering delayed calls for a design for a new capitol for three years. The winner was Gideon Shryock, a native Kentuckian who had studied in Philadelphia. His design was Greek

Revival style, linking Kentucky symbolically to ancient Greece's democratic states. The front of the building was taken from the temple of Minerva Polias in Ionia. Shryock also designed the Franklin County Courthouse, the main building at Transylvania University, and the Orlando Brown home in Frankfort.

Behind the speaker's chair in the Kentucky House of Representatives chamber of the new state capitol hung a full-length portrait of the Marquis de Lafayette, painted by one of the commonwealth's most prolific portrait artists, Matthew Harris Jouett. Born near Harrodsburg, he graduated from Transylvania University in 1808 and began to pursue law. After serving in the War of 1812, he turned to art and studied with the renowned Gilbert Stuart. Over the next eleven years, he produced at least 334 portraits and miniatures, many of Kentuckians. Along with Oliver Frazer, Joseph H. Bush, and Samuel Woodson Price, Jouett made a career in portraiture because portraits sold. As markers of gentility, every person of some status sought to have one. Consequently, there are few paintings of Kentucky's landscape before the Civil War. They just did not sell.

Still, some Kentuckians did purchase animal portraits. Edward Troye became well-known for his paintings of cattle and horses, most notably, his portrait of the great thoroughbred Lexington in 1854. John James Audubon, who arrived in Louisville in 1807 to open a store with Ferdinand Rozier, became a painter of birds. He taught art and painted portraits, but his passion was in animal portraits. His masterpiece, *Birds of America,* was published in four volumes between 1827 and 1838. *Quadrupeds of North America* appeared in five volumes between 1842 and 1845.

Demand for luxuries also sustained craftsmanship. Silversmiths, like Asa Blanchard of Lexington and John Kitts of Louisville, dominated the markets in their respective towns. James S. Sharrard carved out a market for himself as silversmith as well. He sold his silver productions in Henderson, Owensboro, and Paducah. In Madison County, William Campbell became widely known as a master cabinetmaker. In Mason County, Peter Tuttle and his relatives, John Foxworthy and Gerrard Calvert, produced beautiful chests with distinctive legs that made them popular across northern Kentucky. They created sugar chests and sugar desks, which were found almost exclusively in the homes of the well-to-do. Sugar was an expensive food item. Less-affluent Kentuckians used honey, molasses, or maple syrup to sweeten their foods. To protect sugar from insects or theft, sugar chests and desks could be locked. The most important marker of prosperity, however, was the tall case clock. Elijah Warner of Lexington became the state's premier clockmaker. He imported dials from Connecticut and hand-painted faces from Cincinnati.

From furniture, to art, to architecture, the construction of a comfortable and respectable home became central to the formation of the new middle class. As the economy drew men out of the home into new work spaces, the domestic realm became increasingly important as symbols of husbands' success and wives' mastery of the household. *The Kentucky Housewife* counseled women to "discharge each devolving duty with care and precision, fulfilling the station of a housewife indeed, and not a wife only.

. . . by your industry, frugality, and neatness, make him proud, and happy to know that he is in possession of a companion who is a complete model of loveliness and true elegance." The conditions of early Kentucky—from threat of physical attacks to the isolation of farms—had created an image of the Kentucky housewife as rugged and independent. The mythology of their exploits tends to dominate the history: we remember best those who acted least like women were expected to act. But most white women were neither warriors nor determined survivors. They aspired to be good republican wives by supporting their husbands and raising their children. Many died during the protracted war with the Shawnees. Many others were taken captive and never seen again in Kentucky.

Not surprisingly, then, white women in Kentucky were little interested in the national women's movement that emerged in the 1820s. When Frances Wright spoke in Louisville in 1828, she promoted women's education but did so by arguing that, by restricting women, men degraded themselves. In 1838, as one of the few protections provided the first generation of white female Kentuckians, the general assembly empowered widows with school-age children in rural school districts to vote for school trustee. This measure was a very limited recognition of their citizenship. When suffragist Lucy Stone lectured in Louisville in 1853, George D. Prentice expressed concern that "public speaking is generally regarded as implying bold presumption in a woman." Still, most of her audience was male. They refused to let their wives attend.

In 1817, Elias P. Fordham noted, "From the little I have seen, and the much I have heard, I judge they [Kentucky women] are the most spirited women in the world. They are exceedingly fond of dress, and are generally very handsome." "Society is polished and polite," described *Niles' Weekly Register* in 1814. "They have a theatre; and their balls and assemblies are conducted with as much grace and ease as they are anywhere else, and the dresses of the parties are as tasty and as elegant." Commentary regarding upper-class women of Kentucky often contained such observations. Their refinement permitted them to pursue fine clothing, polite society, and the prospect of marrying an ambitious man. Many even received some education in a finishing school. The wealthiest would also have slaves to relieve them of the housework.

Lower-class white women had no access to formal education and toiled for survival. Without the benefits of the consumer revolution, many poorer Kentucky women struggled. "It is rare to see a woman in this [low economic] station who has reached the age of thirty, without losing every trace of youth and beauty," noted Frances Trollope during her visit of 1831. Even motherhood, which bound white women across social ranks, manifested differently for the poor. They had children who were more likely to die in early childhood, and because poorer women worked so much, they spent little time with the children who survived. This contrasted sharply with the experience of motherhood among wealthier women, whose infants were often raised by enslaved nursemaids and whose leisure allowed them more time to nurture their children.

For women who could take advantage of the refined culture emerging around them, entertainment of families and friends was paramount. They gathered in parlors to listen to poetry or sing from sheet music. Some of the most popular regional literature was William Littell's *Festoons of Fancy* (1816) and William Orlando Butler's *The Boatman's Horn and Other Poems* (1821). Amelia B. Welby became the most popular poet in the state. The overly sentimental verses in *Poems by Amelia* (1845) went through seventeen editions. A subscription library that offered books to both investors and students at Transylvania University formed in Lexington in 1795. Within a year, 400 volumes filled its shelves. In 1800, it became the Lexington Library. A group of boys formed the Lexington Juvenile Library, which had 1,135 volumes by 1816 when it merged with the original library. This merger created a collection of 4,000 books for residents to borrow. Over sixty subscription libraries organized throughout the commonwealth between 1801 and 1856. They loaned out books and offered many for purchase based on the subscribers' investments.

Most of the earliest music was religious: *Watts' Hymns, The Pilgrim's Songster, Dupuy's Hymns,* and other imported sheet music. In 1822, John Bradford published the first collection of regional tunes in *Ely's Pocket Companion: comprising a selection of sentimental and humorous songs.* Three years later, T. T. Skillman published *Evangelical Hymns for Private, Family, Social and Public Worship.* Of course, "The Hunters of Kentucky" (1815) was very popular. In the early 1850s, Stephen Collins Foster wrote the first real American popular music, including "Camptown Races" (1850), "Old Folks at Home" (1851), "Poor Uncle Tom, Good Night" (1853; eventually retitled "My Old Kentucky Home, Good Night"), and "Jeanie with the Light Brown Hair" (1854). In the villages and towns, most young women of middling to upper class took piano lessons, although with varying degrees of success. Some trained in flute, harp, or singing.

More public amusements also occupied the leisure time of those Kentuckians who could afford them. Horse races became more popular with the rise of the thoroughbred industry. Agricultural fairs brought in carnival acts and exhibits. Steamboats expanded services beyond shipping goods by catering to passengers with panoramas, plays, and minstrel shows. In the villages and towns, musical performances became common. Between 1805 and 1840, Lexington averaged two major concerts each year. Many charged for admission. The town formed four musical societies: the Kentucky Musical Society, the Handel and Haydn Society, the Harmonic Society, and the Musical Amateurs. "Old Bull" Bornemann, a Norwegian violinist, played in Louisville in 1845. Jenny Lind, the "Swedish Nightingale," offered three concerts in Louisville in 1851. Tickets reportedly sold for as much as $175.

Theatrical performances also became more common. Luke Usher opened the New Theatre in Lexington in 1808 and operated theaters in Louisville and Frankfort within the next two years. Samuel Drake, who managed the Usher theaters, became the primary figure in Kentucky theater for the next two decades. He moved to Louisville, where he promoted the

City Theatre, which hosted over one thousand plays between 1814 and 1843. The theater attracted a wide array of social classes in its audiences, which mirrored those present in the city at large. It had a capacity of seven hundred patrons, with expensive boxes for more refined guests. The gallery was "regarded as a rendezvous for the women of the streets and a convenient place to ply their trade." Drake's theater hosted Anthony Philip Heinrich, considered by many to have been America's first composer. He wrote "The Dawn of Music in Kentucky; or, The Pleasure of Harmony in Solitude." The theater also hosted Thomas D. Rice, a comedian who improvised a song based on having seen an elderly, crippled African American man working at Cincinnati's Crow's livery stable. Each verse ended with "Jump, Jim Crow," as Rice mocked the slave's lameness. He played the character Kentucky Cornfield Negro in a locally written play titled "The Rifle," just one of the many in which he acted in blackface. He always concluded with his "Jump, Jim Crow," which brought the audience to its feet.

A Great Revival and a Greater Awakening

Very early in the market revolution, some Kentuckians condemned the secular entertainments that tempted their neighbors. People seemed more intent on earthly wealth than heavenly salvation. Presbyterian James McGready complained that "All of the conversation is of corn and tobacco, or land and stock. But for them the name of Jesus has no charm, and it is rarely mentioned unless to be profaned." McGready had come to Logan County in 1796, assigned to serve congregations in the Red, Gasper, and Mud Rivers region. His services ran from Friday evenings to Sunday mornings, which forced attendees to camp out for the duration. In June 1800, John and William McGee joined McGready in preaching at one of the camp meetings at the Gasper River. John McGee, a Methodist, in particular, drew spontaneous outbursts of emotions from the congregation. It was the beginning of the Great Revival, which culminated in August 1801 at Cane Ridge in Bourbon County. Presbyterian Barton W. Stone sponsored the Cane Ridge camp meeting, but with thousands in attendance, multiple preachers of various denominations spoke to the crowds. Some worshippers shook with the "holy jerks," their arms and legs flailing about. Others fell with the spirit, later relating out-of-body experiences. Some chased the devil through the woods, barking at him as he climbed up trees.

For many observers, the religious enthusiasms displayed at Gasper River and Cane Ridge were nothing short of heresy against Christianity. Calling themselves the "New Lights," the preachers and participants at the revivals promoted the idea that one could choose to be saved by being "born again." They also openly questioned the need to educate and credential clergy, claiming that anyone could preach when inspired by the spirit. Even women, enslaved African Americans, and children could exercise this privilege. The "Old Light" Presbyterian synod called many of the preachers to explain their support for revivalism, specifically a new theology of salvation through conversion. The Presbyterians revoked some clergy's authority to preach. Other clergy left the church to form their own denominations: the Christian Church, the Cumberland Presbyterian Church, and the Disciples of Christ. As the Presbyterians splintered over revivalism, the Baptists and Methodists tripled their memberships. Both denominations de-emphasized centralized hierarchies that allowed congregations great latitude in their beliefs. They were more democratic, expressing a conviction in equality before God and open salvation for all. It was a theology that appealed to large numbers of the first generation of Kentuckians.

Revival meetings followed throughout much of the Bluegrass and Green River regions, but by 1805, enthusiasm had waned. Some of the converts had undergone life-changing experiences. Others slid back into their more secular lives. When the great New Madrid earthquakes struck in 1811, however, they shook many toward faith again. Centered at New Madrid in the Missouri territory, just across the Mississippi River from what be-

Cane Ridge
Meetinghouse, 1791.
(Cane Ridge Shrine, Inc.,
Paris, KY)

came Kentucky's westernmost point, 3 quakes within a few weeks were so powerful that teacups rattled in Boston. They also reshaped the path of the Mississippi River. Between mid-December 1811 and early February 1812, as many as 3,600 aftershocks shook the region. Revivals again cropped up across Kentucky as people interpreted the tremors as divine signs. But within a few years, the religious enthusiasm had again faded. The *Bedford (Pa.) Gazette* mockingly reported that, the day after the first major quake, residents of Louisville contributed one thousand dollars toward construction of a church. After the second quake, they raised another thousand dollars, as they did again after the third quake. As the aftershocks subsided, they raised seven thousand dollars and constructed a theater.

The religious atmosphere created by revivalism, however, had long-term impacts. Kentucky became known for its variety of religions—a religious marketplace that offered traditional and nontraditional faiths to those seeking salvation. The United Society of Believers in Christ's Second Coming, commonly known as the Shakers, arrived in Mercer County in 1806. Their beliefs were unique. They believed that the millennium had already arrived through the person of Mother Ann Lee, the

second incarnation of the Christ. Their reverence for Mother Ann led to an emphasis on gender equality. They practiced celibacy, pacifism, communal living, and the perfectibility of human beings. By 1808, they had settled over 4,300 acres at Pleasant Hill, a communal farm where they grew hemp, tobacco, rye, and corn, and raised beef and dairy cattle, hogs, and sheep. Another group of Shakers had organized in Logan County, creating the South Union community. Although many Kentuckians viewed the market revolution as an opportunity to purchase or to consume, by the 1820s, the Shakers made hats, brooms, barrels, baskets, fabric, and other domestic productions to sell. Of course, their theology seemed very strange to their neighbors, and rumors constantly spread about the Shakers. During the War of 1812, they were accused of aiding and harboring Native American enemies. In 1812, the Kentucky General Assembly passed a law allowing an individual whose spouse had joined the Shakers to divorce and gain custody of any children. The Shakers were also suspected of being antislavery. Although they took no public position on the institution, Shakers did allow African Americans to join the communities and even vote.

Revivalism exposed slavery as a political issue that threatened religious stability. Like the Shakers, the Baptists, Methodists, and Presbyterians demonstrated discomfort with slavery, although none of the denominations took official stands against it. New Lights in each denomination were more likely to join biracial congregations, and many of those churches were not segregated into the separate seating areas that would arise later. Old Lights remained more conservative on both theology and slavery. The denominations could not remain unified as debates over racial equality before God intensified. In the mid-1840s, many northern Baptists argued that slaveholders were sinful and, therefore, could not serve as missionaries. This position offended many southern Baptists. The denomination splintered into northern and southern branches. The Methodists could not agree whether a slaveholder could be ordained as a bishop.

As theological debates ripped denominations apart, many African Americans created their own churches. Often, they had listened to sermons that proslavery ministers delivered on "Servants, obey your masters." It was scripture that did not speak to them. For African Americans, black churches provided the only "community" institution through which they could implement social, cultural, and educational programs. Peter "Old Captain" Durrett founded the Free African Baptist Church in Lexington as an alternative. A hired-out slave who lived in town with his wife, Durrett was a fiery preacher who drew large audiences. Five hundred parishioners filled the pews by 1810. Old Lights disliked the presence of such a large black church and threw support behind London Ferrell and his First Baptist Church. Ferrell's congregation was a black auxiliary of the white First Baptist Church. It could be watched and supervised. After Durrett died in 1828, the two congregations merged. By 1860, over 2,200 enslaved and free blacks worshiped at the church, by then under the leadership of Frederick Braxton. It was the largest congregation in the commonwealth. In Louisville, free black Henry Adams became the "black" minister at the city's First Baptist Church in 1829. He led black congregants to secede from the church to form their own in 1842. Most towns and some smaller villages had black churches that remained under the watch of white residents, who were leery of black assemblies.

Although the Great Revival awakened religious enthusiasm in Kentucky, as well as throughout the United States, a new spiritual impulse arose after the War of 1812. The Second Great Awakening exploded between the 1820s and 1840s. Baptist and Methodist congregations ballooned. Evangelical theology expanded beyond calling on people to make personal decisions about their connections to God. Emphasis was placed on the individual's role and responsibility to the community. New Light Kentuckians believed they had to effect social change to change their society. Humanitarianism and self-improvement became important aspects of evangelicalism, giving new energy to reform movements. It was a message that reached beyond the churches. It inspired many Americans to address the ills of their society. The idea of self-improvement underlay the rise of reform movements like temperance, public education, women's rights, medical reform, humane treatment of the insane and the criminal, vegetarianism, and the abolition of slavery. Among some Americans, this idea of self-improvement blended with the pursuit of profit and refinement in the form of what Henry Clay called "the self-made man." All of these movements, both religious and secular, gained energy during the Second Great Awakening.

The number of reform institutions that arose during the era was staggering. Temperance societies popped up across the state, the first in Lexington in 1830. The state purchased the Fayette Hospital in 1824 and converted it into the Kentucky Asylum for the mentally ill. A sister institution, the Western State Hospital, followed in Hopkinsville in 1848. Catherine Spalding, who joined two other women in founding the Roman Catholic Sisters of Charity of Nazareth near Bardstown in 1813, opened academies in Lexington, Louisville, and Union County, as well as St. Vincent's Infirmary and St. Vincent's Orphanage in Louisville in the 1830s. In 1841, Maria Cecil Gist Gratz founded the Orphan Asylum of Lexington. The Asy-

Kentucky Institution for the Blind, Louisville, KY. (Richard Deering, *Louisville: Her Commercial, Manufacturing, and Social Advantages* [Louisville: Hanna & Co., 1859], 34)

lum for the Deaf and Dumb was established in Danville in 1822. The Kentucky Institution for the Blind opened in Louisville in 1842.

New emphasis was placed on education. The Kentucky Association of Professional Teachers (1833) and the Kentucky Common School Society (1834) organized to promote public education for all white children. Henry Adams taught black students as early as 1829, eventually developing a school with four teachers. William H. Gibson Sr. started teaching enslaved and free blacks in Louisville in 1847 and was so successful that he organized grammar schools in Frankfort and Lexington. Richard M. Johnson's Choctaw Academy began teaching Native American students in 1821. More educational opportunities appeared for women. In Shelbyville, Julia Ann Tevis's Science Hill Female Academy was founded in 1825. The Green River Female Academy opened in Elkton in 1836, and David A. Sayre's Transylvania Female Seminary was established in Lexington in 1854.

Higher education, too, exploded. In 1819, Presbyterians gained a charter for a college in Danville. It took another eleven years before Centre College opened under president John C. Young, a twenty-seven-year-old minister. Denominational colleges dominated the landscape: St. Joseph's (1819, Catholic), St. Mary's (1821, Catholic), Augusta (1822, Methodist), Cumberland (1826, Methodist), and Georgetown (Baptist, 1829). Transylvania University had broken from the Presbyterians in 1819, al-

though many continued to serve on its board, often fighting with Unitarian trustees. The college flourished in the 1820s under the leadership of Horace Holley, who pieced together one of the best and largest medical colleges in the nation by enticing leaders in the fields: Constantine Rafinesque, Daniel Drake, and Charles Caldwell. William T. Barry and Jesse Bledsoe led the law school. Holley left Transylvania in 1827 when Presbyterian trustees charged him with immorality for being a "warm advocate" of "the Theatre, Ballroom, and Card Tables." In 1837, the Louisville City Council chartered the Louisville Collegiate Institute. Seven years later, it inherited the estate of the old Jefferson Seminary, a school founded in 1798 but defunct by 1829. To finance the Louisville Collegiate Institute, the legislature combined it with the Louisville Medical Institute and created a law school to officially form the University of Louisville in 1846. Between 1834 and 1842, the Kentucky General Assembly chartered over ninety academies, seminaries, colleges, and lyceums. Kentucky had more colleges than any other state.

Among the commonwealth's most visible reformers, however, were antislavery advocates whose motivations, whether religious or secular, arose out of the desire to improve society, improve the lives of African Americans, and, in the process, improve themselves as well. Robert J. Breckinridge supported emancipation out of his Christian faith. When the Presbyterian

Kentucky Synod voted to postpone a decision on whether it would condemn slavery in 1833, he stormed out of the convention, declaring, "God has left you, and I also will now leave you, and have no communication with you." In contrast, Cassius Marcellus Clay seldom used moral or religious arguments, and in fact, he was a wealthy slave owner. Still, he believed that slavery stood in the way of societal and individual improvement and that it injured Kentucky's economy by victimizing working-class whites who could not compete against enslaved and hired-out laborers for jobs.

All of these movements depended upon communication to spread their gospels of improvement. Advances in printing technologies made it easier to produce larger numbers of newspapers that then circulated more widely. Newspapers were sold in markets, carried aboard steamboats and railroads, and discussed in reform associations and political meetings. The *Louisville Journal* began in 1830 as a voice for public education, municipal reform, and the Whig Party that could implement both. In competition with the Jacksonian *Louisville Public Advertiser,* the *Journal's* editor, George D. Prentice, did not hold any punches: "Some newspaper establishments are operated by steam. In others, horse or ass power is employed. Should our neighbor obtain, as he promises, a steam press, he will have a combination of advantages—a paper printed by steam and edited by an ass." Begun in 1845 by Cassius M. Clay, the *True American* published tracts promoting the gradual emancipation of slaves, until Clay rode off to the Mexican War in 1846. William Shreve Bailey published antislavery literature in the *Newport News* (later named the *Free South*) until a mob burned his printing house in 1851. Yet he printed the paper another nine years.

The reformism of the antebellum years had long-term consequences. Young people who came of age in the later reform years carried its lessons with them into adulthood. Born in 1840, George Washington Bain was raised in the New Light Methodist church and became an early advocate of prohibition in the early twentieth century. His wife, Anna Maria Johnson Bain, became president of the Kentucky Women's Christian Temperance Union (WCTU) in the 1880s. Laura Clay, who would be instrumental in both the WCTU and the women's movement in the early 1900s, was born nine years later. May Stone (b. 1867) and Katherine Pettit (b. 1868), also members of the WCTU, became leading reformers in Knott and Harlan Counties in the early 1900s. They not only publicly condemned alcohol and tobacco use but also established settlement schools to improve eastern Kentucky's rural communities.

7

The Age of the Whigs

Rise of the Second Party System

Kentucky's politics reflected the dramatic economic and cultural events that reshaped the commonwealth between the 1820s and the 1850s. Economic, religious, personal, and societal improvements affected nearly every Kentuckian, black or white, female or male. But there was little agreement on how to improve society and self. Even the New Lights, who largely gave impetus to Kentucky's age of reform, fought over whether improvement was the responsibility of the individual or of the larger society. Many believed that their fellow citizens were basically good and well-intentioned. If left alone, in time, they would do what was right. Others believed that people could be trusted only when their character had been transformed, whether by conversion, reform movements, or even government. As one newspaper editor wrote to Henry Clay, the difference between these two views of humanity was the difference between the Whigs and the Democrats: "the former dealt with man *as he should be,* while the latter appealed to him *as he is.*"

Since the 1790s, the First Party System of Federalists and Democratic-Republicans had dominated American politics. The Federalists' political miscalculations during the War of 1812 doomed the party, but they lost traction in Kentucky even earlier. After the war, only the Democratic-Republicans remained, but the economic and political challenges of the 1810s and 1820s gradually splintered them into Democratic-Republicans and National Republicans. By 1828, the former evolved into the Democratic Party. Until 1834, the latter remained disorganized but loyal in opposition to the Democrats. Most of them became Whigs.

Kentuckians split nearly evenly between these two understandings of the nature of humanity and the role of government, and these ideas influenced the outcome of the election of 1828. Thomas Metcalfe was the first of his generation of Kentuckians to run for governor. Identifying as a National Republican, he disdained party politics that pandered to local interests, preferring a national vision of consensus and improvement. He supported tariffs and internal improvements that would bind the nation together. His opponent was William T. Barry, a member of the emerging Democratic Party, which catalyzed around Andrew Jackson, an outspoken critic of large businesses, overreaching national government, and monopolies like the Second Bank of the United States. Claiming the legacy of Thomas Jefferson, Jackson blamed such institutions for the economic depressions that injured the "common men" who supported him. Democrats embraced opportunity unregulated, unhampered, and unaided by government. In Kentucky, many rural citizens, particularly in the far western parts of the state, were Democrats because they saw little relevance for the federal government in their lives. Metcalfe barely beat Barry, 38,930 votes to 38,231.

Metcalfe took over a state deeply mired in the Old Court–New Court controversy and one that was still trying to emerge from economic depression. As a National Republican, he believed road construction, river clearing, and investments in railroads would spur economic development. A former stonemason, "Old Stonehammer" Metcalfe tried to pursue an agenda of economic growth, but he faced a general assembly controlled by Democrats. Despite his ambitions, he remained frustrated throughout his term. His few successes included the Green River Navigation Company, the opening of the Louisville and Portland Canal, and securing financing for the Lexington and Maysville Road after President Jackson vetoed federal funding for the project.

Governor Metcalfe might have had more success had he pursued educational reform. He confessed that he had "experienced all the disadvantages of a neglected education." As governor, he inherited the foundation for a comprehensive educational system. Gabriel Slaughter, governor in the late 1810s, had demanded that "Every child born in the state should be considered a child of the republic, and educated at the public expense, when the parents are unable to do it." His successor, John Adair, had not pursued Slaughter's idea, but the general assembly in 1821 did create a commission to study public education. William Barry, lieutenant governor and future gubernatorial opponent to Metcalfe, led the commission. The report, written by Amos Kendall, editor of the *Frankfort Argus,* recommended a public school system that would serve all white children, starting with elementary education and ending with a state university. The general assembly set up a literary fund to support the project, but the state's continued economic problems doomed the effort.

Had he been inclined, Old Stonehammer would have found a receptive legislature. Barry and Kendall, both Jacksonian Democrats, had led the movement in previous administrations. The Democratic general assembly, therefore, would have followed their lead. In 1829, it ordered another study to develop an implementation plan for a public system. Metcalfe crushed any hopes of passage, however, insisting that the state use its money on internal improvements rather than education. The legislature did authorize county courts to voluntarily establish school districts and to levy taxes to support them, but few counties chose to act. A survey conducted in 1832 revealed that only 31,834 of the state's 140,000 white children between ages five and fifteen attended school. Russell County had one school, and many Kentuckians had access to no schools.

In that year, Henry Clay challenged An-

Portrait of Thomas Metcalfe, by William S. Shackelford, c. 1845-1855. (Kentucky Historical Society Collections, Frankfort, KY)

drew Jackson for the presidency. Jackson's veto of the Second Bank of the United States made him popular among many Americans who blamed the bank for the economic woes of the 1820s. His supporters used "The Hunters of Kentucky" as Jackson's campaign song. Clay's supporters criticized the president's veto power, labeling him as "King Andrew." Although Clay carried Kentucky and five of the smaller states, Jackson won an overwhelming electoral victory. Even in Kentucky, Jackson was popular, garnering 45.5 percent of the vote. It was enough to boost Democrat John Breathitt into the governorship, eking out his victory against National Republican Richard A. Buckner of Green County, 40,715 to 39,473. Still, the National Republicans gained control of the general assembly, and state politics again deadlocked. Breathitt accomplished little before his death two years later. The lieutenant governor was a National Republican, John T. Morehead of Warren County. Upon replacing Breathitt, he became the first governor to have been born in Kentucky and the first to identify with the new Whig Party.

The Whigs, who saw Jackson as "a dangerous man on horseback," formally organized in 1834 with Clay as their leader. Clay had a vision for the nation—a protective tariff to promote American industry, federal subsidies for internal improvements to provide farmers greater access to markets, and a national bank to invest in industry, agriculture, and commerce. His American System appealed to many Kentuckians who lived in the Bluegrass. It also appealed to many residents of the larger villages because these population centers would have benefited from commercial and infrastructure development. Some who lived in rural pockets, like areas of the Appalachians, also appreciated the potential that commercial investment might have had for their communities. With a majority in the general assembly and control of the governor's office, the Whigs installed James Clark as president of the senate and turned to their agenda. The legislature set up the State Board of Internal Improvements, with Morehead as ex officio president. Still, Morehead's administration did not achieve as much as it wished. As a coalescing political party, the Whigs just did not have the organization necessary to enact many of their plans, despite widespread support for their ideas, particularly for internal improvements.

In 1836, James Clark ran for governor as a Whig. His role in striking down relief laws in *Williams v. Blair* as a circuit court judge in 1822 made him rather unpopular among many Democrats. By the 1830s, however, the first generation of Kentuckians dominated state politics, and their inclination to see themselves as part of a larger national polity boded well for the Whigs' future in Kentucky. In contrast to the two previous elections, Clark had little trouble dispatching Democrat Matthew Flourney, 38,587 to 30,491. He laid out an ambitious agenda, pushing for greater fiscal responsibility in the state government, penal reform, laws to curb runaway slaves, and a public school system. The general assembly established a state board of education, provided for a superintendent, and set a mechanism by which public education would be funded. Yet, the state treasurer refused to release money for education in

Portrait of James Clark, by Sophia DeButts Gray, 1908. (Kentucky Historical Society Collections, Frankfort, KY)

1840 because the state had a deficit. By 1843, only $2,504 had gone to the school districts, even though $125,884 had been allocated. Despite the Whigs' intentions, public education again foundered. In late 1847, the *Frankfort Commonwealth* exasperatingly concluded that "the Common School System of Kentucky is a mockery."

Failure to enact their own agenda was not the only problem the Whigs faced. Their party, like the Democrats, was not monolithic, and the governor's actions reflected their ambivalence. On many issues, Clark leaned toward Democratic policies. When the governor, an owner of thirty-six slaves in 1830, asked for a law to prevent abolitionist literature from being circulated in Kentucky, antislavery advocates among the Whigs in the general assembly refused to cooperate. They argued that such measures interfered with freedom of speech. Clark also supported the forced removal of native peoples west of the Mississippi River, a program that most Whigs opposed.

The arrival of thousands of settler colonials in the Green River region had pressured remaining Native Americans into abandoning the last of their Kentucky claims. In 1805, the Cherokees ceded what remained of their northern hunting lands in the Third Treaty of Tellico. That same year, at the other end of the state, the Chickasaws gave up a strip of land at the mouth of the Tennessee River. Still, the Chickasaws held tight to the territory between the Tennessee and Mississippi Rivers, even though most lived in northern Mississippi and Alabama. White settlers encroached on the Chickasaw territory constantly. "This land comes within 7 miles of my door," worried Matthew Lyon. "It is with difficulty the people can be persuaded to keep off from it. Fear of the Indians by no means restrains them, and for my own part I do not think fear of any kind can restrain them long." The Chickasaws came to the same conclusion. In the Treaty of Old Town in 1818, they sold the lands of western Kentucky and Tennessee, between the Tennessee and Mississippi rivers, for $20,000 per year for fifteen years. Andrew Jackson had led the negotiations, and hence the lands acquired in Kentucky became known as the Jackson Purchase.

Only a few months later, Congress created the Civilization Fund, appropriating $10,000 annually to "improve" Native Americans. Richard M. Johnson, a Kentucky congressman and member of the Baptist Missionary Society, received part of the funds to establish an Indian school on his farm in Scott County. After stalling for several years, the society's missionaries began actively recruiting students, finding their greatest success among the Choctaws. In October 1825, 21 students arrived at the Choctaw Academy near Georgetown. By 1834, the Chickasaws too sent a dozen or so students. The student body averaged 120 annually, although at times, it approached 200. The students learned English, "American" habits and morals, and crafts such as blacksmithing, wheelwrighting, and shoemaking. But as a Democrat, Johnson's embrace of civilization policy clashed with the removal policy advanced by his party.

In the mid-1830s, President Jackson ramped up removal efforts. In 1835, a contingent of Cherokees signed over much of their lands in the Treaty of New Echota and agreed to relocate west of the Mississippi River within two years. Some did leave, but most Cherokees refused to acknowledge the treaty. So, in 1838, the US Army rounded up Cherokees and crowded them into internment camps in anticipation of forcibly removing them west of the Mississippi. About 2,800 Cherokees traveled by flatboats down the Tennessee River. They crossed western Kentucky and arrived at Paducah, before continuing their journey down the Ohio and Mississippi Rivers. Months later, another exodus began. US troops forced about 13,000 Cherokees along different routes in what became known as the Trail of Tears. By March 1839, over 4,000 had died, many as they crossed Kentucky. Chiefs Fly Smith and Whitepath were buried in Hopkinsville. Thousands quenched thirsts at Big Spring because the army failed to supply them with necessities. Ferries at Mantle Rock and Columbus were to transport the refugees across the Ohio River, but icy conditions forced them to camp along the riverbanks during freezing weather. They suffered exposure, disease, and death. Defeated by removal, native peoples slowed their support for the Choctaw Academy. It declined over the 1840s and closed in 1848.

In August 1839, Governor Clark died. Lieutenant Governor Charles Anderson Wickliffe, who followed Clark, was a Whig. He, however, opposed many of Henry Clay's policies and had occasionally supported Jackson. As he became governor, another economic depression was under way. The Panic of 1837 hit Kentucky hard. During Clark's last year in office, the state debt ballooned to $42,000. Wickliffe asked for a small property tax increase, but the legislature insisted on borrowing money to offset the debt. As a Whig, he advocated for river improvements and public education. Unfortunately, because he was completing Clark's term, he did not have enough time in office to leverage such measures through the legislature. Wickliffe's most notable accomplishment was preservation of the state archives. A state library had been established in 1809 under the control of the secretary of state. It collected materials to provide legislators with resources for

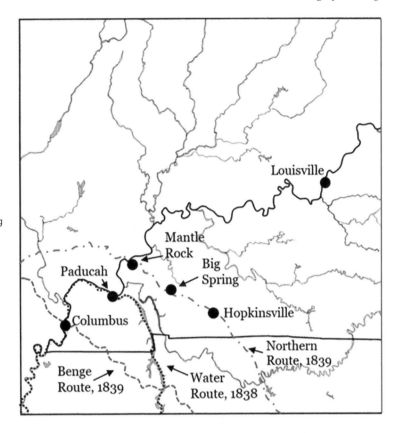

Map of the Trails of Tears. (Courtesy of Craig Friend.)

making knowledgeable decisions. In November 1824, the state capitol, where the library was housed, had burned. It took another six years before a new capitol was constructed, but the library was not restored. Wickliffe used his influence to secure a new library, which became the foundation for the state archives.

Kentucky's first Whig governors—Metcalfe, Morehead, Clark, and Wickcliffe—had rather mediocre records. During the terms of the latter three, from 1832 to 1840, the Whigs dominated the general assembly. Nevertheless, large Whig projects like public education languished. Yet the legislature spurred economic development by chartering companies to create roads, clear rivers, invest in railroads, address the safety issues of town life, and charter businesses. The list of companies chartered for business and urban development between 1834 and 1841 related well the Whig vision for economic improvements.

The problem that the Whigs increasingly faced, however, was also evident in this list. Rural Kentuckians saw the Whigs' attentions drawn primarily toward cities and towns. Who would represent the agrarian interests of the common Kentuckian?

Kentucky and the Nation

The Whigs argued that Henry Clay would protect the interests of the American farmer. During the 1830s and 1840s, Clay was the face of the Whig Party. He ran for president four times, receiving his party's nomination in 1832 and 1844. His American System appealed to northeastern factory laborers and western rivermen. Charleston, South Carolina, citizens praised him for defending sailors' rights. In Pottsville, Pennsylvania, he was known as the champion of coal miners. Everywhere, mobs thronged to see Henry Clay, among them thousands upon

Table 7.1. State-Chartered Companies, 1834–1841

1834	
Covington & Cincinnati Manu. Co.	Lincoln County Steam Mill Co.
Lewis Pottery Co.	Maysville & Mason County Hemp Manu. Co.
Louisville Museum Co.	Maysville Neptune Water Works Co.
Paducah Dock Co.	
Richmond Fire Co.	**1837**
Versailles Hotel Co.	American Cannel Coal Co.
	Bourdon County Agricultural Society
1835	Cynthiana Fire Co.
Campbell Co. Silk Culture & Manu. Co.	Harlan Museum Co.
Covington Dock Co.	Jefferson Gardening & Silk Co.
Covington Hotel Co.	Jefferson Pond Draining Co.
Eddyville Hotel Co.	Kentucky Assoc. for Improving Breed of Stock
Fleming White Sulphur Springs Hotel Co.	Kentucky Silk Manu. Co.
Franklin Minting & Smelting Co.	Louisville Gas & Water Co.
Georgetown Accommodation Co.	Louisville Manu. Co.
Kentucky Mining Co.	Rough Creek Manu. Co.
Kentucky Silk Culture & Manu. Co.	
Lexington Fuel Co.	**1838**
Lexington Hotel Co.	Bowling Green Water Co.
Louisville Dock Co.	
Mansion House Co., Frankfort	**1839**
Maysville Hotel Co.	Louisville Pottery Co.
Mills Point Warehouse Co.	Maysville Athenaeum
Newport Manu. Co.	Mills Point House Co.
Union Agricultural Society	
Union White Sulphur Springs Co.	**1840**
	Elizabethtown Fire Co.
1836	Green River Iron Manu. Co.
Adairsville, Russellville, & Muddy River	Louisville Cotton Manu. Co.
Transporting Co.	Louisville Iron Manu. Co.
Blue Lick Hotel & Water Co.	Louisville Pilots' Benevolence Society
Breckinridge Tar & White Sulphur Sprgs Co.	Marion County Agricultural Society
Covington Ferry Co.	Pond Creek & Green River Coal Co.
Covington Fire Co.	
Eutaw House Co. (Maysville)	**1841**
	Greenup Iron Manu. Co.
	Sandy Iron Manu. Co.

thousands of farmers. The *Frankfort Commonwealth* concluded, "Mr. Clay, undoubtedly, is infinitely the most popular man in America and he certainly is the greatest of American orators and Statesmen."

Kentuckians never seemed to grasp his immense popularity outside the state or how he replaced Daniel Boone as Kentucky's symbolic hero in the national mind. Kentuckians knew too much about Clay: his duels and card playing, rumors of his wild youth, and his long-running feud with Jackson, whom many Kentuckians admired. Still, he was a favorite son. Kentucky artists and writers swarmed to him. Matthew Jouett painted Clay's portrait in

1825. George Prentice, editor of the *Louisville Journal*, wrote *The Biography of Henry Clay* in 1831. Joel Tanner Hart sought Clay out to create a bust in 1847.

Beyond Kentucky, however, John Neagle, a Philadelphia acquaintance of Jouett, painted the most important portrait of Clay. His full-length portrait, produced in 1842, embodied Clay's political vision. Symbols of Clay's role as champion of American industry and agriculture sit to the left: a weaver's shuttle and the anvil as tools of domestic production, the plow as a sign of agriculture, the cow representing herding, and the ship indicating international trade. When the portrait was displayed

Henry Clay, lithograph from 1842 portrait by John Neagle. (Library of Congress Prints and Photographs Division, Washington, DC)

in Frankfort the following year, the *Frankfort Commonwealth* declared it "indeed a great masterpiece, a most perfect likeness, embodying with the highest and most truthful effect the full action and animation of debate, the dignity and majesty of the intellectual greatness of the distinguished subject." Richard M. Johnson commended Neagle for situating Clay "in a portico, upon a plain Republican platform of Kentucky marble, with the pillar of Constitutional Liberty upon his left." Clay and his dedication to the development of *all* aspects of the American economy had been immortalized. As engravings of the painting were sold and hung on the walls of private homes throughout the nation, this was the image of the statesman that most Americans embraced.

There was another image that also circulated widely: Clay the hero. Promoting Clay for the presidency in 1844, *Harper's Weekly* published a political cartoon that labeled Clay "the Hunter of Kentucky." It portrayed him in fringed buckskin and a coonskin hat, hardly the fashion of Daniel Boone but reminiscent of

"The Hunter of Kentucky," lithograph, 1844. (Library of Congress Prints and Photographs Division, Washington, DC)

Kentucky's colonial years nonetheless. Standing on the trunk of a felled, old hickory (an allusion to Andrew Jackson), Clay displays his trophies: the Van Buren fox, the Polk goose, and the Tyler rattlesnake. An eagle hovers above, holding a banner with the Whig campaign slogan, "Honor to Whom Honor Is Due." And so Clay, who never served in the military, became associated with the Hunters of Kentucky and Boone and the myths of early Kentucky. It was an effective campaign designed to make him appear more of a common man. But he still lost the election. Clay later made a convincing argument that vote fraud in New York cost him the presidency.

Although other politicians shared the spotlight on occasion, Clay dominated the national political landscape from 1811 through 1850. His unwavering commitment to union and compromise made all Kentuckians appear less polarized in national politics. He crafted the Missouri Compromise in 1820, found a solution to South Carolina's nullification threats in 1832, and wrote and presented the resolutions that became the Compromise of 1850. Like most of his generation, he placed nation before section or state. "If Kentucky to-morrow unfurls the banner of resistance unjustly," he wrote, "I will never fight under that banner. I owe a paramount allegiance to the whole Union—a subordinate one to my own State." His fellow Kentuckians agreed. When delegates from the slave states gathered at the Nashville Convention in 1850, the Kentucky General Assembly refused to send representatives. The previous year, the builders of the Washington Monument in the District of Columbia had called upon each state to donate engraved stones for the interior of the monument. Kentucky's stone read: "Under the auspices of Heaven and the precepts of Washington, Kentucky will be the last to give up the Union."

With Clay at the fore, Kentucky appeared positioned for national leadership. Other politicians like Richard M. Johnson and John J. Crittenden added to the state's political influence. Born in 1781, Johnson attended Transylvania University, practiced law in Scott County, served in the Kentucky General Assembly

beginning in 1804, and was elected to the US House of Representatives in 1807. A war hawk, Johnson joined the US Army when the War of 1812 began. Although severely wounded at the Battle of the Thames, he emerged a war hero, reportedly the man who killed Tecumseh. After the war, he returned to the US House before joining the state legislature. In 1819, he was appointed to fill Kentucky's vacated seat in the US Senate, and he remained in the Senate for eighteen years. In 1832, Johnson competed to become President Jackson's running mate, losing to Martin Van Buren. Four years later, he was on the ticket with Van Buren. He served as vice president from 1837 to 1841.

Like Clay, Johnson was a larger-than-life character who captured the American imagination. His association with the death of Tecumseh was politically powerful. In fact, many supporters of Van Buren did not like Johnson. An anecdote of the era related how a "thoroughgoing Van Buren man" was asked if Johnson's nomination "did not choke him in getting it down." The man responded, "I should have preferred [William Cabell] Rives, but I find my powers of deglutition wonderfully aided by the reflection that *Rumpsey—dumpsey, Col. Johnson killed Tecumseh.*" Johnson's status as war hero could overcome any question of his character, including his family life.

Johnson had a common-law marriage to Julia Chinn, an enslaved woman whom he had inherited but never emancipated. Chinn acted as Johnson's wife, not only hosting guests but also managing the household and overseeing his business interests, including the Choctaw Academy, in his absence. The couple had two daughters—Imogene and Adeline—who married well and took substantial dowries of land and slaves into their marriages. In 1828, Johnson's interracial family seemed to doom his political career. He was forced to leave the Senate so as not to ruin Jackson's chances at winning the presidency. Eight years later, when nominated as the Democratic candidate for the vice presidency, Johnson seemingly had overcome the political stigma. The campaign was nasty. Opponents ridiculed his family, including Julia Chinn, who had died during the 1833 cholera

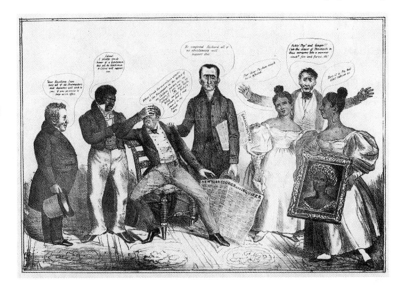

"An Affecting Scene in Kentucky," lithograph, 1836. (Library of Congress Prints and Photographs Division, Washington, DC)

epidemic. A widely popular cartoon portrayed Johnson overcome with grief, as his daughters sought to comfort him with a portrait of their mother. Different constituencies like abolitionists and free blacks promised to support him. Attacks from his opponents did not work, and Johnson became vice president. Rumpsey dumpsey.

Born in 1786, John J. Crittenden may not have recalled his childhood in colonial Kentucky, but he certainly was immersed in its mythology. After attending William and Mary College, he returned to the commonwealth, studied law under George Bibb, and made his reputation as the state's foremost defense attorney. He based his practice in Russellville. Unlike Johnson, who pursued his political career primarily at the national level, Crittenden had a more mixed experience. Elected to the Kentucky House of Representatives in 1811, he served through 1817, when the state legislature selected him to fill a vacancy in the US Senate for two years. He did not engage in public service again until he won a House seat in 1829. He became Kentucky's secretary of state in 1834, returned to the US Senate in 1835, became US attorney general in 1841, and then went back to the Senate between 1842 and 1848.

Whether at the state or national levels, Crittenden was a stalwart Whig who opposed

the Democrats on almost every measure. He was among the greatest orators of the age. As the (*Nashville*) *Tennessean* described, "Grasping with a powerful intellect the strongest views of a subject, and seizing with singular felicity, upon the weak points of his adversary—he guards his own positions with judgment and skill, and attacks those of his opponent with all the weapons of argument, sarcasm, and wit." His character was above reproach. No one questioned his loyalty to the Union, and whether cautioning against speedy resolutions to western problems like Texas, arguing on behalf of the American System, or refusing to give any ground to John C. Calhoun or Andrew Jackson, he remained consistent in his views. Clay may have been a celebrity and Johnson a war hero, but Crittenden was respected, widely. His eulogy in the *New York Times* concluded that, from all Americans, he elicited "the respect which is never withheld from those against whom the breath of slander has never whispered."

The Last of the Whig Governors

In contrast to their predecessors of the 1830s, the Whig governors of the 1840s faced increasingly difficult economic and political circumstances that eventually eroded their political base in Kentucky. When Robert Perkins Letcher easily defeated Democrat Robert French to become governor in 1840, he inherited a terrible economy. He had to pull back from the traditional Whig passion for internal improvements because the state just could not afford them. The financial crisis shut down work on canals along the Licking, Green, and Kentucky Rivers. Letcher resisted any relief bills that would aid individuals in debt, and he curtailed government spending, including reductions in contributions to the school fund. With his thriftiness, the state was able to start using specie payments by 1842, and the economy looked to be recovering.

When William Owsley succeeded Letcher as governor, he thought he could pursue Whig programs again. In the 1844 election, his victory over William O. Butler was closer than expected: 59,680 to 55,056. Many Kentuckians, trying to crawl from under the latest economic panic, remembered Owsley's opposition to relief as an Old Court justice in the 1820s. Despite his election, then, he did not have significant public support and wielded little political influence. He spent much of his term fighting with the legislature to fund the public school system. Owsley decided to start anew symbolically by burning the school bonds. Unfortunately, Kentuckians interpreted the ritual as a sign that Owsley did not care about their children's education. To demonstrate his commitment, he appointed Robert J. Breckinridge as superintendent of public instruction. In his first report to the legislature, Breckinridge demanded and received the $294,000 in interest owed on the burned school bonds. He argued for a property tax of 2 cents per $100 and campaigned for its approval, successfully.

Owsley was very much a victim of his time. By the mid-1840s, the political issue of slavery had begun to erode politics and civility. When Owsley pardoned Delia Ann Webster, who had been found guilty of assisting fugitive slaves, he was widely criticized. When he placed family members into governmental positions, he drew accusations of nepotism. Then, he and his secretary of state Benjamin Hardin engaged in a very public fight over Hardin's authority to make appointments. Owsley removed Hardin after only two years as secretary, but Hardin appealed to

friends in the senate, who upheld his right to remain in office. The Kentucky Court of Appeals later validated Hardin's position as well. Once vindicated, Hardin resigned. As the end of his governorship approached, Owsley announced to the general assembly how it "excites in my breast no emotion of regret."

Just as Owsley's generation had found meaning in the War of 1812, members of a younger generation of Kentuckians had been waiting for an opportunity to prove themselves, and Texas seemed to be calling. A number of Kentuckians, like Mary Holley, had migrated or had ties to Texas, which had separated from Mexico in 1836 and formed the Lone Star Republic. Although the United States recognized Texan independence, it refused to annex the territory. During the election of 1844, Democrat James K. Polk made annexation part of his presidential platform. His victory over Henry Clay convinced the Senate to pass a resolution before Polk took office. When statehood was offered to Texas, Mexico refused to acknowledge the region's annexation into the United States. Polk sent troops into the new state to protect its borders. But the United States and Mexico had very different claims about the locations of those borders. When American troops went into the disputed region between the Nueces River and the Rio Grande, war erupted.

Most Kentuckians welcomed the war as the next step in the United States' Manifest Destiny to spread across the continent. The US War Department asked for two infantry regiments and one cavalry from Kentucky. Governor Owsley, however, rejected the request, partly for financial reasons and partly because he considered the war a political maneuver by the Democratic president. When word leaked of Owsley's refusal, many Kentuckians organized themselves: 105 companies volunteered services. Constrained by insufficient funds, Owsley accepted only about one-third of them, most from the Bluegrass, to meet the state's quota. He had to acquire a $250,000 loan from the Bank of Kentucky and $54,000 from a group of Louisville merchants to pay them. As governor, he also had appointment power over military officers. Clashing with President Polk, who insisted Democrats be in command, Owsley selected Whig allies to fill the positions. (Polk eventually appointed William O. Butler major general of volunteers and Thomas F. Marshall captain of the cavalry.) Owsley's favoritism toward Whigs and the Bluegrass militias outraged residents from the rest of the state who questioned his patriotism.

In August 1847, a second call for two infantry regiments reached Owsley's desk. He approached the regions of the state that he had insulted during the previous recruitment and found eager volunteers who raised twenty-two companies. Paris's *Western Citizen* boasted that "there is something in the very air of Kentucky which makes a man a soldier." It was what had driven their fathers and grandfathers to war in 1812: a desire to prove themselves as worthy Americans. Over 5,100 Kentuckians served in the Mexican War. Many engaged in combat with the major armies that invaded Mexico. They especially demonstrated their mettle in the First Kentucky Mounted Regiment and the Second Kentucky Foot Regiment. Both units fought under Zachary Taylor in the northern reaches of Mexico, making their reputations at the Battle of Buena Vista in February 1847. Among the troops was Henry Clay Jr. Although shot through the thigh as his regiment retreated, Clay encouraged his men to continue without him. His father had given him two pistols, which he handed to a fellow soldier. "Take these Pistols to my father and tell him, I have done all I can with them," he directed, "and now return them to him." His regiment watched at a distance as Mexican troops came upon Clay and lanced him. The very public descriptions of his son's death made Clay even more loved among many Americans. The bodies of young Clay and sixteen other Kentuckians who died in the battle returned to the commonwealth for burial in Frankfort. At the ceremony in 1847, Theodore O'Hara, born in Danville and a graduate of Centre College, read his poem, "Bivouac of the Dead," which included this verse:

Sons of the Dark and Bloody Ground,
  Ye must not slumber there,

"Kentucky War Memorial." (John Warner Barber and Henry Howe, *The Loyal West in the times of the Rebellion; Also, before and Since: Being an Encyclopedia and Panorama of the Western States, Pacific States and Territories of the Union. Historical, Geographical, and Pictorial* [Cincinnati: F. A. Howe, 1865], 65)

Where stranger steps and tongues resound
  Along the heedless air.
Your own proud land's heroic soil
  Shall be your fitter grave:
She claims from war his richest spoil—
  The ashes of her brave.

The following year, the Kentucky General Assembly appropriated $15,000 to raise a sixty-five-foot-tall granite monument over the gravesite. The monument honored war dead from Buena Vista and Monterey in the Mexican War, the Raisin and the Thames battles of the War of 1812, and Tippecanoe, Harmar's Defeat, St. Clair's Defeat, Estill's Defeat, Fort Meigs, and Blue Licks during the Indian wars, connecting three generations of Kentuckians through their military heroism.

When the war ended in 1848 with the Treaty of Guadalupe Hildalgo, the United

States gained most of northern Mexico, including the disputed lands in Texas, the Bear Flag Republic of California, and the future territories of New Mexico and Utah. In return, the United States paid $15 million and assumed responsibility for $3.25 million in claims.

By then, John J. Crittenden had become governor of Kentucky, the last of his generation. A long-time supporter of Henry Clay, during the presidential election of 1848, he surprisingly abandoned his friend. At first, Crittenden believed that Clay would not run, and then when Clay did decide to announce his candidacy for the presidency, Crittenden believed that his old friend could not win. Fellow Whigs accused him of disloyalty, but Crittenden believed the nation needed a war hero like Zachary Taylor. For the 1848 election, he helped Taylor carry Kentucky. Crittenden swept into office on Taylor's coattails, but he made his election about education. He declared that the vote demonstrated that "the difficulty is not and has not been with the people." In 1849, he supported Kentucky education superintendent Robert Breckinridge's efforts to fund the public school system by persuading the legislature to channel turnpike tolls and tolls collected on the Kentucky, Barren, and Green Rivers toward school funding. Before he resigned in 1850 to become attorney general of the United States, Crittenden oversaw reconstruction of the state penitentiary, which had been damaged by fire, funded a comprehensive geological survey of the commonwealth, initiated a sinking fund to pay the interest on the state debt, and urged the legislature to convene a new constitutional convention to modernize the state's governance.

But Crittenden's decision to resign indicated that, like most members of his generation, he always had his eye on the national picture. When John C. Calhoun of South Carolina demanded southern states hold fast against northern efforts to keep slavery out of the territories acquired at the end of the Mexican War, Crittenden delivered a strong rebuke in his annual gubernatorial message of 1848 and again in 1849. He denounced Calhoun's theory of secession and convinced the general assembly to resolve that Kentuckians cherished the Union.

Crittenden's lieutenant governor, John L. Helm, became the last of the Whig governors but the first of the next generation of Kentuckians to serve in the office. Although his term was short—he served for less than a year before the election of 1850—he had a notable impact. To pay interest on school bonds, State Superintendent Breckinridge recommended drawing money from the sinking fund that Crittenden had established. Helm vetoed the bill, but the legislature overrode it. The conflict drew attention to the misuse of the school fund that had forced Breckinridge to make the initial request.

While they dominated Kentucky in politics, Whigs set into motion the economic growth of the commonwealth. In 1840, the state had $5,945,000 invested in manufacturing. By 1860, that figure reached $20,256,000. Industrial output by 1850 was $21,720,000; by 1860, it had climbed to $37,931,000. Kentucky ranked fourth among the slave states. In 1860, it had 3,450 manufactories that employed 19,587 males and 1,671 females, whose wages totaled $6,021,082. But the Whig legacy cannot be measured in numbers alone. Their advocacy for government-supported reform made Kentucky far more progressive than many other slave societies. Kentuckians' support for Whig policies on internal improvements, public education, and economic development allowed northerners, even the most radical abolitionists among them, to think that Kentucky was not so polarized in its politics. It empowered Kentuckians like Clay, Crittenden, and Johnson to be viewed as reasonable and moderate leaders in whom the nation's future could be entrusted.

Romanticism in the Commonwealth

In 1826, Henry Clay proclaimed, "We live in an age of romance." Romanticism was a cultural movement with roots in eighteenth-century Europe that celebrated human emotions and that emphasized creativity and free expression. Romanticism took on many forms. Often, artists and writers situated their subjects in the

Loudoun House. (Carolyn Murray-Wooley color transparencies, University of Kentucky Special Collections and Research Center, Lexington, KY)

wild nature of the American "frontier," where the individual could act free of societal limitations. Young men were often described as Byronic heroes: charismatic and passionate, highly individualistic, solitary, and potentially dangerous. Early histories of Kentucky drew upon such Romantic themes, for example, when they characterized Daniel Boone as a man of heroic simplicity exploring an exotic wilderness peopled by "noble savages." Romantic novels often portrayed young women as unruly and naïve, not yet prepared for the virtuous life of republican motherhood and consequently highly vulnerable. Such themes reflected young Americans' abandonment of older patterns of grace, gratitude, and gentility. They also revealed a growing sense of isolation and a disconnect within a rapidly changing world.

Romanticism was more than artistic, however. The Romantic idea of the self-defined individual seeped into all aspects of American culture. It elevated the importance of individual conversion and emotion during the Second Great Awakening. It energized entrepreneurialism through the ideal of the self-made man. It gave meaning to Democrats' appeal to the "common man" and Whigs' appeal to economic improvement. It allowed reformers to challenge the structures of society and rules that had been framed during the Enlightenment: criminals could be reformed; the insane could be treated; the deaf, dumb, and blind could be aided; women need not be subordinate; African Americans need not be enslaved.

Romanticism's influence in Kentucky manifested most visibly in its architecture and art. Gothic Revival architecture drew from medieval designs to evoke emotion through its grand scale. It was commonly applied to buildings that had religious purposes: Holy Trinity Church in Danville (1830–1831), the Church of St. Peter in Lexington (1835), St. Paul's Episcopal Church in Louisville (1837–1838), First Presbyterian Church in Louisville (1846–1847), Christ Episcopal Church in Lexington (1846–1848), Cathedral of the Assumption in Louisville (1849–1852), and the Abbey of Our Lady of Gethsemani in Nelson County (1852–

"The New Clay Monument, Lexington, Kentucky." (*Ballou's Pictorial*, August 25, 1855, 121)

Capture of Boone and Calloway's Daughters, lithograph, 1852. (Kentucky Historical Society Collections, Frankfort, KY)

1855). The style also appeared in houses like Francis Key Hunt's Loudoun, built in 1850 on the north side of Lexington. The house had towers of irregular heights, diamond-paned windows, and steep roofs. Gothic Revival was also used to design the State Arsenal in 1850 and a memorial to Henry Clay in 1855 that was never built.

Portraiture remained a powerful form of art, and many of the portraits painted between 1820 and 1860 sought to embody Romantic themes of honor, innocence, and family. One of the most famous paintings of the era was George Caleb Bingham's *Daniel Boone Escorting Settlers through the Cumberland Gap* (1852). Bingham used light and darkness to symbolize civilization and wilderness, and Rebecca and Daniel Boone's appearances mimic the biblical imagery of Mary and Joseph headed for Bethlehem. *Capture of Boone and Calloway's [sic] Daughters* (1851), a painting by Karl Bodmer, also became a famous Romantic image of the era. Unruly, naïve girls who had disobeyed their fathers face the dangers of the

untamed wilderness and its uncivilized inhabitants. Other artists copied it for its dramatic portrayal of the clash of cultures. In 1852, it was mass-produced as a lithograph that Americans purchased to display in their homes.

Although most Kentucky artists continued to concentrate on portraiture, Joel Tanner Hart became a sculptor and bridged the shift from neoclassical to Romantic art. As a young man, Hart was a stonemason. He constructed stone walls and chimneys in Bourbon County before moving to Lexington to carve headstones and monuments. He met a Cincinnati sculptor who encouraged Hart's more refined artistic talents. In 1840, he sculpted a marble bust of Cassius M. Clay that initiated his career. Andrew Jackson, John J. Crittenden, Robert Wickliffe, Henry Clay, and Alexander Campbell all sat for Hart's measurements. New Orleans, Louisville, and Richmond, Virginia, hired him to produce statues for public display. In 1845, when he traveled to Florence, Italy, he made it his home. His early works were neoclassical that resembled busts and statues of ancient Greeks and Romans. His best-known works—"Morning Glory" (1869) and "Woman Triumphant" (1875)—evidenced a bit of Romantic influence, however. The former evoked the innocence and virtue of children. The latter, epitomizing the beauty of the ideal woman, stood in the Fayette County courthouse until it was destroyed by fire in 1897.

Romanticism proved most powerful in literature. In 1826, Daniel Bryan wrote "The Mountain Muse" about Daniel Boone's entry to Kentucky's wilderness. His romanticized description of Kentucky consumed thirty pages before he even introduced his Byronic hero:

> With more or higher Virtues is endued,
> Or better qualified to fill the place,
> For which we are about to make a choice,
> Than DANIEL BOONE, th'adventrous
>   Hunter, whom
> I recommend. And he, by knowing well
> The human heart, and having friends,
>   whose souls
> Like his, can dauntless, brave the stormy
>   wilds . . .

Robert Montgomery Bird's *Nick of the Woods; or, The Jibbenainosey: A Tale of Kentucky* (1837) told of the struggle against the Shawnees in the early 1780s. An Owensboro lawyer, James Weir, wrote of outlaws in western Kentucky in *Lonz Powers; or, The Regulators* (1850). Charles Wilkins Webber, of Russellville, produced a collection of short stories in 1852 titled *The Hunter-Naturalist; or, Wild Scenes and Wild Hunters*. Mary Jane Holmes wrote five novels about Kentucky, including *Tempest and Sunshine; or, Life in Kentucky* (1854) and *Lena Rivers* (1856). William Wells Brown, born a slave although his father was white, wrote *Clotel; or, The President's Daughter: A Narrative of Slave Life in the United States* (1853), accusing Thomas Jefferson of fathering children by his house slave. Elizabeth Bryant Johnson, of Mason County, wrote *Christmas in Kentucky* (1862) about an admirable slaveholder who could not escape the system he so despised. Sallie Rochester Ford's *Raids and Romance of Morgan and*

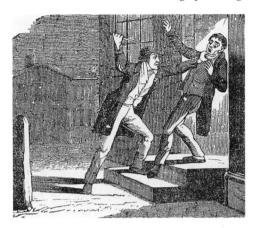

"Jereboam Beauchamp killing Solomon Sharp." (Henry St. Clair, *The United States Criminal Calendar, or, An Awful Warning to the Youth of America* [Boston: Charles Gaylord, 1835], 298)

His Men portrayed the gallantry of Kentucky's cavalrymen during the Civil War. Such works attempted to exalt readers' passions, allowing them to feel and imagine the narratives.

Romanticism also greatly influenced younger Americans and Kentuckians—the children of the first generation. Jereboam Beauchamp, born in 1802 in Warren County, attended Thurston's Academy in Barren County before pursuing a law career in Bowling Green. He admired and sought to study under Solomon P. Sharp, a Bowling Green lawyer who, by 1825, had served in the Kentucky General Assembly, the US House of Representatives, and as Kentucky's attorney general. Five years earlier, rumors had circulated that Sharp fathered a stillborn child with Anna Cooke, a planter's daughter. Not until Sharp ran for election to the general assembly in 1825 did the rumors arise again. Beauchamp, who had married Cooke in 1824, avenged his wife's honor by traveling to Frankfort and stabbing Sharp to death.

As the trial unfolded, the influence of Romantic ideals on nineteenth-century Kentuckians became apparent. Jereboam cast himself as the Byronic hero, a brooding, introspective soul who lived by his own moral code. Anna, charged with complicity in the murder, tried to pass herself as the unruly but doomed heroine. Their ends were as romantically dramatic as one might expect. Anna visited Jereboam in his cell, smuggling laudanum so that they could commit suicide together. They were unsuccessful. The morning of Jereboam's execution in July 1826, Anna revealed a knife, and they stabbed themselves. More seriously injured, Anna was taken to a local house. Jereboam begged to see her. After he watched her die, the guards escorted him to the gallows, where five thousand awaited. As the noose was placed around his neck, he requested a glass of water and for the band to play "Bonaparte's Retreat," a popular reel. The cart moved out from under him, and Jereboam slowly suffocated. Fittingly, the couple had written their own epitaph for the tombstone, which included:

> Daughter of virtue! Moist thy tear,
>   This tomb of love and honor claim;
> For thy defence the husband here,
>   Laid down in youth his life and fame.

Edgar Allen Poe, among the greatest if possibly the darkest of the Romantic writers, used the story for the only play he ever wrote, *Politan* (1835).

The most well-known Romantic story about Kentucky, *Uncle Tom's Cabin* (1852), was by an outsider, Harriet Beecher Stowe. In many ways, Stowe's prose was highly charged with emotion, as one might find in revivalist sermons. She promoted the community of reformers—people bound by Christian love and mutual sympathy. Stowe also reinforced Romantic stereotypes about enslaved African Americans: the mammy, the pickaninny, and the Uncle Tom.* Still, she also wanted to shatter the notion that any slaves were happy. Her narrative described the pain caused by Kentucky's slave trade to the south. In this regard, she was one of the earliest writers in a new cultural movement that was just beginning to spread across the United States—realism. In the United States, *Uncle Tom's Cabin* became the best-selling book after the

Bible. Its popularity transformed Kentucky's image from that of the old western frontier that had inhabited the American mind for so long to the image of a morally corrupt, southern slave society.

Upon reading the novel, Stephen Collins Foster penned "Poor Uncle Tom, Good Night," a song about an enslaved African American's emotional attachment to the beauty of the plantation on which he worked. In the first verse, he referenced the hard times that "comes a knocking at the door" that forced the slave owner to sell his slaves down river. The chorus concluded

> Oh good night, good night, good night
> Poor Uncle Tom
> Grieve not for your old Kentucky home
> You'r bound for a better land
> Old Uncle Tom.

Certainly, when Foster reframed the lyrics for a more palatable song titled "My Old Kentucky Home, Good Night," he drew upon more popular images of southern plantation life. Despite the changes, the sadness and tragedy of the lyrics remained.

Much antislavery literature, like *Uncle Tom's Cabin,* was sentimental, meant to appeal to readers' emotions to elicit outrage over the institution's horrors. Before he wrote *Clotel,* William Wells Brown wrote *Narrative of William Wells Brown, a Fugitive Slave* (1847), a story of his years enslaved between circa 1814 and 1834. It begins:

> I WAS born in Lexington, Ky. The man who stole me as soon as I was born, recorded the births of all the infants which he claimed to be born his property, in a book which he kept for that purpose. My mother's name was Elizabeth. She had seven children, viz: Solomon, Leander, Benjamin, Joseph, Millford, Elizabeth, and myself. No two of us were children of the same father. My father's name, as I learned from my mother, was George Higgins. He

---

* These terms are racially offensive today and should be used thoughtfully in historically appropriate contexts.

Lewis Clarke. (*Narrative of the Sufferings of Lewis Clarke, During a Captivity of More Than Twenty-Five Years*... [Boston: David H. Ela, 1845], frontispiece)

William Wells Brown. (*Narrative of William Wells Brown, an American Slave* [London: Charles Gilpin, 1849], frontispiece)

was a white man, a relative of my master, and connected with some of the first families in Kentucky.

The first paragraph opens with tragedy, emphasizing the lack of individual choice by his mother and the immorality of white men. Lewis Clarke, enslaved from 1815 to 1840, also wrote his story, *Narrative of the Sufferings of Lewis Clarke, during a Captivity of More Than Twenty-Five Years, Among the Algerines of Kentucky, One of the So Called Christian States of America* (1845). The title alone questions the institutions of slavery—as a state of captivity rather than labor—and Christianity. Clarke's story questioned white morality:

I was born in March, as near as I can ascertain, in the year 1815, in Madison County, Kentucky, about seven miles from Richmond, upon the plantation of my grandfather, Samuel Campbell. He was considered a very respectable man among his fellow robbers—the slavehold-

ers. It did not render him less honorable in their eyes, that he took to his bed Mary, his slave, perhaps half white, by whom he had one daughter,—LETITIA CAMPBELL.

Both narratives begin with the words "I was born . . . ," emphasizing the humanness and individuality of the writers.

The Heyday of Antislavery

Since 1816, when Henry Clay became involved with the American Colonization Society, antislavery Kentuckians had been conservative in their arguments against the institution. They generally acknowledged that slavery was immoral, but they envisioned few possibilities for ending it. Little changed over the next three decades. As one Kentuckian wrote in 1849, "There are three parties in this state, the proslavery party—the emancipation party—and the party hostile to both and middle to both, favouring no increase of slavery and no measures to put it beyond future control—but hostile to every thing looking to present action, in the way of emancipation. This third party, is *perhaps,* the bulk of the state." Although there were notable Kentuckians in the first two parties, most residents of the commonwealth did not want to upset the social order—the "peace." Most Kentuckians throughout the 1830s and 1840s seemed paralyzed by the issue of slavery. "I have talked with rich and poor alike on the subject, and find them alike, would be glad if there was not a slave in the state," wrote a recent migrant from Pennsylvania. Slavery remained less critical to the economy than in other slave states, but the institution was entrenched in Kentucky's cultural and social traditions.

And it was embedded in theory that slavery was a "necessary evil." From the nation's and state's inceptions, defenders and even most opponents of slavery accepted that the institution was immoral. Introduced to colonial Americans by the British, however, slavery became institutionalized, shaping economic and racial life throughout eighteenth-century America. Despite African Americans' humanity, more harm than good would arise from ending slavery: property rights would be abridged, labor would be unsettled, racial tensions would increase. The latter was most powerful. "*Prejudice,* unholy prejudice is at the bottom of the whole of it," explained abolitionist John G. Fee. Most white Kentuckians could envision the freedom of their black neighbors, but they could not imagine living side by side as free people. Former Whig governor James T. Morehead echoed this sentiment in 1842: African Americans were "a people between whom and ourselves there never can, in the nature of things, be any possible affiliation—a people, cut off as well by the distinction of color, as by the immutable laws of social order, from all connexion or fellowship with ourselves." Content with colonization or nothing at all, few Kentuckians pushed for ending slavery.

In the 1820s and 1830s, a "positive good" doctrine displaced the necessary evil theory throughout most of the slave states. The new theory justified slavery by forwarding the idea that slavery actually helped to civilize African

Americans by bringing them into contact with white culture and Christianity. Slavery also removed whites from menial labor and elevated the white race. Both of these attributes could be defined as a positive good because they benefited white America. In Kentucky, however, the necessary evil doctrine remained powerful. Slavery touched every part of the state, but only a minority of citizens were invested in it. Their economic pursuits did not require enslaved labor, as did the new cotton kingdom of the Deep South. Yet decades passed, and white Kentuckians held tight to the necessary evil doctrine. To many observers, it became apparent that they did so because they just did not want to live among free black Kentuckians.

By the 1830s, as language of improvement of self and society swept through American culture, some determined antislavery advocates decided to pursue their cause. Voices began to demand a new constitutional convention to revise the Constitution of 1799. In 1833, the Nonimportation Act passed. The following year, a bill to allow for a referendum on a constitutional convention to end slavery failed in the Kentucky House by three votes and in the Kentucky Senate by one. At Centre College and Augusta College, public debates were held on emancipation. In 1835, James G. Birney, a reformed slaveholder from Danville who rejected colonization and demanded the immediate abolition of slavery, led the establishment of the Kentucky Chapter of the American Antislavery Society. Later that year, the Synod of Kentucky published *An Address to the Presbyterians of Kentucky Proposing a Plan for the Instruction and Emancipation of their Slaves.* The winds of change seemed powerful. One abolitionist declared, "It is well understood here that when a convention is called, slavery is gone in this state; and it is also known that a vast majority of people are in favor of calling a convention."

Still, emancipationists could not muster enough political influence to get a convention. Many powerful politicians like Henry Clay, Robert J. Breckinridge, James T. Morehead, and Cassius M. Clay were reluctant to support the effort, as much as they may have sympathized with the cause. A constitutional convention would open the door not only to emancipation but to a variety of revisions that could upset Whigs' hegemony in Kentucky. In an 1836 speech to the house, Cassius Clay openly questioned if it was the time to "deliberately depose of a happy question which involves the political rights of master and slave—the liberties—it may be the lives of one or both parties." When the general assembly authorized a referendum in 1838, only 27 percent of voters approved a constitutional convention.

The Panic of 1837 and the next six years of depression affected many Kentuckians' views of slavery. Comparing themselves with Cincinnati, whose economy had recovered much more quickly, Louisville's town leadership blamed the slow recovery on enslavement as an inefficient form of labor. Their town became the hub of Kentucky antislavery. Its civic, economic, social, and political leaders echoed Cassius Clay's economic critique of slavery, arguing that free labor was morally superior to enslaved labor. Among proslavery advocates, Louisville became the "headquarters of abolitionism and emancipation." Other towns like Covington and Newport appropriated Louisville's position, as did some of the eastern mountain counties, and pockets of the Bluegrass where slavery served minimal purpose. In 1845, emancipationists Ira Root of Newport, William Glover of Louisville, and David Brooks of Bracken County sponsored a new referendum bill that passed the Kentucky House easily but stalled in the Kentucky Senate. In 1847, both houses finally consented to let the people decide whether to hold a constitutional convention. The Constitution of 1799 required two consecutive referenda: in 1847, 67.7 percent approved the measure; in 1848, 72.8 percent agreed. Antislavery advocates rejoiced. Walter Haldeman, editor of the *Louisville Courier*, asked, "What great evil did the people feel pressing upon them . . . if it was not the principle of Emancipation?"

In February 1849, the Friends of Constitutional Reform gathered at the state capitol, where proslavery delegates drew up twelve resolutions on the forthcoming constitutional re-

Cassius Marcellus Clay. (J. Winston Coleman Jr. Collection on Slavery in Kentucky, University of Kentucky Special Collections and Research Center, Lexington, KY)

visions. These resolutions included one that rejected any change to slavery and another that called for supporting free blacks willing to leave the state. Frustrated, Henry Clay, who reluctantly engaged in state politics, wrote an open letter intended for the general public pushing back against the proslavery forces. He laid out a plan for emancipation that would begin in 1855: "slow, cautious, and gradual, so as to occasion no convulsion"; removal of emancipated slaves to a colony; and the cost of transportation to the colony to be defrayed by the profits produced by the slaves. Yet the days in which colonization was a viable option were gone. There were just too many enslaved Kentuckians. Two months later, antislavery advocates gathered in Frankfort specifically to draft a statement on ending slavery in the forthcoming constitution. Unfortunately, the antislavery advocates did not represent a unified front. Some were proponents of gradual emancipation. Others supported abolition, colonization, or coexistence of the races. The several antislavery factions doomed the effort. They could not agree on a platform because they were divided on how best to rid the commonwealth of the institution.

During the summer of 1849, debate on slavery spread across the commonwealth. A visitor noted how emancipation was "more exciting than I supposed and is *the* question of the day overriding all others. . . . It is the principal topic in stage coach and tavern throughout the state." Anticipating the selection of convention delegates, antislavery and proslavery forces whipped up audiences' emotions. Antislavery activists reiterated the economic critique. They argued that the institution's negative effects extended beyond the towns and cities to the countryside, where it undermined white farmers' opportunities by reinforcing landed inequality.

Few antislavery proponents were prepared for the reaction of the proslavery supporters. Proslavery activists responded to the economic critique by appealing to race: "It would ill suit . . . our Southern men, without property, to become shoe-blacks, waiters, and servants of all sorts, who must not sit at the same table with their employers or master, and must hold themselves in submission to them." The Kentucky General Assembly repealed the Nonimportation Act of 1833 to discourage antislavery forces, and then the Kentucky House of Representatives resolved unanimously that they were "opposed to abolition or emancipation of slavery in any form or shape whatever, except as now provided for by the Constitution and laws of the State."

As selection of delegates began, emotions ran high in the commonwealth. When Cassius Clay debated Squire Turner at Foxtown in Madison County in June 1849, he had the best of his opponent. He offended Turner's son, Cyrus, who confronted Clay and called him a liar. Clay pulled a Bowie knife, but a mob surrounded and clubbed him. He was stabbed in the right chest, but wrestled the knife from his attacker, turned on Cyrus Turner, and plunged the knife into his abdomen. The two men were carried to a nearby house where Turner died. Clay survived. A month later, James Campbell shot and killed his antislavery opponent, Benedict Austin, at a Paducah debate. On the first day of balloting for delegates, several antislavery voters in Louisville were beaten. The *Louisville Examiner* described the scene: "Mr. S. attempted to make his escape from the crowd. Means and several others puersued him, and while running, Mr. S. turned partly round and fired at Means who was nearest to him. Both fell. A. J. Ballard, Esq., then fired at a man who was beating Mr. S. as he was lying on the ground. This probably saved Mr. Seymour's life. The man who was shot at turned from Mr. S. to fire at Mr. B. Another gentleman also fired a pistol.—During the affray, a little boy was shot. All the parties are now recovering." Louisville residents prepared for more violence on the second day.

When the delegate ballots were tabulated, only two emancipationists—one from the Knox and Harlan County district and one from Newport—had secured seats, although antislavery candidates came close in Louisville and in Logan and Crittenden Counties. Democrats, most of whom had little interest in abolishing slavery, held a narrow majority of the seats (52) over Whigs (48), who were more inclined to consider antislavery arguments. As delegates arrived in Frankfort in late September 1849, the antislavery movement seemed to die.

The Constitution of 1850

The constitutional convention opened on October 1. Forty-two lawyers and thirty-six farmers dominated the delegation. There were notable absences. Henry Clay and John J. Crittenden had rejected invitations to run as delegates. Robert J. Breckinridge had lost his election. Still, some prominent Kentuckians served: former Whig governor Charles A. Wickcliffe, former Secretary of State Ben Hardin of Nelson County, Democratic US congressman Beverly L. Clarke of Simpson County, Squire Turner who had lost his debate and son to Cassius Clay, and Jefferson County Democrat and former member of the Kentucky House of Representatives David Meriwether. As the *Louisville Journal* reported, "It contained men remarkable for their information, and others remarkable for their want of it." Many delegates never spoke except to vote. Having learned from the lack of information about Kentucky's previous constitutional debates, the convention did keep an official record that was printed as a 1,129-page report.

With momentum on their side, proslavery delegates decided to bring a permanent end to the debate over slavery. Garret Davis, a Whig from Mount Sterling and later Paris, proposed an article that declared that "the right of property is before and higher than any constitutional sanction, and the right of the owner of a slave to such slave and its increase is the same and as inviolable as the right of any property whatsoever." The constitution also directed legislation forcing any future emancipated African Americans, or any who might arrive in the state as free men, to leave or face imprisonment. Delegates inserted elsewhere that a majority of citizens, no matter the number, could wield power over the "lives, liberty and property of freemen." It also dictated that the general assembly had to compensate for the removal of any slaves.

In the months leading to the convention, antislavery proponents had grossly miscalculated the issue of slavery as the "great evil" that Kentuckians wished to address with a new constitution. The reality was that other issues were more important to most white Kentuckians. Many critics wanted more democratic control over the government. Some complained that county court justices, appointed for life terms, dominated and dictated local law and implementation of state laws. Others thought the governors' appointment powers were too vast. The convention decided to make most state and local offices, including judges, elective positions with fixed terms. Still other citizens wanted the state to formally assume responsibility for education. Pro-education delegates successfully pushed forward a provision recognizing public education as an essential function of government, despite opposition. As a result of the changes to the governor's appointment

powers, the office of state superintendent of education became elective.

The bulk of constitutional work, however, went into restructuring the Kentucky General Assembly. Over the previous two decades, the Whig-dominated legislature had exerted great influence. A Democratic-dominated constitutional convention decided to curb its powers. All house members would be elected at the same time every two years. Half of the senate would also be up for election every two years. All officeholders were expected to be exemplary citizens: a constitutional oath was inserted into the constitution, including a prohibition on dueling. A census would be taken each eighth year to adjust for representation, and plans were made to accommodate urban representation. Minor but time-consuming legislation, such as considering divorce petitions and making name changes, became the responsibility of county courts. The sinking fund that Governor Crittenden had established to pay interest on the state debt was protected from poaching. The general assembly was restricted from contracting debts of more than $500,000 except "to repel invasion, suppress insurrections, or, if hostilities are threatened, provide for the common defense." Such loans would have to be accompanied by taxes to pay off the debt within thirty years. And the majority in each house had to approve all appropriations of more than $100,000.

The convention also sought a process for replacing a governor who died in office or resigned, which had happened three times. If the governor vacated the office within the first two years of his term, a special election would be held to fill the remainder of the term. Previously, lieutenant governors had just completed the terms. The constitution of 1799 had also restricted governors from running for reelection. It required that they wait seven years to run again. The 1849 convention revised the wait period to four years. The convention concluded its work in December. Recognizing the Democrats' success in checking Whig power, Ben Hardin sarcastically commented, "We promised to fix the constitution so that a majority could not oppress a minority, and we have done so."

Kentuckians would vote in early May whether to approve the document or keep the 1799 constitution. During winter and spring 1850, newspapers, taverns, and other public venues filled again with political debate. Many Whigs interpreted the new constitution as a Democratic intercession in the Whigs' dominance of state politics. George Robertson, a former Kentucky chief justice, objected to the idea of an elected judiciary, but he also found complaint with the amending process, which had not been revised. To enact further constitutional change, a new convention would need to be called and voters would have to approve the measure in two consecutive elections. Whigs Garrett Davis, Lieutenant Governor John L. Helm, and Thomas F. Marshall of Louisville wrote a lengthy critique of the proposed constitution. Five thousand copies spread across the commonwealth, which were read from courthouse steps and in taverns and coffeehouses. But when the voters spoke at the ballot box, support for the new constitution was overwhelming: 71,635 to 20,302. On June 11, 1850, the reassembled convention signed the new constitution into law.

Ratification brought change to Kentucky politics, particularly the politics of slavery. Antislavery advocates would never seriously challenge the institution again. Appeals to the necessary evil theory of enslavement faded, and Democratic and Whigs alike politicized the protection of slavery as a positive good for their own gains. Kentucky now found itself, more than ever before, aligned with the national debates over slavery that would rend the nation (and the commonwealth) in half within a decade.

The new constitution also represented the rebirth of Kentucky's Democratic Party. The first generation of Kentuckians had dominated the commonwealth through the Whig Party for two decades. By 1850, a new generation of politicians challenged their elders for political seats and power. Louisville's James Guthrie (b. 1792) served in the Kentucky House and Senate and became president of the University of Louisville in 1847. Linn Boyd (b. 1800) of Calloway County was in the US House of Representatives for eighteen years and was in-

strumental in the annexation of Texas. John C. Breckinridge of Lexington (b. 1821) was just entering politics in the late 1840s, having actively campaigned for the Democratic presidential tickets in 1844 and 1848. When Fayette County elected him to the state house of representatives in 1849, it was the first time a Democrat had seen such success in that county. Lazarus Powell (b. 1812) of Henderson joined the Kentucky House in 1836 with an upset victory in a Whig district, and in 1848, he ran as the Democratic gubernatorial candidate against John J. Crittenden, to whom he lost. Three years later, he ran again and scratched out a victory against Archibald Dixon by 850 votes. If Cassius Clay had not run as a third-party Emancipation Party candidate, drawing votes from the Whigs, Powell may have lost. Regardless, he was the first Democrat in twenty years to win election to the governorship. (His predecessor, Whig John L. Helm, had not been elected but had ascended to the position when Crittenden resigned.)

The growing prominence of Democrats may have arisen from their association with the popular new constitution and their ability to use the constitutional convention to weaken their political opponents. However, they also appropriated many of the positions that traditionally had been held by Whigs. John C. Breckinridge supported internal improvements and colonization. And Powell, although facing a Whig legislature that rejected much of his agenda, worked with Robert Breckinridge to increase property taxes to fund public education. Education had improved dramatically under Robert J. Breckinridge's guidance since 1847. When he stepped down as superintendent in 1853, enrollment had increased from 20,402 to 201,223. By 1853, only North Carolina surpassed Kentucky in educational progress among the slave states.

Democrats also benefited from national politics. In 1848, the Whigs had abandoned Henry Clay, choosing Zachary Taylor as the presidential candidate. Clay, as a unifier and national compromiser, faded as the dominant face of the Whig Party. As one former supporter explained, "I have voted for Mr. Clay all the time, have *bet* on him, and lost, until I am *tired*, and have finally concluded that Mr. Clay is *too pure a patriot* to win in these demagoguery times." Clay instead ran for the US Senate. He found the nation once again in crisis and desperate for compromise. California had applied for statehood, potentially upsetting the balance between slave and free state representation in the Senate. Clay devised an omnibus bill and on July 22, 1850, held the floor for three hours as he discussed his ideas, answered questions, and appealed to Americans' nationalism. He failed. Democrats and Whigs were too much at odds, as were proslavery and antislavery proponents. Stephen A. Douglas of Illinois did most of the work to get the compromise enacted by dividing up the bill and lobbying different constituencies to support different aspects of the compromise. Most notable among the bill's provisions was a new fugitive slave law that required residents of free states to cooperate in the capture and return of runaway slaves.

When he arrived home in early October, Clay met a huge crowd that demanded a speech. After speaking for several minutes, he apparently realized the fading of his political career. He abruptly interjected that "for, strange as it may seem, there is an old woman at Ashland whom I would rather see than the all of you." The next summer, he penned his will, providing that enslaved children born on his plantation after January 1, 1850, would receive their freedom and money to be colonized in Africa. He tried to return to the Senate in the summer of 1851. At that point, however, he was too ill to work. In June 1852, he died in the National Hotel, in Washington, DC. He was seventy-five years old. Thirty thousand Kentuckians welcomed his coffin home to Kentucky. Abraham Lincoln eulogized that Clay "loved his country because it was his own country, but mostly because it was a free country; and he burned with zeal for its advancement, prosperity and glory, of human liberty, human right and human nature."

8

Antebellum Kentucky

The Slaves' Cause

Emboldened by their success in the constitution, proslavery Kentuckians pushed the general assembly to pass stronger laws to buttress slavery. In 1850, the legislature reinstated a law forbidding alcohol sales to enslaved African Americans. Six years later, the prohibition extended to free blacks unless they had written permission from "some white person of respect or character." In 1851, legislation passed that all future emancipated peoples had to leave the state, and that free blacks entering Kentucky could stay only thirty days before being arrested and imprisoned for a year. And in 1852, the legislature reinforced the status of slaves as "personal estate," protecting slave owners' chattel slavery from creditors until all "real estate" had been exhausted.

Antislavery advocates, disheartened by the constitutional convention of 1849, were silenced for a while. Arguments for moderate emancipation had not rallied Kentuckians against slavery. In the lull, more radical voices of abolition arose. Some, like New England teacher J. Brady, saw Kentucky as a good location from which to launch abolitionist newspapers. Arriving in Lexington in the mid-1850s, Brady unwisely announced his intentions, and a mob ran him out of town. The general assembly passed legislation a few years later making illegal any publications that would "advise or incite negroes in this State to rebel or make insurrections." The law did not slow William Shreve Bailey, a cotton machinist and steam engine builder in Newport. As early as 1850, in the pages of the local *Newport News*, he had written articles that demanded the immediate abolition of slavery. They drew attention and

anger. The owner and editor soon sold the operation to Bailey, who issued his first paper in March 1850 with the motto "Liberty and Equality." In autumn 1851, his machine shop was set afire, and the type and press were destroyed. Six months later, he reopened with the *Kentucky Weekly News*, traveling repeatedly to New England through the 1850s to raise funds for his publication. He promoted the new Republican Party when it formed in the mid-1850s, and he hosted parties in his home for local slaves. In 1858, he initiated a new paper, *The Free South*. He defended John Brown's raid in its pages the following year. Rumors circulated that Bailey had corresponded with the abolitionist. Over the course of two days and evenings in October 1859, a mob attacked and ransacked his print shop. They threw his presses and printing materials in the Ohio River and then wrecked his home. He and his family were warned to leave town. With financial assistance from friends in Cincinnati, Bailey persisted. When he traveled to England later that year to raise more funds, he met abolitionist Anna Richardson. Upon hearing his story, she wrote *Little Laura, the Kentucky Abolitionist* (1859), about Bailey's young daughter who had helped set the type in the presses. It became a popular book for parents hoping to inspire their children into abolitionist activism.

Cassius M. Clay, who had published the antislavery *True American* out of a heavily barricaded newspaper office in Lexington in the mid-1840s, had moved his enterprise to Cincinnati after a mob destroyed his printing office. When he returned from service in the Mexican War, however, Clay did not go back to printing. Instead, he turned to politics. In 1851, he declared he would run for governor as

"Slave State Free State." (*Narrative of the Life and Adventures of Henry Bibb, an American Slave* [New York: author, 1849], 71)

the candidate of the new Emancipation Party. He had no reason to think he could win, but he hoped for a strong enough showing to demonstrate abolitionism's appeal to Kentuckians. After all, in the months before the constitutional convention, over ten thousand Kentuckians had supported antislavery delegates. But in the gubernatorial election, only 3,621 citizens voted for him. Determined, Clay turned to cultivating a grassroots campaign to abolish slavery. He decided to begin in southeastern Kentucky, where slaves were few and antislavery sentiment was relatively strong. There he became involved with John G. Fee.

Born in Bracken County, Fee attended Ohio's Lane Seminary, where he came to realize the ethical dilemma of his family's slave ownership. His father was furious: "I have spent the last dollar I mean to spend on you in a free state." In 1845, Fee started an interracial church in Lewis County that promoted equality among black and white congregants. Partially supported by the American Missionary Association, he established other churches and published *An Anti-Slavery Manual, or the Wrongs of American Slavery Exposed by the Light of the Bible* (1851), appealing to a "higher law" than the commonwealth's constitution. Clay offered Fee ten acres of land in a remote part of Madison County, and Fee built an antislavery church on a ridge he named "Berea." In 1855, he constructed a one-room schoolhouse. For Fee, the school represented the beginnings of what he hoped would "be to Kentucky what Oberlin is to Ohio, anti-slavery, anti-caste, anti-rum, anti-sin." Joined by John A. R. Rogers, Fee imagined a college that would serve black and white students equally, while providing them with work so that they could pay expenses. Still, Fee regularly faced down mobs as they attempted to drag him from pulpits and threatened the college. He responded by publicly praying for them. A daughter later recalled, "We children never thought anything more about mobs than about thunderstorms. We supposed everybody had mobs." When Clay and Fee differed on the best way to end slavery, however, Clay's protection and patronage disappeared. When proslavery neighbors demanded that Berea close, Beriah Magoffin, the new governor of Kentucky, refused to intervene. Fee and his followers moved to Cincinnati. Not until after the Civil War did Berea rise again.

Through newspapers, politics, and education, abolitionists worked to end slavery. Others became activists in the most immediate sense of the term. The Fugitive Slave Law that passed as part of the Compromise of 1850 infuriated many antislavery proponents. They believed that it stomped upon their personal liberties. Delia Ann Webster, a Vermonter, had moved in the early 1840s to Lexington, where she became principal at the Lexington Female Academy. In 1844, she and a friend, Reverend Calvin Fairbank, were tried, convicted, and jailed for conspiracy to assist runaways. Governor William Owsley pardoned her after two months. Her incarceration did not curb her activism. In late 1852, she bought a farm in Trimble County from where she aided runaways again. The house overlooked the Ohio River, and as local slaves began to disappear, she became the prime suspect. In 1854, a "mock trial" placed her in the Trimble County jail, but a technicality led to her release. When magistrates indicted her on an issue related to the 1844 episode, she escaped to Indiana and never returned to Kentucky.

One should be cautious, however, in looking only to white abolitionists as the leaders of the antislavery movement in the 1850s. They did not act alone, and in many cases, the work of enslaved and free African Americans, who fought for their own cause and often paid with their lives, inspired white abolitionists' actions. In 1849, Cassily, a Fayette County slave, received the death penalty for putting broken glass in his white family's meal. In October 1859, a Woodford County grand jury indicted Willis Lago, a free black man, for helping a slave named Charlotte escape. Jullett, a free woman who had moved from a Bracken County farm to Ohio with her free children, returned to Kentucky on the eve of the Civil War to save the children to whom she had given birth while she was enslaved. As she led her children and grandchildren toward freedom, slavecatchers overtook them. She went to prison. Her entire family was sold down river.

Among those Kentuckians who successfully escaped slavery, some, like William Wells Brown of Montgomery County, became important abolitionist voices. Lewis Clarke of Madison County, the son of a white American Revolutionary War veteran, was to have been freed upon his father's death. But his white

Henry Bibb. (*Narrative of the Life and Adventures of Henry Bibb, an American Slave* [New York: author, 1849], frontispiece)

half-siblings did not follow their father's wishes and laid claim to his slave property. Instead of giving Clarke his freedom, they broke up his family. After he fled slavery in 1841, Lewis reunited with his brother, Milton, and together they pushed for the end of slavery. Louis Hayden, born into slavery in Lexington in 1811, watched as Henry Clay purchased his wife, Esther Harvey, and their son. Clay eventually sold them down river, and Hayden never saw them again. The story may or may not have been true: Clay denied it. A decade later, Hayden met Calvin Fairbank and Delia Webster, who helped him, his second wife, and her son escape to Ohio—the event for which Webster and Fairbank were arrested and jailed. Hayden became a voice of abolition as a speaker for the American Anti-Slavery Society and raised enough money to free Fairbank after he completed four years of his fifteen-year imprisonment. Henry Bibb of Oldham County married Malinda and had a daughter. When he escaped nine years later, the slave owner sold his

Table 8.1. Migrations of Enslaved Kentuckians

	In-migrations	Out-migrations	Total enslaved population	As % of total population
1810s	17,809	3,166	126,732	19.8
1820s	11,164	8,251	165,213	29.2
1830s	4,407	26,925	182,258	23.3
1840s	3,588	22,283	210,781	21.4
1850s	3,838	37,042	225,483	19.5

Source: "The Forced Migration of Enslaved People: 1810–1860," *American Panorama*, http://dsl.richmond.edu/panorama/.

wife. The sale would have made it impossible for Bibb to purchase her freedom, but he instead turned to abolitionism. *Narrative of the Life and Adventures of Henry Bibb, an American Slave, Written by Himself* (1849) became one of the most famous and important narratives of the era. By 1851, Bibb had moved to Canada, where he established the first black newspaper, *The Voice of the Fugitive.*

Despite these prominent examples, it is easy to overstate the success of Kentucky runaways. In 1850, only 96 fugitives were reported out of 210,751 enslaved people. A decade later, only 119 of 225,483 escaped. Many who were successful shared experiences with Brown, the Clarke brothers, Hayden, and Bibb: they benefited from the opportunities found in Kentucky slavery. Even though the Constitution of 1850 had legally strengthened the institution, economically, slavery was weaker than ever in Kentucky. Slave owners desperately hired out their slaves to make money from their investments. Brown, the Clarke brothers, Hayden, and Bibb all had experienced life beyond plantations. Not only did they meet people with stories of freedom, they developed greater senses of themselves as worthy of it. William Wells Brown spent time in St. Louis, working on steamboats and listening to white Americans debate slavery. Louis Hayden later noted how, when the Marquis de Lafayette visited Kentucky in 1825, the American Revolutionary hero tipped his hat to the young man, which inspired him to believe that he deserved respect.

After repeal of the Nonimportation Act of 1833, the slave markets exploded throughout Kentucky. At Cheapside in Lexington, auctions continued to drain enslaved blacks from central Kentucky. In Louisville, immediate access to river transportation naturally made the city a center of slave trading. Matthew Garrison and the Arterburn brothers advertised in Kentucky newspapers. They offered to pay cash for slaves and then imprisoned them in slave pens until a boat could transport them southward. During the 1850s, as slavery became increasingly profitable through the sale of slaves to the southwest, the pace of their exportation increased. More black Kentuckians were sold down river, more families were destroyed, and enslaved people became more active in protecting their families and themselves. "Slavery is the greatest curse on earth," a Trimble County slave told an interviewer in 1856. "Nothing exceeds it for wickedness."

Although many black Kentuckians fought against slavery from beyond the commonwealth, most remained in bondage. They made dramatic points often through tragic circumstances. When newspapers reported these stories, they forced white Kentuckians to confront the institution. The most infamous episode involved Margaret "Peggy" Garner, a slave on the Maplewood Plantation in Boone County, who escaped with her family across the frozen Ohio River in January 1856. US marshals, acting under the 1850 Fugitive Slave Law, tracked down the family and stormed the house where they were hiding in Cincinnati. Hoping to spare her children a life of enslavement, Peggy killed her two-year-old daughter with a butcher knife and wounded her other three children before she was captured. During the trial, the judge decided that Peggy, her husband, and a child had to return to their

"The Modern Medea—The Story of Margaret Garner," wood engraving, after a painting by Thomas Satterwhite Noble. (*Harper's Weekly,* May 18, 1867)

owner in Kentucky. When Ohio officials tried to find her to try her for murder, they discovered that her owner moved her from Covington, to Frankfort, to Louisville to avoid them. He finally sent her to an Arkansas plantation that belonged to his own brother. She ended up being sold to a New Orleans family and then to a Mississippi planter. In 1858, she apparently died of typhoid fever at twenty-five years of age.

Although white Kentuckians had settled on slavery as a beneficial institution, they knew its immorality and brutality. They became increasingly paranoid about slave insurrection, although not without reason. In 1848, over forty enslaved people armed themselves and walked northward from Fayette County, as they attempted to escape to Ohio. In Bracken County, one hundred white patrollers confronted the runaways and fired upon them. About thirty-five were captured and returned to their owners. The rest fled into the woods. A white college student accused of assisting them received twenty years hard labor in the state penitentiary. Yet this was the largest threat of the era, and future fears among the white population arose from imagination rather than reality.

In Hopkinsville, rumors circulated in 1856 that six hundred slaves from Tennessee might attack nearby Lafayette, to the south along the Tennessee border. Panicked, patrollers scoured the region for suspicious African Americans. They

eventually hanged or shot several and whipped to death the white man they assumed had instigated the rebellion. In the end, no evidence of an insurrection surfaced, but fears of slave revolt still spread to Henderson, Taylor, Bath, and Carroll Counties. Similarly, in 1861, white residents of Owen County panicked over a supposed rebellion of four hundred slaves. Such rumors repeated the same themes: telegraph lines had been cut to keep whites from calling for help, the numbers of blacks were overwhelming (and they always seemed well armed despite the improbability of that), and a white man was always ultimately responsible. As in Lafayette and Hopkinsville, an insurrection never manifested in Owen County. A white woman who saw two African Americans with guns started the rumor. She had notified her minister, who then sounded—and exaggerated—the alarm.

Many enslaved peoples, resigned to their status, did not turn to violence but sought to improve their circumstances and lives. In 1845, Elisha Green approached the white Baptist church of Maysville to allow him to "exercise his gifts" as a preacher. Three years later, he founded the First African Baptist Church of Maysville, followed by the First African Baptist Church of Paris in 1855. In Louisville, some of the city's eight independent black churches sponsored schools for enslaved and free black students. Similar schools appeared in Lexington, Bowling Green, Maysville, and Richmond, as well as in eleven counties. By 1860, an estimated 56 percent of adult free blacks were literate. Almost every African American knew at least one fellow African American who could read and write. As fears over insurrection peaked in the mid-1850s, however, white Kentuckians became more vigilant. They suspected churches and schools of conspiracy. A mob ransacked John Fee's Madison County school. In Georgetown, a white man interrupted Elisha Green's sermon to demand that the all-black congregation disperse. Paris prohibited night services. Lexington appointed white citizens to "superintend" black church services. As Kentucky's black population declined and Kentucky became whiter, efforts to control and constrain African American opportunities increased.

Sectionalism and the Rise of the Democrats

When Henry Clay died in 1852, the unity that he symbolized in the Whig Party seemed to die as well. Proslavery southern Whigs distrusted antislavery northern Whigs. The first signs of trouble for the party in Kentucky were the state elections of 1851 when Democrat Lazarus Powell upset Linn Boyd in the gubernatorial election. In addition, John C. Breckinridge shocked everyone by winning the state legislative seat in Henry Clay's old Ashland district. Still, the Whigs remained powerful. They held both houses of the Kentucky General Assembly. In the national election of 1852, Kentucky's electoral votes went to the Whig candidate, Winfield Scott, who had pledged to uphold the Compromise of 1850. However, the tide was slowly turning against Kentucky's Whigs. "A complete triumph must and will be theirs," declared the pro-Democratic *Kentucky Yeoman*, "the times have altered—whiggery is on the wane—a few years ago one could scarce find, except on election days, a corporal's guard of democrats, but now they need not be hunted for, they are met on every turn—on every hill—in every hollow, by-path and high road of the country."

When the Kansas-Nebraska Act was introduced in Congress in 1854, few politicians

who identified as Whigs remained to challenge the bill. The proposal's author, Stephen A. Douglas, advocated for popular sovereignty, the idea that residents of a territory should determine for themselves whether their future state would embrace or reject slavery. The Whig Party, divided between southern and northern constituencies, could not survive the debates. The abolitionist and proslavery proponents that existed within it ripped the party asunder. The Democratic Party similarly struggled to appease northern and southern constituencies. As both the Whig and Democratic parties shattered, many former Whigs formed the Republican Party with a singular platform: slavery should not expand into any new territory, including Kansas. Unlike the Democrats, the new Republican Party was a regional party that appealed almost solely to northerners. It, therefore, could take a hard line on the expansion of slavery. In contrast to the Whigs and the Democrats, the Republicans did not have to compromise with southern members.

The *Kentucky Yeoman* celebrated the demise of its opposition: "The Whig party is extinct, its materials in the North are to be made the nucleus of a great overshadowing abolition party, while the conservative whigs of the South may go over to the new democratic party, to the administration, or to the devil, as soon as they like." Many Kentucky Whigs did not like any of those choices, so they turned to the Native American, or Know-Nothing, Party, which had organized in the state in 1845. Many white Kentuckians viewed the thousands of German and Irish immigrants of the late 1840s as threats to job security and cultural integrity. Catholics too became targets of anti-immigrant sentiments. During the constitutional convention of 1849, Garrett Davis had proposed limiting the political rights of foreign-born citizens, a motion that was denied eighty to six. The strains between native-born and foreign-born became most evident in Louisville, Covington, and Lexington, where new arrivals often migrated to find work and formed small communities that drew attention. For example, three German-language newspapers arose in Louisville. George Prentice's *Louisville Journal* pushed back against the situation.

He declared that the "general issue is between Americanism and foreignism." By election day, August 6, 1855, tensions in Louisville were so high that the Know-Nothings placed armed guards at polling sites. They, thus, deterred hundreds from voting. They also launched a series of attacks on German and Irish peoples and businesses. When a row of frame tenement houses along Main Street was set afire, tenants fleeing the blaze were gunned down. At least twenty-two people died. "Bloody Monday" initiated years of migration from Louisville that weakened the city's economy.

The Know-Nothing gubernatorial candidate in that year was Charles S. Morehead, who seemingly had little chance of defeating Democrat Beverly L. Clarke. The Know-Nothings did not have the political organization to compete with the Democrats, and they faced problems with temperance reformers inside the party, who were led by Robert Breckinridge. Still, Morehead campaigned by avoiding the divisive slavery issue and by focusing on the commonwealth's small immigrant population. He won largely because most Kentuckians rejected the Democratic message that slavery be protected at all costs, even if it destroyed national unity. Upon his inauguration, however, Morehead seemed to step back from his anti-immigrant rhetoric. He instead called for "perfect equality" among all naturalized citizens. As a former Whig, he shaped an agenda that pursued familiar reforms: funding for a Kentucky state fair, organizing the Kentucky State Agricultural Society, doubling the mileage of railroad lines, funding teacher preparation for the public schools, transforming Transylvania University from a private institution to a state-supported university, and expanding and improving the state penitentiary at Frankfort. In connection with the state penitentiary, he also renegotiated the state's contract with the penitentiary warden, which allowed the warden to collect income from convict labor. When another depression struck in 1857, Morehead supported reform of relief to the poor.

In 1856, a national election again challenged Kentuckians to face the divisive politics of their era, but they had few options. Despite

John C. Breckinridge: Vice President of the United States, lithograph, 1857. (Library of Congress Prints and Photographs Division, Washington, DC)

their gubernatorial success, the Know-Nothings had an ineffectual campaign. The Republicans more actively pushed their candidate, but fears circulated that the party's radical and unwavering stance on slavery would throw the nation into war. "Kentucky can never rejoice that the day of compromise is past," wrote a resident of Maysville. "To do so would be false to her history, her position & her dearest interest." The Democrats, confident in having secured slavery in the state constitution, portrayed themselves as dedicated to union. Their nominee, James Buchanan, had selected John C. Breckinridge as his vice presidential candidate. The campaign song celebrated that

> Oh! Buck and Breck are bound to win—
> No power can stop their coming;
> The Pennsylvania steed is lucky;
> And so the one from Old Kentucky
> Pennsylvania is safe and lucky
> So's the hoss from Old Kentucky.

"Buck and Breck" turned Kentucky Democratic for the first time since 1828, when Andrew

Jackson had carried the commonwealth. Breckinridge, at age thirty-six, became the nation's youngest vice president. The Republican Party mustered little interest beyond the northern states. The Know-Nothing Party, however, was the real loser of the election of 1856. It never recovered.

Even as his Whig Party collapsed, John J. Crittenden remained a powerful voice against the rising Democratic Party. He enjoyed much of the popularity that had once been reserved for Henry Clay. In the US Senate, he was a constant voice against the Kansas-Nebraska Act. He insisted that Kansas enter the union as a free state. It was clear that many if not most Kentuckians agreed with him. Upon a return visit to Kentucky in 1858, huge and rowdy crowds greeted him, demonstrating the extent of his popularity. Crittenden's political influence was so strong that Abraham Lincoln blamed Crittenden's endorsement of Stephen A. Douglas for his US Senate loss to Douglas in 1858. Nevertheless, Crittenden was now a man without a party: he could not join a Republican Party that so openly condemned slavery.

As American politics became more contentious, the political party system became dysfunctional. The Know-Nothings largely had disappeared. The Republicans were a northern party. The Democrats, therefore, seemed poised to dominate nationally and in Kentucky, with little opposition. In the state election of 1857, they gained control of the Kentucky General Assembly and won eight of Kentucky's ten seats in Congress. Still, the Democratic Party faced internal divisions. President Buchanan's failings made Vice President Breckinridge more popular and bolder in his defense of slavery. He supported a federal slave code and endorsed the principle of secession. Yet Breckinridge knew the political dangers of appearing too extreme. During a visit to Frankfort, rumors of his loyalty to the South forced him to proclaim publicly, "I am an American citizen, a Kentuckian who never did an act nor cherished a thought that was not full of devotion to the Constitution and the Union."

In a forthcoming Kentucky Court of Appeals election, Breckinridge predicted a Democratic win over an elderly candidate from the Constitutional Union, a political party organized by a group of former Whigs and Know-Nothings that was dedicated specifically to preservation of the union. "Nothing short of a defeat by 6,000 to 8,000 would alarm me for November," he declared. But Breckinridge had become overly confident in Democratic victory in Kentucky. Although the Constitutional Union Party was disorganized, the Democrat lost by more than 23,000 votes!

As the presidential election of 1860 loomed, many Kentuckians supported Crittenden as candidate for the Constitutional Union Party. At age seventy-three, however, Crittenden wanted to retire and orchestrated the selection of John Bell in his stead. The Democrats divided: northern Democrats backed Stephen A. Douglas; southern Democrats selected John C. Breckinridge. Breckinridge had shunned the nomination for months, but when finally pushed, he took the opportunity to pursue his political fortunes. "It is well to remember that the chief disorders which have afflicted our country have grown out of the violation of State equality," he wrote, "and that as long as this great principle has been respected we have been blessed with harmony and peace."

Shocked by the Kentucky Court of Appeals election results and hoping to shed the radical rhetoric of state's rights that he thought doomed his presidential candidacy, Breckinridge planned a barbeque outside Lexington in early September 1860 to woo his constituents. He appeared before a crowd estimated between eight and fifteen thousand people. In his speech to the crowd, he denied that the Democrats were indifferent to breaking the Union apart: "I presently challenge the bitterest enemy I have had on earth, to point out an act, to disclose an utterance, to reveal a thought of mine hostile to the constitution and union of the States." He pointed a finger at the Republicans as the true threats to union, claiming their attacks on southerners' constitutional rights endangered the harmony and unity of the American nation. It was not enough. Across Kentucky, citizens gathered in meetings to express their discontent with Breckinridge and the language of the Democratic Party. Union sentiment remained strong in the commonwealth, and in the end, Kentuckians chose Bell and the unionist course. They rejected Breckinridge, the Republican Abraham Lincoln, and the northern Democrat Stephen A. Douglas. The Constitutional Union Party appealed only to residents of the upper South, however, and Lincoln eked out the presidential victory.

Led by South Carolina, much of the South reacted to Lincoln's election by threatening secession. The US House of Representatives formed a Committee of Thirty-three, with a member from each state, to address South Carolina's challenge. Francis Marion Bristow of Elkton represented Kentucky on the committee, which recommended enforcement of the Fugitive Slave Act and a constitutional amendment that would prevent federal interference with slavery in states that permitted it. Congress approved the plan, but the amendment went unratified by the states. The Senate set up a Committee of Thirteen on which John J. Crittenden served. But the new Republican president-elect warned that he would not budge on his promise to restrict the expansion of slavery. The committee's work faltered.

In mid-December 1860, Crittenden proposed six constitutional amendments to assuage slave owners' anxieties and permanently protect slavery where it already existed. These amendments would reinstate the Missouri Compromise line, guarantee slave owners' property rights regardless of where they took their slaves, and strengthen the Fugitive Slave Law. Finally, by making it impossible to amend the Constitution to change any of the proposed amendments, one of Crittenden's recommendations, if passed, would have insured that slavery would never again be questioned. At the same time, Governor Magoffin circulated his own set of concessions among his fellow slave state governors. He hoped to unite them while avoiding war. Elected in 1859, Magoffin was a vocal supporter of state's rights and slavery. Yet the slave state governors rejected his overtures. Crittenden fared no better in the US Senate. Republicans blocked some of his proposals as Democrats rejected others. Outgoing vice pres-

Democratic Ticket, 1860 Presidential Election, lithograph. (Library of Congress Prints and Photographs Division, Washington, DC)

ident Breckinridge had supported Crittenden's compromise, but as a lame duck, he no longer wielded the political clout to push it through Congress. As Mississippi, Florida, Alabama, Georgia, Louisiana, and Texas followed South Carolina into a new confederacy, ironically, Breckinridge, as president of the Senate in February 1861, announced Lincoln as the winner of the electoral college vote.

Despite his political stances, Magoffin continued to reject secession as a reasonable reaction to Lincoln's election. When representatives from Alabama and Mississippi visited Frankfort in late December 1860, he refused to consider secession. He convened a special session of the Kentucky General Assembly to appoint six delegates to a Peace Convention. In the meantime, Kentuckians who had supported the short-lived Constitutional Union Party and Douglas's northern Democratic Party found common cause in arguing for moderation and patience. They formed the Union Party and called for adoption of Crittenden's compromise. Democrats in the commonwealth also tried to take a more moderate position. Magoffin wanted a convention to determine Kentucky's future, but not all Democrats thought a convention a good idea, including Breckinridge. When he addressed the general assembly in April 1861, the former vice president acknowledged the constitutional right of secession but insisted that Kentucky should continue to work to reconcile the nation. If no state convention assembled, secession could not be voted upon. Only if reconciliation failed should Kentucky then be "free to pursue whatever course her people may think consonant with her interest and her honor."

The Politics of Neutrality

The Civil War exploded when, on April 12, 1861, South Carolinians fired on Fort Sumter, where a Kentuckian, Major Robert Anderson, was in command. President Lincoln sent Governor Magoffin a request for four militia regiments. "I say, *emphatically,* Kentucky will furnish no troops for the wicked purpose of subduing her sister Southern States," Magoffin thundered to Lincoln via telegram. The Union Party supported the governor's position but insisted he reject Confederate requests as well. They asserted that Kentucky *"ought to hold herself independent of both sides,* and *compel both sides to respect the inviolability of her soil."* When, a week after Lincoln's request, the Confederate secretary of war asked for Kentucky troops, Magoffin similarly refused him.

Kentuckians were uncertain of their path. George Prentice declared in the *Louisville Journal*: "KENTUCKIANS! YOU CONSTITUTE TODAY THE FORLORN HOPE OF THE UNION." As Virginia, Arkansas, Tennessee, and North Carolina left the union, a State's Rights Party formed in Kentucky to counter the Union Party. It again raised the call for a convention to consider secession. As politicians and newspaper editors

John J. Crittenden, Senator from Kentucky, Thirty-fifth Congress, photograph by Julian Vannerson, 1859. (*McClee's Gallery of Photographic Portraits of the Senators, Representatives, & Delegates of the Thirty-fifth Congress* [Washington, DC: McClees & Beck, 1859], 216) (Library of Congress Prints and Photographs Division, Washington, DC)

wrestled with the situation, many Kentuckians began to choose sides. Some enlisted in Confederate units in Tennessee; others joined Union forces in Indiana and Ohio. John Hunt Morgan of Lexington wrote Confederate president Jefferson Davis, pledging "twenty thousand men can be raised to defend Southern liberty against Northern conquest." "Do you want them?" he asked.

Magoffin continued to gently push the general assembly to call a sovereignty convention, but the legislature chose to remain neutral. It created a committee to negotiate a path for the state, composed of Union Party representatives—Crittenden, Archibald Dixon, and S. S. Nicholas—and State's Rights representatives—John Breckinridge, Richard Hawes, and the governor himself. When the Union Party representatives rejected any prospect for a convention, the committee settled on a resolution of neutrality and designed a five-man military commission to oversee arming the state against invasions. When the State's Righters insisted on placing Magoffin on the commission, however, the Unionists withdrew support, and the plan collapsed. Only the resolution of neutrality went before the legislature. On May 16, the Kentucky House voted sixty-nine to twenty-six that "the State and the citizens thereof shall take no part in the civil war now being waged, except as mediators and friends to the belligerent parties; and that Kentucky should, during the context, occupy the position of strict neutrality." Four days later, Magoffin issued the commonwealth's proclamation of neutrality. He warned both sides against violating Kentucky's neutrality and encouraged Kentuckians to refrain from joining in the war. The Kentucky Senate followed, approving neutrality four days later by a vote of thirteen to nine.

Still, many Kentuckians distrusted Magoffin and his well-known sympathies for the Confederacy. When Lincoln called a special session of Congress on July 4, 1861, Kentucky held a special election several weeks beforehand to elect new congressmen. Unionist candidates won nine of Kentucky's ten congressional districts. Only Henry C. Burnett of the Jackson Purchase won as a State's Rights candidate. Another election for the Kentucky legislature was scheduled for August. Joseph Holt, a Louisville resident who had served in President Buchanan's cabinet, determined to keep Kentucky in the union. He vigorously campaigned for Unionist candidates, which resulted in a two-thirds majority in both houses. In both elections, disheartened State's Rights voters stayed away from the polls. Still, the electoral results indicate that Kentuckians sought to balance Magoffin's secessionist tendencies. For his work, Holt had a Union army camp named for him, just across the Ohio River from Louisville.

Kentucky was not alone in playing the politics of neutrality. President Lincoln, too, had to balance his goals carefully. Kentucky was not only a border state but the land of his birth. "I have no purpose, directly or indirectly, to interfere with the institution of slavery in the States where it exists," he assured in his First Inaugural Address. "I believe I have no lawful right to do so, and I have no inclination to do so." If Lincoln had promoted emancipation, he risked losing Kentucky and other border states. When General John C. Frémont began freeing slaves in Missouri, the president reined him in, fearing the action would "perhaps ruin our rather fair prospects for Kentucky." Still, President Lincoln also worried that Kentucky and other slave states that had not seceded could prolong the war by giving hope to the Confederacy that they might still join in secession. He developed a scheme of compensated emancipation. This program would pay owners four hundred dollars for each slave if a state committed to ending slavery by a definite date. Lincoln warned border state representatives that, if they did not accept the plan, they risked losing all of their slaves without compensation: "It will be gone, and you will have nothing valuable in lieu of it." During a meeting in early 1863, members of the Montgomery County Union Party retorted, "Kentucky does not desire to sell her slaves to the government of the United States at any price."

Federal and Confederate armies respected Kentucky's demand for neutrality for several months, for fear of frightening Kentuckians into the opponent's camp. But the commonwealth was far too valuable to be ignored for long. Its population was the ninth largest of the thirty-three states, and its economy ranked fifth in livestock, seventh in farm values, and fifteenth in manufacturing. Lincoln knew Kentucky's value: "I think to lose Kentucky is nearly the same as to lose the whole game. Kentucky gone, we cannot hold Missouri, nor, as I think, Maryland. These all against us, and the job on our hands is too large for us. We would as well consent to separation at once, including the surrender of the capital." If Kentucky joined the Confederacy, the Ohio River offered an ideal defense line. Southern troops could push into the Old Northwest and force the Union to defend itself. Jefferson Davis, too, wanted to "treat Kentucky with all possible respect." Still, many Confederates interpreted Kentucky neutrality as spinelessness. An article printed in the *New Orleans Delta* revealed many southerners'

"Governor Magoffin's Neutrality" (*Harper's Weekly,* June 29, 1861)

attitude toward Kentucky's stance of neutrality: "We want no corn, no flour, no swill-fed pork, no red-eye, no butter or cheese from the great Western Reserve, no 'sass,' no adulterated drugs, no patent physics, no poisoned pickles. And we will not pay the 'Blue Grass' country of Kentucky for its loyalty to Lincoln by opening our markets to its hemp fabrics. Let it lay in the bed it has chosen until it awakes to a sense of duty as well as its interest."

In order to protect Kentucky, the commonwealth organized the State Guard under the leadership of Simon Bolivar Buckner of Louisville. The state militia, which had been inactive for years, revitalized in March 1860, drawing from all white, able-bodied males between ages eighteen and forty-five. Buckner selected militiamen to form the State Guard. By the beginning of 1861, he had sixty-one companies ready to confront invaders from either side, although many Kentuckians suspected that he would only use the militia against Union troops. In response, Unionists organized their own Home Guard, supplied by five thousand covertly imported "Lincoln guns," distributed by William "Bull" Nelson of Maysville.

Yet militia troops could not protect Kentucky from a more immediate foe. "Kentucky and the West must be made to feel this war, and feel it until they cry peccavi," the *New Orleans Delta* concluded.[*] In May 1861, the Con-

federate Congress prohibited cotton shipments down the Mississippi River, except through Confederate seaports. Confederates in Memphis disrupted steamboat trade. In June, a Southern Boatmen's Convention resolved that "no boat, not owned within the limits of the Southern Confederacy, should be permitted to sail on Southern waters." In August, the Confederacy expanded its list of embargoed products to include tobacco, sugar, rice, molasses, syrup, and naval stores. But rather than force the Kentuckians' hand, the embargo agitated them against the Confederacy.

Neutrality could not be sustained, neither in Kentucky nor among Kentuckians. Simon Buckner made agreements with Union general George B. McClellan and Tennessee governor Isham Harris to keep their respective militaries out of Kentucky, and he visited President Lincoln to gain his assurance that Kentucky neutrality would be honored. The president responded that he had no "present purpose" to invade the commonwealth, but "I mean to say nothing which shall hereafter embarrass me in the performance of what seems to be my duty."

Nevertheless, both sides actively recruited Kentuckians. The federal war department designated one of its military commands under a Department of Kentucky, and recruiting centers arose at Camp Joe Holt and Camp Clay. "Bull" Nelson visited southeastern Kentucky to

---

* "Peccavi" means to confess guilt.

recruit three regiments. After Unionists dominated the elections of August 1861, Nelson established Camp Dick Robinson in Garrard County as an active recruitment camp. Magoffin demanded the camp close, but Lincoln refused, claiming Kentucky Unionists wanted federal assistance and that Magoffin did not appear interested in preserving the Union. Confederate recruiters also had been active. They enticed pro-Confederate Kentuckians to Camp Boone in northern Tennessee. In late August, the Confederate Congress voted to recruit actively in Kentucky, appropriating one million dollars "to aid the people of Kentucky in repelling any invasion or occupation of their soil by the armed forces of the United States."

Kentucky's August elections had not gone unnoticed. The results suggested that much of the state leaned toward the Union, and Confederates had to do something. General Leonidas Polk demanded to know from Magoffin whether the State's Rights Party in Kentucky had any intention to push back: "I think it is of the greatest consequence to the Southern cause in Kentucky and elsewhere that I should be ahead of the enemy in occupying Columbus and Paducah." Both towns sat in the Jackson Purchase, where control of the Mississippi, Cumberland, and Tennessee Rivers was of strategic importance. In late August, Buckner persuaded Confederate general Gideon Pillow to refrain from invading Columbus. He did not know that Union general John C. Frémont had instructed Ulysses S. Grant to take the town.

When Federal troops occupied Belmont, a loading spot across the Mississippi River from Columbus, Polk ordered Pillow to take Columbus. The governor of Tennessee and the Confederate War Department denounced the invasion. President Davis, however, sanctioned it. He decided "the necessity justified the action." In reaction, Grant occupied Paducah, Louisville, and other Ohio River towns. Alluding to Camp Dick Robinson and the Union's active recruitment within the commonwealth, the *Kentucky Yeoman* declared, "If Kentucky suffers one of the belligerents to occupy our soil, she cannot expect the other to keep off." By the second week of September, Confederate troops

under General Felix Zollicoffer moved through the Cumberland Gap and occupied parts of southeastern Kentucky. They intended to keep Nelson and other Union recruiters from infiltrating southward.

Even as the Peace Convention met on September 10, in Frankfort, to find ways to keep Kentucky neutral, legislators just down the street debated the issue. The following day, they voted seventy-one to twenty-six to order the Confederates to withdraw from the state. A substitute motion that both Federal and Confederate troops be forced to leave was defeated twenty-nine to sixty-eight. The Senate approved the Confederate-only bill, twenty-five to eight. The Unionists clearly had the day and sent the bill to Magoffin, who vetoed it. The general assembly then overrode his veto. Magoffin, faithful to his role as governor, issued the order as directed. A week later, the general assembly again demanded Confederate troops leave Kentucky. The legislature also authorized General Robert Anderson, head of the Department of Kentucky, to take command of the state's volunteers. He moved his headquarters to Louisville. The *Louisville Journal* celebrated that "we at last have weighed anchor and set out for the haven of safety and honor."

Union, Secession, and the Kentucky Belle

Men fought over secession and neutrality in the Kentucky General Assembly, the US Congress, and in more common public milieus—taverns, political clubs, and newspapers—as well as on the battlefield. War was a masculine enterprise: men could earn fame through victory, or they could be honorably memorialized in death. Although the public voices were masculine, white women of the commonwealth had very personal investments in the decision. Privately, women engaged their husbands on political affairs, hoping to exert influence indirectly. Sarah Jacobs of Oldham County spent evenings with her husband discussing "the right to secession and fattening hogs." Whether Kentucky seceded was an important decision, for should the commonwealth join one side or the other, women would watch their husbands and sons march off to war. When Ellen Wallace of Christian County heard that Virginia had seceded, she worried, "Kentucky it is feared will soon follow. She has all to lose and nothing to gain by such a course but ruin."

For women, war was a disruption to a way of life. Since the days when women holding sticks atop Fort Boonesborough had pretended to be men holding guns, women's lives had transformed dramatically in Kentucky. Religious enthusiasm had elevated women's status, as Mary Rhodes discovered in 1811 when she initiated the Sisters of Loretto in Marion County. A Roman Catholic religious order, the Sisters became the first American order of nuns the following year. Reformism had increased educational and occupational opportunity, like that of Rosa Vertner Jeffrey, who arrived in Lexington in 1838 when she was ten years old, received an education at a local women's seminary, and became the first "southern" woman to find success on the American literary market. Medical improvements had advanced women's life spans. For example, Jane Todd Crawford of Green County, having failed to deliver the twins with which she had been diagnosed in 1809, traveled to Danville, where Dr. Ephraim McDowell removed a twenty-two-pound ovarian cystic tumor and saved her life. McDowell performed the first successful ovariotomy on Crawford and did eight more over his career. Economic growth expanded women's enterprise. In Lexington, between 1806 and 1860, women—white and black—listed as *femes sole* rose from 6.8 percent to 20.3 percent of the town's heads of household. Finally, refinement had brought women, specifically wealthier white women, more comforts and some luxuries. Most important, it provided spaces in which they displayed their wit, sophistication, and status, as in the life of Sallie Ward.

Born in Georgetown in 1827, Ward was the daughter of Robert Johnson Ward, a planter and former speaker of the Kentucky House of Representatives. She enjoyed the comforts of elite life, including having enslaved African Americans at her service. She attended French finishing school in Philadelphia, trav-

Portrait of Sally Ward Lawrence Hunt Armstrong Downs, 1860, by George Peter Alexander Healy. (Speed Art Museum, Louisville, KY)

eled among the wealthiest of southern society, married into the Boston elite, and earned the praise of George Prentice: "Genius comprehends all the loveliness of woman, and to be a famous belle one must be a genius." Her fashion was cutting edge. She wore makeup, which drew the condemnation of her husband's Boston Brahmin family. They denounced her "frequent and free use of paints and other cosmetics." As her marriage to her first husband fell apart, she wore a dress resembling Amelia Bloomer's rational women's clothing to a Boston ball, which outraged the elite. The divorce was a national scandal. The *New York Herald* explained it as a culture clash: "In Boston, all is sober, discreet, staid, formal, cold and intellectual. In Louisville, all is impulsive, wild, free, unreserved, warm and lively. Boston delights in lectures and orations. Louisville runs into the frolics of balls and masquerades." In 1852, she married Robert P. Hunt of Lexington. They resided in New Orleans, where she became a fixture in local society as a renowned horsewoman and used her celebrity to host charity balls to aid the poor. When the Civil War exploded, her husband joined the Confederate army, initially serving as a surgeon before dying in battle in 1864. Ward remained loyal to the Union and returned to Louisville.

In other ways, however, women's lives had changed little since the colonial settler days. With exceptions like the Sisters of Loretto, childbearing and childrearing were central to women's identities as wives, mothers, and civic contributors. The role was so important that women knowingly risked their health to fulfill motherhood. Elizabeth Underwood of Bowling Green feared childbirth as "the event most dreaded and terrible to the inexperienced young wife." Many women died in childbirth. Others resented the pressure to continue to have children. "I think our present number makes a snug little family," Underwood responded to her husband's overtures, "& am liberal enough to wish my neighbors all the rest." Childcare demanded women's attentions and time. Unlike many of their peers in the new Confederacy, very few Kentucky women— only the wealthiest—had enslaved midwives to raise their children. For many white women, children became their obsession: educating, clothing, feeding, and healing defined motherhood. Most also knew too well the pain of losing a child, often within the first year, the child having been "lent for a season."

Coverture remained the legal structure of marriage, and men had authority over their wives' dowers. A compendium of Kentucky laws in 1859 included the context that "Marriage operates as an absolute gift to the husband, of such personal property as is in the possession of the wife at the time of the marriage." In a divorce suit that same year, Sarah Burnam of Madison County accused her husband Harrison of misusing her property, although he was fully within his legal rights "to rent real estate for not more than three years at a time, and hire slaves in like manner for not more than a year, and receive the rent and hire." Like many men, he did as he pleased with his wife's land and slaves, which included hiring enslaved laborers to others to make a profit. Even as other states both northern and southern passed Married Women's Property Acts that allowed married women to hold real and personal estates, Kentucky lagged behind in recognizing legal rights for women. Because *femes covert* could not own property, they could neither sue nor be sued. If a woman took a job, her husband had all rights to her wages. Married women's rights would not change in the commonwealth until 1894.

So, as secession rent the nation apart, white Kentucky women saw the stability of life begin to unravel. "The times are so exciting I can't half describe anything," wrote Josie Underwood of Bowling Green in June 1861, "all thought of ordinary things is upset—and we are living in a state of nervous tension that makes everybody excited and restless." Although the Underwoods owned twenty-eight slaves, they were loyal Unionists. Her mother swore never to "be driven out of the Union and give up the Flag and all it stands for, for which her father and forefathers fought." Still, as anxious as she and fellow whites were, Underwood noted that "the negroes—naturally too—can't half do their work. They, poor souls, have more reason perhaps than anybody to be anxious and eager for news." Underwood seemed oblivious to the consequences of the news that might come. Many white women benefited from enslaved labor and found security in white authority over African Americans. They, therefore, resented any disruption to the lives they knew. Frances Dallam Peter of Lexington and her family preferred union because they wanted to preserve the status quo. They feared that war would result in destruction of the southern landscape and economy, including the end of enslaved labor.

Whether they owned slaves or not, many white women anticipated the threat that emancipation would bring to their lives. When President Lincoln issued the Emancipation Proclamation in 1863, Ellen Wallace wrote what many white women thought: it was "not a military necessity, but procedes from the vileness weakness & corruption, of this, base, contemptible, negro equality, negro loving administration." Insurrection scares of the 1840s and

1850s magnified in the midst of war. "Servile insurrection will be the consequence unless the strong arm of the nation prevents it," Wallace continued, "and the blood of helpless women and children will flow in torrents, if his wicked and fanatical policy is not over ruled." The racial and gendered dynamics of wartime Kentucky seemed to turn upside down: "I think if affairs go on as they have been doing, the white women in town and country will find it necessary to carry daggers and revolvers in their girdles in place of pin cushions & scissors. . . . Negroes passing on horse back in squads of three or four yelling and laughing as they prance along on fine horses, as if they had in reality changed places with the white man."

White women in Kentucky wrestled with the meanings of secession and union, and the complexity of their responses may have been embodied best in the nation's most prominent woman: Mary Todd Lincoln of Lexington. Like Sallie Ward, Mary Todd received the training of a Kentucky belle: raised in comfort and refinement, attended by enslaved African Americans, and educated in a French finishing school. At twenty-one years of age, she joined a sister in Springfield, Illinois, where she eventually met and married Abraham Lincoln in 1842. Over the next decade, they had four sons. Mary Todd Lincoln played well the role of belle in Springfield, which celebrated the same type of "impulsive, wild, free, unreserved, warm and lively" society that one would have found in Louisville or Lexington. When her husband became a congressman in 1847, Mary Todd Lincoln accompanied him to the nation's capital and found herself in a much different society. She did not adjust well to living in a boardinghouse, which she considered more meager than she deserved. So, she returned to Lexington for pampering.

When her husband won the election of 1860 and the country began to dissolve, Mary Todd Lincoln struggled with the same issues with which most white Kentucky women dealt. Her husband, of course, sought reconciliation first peacefully and then militarily. Her slave-owning family in Lexington, however, supported secession. Her brother, George,

Photograph of Mary Todd Lincoln, by Mathew B. Brady, 1861. (Library of Congress Prints and Photographs Division, Washington, DC)

and three half-brothers fought in the Confederate army. Two died in battle. Mary Todd remained loyal to her husband and union, forsaking the southern culture that had made her a belle. No slaves worked in the White House. She befriended Elizabeth Keckley, a free African American seamstress who became the first lady's confidante. Mary Todd Lincoln determined to be a belle in Washington. She tried to reconcile the splintering nation by opening the White House to grand entertainments. Washington society was unreceptive. Harriet Lane, President Buchanan's niece and hostess, described her successor as "awfully western, loud and unrefined." Washingtonians laughed at her fashion, condemned her renovation of the White House, and questioned her loyalty to both the Union and to her husband. When she invited Stephen A. Douglas to the White House, she angered her Republican allies, which made her a political target for the rest of her tenure as first lady.

Whether living in the commonwealth or

beyond its boundaries, white Kentucky women found the threat of war difficult to negotiate. They were like women throughout the nation, but Kentucky's dedication to neutrality provided an early, but ultimately false, sense of security. As the war infiltrated the commonwealth, white women found themselves at war as well.

The Invasions of Kentucky

As the Peace Convention met in Frankfort, General Albert Sidney Johnston of Mason County, commander of Confederate Department No. 2, ordered Simon Buckner to occupy Bowling Green. When the Confederates marched into Bowling Green eight days later, they found that many of the Unionists had fled. One elderly lady who approached them clutched her Bible and declared that she was "prepared to die." In October, Johnston moved his headquarters to Bowling Green because he assumed that the Louisville and Nashville Railroad and the Louisville-Nashville turnpike would be primary routes for any Union movements. Bowling Green would be a critical battle site. Johnston had to be deliberate. With too few soldiers along the Confederate's defensive line, he needed to place troops strategically across the southern part of Kentucky, stretching them from Cumberland Gap to Bowling Green to Columbus. Forts Henry and Donelson, constructed on the Tennessee and Cumberland Rivers in northern Tennessee because of Kentucky's neutrality, were not well situated to supply the troops along the length of the line.

In late October 1861, a convention of pro-Confederate Kentuckians gathered in Russellville, along the defensive line. Most of the delegates decided to attend with no appointment or directives. Henry C. Burnett of Trigg County presided. The men proclaimed the people's right to "alter, reform, or abolish their government, in such manner as they may think proper." They called for a sovereignty convention to take place three weeks later. George C. Johnson of Scott County, John C. Breckinridge, and Humphrey Marshall comprised the planning committee.

Photograph of George W. Johnson, 1861. (Kentucky Historical Society Collections, Frankfort, KY)

Johnson was a fifty-year-old farmer who blamed the rupture of the "Old Union" on radical northern abolitionists. Like so many Kentuckians, he viewed secession as an extreme reaction to Lincoln's election and had hoped that compromise might save the union. When eleven states left the nation, however, Johnson reasoned that if Kentucky joined the Confederacy, the sides would be fairly matched. He believed that secession of the commonwealth would force the two republics to negotiate diplomatically to the benefit of both. He joined the State's Rights Party. He became so prominent in the cause that he had to flee his home in the Bluegrass as neutrality collapsed. When Confederate troops occupied Bowling Green, he volunteered as an aide to General Buckner.

On November 18, the second convention met again in Russellville. It severed relations with the United States and declared Kentucky an independent state. Forming a provisional government with a governor, a council of ten members from each of the congressional districts, and judges and other needed officials, the convention selected Bowling Green as capital

Photograph of Simon Bolivar Buckner, c. 1862. (Library of Congress, Prints & Photographs Division, Civil War Photographs, Washington, DC)

of the newest Confederate state. George Johnson became governor. In case of military invasion of their capital, Johnson and the council received permission to "meet at any other place that they deem appropriate." Then, the convention applied for admission to the Confederacy, which was granted on December 10, 1861. Of course, the Kentucky General Assembly still sat in Frankfort, and Governor Magoffin denounced the shadow government, while stressing that most Kentuckians were Unionists. "Self-constituted, as it was, and without authority from the people," Magoffin wrote to the *Louisville Journal*, "it can not be justified by similar revolutionary acts in other States, by minorities to overthrow the State Governments. . . . My position is and has been and will continue to be, to abide by the will of a majority of the people of the State." Still, Confederate Kentucky existed, but only in the space that the Confederate army could carve for it.

The Confederates were determined to expand that space. The Green River country be-

came a sort of no-man's land as small skirmishes broke out along the defensive line. On October 21, at Rockcastle Hills in Laurel County, Confederate general Felix Zollicoffer attempted to push into central Kentucky, but General Albin Schoepf's Union forces checked him. Two weeks later, General William "Bull" Nelson confronted Confederate troops under Colonel John S. Williams at Ivy Mountain. He forced them to retreat from the Big Sandy Valley. When Confederate colonel Benjamin Franklin Terry died in the Battle of Rowlett's Station on December 17, his men renamed themselves "Terry's Texas Rangers" to commemorate their fallen leader and home state. Over late 1861 and early 1862, Union and Confederate forces clashed as well at Sacramento, Hazel Green, West Liberty, Saratoga, Morgantown, Woodbury, and a score of other localities.

Zollicoffer became convinced that the Federals would attack somewhere west of Cumberland Gap. So, he shifted most of his troops to Mill Springs, a tiny community on the southern bank of the Cumberland River. He crossed to the north side of the river after he received intelligence that General George H. Thomas was advancing. Zollicoffer had been unwise, positioning his troops with a flooded river at their banks, leaving no escape should they have to retreat. George B. Crittenden took command of the Confederate troops and decided on January 19 to attack the enemy before Thomas had organized them. In the confusion of the state's first sizable battle, Zollicoffer rode into Union lines and was killed. After fierce fighting that resulted in 522 Confederate and 262 Union casualties, Crittenden managed to withdraw across the river. Confederate Kentucky's government watched these battles with anticipation. The council changed the name of Wayne County to Zollicoffer County to honor the Confederate general, but that was the extent of the government's effectiveness. Governor Johnson could not deliver the 46,000 troops that he had promised the Confederacy.

Near the end of January 1862, the Union turned its attention to western Kentucky. Ulysses Grant moved against Forts Henry and Donelson to undermine the military supply lines

"Battle of Mill Spring, Ky., January 19th, 1862." (*Harper's Weekly*, February 8, 1862)

northward. Fort Henry fell quickly. The small garrison fought a rearguard action as their comrades escaped to Donelson, and the fort surrendered before Grant's full army arrived. Albert Sidney Johnston sent generals John B. Floyd, Gideon Pillow, and Simon Buckner southward to save Fort Donelson. On February 8, he, however, admitted to Floyd that he really did not have a strategy for a counterattack: "I cannot give you specific instructions and place under your command the entire force." Putting the entire force under Floyd's command was a foolish decision. Although he was a successful politician, he proved to be an incompetent general. He hesitated to attack Grant's outnumbered force before it was reinforced. As Federal troops overwhelmed them on February 15, hard-fighting Confederates had almost opened an escape route to Nashville when Floyd ordered them to return to their positions. Realizing his incompetence, Floyd handed command over to Pillow and escaped on the only available steamboat. Pillow then shirked his responsibilities. He turned command over to Buckner and escaped in a rowboat. Buckner endured the shame of accepting Grant's demand for the unconditional surrender of sixteen thousand Confederates. (As evidence of the conflicting emotions that the war raised during the surrender, Grant, who had been a year ahead of Buckner at West Point, took Buckner aside and offered him money if he needed any. And years later, Buckner would be a pallbearer at Grant's

funeral.) Nathan Bedford Forrest, who had led a successful Confederate cavalry charge at Sacramento, rallied nearly four thousand Confederate troops, who escaped the surrender.

Meanwhile, Johnston realized that he could not hold Bowling Green after the losses at Mill Springs and forts Henry and Donelson. Union gunboats patrolled the Cumberland River, cutting off any retreat to the west. Fires broke out as Federal artillery shelled the city from the north. Evacuation began on February 11. The Confederates destroyed two Barren River bridges, the railroad depot, and equipment and supplies that they could not remove. As General Johnston's army evacuated Bowling Green, Governor Johnson and the council had to go with it. The *New Orleans Picayune* reported "the capital of Kentucky now being located in a Sibley tent." Union troops occupied Bowling Green for most of the rest of the war. As Forts Henry and Donelson fell, the Union took control of the lower Tennessee and Cumberland rivers, allowing Federal troops to outflank Columbus. The Confederates abandoned the town on February 27.

Johnston could not make a stand in Nashville. Union gunboats on the Tennessee River could cut his supply line, in the same way gunboats on the Cumberland River had endangered his position at Bowling Green. Many of the supplies massed at Nashville had to be burned, and criticism of Johnston increased. Jefferson Davis resisted demands that he re-

"Bowling Green, Ky.—Burned After the Confederates Marched Out." (*Harper's Weekly*, March 15, 1862)

move his friend from command. "If Sidney Johnston is not a general," Davis told a critic, "we have no general." Determined to stop Grant's march southward, Johnston concentrated his army at Corinth, Mississippi, joined by Generals Braxton Bragg's and Pierre G. T. Beauregard's reinforcements. With approximately 44,000 men, Johnston planned to strike Grant's 39,000 troops before 36,000 more Federal troops arrived under Don Carlos Buell.

They met at Shiloh. Johnston planned poorly, the attack was delayed, but the Confederates surprised the Federal troops on April 6. "Tonight we will water our horses in the Tennessee River," Johnston declared, and for a time it appeared he just might. His army surprised Grant's troops, shattering the Union line. But Union artillery and gunboat fire, in turn, inflicted heavy losses on the Confederates. Although they eventually had to surrender, General Benjamin Prentiss's Union troops rallied long enough to give Grant time to recover from the initial surprise assault. By then, Johnston was dead. A bullet had severed an artery in his right leg. Although he applied a tourniquet, he was dying before anyone realized that he had

been seriously wounded. General Beauregard continued the attack, but the battle ground to a standstill as night arrived. Overnight, Buell's troops began to reach Shiloh, and the Union army reorganized. At dawn, they counterattacked and soon recovered ground lost the previous day. By early afternoon, the Confederate army was in retreat. The expected battle of Bowling Green had been fought at Shiloh in Tennessee. The Confederates lost.

Confederate Kentucky governor Johnson had enlisted as a private in Company E of the Fourth Kentucky Infantry as it prepared for battle at Shiloh. The next day, he was mortally wounded. Found by a Union general who was an acquaintance of Johnson, the governor lay dying on a Union hospital ship. "I wanted personal honor and political liberty and constitutional state government," he explained on his deathbed, "and for these I drew the sword." The council elected Richard Hawes of Paris, who had also been heavily active in the State's Rights Party, to replace Johnson. But he was a governor without a state. Confederate Kentucky's government had moved to Mississippi!

9

The Civil War in a Border State

Despite the romanticism that often surrounds it, the American Civil War was horrendous. The Confederacy insisted on its right to self-rule, particularly when it came to protection of the institution of slavery. The Union determined to keep the United States intact and, as the war progressed, to emancipate enslaved African Americans. Many Americans seemed detached from the realities of war. Confederates bragged that they would whip the Federal armies within months. Northerners packed picnics to sit on hillsides and observe battles. Few seemed to recognize the permanent damage that war would inflict upon the nation. Kentuckians found themselves in the middle, a border state trapped between North and South, between a heritage of freedom and the economic and social benefits of a slave society.

Between 25,000 and 40,000 Kentuckians fought for the Confederacy, all as volunteers. Many enlisted in the war's early days when the commonwealth attempted to remain neutral. The best known of the Confederate units was the "Orphan Brigade," six infantry regiments originally organized under Major General John C. Breckinridge, the former vice president of the United States. Between 90,000 and 100,000 Kentuckians fought for the Union, among them nearly 24,000 African Kentuckians. Like their pro-Confederate neighbors, many volunteered, but many others were drafted beginning in 1863. Colonel Frank L. Wolford's First Kentucky Cavalry, called the Wild Riders, was probably the state's best-known Union military unit. Until 1865, practically all Kentuckians who fought in the Civil War did so in the western theater. Only after the fall of Atlanta, as Federal forces pushed lingering Confederate units eastward, did some Kentuckians engage in the East as well.

The Confederate Occupation

Reeling from the Union push through Kentucky and Tennessee, the Confederate army reacted slowly. The defensive line that had stretched from Columbus to Cumberland Gap was tattered. The Union victory at Mill Springs had been ominous. Columbus and Bowling Green had fallen. And in June 1862, as one final insult to the Confederates' plans, Union General George W. Morgan easily overwhelmed Confederates at Cumberland Gap, forcing them to withdraw. The dissolution of the defensive line ironically freed Confederate troops to be more aggressive with Kentucky.

The aggression began as small raids under John Hunt Morgan from Lexington. Born in Alabama, Morgan had come to Lexington with his family when he was five. After attending Transylvania University, he fought in the Mexican War, then became a successful Lexington businessman and community leader. When the state's neutrality ended, Morgan led his elite company, the "Lexington Rifles," to Bowling Green. Even before being mustered into Confederate service, he began the scouting and raiding that became his trademark. Promoted to colonel in April 1862, he led the Lexington Rifles to Shiloh, but so many died that the squadron had to be reorganized as the Second Kentucky Cavalry. His second in command, brother-in-law Basil W. Duke, along with an eccentric Englishman, George St. Leger Grenfell, supplied the discipline and training the men needed. In May 1862, Morgan returned

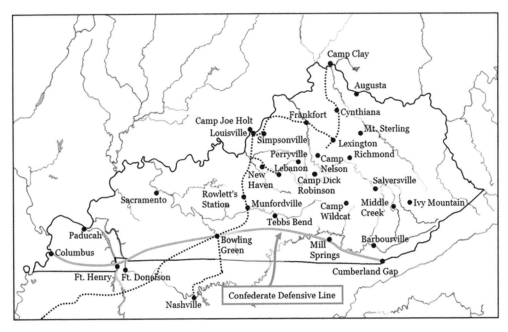

Civil War Kentucky. (Courtesy of Craig Friend).

Table 9.1. Major Civil War Engagements in Kentucky

Date	Battle	Killed, wounded, captured, missing (est.)	
		USA	CSA
19 Sept. 1861	Barbourville	15 (Home Guard)	5
21 Oct. 1861	Camp Wildcat	25	53
8 Nov. 1861	Ivy Mountain	30	263
17 Dec. 1861	Rowlett's Station	40	91
28 Dec. 1861	Sacramento	5	23–135, disputed
10 Jan. 1862	Middle Creek	27	65
19 Jan. 1862	Mill Springs	232	439
29–30 Aug. 1862	Richmond	4,900	750
14–17 Sept. 1862	Munfordville	4,148	714
27 Sept. 1862	Augusta	150 (Home Guard)	0
8 Oct. 1862	Perryville	4,211	3,196
30 Dec. 1862	New Haven	0	1
4 July 1863	Tebbs Bend	80	29
5 July 1863	Lebanon	41	unknown
7–9 Sept. 1863	Cumberland Gap	0	2,300
25 March 1864	Paducah	90	50
13–14 Apr. 1864	Salyersville	74	unknown
8–9 June 1864	Mt. Sterling	14	21
11–12 June 1864	Cynthiana	1,092	1,000
25 Jan. 1865	Simpsonville massacre	28	unknown (guerrillas)

to Kentucky with a small detachment. He ambushed trains on the Louisville & Nashville Railroad at Woodburn and Cave City before returning to Tennessee.

Again, in early July, Morgan swept into Kentucky from Nashville, striking as far north as Cynthiana. Among his 876 troops were some 370 Kentuckians. Some made hasty visits to their families during the raids. The cavalry moved rapidly. George "Lightning" Ellsworth aided their progress. He purposely sent misleading telegrams that were intended for interception by Union troops. The Confederates' misdirection was so successful that Abraham Lincoln wired General Henry Halleck, senior Union army commander in the western theater: "They are having a stampede in Kentucky. Please look to it." Over three weeks, "Morgan's Men" seized seventeen towns, captured and then paroled 1,200 Union soldiers, dispersed fifteen hundred members of the Home Guard, and used or destroyed great quantities of supplies. They recruited 300 men but lost only 90 from their own ranks. As a result, Halleck had to station thousands of Union troops far behind the front lines to guard supplies and infrastructure, like the railroad bridge across the Green River at Munfordville. Back in Tennessee, Morgan's glowing accounts of his success encouraged others to consider invading Kentucky.

Frustrated over Morgan's raids, Union brigadier general Jeremiah T. Boyle clamped down on Confederate sympathizers in Kentucky. Governor Beriah Magoffin openly criticized Boyle's treatment of Kentuckians and the Kentucky General Assembly's refusal to sustain Kentucky's neutrality. He called a special legislative session stating, "I am without a soldier or a dollar to protect the lives, property and liberty of the people, or to enforce the laws." Unionists in the general assembly took advantage of the situation. They decided to force Magoffin out of office by leveraging his frustrations against him. He agreed to resign if his successor would be a "conservative, just man . . . conciliatory and impartial toward all law-abiding citizens." Through a series of political machinations, the legislature arranged for James F. Robinson of Georgetown to become next in line as speaker of the Kentucky Senate (and therefore, next in line to become governor since the lieutenant governor had died in office). On August 18, Magoffin resigned.

Robinson was a moderate. He had opposed secession and abolition of slavery. Like his predecessor, Robinson made Kentucky's neutrality his priority. Morgan's raids had dismantled the Home Guard. Robinson, therefore, worked with the general assembly to raise taxes to revive the state militia. He also came to recognize that Magoffin had been right: the Federal government did not treat Kentuckians well. It imposed martial law on the commonwealth and suspended the right of habeas corpus. Such oppression, he declared, underscored the Lincoln administration's approach to war: "that *military necessity* is not to be measured by *Constitutional* limits, but must be the judge of the extent of its powers." Robinson rejected that philosophy and warned, "If military necessity is not to be measured by Constitutional limits, we are no longer a free people."

Some Confederates believed that the Federal government's poor treatment of Kentuckians would push the commonwealth toward the Confederacy. As Morgan's recruiting success demonstrated, all that was needed was opportunity to display their true sympathies. At the end of July, Confederate major general Edmund Kirby Smith, commander of the Department of East Tennessee, presented a bold plan to his superior, Braxton Bragg. Smith would enter Kentucky through Cumberland Gap; Bragg via the Louisville & Nashville Railroad. Once in Kentucky, they would combine forces to infiltrate farther and liberate Kentucky from Federal control.

Smith and his men started through the Cumberland Mountains in mid-August 1862 and captured Barbourville on August 18. Yet, once inside Kentucky, Smith found few supplies to sustain his army and decided to advance into the Bluegrass without Bragg. When he learned that Union reinforcements were organizing around Richmond, south of Lexington, he planned to attack and take the town. "Bull" Nelson had intended to defend Richmond with Union troops along the Kentucky

River, but General Mahlon Manson advanced his Union regiments south of Richmond to give battle. After several hours of hard fighting on August 30, the Union line collapsed. Nelson, who had rushed his troops to the scene, tried to establish another line. Hoping to inspire his men, he proclaimed, "If they can't hit me, they can't hit anybody!" Then he was struck twice, although not mortally wounded. The rout was on. The Union lost over 75 percent of the sixty-five hundred men engaged.

The Confederates marched on: taking Lexington on September 2, and on the next day, Frankfort, the only capital of a loyal state captured by Confederates during the war. Kentucky's government fled to Louisville. Panic had already set in there, and it began to spread among other Ohio River towns like Newport, Covington, and Cincinnati. Smith's army cut the Union supply line to General George W. Morgan's eight thousand soldiers at the Cumberland Gap, which forced them to evacuate. Expecting Morgan to retreat northward along the good roads in the eastern Bluegrass, Smith moved his main force of some twelve thousand men to Mount Sterling to reinforce three thousand troops that Brigadier General Humphrey Marshall had relocated from western Virginia. John Hunt Morgan scouted the Federal movements and harassed the Union soldiers in their flight northward. George Morgan, however, conducted a brilliant retreat through the mountains to Greenupburg on the Ohio River. Still, Smith had reopened the Cumberland Gap route for the Confederates.

In the meantime, Bragg had not left Chattanooga until August 28. When he reached Glasgow, he learned that Union troops under Don Carlos Buell were moving rapidly from Nashville toward Bowling Green. Bragg should have hastened to join forces with Smith, but he wasted three days at Sparta, Tennessee. He spent yet another three days at Munfordville, where a Union detachment under John T. Wilder guarded the vital railroad bridge across the Green River. Bragg had not wanted to delay, but he decided that the position had to be taken. By mid-September 1862, four thousand Federal troops found themselves surrounded

Photograph of General William "Bull" Nelson of Kentucky, c. 1861. (Library of Congress Prints and Photographs Division, Washington, DC)

by twenty-two thousand Confederates. When told to surrender to avoid the slaughter of his troops, Wilder retorted, "If you want to avoid further bloodshed, keep out of the range of my guns." Unwilling to risk civilian lives or damage the bridge, Bragg again demanded surrender rather than shell the Federals. Under a flag of truce on the evening of September 16, Wilder met with Simon Buckner and asked the Confederate, whom he had never met before, what was militarily correct under such circumstances. Caught up in the Union officer's recognition of his rank and stature, Buckner escorted the colonel and an aide around the Confederate lines so that they could see that they were hopelessly outnumbered. The next morning Wilder surrendered.

In late September, Bragg turned toward Bardstown, where he expected to join with Smith. But Smith failed him. So too did the expectation that Kentuckians would rally to the Confederate cause. Bragg and Smith found re-

"The Battle of Perryville." (*Harper's Weekly*, November 1, 1862)

luctant Confederate sympathizers in Kentucky who wanted to see victories before they committed. "Their hearts were evidently with us," Smith wrote Bragg, "but their bluegrass and fat-grass [cattle] are against us."

Bragg's delays in Munfordville and Bardstown gave Buell more time to reach Louisville, where his army found reinforcements and supplies. The Federals left Louisville on October 1. Three columns advanced toward Bardstown, as a fourth moved toward Frankfort. Bragg had left Bardstown, however, to meet with Smith and the new Confederate governor, Richard Hawes, in Lexington. The Confederates agreed to install Hawes in Frankfort on October 4, a ceremony that they hoped would inspire Confederate sympathizers who had hesitated to enlist under Union occupation. Making Hawes the official governor would also make possible enforcement of the Confederate conscription law that had passed in April. If Kentuckians would not volunteer, Bragg would draft them. Shortly after noon on a rainy October day, Bragg introduced Hawes to the crowd that packed the Kentucky House of Representatives and overflowed into the streets of the capital. The governor assured his fellow Confederate Kentuckians that the capital would never again

fall into Union hands. But the Federals replied later that afternoon, bombarding the town. The Confederates lasted three days in Frankfort. They burned the bridges over the Kentucky River as they fled the capital.

By October 7, some 55,000 Union troops under Buell encamped near Perryville. Another 20,000 Union troops stationed around Frankfort. Distracted by the force at Frankfort, which he thought was actually the larger army, Bragg ordered one of his major generals, Leonidas Polk, to attack and defeat what he thought was the smaller Union force near Perryville. Once Polk had defeated the Federals, he was to return to the main army so that they could consolidate with Smith's army and attack the main Union force. Bragg's intelligence was faulty. When Polk arrived outside Perryville, he realized he was outnumbered but did not know by how much. He defensively bunkered down. Not hearing the sounds of battle, Buell rode from Harrodsburg to Perryville to discover the Confederates in disarray. He reorganized them and sent three divisions along a north-south line to strike. Their aggression surprised the Union First Corps, pushing it back more than a mile. Confederate cavalry checked the Union Second Corps, and a Confederate bri-

"Reception of the Ninth Indiana Volunteers at Danville, Kentucky, after Driving Out the Rebels." (*Harper's Weekly*, November 8, 1862)

gade engaged the Third Corps. When Buell realized the plight of his First Corps, he sent reinforcements that, along with darkness and fatigue, halted the Confederate advance. In the state's bloodiest day of the war, the Union had 894 killed, 2,911 wounded, and 471 missing. The Confederate losses were 532 dead, 2,641 wounded, and 228 missing.

That evening, Bragg finally realized the odds that his men had faced and decided to withdraw to Harrodsburg to unite with Smith. Yet retreating to Harrodsburg was not far enough for comfort, and neither was Bryantsville. He, therefore, ordered a retreat through Cumberland Gap. Although Joseph Wheeler provided effective rearguard protection for the retreating army, the Federals were lackadaisical in their pursuit, and the Confederates escaped through the difficult terrain. A Tennessee soldier, who was among them, later recalled that he did "not remember of a harder contest and more evenly fought battle than that of Perryville. If it had been two men wrestling, it would have been called a 'dog fall.' Both sides claim victory—both whipped." Humphrey Marshall remained in the eastern Bluegrass until Buell turned his attention on the lingering Confederate army. He retreated to the western Virginia mountains, where he could hide from both Union troops and Confederate military authorities. (Marshall

preferred his independence as a military leader. When a friend once asked if he was hiding from the Federals, Marshall replied, "No, from Confederate major generals.")

Although Buell outlasted Bragg at Perryville, he could hardly claim victory. He had not pursued the retreating Confederates, which infuriated President Lincoln. General Halleck wrote Buell that the president "does not understand why we cannot march as the enemy marches, live as he lives, and fight as he fights, unless we admit the inferiority of our troops and our generals." Buell was soon removed from command and ordered to Indianapolis to await orders that were never sent. As the Confederate military retreated southward, so too did Kentucky's Confederate government. It abandoned the commonwealth for good. Hawes pleaded with President Davis to strike Kentucky again since "our cause is steadily on the increase," but Davis refused to dedicate military troops or money. When the Confederacy collapsed in the spring of 1865, Kentucky's Confederate government just disappeared.

The Romanticism of Raiding

Confederate armies would not again invade Kentucky. Although the state was often hundreds of miles from the main scenes of fighting, raiding parties continued to harass Federal troops and civilians throughout the rest of the war. Union forces that otherwise might have been committed to fighting on the major battle fronts had to remain in Kentucky to guard against the raids. Raiders disrupted Union supply lines, inspired pro-Confederate Kentuckians to join the cause, and helped to secure horses and supplies. This duty gave some fighting Kentuckians opportunities to see family and friends, however briefly.

John Hunt Morgan became the face of raiding and guerrilla tactics. For many Kentuckians, even those who rejected the Confederacy, Morgan was a symbol of Kentucky gentility and manhood. Six feet tall with sandy hair and gray eyes, Morgan was dashingly handsome, and he projected a chivalrous air. "His form was perfect," his brother-in-law, Basil Duke, wrote of him after the war, "and the rarest combination of strength, activity, and grace." Popular images of him echoed the Romanticism of the era. He became known as "The Kentucky Lochinvar," drawn from the poetry of Sir Walter Scott, possibly the greatest writer of chivalric romances. Scott's poem "Lochinvar" begins

> O young Lochinvar is come out of the west,
>   Through all the wide Border his steed
>   was the best;
> And save his good broadsword he weapons
> had none,
>   He rode all unarm'd, and he rode all
>   alone.
> So faithful in love, and so dauntless in war,
>   There never was knight like the young
>   Lochinvar.

And there was never a raider like Morgan. As Bragg's army retreated, Morgan pushed through Kentucky. He commanded his brigade on a long sweep through Lexington, Bardstown, Elizabethtown, and Hopkinsville, which unnerved Buell's army. In early December, he led his troops into victory at Hartsville, Tennessee, and was promoted to brigadier general. Fresh off this success, a week later, he married twenty-one-year-old Martha "Mattie"

Photograph of Brigadier General John Hunt Morgan, CSA, 1864. (Hunt-Morgan House Deposit Photographs, University of Kentucky Special Collections and Research Center, Lexington, KY)

Ready of Murfreesboro, Tennessee. Leonidas Polk performed the ceremony—the wedding of the war. Bragg and other military officers were in attendance. John C. Breckinridge was also there.

Then, a week later, Morgan was off again, on his "Christmas Raid." In two hectic weeks Morgan's men covered four hundred miles across central Kentucky. "I come to liberate you from the despotism of a tyrannical faction and to rescue my native state from the hand of your oppressors," he gallantly declared. "Everywhere the cowardly foe has fled from my avenging arms. My brave army is stigmatized as a band of guerrillas and marauders. Believe it not. I point with pride to their deeds as a refutation to this foul aspersion." Then they destroyed twenty miles of railroad track and approximately two million dollars' worth of supplies. They fought four engagements and numerous skirmishes. While they captured and then paroled 1,857 prisoners, only 2 of Morgan's men were killed,

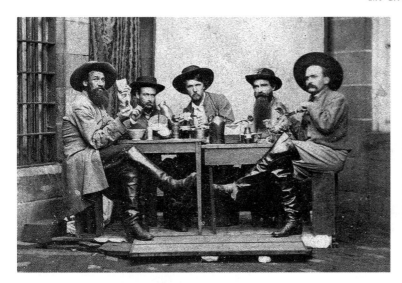

"Morgan's Men," while prisoners of war in Western Penitentiary, Pennsylvania, photograph, 1863. (Hunt-Morgan House Deposit Photographs, University of Kentucky Special Collections and Research Center, Lexington, KY)

and 24 were wounded. Another 64 were counted among the captured or missing.

In summer 1863, Morgan received permission again to raid Kentucky. The target was Louisville, which had never been attacked. His venture might also distract attention from Bragg's army as it shifted toward Chattanooga. The raid started poorly. The 2,460 men struggled to cross the swollen Cumberland River on July 2. They collided with a Union detachment at Tebbs Bend near Columbia, costing 71 casualties. Then Morgan decided against raiding Louisville. He ignored Bragg's order not to cross the Ohio River and invaded Indiana and Ohio. His hope had been to divert Federal forces away from the Confederates' operations at Vicksburg and Gettysburg, but Home Guards were ready to meet his raiders. "Morgan's Raid" ran into hornets' nests across the Ohio Valley. By the time Morgan surrendered in Ohio on July 26, only 363 men remained with him. Hundreds of Morgan's men had been captured and remained imprisoned for the remainder of the war.

By November, Morgan and six of his officers found themselves in the Ohio Penitentiary. They managed to escape, and Morgan returned to command, although his violation of direct orders tarnished his reputation. Anxious to redeem himself, Morgan led his fourth raid in June 1864. Yet, his men were not the disciplined ranks that he had once commanded. He lost control of his troops as they pillaged and burned several Kentucky towns. A Mount Sterling bank was robbed of some seventy-two thousand dollars. When Morgan's senior colonels pressed for an immediate investigation and punishment of the guilty, the commander replied that there was not time. A brief moment of glory came at Cynthiana, on June 11, when the Confederates captured some nine hundred Union soldiers, but that moment faded quickly. At dawn the next morning, Union forces surprised and shattered the brigade. Only a few of the Confederates escaped.

Morgan's daring northern raid became legend quickly. In 1863, "Morgan's Northern Raid Song" was a favorite among Confederate soldiers. In 1864, "Three Cheers for Our Jack Morgan" was published widely and became a popular song in Confederate homes:

Jack Morgan is his name,
   The fearless and the lucky;
No dastard foe can tame
   The son of old Kentucky.
His heart is with his State,
   He fights for Southern freedom;
His men their General's word await,
   They'll go where he will lead 'em.
Gather round the camp-fire,
   Our duty has been done;

Let's gather round the camp-fire,
    And have a little fun;
Let's gather round the camp-fire,
    Our duty has been done,
'Twas done upon the battlefield,
    Three cheers for our Jack Morgan.

Among Union soldiers, however, Morgan was nothing more than the "King of the Horsethieves":

John Morgan's foot is on thy shore,
His hand is on they stable door.
You'll see your good gray mare no more.
He'll ride her till her back is sore,
And leave her at some stranger's door.

And Morgan's cavalier leadership angered his superiors. Bragg never trusted him again. By late August 1864, resentment over Morgan's rogue methods culminated in loss of his command. As he awaited a court of inquiry in western Tennessee, Morgan learned of an approaching Union force and decided, against direct orders yet again, to organize a raid against the Federals. On September 4, the Federal troops surprised him, and Morgan was killed.

Morgan was only the most famous raider. Adam Johnson of Henderson County had an exciting career in Texas before returning east in 1861, when he became a scout for Confederate general Nathan Bedford Forrest. In the summer of 1862, as he recruited behind Union lines in Kentucky, Johnson decided to strike out on his own. On June 29, he led two men in an attack on a Union detachment at Henderson. They killed an officer and wounded ten others before they fled. Six days later, with an enlarged force of six men, Johnson assaulted the six-hundred-man Federal camp at Madisonville. He drove the enemy out of the camp and inflicted several casualties before having to retreat. Two weeks later, leading an army of thirty men, Johnson returned to Henderson. He was disappointed that the Federals had already left.

When Johnson learned of a small arsenal at Newburgh, northeast of Henderson on the Indiana shore of the Ohio River, he fashioned two "cannons" by mounting a piece of

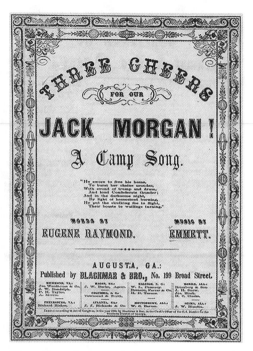

"Three Cheers for our Jack Morgan," 1864. (Library of Congress, Music Division, Washington, DC)

stovepipe and a length of charred log on old wagon wheels. He and 2 men rowed across the river and demanded the surrender of 80 men who initially confronted him. When 350 Home Guards arrived to save the town, Johnson warned them of the battery across the river. If they interfered with his gathering of supplies, he said, "I'll shell this town to the ground." By then, the rest of his raiding party had arrived via a ferry. The Confederates loaded wagons with weapons and medical supplies and then departed as the Home Guard stood aside. "Stovepipe" Johnson became a Confederate hero.

Forrest, too, organized a raid into Kentucky. He needed horses and supplies for his troops in western Tennessee and northern Mississippi and learned that both were available at Paducah. In March 1864, he led twenty-eight hundred men into western Kentucky to capture them. Surprising the Union troops who bunkered in a fort, the Confederates easily gathered the needed supplies, even as Federal gunboats fired upon them. The Federals did not directly engage the Confederates, so the raiders retreated leisurely to Tennessee. Newspaper accounts of their foray actually caught up with them. One story gleefully reported that the Confederates had missed a consignment of especially fine horses destined for the Union cavalry. Confederate general Abraham Buford, owner of a fine stock farm near Versailles, turned his brigade to Paducah. On April 14, they drove the Federals back into the fort and found the 140 excellent horses where the newspaper had reported them.

Like Adam Johnson's and John Hunt Morgan's incursions, most Confederate raids were quick slash-and-run affairs intended to avoid Union forces that could cut off the raiders' escape. Some raids lasted longer. One was led by Colonel Roy S. Cluke, commander of the Eighth Kentucky Cavalry. In mid-February 1863, he led some 750 men into the eastern Bluegrass around Mount Sterling. Most of the men were from the region, and Cluke allowed many to briefly visit their homes, expecting that they would return with horses and clothing. Small detachments struck out in different directions to confuse nearby Federal units. Although many of his troops were ill, Cluke remained in central Kentucky for more than a month. He finally returned southward with 18 more men than he had at the start of the expedition. Cluke's raid and similar expeditions embarrassed Union commanders, but they did not want to reassign troops from major campaigns to stop the incursions.

Beyond gathering supplies, stealing horses, and recruiting soldiers, raiders often engaged in guerrilla warfare. They usually disrupted communication and supply lines, destroyed military property, and struck small outposts and isolated units. Federal troops seldom distinguished between regular Confederate army units that carried on such activities and true guerrilla groups, who operated without official sanction. Unionists often called John Hunt Morgan a guerrilla, but he led a regular unit in the Confederate army that employed guerrilla tactics. Less definitive was "Stovepipe" Johnson's Tenth Kentucky Cavalry, which operated for more than a year in western Kentucky as a group of partisan rangers. Others, sometimes

called "war-rebels," had some association to the Confederate military, although the links were often tenuous and Union authorities seldom recognized them. Then there were outlaws who took advantage of unsettled conditions to operate on their own. They preyed upon anyone, regardless of allegiance to the Union or the Confederacy. During the last two years of the war, and even beyond the war's end, such men terrorized much of the commonwealth.

Most notorious of the guerrillas was William Clarke Quantrill, who had gone through an apprenticeship in "Bleeding Kansas" in the mid-1850s. In January 1865, he led several dozen followers into Kentucky near Canton, striking Hartford, Hustonville, and Danville as he worked his way eastward. When Federal troops failed to catch Quantrill, Edwin Terrill, a leader of Union guerrillas in Spencer County, took up the task. He cornered Quantrill near Bloomfield on May 10. Seriously wounded, Quantrill died in a Louisville military prison in early June before he could be hanged. The last of his men surrendered three weeks later.

Some guerrillas had been members of Morgan's men. They found new ways to occupy themselves after the regiment faltered. Henry C. Magruder of Bullitt County was one of them. He survived Morgan's raid into Ohio and returned to Kentucky. He located other escaped Confederates and led them in raids around Louisville. In mid-February 1865, he was ambushed by Federal troops, shot in the arm, back, and through a lung. He avoided capture for weeks. Once imprisoned, he was allowed to heal from his injuries before standing trial. He was hanged on October 29 at twenty-one years of age.

Successful guerrillas were assisted by civilians, and this proved a particularly difficult problem for Union authorities. Early in the war, the general assembly passed a number of laws restricting Confederate sympathizers. They required loyalty oaths of teachers, ministers, jurors, and public officials. Several ministers were arrested and imprisoned in northern jails, as was former governor Charles S. Morehead. Kentuckians who enlisted in the Confederate armies encouraged others to enlist. Oth-

Slave pen converted into military prison, photograph, n.d. (J. Winston Coleman Jr. Collection on Slavery in Kentucky, University of Kentucky Special Collections and Research Center, Lexington, KY)

ers left the commonwealth with the intent to return and invade it. If caught, they were subject to severe penalties. In June 1862, Boyle, the military commander about whom Governor Magoffin had complained, announced that disloyal persons—not just guerrillas, but anyone who leaned Confederate—would pay for damages done to loyal citizens. He ordered provosts marshals in each county "to fit up quarters for the imprisonment of such disloyal females as they may find it necessary to arrest." He even had a Newport prison prepared for "rebel females," who would be required to sew for the Federal troops.

During the 1863 gubernatorial election, disloyal citizens were forbidden from voting which kept an estimated one-third of potential voters from the polls. General Ambrose E. Burnside declared martial law in the state just before August 3 "for the purpose only of protecting the rights of the loyal citizens and the freedom of election." The Unionist candidates won easily. Thomas E. Bramlette, who resigned his commission as a major general to accept the Union Democrats' nomination for governor, defeated regular Democrat Charles A. Wickliffe, 68,422 to 17,503. Bramlette initially supported the Union's extreme measures. But he began to show discontent with his allies when a former justice of the Kentucky Court of Appeals was stricken from the ballot in the 1864 election simply because he sympathized with the Confederacy. Two years earlier, Boyle had issued an order that "no person hostile in opinion to the government and desiring its overthrow, will be allowed to stand for office in the district of Kentucky." As chief civilian officer of the commonwealth, however, Bramlette could not abide such suppression. He wrote to President Lincoln complaining that the interference violated "the most sacred rights of a free and loyal people."

Still Bramlette supported other extreme measures, like requiring pro-Confederate Ken-

Portrait of Thomas E. Bramlette, by William Ver Bryck, 1874. (Kentucky Historical Society Collections, Frankfort, KY)

tuckians to compensate for damages that Confederate raids inflicted. In January 1864, he ordered five rebel sympathizers to be held hostage for each loyal citizen carried off by guerrillas. By August, alleged Confederate sympathizers in and near Morganfield in Union County were assessed thirty-two thousand dollars to cover such damages and losses. Two months later, individuals considered disloyal within ten miles of Caneyville had to raise thirty-five thousand dollars.

During those months, Union general Stephen G. Burbridge of Georgetown earned the nickname "The Butcher of Kentucky" because he ordered the deaths of four guerrilla prisoners for each Union man who was killed by guerrilla activity. As a result of his order, as many as fifty men may have been executed, several of them legitimate Confederate prisoners of war. In October, Burbridge warned that "hereafter, no guerrillas will be received as prisoners." But he also planned to suppress the vote in the November presidential election, having supporters of Democrat George McClellan arrested so Lincoln would win Kentucky and reelection.

McClellan, who had been a ranking Union officer until he was removed from command, defeated Lincoln in Kentucky by 64,301 to 27,786 popular votes and won the majority of the state's soldiers, 3,068 to 1,203. Yet, Kentucky, Delaware, and New Jersey were the only states that McClellan won. When McClellan carried the commonwealth despite Burbridge's attempts to suppress votes for him, a clearer message could not have been sent: Kentuckians, even those who were adamant Unionists, resented the heavy hand of the Union military.

George Prentice, a stalwart Unionist, was among the disillusioned and created a partially fictional persona to mock the Union commander in his newspaper. "Sue Mundy" was a female Confederate guerrilla who outmaneuvered Burbridge in the tales that Prentice printed in the *Louisville Journal*. Many Kentuckians, however, interpreted Mundy as real, assuming that Marcellus Jerome Clarke, of Franklin, had inspired the character. Clarke returned to Kentucky after Morgan's death in autumn 1864, forming his own guerrilla band to kill Union soldiers and destroy supplies. Like Prentice's Sue Mundy, Clarke was young, smooth-faced, and wore long hair. When the Thirty-Seventh Kentucky Infantry confronted Clarke in Bardstown, the commander reported that the "notorious Sue Mundy and ['One-Arm' Samuel] Berry are said to be the ones who were wounded and made their escape. Sue's fine pipe fell a trophy to my men, and various other articles." By February 1865, Clarke had joined forces with Quantrill and burned the railroad depot and freight cars at Lair Station. In March, Federals captured him in Breckinridge County and took him to Louisville for trial. He insisted he was regular Confederate military and deserved to be treated as a prisoner of war, but the court concluded he was a renegade guerrilla and sentenced him to death. He died in a public hanging at twenty years of age.

Considering his fame, Clarke's hanging was quite a scene. It was held at the corner of Eighteenth and Broadway in Louisville, intended to be a public spectacle. After his body was lowered from the gallows, some in the crowd cut buttons from his coat. Three men were ar-

Portrait of Marcellus Jerome Clark, c. 1855. (The Filson Historical Society, Louisville, KY)

jail, she called out to the captive, "Good morning, Dr. Watkins. You look like Jesus Christ between two thieves."

Raids and guerrilla attacks were unpredictable. They often paralyzed civilians who could not anticipate when the war might crash into their lives. Josie Underwood of Bowling Green feared traveling lest "John Morgan might make one of his daring raids and tear up the railroad tracks and something happen that I couldn't get back home." Frances Dallam Peter in Lexington "kept our house shut and door locked from the day Morgan came in, afraid of the house being searched." When raiders stormed Esther Frogg's Clinton County home, Confederate guerrilla Champ Ferguson found her husband sick in bed. Accusing William Frogg of supporting the Union, Ferguson shot the man twice as he held his five-month-old child, leaving Esther a widow.

Although occupying armies were not as cavalier as raiding parties, they could wreak havoc on the homefront. When the Confederates occupied Hopkinsville, Ellen Wallace noted how residents feared the "conscription act being forced up on the people." "Private rights are not in the least regarded," she complained. "The soldiers walk into any store or house and take whatever they need. . . . There are great many armies of both sides now trying to out general each other in Kentucky." When the Confederates occupied Bowling Green, the pro-Union Underwoods fled, fearful of mistreatment by the enemy. They returned to find "the trees and the house were all charred and burned and that only the gable end of the house was standing . . . both orchards were cut down . . . not a fence left on the entire 1,000 acres only the barn and two cabins left of all the buildings." They never recovered from the destruction. As Bragg's Confederate army approached Louisville, residents stampeded along the roads and filled steamboats to escape the bombardment.

To avoid such damage and danger, many women tried to work with occupying troops to protect their families. Josie Underwood's mother had taken such a tact initially. When "three or four soldiers in gray . . . reached our

rested for fighting over his hat. Sue Mundy was so popular an image in the Kentucky mind that, before his own hanging, Henry Magruder claimed the persona as his own, titling his memoir *Three Years in the Saddle: The Life and Confession of Henry Magruder, the Original Sue Mundy, the Scourge of Kentucky* (1865). The following year, Prentice confirmed in his chronicle of the war in Kentucky that Sue Mundy was indeed his alias for Jerome Clarke.

War on the Homefront

The tug of war between Unionists and Confederates in Kentucky permeated all corners of the commonwealth, including households and families. Margaret Ray of Owensboro supported the Confederacy, despite her husband's position as a Union provost marshal. When her husband had a local physician arrested for spying and two Union soldiers escorted him to

"The Women and children of Louisville, Kentucky, leaving the city," 1862. (Library of Congress Prints and Photographs Division, Washington, DC)

porch," her mother provided them "cold ham and biscuits and milk and gave them fruit." As the war dragged on, even Unionists began to sympathize with the Confederate soldiers who seemed to be chasing a lost cause. "My heart goes out to them in pity," Underwood wrote, before realizing what she had written. She pleaded, "Treason! Treason! I acknowledge my weakness." Still other women felt no charity toward the enemy. Frances Peter related how, when a woman arrived in Lexington without clothing or money, she was asked about her loyalties: "Ma told her that in times like these people had to be very cautious how and to whom they gave money . . . and refused to give her anything."

Still, white women in Kentucky not only sought to protect their families but contribute to the war effort as well, whether that effort was on behalf of the Union, the Confederacy, or neutrality. The Lexington Ladies Aid Society made socks and clothes for nearby Federal regiments. Pro-Union women regularly visited military hospitals. On one occasion, when hospitalized Confederate soldiers asked to share in the goods that the women brought to the Union soldiers, Frances Dallam Peter replied,

"Poor wretches! The Confederacy hasn't done much for them!"

Union occupation of Kentucky was not welcomed by all, however. Elizabeth "Lizzie" Hardin was among those "rebel females" who refused to cooperate with Union armies. Born and raised in Harrodsburg, Hardin remained a stalwart and vocal Confederate sympathizer throughout the war. She was arrested and placed on trial: "Now we had all been vs. the United States for some time but were anxious to know the particular reason the U.S. had for assuming its position towards us." The reason was her family's refusal to take a loyalty oath. Hardin found herself eventually imprisoned in Louisville. Union prison officers, uncomfortable with the presence of women in the military setting, persisted in asking her to take the oath. She refused. "I was born a Southerner and if God will give me the strength I intend to die a Southerner," Hardin declared.

Some women immersed themselves in the military effort. Harriet Wood, whose stage name was Pauline Cushman, made her debut in 1862 at Woods' Theatre in Louisville, then occupied by Union troops. During a performance in which she was to offer a toast, Cush-

191

Pauline Cushman, photograph by Mathew Brady Studio, c. 1862. (Pauline Cushman, Mathew Brady Studio, Glass plate collodion negative, Frederick Hill Meserve Collection, National Portrait Gallery, Smithsonian Institution, Washington, DC)

Rebel soldier I have been." Her mother chalked up Clark's enlistment to two nervous breakdowns precipitated by a physically abusive husband, who divorced Clark, abandoned her and their two children, fled westward, married another woman, and announced his intentions to return to Kentucky with his new family. After her capture at the Battle of Richmond, Union troops discovered her identity and released Clark. They provided her with a dress and insisted that she live as a woman, and she did, rejoining the Confederate army *as a woman.* One soldier described her as "somewhat brazen . . . but sharp as a steel trap." Another wrote home that "among all the curiosities I have seen since I left home one I must mention, a female Lieutenant." Of course, in a war as romanticized as the Civil War, female soldiers had to be explained away. A Mississippi newspaper lauded Clark as "heroic and self-sacrificing" but could not accept that she had enlisted on her own: "Mrs. Clarke volunteered with her husband as a private, fought through the battles of Shiloh, where Mr. Clarke was killed—she performing the rites of burial with her own hands." None of it was true, but in a war that served to bolster manhood, how were female soldiers (who hated their husbands) to be understood? The editor of the *Mississippian* decided to transform Clark into the loving, dedicated wife. Over four hundred women fought as soldiers during the Civil War, but Clark may have been unique. Like Clark did initially, most masqueraded as men. Others who served openly as women often fulfilled non-fighting roles like carrying regimental flags.

Like Mary Ann Clark, many Kentuckians tried to negotiate their desire to remain in the Union with their hopes to retain slavery. As Union occupation and new racial policies began to transform their lives, however, many began to support the Confederacy openly. By late 1864, a Federal War Department agent concluded that "a large majority of Kentuckians are today undoubtedly disloyal." Even loyal Unionists like Josie Underwood denounced the treatment of their families as troops moved from house to house "demanding food and in one or two instances treating Union women

man raised a glass to Jefferson Davis, ingratiating herself to Confederates but losing her job. Apparently collaborating with the Union military, Cushman became a Confederate camp follower before she donned a transsexual disguise and infiltrated the Confederate military. As she attempted to steal battle plans in 1864, she was caught and sentenced to death, but she escaped the gallows. Federal troops forced the Confederates to retreat from western Tennessee and leave Cushman behind.

Mary Ann Clark disguised herself as Henry Clark and enlisted in Bragg's army. She had many reasons for joining the Confederate cause: Kentucky's Home Guard had murdered her pro-Confederate brother-in-law, and she was loyal to the Confederacy. She requested that a friend inform her mother "what a good

with a great deal of rudeness calling them 'Dam Rebels' and ordering them to get something to eat 'damn quick.'" Such actions "destroyed in a few days more Union sentiment than the Rebels had been able to do in six months."

Confederate propaganda regularly pointed out Union arrests of white women as evidence against Kentucky's honor and neutrality. Although complaints focused on Boyle and Burbridge, local military authorities often were greater threats. Stationed at Paducah, General E. A. Paine was put in charge of the western end of the state in July 1864. The next seven weeks were a "reign of terror." Paine taxed Kentuckians to raise one hundred thousand dollars to benefit the families of Union soldiers. Pro-Confederate residents—and there were many in western Kentucky—had a 25 percent tax levied on their cotton. Confederate sympathizers faced exile, unless they purchased freedom from the charges. And then the money just disappeared. Paine had several persons executed on his orders without trial, including a seventeen-year-old boy whose crime was having two brothers in the Confederate army. The young man met death bravely: "I have got enough nerve to face the music; do not tie my hands, do not blindfold me." In early August, Paine ordered construction of a fort in Mayfield's town square. It was less a defensive structure than a scheme to get local men to pay three hundred dollars to avoid working on the structure. Complaints led to investigation, and Paine fled to Illinois. A reprimand was his only punishment.

Federal officials and policies generated animosity that turned many Kentuckians against the national administration. For decades after the war, Kentucky consistently voted with the former Confederate states. By the end of the war, many women also found it difficult to reconcile their sentiments for union with the treatment that they had received. Following the Emancipation Proclamation on January 1, 1863, Ellen Wallace of Hopkinsville expressed her anger: "Lincoln has trodden underfoot the laws of our state and usurped the entire control, he has made the negro master of the white man as far as his power putting arms into their hands, stationing negro pickets at the toll gates and bridges where they defy their former master to pass at peril of their lives. . . . Lincoln is a greater traitor than Jeff Davis because he pretends to support the Constitution by the very means he take to destroy it. We look upon him as a wretch only fit to rule over the most degraded part of the Negro population."

Not since the prolonged struggle with the Western Confederacy of Native Americans between the 1770s and 1812 had Kentuckians experienced the type of intense and intrusive warfare that the Civil War ushered into their homes and communities. As Josie Underwood lamented soon after the war erupted, "I never dreamed it possible we could have a war in this country, brother against brother, friend against friend, as now."

African Kentuckians and the End of Slavery

Military confiscations of supplies and food, destruction of homes and farms, and the arrests of civilians for all sorts of wrongdoings disrupted home life in Kentucky. As Ellen Wallace's words confirm, however, the breakdown of slavery had the most notable impact on the homefront. She accused Lincoln most severely of overturning the nation's racial dynamics. She had seen it coming. Many of the enslaved African Americans who worked her family's plantation fled and "what few slaves remain do just as they please, fine grain fields given up." Only two enslaved men had stayed "& have planted a large crop of tobaco but we are looking for them to leave daily not that they wish to go if left to themselves . . . but the pressure from the abolitionist is so strong that I fear they cannot resist it long." A few months later she noted, "What we have so much dreaded has at last occured. Hopkinsville is now a recruiting rendezvous for negroes a number enlisted to day coming in from the plantations leaving the tobaco crop to take care of its self."

Lincoln's Emancipation Proclamation did not even apply to Kentucky and other border states. It instead pertained only to the states in rebellion. Moreover, changes had begun long before. Many slaves freed themselves without waiting for the federal government to do so. Upon Lincoln's election in 1860, rumors began to circulate about the end of slavery. The rather uncommon level of literacy among African Kentuckians empowered freemen, like Elijah Marrs of Shelby County, to read newspaper accounts of the war to enslaved friends. News spread of Confederate retreats and Union occupations. Amid the confusion, enslaved people took the opportunity to express their hopes. In December 1861, about fifty slaves in New Castle marched through the town, stopped in front of pro-Confederate houses, and sang and shouted for Lincoln. But the volatile conditions also created dangerous situations. Louisville police officers invaded black homes searching for fugitives and weapons. The Home Guard acted as a slave patrol. They used vagrancy laws to punish blacks. Slavecatchers operated with little legal restriction as they chased runaways across the commonwealth.

In the early years of the war when Confederate armies occupied southern Kentucky, many slaves were impressed into service. They dug trenches, built fortifications, cooked, nursed injured or ill soldiers, and washed clothes. As Federal troops pushed the Confederates out of the commonwealth, enslaved blacks offered to help in the military camps, building roads, repairing bridges, laboring on Federal boats, and often entertaining the troops. Having earned a little money, they returned to their owners' farms afterward. But the interactions inspired many to see the Federal armies as refuges. By 1862, slaves were pouring into the camps for work. At Camp Nevin in Hart County, slaves arrived on the average of one per hour. When Buell marched his Union army northward out of Tennessee to counter Bragg and Smith's Confederate invasion in 1862, he brought a thousand contrabands, slaves from the seceded states, with him, requiring them to serve the troops. Louisville officials put another thousand to work as a "spade and shovel brigade" to fortify the town. Black Kentuckians and contrabands from other states provided most of the labor that made Federal occupation of Kentucky possible.

There was only so much work to be done, however, and the flood of slaves swelled regiments to sizes that became difficult to manage. Union officers like William T. Sherman ordered subordinates to return slaves to their owners. "We have nothing to do with them at all and you should not let them take refuge in camp," he directed. Only contrabands received protection from the Federal armies. Many Union soldiers struggled to obey directions to abandon Kentucky slaves. Although most were not abolitionists, they observed slavery for the first time as they marched through the state, and it was a disturbing sight. When slave owners showed up at Union camps demanding the return of an enslaved human, they often whipped that person in front of troops. Increasingly, Union troops became protective of all slaves and turned away slave owners and slavecatchers.

Although President Lincoln authorized use of black troops in late 1862, he purposefully exempted Kentucky from the order so as not to alienate white Kentuckians. Still, many African Americans escaped enslavement and enlisted either at Union camps north of the Ohio River or in occupied Tennessee at Fort Donelson, Nashville, and Gallatin. Indiana officials reported that enslaved Kentuckians passed through the southern part of their state regularly, headed for recruitment centers.

When Lincoln issued the Emancipation Proclamation, it raised a storm of protest across Kentucky. Many white Kentuckians believed, as the *Louisville Journal* had stated at the beginning of the war, that the "two races . . . cannot exist in the same country, unless the black race is in slavery." Despite the fact that the proclamation did not apply to Kentucky and therefore did not free any enslaved African Kentuckians, white Kentuckians could see the writing on the wall. "Be assured that a large majority of the people of the United States are for the Union as it was," warned the *Lexington Observer and Reporter*. About enslaved laborers, the editor declared that his fellow Americans were "resolved to preserve them against the continued assaults of abolitionists and secessionists." As late as autumn 1863, Lincoln assured Governor Bramlette that the Federals would not recruit slaves in the Federal Military Department of Kentucky. Still, the Federals took a census of military-aged Kentuckians, and the 40,285 black men who could be recruited were too important a source of manpower to ignore. In the Military Department of Tennessee, which controlled Kentucky's six westernmost counties as well as Columbus and Paducah, recruitment began in January 1864. Within a month, representatives from the border states convened in Louisville to approve a constitutional amendment that abolished slavery, sanctioned enlistment of African Americans, and recognized the reelection of President Lincoln. With momentum building in support of the recruitment of African Kentuckians, Bramlette, former senator Archibald Dixon, and Albert G. Hodges, editor of the *Frankfort Commonwealth,* traveled to Washington, DC, in March and met with Lincoln to dissuade him from recruiting slaves as soldiers. Lincoln refused their appeal stating, "I am naturally anti-slavery. If slavery is not wrong, nothing is wrong. I can not remember when I did not so think, and feel. And yet I have never understood that the Presidency conferred upon me an unrestricted right to act officially upon this judgment and feeling." Still, it was not to be a traditional draft: only free blacks and slaves who applied for service would be enrolled. Slave owners who had remained loyal to the Union and now lost slaves to enlistment were to be compensated up to three hundred dollars a recruit. Despite the conciliatory policy, bitter protests arose. Colonel Frank L. Wolford of the First Kentucky Cavalry stood at a public banquet in March and remarked, "What with Abe Lincoln on one side and Jeff Davis on the other, our poor distracted country reminds me of Christ crucified between two thieves." He was dishonorably dismissed from the Union army.

The moderate recruitment policy did not last long. By summer, the Federal army accepted any able-bodied slaves, regardless of their owners' wishes, and military camps arose in Paducah, Owensboro, Bowling Green, Lebanon, Louisville, Covington, Louisa, and at Camp Nelson to train and protect the recruits. The

concentration of slaves in the Bluegrass transformed Lexington into a recruitment center, as escaped slaves from the surrounding counties arrived to volunteer for service. In Jessamine and Marion Counties, enough blacks signed up to fulfill each county's draft quotas. For many, it was not only their first taste of freedom but also their first sense of equality. They trained to become soldiers, just like the white troops whom they had seen marching across Kentucky.

The enthusiasm of early summer 1864, however, waned by autumn. Mobs of angry whites in Boyle, Green, Taylor, and Adair Counties tracked down and whipped black volunteers. In Marion County, two recruits had their left ears cropped off. Eight recruits were murdered in Nicholas County. Fearful for their lives, many potential recruits abandoned Kentucky to enlist elsewhere. Union adjutant general Lorenzo Thomas, charged with raising black troops, concluded that he would have to send armed patrols through the counties to impress slaves into service in order to meet the quota. Although impressment had been used in western and southern Kentucky for some months, it accelerated in the summer, as US Colored Troops rounded up slaves in Henderson and Union Counties and forced them to enlist. The practice continued for the remainder of the war.

The migration of black men into the Federal military during the summer of 1864 inspired families to follow. Women and children moved en masse to Union camps. In March 1865, Federal law freed the wives and children of soldiers, which increased pressure on Union camps to accommodate civilians. Some men, like Mary Fields's slave, Ed, enlisted specifically to free their wives and children. When Lucinda, a slave in William Pratt's Lexington home, learned of her freedom through a letter from her husband, who was training at Camp Nelson, she continued to work for Pratt for two weeks until, one morning, he awoke to find "the Kitchen cleaned up, the bread . . . ready for baking & kindling at hand to start a fire." But Lucinda was gone.

The Union camps were not friendly to blacks, however. At Fort Anderson in Paducah,

Barracks, cottages, tents and huts at the Home for Colored Refugees at Camp Nelson, 1864. (Camp Nelson Photographic Collection, 1864, University of Kentucky Special Collections and Research Center, Lexington, KY)

many died of starvation. Thousands congregated around Camp Nelson seeking refuge. Brigadier General Speed S. Fry refused to feed the masses and insisted they stay out of the camp. He actively sought out escaped slaves who had no legal right to be at the camp and returned them to their owners. When he had one woman arrested and held, she begged him to shoot her rather than return her to enslavement. Some of the soldiers eventually rescued her.

Living conditions were horrible. "Nowhere in the whole range of my observation of misfortune and misery occasioned by the war have I seen any cases which appealed so strongly to the sympathies of the benevolent as those congregated in the contraband camp at Camp Nelson," noted a US Sanitary Commission worker. In late November 1864, as temperatures plummeted below freezing, Fry's troops pushed four hundred women and children from the camp and destroyed the shantytown. Joseph Miller, a Lincoln County recruit, went in search of his wife and four children:

> They were in an old meeting house belonging to the colored people. . . . I found my wife and children shivering with cold and famished with hunger. They had not received a morsel of food during the whole day. My boy was dead. He died directly after getting down from the wagon. I know he was Killed by exposure to the inclement weather. I had to return to camp that night so I left my family in the meeting house and walked back. . . . Next morning I walked to Nicholasville. I dug a grave myself and burried my own child.

Joseph Miller's son was one of 102 people who died of exposure in the days following their expulsion from Camp Nelson. African Kentuckians fared little better in other refugee camps. Disease ravaged the families gathered on the outskirts of Louisville, where a Colored Soldiers' Aid Society was established among black residents to assist recruits and their families, collecting money, clothes, and supplies to ease the suffering. Ellen Wallace mourned the circumstances of Christian County blacks: "the poor Negro is the innocent victim of this war. They are departed from their homes by promises of freedom and then left to starve and die with out shelter or any earthly comfort in the most miserable manner by thousands and tens of thousands." Despite the hardships, black Kentuckians risked it all to seek freedom.

As African Americans left farms they knew for unfamiliar camps and towns, they became targets of slavecatchers. Inside Louisville, hundreds of blacks were imprisoned in slave pens. Reverend Thomas James, a black representative of the American Missionary Association, worked to free them. Not until February 1865, however, did he have a local military commander willing to help. Over a couple of months, prisoners in all of Louisville's slave pens were freed, including 260 in Matthew Garrison's infamous jail. James then turned his attention to less conspicuous imprisonments, like 9 slaves held by a slave trader at the National Hotel. They were immediately enlisted.

By March 1865, 23,703 black Kentuckians had enlisted, providing about 13 percent of the total US Colored Troops. Several regiments fought in major battles outside the commonwealth: at Petersburg, Virginia, and Nashville, Tennessee. Some patrolled within Kentucky, skirmishing with guerrillas. Others garrisoned towns like Owensboro and Louisville. The most notorious episode to involve Kentucky's US Colored Troops was at Simpsonville as 80 members of the Fifth US Colored Cavalry drove nearly 1,000 cattle to Louisville. Confederate guerrillas, supposedly under Henry McGruder, attacked from the rear. They killed 22 immediately and left 6 others to die. The white officers at the head of the regiment led the rest in flight to Camp Nelson. The massacre was an embarrassment, and Brigadier General Hugh Ewing demanded to know "if any officers were in command of the guard; if so, arrest and bring them to these headquarters." No charges were ever brought.

When the Civil War ended, nearly 71 percent of African Kentuckians were free, by virtue of their military service or their husbands' or fathers' military service. Still, many remained in Kentucky as servants to their former owners. They had no other place to go. Some sixty-five thousand remained enslaved as stubborn slave owners persisted in believing that somehow slavery would be reinstated after the war. Ironically, given Kentucky's long but shaky relationship with slavery, the state became one of the institution's last strongholds. Even after the fall of the Confederacy, slave sales continued in the commonwealth. Although the Thirteenth Amendment to the US Constitution was ratified by the requisite number of states by mid-December, the Kentucky House of Representatives rejected it, a purely symbolic act since slavery had become illegal nationally. They remained obstinate on the Fourteenth and Fifteenth Amendments as well. Over a century later, in 1976, the Kentucky General Assembly finally ratified the three amendments, recognizing that "this Bicentennial Year is an appropriate time to erase the shadow on Kentucky's history."

Corporal Kager Mays, 108th US Colored Infantry. (Library of Congress Prints and Photographs Division, Washington, DC)

The Price of War

The dismantling of slavery was the major economic loss of the war. Assessed at $107,494,527 in 1860, Kentucky's enslaved property was worth only $7,224,851 by 1865. More important than slaves' property value was the collateral damage, as black Kentuckians escaped slavery. Agricultural production plummeted. Cultivated acreage declined by some four million by 1865. Hemp production fell by over 80 percent, wheat by 63 percent, tobacco by 57 percent, and barley by 15 percent. Occupying armies contributed to the destruction of crops and the confiscation of livestock. There were 89,000 fewer horses, 37,000 fewer mules, and 172,000 fewer cattle in Kentucky in 1865 than at the start of the war. Chickens and pigs disappeared, as did fields of corn and silos of grain. Fences were destroyed for firewood. A Unionist who lost property to Union occupation had some hope of receiving compensation. Miles

Kelly of Warren County had Federal troops on his property for seventy days, and he filed claims of $17,755.80 with the government. Confederate sympathizers had no hope of recovering the value of lost property, no matter who had taken it.

Across the commonwealth, income declined as prices increased. If 1860 prices in Kentucky are considered to be at 100, the index figures for the next five years were 97, 112, 147, 210, and 192. Especially hard hit were soldiers' families who had to survive on what their soldiers could send them. Union privates were paid thirteen dollars a month for most of the war. Beginning in May 1864, they received sixteen dollars, but pay was often months in arrears. Regardless of the amount, the pay of a Confederate soldier became almost worthless as the value of Confederate money depreciated.

During neutrality, Kentucky enjoyed trade with the South, as the Confederates hastened to acquire war materials as rapidly as possible. The Mississippi, Cumberland, Tennessee, and Green Rivers enjoyed brisk trade at the beginning of the war. Then, hoping to pressure Kentucky into choosing a side, the Confederacy began to restrict Kentucky productions. Confederate officials limited the export of cotton, tobacco, sugar, and other items. Pressure came from the Union as well. Indiana and Illinois initially cut off trade with Kentucky to restrict the movement of goods into the Confederacy. A federal order limited river shipment from Louisville for delivery to Unionists. Customs officials issued the required permits. Kentuckians who were less loyal began to smuggle their goods to markets. They sent loaded wagons overland to Franklin and Hopkinsville from where they were carried into Tennessee.

Federal orders like the one that limited shipping typically were intended to benefit Union troops. Why should Louisville merchants profit from sales to the Confederacy when Federal armies needed the supplies? In 1864, as the price of pork skyrocketed, a Louisville depot commissary convinced General Burbridge that he could buy hogs directly from farmers and pack the pork without using the usual contractors. On October 24, Bur-

bridge responded by prohibiting the export of hogs without permits. Outraged, hog farmers demanded the orders be rescinded, and Burbridge complied a month later. Only enforced for one month, the "Great Hog Swindle" saved the federal government at least two hundred thousand dollars, but according to Governor Bramlette, it cost Kentucky farmers over three hundred thousand dollars.

As the Union and Confederacy fought over control of the Mississippi River, the Louisville & Nashville Railroad became the main artery for Kentucky trade. The railroad was not in good condition. Its 30 locomotives, 28 passenger cars, and 297 freight cars were inadequate for the increased traffic. And when the trains went south loaded with Kentucky goods, they returned empty. Little could be sent northward. As the L&N became more important to Union military movements, Confederate raiders made the railroad a major target. They hit the trestles near Elizabethtown and the Green River bridge at Munfordville. Albert Fink, the company's engineer and superintendent of roads and machinery, tried to keep crews on call to repair tracks. The Union deployed thousands of troops along the rail lines to keep the trains operating. Between July 1862 and June 1863, the L&N was open along its entire length for only seven months and twelve days. Amazingly, despite the damage done by Confederate raiders, the L&N did not suffer much during the war. It profited more than six million dollars.

Neither did manufacturing suffer. Much of Kentucky's industry transformed farm products into whiskey, chewing tobacco and snuff, and flour. As long as farmers could deliver, distilleries and factories continued to produce, and the Union army and Confederate raiders had an insatiable demand for such goods. Major manufacturing facilities in Louisville went untouched, as did most banks. Until 1863, state banks continued making specie payments, even after major institutions in Boston, New York, and Philadelphia had suspended them. The National Banking Act, passed in that year, required banks to obtain a national charter by investing at least one-third of their stock in national bonds. They could issue paper currency worth up to 90 percent of the value of the bonds, but they had to pay a federal tax of 10 percent of the value of their banknotes. The new regulations drove banknotes out of circulation, leaving national greenbacks as the standard currency.

Although many Kentuckians struggled personally, railroads, manufacturing, and banking did fairly well during the war. The stability of Kentucky's economy allowed the state government to reduce its debt from $5,698,000 in October 1859 to $5,254,000 by 1865, despite spending $3.5 million for military needs. The sinking fund, created a decade earlier, became adequate to handle debt payments as they came due.

The cost of war was more than economic, of course. There was an emotional cost that proved far more detrimental. Families broke up, as husbands, sons, brothers, and lovers went off to war. Many never returned. Malvina Harlan of Louisville counselled her husband John Marshall Harlan as he agonized over leaving her: "You must do as you would if you had neither wife nor children. I could not stand between you and your duty to the country and be happy." War took an inordinate toll on men between eighteen and twenty-five years of age. Thousands died on battlefields or in hospitals. Those who returned were psychologically and physically traumatized. An entire generation was lost.

Churches that had weathered the sectional tensions of the 1840s and 1850s struggled in the midst of war. Fearful to travel to church services because of raiders and guerrillas, many Kentuckians just stopped attending. Churches that had survived for years as interracial congregations began to decline toward the end of the war, as black members abandoned communities. And the war raised strange theological issues. Until May 1863, Methodist minister George R. Browder of Logan County refused to take the loyalty oath, believing it contrary to the spirit of neutrality: "Ought a Christian man to swear against his conscience to avoid suffering any more than to obtain a desired good?" As Confederates occupied Bowling Green in September 1861, Samuel Ringgold, pastor of Christ Episcopal Church, worried whether he should include the Confederates in his liturgical prayer for those in authority.

Education suffered as well. Most college students were of military age, so campuses emptied. Georgetown College and Augusta College had to close. Confederates occupied Centre College in 1862. They turned the main college building into a hospital. Berea College closed in 1859 and would not open until 1866. The war also slowed the progress made in public education over the 1850s. The superintendent of public instruction reported that, in 1861, the number of school children dropped from 165,000 to 90,000. Many teachers went into military service. Local and state funding dried up.

In the midst of so much death and destruction, many Kentuckians sought escape, finding it in the social affairs that accompanied military occupations. Elizabeth Patterson, wife of a Centre College math professor, described how "the college campus would be lighted up by cheerful campfires around which the soldiers at the hospital would gather, sitting upon logs of firewood and singing rebellious songs, such as 'Dixie.'" Typically, only civilians loyal to the occupying forces participated. Confederate sympathizer Agatha Strange later wrote wistfully of Albert Sidney Johnston's occupation of Bowling Green, when it served as the capital of Confederate Kentucky: "Our house in those days was visited and made the home of by the intellect and chivalry of the South. . . . These were days of happiness and never can be erased from my memory." Although some events such as county fairs were discontinued, the need to escape war made entertainments like plays and musical productions popular in the larger towns. Picnics, frolics, and dances were popular in villages. Proceeds from larger affairs often went to benevolent organizations like the Ladies' Military Benevolent Association of Lexington and the Colored Soldiers Aid Society in Louisville.

How Kentucky Became Confederate

In 1868, John Hunt Morgan's body returned to Kentucky. After his death in 1864, he had been buried in Richmond, Virginia, but his family had him disinterred and relocated to the Lexington Cemetery. Union and Confederate veterans accompanied the hearse from the church to the burial site, laying wreaths and a small Confederate flag atop the casket. The military war may have ended in 1865, but the Civil War as a struggle over the hearts and minds of Americans did not. Indeed, many might say it continues today.

Although most white Kentuckians remained loyal to the Union, as the war came to a close, they became alarmed by their treatment by Federal authorities, the end of slavery, and the heavy presence of US Colored Troops in the commonwealth. A visitor in 1863 expressed surprise that "since the emancipation proclamation the people of Kentucky are all secesh except at Louisville and along the river at Covington." As the *Lexington Observer and Reporter* acknowledged in May 1867, "a majority of her voters believe the war for the Union was wrong and that their hearts as well as their voices [are] in sympathy with the 'lost cause.'" A year earlier, Edward Pollard had written *The Lost Cause: A New Southern History of the War of the Confederates,* followed two years later by *The Lost Cause Regained.* Both books sought to explain why Confederates had gone to war. Drawing upon ideas of white supremacy and romanticized ideas of southern chivalry, Pollard argued that the war had always been about state sovereignty—the right of whites to rule themselves, including sustaining the institution of slavery. Defeated Southerners could redeem themselves by returning to those ideals, restoring honor by rejecting racial equality. Disgusted by the dramatic changes wrought to their world, many Kentucky Unionists found in the Lost Cause a common, if rather mythical, past for them to share with family, friends, and neighbors who had supported the Confederacy. When the general assembly refused to ratify the Thirteenth Amendment, then, it was just the first act in Kentuckians' embrace of the Lost Cause.

The Lost Cause was about memory, and many white Kentuckians struck out to shape the state's memorial landscape. The reshaping began in cemeteries and battlefields where the dead lay. Families sought their dead soldiers. Sometimes they went across state lines so that they could rebury them in the commonwealth. The federal government assisted with the burial and reburial of Union soldiers. In 1862, the Union had established a cemetery outside Lebanon to inter casualties of its military hospital. Over 865 troops, many from the Battle of Mill Springs, were buried there. In 1867, the burial yard was designated a national cemetery, but it was not big enough. A year earlier, the US government expanded the small cemetery adjacent to Camp Nelson. By the end of the war, it held 1,180 men, many of them US Colored Troops. By summer 1868, 2,023 remains had been removed from Frankfort, Richmond, Covington, and London and reinterred at the new national cemetery. At the same time, the remains of Confederate prisoners of war were purged from the cemetery, either moved to Nicholasville's cemetery or to private family plots.

No government assisted Confederate Kentuckians in burying their loved ones. Many faced insurmountable financial and logistic burdens. By the early 1870s, Kirby Smith, who had once invaded Kentucky militarily, infiltrated the state again with the Confederate Burial Memorial Association, with the aim of reburying Confederate soldiers and erecting monuments to the Confederate dead. Most of the work fell upon individual families, driven by the desires of women to locate sons, brothers, and husbands. The task was daunting and often impossible. After the Battle of Perryville, for example, the Union army buried its dead in regimental plots. They were later reinterred at Camp Nelson National Cemetery. Because the Confederates had retreated, their dead lay unburied. Their bodies remained where they fell until a local farmer, his slaves, and neighbors found and buried them. They placed around two hundred Confederate casualties in two large pits, most without any identification.

Unable to identify and honor many of their soldiers, Confederate Kentuckians created collective memorials. In 1869, the Cynthiana Confederate Monument Association raised funds to erect a white marble obelisk with the representation of a Confederate flag over the

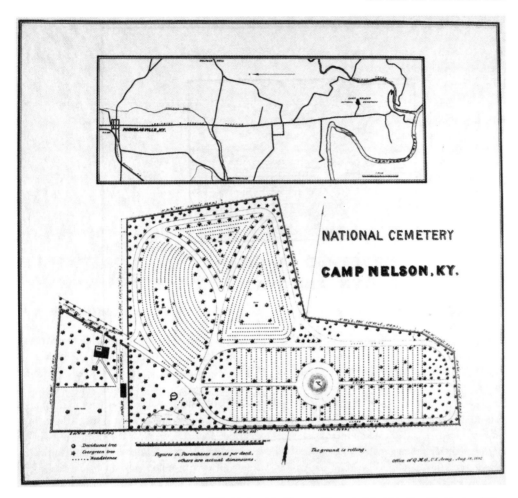

Site plan of Camp Nelson National Cemetery, 1893. (National Archives and Records Administration, Washington, DC)

top. A verse from Theodore O'Hara's "Bivouac of the Dead" was inscribed on one side. Forty-seven Confederate corpses, some of whom had died during Morgan's raid of the town, were relocated to encircle the monument. On May 27, a parade directed celebrants to the memorial site, where William Campbell Preston Breckinridge, once a colonel in John Hunt Morgan's cavalry, extolled the virtues of the Confederate cause and its soldiers.

Similar monuments with similar origins arose across Kentucky. In 1870, a monument to Confederate soldiers from Union County was erected in Morganfield. In Lincoln County, another was placed near Crab Orchard in 1871. The inscription ended, "They fell among

strangers, unknown, unfriended, yet not unhonored for strangers' hands have gathered their ashes here and placed this shaft about them. That constancy, valor, sacrifice of self, though displaced in fruitless enterprise, may not be unremembered." The following year, a monument in Taylor County honored the Confederate dead of the Battle of Tebbs Bend. In 1875, another monument commemorated Confederates who died at Dutton's Hill in Pulaski County. The Warren County Monumental Association formed to create a monument in Bowling Green in 1876. The design included a bas-relief of Henry Mosler's "Lost Cause," a popular painting of the era. Some seventy Confederate soldiers were reburied around its

Bas-relief of Henry Mosler's *Lost Cause*, on Confederate monument in Bowling Green, KY, 1876. (Courtesy of C. Bedford Crenshaw)

base, and ten thousand people attended a large dedication ceremony to hear W. C. P. Breckinridge speak. A year later, Versailles erected its own monument, a hexagon on which the names of Confederate veterans were inscribed. In 1880, Mt. Sterling built a monument layered with verses from "Bivouac of the Dead." And in 1888 in Georgetown, the Ladies Monument Association dedicated a memorial, reinterring eighteen fallen Confederates around the base. Again, thousands attended to hear a dedication speech, this time by Dr. John A. Lewis, a local physician who had served in the Confederate army.

Almost all monuments were located in cemeteries, reasonable locations in an age before public memorial spaces, and we often mistake them today for grave markers. Three memorials of the era stood out. In 1874, the Ladies Memorial and Monument Association of Lexington commissioned a monument that *Frank Leslie's Illustrated Newspaper* proclaimed "probably the most perfect thing of its kind in the South." Sculpted as a wooden cross on a mound of rocks framed by an empty scroll and a broken sword, the memorial echoed themes of grief rather than pride: "It tells its own story— the tragic story of the Lost Cause—without the use of a single word." Although the Lexington monument commemorated fallen Confederates, two others remembered the dead not as

honorable soldiers but as victims of Federal oppression. In 1864, residents of St. Joseph memorialized two Confederate soldiers who were executed under Union general Stephen Burbridge's order that four Confederate prisoners be killed for the death of one unarmed Union civilian. Six years later, citizens of Eminence erected a monument to three men whom Burbridge had executed for the deaths of two US Colored Troops. Residents of Midway and Jeffersontown installed their own martyrs' monuments in 1890 and 1904, respectively. Such martyrs' memorials were unique to Kentucky, where Federal policy clashed with citizens' loyalties. Whether it was represented as a bas-relief or in inscriptions, in O'Hara's poetry or Breckinridge's dedicatory speeches, the Lost Cause permeated Confederate Kentuckians' memorial culture as they honored their dead.

Shaping the memory of Kentucky also required attention to the records of the Old South. In 1869, Simon Bolivar Buckner joined eight others in forming the Southern Historical Society, an organization dedicated to gathering and publishing the archives of the Confederacy to justify its war record. By 1878, a chapter had formed in Lexington, with Buckner as president and John C. Breckrinridge as vice president. Two years later, Basil Duke and others organized another chapter as the Southern Historical Association of Louisville. In 1882,

Ladies Confederate Memorial, Lexington, KY. (Courtesy of C. Bedford Crenshaw)

the Louisville chapter published its first issue of the *Southern Bivouac*, a monthly journal of stories, poetry, recollections of battles and skirmishes, and notices and reports from reunions. Unlike many other southern publications, the *Bivouac* proved far more conciliatory. It appealed to fellow Kentuckians who supported the Union, particularly after 1885, when Duke became the editor. Yet, among the tales of heroism and honor, emerged sentimental, romanticized tales about contented "darkies"* who had served caring, paternalistic owners, making the argument that enslaved African Americans had been dedicated to the Old South as well. "In communities where the bulk of the able-bodied white males had departed for service in the army, on the plantations where no white persons remained save women and children, or sometimes an overseer," an editorialist opined in April 1887, "the blacks remained quietly and obediently at work."

In the aftermath of the Civil War, some of the Confederacy's former military leaders took the lead in framing how Kentuckians would remember the war. Kirby Smith's work with Confederate reburials, Simon Buckner's efforts to preserve Confederate archives, W. C. P. Breckinridge's oratory, and Basil Duke's *Southern Bivouac*—men who had fought to preserve the Old South now worked to resurrect it. But they did not work alone. White women of comfortable means populated most of the memorial associations that raised funds for the monuments. Mary Burch Breckinridge, the former second lady of the United States, founded Lexington's Ladies Memorial and Monument Association. Susan Marshall Preston Hepburn, William Preston's sister and Albert Sidney Johnston's sister-in-law, organized Louisville's Kentucky Women's Confederate Monument Association in 1890.

Unionist Kentuckians also developed a memorial culture, although it was not as prevalent as the Confederate memorial culture. The Union, after all, had won, and Unionists did not need to prove the justness of their cause. But Union memorial culture also faced racial obstacles. When the Grand Army of the Republic (GAR) organized in 1867 as a veterans' association, tensions emerged between white and black members. Some white chapters refused to sit alongside black chapters when the GAR held state reunions. Most white Unionists had always been rather conservative about abolition, and the presence of black veterans only reminded them of what many considered to be Lincoln's treason.

So, few Union monuments arose in Kentucky. The first was in Columbia, which memorialized Frank Wolford, leader of the Wild Riders. Of course, Wolford had opposed abolition and been dishonorably discharged for denouncing Lincoln's decision to enlist black troops. The conservatism of white Kentucky Unionists opened the way for reconciliation with their white Confederate neighbors and family members. Former Kentucky governor Beriah Magoffin extended the hand of for-

---

* This term is racially offensive today and should be used thoughtfully in historically appropriate contexts.

Thompson and Powell Martyrs Monument, St. Joseph, KY. (Courtesy of C. Bedford Crenshaw)

giveness at a fund-raising dinner, declaring the "fame of American soldiers and sailors, whether rebel or federal, is the common heritage of our people." "Our people" did not include African Kentuckians or Appalachian Kentuckians.

White residents of Appalachia, who had remained overwhelmingly Unionist during and after the war, eyed the reconciliation throughout the rest of Kentucky cautiously. In the northernmost reaches of eastern Kentucky at Vanceburg, a very different Union monument arose in 1884. A Federal soldier, clothed in his heavy winter coat and kepi hat and holding his rifle, looks northward across the Ohio River. The inscription read: "To communicate the bravery and patriotism of our soldiers who lost their lives in the war for the preservation of national unity . . . the war for the Union was right, everlastingly right, and the war against the Union was wrong, forever wrong." Residents of Appalachia rejected the Lost Cause narrative taking root in the rest of the state, even laying claim to Abraham Lincoln as the prototypical eastern

Kentuckian (despite the fact that he was not from eastern Kentucky but rather was born and raised near Hodgenville before moving to Indiana when he was seven years old). In 1888, promotional literature declared, "No truer type of manhood can be found than is found in the mountains of Kentucky—the same region that gave birth to Abraham Lincoln." Although eastern Kentucky had always developed differently from the rest of Kentucky, as the Lost Cause grabbed the imagination of most white Kentuckians, it became deplorable to those living in Appalachia.

African Kentuckians also found the formation of Lost Cause ideology and white Kentuckians' appropriation of it disturbing. As Kentuckians with more money erected monuments, black Kentuckians developed a humbler memorial culture, appropriating July 4 as a holiday that applied to them as well. On Independence Day in 1865, much of the commonwealth was quiet, but at Camps Nelson and Dick Robinson, freemen and freewomen celebrated. In Louisville, US Colored Infantry led nearly ten thousand African Kentuckians through the streets, breathing the "fresh air of freedom."

Black Kentuckians, too, wanted to shape the narrative of the Southern past. William F. Butler of Jefferson County took the lead in offering an alternative to Confederate Kentuckians' revisionist history. "First we had the cartridge box, now we want the ballot box, and soon we will get the jury box," he announced at the first convention of the Negro Republican Party in Lexington in 1867. Elisha Green, once interrupted during a sermon in Georgetown by a white man demanding the congregation disperse, became vice president of the Kentucky branch of the party. As Emancipation Day became more important in black Kentuckians' memorial culture, they used it to promote their vision of the South's past. They invoked war memory to reject the docile slave imagery that had emerged in Confederate literature. The men

and women who had sympathized and fought for the Confederacy were not friends to blacks. At Louisville's 1866 Emancipation Day celebration, Union military governor John M. Palmer elaborated on how, after the issuance of the Emancipation Proclamation, many Americans demanded Lincoln revoke it: "None did so more earnestly than citizens of Kentucky, and many men went away from the cause of the Union sorrowful, for they had many 'niggers.'"* Slavery had been a burden that kept African Kentuckians from achieving their potential as Americans and as humans. "We only ask you take your hand off the black man's head and let him grow to manhood," demanded Butler at Louisville's 1867 Emancipation Day ceremony.

The Civil War did not end in Kentucky in April 1865. It continued to be fought in the imaginations of Kentuckians, black and white, Unionist and Confederate. Their competing memories added to the difficult task before Kentuckians as they tried to heal from the war.

---

* This term is racially offensive today and should be used thoughtfully in historically appropriate contexts.

10

1865 and After

The Kentucky World of 1865

One Kentuckian remembered the April day vividly: "When we heard of Gen. Lee's surrender pandemonium broke loose and everyone acted as if the world was coming to an end." For people in the state in 1865, one world was in fact ending, and a new, uncertain world built on the wreckage of war was replacing it. But what kind of new world would it be? Would it replicate the old in most fundamental respects, or would it be vastly different? Change, confusion, and chaos often follow war, but this conflict, this civil war, was more destructive and disruptive than any experienced by Americans before or since. More than 700,000 had died or would soon die. Among Kentuckians, perhaps as many as 1 in 7 who left to fight—some 20,000 out of as many as 140,000—never returned. Their graves were scattered across a large, war-ravaged area. As one who fought noted, "A large part of the best of the youth perished."

Thousands more were wounded, marred for life by bullets or by unforgiving memories of battlefields. Empty sleeves, legless bodies, permanent damage to the mind—all these came home with the veterans of combat, black and white. An entire era had been blighted. What leaders had the state lost among its dead? What art, literature, or statecraft would have resulted from those lives? A generation grew to maturity without those talents. The war exacted a personal toll that could not be replaced. Kentucky's future would be one filled with bitter memories, wartime scars, and long-felt hurts.

The war's effects, however, went beyond the casualties. Perhaps more so than any other state, Kentucky had been sharply divided between the two causes. The conflict had been a brothers' war, as whole families were torn asunder. Friends warred on each other; Kentuckians had looked down their gun barrels at other Kentuckians; churches and communities had split. In time, many of those who wore the Blue or the Gray would grow to respect their former enemies, and the healing would begin. For others, however, the fabric of life, rent by the war, was never mended. The memories remained too strong. A bitter feeling between neighbors still prevailed, and this situation made compromise and cooperation difficult and intense violence likely. A soldier of the conflict wrote later of "hearts thus hard and stern and seared by war." Those dormant seeds of animosity deposited by the Civil War would spring to life later, bringing forth harvests of more bloodshed.

The conflict left behind its toll of physical destruction as well, for crops had been lost, livestock taken, and property destroyed. The amount of land under cultivation declined drastically. Despite wartime inflation, land values in places like Lexington decreased one-fourth between 1862 and 1872. A soldier returned to an eastern Kentucky town and was welcomed by "neglected farms . . . roads and paths overgrown with weeds, and almost no business of any kind being carried on." Homes had been destroyed, river locks and salt works damaged, and crops disrupted. But that sense of economic setback could be—and would be—easily overcome, for in truth Kentucky had not suffered as greatly as the states farther south. In fact, some locales, such as Louisville, had actually prospered during the war. The commonwealth thus emerged from the conflict hobbled, but strong enough to move ahead, to grow rapidly, even to take a leadership role in

Camp Nelson National Cemetery in Jessamine County is the final resting place of many soldiers, black and white, who died in the Civil War. (kentuckydaytrips.org)

a region where other states had much greater handicaps and devastation to overcome.

More damaging than the economic costs was the war's effect on the psyche of the populace. So much of what had once been was no more. The optimism that drove settlers to frontier Kentucky now seemed a rare commodity. Uncertainty caused citizens to wonder just what this postwar world would hold for them. What was their life going to be like now? They knew already that the War between the States—as southerners preferred to call it—had left an indelible mark on their lives and would likely do so for decades to come. The keys to understanding future developments in Kentucky would be the war, the war, and the war. For example, even before the Civil War, the death of Henry Clay's Whig Party in the 1850s had left the political arena confused. Considering actions taken since then, now what would occur? What would become of the state's educational system, which had made some important progress before the war, but had 75,000 fewer students in 1861 than the previous year? It had been hit hard. Could it recover? Would the commonwealth retain its status as one of the nation's leading agricultural states, or

would new trade and industrial growth dominate? Kentucky was a land of worry, distrust, and fear, as well as a place of hope, hospitality, and confidence. With so many questions and so few clear answers, the year 1865 seemed an uncertain time indeed.

Yet with all that, one other question seemed in some ways the most important of all at the time. The single most crucial issue, the one topic that filled the pages of the state's newspapers, concerned the place of African Americans in the postwar world. For blacks themselves, the debate was simply resolved: Free us from slavery, give us the rights of other American citizens, let us enjoy those freedoms without hindrance, and allow us to go on with our lives as we too seek a better future. Not a single one of these actions, however, would occur without dispute or restriction.

White Kentuckians ruled the state, for only one of every six people in the commonwealth was black in 1870. The former slaves did not compose close to a majority and could not threaten white dominance except in a very few locales. Yet the issue was never fully a matter of numbers. Slavery had been not only an economic institution but also one of social and racial controls, in which one group ruled another. For many generations it had been emphasized that slaves were not at the same level as the white people around them. Few white Kentuckians—or white Americans, for that matter—could conceive of accepting the idea that blacks were their equals. The world built on that set of racial values was under attack and in danger of being overturned, as political and social equality became the sought-after goal. In large part, white Kentuckians refused to replace the scheme of dominant and subordinate statuses with a system of equality. One newspaper writer would not "submit to a social association perfectly revolutionary to all sensible persons." Such attitudes would breed resistance and cost many lives over many years. For more than a century justice would war against prejudice in a fiercely fought, decidedly uncivil conflict.

The question of civil rights added yet another ingredient to a mix that was already boiling over in the South and in Kentucky in 1865. The attempt to reconstruct a society split by war was difficult enough. With the issue of race and the ferocity of reaction then added, smooth transition into peace became almost impossible. At one extreme, some in the North called for harsh treatment of the South, even for the death by hanging of "traitorous" southern leaders, like Kentucky's John C. Breckinridge. At the other extreme, some southerners seemed unable to accept the fact that they had lost the war and must accept the consequences. Feelings grew so bitter that various commentators wondered aloud if the war or some guerrilla resistance would begin again. A Kentucky woman wrote that "the war was not over in Kentucky, a state divided against itself." The *Elizabethtown Banner* asked if the country might "be convulsed with the throes of a new revolution, involving the North and South alike, in common ruin." When the former slaveholding states, including Kentucky, refused to accept blacks as free men and women, not to mention as voters or as equal citizens in society, and when they used force to reinforce that stand, northern Republicans responded with stronger actions. Some of them raised serious constitutional questions. Those in opposition compared such moves to those made by the radical Jacobins of the French Revolution and predicted equally bloody consequences. The *Bardstown Leader,* in its arguments against implementation of the national Civil Rights Act of 1866, editorialized that "precious blood has been poured out like water; precious lives have been ruthlessly sacrificed. . . . Now for the sake of three millions of negroes, the white people of this country are asked to submit to the abrogation of the Constitution." Other writers quietly counseled acceptance of the postwar situation and asked their fellow citizens to direct their attention and energies to rebuilding out of the destruction of war, to create a New South, a new Kentucky.

If trying to repair wartime damages, seeking to reintegrate returning soldiers of both armies into society, and working to find a racial arrangement that would satisfy all was not enough to deal with, Kentuckians also had to face what appeared to be serious breakdowns in the legal system. During the war one Christian County diarist had written that young people "seem to think the war will never end & they might as well enjoy them selves as they can." This uncertainty frequently combined with the absence, or loss, of one parent to produce generational conflict. Now in the postwar world those same young adults continued to face an unknown, confused future—as did their elders—and seemed to be searching still for answers and direction. Newspapers printed disapproving stories about bands of roving adolescent boys who drank, stole, fought, and committed acts of violence. The same virus of dissatisfaction struck wartime veterans, some of them little more than boys themselves. They, too, found it hard to adjust to a peacetime situation. Former Union captain John W. Tuttle of Wayne County would later be a successful attorney, but he recalled that when the fighting ended, he "contracted a hearty contempt for useful employment of any kind whatsoever so I passed most of my time in gambling, drinking, and rollicking around with . . . the boys." Add to that mix the new status of the former slaves and the movement of many of them from farm to city, and general unrest and significant uncertainty seemed to characterize postwar civilization.

Violence exacerbated the problems and appeared ever present to Kentuckians of the era. During the conflict, the state had been infested with lawless guerrilla bands, made up of outlaws and outcasts from both armies. Many normal protectors were off fighting the war, and little slowed the guerrillas. One Monticello resident recalled:

Lawless bands were continually prowling about through this region of country stealing, robbing, plundering, burning, and committing all manner of depredations, cruelties, and atrocities upon helpless and unoffending citizens. . . . They howled about the streets like demons, shooting at every man that showed himself on the streets. . . .

It may seem strange that a town . . . should suffer such a gang to run rough shod over it in that manner, but the people knew if they shipped one gang out another larger one would come and destroy the town and perhaps massacre its inhabitants. . . .

Taken all together there is little connected with this period of time that is pleasant to look back upon or desirable to remember.

Such lawlessness did not end with Lee's surrender at Appomattox, and one person who lived in Kentucky during that time recalled later that a virtual reign of terror prevailed in the state from 1865 to 1868. Those who had supported the opposing side and still had a score to settle ambushed a few returning soldiers. More commonly, criminal bands simply made life dangerous for everyone. One boy remembered that his father slept with two pistols, two rifles, and a machete by his bedside. In Washington County, break-ins were so likely that the bank refused to take deposits. The sheriff himself was robbed of county tax receipts. Across the commonwealth, vigilantes, the Ku Klux Klan, and individual groups killed and lynched blacks with seeming impunity. All that lawlessness caused some of both races—including bright, ambitious people that the state could ill afford to lose—to see little hope in the "unsettled state of society" and to leave the commonwealth entirely. Those who remained would find it very difficult to eliminate the influence of violence on their lives.

Continuity and Change

Kentucky author James Lane Allen, who could be both an astute critic and an undiscerning onlooker, wrote that out of the postwar period "of upheaval and downfall, of shifting and drifting," his state emerged with "so much the same." Yet Allen in the same book also noted that the war changed things drastically. It was "a great rent and chasm, down into which old things were dashed to death, and out of which new things were born into the better life." Former Confederate Basil W. Duke looked back on the postwar era with its physical and mental destruction, its racial struggles, its violence and unrest, and said of Kentucky and the region that "the life of the post-bellum South no more resembled that of the other than the life of the early settlers . . . was like that they had left on the other side of the ocean." Just as the first Americans had discovered a new world, so too, he argued, Kentuckians after the Civil War found themselves in a new era, in a place vastly different from the one they had known before.

Was life in postwar Kentucky, then, fundamentally a continuation of the earlier lifestyle, or was it profoundly different? Obviously, the knowledge that numerous exceptions exist to any broad statement must temper any generalization about the identity of a physical place bounded by political lines. There were, for example, rural Kentuckys and urban ones, Kentuckys of black and white, rich and poor, young and old. People who lived in the eastern mountains seemed a world away from those in western Kentucky, and people in the countryside had vastly different lives from people in the cities. Divisions of class, gender, race, ethnicity, region, and socioeconomics partitioned the state. To complicate the matter further, little unity existed within each major group. The urban poor, either black or white, might find they had more in common with their rural counterparts than with upper-class society in their own cities. On the other hand, some issues would cause such alliances to break down, and farmers, rich and poor, might join together against urban dwellers. Over the years there would be many Kentuckys, constantly shifting with the various issues that united or divided them.

The state would change as the decades passed, but the degree of change, and its timing, would vary widely across the commonwealth. Each locale had to weigh the costs of every decision, as citizens asked which of the current institutions should be retained and which should be discarded. Each change, no matter how positive it might seem, would affect the way of life that had once been known. The coming of the telephone from 1879 on, for example, allowed merchants to conduct business better, helped bring aid quicker in emergencies, and permitted easier communication among people in a community. Yet the telephone might also cause neighbors to visit less in person; it might add to the impersonal feeling of a growing nation. In the twentieth century, when the dial phone replaced the system in which a local operator made the calls, then the operator's intimate knowledge of the community would be erased. Few questioned the desirability of the telephone or the modifications in it that added to the convenience of the users, but each change made a subtle difference in the way a community worked. The question was one of balance, and in this case the scales easily tipped toward accepting the telephone. But when larger issues arose that had greater consequences, the decisions would not be so simple.

While some places and certain communities embraced new ideas and different outlooks almost immediately, others remained virtually unchanged for more than a century. In 1865 many people all across the state lived on a lingering frontier, isolated and ignored. The nineteenth-century experience of a man who grew up on a farm and by the age of seventeen had never seen a town, not even his county seat, was not that rare. In the first third of the twentieth century, as another Kentuckian recalled, young boys and girls lived within view of the small creek that dominated their lives and went to a small hamlet only a few times a year, "and only then if it didn't rain." By the middle of the twentieth century, despite all the improvements in transportation, a rural high school graduate noted that he had been no farther than the next county. An intense provincialism resulted from such isolated and limiting situations. As one writer remembered, "The conversations of the people were of local subjects. Their intelligence never soared across many watersheds; beyond many streams."

In many such places after the war, the inhabitants could not read—more than one-fourth of Kentuckians over the age of ten were illiterate in 1870—and even in literate homes, books and newspapers might be scarce possessions. Oral traditions were passed down, and with them stories and beliefs of an earlier time. Fears and superstitions made a sweeping 1866 rumor believable. Accounts spread that the end of the world was near and that the devil was unchained. A lawyer wrote in his diary that "there was considerable excitement on the streets all day about the coming of the Devil. . . . Some seemed to believe the preposterous stories afloat, some were actually scared." Accounts of ghosts and witches were widespread, and to many people these beings seemed real. In 1869 an Owen County woman was presented to a grand jury on the charge of being a witch. She was not indicted. (Later, in 1898, a woman was supposedly burned as a witch in Fleming County.) The world of many Kentuckians featured limited learning, narrow geographic boundaries, and restricted mental horizons. Places of finite options and confined imaginations would long survive.

Yet so too would another, very different world, one peopled by Kentuckians who had broad education and strong vision. They had traveled widely, read well, and learned much. In their own way, they had weaknesses and prejudices, and sometimes they could be just as provincial and limited in outlook as their more place-bound fellow citizens. Still, their lives proved very different. Between these two extremes existed almost all variations, and people in practically every group agreed that their own beliefs should be guiding the entire commonwealth.

Despite the differences among Kentuckians, however, certain overall characteristics were evident. First of all, mid-nineteenth-century citizens worshiped an agrarian ideal. Increasingly that would not be so, for an urban ethos quickly would make inroads, and the goals of business leaders would replace those of country gentlemen. But in the nineteenth century, the ties to the land remained strong and binding. A web of traditions linking physical things—the ridges and rivers, the hills and hollows—created a particular "landscape of the mind," a dignity, a strong sense of place. People walked the land they farmed, felt it beneath their feet, knew how it looked, understood its vagaries and variations. They had a camaraderie and partnership with the soil. The bond was often a hard one, but intimate nevertheless. As one Appalachian resident wrote later: "I don't remember even seeing a Van Gogh or Rembrandt . . . but I remember beauty. . . . There was natural beauty enough to fill the eyes and the soul."

Conservatism and a tendency to resist change surfaced as a second characteristic of the time. Many Kentuckians, particularly the well-to-do, the established, and the landed, believed that there was little need to reexamine the basic arrangement of their lives. They were not reactionary, for they could support improvements, such as in technological matters, for instance. They simply did not see the need to modify the system they knew. That attitude was not restricted to just one class, for many citizens accepted a stable way of life they did not consider terribly bad. Even the poor and landless did not often offer challenges because such behavior was too dangerous—blacks might lose their lives, poor whites their jobs. Others showed a kind of resignation. They knew only one way of life, and a hard, unlettered existence left them little time to contemplate options or to put ideas into effect. Still others, of both races, believed that a better life awaited them after death and expected their reward in another world. Such fatalism and passiveness allowed people to accept misfortunes in this life but also created an outlook that resisted change. Indifference and complacency resulted. Amid the uncertainty of postwar Kentucky and beyond, such citizens rarely challenged authority.

Although contradictory, a rising demand for change and reform of existing ways also marked the era. Some people spoke out for the idea of progress—whatever that meant to them—because, in their eyes, justice demanded it. Others did so because they and their children had few future prospects under the current system. Thus, throughout the next tumultuous half century—and beyond—various Kentuckians would attempt to alter the status quo. Occasionally such reformers might focus on less vital questions, such as fashion, but more often they dealt with major issues. Questions of politics, race, women's rights, and agrarian change would all demand answers. The struggles to find these answers would be long, hard, controversial, and divisive.

Rural and Small-Town Life

One historian astutely termed Kentucky a "land of contrast." In 1865, however, the state's population presented less social contrast than at any time since the frontier period. The end of slavery loosened the legal bonds that tied one group to another and at the same time seriously weakened the financial condition of those who had held slaves. Millions upon millions of dollars had been invested in human property. Early in the Civil War, Kentucky had rejected Lincoln's offer for compensated emancipation. Then, belatedly, state political leaders sought compensation for freed slaves—more than $108 million—but it was not forthcoming. Families that had been, at least on paper, quite wealthy now became quite poor in fact. A leveling had taken place. In Franklin County, the seat of the state capital, only thirty-six people had incomes of more than one thousand dollars in 1867. On the other hand, blacks began a slow process of gaining wealth and status. For former slaves with little or no money or land, any financial gains would constitute an improvement on the poverty of slavery—and the poverty of the spirit that such bonds had brought as well.

There were still wealthy Kentuckians and still very poor ones. As Allen noted, "a spirit of caste" existed everywhere, and each town of any size had what one woman called "Society . . . with a capital S. . . . You were either in it or out of it." Great racial and gender inequalities continued as well. Yet less wealth existed than before, and the formal divisions made evident by slavery and slaveholding were gone. In a society in which rural interests still dominated, the lack of money was also less evident, and thus the distinction of class was less clear. Even the Appalachian Highlands, an area later associated with poverty, did not differ so greatly from the rest of the commonwealth at the time. At least for the moment, the people of post–Civil War Kentucky lived in a relatively less financially defined society and a more classless one.

They also lived in an increasingly homogenous society. Their state declined in population relative to the United States. Kentucky's growth, from 1,321,011 people in 1870 to 2,147,174 in 1900, trailed the nation's expansion. The state population had increased more

slowly than that of the country as a whole since 1830 and would continue this trend, with two exceptions, into the twenty-first century. Eighth largest of the states in 1850, Kentucky fell to twelfth by 1900.

Part of that relative decline resulted from an out-migration of residents, many of them African Americans. Overall, the number of black Kentuckians declined from nearly 17 percent of the population in 1870 to over 13 percent in 1900. Likewise, fewer new faces, particularly of the foreign-born, were arriving in the commonwealth. At a time when great waves of new immigrants flooded America's East and North, Kentucky remained almost untouched, except for a few instances in the coalfields.

Kentucky had a small immigrant presence. In 1870 only one in twenty citizens had been born outside the United States. Concentrated along the Ohio River cities—Covington, Newport, and Louisville all had 20 percent or more foreign-born—these immigrants consisted chiefly of Irish and Germans who had arrived before the war. In those places, German would be spoken in churches until the 1910s, and Irish and German newspapers would be printed for decades beyond that. Yet other parts of the commonwealth had no for-

Table 10.1. Population of Kentucky, 1870–2010

Year	Population	Kentucky Growth Rate	US Growth Rate
1870	1,321,011	14.3	24.0
1880	1,648,690	24.8	30.1
1890	1,858,635	12.7	24.9
1900	2,147,174	15.5	20.7
1910	2,289,905	6.6	21.0
1920	2,416,630	5.5	15.0
1930	2,614,589	8.2	16.2
1940	2,845,627	8.8	7.3
1950	2,944,806	3.5	14.5
1960	3,038,156	3.2	18.5
1970	3,220,711	6.0	13.3
1980	3,660,324	13.6	11.4
1990	3,686,891	0.7	9.8
2000	4,041,769	9.7	13.2
2010	4,339,367	7.4	9.7

Source: P. P. Karan and Cotton Mather, eds., *Atlas of Kentucky* (1977), 17; US Census; *World Almanac and Book of Facts, 1992* (1992); *1996 Kentucky Deskbook of Economic Statistics* (1996).

eign-born residents whatsoever. With few new immigrants and with little in-migration from other states, Kentucky became more and more self-contained. Different ideas and lifestyles brought from outside would prove scarce. By 1910 nearly 90 percent of those living in the state had been born there, the fifth highest percentage nationally.

In the half century after Appomattox, then, the core of life of the average Kentuckian changed only slowly. A resident's lifestyle might vary considerably from class to class, from city to small town, and from small town to farm, but at root it remained relatively static. At the center of life stood the family. There, children learned cultural patterns and ethical norms. The family shaped character in ways both open and subtle, and it imparted duties and expectations. Kentucky in 1870 had the highest average number of people per family in the nation—5.7 persons. Each decade that average would fall, so that by 1910 the state's average of 4.6 per family only barely exceeded the national figure of 4.5. Yet larger families remained the norm for the commonwealth during that period.

Families, both black and white, usually lived in a rural setting. As late as 1910 four of five Kentucky families belonged in that category. People typically would rise early after sleeping on beds stuffed with goose feathers, straw, or cornhusks. Upon waking, they seldom looked at a clock to find the time, for few timepieces existed in poorer homes. One Caldwell County resident recalled, "I never saw a clock until I was nearly grown." An eastern Kentuckian noted that he never needed a watch: "Got up at light and to bed at dark." Other families might have a cheap timepiece sold to them by a traveling peddler, but nature's hours still remained primary in ruling their lives. If they rose before daylight, they lit kerosene or oil lamps. (Not until the 1940s or 1950s would most rural Kentuckians have electricity in their homes.) On cold days many would jump from the warmth of their beds and rush to a place with heat. Many homes, mostly uninsulated, might offer only a single fireplace. Parts distant from that central source

could feel virtually unheated as the wind whipped through the walls. Family members would undress by the fire at night, jump into their nightclothes, and rush off to the feather bed and stack of quilts designed to keep them as warm as possible in a cold room, where they could see their breath on a moonlit night. In the morning the mad dash to the fire would be reversed.

A family member charged with bringing in the wood or coal to start the day's fire would have to make certain that embers from the previous day had been preserved, so a new flame could begin. If the embers had died, a trip to a perhaps distant neighbor "to borrow fire" was necessary because matches remained rare luxuries in many homes until late in the nineteenth century. Warmer weather freed the family from the fire-making chore but brought other problems. Feather beds were hot in summer and might attract fleas. Some families slept outside at night to escape the extreme heat. Glass was too expensive for many families, and mesh screens were not typical. Open windows, therefore, were the usual option for cooling the interior. This option, however, meant a thin layer of dust often coated the interiors of homes. It also allowed a variety of flies and other insects to invade the premises. Strips of sticky flypaper hung in some houses in an attempt to reduce their numbers. Air conditioning would begin to be used in limited form, such as in theaters, by the 1930s, but not for three or more decades after that would it become commonplace. Until then, handheld and, later, electric fans, open windows, and cooling breezes would be the answers to summer's heat. For a long time in Kentucky, heating and cooling depended as much on nature as on artificial means.

Whether the weather was warm or cold, water for cooking or washing came from outdoors. Indoor plumbing was not prevalent in nineteenth-century Kentucky, and a well or nearby creek often provided water for all uses. Otherwise, rainwater was collected in barrels or cisterns. Sanitary quality varied. Even urban dwellers in Louisville drank unfiltered water straight from the polluted river until 1909. As one resident recalled, "No family was without its case of typhoid." Those fortunate enough to have a water tank attached to a kitchen stove had hot water readily available, but most people started the morning by washing in cold water instead. Similarly, using a chamber pot indoors or taking a trip to an outside privy—an outhouse—or even to a secluded spot in the woods were the only ways to answer what was euphemistically termed "nature's call."

Many Kentucky families lived almost self-sufficient lives. As in earlier times, people washed themselves and their clothes with a rough homemade lye soap produced from fat waste, wood ashes, and water. They wore clothes made with thread woven at home on a spinning wheel. Yarn, all colored with dyes fashioned from tree bark or berry juice, was used to knit stockings, socks, and scarves. Sheep represented a vital part of the cloth-making process, for their wool would be sheared, washed in a nearby stream, and then either made into cloth on the premises or shipped to a distant mill, to be returned later. Straw was braided to make men's hats, and leather was formed on stocks to make shoes—although most children went barefoot during the summer months.

Food on the family table came from nearby sources. Hunting and fishing provided some food, while chickens and hogs offered a more constant feature on most farms. With cool weather came "hog-killing" time, and neighbors gathered to help each other. The animals would be shot or axed, their bodies placed in scalding water to remove the hair, and then the carcasses were hung upside down so that the blood could drain out. Finally the meat would be cut up. Some went into sausage—"Unless you have tasted sausage made on the farm," said many, "you have never tasted sausage." The rest would be preserved by salting or smoking, to keep out worms. Chickens provided eggs, while cows furnished milk, both for drinking and for making into butter. While some towns had ice companies that made daily deliveries, most places kept food cool only by placing it in a spring or in a specially designed "well house."

Fruit trees and vegetable gardens provided a variety of foods, preserved in many ways. Cellars sheltered potatoes, cabbages, and dried items such as apples, green beans, and peppers. Canning in sterilized jars became common at different times across the state, usually after the turn of the twentieth century. It offered a good way to preserve beets, corn, tomatoes, berries, and similar items. Honey from beehives kept on some farms, as well as molasses made from cane, gave further variety to daily fare. The only food items that many people purchased with regularity were salt, sugar, coffee, and flour. Across Kentucky, many people lived in or near self-sufficiency, but this life was one based on long, hard work. As a woman wrote about her twentieth-century life, "Although we were self-sufficient and resourceful . . . we lived in a state of psychological poverty. . . . We were country folk. We didn't ordinarily go on vacations because there were cows to milk, chickens to feed." She added that the farm "held us back with invisible fences as confining as the real barbed wire bordering our pastures." Or as a teacher observed of the people in a mountain county in the early part of that same century: "The mothers were tired, the children were tired, the men were tired trying to make out a living on those steep hillsides. And the land itself was tired . . . with no crop rotation." When other, easier options became available, many would be seized eagerly.

The nutritional value of the meals prepared in rural residences fluctuated. Those who had access to all the dietary possibilities—the many fruits, the numerous vegetables, the different meats—did quite well. One person recalled a bountiful breakfast of biscuits, sausage, gravy, fried apples, strawberry preserves, butter, and milk. Others remembered equally plentiful dinners (the noon meal) and suppers. Yet some Kentuckians faced meals of little variety, few options, and no luxuries. Their diets more typically consisted of salt pork, corn, coffee, and cornbread. Still others found out that hunger continued to stalk this land of seeming plenty. In the early twentieth century a woman was asked if she had ever been hungry: "Yes, many a time. . . . Some mornings we had just enough meal in the house to make one hoecake. . . . And we had to divide that ten ways."

Whether the meal a family consumed was

A Lexington baptism performed by the Reverend Sanford Howard in the 1890s. (Bullock Photograph Collection, Transylvania University Library, Lexington, KY)

makeshift or full, women likely prepared it, for a clear division of labor based on gender existed in Kentucky. Young boys might bring in wood for the fire, carry water to the house, and do minor farm chores, such as clearing out chicken houses or feeding pigs. Girls might gather eggs, skim milk, churn butter, roll candles, and generally assist their mother. Grown women faced myriad tasks, ranging from making and mending clothes to washing and ironing them, from cleaning house to caring for the garden. They stored and canned food and prepared meals three times a day. If the family was large and local custom strong, women might well not eat until the men of the household had been served, or they might sit with the children for meals. One man, remembering how his mother balanced all of her work while also raising nine children, concluded simply: "She didn't have much time left." Men, meanwhile, usually worked all day in the fields when weather permitted, plowing, weeding, harvesting. They kept buildings repaired and conducted most of the formal business. In providing food for the table through hunting and fishing, males did have the oppor-tunity to venture away from home more than women did. Women's activities tended to restrict them more to the household.

For women and men, girls and boys, two institutions provided the opportunity to meet and interact with other Kentuckians of the area. No matter the location or relative isolation of the neighborhood, people would gather at church or at the country store. Churches had a threefold purpose. One obviously was religious, at a time when religion dominated people's thoughts and words. Although members of some denominations would deny it, the church also offered a kind of entertainment. For isolated Kentuckians, the discourses and music heard there might represent the only group exposure to the arts. Finally, the churches offered people a place to meet and talk. There new friendships were made or older ones renewed. Many young men and women met their future spouses at the country church. Even when seating was segregated by sex, as it was in places, picnics or walks home afterward provided opportunities for interaction. The church was a social, cultural, and spiritual center.

In a different manner, the country store was just as central a part of people's lives. For an isolated populace, tied to family and home on most days, a trip to the country store seemed almost a journey to grandeur. Each business varied, but most seemed to have a little of everything. On entering, the first sense to be assailed would be the nose. The smell of oiled floors (oiled to keep down dust) mixed with the odor of tobacco smoke, combined with the scent of leather and the fragrance of dried herbs. These joined with the aroma of a mix of foods—cheese, coffee, and fruits—to alert visitors to what might lie within. Sounds of delighted children or bargaining customers blended with voices of a local politician seeking votes. The eye could barely take in all that was there. A counter showed off everything from candy to candles. Nearby might be stoves for sale, or harnesses for horses. One Jessamine County resident noted that the owner of the store near him was postmaster as well as proprietor, and he dispersed "smiles, local news, reminiscences, and everything from hay-rakes to headache pills; from cedar posts to shoes; from ten-quart tin-pails to pencil sharpeners and old-fashioned peppermints." The country store functioned as grocery, clothing store, voting place, credit center, hardware business, post office, and information distribution center. People bartered eggs for canned sardines, mailed and received packages, and traded gossip for more gossip. Front-porch rocking chair debates in summer or spittoon discussions around the pot-bellied stove in winter solved, in the participants' view at least, most of the concerns of the neighborhood, or the world.

Country stores existed well into the twentieth century, for they lived and died based on the isolation and mobility of those around them. But they were never again so central a part of people's lives as they were in the late 1800s. With better highways and the coming of the railroad, some stores declined. Others lost trade when mail-order houses brought goods to the doorstep through rural free delivery, particularly after about 1901. Finally, their place at the center of social life and the rural economy went to other institutions.

Improved transportation brought small county seat towns within easier reach of many rural residents. As a result, county court days became as important as the country store to some Kentuckians. On court day, whole families would arrive in town by horse or wagon. Women and girls went to the small selection of stores and shops, while men and boys mingled with the mob that comprised something that was part folk gathering, part festival, and part marketplace. A minister visited Winchester's court day in 1880 and wrote in his diary: "Pavement as thickly thronged as Broadway, New York. A perfect Babel with the various auctioneers, shouting themselves hoarse, the cattle lowing, horning, hoofing, crowding each other; the drivers yelling . . .; the various bargainers, buyers, and sellers gesticulating, arguing, protesting; loafers strolling up and down eating peanuts, apples, pawpaws, and enjoying the sights and sounds." Across Kentucky, items as diverse as baskets and bulls, patent medicines and pickles, furniture and farming implements, were presented to wary buyers. Wealthy merchants talked with tenant farmers, well-to-do estate owners rubbed elbows with laborers, and social distinctions seemed less important than the ability to bargain for a good price. But like the country store, court day saw its glory fade as the nineteenth century died. Although a few examples lived on, the institution had seen its heyday by the time Lexington abolished its court day on Cheapside in 1921.

The Urban Commonwealth

The smaller county seats and other similarly sized towns barely deserved the designation "town," for they frequently remained rough and primitive outposts in the rural landscape well into the twentieth century. Elizabethtown, on the railroad and not far from urbanized Louisville, still was described in the 1880s as a place where hogs roamed the streets, sleeping in the courthouse at night. Only the business section had sidewalks. The rest of the town featured dusty or muddy walkways, depending on the weather. The lack of streetlights meant that people had to carry lanterns if they moved

Court day in Lexington, 1897. (Wilson Family Photographic Collection, University of Kentucky Special Collections and Research Center, Lexington, KY)

about after dark. When Hopkinsville decided to deal with its own problem of unattended hogs and cows and outlawed the practice of allowing livestock to roam at large, "the community was thrown into an uproar." As late as the 1940s, Hyden in the eastern Kentucky mountains was described as "a slop hole," a "drab and dreary" place filled with roaming bands of cows, hogs, and mules, traveling freely over dirt streets pocked with enormous holes. In 1910 only thirteen cities in the state had more than six thousand people.

Yet for all their roughness, such places gradually brought to rural Kentuckians new technologies, different ideas, and fresh styles. At varying times, depending on the towns' isolation, they introduced their locales to the wonders of electricity, telephones, indoor plumbing, and much more. A young Muhlenberg County girl arrived in one such urban place in the first decade of the twentieth century and recalled that in the next few weeks she experienced "the first brick paved streets I ever saw, first electric lights, first gas lights, first bathroom and toilet, first board house, first concrete walks, first streetcar, first movies, . . . first pipe organ, first tunnel, first x-ray machine, first love." All was wonderment and ro-

Table 10.2. Kentucky's Largest Cities, 1910 and 2010

1910		2010	
City	Population	City	Population
Louisville	223,928	Louisville	597,337
Covington	53,270	Lexington	295,803
Lexington	35,099	Bowling Green	58,067
Newport	30,309	Owensboro	57,265
Paducah	22,760	Covington	40,640
Owensboro	16,011	Hopkinsville	31,577
Henderson	11,452	Richmond	31,364
Frankfort	10,465	Florence	29,951
Hopkinsville	9,419	Georgetown	29,098
Bowling Green	9,173	Henderson	28,767

Source: 1910, 2010 US Census.

Many Kentuckians in the nineteenth century still lived in houses that resembled this homestead in Eddyville. (Kentucky Historical Society Collections, Frankfort, KY)

mance. As towns grew in size and became part of a real urban setting, however, they faced new concerns. Soot from hundreds of chimneys caused "the smoke nuisance." Gatherings at the saloons of the city led to disorder, and crime erupted. Cities constantly struggled to keep streets free of the tons of manure and gallons of urine deposited daily by horses and mules. Small-town Kentucky gradually emerged into urban Kentucky and found both benefits and problems in that transformation.

For a very long time, however, the agrarian ideal lived on, even in parts of the urban commonwealth. In the heart of the Bluegrass, for example, where "the horse is the first citizen," out-of-state observers usually focused on the country estates and thoroughbred farms with their pastoral ethos. They noted that Lexington had an English, aristocratic, preindustrial tone. One visitor thought Lexington characteristic of all small Kentucky towns, "slow, easy going and taking but little thought of tomorrow." Native son James Lane Allen described Lexington and its surroundings as a place where an honored name brought instant respect, where the ideal of the rural gentleman prevailed, and where love of the land dominated the industrial mindset. Lexington and other Kentucky cities, such as Paducah, Owensboro, or Ashland, found that an almost rural orientation would long war with the outlook of urban boosterism.

In late nineteenth and early twentieth-century Kentucky, the urban frame of mind ruled only in two areas—Louisville and the communities near Cincinnati. The state's only real metropolis was Louisville. At the beginning of the twentieth century, when only one of every five state residents lived in places with populations greater than twenty-five hundred people, nearly half of all urban dwellers in Kentucky lived in Louisville.

Even then, the urban life of Louisville retained many small-town aspects. Local shops functioned like country stores, poorer areas had outdoor toilets—Louisville had twelve thousand as late as 1935—no sewage disposal existed, and neighbors helped neighbors. Even the clothes worn by some urban dwellers might resemble those of their rural counterparts. Men dressed in formless brogan work shoes that fit either foot (until the 1880s), unbleached jeans and overalls, and rough shirts. No underwear or shoes would likely be worn in summer. Women typically wore long, shapeless dresses, except for church. Yet clothing patterns did demonstrate the city's differences from rural Kentucky, for a stroll down any well-to-do street would reveal fashionable women wearing tight corsets, wire bustles, high-top shoes, and heavy skirts that brushed the ground. Since a glimpse of a woman's ankles was considered almost scandalous, unseen legs were quietly covered by more utilitarian stockings. These women's male companions might escort them while outfitted in hot, highly starched detachable collars and cuffs, a fancy vest with a watch fob, and a derby or straw hat. Styles would vary, but not until the 1920s would drastic fashion changes take place.

Louisville's size made it different from rural areas, not only in fashion, and magnified the distance between urban and agrarian Kentucky. With two hundred thousand people in 1900, the city at the Falls of the Ohio was the eighteenth largest city in the United States and was five times larger than any other Kentucky place. In some ways, the characteristics of Louisville that visitors observed were simply those of Kentucky writ large. A voting scandal involving a dozen people in a small town might not even be noticed; one in Louisville, involving hundreds, would make front-page news. A dispute between workers and one business in a smaller Kentucky city might never be known, but a labor strike in Louisville would be widely discussed. Brothels or a "fast" woman might exist in almost every small town, but in the Falls City, the houses of prostitution operated so openly that they even published the innocently titled *Souvenir Sporting Guide*, which touted for visitors the attractions of such establishments as those of Madame LeRoy, Lizzie Long, and Mother Mack. A Harrodsburg preacher in 1888 confessed to his diary that three "large, healthy, handsome . . . whores" had accosted him in Louisville, and one "was so kind and cordial, I should have yield[ed] to my low passion. . . . But I escaped." If labor problems, election fraud, and charges of moral laxity resulted in part simply from the city's size, other differences made Louisville more unique. It was urban; a majority of the state's population would not live in urban areas until 1970. It was prosperous; much of Kentucky was not. Its population included large numbers of blacks and foreign-speaking immigrants; the commonwealth had few such persons in most areas. Louisville could offer those who lived in its environs such things as street vendors, home deliveries of milk

and beer, and fresh ice. It also provided easily accessible public schools, fine restaurants, convenient banking, much industry, diverse entertainment, plentiful jobs, and more. Most Kentuckians did not have such options. And if all these benefits came with a price tag that included greater vice, more pollution—the city was the sixth dirtiest in the nation as late as 1931—less personal stature, and a dependence on others for livelihood and food, more and more Kentuckians seemed willing to pay that price for urban living as the years passed.

Leisure Time

All across Kentucky, in urban places and rural ones, among all races and both sexes and all classes, people continued to find release from their work and woes through a wide variety of entertainment. After the war's end, Kentuckians in the main still followed long-established patterns but eagerly adopted a few new ones.

Little changed in the home, for people looked to themselves for entertainment. They either told stories, sang songs, or listened to music played on banjos, fiddles, or perhaps a piano. In other homes, reading individually or aloud to the family proved popular. One woman remembered that, as a result, "the printed word was sacred to us." Kentuckians played board games, such as checkers or Parcheesi, as well as card games. Many families frowned on dancing, but others enjoyed it with passion. They would have "dance parties" in their yards or would form a club that had dances on a regular schedule. Such goings-on disturbed a Livingston reporter, who wrote that "there is a hop every night, the boys and girls seem to have the devil in their heels but nothing in their heads." Yet for all that, the most common form of entertainment was simply conversing with neighbors, relatives, and friends. A young Madison County woman told how she and a visiting friend had spent an enjoyable and simple day, walking in the forest. They had gathered some flowers, stopped and talked, while listening also "to the warble of the birds . . . and the lowing of the cattle in the distance." Plucking a few dogwood blossoms for their hats, they then heard the dinner bell calling them home. Such pleasant and slow-paced pleasures sometimes came at a cost, for certain places seemed to have an endless parade of visitors, who gave tired hosts no rest or time alone. After a period of two months of constant visitors, an exhausted Woodford County woman cried out, "Talk, talk, talk until I was nearly *dead*." Yet for some people in the state, that talk—in reasonable amounts—might be their favorite entertainment.

For others, however, entertainment choices were varied. Food-oriented pursuits, such as hunting and fishing, or work-oriented ones, such as cornhuskings, offered opportunities to meet people and socialize. Picnics, hay rides, and sleigh rides produced similar results. On a more formal scale, an activity presented as educational—the Chautauqua—did much of the same thing. Most medium- or large-sized Kentucky towns had a parklike Chautauqua grounds, where for a two-week period each summer gatherings would take place. Participants lived in rented cottages and tents amid landscaped walks and lagoons. A dining hall, a library, and an auditorium were also on the grounds. Mornings offered temperance addresses, Bible classes, music lessons, teacher workshops, and talks on civic betterment, while afternoon fare included concerts or education-oriented lectures. In the evening, a featured speaker regaled listeners, who then went on in the cool of the twilight, strolling and

hearing more music in the distance. Owensboro's Chautauqua featured a twelve-thousand-seat auditorium, a bowling alley, and train delivery to the grounds. In 1903 popular orator William Jennings Bryan of Nebraska delivered its main address, and the next year Louisville editor Henry Watterson presented his talk on "Money and Morals." But by the 1910s smaller traveling tent Chautauquas had replaced the more permanent ones. Two decades later a once-formal part of Kentucky life had vanished, a victim of the increased mobility of the people, who traveled to entertainment; of newer challenges, such as radio and motion pictures; and of difficult monetary times. At its peak, however, the Chautauqua provided not only a local out-of-school educational opportunity but also many societal diversions.

Small tent shows, carnivals, country fairs, "Wild West" shows, circuses, and showboats (for those on navigable waterways) also brought audiences a variety of offerings right in their own communities. Performers—who in the absence of access to national models for comparison seemed wonderfully talented—strange animals, hot-air balloons, daring games of chance, fortune-tellers, races, exhibits, prizes—all these things made such shows the high point of the season at many places. Those Kentuckians who could travel to Louisville saw even greater fare. In 1883 the Southern Exposition provided a regional exhibition. In a building that covered thirteen acres, the exposition's

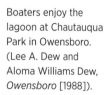

Boaters enjoy the lagoon at Chautauqua Park in Owensboro. (Lee A. Dew and Aloma Williams Dew, *Owensboro* [1988]).

A carnival in Somerset attracted customers with rides and sideshows. (George Tuggle, *Pulaski Revisited* [1982]).

one-hundred-day run brought seven hundred thousand visitors, including the US president. Such popularity made the exposition an annual fixture over the next several years. In 1902 Kentucky began its state fair.

Travel was required for attendance at another popular place—the springs and spas of Kentucky. In relative decline from their antebellum prominence, such places still continued to hold great appeal for middle- and upper-class Kentuckians as places to "flirt, freshen, and fatten." Whether at Dawson Springs in Hopkins County in western Kentucky, Rockcastle Springs in Pulaski County to the east, or Crab Orchard Springs in Lincoln County in the central part of the state, the story was similar. Large, spacious hotels in rural settings offered visitors comfortable chairs, handsome lodging, fine dining, and beautiful ballrooms. Outside, horseback or carriage rides, walks in the woods, swimming in the lake, boating, fishing, tennis, croquet, or visits to the mineral waters all appealed to visitors. Well-dressed Kentuckians danced late into the evening and began their activities again in the morning. But new challenges brought an end to the appeal of the springs, as better transportation took families outside the state, and patent medicines made the water "cures" more readily available. By the early twentieth century most spas had expired.

New forms of entertainment appeared throughout the era, replacing or supplementing the old. Most any town of size, for example, had an opera house, where traveling troupes brought plays and actors who performed both

drama and comedy. Minstrel shows featuring white actors in black makeup, vaudeville acts of comedy and singing, and burlesque shows made the rounds as well. By the first decade of the twentieth century, however, one of the results of a new technological revolution in communication—the motion picture—challenged that popular fare. By 1910 most accessible medium-sized communities had theaters devoted chiefly to showing reasonably priced silent movies. Despite occasional outcries about the "immoral pictures," the new medium had arrived.

Similar changes took place in the field of sports. Some older individual physical exercises continued in the form of swimming, riding, and skating, but the late nineteenth century saw the introduction and acceptance of new sports. By the 1880s bicycling, lawn tennis, and croquet had become popular, and the 1890s saw table tennis and golf begin to make headway, particularly among middle- and upper-class women eager to show their healthfulness.

For the first time, people also became significantly involved in team sports, both as participants and as spectators. The Civil War had spread baseball's popularity, and organized clubs sprang up across Kentucky. The Louisville Grays, a charter member of the National League, had a checkered existence but remained part of the major leagues until 1899. For almost a century, however, smaller clubs formed the heart and soul of the sport. At a time when other team sports were more school oriented and few such institutions existed across Ken-

221

tucky, baseball offered communities a variety of amateur, club, and professional teams around which they rallied and cheered. Unlike many other sports, baseball involved all classes.

Football, a college game at the start, was played in Kentucky as early as 1880, when Kentucky University (present-day Transylvania) defeated Centre College 13 3/4 to 0, under rules very different from today's. One historian has called that game "the first intercollegiate football match in the South." Despite attacks on its violence and use of professional players, football gained much support in the state, and games won front-page headlines by the 1890s.

The newest and least popular of the three major team sports in Kentucky at the start of the twentieth century was basketball. Played chiefly after 1900 and initially by women as much as men, it would grow slowly. It only became very popular after the 1920s, with the development of high schools and the prominence achieved by coaches at the college level in the state.

For those living in the years after the end of the Civil War, then, Kentucky seemed always changing, with new racial rules, new activities, and new technological developments. The slow death of familiar activities, such as visits to the Chautauquas and the spas, added to the sense of change.

Diaries kept by two young Kentucky women during the post–Civil War period demonstrate just how diverse lives could be in the state. From 1900 to 1914 upper-class Lexingtonian Margaret Preston described times filled with games of cards, tennis, croquet, table tennis, and golf and with seemingly endless visits to friends or picnics or visits from her suitors. Days spent reading or listening to phonograph records were followed by nights at concerts, parties, plays, minstrel shows, or club meet-

ings. The presence of maids and a cook freed her to go, by 1910, on "motor-car" rides, football game excursions, and motion picture visits. Only occasionally—such as when her pet bird was eaten by a rat—does the darker side of life appear in her pages.

Twenty-four-year-old Nannie Williams of Graysville, however, told her 1870 diary how she rose at 4:00 a.m. to clean the house before breakfast, then ironed dresses throughout the morning before setting the table for noon dinner. In the afternoon she sewed, then went to the fields to stack a shock of wheat. Married that year to a poor, widowed farmer with four children, she would bear him six more offspring before her twenty-eighth birthday and would raise all ten children. By 1880 the couple's Todd County farm yielded poor crops, and the debt hanging over them caused Nannie to despair that it "is a canker worm that eats the bud out of the flower of happiness. Something will have to be done to pay off or we will suffer." Devoted to her husband and children but frustrated by money problems, she wrote in 1886 that her life involved "cares, duties, suffering on one side, Love, faith, and enduring confidence on the other." Her days of hard work broken by churchgoing and a few visits made up a life not unlike that of her mother and grandmother before her.

In the half century after Appomattox, citizens of the commonwealth would live through times of transition and wondrous discovery. But currents of change only touched some, and then only lightly. Most people still worked and lived in long-established patterns whose roots were more firmly planted in the antebellum world than in the world of the twentieth century. In the main, Kentuckians' lives had not changed a great deal after all in that half century. But change was just over the horizon.

11

Reconstruction, Readjustment, and Race, 1865–1875

Despite much continuity in the postwar lives of Kentuckians, some major changes occurred immediately, chiefly in the areas of race relations and politics. The end of slavery destroyed many of the old racial rules, and new relationships developed. In the defeated South these new relations were forged under the aegis of federal Reconstruction. But Kentucky had officially been a loyal, Union state and did not fall under those controls. Many of the same problems and concerns existed in the commonwealth as in the states of the former Confederacy, but solutions resulted from a different set of circumstances. Kentucky's example suggested what might have occurred in a South without Reconstruction. The results proved discouraging. In the end, the federal government did have to intervene, to ensure that blacks received basic rights in this new postwar world. Under these circumstances, Kentucky went through a period not of Reconstruction but of Readjustment.

Freedom

Many problems grew out of the piecemeal way slavery ended in Kentucky. The Emancipation Proclamation of 1863 had not affected the commonwealth, since the wartime order applied only to states in rebellion. That fact did not keep some sympathetic Union soldiers and officials from encouraging Kentucky slaves to leave their masters, but equally unsympathetic local and state courts ordered their return. Since enforcement of such court decrees could be sporadic, a kind of de facto freedom existed. Slaveholders in Kentucky had had the

opportunity to grasp emancipation with compensation but had totally rejected that course. They could not envision a world without slavery. But had such a route been taken, much of the heartbreak that followed could have been avoided.

In March 1865, shortly before the war's end, the US Congress passed an act proclaiming that all slaves serving as Union soldiers "are made free," and their wives and children were freed as well. Kentucky law did not recognize slave marriages, however, so the whole matter became very complicated. Circuit judges in the state quickly declared the law that applied to spouses and offspring unconstitutional, and the case went to appeal before the state's highest court. That process would take eight months. In the interim, Kentucky-born general John M. Palmer of Illinois, as Federal military commander of the commonwealth, consciously disregarded the circuit court ruling and enforced the congressional decree instead. As a result of that and other actions, an estimated 70 percent of the 225,000 slaves in the state considered their bondage terminated. Most white Kentuckians refused to acknowledge the legality of that situation, and the status of blacks in the commonwealth remained unclear. Were they fugitives or free?

Unquestionably, however, some sixty-five thousand Kentucky slaves remained in bondage after the war concluded. Kentucky and Delaware had not ended slavery, and the institution remained legal in those two states longer than anywhere else in the country. Determined to deal with the situation by action if not by law, General Palmer used his powers under the martial law still in force in Kentucky and in May 1865 issued what became known as "Palmer passes." These permits lifted the tight travel restrictions of the old slave codes and permitted virtually free movement. Some ten thousand or more slaves took matters into their own hands—or feet—and simply walked to a boat and crossed the Ohio River to a free state. Others went to Federal army camps, where a forced return to their owners would be less likely. At a July 4 rally, General Palmer was understood to have told a massive crowd of twenty thousand African Americans that they were free, and they took him at his word. Again, most white Kentuckians bitterly opposed the words and the passes as arbitrary and illegal actions. A Louisville court indicted the general for violating the slave code. As one author accurately concluded, "Slavery died hard in Kentucky."

In an attempt to provide some order to the chaos as well as protection to blacks, the state remained under martial law for five months following the surrender of the last Confederate army. On October 12, 1865, however, President Andrew Johnson ordered the end of military rule in the state. This was one of the few federal actions white Kentuckians applauded. Some African Americans still remained slaves, and others lived in an uncertain legal status, awaiting court decisions to uphold the freedom they understood they had. Now they all lacked the protection of the US Army. Moreover, on December 15, the Kentucky Court of Appeals upheld the earlier lower court decision declaring illegal the federal law regarding the emancipation of black wives and children. These people were still slaves, according to the state decision, and could be returned to their owners. Three days later, however, the entire issue became moot. On December 18, 1865, seven months after the war's end, when the Thirteenth Amendment to the Constitution was declared ratified, all Kentucky slaves became free. It affected really only the two states in which slavery remained legal. One was Kentucky. But the legal question of slavery or freedom had at last been answered.

Yet the question of black rights persisted. Finding answers would take a century or more.

Still, for former slaves, the immediate fact was that they were free at last. Liberty came in degrees, in different ways and at different times at various places across the state. In some isolated areas news came slowly, and it might be presented in confusing ways or withheld entirely. As late as 1867 cases were reported of children who were still held in bondage. One woman remembered finally hearing the news: "I got happy and sung, but I didn't know for a long time what to be free was." She learned.

When freedom did come, former slaves generally experienced similar emotions: "When the news came we were free every body was glad," one remembered. A contemporary observer wrote that "the *consciousness* of *freedom* has got hold of them and abides with them." Some white families, long convinced of the loyalty of their slaves to them, were genuinely shocked when they arose not to the smell of breakfast being prepared by slaves but to the silence of an empty house. Their servants had slipped away in the night. One man who lived at the time remembered that in his area only a very few slaves did not leave. Such changes added to labor problems and angered white Kentuckians. The situation in some households changed little, however, as former slaves willingly stayed on, working for wages and continuing close relationships with white families. But there was a crucial difference: they stayed because they had chosen to do so and could leave when they desired. The working situation may not have been openly modified on the surface, but everyone knew it was different. The former slaves were free.

Freedom brought with it a mobility unknown under slavery, and African Americans flocked to towns and cities to get away from former masters, rural violence, and unpleasant memories. Like others, they sought new lives and better opportunities in an urban setting. As a result, the black population of Lexington, for instance, increased over 130 percent between 1860 and 1870. During that same time, the city's white population grew only a little over 20 percent. Black migrants lived wherever they could—integrated into white areas through housing in back alleys, out-of-

A black family in Glasgow in the post–Civil War period. (J. Winston Coleman Photographic Collection, Transylvania University Library, Lexington, KY)

the-way streets, and older houses, or self-segregated in newly built shantytowns on the city's edge. The same pattern developed in Louisville and in most towns across the state. But the independence blacks found in cities and towns came at a high cost. They lived in dilapidated housing, endured inadequate food and fuel, and suffered widespread disease. Fever took its toll in Owensboro, where a quarter of its population was African American by 1880, and in Paducah, where a third was. Destitute people died in the streets. Some white Kentuckians provided aid and support, but anger directed at the newly freed slaves represented a more typical response. Black attempts at self-uplift were viewed almost as an attack on the status quo. When desperate former slaves stole food in order to survive, whites condemned them, and this condemnation became a part of a self-fulfilling prophecy. It seemed as if many whites wanted to prove slavery had been good by seeing former slaves fail.

Strong black families, however, helped the former slaves survive and succeed in the end. First of all, freedmen who had been separated by sales or distance from spouses and children searched them out and reunited their families. A study of housing in Louisville showed that 70 percent of black children lived with both parents by 1880, a figure similar to the white average. Since the law had not recognized the

marriages of slaves, those who had been living together before the war sought to solemnize their relationships. An 1866 Kentucky law prohibited interracial marriages, with a five-year jail term as penalty, but it also allowed former slaves to purchase marriage certificates. The law, therefore, recognized antebellum cohabitation as a legal marriage and offspring as legitimate. Many, many Kentucky blacks paid with scarce money to formalize their marriage ties. In spite of all the family divisions and disruptions as a result of slavery, black families within a half decade after war's end were basically similar in structure to white families.

The 1866 marriage law proved to be one of only a few concessions made to the former slaves. A white minister in western Kentucky, on hearing of a black barn dance, remarked in his diary, "This is almost an insult to the moral sense & sentiment of our community." Such attitudes were prevalent. Whites had been reared on stories about the anarchy that would result from the removal of the guiding controls of slavery: blacks would rise up and kill whites, so the stories went, or intermarry with them, or utterly disrupt the labor system. But none of that happened on the scale predicted, and one farmer wrote two years after the end of slavery that "we have tried the system of Free Negro labor . . . and they are doing better than the most sanguine of us had hoped." Yet despite evidence to the contrary, white Kentuckians continued to paint dire pictures of the awful consequences should blacks have anything but a subordinate, slave-like status. As a result, one race had public education; the other did not. One race could sit on juries; the other could not. One race could testify against the other in court; the other could not. And one race could use violence to oppose any action that sought to advance black equality.

Kentucky was a violent state for both races in the 1860s and beyond, but the intensity of the actions directed against former slaves exceeded anything experienced by whites. Sometimes white antagonism emerged as economic opposition, such as a refusal to sell land to blacks for them to build schools or churches. At other times and places threats preceded violent outbursts, and blacks were forced to leave whole areas of the state. A band of five hundred whites in Gallatin County, for example, drove hundreds of blacks to flee across the Ohio River. Finally, white hostility could explode directly into physical force. During a two-week period in 1867 some sixteen whites in Kentucky were arrested on separate charges of beating former slaves. The next year brought the account of a black woman who accidentally brushed against the dress of a county judge's wife and was caned so hard by the judge that she acquired a scar. Such events unfortunately were not rare. In a single month in 1868 a black school was destroyed in Monroe County, a school and two churches were burned in Bullitt County, and a teacher of a black school in Mayfield was driven from town by a mob.

Hatred also brought death. Between 1867 and 1871 more than one hundred blacks were lynched in Kentucky, and dozens more were killed by other violent means. As author Robert Penn Warren later wrote, "To a certain number of contemporary citizens the Civil War seemed to have been fought for the right to lynch without legal interference."

Groups of self-styled "Regulators" virtually controlled the central Kentucky counties of Anderson, Mercer, Marion, Lincoln, and Boyle. Groups called Skaggs Men, the Crab Orchard Gang, and the Bull Pups, often numbering well over a hundred each, used violence to try to give them control over a new world they did not want. They lynched people of both races and drove off entire communities of blacks. A harried farmer pleaded for aid from the governor: "We cannot lay down at Night in peace we are aroused Shooting and yeling like mad or Deranged men." All across the state such groups or even more formal bands of the Ku Klux Klan terrorized the countryside. A Freedmen's Bureau teacher in Bowling Green received a warning: "KU KLUX KLANS! Blood! Poison! Powder! Torch! Leave in five days or hells your portion!" A study of Klan violence in the period concluded that "outrages in Kentucky equaled those elsewhere in size, frequency, and brutality," and a historian recently noted that the commonwealth was the only one of the non-seceding states that had any significant KKK violence. In July 1869, a newspaper reported that the Klan had hanged twenty-five people within a central Kentucky area that was twenty-five miles in diameter and had beaten a hundred more during the previous two years. While some leading citizens and newspapers attacked such extralegal violence, and towns like Henderson outlawed the wearing of masks, others in the state media praised "Judge Lynch." People often remarked in stories they wrote that "many of the best citizens of the city were members of the clan." In Central Kentucky state militia forces operated as a political paramilitary to intimidate blacks, especially when African Americans got the ballot.

It is little wonder that African Americans such as former Union soldier Elijah Marrs formed Loyal Leagues for protection. Living at the time in Henry County, a place "overrun with the K.K.K.," Marrs had windows broken in his house, but by sleeping with a pistol under his pillow, a rifle by his side, "and a corn-knife at the door," he remained unharmed. Marrs would go on to be a teacher, minister, civic leader, and political activist, speaking out later against segregation. But an atmosphere of violence like the one in which he lived could only beget more violence.

The bitter, unrelenting opposition to black

education, advancement, or rights—indeed, to anything that hinted at the possibility of equality—brought forth a response from the federal government. The extent of the resistance to black self-help efforts and the defiant hostility to efforts at economic independence necessitated outside aid if blacks were to have any reasonable opportunities. The Bureau of Refugees, Freedmen, and Abandoned Lands had been organized to deal with the former Confederacy, but its jurisdiction did not extend to Kentucky. With the state's recent history, however, the head of the organization, General Oliver O. Howard, directed that it supervise the former slaves of Kentucky as well. Opposition was immediate, for the Freedmen's Bureau, aided by a few soldiers, quickly took a limited but active role in trying to secure fair contracts and proper treatment for the state's blacks. Between 1866, when the organization began to operate in the state, and 1869, when its main duties ended, the Freedmen's Bureau proved to be about the best friend former slaves had.

The always underfunded and understaffed Freedmen's Bureau, which never had more than fifty-seven officials for what was then the 110 counties of the state, provided small amounts of food and clothing to destitute blacks. It operated a hospital in Louisville, and it supervised and, if necessary, voided apprenticeship contracts, which seemed almost an attempt to reestablish slavery. One such typical 1866 contract in Warren County ordered that James Watthall, "a freed boy of color of the age of seven," be bound to a white man "until he arrives at the age of 21 years, to learn the trade, art, or mystery of farming." Most important, however, the Bureau helped establish schools across Kentucky, which were in most instances the only educational facilities available for blacks. By November 1867, 97 schools, employing 117 teachers, had 5,610 pupils; a year and a half later, nearly 250 schools had an attendance of 10,360. Unlike the situation in the former Confederacy, where white northern teachers tended to predominate, 80 percent of the teachers at the Freedmen's Bureau schools in Kentucky were African American. Among the seventeen states where the Bureau operat-

ed, Kentucky usually ranked third or fourth in attendance and first or second in the percentage of school-age blacks in school. In fact, by 1869 probably a greater part of the black student population attended classes than did the white. Freedmen's Bureau schools provided basic instruction only, but they fulfilled a fundamental need for former slaves.

It is remarkable the Freedmen's Bureau schools did as well as they did, for almost every effort met resistance. An agent was murdered, schoolhouses were burned, teachers were beaten, and students were threatened and killed. Reports repeated the same story over and over: in 1867 former slaves had been the victims of 20 killings, 18 shootings, 11 rapes, and 270 other cases of mistreatment; in January 1868, "there is certainly a very determined and a very bitter opposition to the education of the negro"; in November, "Armed and Masked bands of men exercise unlimited sway."

The Freedmen's Bureau had been established in Kentucky because the state's citizens had not accepted "responsibility for the human needs of freedmen." The commonwealth's inaction or opposition had brought federal intervention, but the Bureau itself grew to be so hated that even greater violence resulted. The organization became both part of the solution and part of the problem. One study concluded that "Kentucky had the dubious distinction of being in the forefront in its violent opposition to the activities of the Freedmen's Bureau."

Whites who were already angry over military rule, federal resistance to state court decrees, and what they perceived as unconstitutional actions concerning slavery struck out against the Bureau as yet another interference in their lives. Unfortunately, white Kentuckians did not see that they could have avoided much of the tragedy that they brought on themselves through some basic humanitarianism and fairness. But for black Kentuckians, without some of the rights provided in the North and without the federal protection given to African Americans in the defeated South, they existed in what one historian called "a new, raw kind of middle ground both north and south of freedom and equality."

Political Decisions, 1865–1868

If racial adjustments constituted a major part of the shifting ground that made up postwar Kentucky life, political readjustments took place almost in quicksand. The fluid political situation was uncertain, unstable, and unsteady, and for a time Kentuckians tried to make sense of a world that featured three virtually new political parties.

In antebellum times, the Whig Party of Henry Clay had dominated, but with Clay's and his party's death in the 1850s, new challenges had come forth. These were not met before the war came, and the conflict changed all the rules. Now, three groups—former Whigs, former Unionists, and former Confederates—were the prizes the parties sought to gain. Even the causes prewar Democrats had supported, North or South, divided them. In the political card game, all earlier bets were off, and new hands were being dealt. All parties wanted to make certain they could win.

What were really all-new parties emerged. The Union Party, as it was sometimes called, had the best-defined principles and was the most stable. It soon became known as the Republican Party. Representing the victors in the war and the party that controlled national policy, Kentucky Republicans supported Reconstruction in the South and the adoption of the Thirteenth, Fourteenth, and Fifteenth Amendments, giving former slaves rights as citizens and voters. They also early waved the "bloody shirt" and reminded voters that theirs was "the party of the patriot soldiers who saved the government . . . the party of the widows and orphans," whose husbands and fathers had died putting down the rebellion. Consisting chiefly of former Unionists, and with some former Whigs in its ranks, the state party consciously adopted more moderate stances than did the Radical Republicans at the national level. Yet it also sought to have Kentucky perceived nationally as a loyal state deserving of rewards. Republicans in the commonwealth saw themselves as the progressive, "modern" force in the state, the faction that would reshape Kentucky along the lines of the developing North.

Opponents sought to tar Republicans with the brush of radicalism. Calling them Red Republicans, Radicals, Radical Abolitionists, or Jacobins (referring to revolutionary France), those in opposition pictured Kentucky Republicans as bloodthirsty militarists who were seeking, as the *Flemingsburg Democrat* stated, a nation "where liberty is swallowed up by . . . anarchy." Attackers proclaimed that these radicals wanted black suffrage, even racial equality, and would support any actions, constitutional or otherwise, to destroy the rights of white southerners and to promote black privilege.

The Conservative or Southern Rights Party, as it was sometimes termed but more often simply identified as the Democratic Party, spearheaded this attack. A Frankfort paper said the group was led by rebels "*subdued,* but not *repentant.*" Called "the secession Democracy" by its enemies, the party did include many former Confederates and their supporters. But from the beginning it also numbered in its ranks former Unionists who had turned against the national administration over questions involving military, constitutional, and racial matters. Both Democrats and Republicans had former Whigs and former Unionists in their parties, and both parties attempted to attract those former voting blocs. Democrats made their appeals by calling for what amounted to a return to the past, as they opposed, in general, all the constitutional amendments, and fought at first any movement toward extending black rights. They also indicated that they—and Kentucky—must speak for the South because only their "free" and "unconquered" state could represent southern interests against the national radicals. While Republicans looked northward for their model, Democrats looked southward. The *Kentucky Gazette,* published in Lexington, presented the Democratic arguments clearly in its July 4, 1866, issue. It proclaimed that the question was "whether we will yield up the last vestige of the institutions reared by Washington and Jefferson, and bid adieu to that constitutional liberty . . . or whether we will listen to the syren song of the Jacobins [Republicans], and . . . overturn the Constitution of the country." In response, Kentucky Republicans praised their martyred hero Lincoln and said that his more modern vision must be followed, rather than that of the recent traitors who had sought to destroy the Union.

In all this, however, a third party lurked, seeking votes. Called the Conservative Union or Constitutional Union Democratic Party, it sought to build its base among former Whigs who disagreed with both the "radical" policies of the Republicans and the reactionary ones of the Democrats. It also wooed Unionists who could not stomach alliance with either the increasingly Confederate-dominated Democrats or the black-oriented Republicans. Samuel Haycraft, in a May 1866 letter to a newspaper editor, spoke for those who feared, as he did, voting for an "Abolition" party or a secessionist one. He belonged to "a class of men, old-line Whigs and Democrats" who had supported the Union, but not the end of slavery as it was now occurring. Should either the Democrats or the Republicans adopt extreme stances, then the Constitutional Unionists might develop into a major force.

The three parties engaged in a propaganda war to sell their viewpoints to undecided voters, and the issues were chiefly national ones—Reconstruction in the South, racial concerns, and constitutional matters. Kentucky's political future was being shaped not on state questions but on even broader ones. Citizens had to decide what they wanted their future to be. They made their choice very clear, very quickly.

The initial opportunity to test the strength of the various groups came in the state election held in August 1865. (Some federal elections were held separately, in November.) Some months earlier, the Kentucky General Assembly had rejected the Thirteenth Amendment freeing the slaves, by a vote of fifty-six to eighteen in the house and twenty-three to ten in the senate. The only support for it had come from northeastern and southeastern Kentucky. The Thirteenth Amendment remained a key issue; Unionists (Republicans) supported it, and Conservatives (Democrats) opposed it. The state continued under martial law, and the military did influence the vote in some places, but overall the Conservatives carried the day. They

elected a state treasurer, five of nine congressmen, and a majority of the legislature. Republicans were worried.

Well might they be. The new general assembly again refused to ratify the Thirteenth Amendment, then angered some Unionists by repealing the Wartime Act of Expatriation, which had deprived Confederates of political and civil rights. As a result, former Confederates suffered no reprisals, and the governor began granting pardons to soldiers under indictment for actions taken during the war. Former Confederates quickly began to retake leadership posts in their communities and state. An official of the Freedmen's Bureau noted that in Christian County, nothing had been done about the shooting of a former Union soldier because "our county officials are all rebel." At the state level, the next six governors would either be former Confederate soldiers or men who had been wartime southern sympathizers. The new heroes were not those who had victoriously defended a now less-popular vision, but rather those who had waged war against it. The pro-Union narrative faded; the victors lost the peace. And in the longer struggle over interpretation and memory, the southern version won out as well.

That fact became even clearer in what would normally have been a minor, off-year race, the race for clerk of the Kentucky Court of Appeals in 1866. Instead it became a testing ground regarding the meaning of the conflict, with the Democrats running Judge Alvin Duvall of Georgetown. He quickly attacked the "Yankee agents" of the Freedmen's Bureau and that group's "vile usurpation" of state powers. Both the Conservative Union Party and the Union (Republican) Party had candidates in the field, but just five weeks before the election, the two parties united behind former Union general Edward H. Hobson of Greensburg, a man who had captured the Confederate John Hunt Morgan. But Unionist hero status meant less than Hobson's advocacy of the Thirteenth and Fourteenth Amendments, and Democrats labeled him a radical who had supported the "robbery" of one hundred million dollars' worth of slave property through uncompensated emancipation. Bitterness erupted on election day, and some twenty people were killed in disputes across the state. Democrat Duvall won a convincing victory, obtaining 95,979 votes compared with Hobson's 58,035. The pro-Union *Frankfort Commonwealth* summarized accurately the results: Unionists "have been out-numbered or out-generaled, the great engine used against them having been, as usual, the negro."

This election was but one of several preliminary skirmishes before the 1867 battle for major political office, the governorship of the Commonwealth of Kentucky. The victories went consistently to the Democrats. First, the legislature of January 1867 overwhelming defeated, by votes of sixty-two to twenty-six and twenty-four to seven, the proposed Fourteenth Amendment to the US Constitution, giving blacks citizenship and certain other protections. Next, in a three-way fight that ended with the Constitutional Union forces combining this time with the Democrats, incumbent US senator Garrett Davis of Bourbon County won reelection for a six-year term. A former Whig and former Know-Nothing, Davis had become a wartime Democrat, and he made the transition to peacetime victory. Then in May 1867, in a special congressional election, Democrats won all nine seats in races that frequently featured all three parties. A disgusted Republican wrote, "Kentucky is today as effectually in the hands of rebels as if they had every town and city garrisoned by their troops. . . . What is to become of the poor blacks and loyal white men God only knows."

The answer become common knowledge with the gubernatorial race decided in August 1867. Sixty-five-year-old Democratic nominee John L. Helm of Elizabethtown had been a Whig governor of the state in the 1850s. One of his sons had been killed fighting as a Confederate general in the Civil War. While the rest of the ticket included one former Union officer, it also featured a Confederate who had ridden with Morgan and several wartime southern sympathizers. Terming this ticket a "theft of all the offices by the rebels," old Unionists, including current governor Thomas E. Bramlette

and Lieutenant Governor Richard T. Jacob, organized a third-party convention, called themselves the Conservative Union Democrats, and nominated William B. Kinkead of Lexington. Both groups chastised Radical Reconstruction policies and opposed granting further rights to blacks. The main difference seemed to be that the Conservative Unionists wanted recognition of their wartime accomplishments and a limit on the growing strength of former Confederates in the Democratic Party. Republicans had been unable to forge another merger with the so-called third party, for their differences on policy were too great, and the Republicans offered instead a slate headed by former Union colonel Sidney M. Barnes of Estill County. His support for the unpopular Fourteenth Amendment overshadowed moderate words that suggested a quick end to military rule in the South. The results indicated how Kentuckians felt: "We have met the enemy, and—we are their's," wrote the editor of the *Maysville Republican*. Democrat Helm won 90,225 votes, Republican Barnes got 33,939, and Conservative Unionist Kinkead polled but 13,167. Two-thirds of the voters had gone Democratic, and Republicans won only 17 seats in the 138-person general assembly. Happy Democrats rejoiced that they had rid the state of "the Curse of Radicalism." Republican editor William O. Goodloe of Lexington's *Kentucky Statesman* spoke for his side when he angrily cried out, "What [Confederate general] Bragg failed to do in 1862, with his army and banners, the people of Kentucky, five years later, have done; they have given the State over into the hands of those who are and have been the enemies of the Union." Others lamented that "the foulest and most inexcusable treason is rewarded." Some of the party called on Congress to bring in the military and initiate Reconstruction policies. The *Frankfort Commonwealth* confessed, "The 'Lost Cause' is found again in Kentucky."

Republicans erred in attributing Democratic success totally to the former Confederates in that party. The scope of the Democratic victory showed that many former Unionists simply could not support Republican policies on race and other issues. These "belated Confederates" had joined the opposition instead. In the fight for the former Whigs, both parties had made gains, but that was not enough for the Republicans. To forge a winning coalition, they had needed to bring in even more Whigs. A study of Caldwell County in western Kentucky showed that, of those who had opposed the Democratic Party as Whigs in 1848, only 41 percent voted against the Democrats twenty years later. Similarly, a statewide survey of two dozen prominent prewar Whigs found that thirteen had become postwar Democrats and eleven had become Republicans. In short, the powerful former Whig block had divided fairly equally. Of the twenty counties that had voted Whig consistently before the 1850s, only five— all in the Unionist Kentucky mountains—had voted Republican in 1867. In the struggle for the hearts, minds, and votes of Unionists and Whigs, the Republicans had met defeat.

The year 1867 marked the effective demise of the Conservative Union third-party movement. Ironically, it also marked the death of the man responsible for their immediate defeat. Ill during the campaign, Governor Helm could not leave his home and was sworn in there. Just five days later, on September 8, 1867, Helm died, and his lieutenant governor, John White Stevenson, took over the gubernatorial term. A wealthy, fifty-five-year-old attorney from Covington, Stevenson was the son of a Speaker of the US House from Virginia and had followed his father's path into Democratic politics as a Kentucky congressman and southern sympathizer. Now he inherited a state divided on race, inundated with violence, and mired in debates about federal-state relations. But his immediate task was to win a special election to fill the rest of the unexpired term, a contest that took place in August 1868. Even though the new governor proved to be a less-than-dynamic speaker, he had no third-party opposition, for a change, and numerous national issues to attack, as usual. The result was a landslide victory over Republican R. Tarvin Baker, on a vote of 115,560 to 26,605. Winning more than 80 percent of the vote, the Democrats ruled supreme in the state. For almost the next three decades they would continue to do so.

Bourbons and New Departure Democrats

Democrats forged an uneasy alliance, however. They could usually unite at election time and win victories, but many cracks and blemishes developed in their armor.

Part of the problem lay in divisive sectionalism and the divergent interest groups operating in Kentucky. People in different regions of the state—western, central, northern, and eastern—had varied interests and sought to protect and advocate their own positions. Commercial forces struggled with agricultural ones. City competed with city, and leaders with leaders. The old hemp-growing Bluegrass and the new tobacco-growing western Kentucky areas, the railroad towns and those without rails, the old power blocs and the new all contested for power within the party.

Philosophical differences also arose, and, for a time, two major factions split the party. Yet it would win almost all the elections for nearly thirty years. On one side stood the so-called Bourbon Democrats. Like the Bourbon royal family of France, they forgot nothing and learned nothing. Led by conservatives, like J. Stoddard Johnston of Frankfort's *Kentucky Yeoman* and former Whig George Washington Craddock, the chairman of the Central Committee, they initially controlled the Democratic Party and opposed almost any variations from the old, prewar order. They sought security from the chaos of the present by seeking to return to earlier ways, refused to recognize change brought about by Reconstruction, and, according to one writer, "seemed to worship at the shrine of the dead past." On racial issues, they agreed with the 1867 assertion of the *Kentucky Gazette* that an African American was only capable to be "a hewer of wood and a drawer of water to the white man." Strong advocates of low taxation and limited state aid to education, the Bourbons supported an extremely restricted role for government in the lives of Kentuckians.

The New Departure Democrats opposed them. So named because they sought to break away from old issues and forge a new Kentucky, the New Departure forces counseled acceptance of the federal amendments so that Reconstruction could be hurried along and ended. They wanted not to refight the war in the press but to put it all behind them and move ahead. Supporting a state and federal role in government and the economy that harkened back to the philosophy of the old Whig Party, they advocated a vision that included support for industrialization, education, and, to a much more limited extent, some black rights. The Bourbons referred to "the humiliation of this new departure, which is a surrender of the whole subject to radical usurpation and revolution." But able New Departure leaders answered that charge easily. On November 8, 1868, major Louisville papers merged and formed the *Courier-Journal.* Led by its young editor Henry Watterson, it soon became the leading newspaper in the South and made Watterson a national spokesman for his party and his region. In the Bluegrass another former Confederate soldier, William Campbell Preston Breckinridge, already was editing the *Lexington Observer and Reporter.* Both men used their papers to spread the New Departure word. Neither man necessarily favored the federal Reconstruction policy, and neither was a racial egalitarian. But both called for acceptance of the amendments, both spoke out against the Klan and violence, and both promoted internal improvements. In October 1866, W. C. P. Breckinridge issued the call for a New South and a new Kentucky: "Extend her railroads; open up her rivers . . .; dig into her mountain sides and develop her inexhaustible mineral wealth; erect mills and manufactories, and with zeal and energy compete with other parts of the country." More agrarian-oriented Bourbons attacked that vision as only a pale reflection of Republican philosophy, and the factional fight was on.

The Stevenson Administration and Black Rights

The new governor, John W. Stevenson, represented a party that totally controlled the state. The selection of conservative Democratic attorney Thomas Clay McCreery of Daviess County

to fill an unexpired US Senate term, the election of Democrats to all nine congressional seats in the 1868 fall elections, and the presidential vote that year all showed trends. On national issues, Kentucky stood firmly with the southern Democratic viewpoint. As a result, war hero and Republican presidential candidate Ulysses S. Grant received but 39,566 Kentucky votes in the 1868 race, while Democratic hopeful Horatio Seymour of New York carried the state with 75 percent of the vote, a total of 115,889. Kentucky was one of only eight states that supported Seymour (three southern states did not vote in the election). President Grant brought the hated Radical Republican banner to the White House.

Overall, Governor Stevenson tried to steer a middle-of-the-road course between his party's two factions. The chief executive dispatched the state militia to various locales in a largely fruitless effort to stem violence. He favored the establishment of a house of reform for juvenile delinquents and supported a successful school referendum that provided more tax money for education. The New Departure group supported all these moves. Yet at the same time Stevenson opposed almost all attempts to expand black rights and did not speak out against initiatives designed to limit those rights even further, actions the Bourbons advocated. On the question of black testimony, for instance, Stevenson first took the conservative stance. By Kentucky law, blacks could not testify in court against whites. But under the US Civil Rights Act of 1866, when African Americans were denied their right to testify, the cases could be taken to federal court, where black testimony would be allowed. Republicans and some of the group that would be called New Departure Democrats advocated that Kentucky pass legislation allowing black testimony, thus returning Kentucky cases to Kentucky courts. The bill failed in 1867, and that year the state's highest court declared the Civil Rights Act unconstitutional in regard to the issue of testimony. Once again the national and state judiciaries stood in conflict, as a federal lower court soon upheld the Civil Rights Act as constitutional. In 1869 the legislature once more refused to modify the state law, and Governor Stevenson supported a move to take the issue to the US Supreme Court. State action thus was delayed for two more years.

Meanwhile, individuals took stands on the issue, often at great political cost. New Departure leader W. C. P. Breckinridge, for instance, ran for commonwealth's attorney in 1868 and at a gathering was accused of supporting black testimony. He responded: "Fellow-citizens, the charge my opponents urge against me is true. I am aware that this avowal will most likely defeat me in this canvass, for you are not ready to view this question calmly and dispassionately. Your prejudices blind your judgement. . . . In the after days, when the passions of this hour shall have cooled, when reason shall assert her sway . . . in that hour you will approve though now you condemn me." Facing certain defeat after that open acknowledgment of his views, he withdrew from the race. Not until 1871 did Governor Stevenson support black testimony, but his last legislature defeated it once more. With local judges now being indicted in federal court for denying black testimony, however, the Kentucky General Assembly in 1872 finally passed a bill giving blacks the same legal rights held by whites in the state's courts. Ironically, only a few months later the US Supreme Court gave some support to Kentucky's appeal, but the matter had been decided by then.

In the meantime, an even greater fight was going on. The proposed Fifteenth Amendment to the US Constitution gave black men the right to vote, but the state legislature in January 1869 had rejected the proposed measure by votes of twenty-seven to six and eighty to five. Yet as each month passed, more and more states ratified the amendment, and it was only a matter of time before the proposition became the law of the land. The *Covington Journal* protested the "infamy" of the idea, the *Paris True Kentuckian* called the proposal "a villainous innovation," and Bourbon leader Craddock termed it unconstitutional. Angry Democrats said that theirs must be "a white man's party," free of any black voters. When declared ratified on March 30, 1870, the amendment enfranchised thousands of blacks, most of whom were expect-

Kentuckian and US Supreme Court Justice John Marshall Harlan. (Library of Congress Prints and Photographs Division)

ed to vote Republican—if they could. Some towns and cities imposed lengthy residence requirements for voting or changed their boundaries to omit areas of significant black population and thus remove potential voters. Those subterfuges eventually failed. More commonly blacks voted, amid some violence but without major problems. A few scratched the Democratic ticket, but most voted for the party of Lincoln. They and their descendants continued to do so for the next seven decades. Many previously Democratic areas with sizable black populations suddenly saw a two-party system develop overnight, as blacks began to vote Republican. In the 1870 election in Danville, for example, the winning Republican count of 276 consisted of 59 votes from whites and 217 votes from blacks. The losing Democrats had 203 votes; only 5 of these came from black voters.

Governor Stevenson would not have to face these new voters directly in the future, for he had been selected by a joint vote of both houses of the legislature to replace incumbent McCreery as US senator from Kentucky. Since senators continued to be elected by the legislature and not by popular vote, and since the Kentucky General Assembly remained heavily Democratic for decades, the US senatorship would stay solidly in that party's hands. In February 1871 Stevenson resigned as governor to take up his new position the next month, leaving behind an administration constantly troubled by turmoil and conflict. Since Stevenson had vacated the lieutenant governor's post to become governor when Helm died, the president of the Kentucky Senate, Preston H. Leslie, now became governor—the third person to fill the office in the four-year term.

The Leslie Years, 1871–1875

Facing an August 1871 election for a full four-year term, Governor Leslie tried not to alienate either faction of his party, thus to ensure his re-election. He had usually followed such a path. Born in present-day Clinton County, Leslie had overcome poverty and a limited education to enter the legal profession. A successful Whig legislator, Leslie had turned to the Democrats after Clay's death. He had gone through the war years as a slaveholder opposed to secession but sympathetic to the southern cause. Now in 1871, he ran on a states' rights platform that opposed the "revolutionary" spirit of the "unconstitutional" Fourteenth and Fifteenth Amendments and just about everything connected with the Republican administration of U. S. Grant.

With African Americans voting in a governor's race for the first time, Republicans voiced more optimism, particularly once their gubernatorial choice was made. John Marshall Harlan represented the "new" Republican of the commonwealth, although he came from an old Kentucky family. Son of a Whig congressman, he had been a prewar Whig state adjutant general at age eighteen. When war came, the well-educated and capable Harlan had joined the Union Army, then resigned later to accept election as attorney general of Kentucky. A slaveholder who opposed the Thirteenth Amendment and

the Freedmen's Bureau, he had first joined the postwar third-party forces but with their demise went to the Republicans. Harlan was one of those leaders who matured in politics. When his earlier, conservative racial stands were pointed out, he replied simply: "Let it be said that I am right rather than consistent." He soon was recognized as one of the most able Kentuckians and would be named to the US Supreme Court in 1877. In his thirty-three years on the bench there, Harlan became known as the Great Dissenter, famous for his defense of minority rights—a stance perhaps influenced by the fact that he had grown up with a mulatto man who may have been his half brother. "The People's Judge," Harlan took courageous stands and spoke for the future with dissents that stressed "Our Constitution is color-blind, and neither knows nor tolerates classes among its citizens." He would later be named one of the Supreme Court's dozen greatest justices.

By the 1871 governor's race, the Republican Party, like its Democratic counterpart, had finally stabilized and had taken on the characteristics it would retain for the next several decades. The Republican Party was a party of contrasts, made up chiefly of economically disadvantaged blacks and eastern Kentucky whites, but led by wealthy and pro-business urbanites such as James Speed and Benjamin H. Bristow, both of Louisville. The combination also included what were termed Post Office Republicans, who joined the party primarily to benefit from the patronage of what were usually Republican administrations in Washington. Some two thousand federal jobs came to the state. But fights over the spoils of office would divide the party, as would disagreements over the role of African Americans. In the end, votes of blacks were accepted and sought, and some further rights were advocated, but Republican candidates statewide remained as white as those the Democrats proposed. Even then, for some in the commonwealth Republicanism was akin to heresy. One politician noted much later that in one Democratic stronghold, "If Christ came to Earth, even the strong Baptists up there wouldn't vote for him if he were on the Republican ticket."

In the 1871 election Harlan appealed to the New Departure Democrats on mostly state issues, as he called for support for education and railroads, an end to lawlessness, and acceptance of the federal amendments. Tall, muscular, and a strong speaker, the red-haired Harlan dominated his bearded friend, the less oratorical and less imposing Leslie, in joint debate, but, in the end, it did not matter. The Democrat began to take more moderate stands, stressed federal instead of state issues, and found that most Kentucky voters simply could not bring themselves to endorse the Republican record nationally. By a vote of 126,455 to 89,299, Leslie won the race. Even with a strong candidate and the support of black voters, the Republican Party could not break free of the shackles of the war and Readjustment. The Republicans' immediate electoral future seemed clear—continued defeat.

A Lexington newspaper had editorialized earlier that "the Kentucky Democracy is a party that hangs very loosely together. The least difference, the smallest dissatisfaction creates a split." Governor Leslie quickly discovered the truth of that conclusion, as a major conflict split not only his party but also the state.

At issue was the Cincinnati Southern Railroad bill, which would support building a line through the central part of Kentucky and tying that area to the South via Chattanooga. Sectionalism quickly arose as supporters of the powerful Louisville and Nashville Railroad opposed this challenge to their near monopoly of the state's rail system. They especially resisted a challenge led by "Yankee" commercial rival Cincinnati. The question was one of power, money, and sectional dominance, and the bitter battle lines divided parties and factions. Some usually pro-railroad New Departure leaders, such as Louisvillian Henry Watterson, opposed the bill, while more conservative central Kentucky Bourbon Democrats favored it. But in 1870 and 1871 votes, the legislature had rejected the bill, despite pleas from one-time presidential candidate and lionized Confederate hero John C. Breckinridge of Lexington. Now in the 1872 Kentucky General Assembly, Leslie opposed the measure. It, neverthe-

less, passed the Kentucky House and gained a tie vote in the senate. Lieutenant Governor John G. Carlisle of Covington cast his deciding ballot in the bill's favor, and it became law. Sectionalism and the L&N had been defeated. That would not always be the case.

Despite passage of this bill that he did not support, Leslie usually collaborated well with the legislature during his term of office. Some much-needed legislation was enacted. Laws passed during his tenure allowed black testimony, increased funding for asylums and correctional institutions, implemented more stringent laws against violence, established a geological survey to determine the state's resources, created a pharmacy board, and, in a particularly important action, began a public system of "colored" schools. An advocate of temperance who did not serve liquor at state functions, the "Coldwater Governor" also signed a law providing for local option elections to decide whether intoxicating drink could be sold.

Politically, Leslie's administration held few surprises. Former Confederate congressman Willis B. Machen of Lyon County was selected to fill an unexpired term in the US Senate, and on-again, off-again Senator McCreery won a full term in 1872. Democrats continued to control the congressional and legislative delegations. The only confusion appeared in the 1872 presidential election, when reform-minded Republicans at the national level rejected what they saw as Grant's scandal-ridden administration and nominated former Whig Horace Greeley of New York as their candidate. They called themselves the Liberal Republican Party. Nationally, the Democratic Party recognized that it could not win the election and endorsed Greeley as well. Henry Watterson led a reluctant Kentucky into the Liberal Republican fold, but to no avail. Greeley carried the commonwealth by a vote of 100,212 to 88,816, but of the thirty-seven states, he carried only five others.

At the conclusion of the Leslie years in 1875, then, the patterns for the next decades seemed established. The Freedmen's Bureau was gone, and Reconstruction was fading as an issue. The third-party movement had died, for the moment. Party factionalism appeared to be receding, and the divisive Cincinnati Southern issue had been re-solved. All the voting blocs were now securely attached to one party or another. In short, many of the concerns troubling Kentucky in the Readjustment years now seemed solved.

Much had been decided, but the role of African Americans had not. In some areas gains had been made. Whites in Kentucky now begrudgingly accepted blacks as citizens and as voters and would not deprive them of their voting rights (unlike the situation farther south). Blacks could now testify in court. By 1876 they sat on some federal juries, and by 1882 on state ones (although that would change). Black lawyers Nathaniel R. Harper of Louisville and George A. Griffith of Owensboro were accepted to the bar in 1871. A new cadre of leaders came to the forefront, including Dr. Henry Fitzbutler, Kentucky's first black physician and editor of Louisville's *Ohio Falls Express*. In Louisville, protests in 1870 caused the city streetcars to be open to all, and they remained so. African Americans could attend an integrated institution at Berea College, where the 237 students enrolled in 1875 included 143 blacks. Blacks also lived physically among whites in cities across the state. Louisville in 1870 had black families residing on three of every four blocks on average. People of color began to run for and win minor political offices. In Hopkinsville, for example, a black man sat on the city council from 1895 to 1907, and others of his race served as deputy sheriff, county coroner, and county physician. In Mount Sterling between 1901 and 1918, at least one African American won election to the city council. In certain locales, blacks and whites sat together at religious services and worked beside each other in coal mines. The integration of blacks into some facets of Kentucky life had occurred.

Yet as the years wore on after 1875, segregation increased in other areas. There were no sudden changes, and just about every community had its own rules and exceptions. But some communities used vagrancy laws to enforce a status for blacks not dissimilar to slavery. More formally, the state penitentiary in 1882 segregated the races at its church services. Two years later, the Kentucky Institution for

Nathaniel R. Harper, admitted to the bar in 1871, practiced law in Louisville. (A. P. Lipscomb, ed., *The Commercial History of the Southern States . . . Kentucky* [1903])

the Education of the Blind set up a separate "Colored Department." Public schools started out segregated and remained so. Residential integration grew less prevalent, and increased segregation in all areas seemed the future for Kentucky blacks. That situation and the continued presence of violence stimulated an out-migration of thousands of black residents, particularly to places like Nicodemus, Kansas, in the late 1870s. The promised land lay elsewhere.

With all that, black and white children continued to play and eat together all across the state. Strong bonds remained between some adults in both races as well. But only an optimistic leader such as W. C. P. Breckinridge could look beyond a present without great hope for blacks to a time when "barriers will be removed, prejudices will die, class distinctions be obliterated. Not at once; not in our day; not without fierce contest; not without heroism and sacrifice; but yet slowly, surely [that] day grows stronger."

12

Decades of Discord, 1875–1900

Politically and socially, the first fifteen years of the last quarter of the nineteenth century were relatively static, save for a scandal here and there. But the last decade of the era proved to be one of the most turbulent in the state's history. Throughout the period from 1875 to 1900, Kentucky unfortunately developed a reputation as one of the most violent places in the United States. Feuds grew almost commonplace, and an Appalachian stereotype entered the American consciousness.

Despite the decades of discord, the state's political order displayed the characteristics that would form the core of the system for many decades into the twentieth century. It was a world of patronage and personal politics, localism and sectionalism, lobbies and little kingdoms, voting blocs and bosses.

The Political System

In a general sense, party affiliation defined how people voted more than anything else. On occasion it ruled individual lives, for some families simply did not associate much with other families of a different political faith. Yet at the local level, when it came to specifics, politics was first and foremost personal. The *Henderson Journal* remarked, "No people in the world are more given to confidence in the value of family strains than our people." While an exaggeration, the comment did indicate the importance of family to voting. Past leaders tended to perpetuate their families in office; families often voted as a bloc. Winning candidates combined as many of those families as possible. Kinship ties remained a key to political success.

Rewards were expected for political support. Voters did not cast their ballots necessar-

ily because of a particular candidate's qualifications or fitness for office. Many understood the system to be one in which those who favored the victor should receive benefits for their aid. At the local level, few challenged a winning candidate's right to name family members to office, and nepotism ran rampant. Fewer still questioned a victor's right to place supporters in appointive offices, even though this practice meant frequent turnover and little opportunity to develop a professional staff. Each community had its leaders around whom voters gathered; each had strong kinship connections that had to be recognized; each had particular local interests to protect.

Added to that localism was a system of county government that made those units semiautonomous, or as Robert Ireland has called them, almost "little kingdoms" unto themselves. Each officer had important powers at a time when relative isolation made the county about the only place where citizens had any contact with government. The county judge, for example, could dispense liquor licenses at his discretion, the sheriff gathered taxes, the justices of the peace—there were two thousand in the state in 1889—served as local jurists hearing cases concerning petty crime, the county clerk recorded legal documents, and the county assessor evaluated property for tax purposes. Local government—not state—built most roads, enforced most laws, collected most taxes, and dispersed most poor relief. It did not always do so fairly or effectively, but it did so locally. By the time of the creation of Kentucky's last county (McCreary) in 1912, Kentucky counties were, on average, the second smallest in area in the United States. Citizens therefore had a very intimate connection with the officials they elected in the state's 120 counties. Elections became even more personal and important. As a minister wrote in 1886: "Politics is the all absorbing question."

Some questions transcended local issues, however. Race could always be pulled out as an issue at election time, for example. But more than that, the state's growing surrender to a pro-southern memory proved potent. The trickle of monuments that arose after 1866 became a flood between 1895 and 1925. Some twenty-three Confederate monuments were erected: only three Union ones went up. In 1901, the Lexington chapter of the United Daughters of the Confederacy placed pictures of Robert E. Lee in each Lexington school. A year later, the legislature funded a home for ex-Confederates at Pewee Valley, then four years after that, prohibited the showing of any play that showed "antagonism . . . between master and slave." By contrast, during the same time, support for a monument to Abraham Lincoln at Hodgenville came mostly from outside the state. Only slowly would Kentuckians belatedly reclaim Lincoln. But Confederate president Jefferson Davis's monument received four times the state support as the meager aid given the Lincoln one, and his birthday would long be a state holiday. Many still worshipped the civil religion of the Lost Cause.

But other, less issue-oriented political forces operated on a somewhat different stage. In Louisville, for instance, "Papa John" Whallen, and to a lesser degree his brother James, built a powerful machine by the 1880s, one based in the Catholic and Irish population centers of the Falls City. By providing jobs, particularly in the police force and city government, assisting those in need with rent or meals, and giving baskets of food and clothes on special occasions, the Whallens built a supportive network, one whose votes they could control. Their Buckingham Burlesque Theater offered scantily clad showgirls and a popular saloon, but behind those areas, in the green room of "the Buck," political careers could be made or broken by the "Buckingham Bosses." In Lexington, Irish immigrant Dennis Mulligan similarly dominated government into the 1880s.

Almost every smaller town and city had its own version, perhaps with a different base but with the same goals—to control votes and win elections.

Various forces could disrupt that local power, particularly powerful lobbies. The most powerful of those in the late nineteenth century was the Louisville and Nashville Railroad. The L&N paid 40 percent of all rail assessments in the state in 1900. Its longtime chief executive officer, the capable and cold Milton Hannibal Smith, openly stated that "all legislative bodies are a menace. In action they are a calamity." He thus determined to reduce the perceived risk to his lines by controlling such bodies as much as possible. Numerous legislators were on the payroll of the well-organized and wealthy L&N as its attorneys in counties through which its lines passed. Others received free travel passes for themselves and their families. Still more benefited from L&N's "suggestions" to its numerous workers on how they should vote in elections. Almost all partook of the railroad's lavish entertainment for legislators, being "freely furnished with whiskey, &c." It is little wonder that one observer noted in 1900: "A man could not be elected justice of the peace or school trustee without the sanction of the Louisville and Nashville politicians."

Other lobbies would come and go. An active lobby for the lotteries, for example, existed through the 1880s, and various agricultural forces asked for legislative support. In the early twentieth century the coal interests and the thoroughbred groups each developed strong forces in the legislature as well.

The lobbies, the localism, the racism, and the expectation of rewards for votes—all created an atmosphere that tacitly accepted or condoned corruption in the voting booth. In 1879 a minister visited a Simpson County canvass and told his diary: "Oh the rabble . . . men aspiring to high offices treating to whiskey & buying up votes." Vote buying, said one observer, "is as common as buying groceries." Even after Louisville became the first American municipality to adopt the use of the secret ballot in 1888, problems continued to grow. One 1909 estimate indicated that up to one-fourth of all votes in the average Kentucky county could be purchased. Two years later a gubernatorial candidate suggested that seventy thousand ballots were bought each year.

The practice went on far into the twentieth century. One county judge recalled that in his mountain county, up to half of the votes would have to be paid for, usually for a dollar or some whiskey. His counterpart in another area recalled voting before friendly election officials when he was but fifteen. Later, he reported, he would pay black transient miners to vote for his party, then would take them en masse to another precinct and have them vote a second time. After that he would have them change their clothes and vote a third time elsewhere. A white voter in another eastern locale remembered selling his vote for four dollars, but, he said, "I was thoroughly rebuked by my father . . . for not holding out for the going rate of seven dollars and a half pint of Heaven Hill bourbon." Fraudulent activity did not end with the buying of votes. Until 1936, the practice of counting the ballots at 10:00 a.m., the next weekday after the election, gave time for returns to be "fixed." As one county judge noted, it was standard practice to call party headquarters to see if the election was tight "and ask them how many they need." In close races, each party held back local totals as long as possible to counter suspicious late results favorable to the other party. Democracy in Kentucky often had several helping hands on election day.

General Violence

Elections took place in a state plagued by violence. Reports make it appear that almost every voting area featured fights and gunplay on the day the votes were cast. The commonwealth seemed immersed in a culture of violence. Once unleashed, the violence that had become so prevalent in the immediate postwar period would not go away. Formally constituted lawless groups, such as the Ku Klux Klan, did not long survive the time when black rights were under debate. The Klan's name, however, often would be attached to more informally organized, self-styled "Regulators," who operated for the rest of the nineteenth century and tried to place their own interpretation of the law on those around them. In a few instances, Regulators may have given some order to isolated counties with ineffective law enforcement, but that result was atypical. Such groups usually contributed to the lawlessness. While they sought to justify their actions by suggesting that they were merely implementing justice, they in fact decided guilt and inflicted punishment arbitrarily and willfully. They allowed no trial by one's peers, heard no evidence, and offered no appeal. Each time they acted, justice in Kentucky became a little more lifeless.

Threats and beatings became commonplace where Regulators ruled, and lynchings sometimes occurred. Between 1873 and 1900, at least 166 lynchings took place. Two-thirds of the victims were black. Mobs murdered with impunity. In October 1899, for example, a Maysville mob took accused killer Richard Coleman from the sheriff, who did not resist. As hundreds watched and then fed the flames, Coleman was set on fire and died a slow death. Later the mob dragged the body through the streets, and people cut off the fingers and toes as souvenirs. No one wore masks; everyone knew who was involved. But no charges were filed, and the lesson for Kentuckians was that the law was not supreme.

Many other examples supported that conclusion. The production of whiskey at home stills had been commonplace and legal for many years, but in 1862 a new federal tax on whiskey production changed that. Failure to pay the tax made "moonshining" illegal, and revenue agents began to try to seize illegal stills and place violators of the law in custody. In 1881, for example, 153 arrests were made. But many communities tacitly accepted the moonshiner. A wall of silence often met the attempts of the revenuers at law enforcement. One county newspaper in 1881 openly proclaimed that "shooting matches and moonshine whiskey are as common as corn bread." Once more, community mores seemed more powerful than established law.

That supposition became even clearer in the way certain communities reacted to individual acts of retributive violence. If a gentle-man's honor and reputation were challenged, deadly responses seemed acceptable. In April 1883, for example, Congressman Philip B. Thompson Jr. of Harrodsburg killed a man he claimed had "debauched" his wife. A jury eas-ily acquitted him. A few years later, *Louisville Times* journalist Charles E. Kincaid report-ed that married congressman William P. Taul-bee of Magoffin County had been found "in a compromising way" with a young woman in the US Patent Office. The story ended Taul-bee's career, and when he encountered Kin-caid in Washington, DC, in 1890, the two ar-gued, and threats were made. Two hours later they met again, and a shot rang out in the halls of the US Capitol. The unarmed Taulbee had been wounded, and he died some days after-ward. Kincaid confessed but was found not guilty in a District of Columbia court on the grounds that he had reacted to threats as a gen-tleman would. In a similar instance, an irate husband discovered his wife with the son of former governor John Young Brown in Lou-isville in the 1890s. He killed both of them but was acquitted under the "unwritten law" that in essence permitted personal revenge in such cases. Many elements of Kentucky society seemed, then, to approve of individual retribu-tion, Regulator violence, and illegal moonshin-ing. The law took second place.

The poor condition of the legal process itself made the challenges to the system even more accepted. In some places the entire judi-ciary was tainted. A Kentucky attorney general found one county's grand jury "made up of the criminals, their close kin, and steadfast friends and admirers." Other locales saw one party or faction or family firmly in control of the whole system, and those in opposition could find little justice. Grand juries that would not in-dict, or courts that would not convict, resulted. Even if a conviction did occur, governors of-ten rewarded political allies by pardoning their friends in the penitentiary. Convicts seemingly incarcerated for life might be free in a matter of months.

Being an enforcer of the law also became dangerous. Even the justices of the common-wealth's courts were vulnerable. In March 1879 Thomas Buford of Henry County approached John Milton Elliott, a former US congressman and now a judge of the state's highest court, on the streets of Frankfort. Upset over a judicial decision of Elliott's, Buford shot him at point-blank range with a double-barreled shotgun. Declared not guilty by reason of insanity, Bu-ford later escaped from an asylum, fled to Indi-ana, and remained free from Kentucky law for two years before he returned voluntarily to the asylum, where he died. In 1884, an attorney who erroneously thought Superior Court Judge Richard Reid of Mt. Sterling had injured his honor in a court decision, whipped and severe-ly beat Reid. A man of the law and a "Chris-tian Gentleman," Reid did not resort to per-sonal vengeance, as even the law allowed, but decided to support legalism over violence. His society, however, generally refuted that course of action. With his support groups gone, his manhood impugned, and his long-held beliefs under attack, the judge committed suicide. The Cult of Honor had claimed another victim.

Group support of the law was shown to be dangerous as well. After three men in Ash-land were arrested for some brutal murders, a mob lynched one of them. The state militia was called out in 1882 to protect the remaining two, and officials were in the process of moving them by water to a safer place when a mob fired on them from a boat and from the shore. Af-ter a furious hail of bullets, the "battle of Ash-land" ended with several wounded soldiers and at least four dead civilians.

Some commentators recognized the effect that all the lawlessness was having on the state. A central Kentucky editor in 1878 called for "a revolution in the moral sense of the com-munity, so that the man-slayer instead of be-ing exalted as a sort of hero, and actually wor-shipped for the very qualities which ought to make all men shun him, will be esteemed for his real worth, and blood guiltiness be regard-ed as it is—as the worst and blackest of crimes against nature." Four years later, after the Ash-land tragedy, another editor in the common-wealth found that little had changed: "Mur-ders are more frequent, punishment is lighter, pardons more numerous, and abuses are more flagrant. . . . The most alarming feature of all is the indifference of the public. . . . Shocking tragedies at their very doors do not startle them to a realization of the evils that are cursing Kentucky . . . and presenting us to the eyes of the world as a reckless, God-defying, reeking band of law-breakers and murderers." In truth, the violent situation these writers decried did not differ markedly from the situation in the South generally at the time. The partisan *New York Times* recognized that fact, even as it unfairly declared that the Elliott assassination "could scarcely have taken place in any region calling itself civilized except Kentucky, or some other southern state." The commonwealth partook of a regional subculture heavily oriented to violent behavior. So it was violent but not unique. In the three decades after 1875, however, another form of Kentucky-centered violence identified the state with a particular, almost unique, kind of killing. Feuding created a stereotype that would curse Kentucky for a century or more.

Feud Violence

One definition of a feud is "a lasting state of hostilities between families or clans marked by violent attacks for revenge." In short, feud violence must take place over time, must involve family, and must have the motive of revenge. Often, actions labeled as feuds did not meet these criteria, and the term was carelessly applied to violence that differed little from that taking place elsewhere. Moreover, much of the so-called feud violence resulted less from family vendettas than from personal, economic, or political causes. Even if wrongly defined and misnamed, however, what was called feud violence did exist aplenty in Kentucky. Place after place saw lives snuffed out and families destroyed.

Most of the feud violence took place in Appalachia after the Civil War, but one of the earliest identifiable feuds did not. The Hill-Evans feud of Garrard County traced its roots back to an 1820 controversy but erupted in full force in the 1850s. It was renewed during the Civil War and finally concluded in 1877, when, according to one report, only one male participant remained alive.

Confused and biased reporting of all the feuds makes a clear picture of what happened elusive. The so-called Underwood-Stamper-Holbrook feud in Carter County, for example, may have been more a struggle between outlaws and Regulators than a feud. But the fighting erupted out of an "old grudge," Civil War antagonisms, and an earlier "Kinney-Carter war." Defending themselves in "Fort Underwood," that family faced, at various times, the Stampers, a law-and-order citizens' group, and a state militia force. Various arrests ended with few convictions. As many as thirty deaths may have occurred. A brief period of calm ended by 1880, when reports once more filtered out of the hills, telling of a band of two hundred Regulators who enforced their clan's version of justice. By that time, though, events in a neighboring county were seizing the headlines.

The Rowan County War of the 1880s, or what some termed the Martin-Tolliver-Logan feud, resulted in at least twenty murders and sixteen other casualties during just a three-year period, in a county whose population never exceeded eleven hundred. Only one conviction occurred. Beginning with some political disagreements in the 1870s, the fighting erupted in an 1884 election dispute that left one man dead and two more, including John Martin, injured. A former Underwood ally, Martin met "Big Floyd" Tolliver in a saloon months afterward, accused him of the earlier shooting, and killed him. Eight days later the Tolliver faction seized Martin from the authorities with a forged order and fired numerous shots into his body.

On one side stood the Tollivers and the Youngs, on the other the Martins, Humphreys, and the Cooks. Each side took turns with retaliatory killings, but the Tollivers gained virtual control of the city of Morehead and of the court system. Finally Daniel Boone Logan, whose father had been killed in the Underwood "War," and who himself initially had been more sympathetic to the Tollivers, was pulled into the violence when he learned that his two cousins had been killed after they had surrendered to the Tollivers. When he confronted Craig Tolliver, he was told to leave town or be executed. If his wife remained, Tolliver said, she would be hired out. An attorney, Logan first requested aid from the governor. When the chief executive rejected his request, Logan sought justice in his own manner and purchased rifles and ammunition. He then armed a group variously estimated at from sixty to two hundred men and surrounded the Tollivers and the town. In a western-style shoot-out in June 1887, the Tollivers were forced to flee a burning building. They were caught in a crossfire, and their leader and three others were killed. Pardons were issued to the Logan faction. In quieter times, a legislative investigating committee called officials in the county inept, inefficient, corrupt, and "depraved." The committee recommended that Rowan County be abolished, but this partial solution was rejected.

Deeper in the mountains, three more feuds also attracted much attention in the 1880s. The Howard-Turner feud in Harlan County had its origins in the pre–Civil War period, and isolated murders had occurred during the 1870s. By June 1889, however, hostilities had become so open that a pitched battle took place, and the Turners withstood a long siege in the courthouse. By the end of the month it was estimated that fifty people had died over the decades of the "troubles." Similarly, the French-Eversole feud in Perry County grew out of a business rivalry and eventually saw the two opposing bands meet in a two-day battle in the streets of Hazard in 1880. By the 1890s the violence had declined, but it left a legacy of bullet holes and empty buildings, forty to fifty deaths, and nearly fifty orphans.

Ironically, what would become the best known of the feuds was not the bloodiest, the longest-lasting, or even the most spectacular of the family "wars." The Hatfield-McCoy feud, nevertheless, received much attention from the media, involved two state governments in its dispute, and became synonymous with feuding. In many ways, the "war" was not unusual: Randolph ("Old Ran'l") McCoy led the Pike County, Kentucky, clan; William A. ("Dev-

il Anse") Hatfield directed the West Virginia group, who mostly resided across the Tug Fork. Disputes concerning the Civil War, failed justice, a hog, economics, and a romance were all prelude to what resulted on election day in 1882. A fight between a Hatfield and three McCoys left the Hatfield mortally wounded. Angry members of his family, distrustful of Kentucky justice, seized the three McCoys, tied them to bushes, and, in an almost ritualistic manner, riddled their bodies with some fifty bullets. One fifteen-year-old's head was virtually blown away by a shotgun blast. Scattered violence took place over the next five years. Then on New Year's Day in 1888, Old Ran'l McCoy's home was surrounded and burned, and a son and daughter were killed. An illegal raid by a Kentucky deputy sheriff ended in some Hatfield deaths and arrests and a court case that involved the governors of both states and eventually the US Supreme Court. A lawful execution by hanging took place in 1890, and some semblance of peace followed. Overall, from twelve to twenty deaths had resulted from a feud that the *New York Times* said "caught the attention of the whole nation."

As that feud faded, a conflict heated up in Clay County. Involving the leading families in the county—the Whites and the Garrards— the violence erupted in the 1880s over longtime business and political rivalries. Each side had various families tied to them by economic, legal, and political alliances—the Bakers and Philpots to the Garrards and the Howards to the Whites. As two students of the conflict wrote, those dependent armies "made it possible for elites to engage in sustained violent conflict through intermediaries." As a result, in 1899 alone, an estimated twenty died violently in the county. Two years later, a truce ended most of the killing, but aspects of the conflict went on for another three decades. A 1932 investigation called for the abolishment of the county as the only way to establish order.

The final major Appalachian violence termed a feud was one of the longest lasting. Violence had plagued Breathitt County since the "little hell" that was the Civil War there, and the so-called Amis-Strong-Little feud

Stock images, such as this one showing members of the Hatfield clan posed around "Devil Anse" Hatfield (*seated, at center*), helped shape the conception of the feuding mountaineers. (West Virginia Archives and History, Charleston, WV)

marked the formalization of the killing. Growing out of Civil War, racial, and political rivalries, as well as family lines, fighting continued for four decades. In 1874 one faction fortified the courthouse, and the militia was called in. Four years later a member of the Little family was arrested for murdering his pregnant wife. As he was being taken to trial, ambushers killed the county judge. The circuit judge disappeared.

A mob again seized the courthouse, several were wounded, and virtual anarchy reigned. Once more the militia marched in and enforced an uneasy peace in a county, where some said a hundred had already died. Religious mountain missionaries, like George Barnes, John Jay Dickey, and Edward Guerrant, began to make their way to what they saw as an ungodly place. Still, the new generation of leaders that had come to the fore in Breathitt County by the 1890s seldom followed the Golden Rule.

Out of the Amis-Strong-Little feud grew its successor, the Hargis-Marcum-Cockrell-Callahan feud. Democratic county judge and businessman James Hargis, aided by Sheriff Ed Callahan, led one group; Republican attorney James B. Marcum and town marshal Tom Cockrell led another. Each group had ties to the earlier feud, some had been involved in economic disputes, and several had connections to families and politicians on both sides. In separate fights Hargis's brother and half-brother were killed; in July 1902 Cockrell's brother Jim was murdered as Hargis and Callahan watched. By November of that year numerous houses and businesses had been burned, and nearly forty deaths had resulted. Marcum would not venture out in public without a young child in his arms, for he knew his enemies would not risk killing a baby. But in May 1903 an unescorted Marcum was shot in the back, then in the head. Two convictions followed, but neither Hargis nor Callahan was found guilty in criminal trials. Their punishments came in other ways. In 1908 Hargis was killed by his drunken son. Later, on an anniversary of Marcum's assassination, Callahan stood by a store window and was wounded by an assassin's bullet. On the ninth anniversary in 1912, a shooter succeeded, killing Callahan as he spoke on the telephone. In essence the feuds in "Bloody Breathitt" and other Appalachian counties had ended. But people went on paying the costs, and like a ghost haunting the state's hills and hollows, the bloody specter of the feuds would long bedevil the people of Kentucky.

243

Kentucky Images and Appalachian Stereotypes

While each so-called feud differed in details and causes, several characteristics did stand out. In the first place, many of the leading citizens of a county were often involved. Entrepreneurial business types often headed one or both factions, although, conversely, virtual outlaws sometimes served as feud leaders. In either case, what one observer called almost "a large, paid army" operated under the guidance of a person who functioned mainly as a medieval feudal lord caring for his men. The fighters might center around a family or political allies but could include others who were little more than "hired guns."

A second characteristic, which writers of the time sometimes submerged by describing the "code of honor" of the mountains, was that the actions taken were generally cruel and cowardly. Honor seldom appeared when ambushes and assassinations proved the favorite method of murder. Pitched battles, usually centered around the symbol of justice, the courthouse, did occur, but usually only because one side found itself trapped and outnumbered. Young boys tied to bushes and executed, unarmed women beaten or shot as they fled a burning house, men shot in the back—these kinds of violence left deep mental scars with the living and produced deeper desires for further revenge.

Finally, while causes of the "wars" differed, a few key elements appeared in what people of the region called "the troubles." Anger escalated into violence because of such factors as Civil War memories, the presence of whiskey at elections, political partisanship, economic rivalries, the ready prevalence of weapons, and an intense localism fed by a restrictive isolationism. Even though the mountains were less static and more nuanced than portrayed at the time, some areas remained very remote. A kind of urban-rural conflict, where external forces intervened adding fuel to more local and traditional ones, may have been a factor as well. But in the end, the ineffectiveness of the law and the consequent lawlessness in a subculture of violence provided the main source of feuds. When no responses or legal redress could be obtained from a biased legal system "rotten to the core," other answers would be sought. A form of culturally approved vigilantism developed, one in which interwoven ties, fed by a limiting environment, produced a bloody personal code. Each resulting act only worsened the situation, and revenge, not justice, soon guided most actions. A widow from the Clay County violence explained how her "chief aim" in life became the avenging of her husband's death: "Each day I shall show my boys the handkerchief stained with his blood, and tell them who murdered him." The circle of violence grew wider with each generation.

The result of what some termed as feud violence for Kentucky and Appalachia would be broad and far-reaching. The immediate effect of most violence proved to be an out-migration of some citizens, a business depression in the affected counties, and suspended growth. While partisan political institutions may have resulted, overall, other effects usually did not last because the great coal boom that struck the region gave some feud-desolated places a rebirth of sorts.

More crucial long-range results grew out of the publicity the feuds generated and the stereotypes that developed. Once almost forgotten by Kentucky and the nation, Appalachia now was suddenly "discovered," and two somewhat contradictory images grew out of the resulting deluge of print stories and silent movies. One stereotype presented the mountain people as "our contemporary ancestors," a people from frontier times, cut off from the world by isolation. As a result, they spoke—so sayeth the commentators—"the English of Shakespeare's time," maintained the earlier ways of life, and preserved old customs. In this benign and pastoral view, hospitable mountain people lived self-sufficient and happy lives as they sat in front of their quaint log cabins, produced quilts, sang ballads, and played their dulcimers. This image perpetuated the past and represented a hope for the future.

A second, much starker and darker stereotype presented Appalachian people as ignorant and immoral, backward and bloodthirsty, poor and primitive. It featured not the home-spun pioneer but a gaunt, bearded feudist with moonshine jug in one hand, rifle in the other, and murder in his eye. That image grew over time into a picture of a people who chiefly "fuss, feud, and fornicate." By 1934 historian Arnold Toynbee concluded that "the Appalachian 'Mountain People' at this day are no better than barbarians."

That stereotype expanded to include all of Kentucky, and the commonwealth as a whole began to be labeled as a violent, lawless place that should be avoided. Between 1878 and 1883, for instance, the *New York Times* called Kentuckians "unreclaimed savages" and "effective assassins," proclaimed the state a "delightful" place to live, "especially if one enjoys anarchy and mobocracy," and concluded that "there is no state in which lawlessness and bloodshed prevail to such an outrageous extent as in Kentucky." The *Chicago Tribune* in 1885 said the commonwealth's civilization had been tested "and found to be barbarism," while an article in *Leslie's Popular Monthly* in 1902 described the author's trip to bloody feudist country "where the sun set crimson and the moon rose red." The stories went on and on, so that the stereotype of violent Kentucky became firmly embedded in the national consciousness.

Both images—the forgotten pioneer and the violent hillbilly—had a basis in fact. Some elements of the romantic view did exist. Kentucky was also a very violent state, comparatively, until at least the 1940s. But neither stereotype represented Appalachian Kentucky fully or fairly. Many writers, for example, based their accounts on a quick trip to the area, "popped in, popped out, and then popped off," and their resulting stories often ignored the region's complexities. As one 1901 article noted, correctly, "very great differences exist among the people." While there was poverty, there was also wealth. While there were log cabins, there were also houses that would have been fashionable in upper-class urban settings. While there was a traditional society, there was a coexisting modern one. That "other" Appalachia seldom appeared. What writers have called an "urban provincialism" often colored the attitudes behind the stories, and a cultural colonialism shaped the results. Once established, however, the stereotypes would prove to be extremely hard to demolish. While later, some might agree that "it's crude to feud," there may have been some truth to the lament in the *Hazard Herald* that "one little crime in the mountain section will receive more front page comment than a dozen murders . . . in the cities." A congressman complained that authors "make a universality out of an incident." Whatever the correctness of that view, there was still little doubt that in the late nineteenth century Kentucky garnered a stereotype of violence. In that same atmosphere, Appalachia gained several stereotypes. All of this hurt the state's and the region's image and subsequent development for decades to come.

The McCreary Administration and Health Care, 1875–1879

Violence stood out as one of the key issues in the gubernatorial campaign of 1875. Democrats pledged to contain the violence while Republicans criticized them for failing to do so. But that was but one of many issues, as the party of Lincoln again put forth its strongest candidate and best speaker, the young attorney and former Unionist John Marshall Harlan. Opposing him was an even more youthful barrister, former Confederate colonel James B. McCreary of Madison County. McCreary—like his predecessors and successors—played on his ties to the South, as did many candidates for local offices. One nineteenth-century observer noted that "worthy and capable ex-Confederate soldiers (especially if maimed)" would "invariably" be elected, and Alben W. Barkley exaggerated only a little when he wrote that "for years after the Civil War, a candidate for political office in our part of Kentucky who had not had at least one limb shot off while fighting for the Confederacy might as well have whistled down a rain barrel." While Harlan hammered state issues, McCreary focused on national ones. He centered his attention on Reconstruction and successfully reiterated his

Confederate ties and won by a vote of 130,026 to 94,236. Governor McCreary came to office as the youngest governor ever elected up to that time, and he quickly found new issues awaiting him, matters that created conflict and controversy for the next quarter century.

Labor demanded a larger voice in the state, and the outcry came both from the farm and the city. The more numerous agrarians saw much of the attention devoted to railroad and business issues, they saw the value of farm products decline in the state by 27 percent during the 1870s, and they saw their people—"the very bone and sinew of our country," one Kentuckian called them—their world, their ideal, under attack. They struck out against that change.

The first formal organization to expound the agrarians' view was the Patrons of Husbandry, more commonly called the Grange. While conservative in many of its demands, the Grange also called for actions that were deemed radical at the time. The Grangers sponsored the formation of farmers' cooperatives in the form of stores and warehouses. They also supported a revision in the nation's financial structure, which they argued favored business. Such appeals found favor in Kentucky, and in 1875 the commonwealth had some fifteen hundred Granges with more than fifty thousand members, one of the largest state totals in the South. The organization had planted the seeds of agricultural discontent that would grow over the decades. Sometimes that dissatisfaction spilled over into politics, as farmers supported first the so-called Greenback Party, which advocated the printing of more money, thus creating an inflated currency. By the 1880s the Agricultural Wheel and the Farmers' Alliance took up the cause as well, calling for a money policy of inflation and a political policy of agrarian pride. Tightly organized and sometimes almost evangelical in their fervor, the various agrarian groups represented a threat to the existing political order in Kentucky. Just when the old Democratic Bourbon–New Departure divisions seemed to be healing, the party now had to face angry farmers, who might bolt the Democrats or even form their own party if their wishes

were not met. The problem for McCreary and his successors was how far to go to meet those demands without alienating the other forces in the often-fragile Democratic coalition.

At the same time, labor unrest in the cities developed, particularly in connection with a prolonged "long-wave" depression that lasted much of the rest of the century. When the L&N and other railroads slashed wages in 1877, workers struck in protest in Louisville. In July the militia was called out, but no further conflicts of any significance developed. The formal organization of unions increased, however, and by 1880 the Knights of Labor had thirty-six assemblies in Louisville. During the next two decades, that city alone experienced at least 140 strikes, chiefly over wages. In 1887, for example, working women struck the Louisville Woolen Mills, but lack of funds or laws sympathetic to labor doomed their effort. Similarly, a depression in 1893 left an estimated ten thousand women and men unemployed in Louisville and many more suffering from wage cuts. A two-month strike to better that situation failed. Labor won few victories over management in the nineteenth century, but workers increasingly coalesced as an important voting bloc. They too represented a fresh force that the dominant Democratic Party had to face.

Despite the new threats, Democrats continued to win state elections. In the 1876 presidential race, Kentucky editor Henry Watterson emerged as perhaps the leading national advocate for Democratic nominee Samuel J. Tilden of New York. For the first time in two decades, it appeared that state Democrats might be on the victor's side in a presidential canvass. Republicans considered as a possible presidential choice a native Kentuckian. Benjamin H. Bristow of Elkton had had a distinguished career as a Union soldier and had been the secretary of the Treasury. But Rutherford B. Hayes won the nomination and, in a controversial way, the election. Democrats carried Kentucky by a vote of 160,445 to 98,415, won all ten congressional seats (through some resourceful gerrymandering of the districts), and believed they had elected Tilden as president. When questions arose over the count, Kentucky party members passed resolutions asserting that "an appeal to arms is the last desperate remedy of a free people in danger of being enslaved." An angry Watterson called for ten thousand Kentuckians to march to Washington to show their displeasure at events. Wiser heads prevailed, violence was avoided, and a compromise put Hayes in the White House. But Kentucky Democrats, feeling cheated of victory, put the election of 1876 in their campaign arsenal to be used against Republicans.

In state politics, the Democrats still ruled in the legislative halls. Since the Grange had a dominant voice, though, many of the laws passed during McCreary's tenure had an agrarian orientation. Various acts established the Kentucky Bureau of Agriculture, reduced the property tax—the main source of state revenue—by some 11 percent, lowered the maximum interest rate to 6 percent, instituted a conservation measure for fish, and made the Agricultural and Mechanical College (later the University of Kentucky) an independent school. Almost ignored in all that activity was a bill creating a State Board of Health, one of the first in the nation.

Such an action was desperately needed, for Kentuckians did not live in a healthy state. Major epidemics of cholera, smallpox, yellow fever, and typhoid left thousands dead. Drinking unsterilized milk or contaminated water (which might come directly from a sewage-polluted source) or eating food prepared in the absence of health regulations added to the incidence of disease. One study of a meat slaughterhouse found "conditions barbaric in the extreme. . . . The meat is dressed by unwashed hands, covered with flies . . . [and] hung upon hooks that are never cleaned." Lack of sanitation in the home, where whole families drank from the same water dipper, spread diseases quickly; the absence of shoes on summer feet resulted in bodies riddled with hookworm; poor ventilation in homes added to the high rate of tuberculosis. As late as the 1910s perhaps one-third of all Kentuckians had hookworm, and one-fourth of those in some areas had trachoma, a disease that could cause blind-

ness. The river town of Paducah in 1900 had the nation's second highest rate of typhoid fever and the third highest level of malaria.

Medicines available to treat these diseases ranged from adequate to ridiculous. With little or no regulation of drugs, patent medicine firms covered newspapers with their advertisements, offering "cures" for virtually everything. For one dollar a bottle, for example, Dr. Radway's Sasaparillian Resolvent claimed to cure tuberculosis, syphilis, ulcers, sore eyes, skin diseases, ringworm, "female complaints," and "nocturnal losses." Most such offerings proved to be either heavily alcoholic or a laxative. Other Kentuckians innocently sought relief through morphine, cocaine, and opium, which were sold legally in many drugstores in the nineteenth century. Unexpected addictions brought other newspaper advertisements for more "cures" of "the habit." The cure often proved worse than the problem.

The new Kentucky State Board of Health, under the longtime direction of Dr. Joseph N. McCormack of Bowling Green, and then his son Arthur, sought to improve that situation, although its annual budget never exceeded five thousand dollars until 1901. The board began by addressing the question of medical preparation. An 1878 study found that one thousand of the commonwealth's five thousand doctors had never attended a medical school. Another report conducted a few years later termed Kentucky "the worst quack ridden State in the union" and called physicians little more than "ignorant vampires." Even attendance at a medical "college" might be meaningless, for, without regulation, some institutions served more as diploma factories than places of instruction.

The quality of the food that Kentuckians ate presented a second concern. By 1898 a state Pure Food Law—later revised and strengthened—brought inspection of processed and prepared items. Through the efforts of people like Robert McDowell Allen, who became a national leader in the field, major change soon occurred. One sampling of certain foods, for instance, found that 80 percent were adulterated in some way. Punishment of violators quickly reversed the situation, and by the first decade of the twentieth century good medical education, stronger food and drug laws, along with a better-educated citizenry, began to make positive differences in the health of Kentuckians. By the 1920s, the state would be a pioneer in public health.

The Blackburn Governorship and the Prison Issue

Plagued by statewide violence and by political infighting within his own party, Governor McCreary had served amid a climate of financial retrenchment and limited initiatives. Either the young Republican nominee, former Union soldier Walter Evans of Louisville; the Democratic choice, Dr. Luke Pryor Blackburn of Woodford County; or the National (Greenback) Party candidate, C. W. Cook, would face these concerns as his successor in 1879. Cook, representing the agrarian and labor interests, eventually polled more than 8 percent of the vote, supported chiefly by those usually in the Democratic ranks, but Blackburn still won easily over Evans by a count of 125,799 to 81,882.

New governor Luke Blackburn came to office amid controversy and remained mired in strife throughout his term. During the campaign one issue had been physician Blackburn's earlier unsuccessful attempt to aid the Confederacy by infecting northern cities through biological warfare. However, his postwar humanitarian efforts to fight disease across the South balanced this perfidy. His work during an 1878 yellow fever epidemic in Kentucky won him the appellation the "Hero of Hickman" and brought the former Whig legislator the gubernatorial nomination and the election victory.

Most of Blackburn's subsequent work as governor focused on a single issue—prison reform. At the time Kentucky's prison population lived—and died—in miserable conditions. Seeking to operate the system as a business, the state government leased the penitentiary at Frankfort and its inmates to the highest bidder. Maximizing profits, each lessee kept expenses low, worked convicts hard at various tasks, such as chair making, and sold the products. With literally a captive labor force, lessees ignored

the human element, and the existence of what one paper called a system of "absolute slavery." As a result, the penitentiary became a place of slime-covered walls, open sewage, "graveyard coughs," and general unhealthiness. An 1875 study had found that 20 percent of the inmates had pneumonia. The year Blackburn took office another report revealed that three of every four prisoners had scurvy, owing to poor diet. More than 7 percent of the nearly one thousand prisoners had died during the year. Others had lived on in a hellish existence, with two prisoners per poorly heated, disease-ridden, rat-infested cell. Each of these cells measured less than seven feet long and four feet wide. In the women's quarters, located in marshy ground, their cells stood ankle-deep in water for days after a rain. Untrained guards owed their jobs to political patronage, and these officials changed as frequently as the administration. Prison lessees sought favor with the legislators, whose votes would select them, by providing the lawmakers with cheap washing, free meals, and other benefits. Legislators, in turn, averted their investigative eyes from the frequent whippings of prisoners, the cockroaches in the food, the rodents in the hallways, the thumbscrews, the sicknesses, and the deaths.

With no parole system in existence, the only way a prisoner could be released before the full sentence was served was to die or to be pardoned by the governor. The gubernatorial power to grant pardons had previously been much criticized, for the friends of political allies, or those whose families contributed to campaigns, seemed to receive a disproportionate share of them.

Luke Blackburn examined the "degrading" situation in the state prison, concluded that something had to be done immediately or more deaths would follow, and began an unprecedented pardoning policy. The net effect was to relieve overcrowding and to provide a second chance for prisoners previously without hope. In practice, however, his decision earned him widespread criticism as "Lenient Luke." Before his term ended, the governor had pardoned more than a thousand people, including nearly four hundred Regulators from eastern

The Kentucky State Penitentiary in Frankfort. (Kentucky Historical Society Collections, Frankfort, KY)

Kentucky. Such actions, amid increasing state violence, angered many.

Attempts at reform took place in the legislature as well, for the 1880 session authorized but did not fund a new prison (eventually located at Eddyville), set up a warden system in which responsibility for prisoners rested with the commonwealth and not the lessee, and provided for a crude system of parole. But one supposed reform only added to the woes of the prisoners. In an attempt to end overcrowding immediately, the general assembly allowed contractors to lease out convict labor—at $50 per convict per year in 1880—and to employ the inmates on public works outside of prison walls. Abuses arose at once, for contractors had no one supervising their handling of the prisoners. At one camp, half of the fifty leased convicts perished; at another, inmates officially reported as escapees had, in fact, died of malnourishment, overwork, and beatings. Attempts to regulate the contractors failed, chiefly because there was no longer any place to put the prisoners should they be returned to the penitentiary. Laboring at mines, railroads, and reservoirs, inmates continued to live in virtu-

al death camps until the 1890s, when the new state constitution prohibited convict leasing.

So in the end, Blackburn's efforts at prison reform only partly succeeded: the governor's free use of pardons still had not helped the overcrowding a great deal, the new penitentiary would itself be full almost immediately, and the convict leasing system represented a step backward. Over the coming decades, more prison investigations would find more problems, and the same story would be repeated.

By the conclusion of his four-year term, the politically inexperienced and somewhat naive Blackburn had almost no allies. His own party shouted him down and booed him as he sought to defend his record. Democrats, after all, had once more carried the state in the 1880 presidential race, this time for Winfield Scott Hancock, and had reelected US senator James B. Beck. Besides reforming prisons, Blackburn and the legislature had raised property taxes, cut state salaries by one-fifth, improved river navigation, and reorganized the court system. The press ignored most of these achievements, however, and instead wrote about the pardon record of the man whom one paper called "the old imbecile." In truth, Blackburn's overall accomplishments varied little from those of most other governors of his era. His tenure saw some reform, some financial actions, and some problems with violence. If his reform agenda had been limited, at least he—unlike some others—had tried to do much more.

Knott, Buckner, and "Honest Dick" Tate, 1883–1891

Some Democrats worried that the unpopularity of the Blackburn administration would hurt their party's chances of retaining the governorship, but that concern proved needless. Republican nominee Thomas Z. Morrow, a former Union officer and attorney from Somerset, faced a difficult race because his Democratic opponent was the popular six-term congressman J. Proctor Knott of Lebanon, who had narrowly defeated former congressman Thomas L. Jones of Newport in the primary. Knott owed much of his political fame to a very witty speech made in 1871, in which he sarcastically commented on a federal project near Duluth, Minnesota. In an era that praised oratory, and at a time when average people could become major leaders on the strength of their speaking abilities, Knott's "Duluth speech" garnered him national acclaim. It also helped propel him in 1883 to the governorship, which he easily won by a vote of 133,615 to 89,181.

Between the end of the Civil War and the turn of the twentieth century, virtually all Kentucky governors made recommendations to their legislatures that proved to be far more reform oriented than their administrations turned out to be. The influence of powerful lobbies, party factionalism, and the limitations of a local-oriented mindset all combined with the presence of mostly conservative legislators, so that the Kentucky General Assembly did little. Stronger chief executives could have challenged that situation more, but in the end their limited vision and restricted philosophy of government held them back.

Proctor Knott was no exception. A learned, intelligent, and well-liked individual, he still could do little regarding the violence in

Rowan County and other areas of eastern Kentucky. He also continued to pardon large numbers of prisoners, and he usually advocated local actions over state ones. His administration did create the Kentucky State Normal School for Colored Persons in Frankfort (now Kentucky State University) and enacted a major overhaul of the educational system, but Knott's major achievement lay in the area of revenue reform. A new law not only fixed new taxes and raised the property tax but also established more uniform assessments, providing, for example, that railroads and other corporations be taxed at the regular property rate. The action concerning corporations alone added $90 million of property to the taxable property lists. As a result, state government revenues increased to $3.6 million by 1890, representing 50 percent growth over the 1880 figure. All this had occurred despite one other fiscal action during the Knott years. The governor opposed but the legislature enacted a bill backed by the L&N that granted newly constructed rail lines—about one-fourth of those operating—a five-year period free of taxes. Powerful forces still operated in the general assembly.

For the Democratic Party of Proctor Knott, perhaps the greatest achievement took place outside Kentucky. In the 1884 presidential election, the issues varied only in detail from before: Democrats attacked the "horrors" of Republican Reconstruction and the character of Republican nominee James G. Blaine of Maine (a man who had once taught in Kentucky), while calling for a low tariff on foreign goods so workers would have access to cheaper merchandise. Republicans, in turn, countered with the observation that the character of the Democratic nominee, Grover Cleveland of New York, hardly seemed pure, given the fact that he had acknowledged paternity of an illegitimate child. They also defended a high protective tariff, arguing that it allowed American manufactures to grow. Such issues mattered little, it appeared, for the commonwealth followed its usual pattern and went Democratic—as it had for twenty years—by 152,961 to 118,122 votes. This time, however, Republican divisions and mistakes at the national level proved fatal, and Cleveland won. Kentucky Democrats looked forward to long-delayed political rewards from a president from their own party.

The Knott administration was nearing its end. Would the Democratic Party be able to hold the reins of office in the commonwealth in the gubernatorial contest of 1887? Republicans put forth a strong candidate for governor, forty-year-old attorney William O. Bradley of Garrard County. A strong orator, "Billy O'B." openly called for black support. His opponent, the stereotypical goateed southern gentleman Simon Bolivar Buckner of Hart County, brought both strengths and weaknesses to the race. A former Confederate general who had grown wealthy from business ventures after the war and had been a pallbearer at Grant's funeral, Buckner had never held political office. His advocates seemed willing to forget political records and praised instead the family record of the sixty-four-year-old general, his thirty-year-old wife, and their newborn son. Ignoring the fact that Buckner's wife's name was Delia, they cried out, "Hurrah for Bolivar, Betty, and the baby!" Despite a sizable Union Labor Party vote in northern Kentucky and a strong race by Republican Bradley, the Democratic appeals were enough. The "Confederate Dynasty" continued—barely. In the closest contest since the war, Buckner won with 51 percent of the vote. He polled 143,466 votes against Bradley's 126,754, and more than 12,000 more ballots went to third-party candidates. The vote showed that the long-successful Democratic coalition had developed serious problems.

Those problems grew worse under Buckner. Dominated by rising agrarian interests in the form of the Farmers' Alliance, his legislatures successfully pushed for a property tax reduction that left the commonwealth so short of cash that the governor had to make a personal loan of more than fifty thousand dollars to the state treasury in order to keep Kentucky solvent. Other laws passed by the general assembly so angered Buckner that he vetoed more than a hundred bills, issuing more vetoes than his ten predecessors combined. At the same time, the actions of the L&N lobby brought forth a

legislative investigation that concluded that the railroad company had used money, passes, and influence in "an extraordinarily powerful effort to dominate the legislature." Additionally, the Hatfield-McCoy feud dragged Buckner into a convoluted legal controversy with the governor of West Virginia, one that had to be settled by the US Supreme Court. Even that issue, however, paled in comparison to a sensational political scandal that suddenly erupted.

Beginning in 1867 and continuing every two years thereafter, Kentucky voters had elected James W. ("Honest Dick") Tate of Frankfort as state treasurer. Praised for his integrity and affability, Tate was so trusted that other state officials did not even bother to carry out their duties and double-check his accounts. On March 14, 1888, Tate packed some bags for a trip to Louisville and Cincinnati. As far as is known, he was never seen in Kentucky again. A few days later, worried officials began to scrutinize his books. They found a chaotic, confused system that seemed no system at all. Bills had been laid aside and forgotten; others had been paid but not so recorded; more seriously, some had been marked paid when they had not been. State funds had also apparently been offered by Tate as personal loans to various friends and officials, including at least one governor. The treasurer had used the commonwealth's money to speculate in land and coal mining ventures of his own. Finally, a clerk recalled that Honest Dick had filled two large sacks with gold and silver coins and had taken a large roll of bills with him on his final trip.

Eventually, investigators found that Tate had embezzled more than $247,000 from the state—about one-tenth of the annual budget. He had doctored bills, deleted accounts, and forgotten transactions in a fairly crude way, but the loose controls had allowed him to continue his fraud for years. Worried about the possibility of a routine check, he finally fled. The Kentucky House of Representatives quickly impeached Tate, and the senate removed him from office. Criminal charges were filed against him in civil court. Belatedly, the legislature created the office of state inspector and examiner.

Behind the scenes, chaos reigned. Worried

officials tried to distance themselves from Tate or to minimize the damages in a scandal that reached the highest levels. Long-unpaid IOUs to Tate were suddenly redeemed. The current state auditor, like his predecessors, had been clearly derelict in his duty, but he got off with only the censure of the public. More uncertain was the fate of a series of wealthy, influential, and trusting people who had signed as bondsmen for Tate, as required by law. Supposedly any fiscal shortage by him would have to be met by them. But given the magnitude of his embezzlement, several people's fortunes would be lost if the commonwealth collected. In the end, the state's highest court, in a decision not openly reported because of political consequences, decided that the bondsmen would not be held liable.

Back in 1876 the Covington city treasurer, a son of former Confederate governor of Kentucky Richard Hawes, had embezzled fifty-seven thousand dollars, only to be among those pardoned during Governor Blackburn's term. The Tate affair thus seemed a continuation of a trend. Distrust of all public officials increased dramatically, and angry critics charged that a cover-up had occurred.

What happened to Honest Dick Tate and the state's money after he left Kentucky? The wife and daughter he left behind, as well as a family friend, said later that for a brief time they received secret letters indicating he had gone to Canada, the Orient, and finally Brazil. No further word came from Tate after that. Whether he returned to the United States under an assumed identity or lived and died in a foreign country is unknown, one of the mysteries of Kentucky history. His actions would have an enduring effect on the state, however, particularly in regard to the new constitution soon to be drafted.

A New Constitution

The constitution of 1850 clearly required at least revision, for it still sanctioned slavery and did not adequately deal with new issues such as corporations and railroads. Calls for a new convention had been made for two decades, but fi-

nally an 1889 vote made that possibility a reality. One hundred delegates, representing each district in the Kentucky House of Representatives, were selected. They convened in Frankfort on September 8, 1890, met for 226 days, and signed the result of their deliberations on April 11, 1891. The process was long, controversial, and not always fruitful.

Not unexpectedly, the delegates were a varied lot. There were sixty attorneys, twenty farmers, thirteen doctors, and seven business leaders. Almost one-fifth of them had been elected as representatives of the Farmers' Alliance and spoke out chiefly on those issues of importance to agrarians—limited government, control of corporations, railroad regulation, and the like. The delegates at the convention included a former governor, the current governor, a future governor, and the uncle and brother of two other governors. About a dozen middle-level political figures formed the core of those involved in most deliberations, however. In short, the group of delegates was competent but not exceptional.

Unfortunately, the delegates often operated like oarsmen in a boat with no one steering. With no particular person to lead and with a piecemeal rather than a considered approach to constitution making, the convention seemed to flounder. Delegates spent long hours offering resolutions or debating procedural or minor matters. What one delegate termed lengthy, "aerial flights of oratory" emanated on virtually every subject. Delegates ignored William M. Beckner's advice that they should fashion a flexible document, to "give posterity a chance." Unable to agree on broad statements, they instead degenerated almost to making laws in the form of a constitution through very specific sections, which, as it turned out, were often quickly outdated. Fresh from the Tate scandal, the delegates did not trust government or its leaders very much. They therefore limited officials' time in office and fashioned a restrictive document that reflected their suspicion of power and those who wielded it.

The document they drafted in 1890 and 1891 would change drastically over the years, as a result of various constitutional amendments. Its chief provisions at the time included the following:

1. The basic Bill of Rights from the 1792 constitution was retained, except for the slavery provision.
2. The general assembly would consist of a house of representatives of one hundred members elected to two-year terms, and a senate of thirty-eight members serving four-year terms.
3. The executive branch would consist of the governor and other constitutional officers, all elected for four-year terms, with restrictions on selection. On the chief executive's absence from the state, the lieutenant governor automatically assumed the power of the office (this provision was later amended).
4. The judicial branch would consist of a court of appeals, made up of five to seven members elected for eight-year terms, and a system of circuit, quarterly, county, justice of the peace, and police courts. The general assembly was forbidden to create any courts other than those in the constitution (later amended).
5. Under more general provisions,
   a. The elected Railroad Commission of Kentucky was given constitutional sanction to help its regulatory powers (later abolished).
   b. Lotteries were abolished (later amended).
   c. Salaries of state officials were restricted to five thousand dollars per year (later amended).
   d. State elections would be held in November instead of August, would be by secret ballot rather than voice voting, and would be limited to males over the age of twenty-one (later amended).
   e. "An efficient system" of schools had to be maintained and must be racially segregated (later amended). The creation of new counties was made more difficult.
   f. For the first time, the governor had the power to line-item veto budget matters.

Almost as soon as it was written, the new constitution attracted critics, including Watterson, who opposed its limitations and restrictions as well as its bundle of statutes disguised as a constitution. Others disliked some of the reform elements, such as the strengthened railroad commission, and the L&N campaigned against adoption. But the framers had reflected the will of a state fearful of power, distrustful of politicians, and careful of prerogatives, and the constitution was adopted by a statewide vote of 212,914 to 74,523. Then, in a strange move, the delegates reassembled for almost a month, made several changes, some of them significant, and signed a new, "final" draft. Not voted on in that form by the people, the document was tested in the courts but was eventually approved. At long last the constitution of 1891 was complete. The problems it would create, however, had only begun.

Populism in the Chaotic 1890s

The postwar Democratic Party consisted of many elements—former Whigs, former prewar Democrats, former Confederates, former Unionists, rural interests, urban interests, wealthy Bluegrass farmers, poorer western Kentucky agrarians, leaders of a Bourbon bent, politicians of New Departure views, and much more. Bonded in a weak philosophical way by a devotion to low tariffs, a limited role for government, and an opposition to Republicans, Democrats had never had a fully united party. One element seemed always in conflict with another, whether it was Bourbon versus New Departure earlier, or agrarians against the established leadership in the 1880s. Over the years, different factions had broken off, either in passive rebellion or in small third-party movements. Now those divisions threatened to grow into full-scale revolt.

Farmers grew even more worried about their place in American life and in Kentucky politics. Many argued that corporations, especially railroads, discriminated against them. Others noted the long-term debt many agrarians owed to bankers or other lenders. Still more complained, as did an 1891 writer in

Rock Bridge, about the "defeated feeling in the minds of the people of this part of the state that they have not rec'd. the recognition they were entitled to, in the division of state offices." Simply put, as a historian noted, "Rural people sought to claim a share of the New South's promise, to make a place for themselves and their children in the emerging order."

Various groups had sought to do that, ranging from the Grangers to the Greenbackers, from the Agricultural Wheel to the Farmers' Alliance. The Alliance had been organized in Kentucky in 1886, with S. Brewer Erwin of Hickman as president. Within five years, the Alliance—under the formal name of the Farmers and Labor Union—claimed more than 125,000 members in some twenty-four hundred sub-unions in eighty-eight counties. Its endorsement was eagerly sought, and its influence on the political scene was important. But all of that power had come about within the structure of the existing two-party system. By 1891 it was not at all clear whether the situation would continue, and in an open letter to Democrats, one agrarian summarized the atmosphere, in a "Word of Warning." He told of the "unrest" in the minds of many who usually voted Democratic, for "this element, chiefly farmers, are honestly impatient as to existing grievances."

The agrarians grew more concerned once the Democratic nominee for governor in 1891 was chosen. John Young Brown of Henderson did represent western Kentucky and helped calm sectional fears, but he also represented the old leadership more than had his defeated party rivals. Disgruntled agrarians who had attended a national farm protest meeting in Cincinnati crossed the river to Covington, founded the People's—or Populist—Party in Kentucky, and offered a slate of officers for the 1891 governor's race. Led by candidate Erwin, the Populists did not stress some of the issues that would be important when the national party organized in 1892, such as a graduated income tax, the direct election of US senators, and greater regulation—even to the point of government ownership—of transportation. Although far from revolutionary in their demands, the Populists

were perceived by the "old guard" of both parties to be quite radical, chiefly because of their stand on the money issue.

During economic hard times, those in debt sought relief. More than sixty years before, conflicts on that issue had erupted in the Old Court–New Court struggle. Now the same kinds of concerns brought forth new responses but similar divisive reactions. Self-described "slaves of the money powers and corporations," the debt-ridden agriculturalists called for the free and unlimited coinage of silver at a set ratio to gold. Perhaps few understood this action in principle, but many knew that it would create an inflated currency. Higher prices for farm products would mean that farmers could use cheaper dollars to pay off old debts. The Republicans and one part of the Democratic Party vehemently opposed the proposal and called for "sound money." A large—and growing—faction of the Democrats cried out instead for "free silver." The fight was on.

Populists began to draw votes from both parties, but the Farmers' Alliance refused to endorse the third party. That decision gave the victory to Democrat Brown, who received 144,168 votes. Republican Andrew T. Wood of Mt. Sterling had 116,087, Populist Erwin polled 25,631, and a Prohibition candidate won 3,292. But the Democrats had not won a majority of ballots cast (only 49.9 percent). The Populists had garnered nearly 9 percent of the vote, and the potential for future problems was clear. The slow erosion of Democratic votes over the years had continued, and the party's western bastion had drastically lessened its support. Of the forty-four counties where Populists had gained more than 10 percent of the vote, most were in the agriculturally distressed western farm belt. Populists had elected at least thirteen members to the general assembly, and the presence of numerous Alliance-backed Democrats gave agrarians a majority in the legislature. Democrats would have to address free silver and agricultural reform issues, or their party could face the rarest of events—future defeat.

Governor Brown presided over a schizophrenic and chaotic administration. Operating under the new constitution for the first time, the legislature had to reexamine old laws. As a result, it stayed in session almost continuously from December 1891 until July 1893, an action that pleased few and earned the body the name the Long Parliament. Brown so feuded with his cabinet and his lieutenant governor that the administration split into two factions, and the political situation in Frankfort grew increasingly bitter. Meanwhile, legislative actions varied between the reactionary and the reform minded. The general assembly passed a much-needed law that at last gave property rights to married women, but at the same time it enacted a segregationist separate coach law.

The most vocal opposition from the black community on the changes taking place occurred in that 1892 fight to segregate railroad cars operating in the state. African Americans fought the proposal—and the leader of the protests, Professor C. C. Monroe, lost his job as a result. Opposed in the legislature by Populist leader Thomas S. Pettit and others, the bill still passed by seventeen to ten and sixty-one to twenty-seven margins and was signed by Governor Brown. Boycotts, books, a lower court's declaration of illegality, and a later governor's call for repeal all went for naught after the US Supreme Court—with Justice John Marshall Harlan of Kentucky the lone dissent—ruled the law legal. (It would remain a state statute until 1966.)

The Kentucky General Assembly also passed a limited but basic coal mine safety act but terminated as too expensive the important geological survey. Brown himself vetoed a revenue bill that would have increased railroad taxes but then turned against the railroads by preventing the merger of the L&N with the second-largest carrier in the state, the Chesapeake and Ohio. Yet at the same time, the governor intervened on behalf of a corporation in a Clay County case involving a New Jersey-based company's request for a reduction in taxes on some thirteen thousand acres of land. No one seemed to be in charge or to know where the state was going.

Similar problems plagued the Democratic Party at the national level. The 1892 presiden-

tial election brought Grover Cleveland back to the White House, a move endorsed by Kentucky voters, who gave Cleveland a 40,000-vote majority over incumbent Republican president Benjamin Harrison. Populists garnered a smaller but still respectable 23,500 votes (7 percent). President Cleveland and his Kentucky-born vice president, Adlai E. Stevenson of Illinois, recognized the role of the Kentucky Democrats by appointing John G. Carlisle as secretary of the Treasury.

Then the most prominent national political figure from Kentucky, Carlisle had studied law under former governor Stevenson. From his northern Kentucky base of Covington, he had won election as lieutenant governor, US congressman for seven terms, and US senator. He had also been Speaker of the US House. Looking cold and austere dressed in his traditional black suit, Carlisle was usually described as intellectual, analytic, and brilliant, and many expected him to use the cabinet position as a springboard to the presidency. But a national depression and the money issue made the Cleveland administration and Carlisle very unpopular, even in Democratic Kentucky, and doomed his political hopes. A sound money man, Carlisle spoke in Covington in 1896, and when free silver supporters pelted him with rotten eggs, he made that occasion his last public speech. Carlisle left the state to live elsewhere, his career having fallen victim to the issues that were dividing the commonwealth.

Political, Tollgate, and Other Wars

In the 1895 race for governor, the money issue and other questions threatened to end the dominance of the Democratic Party in Kentucky. With an unpopular Democratic president and governor, with a depression still ongoing, with the third-party Populists present to siphon votes from the majority party, and with the free silver issue splitting the Democrats further, Republicans could taste victory at last. They put forth their strongest candidate, William O. Bradley.

In a bitter convention fight, Democrats repudiated incumbent governor Brown's choice, selected P. Wat Hardin of Harrodsburg instead, and endorsed the gold standard and sound money. Hardin's plank fell apart quickly, for the Democratic candidate repudiated the party platform and came out for free silver, to try to hold agrarians in the party. Meanwhile, Governor Brown refused to campaign for Hardin, and conservative Democrats abandoned Hardin for the Republicans. Populists put forth a fairly prominent former Democrat, Thomas S. Pettit of Owensboro, and he gained the support of one of the largest black newspapers in the region, Louisville's *New South*. Overall, however, blacks generally remained loyal to the Republicans.

Republican Bradley further divided the already-splintered Democratic ranks by courting the estimated 20,000 to 30,000 votes of the American Protective Association, a secret fraternal group opposed to Catholics and immigrants. The group had been credited with the defeat of a Catholic who was running for Congress in Louisville in 1894, and it now favored the Republicans over the party associated with Catholic ethnic groups. Forty years earlier, similar elements and feelings had erupted in the "Bloody Monday" riots, but the election of 1895 passed with no unusual violence. But what once seemed almost impossible in Kentucky had happened. The Republicans won. Bradley gained 172,436 votes to Hardin's 163,524. Although in decline as a formal party, the Populists had garnered 16,911 ballots with Pettit, and the Populist candidacy made the difference in a race decided by fewer than 9,000 votes.

The election of 1895 marked the beginning of more than three decades of strong two-party competition in Kentucky at the state and national levels. Legislatures and local politics remained solidly Democratic, but Republicans would win four of the next nine governor's races. In the presidential election of 1896, the state went for the party of Lincoln for the first time since the Civil War, as William McKinley defeated the silverite and Populist-oriented William Jennings Bryan by a margin of fewer than 300 votes. To Kentucky agrarians, Bryan was a hero who spoke for them "on behalf of

the masses against the classes." To more conservative elements in the state, he represented a "dangerous," radical spirit. With many of the old key leaders—including Watterson, Breckinridge, Carlisle, and Buckner—in opposition to Bryan, some Democrats left their party for the Republicans, while others gave their votes to the National—or Gold—Democrats. Another splinter third party, the Gold Democrats had as their presidential nominee Kentucky native John M. Palmer of Illinois, and their vice-presidential choice was former Kentucky governor Buckner. They won only 5,108 votes in the 1896 election in Kentucky, but had those ballots gone to regular Democrat Bryan, he would have won the state. Some of the wayward voters would return to Democratic ranks, but others would not.

Similar issues resulted in the rejection of the once-popular US senator J. C. S. ("Jo") Blackburn of Woodford County and the selection—after fifteen months and 112 bitter ballots in the general assembly—of the state's first Republican senator, William J. Deboe of Crittenden County. A realignment of parties was taking place, and as a result the Republicans, once the more reform minded of the two major parties, grew more conservative. On the other hand, Democrats would increasingly be viewed over the next few decades as the reform party of the commonwealth, except in racial matters. Yet in the end, both parties retained reform and reactionary wings, eschewed extremes, and remained moderate.

Despite the string of Republican victories in political races, new governor Bradley did not taste great success otherwise. Much of his time was spent dealing with violence, both legal and illegal. The so-called Tollgate Wars resulted from a system whereby private companies met the need for local roads by building them, then charging tolls to pay off their investment, and eventually earning a profit for their stockholders. By 1890 more than three-fourths of all hard-surfaced roads in the state were under the toll system. But people less able to pay opposed the roads, charging that their rates were exorbitant, especially in such depressed times. The call went up for "free roads." State and local government hesitated to get involved and, faced with inaction, angry agitators began to take matters into their own hands. Tollhouses were burned, gates destroyed, and gatekeepers threatened and beaten. One Mercer County man received a warning which read, in part: "We ask you Not to collect no more tole. You must Not collect one cent[.] if you do we are Going to Destroy your House with fire and Denamite. . . . We want a Free Road and are agoing to have it, if we have to Kill and Burn up everything. Collect No more tole[.] We mean what we say." By 1897, eleven gates had been destroyed in that county, and a keeper had been seriously wounded. A state of siege existed. Other places, mostly in central Kentucky, saw masked Regulators destroy virtually every tollgate in the area.

A kind of class warfare seemed to be occurring, and business leaders spoke of anarchy and communism. An angry Governor Bradley called for retribution toward "lawbreakers" and "outlaws," but a Democratic legislature that may have been quietly sympathetic to the agrarian goal of free roads refused to act against the tollgate attackers, saying the matter was a local one. Such decisions probably encouraged conservative Democratic Party members to look to the Republicans. By the turn of the century the wars had ended because tollgate companies either had sold their stock to local groups, who then opened the roads without charge, or had simply been driven out by the violence. The lesson some people seemed to have learned was that violence worked. It would be a deadly lesson for Kentucky's future.

Kentuckians' desire to channel their violent energies found an outlet in 1898 with the start of the Spanish-American War. Eventually, some 5,590 state soldiers—four Kentucky regiments and two troops of cavalry—served in the conflict but saw little action. Their suffering came not on the battlefield but at army camps in the United States, where official ineptitude, crowded conditions, inadequate clothing, poor sanitation, impure water, and spoiled food all took their toll. With sick soldiers awaiting transportation back to Kentucky, the state government found that it had no funds to pay for the hospital trains needed to return them. Governor Bradley ended up borrowing the money from a bank, trusting the Kentucky General Assembly to reimburse the loan. Eighty-nine Kentuckians did not make that trip back, and their deaths reminded others that the conflict may have been "a splendid little war" with easy victories, but it had a cost even at that.

Goebel!

Governor Bradley had another problem in 1898, and it concerned a person who was becoming the most controversial man in Kentucky. William Goebel seemed a strange leader of the Democrats, for that party had been guided by the Confederate Dynasty; Goebel's father had fought for the Union. In a state that praised its British ties, Goebel had been born to German immigrant parents and had spoken the German language early in life. In a commonwealth whose politicians stressed their long lineage in the Bluegrass, Goebel had been born outside the state. And in a place where hearty greetings, strong oratory, and warm camaraderie characterized most politicians, Goebel displayed none of those traits.

Aloof and cold in public, uneasy when mixing with crowds, and just barely an effective speaker, Goebel overcame his faults by reading widely to become well informed and by winning his victories behind the scenes through a strong organization. Politics was his life, and he had few male friends and even fewer female ones. As a result, his waking moments were devoted to his search for political power. Brilliant and bold, ambitious and audacious, he seldom compromised and won battles by his will, his inner force, and his program. Heading a new group of young Democrats unhappy with the old leadership, Goebel called for aid to the laboring class and greater controls on corporations and their lobbies, particularly the L&N. He was pictured as the friend of the "common man." Such appeals found a ready audience, but Goebel's forceful and antagonistic manner of making them resulted in an equally strong-willed opposition. No one of his

Ambitious and uncompromising, Pennsylvania-born William Goebel was the most controversial figure of his era in Kentucky politics. (Library Special Collections, Western Kentucky University, Bowling Green, KY)

era aroused such passions, and one of his enemies—a former Confederate from his own party—had met Goebel on a street in their hometown of Covington in 1895. Each man drew a pistol and fired one shot. Goebel's opponent fell dead; the widow went to the insane asylum. No indictment of Goebel followed. To those who battled against "Boss Bill," the Kenton King, the shooting was but another indicator of the man's ruthless nature. To them he was a murderer.

Now he sought the governorship of Kentucky, to be decided in 1899. As a Kentucky Senate leader, he pushed through the so-called Goebel Election Law in the 1898 session. The act established a Board of Election Commissioners, with members basically selected by Goebel, that would choose all local precinct officials and would judge disputed gubernatorial races. Furious opposition arose from both parties, as warnings of one-man rule and one-party tyranny came forth. But enough Democrats remained loyal to override Governor Bradley's veto. The act became law.

In the 1899 governor's race Goebel did in fact win his party's nomination but in a man-

ner that so angered his opponents at the turbulent Music Hall Convention in Louisville that some bolted and organized a third party, the Honest Election League. These Democrats soon took a name from their popular nominee, former Democratic governor John Y. Brown, and as Brown Democrats they went on to garner 12,140 votes. A dying Populist Party took 2,936 more. But in the end the election came down to a contest between Goebel and Republican William S. Taylor of Butler County. The state attorney general, Taylor was not the strongest of candidates, but the growing opposition to Goebel plus the financial largess of the L&N gave him a chance for victory. Goebel, meanwhile, continued to attack: "I ask no question and I fear no foe." On election day the count was too close to call. Each side claimed victory and charged the other with fraud. Finally the Board of Election Commissioners, thought to be in Goebel's control, surprised almost everyone by declaring that Taylor had won with 193,714 votes to Goebel's 191,331. Once more the third parties had taken away the votes that could have won the election for the Democrats. In December Taylor was inaugurated as the second governor from the Republican Party, and the matter seemed resolved.

The conflict was only beginning, however. The Democratic majority in the general assembly voted to investigate the election to determine whether fraud and illegal military force had been used. A change of only a few votes could make Goebel governor. An investigating committee was formed, and in what was likely a prearranged drawing, ten of the eleven names picked were Democrats. Republicans expected the committee to recommend removal of enough ballots so that Goebel would have a majority, and then the legislature would approve that finding. Such an action would be similar to measures taken a few years before regarding a Republican governor in Tennessee. Desperate Republicans tried to put pressure on the general assembly and brought in a "Mountain Army" of supporters, a move suggesting that force might be used. Both sides issued threats and counterthreats, and another volatile element was added to an already combustible political mix.

In that atmosphere, Goebel and two of his supporters walked toward the state capitol on January 30, 1900. Within days Goebel might become governor. His long-term desire would at last be realized.

Then a shot rang out.

13

Progressivism, Prohibition, and Politics, 1900–1920

Assassination of a Governor

Goebel had been shot. Mortally wounded from a rifle bullet that had passed through his body, he was taken for treatment to a room in a nearby hotel. Governor Taylor declared that a "state of insurrection" existed, called out the militia, and ordered the legislature to reconvene in a safer location, in this case the Republican stronghold of London, Kentucky. Democratic legislators refused to recognize the legality of that action, but they found armed soldiers barring them from meeting in the capitol or in several other public places in Frankfort. Gathering secretly in the hotel, with no Republicans present, they accepted the contest committee's report regarding the disputed election, threw out enough votes to reverse the results, and on January 31, 1900, declared Goebel governor. He was sworn in, and in his only official act he ordered the militia to disperse and the legislature to reassemble. Soon the new Democratic government called out a friendly militia force to face the Gatling guns staring across the capitol lawn. Republicans in turn cried out about the "steal" of the election and refused to recognize the constitutionality of any of the Democratic actions. Two governments, each with its own force of more than a thousand armed men, faced each other, and the level of tension rose higher and higher. A stray shot could spark bloody violence and perhaps even another civil war, only this time along party lines.

At 6:44 p.m. on February 3, 1900, William Goebel died of his wounds. The only governor in American history to die in office as a result of assassination, he had been chief executive of the commonwealth for three days. The forty-four-year-old northern Kentuckian had survived the assassin's bullet for only a little over a hundred hours. His last words, at least as reported by the Democratic press, ensured that he would live on as a martyr: "Tell my friends to be brave, fearless, and loyal to the great common people."

With the death of the controversial Goebel, more rational discussions began to take place, and the danger of warfare lessened. Goebel's lieutenant governor, J. C. W. Beckham of Nelson County, now took the reins of leadership for the Democrats, and both sides waited for the courts to decide who legally was governor and who was not. Meanwhile, state government ground to a halt, since no one knew who was in charge. Banks refused to honor checks from either side. Finally, in May, with John Marshall Harlan dissenting, the US Supreme Court ruled that it could not examine the issue because no federal questions were involved. Thus the actions of the Democratic majority in the legislature would stand. The Republicans were out, and the Democrats in.

Governor William S. Taylor, under indictment from a partisan jury as an accessory to the crime, fled the state. Numerous others were arrested, and eventually three men were convicted of the assassination: Republican secretary of state Caleb Powers of Knox County, the man said to be the mastermind of the plan; Henry Youtsey, a clerk from northern Kentucky, said to be the aide to the assassin; and James B. Howard, a man involved in the Clay County feud and the supposed assassin. But the whole legal process was flawed. Juries were packed with Democrats, most trial judges had been partisan supporters of Goebel (one had been a Democratic lieutenant governor), and

On January 30, 1900, William Goebel was assassinated outside the Kentucky state capitol. He was sworn in as governor the next day but died on February 3. (*Cincinnati Enquirer*, January 31, 1900)

several witnesses perjured themselves in giving testimony. Two of the three convicted men appealed and won the right to a new trial from an equally partisan high court that had a Republican majority. As a result, Howard went through three trials, and Powers through four, during a seven-year period. The long, drawn-out process only added to the party bitterness and the bad publicity for the state. As one national observer noted: "How deeply the bitterness of the Goebel killing has entered into the life of Kentucky no outsider can fully realize. The animosities engendered by it have brought about literally scores of fatal quarrels. Business partnerships have been dissolved; churches have been disrupted; lifelong friendships have been withered; families have been split; there is no locality so remote, no circle so clearly knit, as to escape the evil influence."

In 1908, eight years after the assassination, after the last Powers trial had ended in a hung jury, the governor pardoned Howard and Powers, and later he pardoned others still under indictment. In 1916 Youtsey was paroled, and he was pardoned in 1919. After Powers went free, he quickly ran for a seat in the US House of Representatives and won. As he liked to say, he then served as many years in Congress as he had in jail. The other two men lived quieter lives, although they were frequently asked, "Did you kill Goebel?" Because of the contradictory evidence and partisanship surrounding the case, the answer to the question of who killed William Goebel still remains mired in mystery and intrigue.

The effects of the assassination on Kentucky are a bit clearer. First, the event strengthened Kentucky's reputation as a violent place. Second, party lines solidified, as each group looked at the other with greater and greater distrust. Republicans would cry out that Democrats had stolen the governor's office from them; Democratic orators would figuratively wave the bloody shirt of Goebel before voters and label their opposition as murderers. A third effect is less clear-cut. Some have argued that the death of Goebel snuffed out the reform spirit in the state. That really was not the case, for reforms did occur and progressive legislation was enacted. Moreover, it is far from certain whether Goebel's record would have been much different from that of some of his predecessors. What the assassination did show, however, was that personality and reform were joined. Bold moves and successful challenges to the establishment could take place, but the tactics had to be carefully chosen. Political bosses who lacked charisma and popularity had to move slowly. The Goebel affair was to the wise politician not a roadblock to action but rather a caution. In that sense it did have an effect on reform in Kentucky.

In the midst of the Goebel trials, with partisanship at fever pitch, a former legislator and judge delighted a 1902 banquet audience with a poem that would be endlessly reprinted over the years. The concluding lines of the last verse of James H. Mulligan's "In Kentucky" summarized the state of politics in the commonwealth not only then but in the future as well:

The song birds are the sweetest
In Kentucky;
The thoroughbreds are fleetest
In Kentucky;
Mountains tower proudest,
Thunder peals the loudest,
The landscape is the grandest—and
    politics—the damnedest
In Kentucky.

Bosses and Beckham

John Crepps Wickliffe Beckham was called the Boy Governor. Coming to office as a result of Goebel's death, J. C. W. Beckham at age thirty was barely old enough to meet the constitutional requirements of the office. In truth, he probably owed his place on the Goebel ticket to the fact that he was what Goebel was not—from an old Bluegrass family. Beckham's grandfather Charles A. Wickliffe had been governor of Kentucky, and his uncle Robert C. Wickliffe, the chief executive of Louisiana. An attorney, Beckham had been speaker of the Kentucky House, and from that position he became the party's nominee for lieutenant governor. Looking as young as his years, he also projected a sense of handsome, aristocratic dignity and reserve. Many were uncertain whether he would even survive a special election in the fall of 1900 to fill the remainder of Goebel's term. As it turned out, Beckham showed very quickly his political acumen and became one of the state's major political leaders over the next three decades.

But was the governor of Kentucky really the ruler of the state? For five or more decades after 1900, a series of political bosses wielded much of the real power, usually behind the scenes. Almost every town and county had someone who could "get out the vote," and electoral success often depended on how many of those key people could be brought into a candidate's camp. Some individuals had influence beyond their small area, and they became the major players. Foremost of those was William Purcell Dennis ("Percy") Haly, who had started out selling newspapers on the streets of Frankfort. He became a confidant of Goe-

J. C. W. Beckham assumed the governorship upon the death of Goebel. Known as the Boy Governor, Beckham was only thirty at the time he took office. (Kentucky Historical Society Collections, Frankfort, KY)

bel's and stayed in the dying man's room day and night. While Goebel had wanted both the spotlight and the power, Haly needed only the latter. With Boss Bill's death, Haly quickly transferred his allegiance and talents to Beckham. The two men became politically inseparable and won numerous victories as a result. Although intelligent and an exceptional planner, Haly was not a good speaker or public figure, and he achieved his aims away from center stage. His only important office was an appointed one, as adjutant general, but "the General" preferred to command votes, not troops. An insomniac who lived in a hotel and never married, Haly devoted his many waking hours to the political game he so enjoyed and mastered.

Numerous other political bosses vied for power all across Kentucky. In the western part of the state, Thomas S. Rhea and then Emerson ("Doc") Beauchamp controlled Logan County and other areas, while the Broadbent family of Trigg County proved important later. Michael J. ("Mickey") Brennan, then "Miss Lennie" McLaughlin, Johnny Crimmins, and the Fourth Street Machine succeeded Louisville's Whallen brothers. Maurice L. Galvin controlled votes in northern Kentucky, as William F. ("Billy") Klair did in Lexington. Bardstown, the home of Beckham, was also home to a bitter enemy of his, "Boss Ben" Johnson, and Johnson's son-in-law J. Dan Talbott. The eastern part of the commonwealth saw Albert W. ("Allie") Young, a man once involved in the Rowan County War and now called the Morehead Manipulator, become a powerful political force, while Marie Turner of Breathitt County filled that place later.

The lives of the various bosses exhibited few common characteristics. All but Galvin were Democrats, for that was the party in power in most local areas. A large number were Catholic: Haly, the Whallens, Brennan, Klair, Johnson, and Talbott all recognized that they could not win statewide office because of their religion. To gain power they had to operate in a less open manner.

Otherwise, differences distinguished the various bosses. Some, like Ben Johnson, were born to wealth, while others, such as Haly, Brennan, and Klair, came from poorer German or Irish immigrant bases. Some used their positions to garner additional funds either for themselves or for their political organizations. Yet in the end, power, not money, motivated most. Klair's contacts brought a large share of the state's insurance business to his firm, while Brennan in Louisville attracted funds from political activity. Brennan told one would-be candidate that, if he paid two thousand dollars, Brennan would ensure that the city precincts would all vote for him. He paid, and they did. In Bourbon County, as one politician recalled, "There was [a lot] of votes you could handle with money, probably a thousand or twelve hundred." Once when a worker indicated to a local boss there that he was having difficulty getting the votes in a precinct because "the sentiment is against us," the boss replied, "Why you silly son of a bitch. That's what the money's for; to fight sentiment."

Some of the bosses sought or held no po-

litical office, while others pursued their own political goals: Rhea ran for governor, Beauchamp was lieutenant governor, Johnson a congressman, Klair a state representative, Young a state senator. Most attained their fame, however, not from the positions they held as much as the power they controlled.

They gained that power by fulfilling a need. In an era of little governmental involvement in relief efforts, the bosses provided aid to destitute families, whether in the form of a pair of shoes, a load of coal in winter, a turkey at Christmas, a loan, or a job. Brennan, for instance, used the funds given him by political candidates and daily took cash from his Louisville bank account and ordered it distributed to the needy. In return for such actions, bosses asked for people's allegiance—and their votes. They could then offer those votes to politicians, in exchange for rewards—usually in the form of contracts or the promise of jobs. Distributing patronage, they gave allies positions in fire and police departments, and later in highway departments, or in prisons or hospitals. If this political circle did not benefit democracy, it did benefit those who were part of the game.

Of course, if the occasion demanded, some bosses were not averse to taking action that made certain their pledges of political victory could be honored. A widely circulated story, for instance, told how Percy Haly manipulated the vote of a Franklin County precinct so that his ally Beckham won by a vote of 219 to 0. On examination of the suspicious returns—so the accounts said—it was discovered that such voters as A. Apple, B. Beans, C. Corn, P. Pear, P. Plum, R. Raspberry, as well as B. Broom, F. Fence, H. Hog, L. Log, R. Road, and R. Rock, had all cast ballots—in alphabetical order! Less ingenious or daring bosses simply used the names of voters who resided in the local cemetery on election day.

Yet for all the corruption and power politics, the bosses provided aid and support when others did not. They often were reform minded, for their constituencies generally were the poor and forgotten, but they would be attacked for the perceived evils they brought to politics. Their influence was mixed, and for half a century or longer their role was all-important. They were the kingmakers.

In the fall of 1900 Governor Beckham faced an election that would decide whether his term would continue. Called to fill the remainder of Goebel's term, the contest—for a change—did not include any significant third-party threat. The Populists had generally returned to the Democratic Party, while many disgruntled Brown Democrats voted Republican. Thus a close vote was expected, as in the two previous governor's races. Beckham and Haly made two shrewd moves that may have been decisive. Openly, a special session of the legislature was called, and it repealed the unpopular Goebel Election Law. That action removed what had become one of the main Republican campaign issues. Behind the scenes, a representative of Beckham's met secretly with a recent and powerful enemy, Milton Hannibal Smith of the L&N, and Smith agreed that if the attacks on railroads ceased, he would support the Democrats. As he noted later, "The procedure suggested was followed." All of this effort was needed, as it turned out, for Beckham still barely beat the Republican candidate, John W. Yerkes, a law professor from Danville, by a count of 233,052 to 229,363. Losing by fewer than 3,700 votes, Republicans charged fraud, particularly in the boss-dominated Louisville precincts, but they did not have the legislative majority that had enabled the Democrats to give a victory to Goebel in 1900. Beckham was elected.

Could he be reelected in 1903? The constitution specified that the governor "shall be ineligible for the succeeding four years after the expiration of the term for which he shall have been elected." A high court friendly to Beckham ruled that since Goebel, not Beckham, had been elected to the original term, Beckham could run again, and he did. In the period since Beckham's first race, the governor and General Haly had together built an effective political machine—this became the issue for Republicans—and had attracted some wayward Democrats back into the fold. One who had not returned cried out against his former party's appeal. "It is pitiful," he said, "to have

William Goebel's wounds torn open at every election and his bones dragged from the grave to secure votes." The result of such tactics, however, was a Democratic victory in 1903, and for the first time in sixteen years that party won a majority of the votes cast. Facing a wealthy Louisville businessman (and son-in-law of former Democratic Governor Buckner), the incumbent's 229,014 votes outdistanced Morris B. Belknap's 202,764. As a result, Beckham ended up serving all but two months of two full terms. He had time to do much.

Beckham's administration left a decidedly mixed record of achievements. Basically the governor hesitated to take strong stands if opposition arose, and he sought to heal many of the wounds left by the Goebel affair. His legislatures passed a child labor law, acts concerning conservation, and a statute regulating insurance companies. Using funds received from the federal government for a long-delayed Civil War claim, Beckham ended the state's debt and began construction of a new capitol. Two new colleges—Eastern Kentucky State Normal School and Western Kentucky State Normal School—were established, chiefly to train teachers. A racing commission was set up to regulate horse racing, and the state fair was begun.

Yet these more progressive actions were offset by others of a less noble bent. The governor's declaration that Kentucky was "exceedingly generous toward her schools" did not help education. Beckham signed legislation that ordered Berea College, the last integrated college in the South, to become segregated. Limited franchise for women came to an end as well. The administration's numerous pardons and its close ties to the Hargis faction in the feuds in "Bloody Breathitt" brought much criticism. In addition, the state's highest court voided the creation of Beckham County because the county did not meet guidelines outlined in the new constitution. The time-honored process of naming counties for governors might finally cease, it seemed.

In some ways, Beckham's chief accomplishment lay in the political arena, for Democrats resurged and won most major elections.

In the 1900 presidential race in Kentucky, a huge turnout—86 percent of the voters—gave William Jennings Bryan a majority over incumbent president William McKinley; four years later Democrats once more carried the state, for Alton B. Parker over Theodore Roosevelt. Again the efforts of Kentucky Democrats proved of no avail, for the Republicans won nationally in both contests. In 1900 Democrat J. C. S. Blackburn took one US Senate seat, and two years later former governor James B. McCreary defeated incumbent William J. Deboe for the other. Near the end of Beckham's term, nine of the eleven members of the US House from Kentucky were Democrats. It appeared that the party had made a comeback. But factionalism, that old devil of the Democrats, had been growing as well. In his quest to build a base of power, Beckham alienated major leaders, including Senator Jo Blackburn, who said that if the "machine" tried to control the party, "there is going to be a black flag fight." Beckham enemy Henry Watterson broke with the "boy Governor" over another issue, one that widened party divisions.

Prohibition and Progressivism

Progressivism meant different things to different people in the first two decades of the twentieth century. Middle- and upper-class Kentuckians of urban and commercial backgrounds, in a sense, took up some of the reforms so long advocated by farm groups, and in their hands they now became respectable ideas, considered worth pursuing. Viewed as more moderate and less disruptive than the agrarians, such reformers found more support and had more success, as they tried to modernize their world while remaining true to many of the traditions of their past. They worried about the current situation, one filled with social unrest and much injustice, but remained optimistic about their generation's ability to change all that. With faith in a future of progress, they were convinced that they could eliminate many of the evils around them.

A historian has written that southern progressivism "was a diffuse, amorphous move-ment, embracing a complex of reforms designed to promote corporation regulation, political democracy, public health and welfare, efficiency, and morality." So it was in Kentucky. Not all interested groups or individuals supported all aspects of the political and social reform movement that gave the period 1900–1920 the label of the Progressive Era. Coalitions shifted, at times crossing party lines, at other times strengthening them. In the end, individual Kentuckians had to decide the extent of their own personal commitments to change.

Putting the ideas and theories of progressivism into practice required that citizens accept a "new interventionism," a different concept of government's role. In reality, this new view meant that trusts would be controlled by regulation of corporations, utilities, railroads, and the like. It meant that corrupt politics and bossism would be offset by laws forcing the direct election of US senators (instead of their being elected by the state legislature), the selection of party candidates through direct primary votes (instead of via political connections in "smoke-filled rooms"), and even, perhaps, the votes of women. Reformers would call out for acts against corrupt practices, more restrictions on lobbyists, and an extended civil service. They advocated social justice through child labor laws, factory safety inspections, and systems of workers' compensation. Food and drug controls for consumer protection, tax reform through a regulated income tax, attempts to fight poverty and give the dispossessed a better life, greater protection of natural areas and natural resources—all these issues were part of some people's progressivism as well.

It was in the area of social control, however, that Kentuckians had their greatest differences regarding progressivism. Some, in large urban areas of the United States, argued that true reform required a restriction on immigration. In the South, the same contention produced so-called voting reforms that resulted in white supremacy and a segregated voting system. Those conservative elements of progressivism had less appeal in Kentucky, for with comparatively few immigrants and blacks in the state, white, native-born residents did not see such groups as threats to the same extent as their counterparts did elsewhere. Instead, progressivism in Kentucky turned its full fury in the area of social control to one other part of progressivism—the prohibition of alcoholic drink.

Prohibition found many allies in the home of bourbon. At the same time that whiskey production in the state was growing from 5,870,000 gallons in 1871 to 30,386,000 in 1882, a strong movement was forming to control "Demon Rum" in the commonwealth. In 1874 the legislature passed a general local option bill that allowed towns, cities, and other legal entities to enact Prohibition if a majority of citizens so voted. Two years later Kentuckian Green Clay Smith ran for US president on the platform of the National Prohibition Reform Party, although he gained only 828 votes in his home state. John Hickman led a powerful temperance group, the Independent Order of Good Templars. Carry Nation, born in Garrard County, soon attracted greater national attention with her hatchet-wielding forays against saloons. In Kentucky, however, such religious-based groups as the Women's Christian Temperance Union (WCTU) and, after 1904, the Anti-Saloon League probably changed more attitudes. Two people led the fight, both operating from Lexington, both strong orators and national figures. George Washington Bain took the early leadership role, as presiding officer of the twenty-four-thousand-member Order of Good Templars and as editor of the *Temperance Advocate* newspaper. Through the active involvement of WCTU president Frances Estill Beauchamp, more than three hundred chapters of her organization were established across Kentucky. Temperance advocates asked citizens to look around themselves, for virtually every town experienced fights and deaths resulting from drunkenness. In 1895, Louisville alone had 840 saloons. The Prohibition forces argued that drinking produced spouse abuse, destroyed families, corrupted elections, and provided power to a "Beer Trust" or a "Whiskey Party." To their minds, drinking ripped apart the social fabric of society.

Those opposed to Prohibition praised the

individual's right to choose whether or not to imbibe alcohol, stressed the recreational benefits of beer gardens to laborers on their days off, pointed out how much money and how many jobs the liquor industry brought to Kentucky, argued that drinking could not be legislated out of existence (as shown by moonshining and bootlegging in "dry" areas), and noted that with the water and milk quality so poor, alcoholic beverages often provided safer alternatives. In a culture where saloons provided not only free meals with drinks but also an almost sacrosanct male meeting place, the Prohibitionists' attacks brought forth spirited defenses in return.

The anti-Prohibition forces, however, found themselves losing fight after fight. In the 1906 legislature a bill passed that permitted an entire county to vote to decide whether to allow liquor sales (and be "wet") or to restrict them (and be a "dry" county). Tardily, Governor Beckham came out in support of Prohibition, and the party split widened. As a result of the county unit law, by 1907, 95 of the state's 119 counties were dry. The fight now turned to statewide Prohibition, and that issue would be very divisive. It also proved to be a very emotional issue, as a political candidate's poster made clear: "Are you willing to redden your hands with human blood by voting to protect the Whiskey and Beer Trust? . . . If it strikes down your own boy, and sends him to a drunkard's grave and a drunkard's hell, how will you answer to the bar of God?" Prohibition and, indeed, progressivism in all its facets provided major defining issues in Kentucky life for many years.

The Black Patch War and the Night Riders

The Progressive crusade attempted to restrict trusts, to bring back Jeffersonian values, and to heal rifts between classes rather than to divide them further. With farmers across Kentucky facing a tobacco trust that controlled them, their actions could be viewed as part of progressivism, but, in reality, the roots of their rebellion lay in the nineteenth-century revolts of Populists, the Farmers' Alliance, the Grange, and other such groups. In those long-distressed areas of western Kentucky, the situation had grown worse and worse. Finally the farmers could take no more, and a massive popular uprising took place, which would spread to other parts of rural Kentucky. It was war.

Tobacco had become the salvation crop for more and more Kentucky farmers, who were attracted by its high prices and strong production from small plots. Whether the new light-colored burley or the dark tobacco of western Kentucky, the crop replaced others on farms, and less diversified production resulted. In good times this system worked well to yield greater rewards; but if prices fell, then all the farmer's fortunes were tied to "the filthy weed." By the turn of the century the agricultural situation was, in fact, becoming almost hopeless. The American Tobacco Company, together with two overseas groups, dominated the market, and the three agreed not to compete against each other when purchasing tobacco. A virtual monopoly resulted and left farmers no choice in selling their crop. They had to take what was offered, which was not much. Prices continued to fall, to levels below the cost of production. Agrarians had long been concerned about their declining economic fortunes in Kentucky, and now they grew desperate. Something drastic had to happen, they believed, or they would not survive.

Their answer proved to be a massive grassroots effort that united tobacco growers in an economic struggle against the tobacco trust. In September 1904 a large number of farmers met at Guthrie and soon formed the Planters' Protective Association (PPA), a two-state cooperative. Agrarians would pool their tobacco and hold it off the market until they were given the price they desired from the tobacco companies. In central Kentucky, the Burley Tobacco Society organized to decrease production and increase demand. But success depended on cooperation, and if significant numbers of agrarians defected, then the pool would not be effective. Some farmers, particularly those strapped for funds, continued to sell to the trust, and these so-called Hillbillies soon became the focus of

violence, particularly in the dark patch tobacco areas of western Kentucky.

Known as the Night Riders, or the Silent Brigade, lawless vigilante bands donned masks, took oaths of secrecy, obeyed the orders of leader Dr. David Amoss of Caldwell County, paid dues, and rode across the region to "persuade" farmers who remained outside the pool. They issued warnings, perhaps tied to a bundle of sticks thrown on a porch. Then they would destroy tobacco plant beds or burn the crops in the fields. If this action did not produce results, these vigilantes beat people—sometimes with thorn bushes—and even killed others. As one person noted, "To join the Night Riders was both fire and life insurance."

The violence spread, and soon Night Rider armies of hundreds of men took over entire towns and burned trust tobacco stored in warehouses. In Todd County and in Princeton, Hopkinsville, Russellville, Eddyville, and elsewhere, flames, bullets, and burned-out buildings represented the Night Rider legacy from 1905 to 1909. Unsupportive county officials either cowed to threats or were beaten. Huge divisions marked western Kentucky, as rural elements fought with urban ones, as Night Riders warred on Hillbillies. Homes became armed fortresses across the Black Patch. With some thirty thousand members in the PPA, more in the burley pool, and an estimated ten thousand in the paramilitary Night Riders, the tobacco farmers formed a formidable group. Many political leaders either openly or tacitly supported the PPA and usually the Night Riders as well. Those who were fighting saw the conflict as a people's war against a monopoly that strangled them, and all means were justified. Others saw property being destroyed and individuals being hurt, and they cried out against the use of illegitimate violence to achieve legitimate goals. When other area elements used the opportunity to harass, beat, or kill black families in the region, the whole movement began to take an ugly racist turn and whirled more out of control.

By the 1907 gubernatorial election, the Night Riders had become a major campaign issue. Governor Beckham, proclaiming that "our people are contented and prospering," had done virtually nothing about the situation. His party's nominee, state auditor Samuel W. Hager, had to bear that fact and the other burdens of his predecessor. Once an ally of Haly and Beckham, Hager disagreed with them during the race, and they offered him only limited support thereafter. Republicans knew they had a good opportunity to reclaim the office of governor. Their nominee, Augustus E. Willson, appeared to have the needed attributes. A sixty-year-old, Harvard-educated attorney from Louisville, Willson had been in a firm with the state's two major national Republican leaders, Benjamin Bristow and John Marshall Harlan. On the negative side, he had once served as a lawyer for the American Tobacco Company, and he had never before won a major elective office. He criticized Beckham's "bossism," pledged to end the violence of the Night Riders, and presented himself as the best choice of Prohibition forces. He won with 51 percent of the vote; 214,481 votes were cast for Willson, and 196,428 for Hager.

As governor, Willson soon activated several state military units and sent them to more than twenty tobacco counties in central and western Kentucky. He also dispatched detectives to uncover more details and even suggested publicly that he would pardon anyone who killed a Night Rider. The irony of a tacit endorsement of vigilantism—against the Silent Brigade—coming from a law-and-order governor was not lost on his critics.

Yet in the end, other actions had more to do with ending the Black Patch War. Finally some court convictions resulted, while in 1909, Kentucky's A. O. Stanley guided a bill through the US Congress that removed an oppressive national tax on tobacco. Two years later the US Supreme Court ruled that the American Tobacco Company had violated antitrust acts. The "cut out" of a whole year's crop—said by one historian to be the only successful agricultural strike in the nation's history—together with the pooling of crops had helped the situation as well. Higher prices for farmers resulted. But internal problems and the inability of agrarians to stay united during prosperity

A masked Night Rider, 1909. (Christopher R. Waldrep, *Night Riders* [1993])

doomed the PPA and the Burley Tobacco Society. Both dissolved. What remained was a Pyrrhic victory, one of temporary gains for agrarians but long-term losses for Kentucky. The violence had again seriously damaged the state's image, and the tobacco issue still had not been settled.

Both sides criticized Governor Willson during the "wars," for doing too much or too little. In some ways that was the story of his administration, which had a decent record of achievement. That achievement, however, came from a general assembly under Democratic control. The major accomplishment proved to be passage of an educational reform act, which established high schools in every county and gave the newly renamed State University needed funds. Limited progressive acts emerged, with a stronger child labor law, a new juvenile court system, a better pure Food and

Drug Act, and an eight-hour day for laborers on public works. The state legislature also ratified the Sixteenth Amendment to the US Constitution, which authorized the federal income tax. But attempts to enact broader laws concerning Prohibition failed, and that issue continued to make or break political fortunes.

The 1908 Kentucky General Assembly by joint ballot would again select a US senator, and hopeful Republicans put forth their colorful former governor William O. Bradley to meet the newly retired Democratic former governor, J. C. W. Beckham. When the votes were counted, seven mostly "wet" Democratic legislators had failed to support their party's "dry" nominee and had voted for others. No one had a majority. Over the next seven weeks, vote after vote was taken, with similar results. Political figures called on Beckham to step down so that another, less controversial party member could unite the Democrats and give them victory. He refused. Finally, on the twenty-ninth ballot, four "wet" Democrats switched to Bradley, and he was elected. Termed traitors, none of the four won reelection; Bradley later hired one as his private secretary.

During that same year, 1908, Republicans won the presidency once more, as William Howard Taft overcame Henry Watterson's colorful characterization of him as "a mess of pottage and a man of straw." With 83 percent of Kentucky's eligible voters casting ballots, the commonwealth had given its electoral votes to old hero William Jennings Bryan, 244,092 to 233,711. The efforts of the Bryan voters were of no avail. It was a Republican, outgoing president Theodore Roosevelt, who laid the cornerstone of the new Abraham Lincoln Memorial near Hodgenville in 1909; it was a Republican who held the governor's office when the new state capitol was christened in 1910. It seemed that a Republican tide had swept Kentucky. As it turned out, however, there was much ebb and flow still in party currents.

The Politics of Progressivism

For a long time many Kentuckians had been concerned about the situation both in the state and in the nation. In the commonwealth, the scandals, like the Tate affair, the party factionalism and third-party movements, the endless violence, the farm revolts, the corruption, and the inequities had all brought some citizens to call for a reform of the political system. Both parties contained elements of that reforming force, but since the invasion of Alliance and Populist elements into the Democratic Party, the Democrats had become increasingly supportive of change. Some party members, however, had either temporarily or permanently left the party, finding the reformist elements too radical. Now, though, different forces led the Progressive movement that was seizing the Democratic Party. These forces were more acceptable to the middle- and upper-class leadership elected by lower-class votes. Reform had become respectable, and both old and new leaders embraced it eagerly and readily.

Representing the old guard was one of the most accomplished political survivors of Kentucky history, former governor James B. McCreary. Since serving as chief executive of the state from 1875 to 1879, the former Confederate colonel had been in many political camps. When governor he had balanced between Bourbon and New Departure factions; as congressman during the monetary debates, he had first supported the sound money faction, then, as the votes changed, the free silver group. Initially opposed to Goebel, he had finally endorsed his campaign. He then became a Beckham supporter and won a US Senate seat in 1902 but lost it later in a primary to one-time ally Beckham. Now, seeking to leap out of political oblivion and gain the governorship in 1911, he once more tied his aging star to young Beckham and General Haly. Given all that waffling, it was no surprise that McCreary was nicknamed Bothsides. According to a popular story of the time, McCreary had once been observing black sheep in a field, and someone remarked on their color. "Well, they do appear to be black on this side at least," he responded. Such extreme cautiousness carried over to his political attitudes. He was asked once how he stood on the divisive question of Prohibition. McCreary replied, "If the people of Kentucky are for prohibition, I'm for it. If the people of Kentucky are against prohibition, I'm against prohibition. Does that answer your question, my friend?" The seventy-three-year-old candidate would seldom lead voters, but he very carefully gauged their wishes, then almost never opposed the views of the majority. With voters supporting reform, McCreary—ironically—followed them into progressivism. As a result, the vain man with the dyed hair, the politician so slippery on issues that he was called "Oily Jeems," became associated with major reform.

Two western Kentuckians represented the younger wave of progressive Democrats—A. O. Stanley and Ollie Murray James. Both men were superb orators; both could descend into demagoguery on occasion; both exhibited little sympathy for African Americans; both supported the Night Rider movement; both advocated numerous reform measures. Although not always united, the two men soon formed a new faction in the Democratic Party, one opposed to Beckham.

A. O. Stanley, the son of a minister who fought for the Confederacy and a mother who was the niece of Whig governor William Owsley, grew up in central Kentucky, but after becoming an attorney he moved to Henderson. There in 1902 he won election, at age thirty-five, to the US House and soon gained huge voter acclaim for his role in repealing a tobacco tax. A fierce opponent of trusts, he became nationally known for his actions in a congressional investigation of the US Steel Corporation. But it was the man rather than his programs that people most remembered. Eloquent, flamboyant, and intelligent, Stanley would stand before an audience, loosen his tie, and start his talk. Then as his passion increased, he would throw off his vest and coat and leave his audience shouting for more oratory. The subject of many of his harangues was his bitter enemy J. C. W. Beckham. Both men drank, but the former governor led the "dry" forces, a move that infuriated Stanley, who opposed Prohibition. Beckham, Stanley shouted, "would sell out the world to go to the Senate. This house is full of squirming cowardly prohibitionists just

like him. . . . I have not been a canting two faced hypocrite." Sparing few words, Stanley called his bête noire "a fungus growth on the grave of Goebel" and painted word pictures of him "with one dimpled hand placed trustingly in the cadaverous clutch of Percy Haly." In addition to their differences on Prohibition, Stanley and Beckham also took different stances toward corporations and trusts. Beckham had allied with the L&N, serving as its attorney, while Stanley had inflicted political damage on tobacco, steel, and railroad companies. Corporations representing all three interests opposed Stanley, with Milton Smith of the L&N calling him "a demagogue" and Beckham "a very good man." In truth, Beckham stood closer to the progressive camp than Stanley indicated, but the personal gulf between the two was too great to bridge. Even their campaign styles exemplified their differences, for Beckham relied on Haly's behind-the-scenes organizational talents, while Stanley trusted in his oratorical gifts. In the end, the only answer was a factionalism that further split the party.

Ollie Murray James, another relative newcomer, joined the Stanley faction. In his Crittenden County home, James lived across the street from one-time Republican US senator William J. Deboe. Elected to the US House the same year as Stanley, James moved to the US Senate in 1913 and supported measures to create an income tax and to elect senators by popular vote. A thorough progressive, he—like Stanley—gained national acclaim for his eloquent and forceful speaking style. Standing six feet, six inches tall and weighing well over three hundred pounds, he was, as one admirer recalled, "an enormous man with an enormous voice." James supported horse racing and disapproved of Prohibition—which placed him in opposition to Beckham on both counts—and he thus joined Stanley. But, in some ways, he went beyond his ally, for James compromised more and left fewer feelings of ill will behind as a result. He gained numerous national allies and in 1912 gave an important keynote speech at the presidential convention. Four years later, speaking as permanent chairman of the Democratic National Convention, he brought forth a large roar and a large demonstration when his booming voice praised the president as a peacemaker who was keeping the United States out of World War I, thus demonstrating "that principle is mightier than force, that diplomacy hath its victories no less renowned than war." Delegates discussed the possibility of James as a presidential candidate in 1920, and he appeared to be a good possibility. Then in 1918, at the age of forty-seven, he suddenly died of Bright's disease. It would be more than a quarter century before another Kentucky politician would again be seriously mentioned as a presidential candidate.

While James was making his impact in the nation's capital, James B. McCreary was doing the same in Frankfort. His election as governor in 1911 had not been easy. At the Democratic convention Beckham and other supporters of McCreary had passed a platform supporting Prohibition, which alienated Watterson, James, Stanley, and other "wets." Moreover, earlier in the race candidate Ben Johnson had dropped out, citing opposition to his Catholicism. The Republicans' own problems, however, offset these moral and religious questions. Their candidate, Judge Edward C. O'Rear of Montgomery County, had supported the law segregating Kentucky schools and thus risked losing the usually Republican black vote. He had also favored several reform measures that made moderates uneasy, while ignoring his predecessor's record. Governor Willson's friends gave him little support. McCreary won with 226,771 votes to O'Rear's 195,436. Northern Kentucky Socialist Party candidate Walter Lanfersiek gained most of the remainder of the ballots, with 8,718 votes.

McCreary's win resulted, in part, from the fact that he had a much better-funded campaign than did his opponent. The reason for that was John C. Calhoun Mayo. Born in Pike County, he settled later in Paintsville and abandoned school teaching for the business world. He traveled across eastern Kentucky, stopping at homes and farms, chatting with the owners, then offering them scarce hard currency in the form of gold coins in exchange for the option to mine the minerals on their land. Using such

"broad form deeds," he collected hundreds of thousands of acres of options, formed companies, and sold options to other major producers of coal. That sparked the development of the Eastern Coalfield. All this made Mayo incredibly wealthy, and he used that power in politics. With timberman Rufus Vansant of Ashland and horseman Johnson N. Camden Jr. of Woodford County, Mayo formed what was called the Millionaires' Club. Its members supported Beckham and Haly and, through them, McCreary. In return, the new governor saw to it that some of Mayo's suspect titles to mineral lands were validated. But Mayo's role as political financier was cut short in 1914, when at the age of forty-nine he died of Bright's disease. At his death, he was reputed to be the wealthiest man in Kentucky. Within the decade, then, each faction had seen one of its major figures die from the same disease—Beckham had lost Mayo, Stanley had lost James.

Despite McCreary's actions regarding the Mayo land titles, his administration had a very good record and justified the accolades he was given as a progressive governor. Legislation passed to give some women the vote regarding school matters. A department of public roads was created and funded, and a mandatory statewide primary system for selecting candidates was established. The legislature created numerous new regulatory groups, the Kentucky Illiteracy Commission, and a stronger child labor law, while funding construction of the new Governor's Mansion, strengthening the local option law, and lengthening the school term. It also rewarded McCreary by creating a county in his honor, which turned out to be the last of the state's 120 counties.

For Democrats, however, perhaps the greatest achievement came outside Kentucky.

The 1912 presidential race saw the usually victorious national Republican Party divided between incumbent president Taft, who had made William M. Bullitt of Louisville his solicitor general, and former president Roosevelt, whose followers eventually formed the Progressive, or Bull Moose, Party. Kentucky Republicans similarly divided, and Democrats had an excellent opportunity for victory. Two native Kentuckians, Oscar W. Underwood of Alabama and Champ Clark of Missouri, pursued the prize, with Clark being the choice of the delegates from the Bluegrass State. But in the end, a man whom an angry Henry Watterson called "cold, nervy, and unscrupulous," Virginia-born Woodrow Wilson of New Jersey, became the candidate, and on his shoulders the Democrats rode to victory. Republicans in Kentucky split their votes, with Taft getting 115,512 votes and Roosevelt 101,766. A particularly strong showing in Louisville bolstered Roosevelt. Socialist Eugene Debs received 11,607 votes, mostly in northern Kentucky. But a united Democratic Party won 219,584 votes, garnering the electoral votes of Kentucky, and Democrat Wilson won the nationwide election.

The race of 1912 proved important to the future of Kentucky political parties. With Woodrow Wilson firmly committed to progressive legislation as president, and with most Kentucky Democrats firmly supporting the chief executive, the party began to take much stronger stands on reform issues than before. At the same time, the more reform-minded elements of the commonwealth's Republican Party—those who had broken ranks and supported Roosevelt's Bull Moose Party—soon found themselves in a second-class status. Increasingly, conservatives would dominate Republican councils. For a time in the 1920s, there would be little difference between the two parties, until the next Democratic president once again made the Democrats the party of change.

A change of gubernatorial administration would take place in 1915, and the race that year turned out to be perhaps the most entertaining in the state's history. Beckham had finally become US senator in early 1915. With him removed as a political possibility, A. O. Stanley won the nomination for the Democrats, to face his close friend, Republican Edwin P. Morrow of Somerset. The son of a defeated Republican candidate for governor and the nephew of former governor Bradley, attorney Morrow was one of the few men in Kentucky who could match Stanley's speaking on the stump. The two men seemed to savor the situation and traveled together to towns and hamlets across the state, verbally ripping each other apart in daytime speeches, then often sharing the same hotel room and, some said, the same bottle at night. In a rollicking campaign marked by little substantial difference between the two platforms, the election came down to oratory and style. Morrow blamed Democrats for corrupt government and called for a Republican administration, since, he said, "You cannot clean house with a dirty broom." Stanley, in turn, criticized past Republican governors as corrupt: "Why a snake in a spasm isn't that crooked." With former Republican gubernatorial candidate O'Rear speaking with Democrat Beckham across Kentucky in favor of "dry" candidates, the liquor issue remained a potential threat to Stanley. Progressives from the Republican camp opposed Morrow and made their support a matter of concern for him. But personalities proved more of a decisive factor. The most widely repeated story told of Stanley's too free imbibing of his favorite beverage. Under the effects of a hot sun, he vomited in full view of the audience, while Morrow was speaking. When it came his turn to talk, a pale and weakened Stanley walked to the podium, then in a strong voice said, "That just goes to show you what I have been saying all over Kentucky. Ed Morrow plain makes me sick to my stomach."

Election day brought no resolution to the contest. The election was too close to call, and each side hesitated to report returns until it saw how many votes were needed to win. A week after the election, knowing that Democrats controlled the legislature and that contesting the results would end in failure, Morrow finally conceded. The official count later showed Stanley had won by 471 votes, 219,991 to 219,520, in the closest governor's race in state history.

Governor Stanley did not acknowledge that the election had been less than an overwhelming mandate for his views, and he proceeded to fashion an excellent record of accomplishments. With his term of office, the Progressive Era reached its apex in Kentucky. The general assembly passed a Corrupt Practices Act, a bill forbidding railroads to offer free passes to public figures, and a state antitrust law. In a special session, the legislators created a state tax commission, set up the first budget, and modernized the revenue system, shifting the burden from property taxes to other forms of taxation. Given more funds, the legislature then appropriated needed fiscal support for education and government. Ironically, the "wet" Stanley recognized the trends and agreed to let the people vote on a state constitutional amendment that would put in place statewide Prohibition. In 1919 the voters adopted Prohibition by a ten-thousand-vote majority, and the home of bourbon became officially dry before the nation did. When national Prohibition went into effect in 1920, under the Eighteenth Amendment to the US Constitution, one divisive state issue seemed settled at last. But other controversial issues had to be addressed as well.

Child Labor, Women's Rights, and Race Relations

Young children often worked long hours, from daylight to dusk, six days a week, on farms and in factories all across Kentucky. Families counted on the labor or meager salaries of children to help alleviate economic want. Youth ended early in such situations, and small bodies wore out quickly.

Reformers who sought to limit child labor argued that the state had a right to protect its future generations when they were powerless to protect themselves. Opponents stressed that children's work was an individual choice and said that the commonwealth had no right to interfere in what was essentially a family matter. As early as 1894 a law had forbidden children to beg or to peddle goods on the streets or to engage in jobs of unusual danger. But that measure left most young laborers untouched. In 1902 the first real child labor law for the state made it unlawful for industries to employ a child under the age of fourteen, except with a parent or guardian's signed consent. Farm work was exempt. A labor inspector, soon after that, found a Maysville factory in which forty children, aged eight to thirteen, worked from 5:45 a.m. until 6:15 p.m., with a thirty-minute break for lunch. All the children had permits; they all were legal under the new law; they all

worked twelve hours. Under these conditions, each child earned twenty-three cents a day.

In 1906 the law was amended to limit child labor to a maximum of ten hours per day and sixty hours per week, with the age raised to sixteen. Eight years later, under Governor McCreary, further changes lowered limits to a forty-eight-hour week and an eight-hour day. No child under the age of fourteen could work during school hours. With that law, Kentucky's child labor statutes were considered to be among the best in the nation. But inconsistent enforcement allowed many places to continue hiring young boys and girls in violation of the law. Kentucky cared better for its children as a result of Progressive Era reform, but it still neglected them all too often.

A much more controversial question focused on the role of women in Kentucky, and that fight had been building for decades. All agreed that there was a double standard for men and women, and the two groups did not share equal rights. In the nineteenth century most Kentuckians also agreed that that situation was how it should be. They defended the status quo with two somewhat contradictory arguments. The starker one simply said that women were not men's equals and should be subordinate to them as their "helpmates." A state senator in 1880 quoted the Bible's saying that wives should submit themselves to their husbands as the head of the family. Then he concluded: "Give me a wife that can love, honor, and look up to me as her lord and shield, or give me separation and death."

The second defense turned that argument around and said that women were subordinate to men in the public sphere but were superior to them in the home arena. Writers waxed poetic about nature's intended place for women. In the words of a governor, women are "but ministering angels in the quiet loveliness of our homes." Under "a cult of woman-worship," women occupied a higher moral plane than men, and to involve them in public life would "overburden" them and destroy their innate superiority. As late as 1914 Senator James—who would eventually vote for woman suffrage—said: "I believe woman should remain in her

273

sphere. Her power is greater where it is, than it would be in the mire and maelstrom of politics." Those who agreed with such perspectives would view any action to change the existing order as revolutionary, as an attack on the home and family and the whole social fabric.

Soon after the Civil War, fledgling and isolated groups began to question the status quo regarding women, probably beginning with an 1867 organization in Hardin County. National leaders such as Carrie Chapman Catt and Susan B. Anthony toured the state after that, and in 1881 the Kentucky Woman Suffrage Association was founded, the first such group in the South. Seven years later it transformed itself into the broader-based Kentucky Equal Rights Association (KERA).

Other women-oriented organizations formed in the same period, and most eventually gave the women's rights movement support in one way or another. The Daughters of the American Revolution, cofounded by Kentuckian Mary Desha in 1890, turned away from equal rights more as time passed, but groups such as the Women's Christian Temperance Union and the Kentucky Federation of Women's Clubs—the latter was founded in 1894—did not. Increasingly, members of such groups saw the vote as a way to achieve Prohibition, educational reform, and other goals.

Changes taking place in society also caused some people to question the "home sphere" argument. In 1884, Mildred Lucas of Owensboro won a special election to fill her murdered husband's unexpired term as jailer, but the state's highest court ruled that since she could not vote, she could not serve. Still, by 1903, a labor inspector wrote that "women in the business world are no longer regarded as intruders," and seven years later some 11 percent of Kentucky factory workers were female—although they received discriminatory wages. A study conducted in 1905 showed that the average daily wage was 87.5¢ for women and $1.63 for men. Still, change was in the air.

The first target was the state's discriminatory laws. Before 1894 Kentucky law and legal rulings allowed divorce for adultery only if the wife was the offender. And once a woman

married, she basically yielded her rights to her husband. While a wife could retain property, she could not sell it without her spouse's consent. If she received rents or earned wages, they went to him. If she wanted to make a will, she had to get her husband's consent. If she wanted to enter into a contract or own property in her name while her husband lived, she could not. Finally, in 1894, laws recognized a wife's separate legal existence, and gave married women property rights and the right to prepare a will. Six years later married women were allowed to keep their wages; a decade after that the state legislature raised the age of consent at which women could marry to sixteen years, up from twelve years.

More and more, the highly symbolic issue of suffrage held the key to opening the doors to full equality. As early as 1882, Congressman John D. White of Clay County had introduced a bill giving women the vote, but it did not come for a vote. Meanwhile, over time, greater numbers of middle-class and upper-class women began advocating their right to the vote, as a simple matter of justice. Because of their involvement in temperance reform, some women wanted the ballot in order to "clean up" politics. Others simply saw it as a way to leave behind a second-class citizenship status. Because of the level of leadership, the crusade became a call for respectable, not radical, reform.

Women such as Josephine K. Henry, of Woodford County, Eugenia B. Farmer, of Covington, and Eliza Calvert Obenchain, of Bowling Green, were important, but the acknowledged leader of the nineteenth-century fight was Laura Clay, of Madison County and Lexington. Ironically, her father, Cassius Marcellus Clay, had been a leading antislavery reformer, but he bitterly opposed women's rights. The inequalities involved in the divorce of Cassius Clay and his wife, Mary Jane Warfield Clay, prompted action on the part of their daughters Laura, Mary, Annie, and Sallie. All four women became strong advocates for the cause of women's rights. For twenty-four years Laura Clay served as president of the KERA. By the 1890s, she also was recognized as the leading southerner in the National American Woman

Laura Clay (*center, with umbrella*) leads a delegation of the Kentucky Equal Rights Association to the Democratic National Convention in 1916. (Laura Clay Photographic Collection, University of Kentucky Special Collections and Research Center, Lexington, KY)

Suffrage Association (NAWSA). Progress came slowly in Kentucky, however, and just as hopes for success grew high in the early twentieth century, Clay left the KERA. Disagreeing with the organization's strategy to seek a federal constitutional amendment and supporting states' rights arguments instead, Clay joined a splinter southern group, which used more racially charged arguments. Sadly, others would have to take up the suffrage banner she had borne for so long.

A younger woman, Madeline McDowell ("Madge") Breckinridge, hardly hesitated and energetically pushed forward to victory. A great-granddaughter of Henry Clay, she had lived part of her life at Clay's Ashland estate in Lexington and then furthered her already strong aristocratic credentials by marriage to Desha Breckinridge, editor of the *Lexington Herald.* He became a convert to the cause of women's rights and made his paper a leading voice for the movement. Madge Breckinridge's sister-in-law, Dr. Sophonisba P. Breckinridge, had probably been the first woman lawyer in Kentucky and served as a national leader in the field of social work as a professor at the University of Chicago. With that support, a reserved but confident Madge Breckinridge began her personal crusade. She did so despite great suffering, however, for at the age of twenty-four she had lost part of a limb to tuberculosis of the bone and wore a wooden leg the rest of her life. When thirty-two, she suffered a stroke and later experienced other unhappiness in her pri-

vate life as well. But as her biographer Melba Porter Hay, notes, "Instead of retreating from the world, Madge began to focus on reforming it." Incredibly active in virtually all the Progressive Era movements, Breckinridge made a difference in children's rights, labor issues, the tuberculosis crusade, educational improvement, racial matters, and more: "The children she never had, the sick, the poor, the women of the nation—all demanded her devotion." In 1912, she became president of the KERA, and vice president of the national group a year later. (She turned down the opportunity to be the national president.) The most influential woman in the state, she used new tactics, such as suffrage marches, as well as her speaking ability and humor, to gain more support. In a strong voice coming from a slim and often weak body, she told audiences to look at male-led Kentucky, with its poor schools, violence, and corrupt politics, and asked if the question should be not whether women were fit for suffrage but whether men were. She criticized one governor for his response to her questions, noting, "Kentucky women are not idiots—even though they are closely related to Kentucky men."

Slowly, gradually, her appeals made headway. In 1902 the legislators had taken a step backward and had repealed, supposedly because of racial arguments, a law that allowed women in second-class cities to vote on school matters. In 1912 the Kentucky General Assembly returned that right to literate women, in

One of the most important women in Kentucky history was women's rights leader Madeline McDowell ("Madge") Breckinridge of Lexington. (Mary Elliot Flanery Photographic Collection, University of Kentucky Special Collections and Research Center, Lexington, KY)

more areas across the state than before. Various attempts to secure a state amendment to allow women to vote failed, but with President Wilson's support for a national constitutional amendment, enough legislators fell in line. On January 6, 1920, Kentucky ratified the Nineteenth Amendment and became one of only four southern states to do so. The commonwealth, and Clay and Breckinridge, had long been leaders in the women's rights fight in the region and set the example to the end.

In November 1920 Kentucky women voted and for the first time had equality in suffrage matters. Within weeks after that election, Madge Breckinridge died at the age of forty-eight. Her tragedy was that she voted but once; her triumph was that she and others had voted, at last.

World War I

While women were fighting for political equality, people of both sexes had been fighting their own battles, both domestic and foreign, in a real war. In 1914 World War I broke out in Europe, and Americans easily adopted a policy of neutrality. Kentuckians experienced some prosperity as overseas demand brought an agricultural boom—farm prices went up 110 percent between 1915 and 1917 in one town, for instance—but overall, they seemed more interested in local political conflicts than in struggles between France and Germany. Bellicose editors Watterson of the *Courier-Journal* and Breckinridge of the *Lexington Herald* cried out for early entry into the war, but immigrant-oriented newspapers in Louisville criticized those appeals. Generally, citizens around the state evinced no real war spirit. Yet when Congress finally declared war in April 1917, most Kentuckians joined the national effort with little hesitancy and much fervor—in fact, almost too much fervor.

On the homefront, anything German became a target, and any action that questioned official policy was viewed as traitorous. Hearing Watterson's editorial advice, "To Hell with the Hohenzollerns and the Hapsburgs," the legislature forbade the teaching of German in schools, an act Governor Stanley courageously vetoed, saying the country was at war with a government, not a language. A minister termed him a "traitor and coward." In Campbell County, a group used the words "disloyalty, sabotage, and treason" to describe his action. Such feelings caused banks in Newport, Covington, and Louisville that had the name German in their titles to change to either American or Liberty Bank, while streets and places of worship also were rechristened. Some of the churches that still had Sunday services in German now ceased that practice, and sauerkraut became "liberty cabbage." Even private criticism of the government—as in the *Schoberg* case in Covington—earned jail terms for some Kentuckians, a pro-German Kenton County farmer was whipped, and those who did not buy bonds to help finance the fight were criticized as "enemies of their country."

Meanwhile, Councils of Defense in each community supervised the war effort at the local level. People sacrificed, with "Gasless" Sundays, "Fireless" Mondays, "Meatless" Tuesdays, or "Wheatless" Wednesdays, and they enacted stronger laws regarding morality. Not only did Prohibition emerge from the war, but many red-light districts across the commonwealth were shut down to protect supposedly innocent soldiers from such professional enticement. And there were many such professionals. A 1915 study of Lexington had revealed that some 188 "inmates" offered their services there; in Louisville the Vice Commission reported an estimated 463 engaged in prostitution. Some houses closed but reopened later; some did not. The most famous brothel in Kentucky, that of Belle Brezing of Lexington, did not survive the war. Belle, perhaps the model for a character in the book and movie, *Gone with the Wind*, had been so famous that when she died *Time* published her obituary and termed her's "the most orderly of disorderly houses."

Change occurred across the commonwealth. In fact, Kentucky in places took on the appearance of an armed camp. Troops patrolled bridges and public buildings. Fort Thomas in northern Kentucky and Camp Stanley in Lexington functioned as staging areas for soldiers sent elsewhere, while Camp Knox opened in 1918 as a training facility for artillery. But the major post became Camp Zachary Taylor in Louisville. Overall, about 200,000 soldiers received training there, including author F. Scott Fitzgerald. Some went on to fight—and die—overseas.

Unlike the situation in earlier conflicts, state identity was not retained in units, so soldiers found themselves scattered in all sorts of organizations. Fifth Regiment colonel (later general) Logan Feland of Hopkinsville and Owensboro, for example, would be the longest serving marine in France in the war, while Willy Sandlin and Samuel Woodfill won Medals of Honor for heroism. Eventually, over 100,000 Kentuckians served in the conflict, and 3,315 gave their last full measure of devotion in a conflict journalist Irvin S. Cobb termed "hideous and utterly awful." Thousands more returned with debilitating wounds or with lungs damaged by poison gas. One Owen County soldier wrote home, telling of the despair, and also the hope, in life in the trenches: "I thought I did not care if I lived or died, but when I would hear one of those big shells coming, and look death in the face, I . . . would decide I wanted to live awhile longer." Finally, on the eleventh hour of the eleventh day of the eleventh month in 1918, it all ended. A Kentucky soldier who survived concluded, "I cried because I was so glad it was all over. . . . We heard the last big roar die away and the world seemed quiet."

The suffering and deaths had not ended, however. In that same fall and winter, Spanish influenza struck Kentucky and the nation. At Camp Taylor the disease struck fourteen thousand soldiers, and an estimated fifteen hundred did not recover. Across the state, the "Spanish Lady" took its victims, and before the pandemic ended in early 1919, some fifteen thousand people had died. Schools, churches, and places of amusements closed; political rallies ceased; industries stopped; even funeral services halted. As one Leslie Countian remembered, "The flu came in here and it killed people in piles." With the epidemic raging across the state at war's end, few celebrations took place. The "war to end all wars" came to a quiet conclusion, and soldiers began to trickle back to their homes.

What had been the result of the war for Kentuckians? First of all, it initially stimulated, then eventually dampened the reform spirit. Women had worked in public campaigns during the conflict, and a few more took jobs as a result of the absence of men. That situation, plus the argument that democracy should extend to both sexes, helped the suffrage movement succeed. For those who viewed Prohibition as a reform, the war sped that movement forward as well. Yet Kentuckians, and Americans, had entered the conflict with the spirit, as one state paper explained, that "we wage not our own, but humanity's war." The Progressive Era had widened the idea of community to extend beyond the locality to the nation, or even the world. As one historian noted, "The war was to be the final crusade, the full flowering of progressivism." Yet it was not to be. Those who returned from the battlefields spoke little of glory; the hardships, the deaths, and then the epidemic at home did not seem rewards for noble actions. Doubts arose about America's mission, and the peace treaty seemed to leave many goals unrealized. As Congressman Alben Barkley—who had visited the trench warfare of the war zone—remarked, "You wonder if anyone ever wins a war." While the draft, Liberty Loan drives, and various other things had caused Kentuckians to see themselves as part of a bigger world, they mostly now turned more inward, back to their locales. In the end, the war wounded the humanist spirit of the people. Their recovery would be slow and uncertain.

Other results were more definite. Some prosperity had occurred, but it would turn out to be fleeting. More lasting was the damage done to schools, which suffered from a scarcity of teachers, and to health care. African Americans became a part of the war effort and participated in broad ways, but they found few new freedoms as a result. Mays Lick–born Colonel Charles Young, the third black graduate of West Point and the highest-ranking African American officer in the army, had been placed on inactive status in wartime, at least partly to prevent his appointment as a commander of white troops. In Fulton County, one African American veteran who had served his country was taken to jail, and then a mob hanged him, with his uniform still on. Another decorated black soldier was warned not to return to his Hickman hometown in the uniform he had honored because the police chief did not like blacks in uniform. This soldier's experience was not uncommon. Improved race relations would not be an outcome of this war. But almost all soldiers, black or white, did return home changed men. They had been to parts of the United States they had never before seen and had experienced foreign lands for the first time. New contacts, new people, new ideas all resulted. Some came back eager to change the land they had left behind. But most appeared more resigned to try to forget the horrors of trench warfare and to retreat into a world of quiet and peace. They had seen too much. Like them, most Kentuckians retreated from reform and retrenched in a reactionary world.

14

Bourbon Barons, Tobacco Tycoons, and King Coal

The Economy, 1865–2015

Agriculture

Before the Civil War, agriculture had been the economic lifeblood not only of Kentucky but also, in large part, of the nation. At a time when farm products formed a major part of economic wealth, Kentucky was a wealthy state. It ranked high or led nationally in the production of hemp, tobacco, corn, wheat, and livestock. Yet in the decades after the Brothers' War, Kentucky slowly lost its leadership position, in part because of decisions made within the commonwealth, in part because of events taking place in the United States. Overall, the country was becoming an industrial nation, and agricultural wealth declined in importance. Kentucky did not match the nation's pace of industrialization. But even in agriculture, problems arose. The opening of the great corn and wheat belt in the Midwest, for instance, introduced that region as a major producer that would soon eclipse Kentucky. Overall, several trends characterize the state's agrarian history between 1865 and 2015: Crop patterns changed and, for a time, were less diverse. Livestock also played a greater role. The involvement of the federal government increased as well. Finally, as agriculture, as a science and a business, professionalized, the agricultural workforce decreased, and the family farm declined.

Changing Crop Patterns

Hemp had been the major cash crop for many antebellum central Kentucky farmers, with its use in ships' riggings and as bale rope and bagging for southern cotton. Kentucky's economic isolation from the South during the Civil War, however, had forced cotton planters to look elsewhere for alternatives. That trend continued after the conflict's end, and jute bagging and iron bands for baling cotton gradually replaced hemp. At the same time, ships began using wire rigging, and another part of the hemp market declined. In 1860 the United States produced almost seventy-five thousand tons of hemp; a decade later the nation grew less than thirteen thousand tons. Kentucky's crop had declined from nearly forty thousand tons to less than eight thousand. Farmers needed alternate crops.

Some hemp growers did turn to other crops. A few held on. By 1890 the commonwealth grew 94 percent of all the hemp produced in the United States, but only a thousand farmers still worked those fields. Their crops yielded a thousand pounds per acre, brought an average price of $96.82 per ton, and gave them earnings of $800 each—for a total value of nearly $1 million. When World War I halted foreign imports, the crop experienced a brief revival, but by 1940 only four Kentucky farms still grew the fiber. The next year, however, another war brought further shortages as a result of the Japanese capture of Philippine jute fields. Encouraged by governmental supports, Kentucky farmers went back to hemp, and thousands of acres once more blossomed over the Bluegrass. A hemp factory was constructed near Winchester as well. The spurt proved brief, though. Buildings were sold as war surplus, and hemp effectively died as a Kentucky cash crop—or so it seemed.

The use of another variety of hemp in the form of marijuana cigarettes had become known by the 1920s. A national tax was instituted in 1937, and World War II hemp production had strict controls imposed on it. Afterwards, it became illegal to grow the crop without a license, and none was issued. For several decades after that, the crop seemed forgotten. Yet James F. Hopkins, the author of *A History of the Hemp Industry in Kentucky*, may have been more prophetic than he knew when he wrote in 1951 that "once more perhaps the distinctive odor of growing hemp will hang heavily in the summer air, and the fields of emerald green may once again add beauty to the Kentucky landscape." By the 1980s hemp was adding not only beauty but also green dollar bills to an underground economy. By then moonshine production had nearly ceased, but the spirit behind it lived on through illegal hemp/ marijuana production. "Wars" between federal and state officials and some Kentuckians broke out once more. In 1988 officials estimated that they destroyed half a billion dollars' worth of the potent "hillbilly pot" plants in Kentucky, but that half of the crop had been harvested and sold, partly by what they termed the "Cornbread Mafia." If so, then hemp may have again become the commonwealth's chief cash crop, for tobacco brought in only $471 million that same year. In 1992 more than nine hundred thousand plants were exterminated. As a result, Kentucky ranked first in eradicated plants in the US, and more than five hundred people were arrested. After that, however, marijuana production generally declined. But by 2014, legal production of industrial hemp—"It's rope not dope"—occurred for the first time in many decades. Despite all attempts to eradicate it, hemp persisted as a part of the state's economy.

The decline of the hemp industry after the Civil War and the growth of other production centers for certain crops helped make tobacco the undisputed ruler of Kentucky agriculture.

Bringing in a sizable return on a small plot, tobacco added dollars to farmers' income, but it also had longer-term effects on the state that would be debated for decades. In 1869, for example, the Columbus (KY) *Dispatch* warned readers of the health hazards of tobacco and asked smokers to restrict their puffing to private smoking rooms.

For all of the nineteenth century and much of the twentieth, however, few people seriously challenged tobacco's place in American life. Through chewing tobacco, pipes, and cigars and then, after the 1880s, through the popularity of factory-produced cigarettes, tobacco consumption rose. By the Roaring Twenties, daring women increasingly smoked. As a brief inspection of almost any motion picture of the 1930s and 1940s indicates, smoking had by that time become accepted in the middle class.

Kentucky farmers sought to fill the demand for tobacco. The work was not easy, and tobacco long proved resistant to labor-saving mechanization devices. But the major change affecting Kentucky tobacco cultivation came soon after the Civil War, apparently by accident. State farmers grew a dark-fired tobacco, "cured" by hickory smoke in tightly enclosed barns. In the 1860s, however, some seeds were planted—first on either a Brown County, Ohio, or a Bracken County, Kentucky, farm—and they unexpectedly matured into a lighter-colored leaf. White burley tobacco was born. From that beginning, the crop spread rapidly across the central Kentucky area, where hemp's decline had left a void. The new variety also began to replace the dark-fired version, since it could be harvested earlier and could be more safely air-cured in barns, where panels could be opened or closed to control moisture. White burley seemed a godsend to farmers increasingly strapped for cash. Gradually, more and more Kentucky farms turned away from a variety of crops and focused on the golden tobacco leaf. In Scott County, for instance, burley tobacco production jumped from 43,000 pounds in 1880 to 3.3 million pounds nine years later. Tobacco fever in Washington County brought an increase from 90,000 pounds in 1888 to nearly 2 million pounds by 1900; the county was producing almost 10 mil-

Tobacco and hemp grow side by side in a Woodford County field, 1931. (Kentucky Historical Society Collections, Frankfort, KY)

lion pounds by 1920. Cumberland County's tobacco crop increased fivefold between 1890 and 1940. The story repeated itself across Kentucky, as good prices made the switch attractive. In more difficult times, however, the increasing dependence on one crop and one price gave agrarians fewer options. For better or worse, Kentucky farmers had made their choice and had to accept the results.

The raising of tobacco continued almost without change, decade after decade. In a difficult, labor-intensive process, farmers plowed the land, sowed a protected seedbed, transplanted the shoots to a larger field, and began the endless weeding of the crop. They periodically "topped" the blooms to stimulate leaf growth, they removed worms, and they watched the weather for floods, hailstorms, and high winds. In late summer the whole family helped cut the crop, bring it to a barn for curing, and then strip the stalks. If the weather held and if prices were high, bills could be paid and income saved. All too often the reverse occurred, and suffering resulted. Yet even

then Kentucky could not bring itself to let go of a plant that held the state hostage and also paid the ransom.

Tobacco production statewide increased steadily from over 105 million pounds in 1870 to 180 million pounds three decades later. From 1865 through 1928 Kentucky led the nation in tobacco production. Yet that position came at a very real cost to farmers. The large amount of tobacco brought prices down, from a high of 13.7¢ per pound to 6.6¢ per pound during a twenty-year period ending in 1894. That decrease in price of over 50 percent offset the advantages of the increased poundage grown and brought angry farmers into the Grange, the Farmers' Alliance, and the Populist movement. When the American Tobacco Company formed a virtual buying monopoly and prices went down even more, the anger spilled over into violence, in the Black Patch and in the burley region. Resolution of these problems proved difficult, but the market seemed to be on its way up by the time World War I began.

Increased demand during the war years brought a 1916 Kentucky crop of 462 million pounds. Prices continued to rise. Farmers grew more and more tobacco, and it all seemed good for the industry. Then peace brought resumed production overseas, and markets suddenly declined. Hope made the 1919 crop the largest the state ever grew. Reality, in the form of overproduction, brought 1920 prices to 13.4 cents per pound, down from 34 cents per pound the previous year. Lower averages the next year shut down the market. Once more, planters lashed out at the invisible enemy of poor prices and formed another cooperative marketing organization. Joint action resulted in higher prices for a time. As in the Black Patch War earlier, however, impatient farmers could not remain united, and the cooperative failed by 1926. Once again agrarians had to turn to auctioneers, whose final cries left them still searching for answers to their financial problems.

Relative stability finally came to the tobacco fields as a result of the governmental controls and supports initiated during the New Deal years of the 1930s. As a result, by 1960, Louisville produced one-half of all American-made cigarettes. Eleven years later, the federal program shifted from an acreage quota to a poundage system, but the premise remained the same—the government would guarantee a stable price in exchange for limiting the crop. Better production methods occurred as well. The University of Kentucky Experiment Station produced or introduced more disease-resistant tobacco plants and pesticides that helped control tobacco worms. In the 1960s, these chemicals, such as MH-30, killed the "suckers" that had to be removed by hand previously. The experiment station also introduced baling rather than tying of the crop for sale in the 1980s. All that made the still-labor intensive crop easier to produce.

Crops and prices steadied to a degree, but in 1964, the United States' Surgeon General found tobacco injurious to health, and federal regulations soon required a warning on cigarette packs. All of which brought a Mt. Sterling paper to proclaim, "We don't need someone to tell us what's good for us. Pass the nicotine please." The warning label had limited effect on production, but smoking, which had once been a frequently copied and almost glorified social activity, continued to come under criticism and increasing restriction.

In 2005, the federal government ended its price supports, while also ending its acreage allotments. To aid Kentucky farmers in the transition to other crops, a $2.5 billion tobacco buyout program provided some support, until it concluded in 2014. With the end of the support system, farmers could grow as much tobacco as they desired, but without the security of price supports. Instead of selling to many buyers at auction warehouses (which disappeared), now growers found themselves selling directly to a single tobacco company at a predetermined cost through a contract system that harkened back to days past, when farmers found themselves at the whim of the manufacturer for the grading and pricing of their crop. All that, coupled with labor shortages, higher costs, and competition from foreign growers, produced smaller crops, on fewer farms. Between 1992 and 2012, farms growing tobacco declined from almost 60,000 to under 5,000, and acreage dropped from 268,000 to 88,000. Production in 2015 was under 150 million pounds—a far cry from the 366 million of 1990. Still, the state remained the second largest producer of the crop, after North Carolina. Tobacco, once a crucial and controversial part of Kentucky's agricultural past, remains a part of its present, but a much less important aspect. In 2015, tobacco ranked only fourth in Kentucky crop receipts, behind soybeans, hay, and corn.

Even in the best of economic times, tobacco had not reigned unchallenged. Various crops sprang up to dispute that dominance, but none offered a sustained value that would bring farmers to abandon tobacco. By 1870, however, before burley's great growth, Kentucky remained diversified, ranking not only first nationally in hemp production but also fifth in rye, sixth in corn, and eighth in wheat. In 1890 the state stood third nationally in apple production. All of those crops, however, faded relatively before tobacco, other states' dominance, and farmers' preferences. Wheat production, for example, doubled between 1870 and 1900, but a decline followed. Only near the twentieth century's end did wheat production in the state climb back to nineteenth-century levels. Oats never did. A crop that in the 1880s had been grown on twice as many acres as had tobacco, oats had become chiefly a cover crop a hundred years later.

Most of the agricultural variety in twenty-first-century Kentucky came from the three now-major revenue crops—hay, corn, and soybeans. Between 1889 and 1907 the acreage devoted to hay increased 40 percent, and annual production approached a million tons by 1909. In 2014, over 2.2 million tons were harvested, ranking the state fourth nationally. Similarly, in 1900 nearly half of the state's six million acres of cropland was planted in corn. This figure would rise and peak in the wartime year of 1917. The widespread use of hybrid seed corn by the 1940s helped increase production from 63 million bushels in 1896 to over four times that figure by 2014—placing Kentucky fourteenth in the US. And the amount of labor required to produce all crops dropped drastically—the labor hours to grow a hundred bushels of corn, for example, fell from 147 in 1900 to only 3 hours by century's end.

The greatest change in the state's agricultural mix of crops came in the growing of soybeans. The crop was virtually ignored for much of the nineteenth and twentieth centuries; only 5,000 acres were harvested in 1928. By 2015, however, over 1.7 million acres produced nearly 84 million bushels of soybeans, valued at over $1 billion. That made soybeans the state's number one cash crop and Kentucky the nation's fourteenth-leading producer. Capable of two crops in one growing season and used in various forms, soybeans appeared the most likely candidate of choice when farmers abandon tobacco.

Livestock

Crops represent only one of the farmer's sources of income. By 2013, in fact, cash receipts from livestock overall, at $2.8 billion, almost matched the money generated from crop sales, $2.9 billion. Yet reaching this level of livestock production—chiefly of cattle, sheep and lambs, hogs, and poultry—had taken a long time and had required drastic changes in the production processes.

Hogs and pigs were early mainstays of Kentucky agriculture, used both for home food purposes and for sale to nearby markets in Louisville and Cincinnati. Like other livestock, swine for many years roamed free on open ranges, to be collected at the time of sale. Soon after the Civil War's end, the state had more than 2.1 million hogs, but a decline followed, and the state had only 325,000 in 2014, down from nearly a million head just a quarter-century before. Sheep experienced even more drastic declines. In 1867 Kentucky had 1.1 million sheep, constituting an important part of self-sufficient farms, where families used the wool to produce homespun materials. As store-bought clothes filled that need more and more and as other markets opened, sheep production almost ceased. By 2015, Kentucky sheep and lambs numbered fewer than 50,000. By then Kentucky ranked twenty-first nationally in numbers of hogs, and twenty-ninth in sheep and lambs. It was a far cry from 1870, when Kentucky had stood fourth nationally in numbers of swine and tenth in sheep.

The new success industry replacing those was poultry. Particularly in rural areas, chickens had long furnished meat as well as eggs, not only for home use but also for barter at country stores and for cash sales. Needs and markets changed, however, and from a high of more than 14 million chickens in 1944, the numbers dropped to 6 million in 1961 and 2 million in 1990. But as large-scale poultry production facilities moved into the commonwealth, production drastically increased, so that by 2015, poultry was the number one agricultural commodity in the state, with a value of over $1 billion.

The cattle industry in Kentucky did not suffer such drastic changes. Damaged by the Civil War, cattle production in the state required almost two decades to attain its prewar level. Then western markets, railroad refrigerator cars that brought western beef to eastern processing centers, and new diseases in Kentucky herds all slowed relative growth. Cattle remained at the 1 million level for nearly four decades after 1886. Better animal feed, improved breeding methods, and increased popularity of Hereford and Angus herds were offset by agricultural depression and the drought of 1930. Major increases began after 1940, and production rose to over 3.7 million head in 1975. But declines followed, to 1 million cattle and calves in 2015. Still, the state had the most beef cattle of any state east of the Mississippi River, ranked eighth nationally, and cattle and calves overall stood fourth among the commonwealth's cash receipts from commodities. In short, even though Kentucky farms and businesses had turned away from hogs and sheep, and more toward chickens and cattle, the livestock industry had experienced inconsistent growth, and its role in Kentucky's future remained uncertain.

Then there were the horses. Almost from the time of statehood Kentucky had been known as a place for quality thoroughbreds and, later, standardbreds. Yet the Civil War had hit the commonwealth particularly hard in regard to horseflesh, quality or otherwise. The census of 1870 showed that the 350,000 horses then in Kentucky represented a decrease in numbers of more than 60,000 animals from a decade earlier, before the war. Mules, which had survived military raids better, made the state a major market for that four-legged beast. Kentucky ranked third nationally in the number of mules in 1870. Three decades later, the state still held an important place, with 190,000 mules within its borders. But by 2013, only 14,000 of the once-commonplace and hard-working mules existed in the state. With increased mechanization in the twentieth century, the need for horses and mules, either to work on farms or as methods of transportation, declined with each passing year. From 450,000 at the start of the twentieth century, the number of Kentucky horses fell to 240,000 over a century later.

Throughout that time, however, thoroughbred farms in Kentucky continued to produce major racing champions. In 1926, 44 percent of the thoroughbred foals registered with the Jockey Club were from Kentucky. But changes soon affected the numbers. Competition from other states, a more unfavorable national tax structure, and other factors lessened the state's dominance of the industry. But in the twenty-first century, the commonwealth regained that position, in part. That was symbolized when the World Equestrian Games made their first North American appearance in 2010 in Lexington. On the business side, by 2013 Kentucky still produced almost half of all the foals registered in North America and ranked first in horse sales and stud fees. Overseas buyers drove up sale prices drastically in the 1980s, when one horse sold for $13.1 million, but those heady days passed. Nationally, fewer foals have been bred; track betting has declined; tracks have closed. The horse industry also competes with other entertainment options that have emerged. And what was once "the privileged . . . primary form of gambling in the U.S.," now faces competition from casinos, online sport betting, and other venues. Although the major tracks in the state have continued to do well, overall, all that had an effect on the industry. In fact, by 2015 horse sales and stud fees stood only third in Kentucky's livestock receipts, behind poultry production and cattle sales. While the state's image nationally remained tied in part to the thoroughbred, some worried citizens grew concerned about the ability of the industry to persevere and grow.

"The Feds," the Family Farm, and Agribusiness

Those who formulated New Deal farm policy in the 1930s recognized that overproduction had long plagued tobacco farmers. Through the Tobacco Control Act of 1934, tobacco growers could vote for mandatory quotas, in exchange for a minimum price (parity) guaranteed by federal funding. State farmers agreed to that scheme, and in 1936, for example, they reduced their harvest by 28 percent while increasing overall income by several million dollars. The limits on acreage (and later poundage), plus the huge increase in demand during the war years—consumption went up 75 percent between 1939 and 1945—brought a boom to tobacco. Ironically, in the forty-year period from 1965 to 2005 the federal government subsidized production while criticizing and limiting tobacco products in the marketplace.

If for years federal policy aided certain parts of the agricultural community, virtually all sectors felt the effects of broader changes in the agrarian world. Generally, farm homes lagged behind the rest of the commonwealth in receiving the advantages of "modern" America—good roads, electricity, indoor plumbing, and the like. As late as 1940, for instance, four of every five rural dwellings in Kentucky had no electricity, no telephones, no refrigeration, and no access to hard-surfaced roads. Ninety-six percent had no running water. As technology and transportation bypassed much of rural Kentucky, particularly the Appalachian area, the ideal of agrarian life seemed unalterably tarnished. Kentucky could not keep its population down on the farm.

In 1880 more than two-thirds of the state's labor force worked on farms (versus a US average of fewer than one in five workers). In 1940 slightly more than one-third of that force still worked in agriculture. But by 2015 less than 3 percent of the state's labor force did. As a result, the number of farms in Kentucky declined from a peak of 270,000 in 1920 to 76,000 ninety-five years later.

Yet despite all that, Kentucky remained a significant agricultural state, if for no other reason than the fact that the mindset of rural areas remained agrarian. After all, compared with the rest of the nation, numerous Kentuckians still farmed. In 2013, the state stood sixth nationally in the number of farms, chiefly because of the small size of average holdings. From the end of the Civil War until the start of World War II, state farm size declined, from an average of 158 acres in 1870 to a low of 80 acres in 1940. But as people left the farms after that, larger farms became more commonplace, and the average farm size increased to over 100 acres in 1955 and some 170 acres sixty years

later. Still, the average farm in Kentucky was about one-third the size of the typical American farm.

In the half-century after the Civil War, Kentucky agriculture had three advantages. First of all, it had survived the Civil War better than agriculture in the South, and in 1870 Kentucky had more acres in agriculture than any southern state, save one. As late as 1900 the value of Kentucky's farm products surpassed that of all southern states except Texas. Kentucky also depended less on tenant labor, comparatively, than did other southern states. At a time when about one-half of most farms south of the Mason-Dixon Line were operated by tenants, only between one-fourth and one-third of Kentucky ones were. Moreover, very few black Kentuckians were tenants—representing only 8 percent of all tenants in the state in 1900—and the chances for racially unfair treatment therefore remained lower. Finally, Kentucky farms remained relatively mortgage free. In contrast to the images of the debt-ridden agrarian, an 1890 report indicated that 96 percent of the state's farmers had no debt on their property (72 percent of the nation's farmers were mortgage free). Twenty years later, at the close of the era of the tobacco wars, 85 percent of Kentucky farmers were without mortgages.

Yet despite all that, the real statistics of importance show the relative poverty of Kentucky farmers, even when they formed the mainstay of the state's economy. Rural Kentuckians did not live on valuable plots—the 1920 average value of state farms was not much beyond one-third of the national mean, and the commonwealth ranked forty-first of forty-eight states in that regard. While the state ranked high compared with the South in the value of farm production in 1900, the South was poor. Overall, Kentucky stood only fifteenth nationally that same year. By 2013 little had changed—the state ranked sixteenth in the United States in net farm income.

But in those years, Kentucky had seen drastic agrarian modifications. In fact, the farmers of 1900 little resembled their counterparts a century later. The earlier era featured small, family-operated farms, with mules or horses pulling plows through unfertilized fields, with acreages little improved by conservation efforts. While a variety of livestock helped make such places more self-sufficient, already a dependence on one crop was the seed for future problems. Farmers lived a life governed by daylight and the weather.

A century and more later, much had transpired to change all that. Terms that had once seemed foreign to Kentucky farmers, such as "crop rotation" and "soil conservation," were accepted without question. The beginning of the state fair in 1902 had helped showcase new agricultural successes. By the 1920s county extension agents, operating under the aegis of the University of Kentucky College of Agriculture, began to have an effect, as they told farmers about new methods and different options. Hybrid plant strains, chemical herbicides and pesticides, education about the values of fertilizer—all had an influence. By the 1980s some farmers did not plow their fields, using chemicals instead in the "no-till" method.

While that made life easier for the farmer, production per acre also drastically increased. Tobacco poundage went up from 550 pounds per acre in 1874 to 1,100 pounds per acre in 1945, and two decades later the figure had doubled again. The average bushels of corn produced expanded from 27 bushels per acre in 1904, to 116 in 1989, and to a record 170 in 2013. Wheat's yield of 4 bushels per acre in 1885 escalated to 71 bushels 130 years afterward. As a result, the shrinking amount of land devoted to farming produced more and more, with less effort. For those who had struggled in the hot summer sun for meager returns, those changes seemed almost miraculous.

In a sense, farming became more professional and less personal. Other labor had replaced that of children on larger farms; tractors had taken the place of mules; mechanization had displaced hand planting; machines, not people, milked cows or fed livestock. No longer could successful large farmers plant the same seeds in the same field, year after year, with little knowledge of outside events and forces. Kentucky farmers had to have global vision,

for the markets for tobacco, live animals (including horses), and feed grains extended beyond national boundaries. In 2013 the state sold nearly $2 billion in agricultural products abroad, representing over a third of state production. Instead of using a stubby pencil to write notes in a worn notebook, farmers now could use a computer tied in to a widespread communications network. They focused on interest rates, investments, and income potential and lived in air-conditioned homes that usually featured all the conveniences of the city. The gap between farm and city had narrowed considerably.

By the first decades of the twenty-first century, Kentucky agriculture had a twofold division. On the one hand, well under half of those who operated farms did so because farming was their primary occupation. They made their living from "agribusiness." The toilers of the soil followed the latest agricultural bulletins, experimented with new hybrids and herbicides, and seemed far removed from the often-provincial agrarians of the century's first decades—those who had trusted the weather and had waited. Chance played a much smaller role in their lives than in those of their ancestors.

Others who identified themselves as farmers were very different. Some 57 percent of the commonwealth's farms had sales of less than ten thousand dollars, and most of the laborers in those fields worked as part-time farmers. For them the agrarian way of life still had importance, but farming was a secondary consideration, providing a supplementary income. The family farm of yesteryear had increasingly disappeared from Kentucky. An ideal of a nation of small, self-sufficient farms whose yeomen formed the backbone of the country seemed as far away as a distant star. Few Kentucky counties depended on farming as the keystone of their economies, but many worried about developers taking more and more of their farmland. Yet those who continued to work a small plot, perhaps in the evening or on weekends, showed that the smell of the earth, the view of crops blowing in a breeze, the feel of the land itself, even yet remained an important part of the Kentucky psyche.

Commerce

Even though Kentucky would long honor the agrarian ideal, residents would increasingly praise the goal of a more commercialized and industrialized commonwealth with each passing decade after the Civil War. Slowly, more and more people in Kentucky accepted the idea that future progress was tied to industrial growth. Few questioned exactly how that growth should occur, or at what price because the United States was developing industrially and state government and business leaders feared being bypassed. City leaders fought to attract new industry to their locales. This urban boosterism pushed the businessman as the new ideal.

Yet Kentucky had great difficulty attaining the commercial success its leaders desired, as two examples indicate. The state's timber, for instance, provided a vast resource, worth millions of dollars. Small subsistence farmers needed cash to pay taxes and bills, and often their only real source of money was the timber around them. They would cut the trees and take them down aptly named "snake roads" to log dumps, where a "splash dam" had backed up enough water to float the logs. Tied together in great booms, which might typically be sixteen feet wide and fifty to a hundred feet long, the logs would be released into the waters of the Kentucky, the Licking, the Big Sandy, the Cumberland, or a few western Kentucky rivers when a high "tide" caused by rains finally occurred. Over the next several days, loggers would guide their rafts through treacherous waters, in a process that cost some loggers their lives. Finally they would reach a mill, at Beattyville, Irvine, Frankfort, Catlettsburg, Ashland, Clay City, Burnside, Paducah, or oth-

Many Kentuckians made money by cutting trees. They tied them together in rafts and floated them down a river. They lived in little shacks, like the one in the picture. (Library Special Collections, Western Kentucky University, Bowling Green, KY)

er places, and sell the logs. In 1890 a sizable raft would yield between $150 and $300. At that time those sums represented one or two years' worth of wages for a laborer. If the loggers could resist the temptation to spend their new cash on the worldly temptations near the mills, they could return home and pay off bills. If not, they at least could come back with new memories of an exciting time.

That system presented many problems, however. Those in poverty needed money and cared little about renewable resources. As a result, whole forests were stripped and never replanted. As early as 1868, the *Bowling Green Democrat* warned that small forests in the area had already been exhausted and others would follow "unless a different system is adopted." In 1887 the governor called on the legislature to reforest denuded land and preserve the remaining timber. No one acted. The head of the Kentucky Bureau of Agriculture, Labor, and Statistics worried in 1905 that state forestlands were being devastated "without regard for the future." Barren County, he reported, remained "nude of even firewood." His successor in 1909 predicted that the "suicidal" cutting of timber resources would strip the state of all good trees within eighteen years. Not only lack of income but also soil erosion and flooding would result.

The timber boom continued for a time. From 1870 to 1920 flush years brought large sales. In the peak year of 1909, over a billion board feet of lumber was sold, and some ten thousand worked in the industry. As predicted, however, the timber began to run out, and in 1927 production had fallen to less than one-third of the previous high. The glory days had passed, and timber rafts became rare sights in the rivers by the 1920s. The huge Mowbray-Robinson Company in Perry, Knott, and Breathitt Counties depleted fifteen thousand acres of timber. By 1922 the area industry that had employed five thousand workers had vanished. The deforested region and a million dollars were donated to the state university, the sawmills were torn down, and the railroad lines were abandoned.

But perhaps the greatest tragedy for Kentucky's economy, other than the exhaustion of the land and the partial devastation of timber as a resource, was the fact that those raw materials did not form the basis for some other home industry, such as furniture building. In a story that would be told and retold in the commonwealth's economic history, many of the benefits of Kentucky's sizable timber industry went outside the state. When by the 1990s the commonwealth made its way back to become the nation's fourth-largest producer of hardwood lumbers—furnishing 11 percent of American production—still three-fourths of that lumber was shipped, unprocessed, to other states.

A second example of the problems facing Kentucky's commercial sector affected the area around Cumberland Gap. For years, Kentucky had been an important producer of iron, through furnaces scattered across the state. The Ashland Furnace, started by John Means, for instance, produced over thirty-five tons daily in 1869. But depletion of ore and timber resources, the middling quality of the local product, and the easier availability of iron to out-of-state buyers through better transportation all hurt the industry. The Boone Furnace in Carter County ceased production in 1871, the Estill Furnace in Estill County stopped blasting in 1874, and the Raccoon Furnace in Greenup County did not operate after 1884. The story was repeated across the commonwealth, as the industry declined from the number three position nationally that it had held in 1830. The dream died hard, though, and in 1886 Alexander A. Arthur looked out at the half dozen houses in a valley near the Gap and saw visions of greatness. As president of the British-owned American Association Limited, he bought huge tracts of untouched coal and iron reserves and started construction of a railroad tunnel under the Gap, to this new place called Middlesborough.

By 1889 the area was being transformed into what was expected to be a major steel manufacturing center in the United States, much on the order of Birmingham, Alabama. In a violent and raucous boomtown atmosphere, Englishmen in silk hats, monocles, morning coats, and spats mixed with upper-class easterners and rough mountaineers in the

"Marvelous City." Steel mills were established, coal mines dug, railroads completed, and businesses built. On a wide main street designed for future growth, ten blocks of stores sprang up; town lots sold at unheard-of prices of more than four hundred dollars per square foot. Impressive stone and brick Victorian homes were constructed on spacious lawns. In this "New Eldorado," a massive hotel served by an electric railroad became the center of social life, while the state's first golf course attracted attention. It was a heady time for investors.

In 1890, though, a fire destroyed the core of the city. That same year a bank failure in England cost foreign investors heavily and left Arthur without the capital necessary to go forward. In the United States, a national business depression struck. Then it was discovered that the iron deposits so central to growth were of a mediocre quality. The boom ended with a thud, and land values fell nearly to nothing. The four banks all failed, and half the population left. Those who remained included people who were once wealthy but now were penniless or even insane as a result of their losses.

Middlesborough's experience in many ways represented the pattern of future development in the state. The capital for growth had come from outside the commonwealth, and that circumstance would characterize Kentucky's economy after 1880. Saying that the state became part of a colonial economy, with control located outside of the commonwealth, may be an overstatement, but the analogy is not too inaccurate. Even though Kentucky-owned businesses continued and prospered, as time wore on the finances directing the state's growth, as well as the stockholders and boards of directors of the major business institutions operating in the commonwealth, increasingly came from outside the state. The wealth went elsewhere, and Kentuckians lost more control of their economic destiny.

What was attempted at Middlesborough took place on a smaller scale at other locales in eastern Kentucky, as new coal communities changed the face of the land. Some towns rose and fell with the fortunes of the minerals; others expanded and grew on their own. Similar-ly, towns all across the commonwealth might spring up and prosper for a time, because of their location along a new railroad line or because of a sudden oil or timber boom in the area. Many of those places, some of which were sizable communities, fell back into quiet obscurity as the boom ended.

More commonly, urban areas in Kentucky grew or declined in commercial activity at a slower pace. Most smaller cities might have an industry or two, but they generally gave the impression recorded by an 1881 traveler: "There are no manufactories in these towns; they make one think of villages in rural England." Most of the growth took place in the larger urban areas. Towns expanding in the late nineteenth century and the early twentieth generally were located in the eastern or western regions of the state. In the east, Ashland's strength in timber, petroleum refining, and iron rolling mills brought a doubling of population to twenty-nine thousand during 1920–1930. In the west, Owensboro, the site of a major wagon company, tobacco factories, and, after 1900, a light bulb manufacturing plant, almost quadrupled in population between 1880 and 1920, reaching nearly twenty-three thousand. At the same time Paducah, then slightly larger than Owensboro, almost tripled in size. Also west of Louisville, Henderson, whose woolen mill produced "Kentucky Jeans," had municipally owned water, gas, and electric utilities. It also had the first electric streetcars in the area, which operated from 1889 to 1923.

Cities in the central and northern parts of the commonwealth grew as well, but at a slower pace. Once at the forefront of commercial activity in what was the New West of the early nineteenth century, Lexington had languished since then, and an 1886 visitor accurately described it as "a pretty village," living on "frequent memories of fugitive greatness," a place whose dreams of glory had passed. By 1900 it had fallen to fourth in population among the state's cities, behind the growing Covington and the static Newport, which both benefited from the expansion of adjacent Cincinnati. Lexington's economic fortunes would change within half a century, but some communities could never adjust from being a supplier to a surrounding agrarian world to being an industrial place. Moreover, the residents of some towns may not have wanted such a change.

In truth, Kentucky had only one truly industrial and commercial city. After all, in 1890 only six cities in the commonwealth had more than ten thousand inhabitants, and commerce in those places concerned relatively small establishments. For most of the nineteenth and much of the twentieth century the only sizable manufacturing center in the state was Louisville.

The Falls City and Urbanization

Virtually untouched by the Civil War, Louisville, in fact, benefited from it economically. The Falls City emerged at war's end as a center of trade for the still-devastated South. Traveling salesmen, called drummers, spread the gospel of trade to small stores and homes across the region, all the time preaching the virtues of Louisville's goods. Those economic missionaries capitalized on Kentucky's southernness and usually introduced themselves by a military title, obviously won in the Rebel cause. They told stories, entertained the locals, and made sales. In 1874, a year in which the Falls City sold 287,000 bales of southern cotton, one paper in Arkansas said that people there knew "no market but Louisville."

Louisville-based J. P. Morton and Company had become "publishers to the Lost Cause," and the *Louisville Courier-Journal* had for a time the largest circulation of any southern newspaper. Capitalizing on these connections, the drummers rode the L&N Railroad, took orders, and sent them back to the Falls City to be filled. There stores such as Bamberger and Bloom, the largest in the region, did the rest. Louisville also had the largest plow factory in the world, B. F. Avery's, and near the end of the nineteenth century the city was the nation's chief producer of cast-iron pipe, the largest banking capital in the South, the chief leaf tobacco market in the world, the second-largest tobacco manufacturing center in the United States, and the home of the largest textile industry west of the Appalachians. The city at one time featured the largest leather market in the United States and served as one of the major paint and varnish centers, as well as a significant liquor headquarters, with thirty-five distilleries on the eve of World War I. It continued to be an important pork-processing center, though economic rivals Cincinnati and St. Louis made inroads there, as in other areas. Still, Louisville's prosperity brought its exuberant spokesman, editor Henry Watterson, to cry out that "a union of pork, tobacco, and whiskey will make us all wealthy, healthy, and frisky."

Notwithstanding the question of the Louisvillian's frolicsome and robust nature, the people and the city certainly prospered. Between 1870 and 1900, the population doubled to more than two hundred thousand, making Louisville the nation's eighteenth largest city. Visitors to the urban metropolis saw a place that had the look and feel of a big and vibrant city. One observer in 1888 wrote that the "friendly" city "has the unmistakable air of confidence and buoyant prosperity." The city celebrated that wealth with a popular Southern Exposition that ran from 1883 to 1887 and included the newly introduced electric lights. Louisville also featured fine theaters, a growing system of parks, designed in part by Frederick Law Olmsted; racing at Churchill Downs; and 175 miles of street railways by the first decade of the twentieth century. The second largest city in the South offered telephones, electric lights, daily ice delivery, and much more, plus a strong literary tradition. In places such as St. James Court and nearby Central Park, a new elite and old families mixed. Later, summer homes grew up away from the core of the city, and then permanent residences connected by street railways broke up the earlier unity to a degree, but the orientation remained toward downtown. Each generation, however, faced the problems of slums, violence, and racism. For better or worse, Louisville was the place where Kentucky first confronted the industrialization of the new United States.

Louisville's growth continued at a less spectacular but still steady rate through the first decades of the twentieth century, and the city ranked twenty-second nationally in the value of manufactured products in 1920. At the end of the twenties, manufactories in or near Louisville provided over half of the value added by state industries. But by the late 1930s one author included the city in a group of five he studied in their "old age." Calling it "a museum piece," untouched by waves of immigrants or by new economic patterns, he concluded that the Falls City was approaching "an ossified dotage." At almost the same time as he wrote, the huge Ohio River flood of 1937 devastated the town. Yet those two events may have helped transform Louisville's psyche, as leaders and the populace worked to rebuild from both a natural and a public relations disaster. Stimulated by World War II, and a new leadership that included Wilson W. Wyatt, Louisville began a rebirth, both culturally and economically. The 1950s became a Louisville decade in Kentucky: General Electric built Appliance Park, the largest such complex in the nation at the time, and the state constructed the Fair and Exposition Center, the largest indoor facility in the US. The city's peaceful racial integration of schools won national praise, while activity in the arts brought further recognition.

Yet Louisville's dynamic spirit of the 1950s did not continue at the same level. That situation was not surprising, for Kentucky cities generally have experienced periods in which businesses, or leaders, or a combination of other forces have for a time made them vigorous and progressive places, attracting energetic men and women. Lexington had experienced such vitality during the state's first decade of statehood but had relinquished its position later. In the 1970s and afterward it would again be revitalized. Northern Kentucky cities had been strong in the late nineteenth century, then had slowed in growth. Paducah, Owensboro, Hopkinsville, and other western Kentucky cities had shown similar trends at different times. Louisville in the 1960s and beyond continued to develop, but at a different and more mixed pace. Older, individually and locally owned firms consolidated with larger, national ones, and at the same time a city whose fortunes had

been tied to the assembly line began to lose jobs. Race-oriented violence in 1968 and 1975 hurt Louisville's image. Labor strikes slowed production, and the growth of suburbs, each constituting its own little municipality, fragmented efforts toward unity and affected downtown trade. At the beginning of the twenty-first century, for example, there were 94 separate incorporated areas in Jefferson County. A merger of many of those communities took place in 2003 and simplified governance. The thirtieth largest city in the nation, Louisville remains the financial and economic core of Kentucky.

Fragile Finances

One of the mainstays of Louisville's—and Kentucky's—economy has been the liquor industry. Aided by habits developed by wartime imbibing and more accessible postwar transportation, whiskey production nearly tripled in the state between 1871 and 1880, and by 1882 thirsty Americans had doubled the 1880 figure again, to more than thirty million gallons. Within the commonwealth, drinking proliferated. By 1886 there was one saloon for every fifty-five adult males in Owensboro, for example. Five years later Kentucky's 172 distilleries had the largest daily mashing capacity in the nation and produced 34 percent of the distilled spirits manufactured in the United States—at a time when the tax on liquor represented the greatest source of income for the federal government. Little uniformity in production existed, however, until acts in 1897 and 1936 defined standards to be followed.

At the same time, the industry faced huge challenges. A national business depression in 1893 drastically curtailed production, while the growing temperance movement added to liquor's problems. National Prohibition in the 1920s and beyond seriously injured the state's manufacturing standing, particularly in relation to southern states not so tied to the spirits industry. Louisville alone lost an estimated eight thousand positions when its distilleries closed, and the state lost 5 percent of its jobs. Farmers lost a market for their grain, newspapers lost advertisers, railroads lost the cost of shipping products, and cork, label, and bottle makers lost a source of income—the effects were widespread. Towns dependent on nearby distilleries almost vanished: Tyrone in Anderson County declined from a place with one of the largest plants in the world and nearly a thousand inhabitants to an unincorporated village. The empty buildings became vulnerable to vandals and the weather.

Ironically, out of another depression came the impetus to repeal Prohibition and provide more employment. In the 1930s the Kentucky distilleries once more filled the air with the aroma of sour mash. The 1937 opening of Seagram's Distillery in Jefferson County, billed as the world's largest at the time, symbolized the new growth. By 1943 the state furnished 68 percent of US liquor production. In 1964, Congress declared bourbon the nation's only native spirit. But a shift in national patterns of consumption soon after that hurt the industry for some decades. A later rebirth of interest in bourbon, fueled by a "Bourbon Trail" in the state, helped the industry rebound and prosper. In the last fifteen years, production has increased over 170 percent. The state distills over 95 percent of the world's supply of bourbon.

The shifting fortunes of the liquor industry symbolized a trend that affected many mainstays of the state's economy. Restrictions have beleaguered all three of the bedrock industries—liquor, tobacco, and thoroughbreds—at one time or another. Prohibition stopped legal liquor production, the federal controls on tobacco increased from the 1960s on, and the racing industry almost ended in the 1920s and continued to face challenges. In addition, a once-strong lumber industry went into decline before later rebounding; certain major factories, such as those that made carriages, disappeared; and the commonwealth's coal industry experienced a decline. The combination of such trends resulted in an uncertain economic future for the state by the late twentieth century. Change seemed a more likely and promising option. To Kentucky's credit, the state economy did move into needed other areas, but often slowly and tardily.

Toward a Twenty-First-Century Economy

By the twenty-first century, some observers argued that Kentucky had always been in a second-class status on economic matters and lagged behind both the nation and the region. Yet the picture they painted did not exactly reflect the reality of the not-so-distant past. Even though post–Civil War Kentucky never stood at the forefront of the nation's industrial states, neither did it always trail. In 1870, for instance, the commonwealth's manufacturing worth placed it first in the South and sixteenth in the United States. Thirty years later it stood in almost the same position. Generally, then, Kentucky entered the twentieth century in a role as a regional leader.

Between 1900 and 1930, however, the state fell further and further behind. During the first decade of the new century, which saw violence in the Black Patch, feuds, and gubernatorial assassination, only two southern states grew slower than Kentucky. Other southern states continued to grow at a faster rate than Kentucky during the World War I years. In that time the commonwealth suffered an absolute drop in manufacturing. The decline of the lumber and liquor industries by the 1920s only added to the industrial decline, and one study showed that by 1930 the southern manufacturing base had expanded three times more rapidly than had Kentucky's. Only Ohio River cities had experienced much prosperity, and between 1920 and 1930 interior counties had actually suffered a decrease in the number of wage earners. The national depression of the 1930s kept Kentucky from falling further behind. However, the increased prosperity growing out of World War II did not benefit the commonwealth as much as it did most of the South. By the mid-twentieth century Kentucky's economic future had dimmed considerably compared with the bright promise of 1900.

Slowly, the state's economy diversified and began to reflect overall national patterns to a greater degree. Kentucky made a largely successful shift from agricultural employment to other sectors. By the 1960s General Electric in

Louisville, International Business Machines in Lexington, and Armco Steel in Ashland represented the most visible aspects of the change. In 1980 the state's largest employers were in the fields of electronics, machinery, textiles, food, metal industries, and chemicals, and by the 2010s Kentucky had about the same percentages of people employed in most work categories as did the rest of the United States. Only in the financial and service areas did the state lag.

Out of these changes came a state economy that led the nation in few new fields, but one still very different from that of earlier years. Kentucky continued to play a significant role in the liquor industry, but it also had become an important automotive center. Kentucky's own attempts at building horseless carriages, such as the Ames, the Dixie Flyer, the Lexington, and the Bowman, had failed. But a plant started assembling Model T's in Louisville in 1913. Aided by better roads, and the improved traffic light—introduced in 1923 by black inventor Garrett A. Morgan (who grew up in Bourbon County and who also patented the predecessor of the gas mask)—the demand for cars grew. By 1955 the Ford Assembly Plant opened, and fourteen years later the Truck Plant began operations in Louisville. Together, they had produced over eleven million heavy and light trucks and utility vehicles in the state by 1998. In 1980 a General Motors plant in Bowling Green became the only factory building Corvette sports cars, and Toyota Motor Company opened its Georgetown factory. In the late 1980s, the new Toyota plant started turning out Camrys, and then Lexus models. Such activity made Kentucky the third-leading producer of motor vehicles nationally in 2013, with over 1.2 million vehicles produced annually by state workers. When coupled with DHL's hub at the Northern Kentucky Airport and with United Parcel Service's use of the Louisville airport as its main air hub—with UPS's Worldport hub employing over twenty thousand employees—then clearly Kentucky has become an important part of the nation's transportation network.

Similarly, the commonwealth advanced as a health care center, particularly with the growth of a new company that started as a simple nursing home, born out of the entrepreneurship of Louisvillians David A. Jones and Wendell Cherry. The enterprise that became the multifaceted Humana Corporation had 2014 revenues of over $41 billion dollars and employed some twelve thousand full-time workers. When coupled with Kindred healthcare in Louisville, that gave the state a significant role in the field.

In the food products line, young businessman John Y. Brown Jr. capitalized on Colonel Harland D. Sanders's product, co-purchased Kentucky Fried Chicken in 1960, and made the company's name an international byword.

Table 14.1. Gross State Production, 2005, 2015

Industry	Amount (millions of dollars)	
	2005	**2015**
Manufacturing	38,790	37,274
Services	30,008	43,963
Government	21,451	27,982
Financial and Real Estate	20,123	29,702
Transportation/Communication	11,173	13,701
Retail Trade	9,639	11,599
Wholesale Trade	9,385	13,124
Construction	6,770	8,479
Mining	4,357	3,043
Utilities	2,338	2,744
Farms, Forestry, and Fisheries	2,223	2,388
Arts, Entertainment, Recreation	720	942
Total	**$146,968**	**$194,942**

Under the name of Yum! Brands it now includes Pizza Hut and other fast-food chains in its Louisville headquarters. Other companies, such as Jerrico (later Long John Silver's), Texas Roadhouse, and Rafferty's were also born in the Kentucky economy. And the nation's largest peanut butter production facility is in Lexington. By 2014, eight of the nation's largest one thousand companies in terms of revenue were in Kentucky—in order: Humana, Yum! Brands, Ashland, General Cable of Highland Heights (wire and cable), Kindred Healthcare of Louisville, Lexmark International of Lexington, Brown-Forman (distilled spirits), and Tempur-Sealy International (bedding) in Lexington.

But the real story of Kentucky's economy remains its global connections. By the 2010s, over four hundred foreign businesses operated in the commonwealth, employing over 75,000 Kentuckians. Conversely, the state's exports reached over $28 billion—up from $10 billion in 2002—with the chief markets being Canada, the United Kingdom, Mexico, China, France, Brazil, and Japan. Overall, Kentucky ranked in the middle of the states in that regard.

Yet those positive economic indicators could not obscure a trend that had perhaps increased in importance as the centuries have progressed: much of the state's wealth still went to companies with headquarters outside its borders. In the banking industry, for example, several sizable and independent state banks in the 1980s and 1990s became part of larger national financial institutions that had their corporate centers in Ohio, Pennsylvania, North Carolina, or elsewhere. Privately held newspapers, with the *Louisville Courier-Journal* and *Herald-Leader* being only the best-known examples, followed the same trend, as did other businesses. Kentucky remained primarily what one scholar has called a peripheral region, where products are processed locally but where dollars flow out of communities rather than into them. Extractive rather than constructive actions more often result. That situation makes even more praiseworthy those Kentucky-based people and companies that

have returned some of their funds to better the quality of life of Kentucky.

King Coal and the Mineral World

When young mountaineer John C. C. Mayo rode across his native eastern Kentucky mountains in the late nineteenth century, he represented, in one sense at least, the future of Kentucky's coal industry. At the time, most coal was produced in small community mines, for local use. As one observer noted on her trip to Appalachia, "We saw coal-mines all along the road, just sticking out of the mountains." Some thirteen hundred of those shaky affairs dotted the region. Only slowly had Kentucky sold coal for shipment outside its borders: in 1870 the state produced just 150,000 tons of coal, but a decade later it had passed the million-ton mark. As late as 1900 some 60 percent of the coal dug in the commonwealth was still used in Kentucky. Early mines generally remained in local hands, and talented immigrants who had had experience with mines overseas were usually involved. The largest operation in Kentucky in 1900, for example, had as its superintendent a man born and educated in Germany, who brought his mining engineering degree to the United States after the Civil War and settled in Kentucky by 1886. The center of coal produced for sale was western Kentucky. In 1884, for instance, 57 percent of all coal mined in the commonwealth came from the Western Coalfield. This area would continue to lead in coal production until 1912.

Mayo sought to change all that. From the end of the Civil War on, people knew about the vast coal reserves in eastern Kentucky, but poor transportation, feud violence, and other factors had slowed development of those resources. But locals like Mayo of Johnson County and Walter S. Harkins of Floyd County saw that many mountain residents were mired in debt "in a permanent state of crisis" and sought ways to change their status. They thus used the so-called broad form deed, which gave the purchaser rights to the minerals on the land in exchange for a set fee. For the sellers, in the short term, their decision to sell seemed a rational

Miners' houses and a coal tipple near Hazard, 1928. (Bobby Davis Museum and Park, Hazard, KY)

decision—they got rid of debt, secured their ownership to the land, and saw little immediate change to the landscape. Mayo and others thus acquired mining rights to hundreds of thousands of acres—and then sold those rights to mostly northern developers. Only several generations later did the full effect of the sales come home to haunt the mountain homeplaces, in the form of strip-mining. As historian Robert S. Weise notes, "Farmers who sold mineral rights may well have saved their farms, but the consequences . . . would be visited on their children and grandchildren."

Mayo symbolized the revolution taking place in eastern Kentucky, one that changed the face of an agrarian region. Railroads inched their way into formerly isolated areas—to Middlesborough in 1889, to Harlan in 1911, to Hazard the next year—and as they did a transformation occurred, sometimes virtually overnight. In Perry County (Hazard), before the railroads, its total taxable property had been listed as some $80,000; a decade later, it had increased to $23 million. The county seat had grown from 250 to 8,000. In Letcher County, a valley containing a lone cabin became in a few

days the booming coal town of Jenkins. That coal camp town featured more than a thousand buildings, including a school, a library, a hospital, an electric plant, and several churches. Tennis courts, playgrounds, motion-picture theaters, and shops added to its appeal. Nearby in Harlan County, the town of Lynch brought forth similar promise: it had ten miles of paved streets for some sixty-five hundred people by 1920. By 1924 nearly two-thirds of the state's miners lived in company housing. The urban world thus came to parts of rural Kentucky with little time for adjustments or evaluation.

To people eking out a subsistence on a farm without electricity, far distant from stores and communities, the new life offered by the coal boom held great appeal. Those who came to the coal camps in the first generation mostly did so eagerly, for they gambled that mining could give them a better life, new opportunities, and a more promising future. As one recalled: "I didn't have any choice. I had a family. They had to eat. There wasn't anything else to do. . . . You couldn't make a living on the farm." And so they came from within the state, as well as from across the region and overseas.

Immigrants and African Americans moved to the mining areas and added an ethnic mix to a population that had previously been almost totally Anglo-Saxon. Still, as the boom times passed, only remnants of those new groups would remain. In the good times, though, most enjoyed the higher wages, the entertainment options, the goods to be purchased, the schools, the medical care, the higher hopes. For those men and their families, a long-established way of life had ended, for they now lived in different homes, surrounded by different people speaking strange languages. They were working different jobs and adjusting to different family structures.

Prosperity often came at a high price, however. The vaunted Appalachian independence, self-reliance, and self-sufficiency now had to be submerged to officials who ran company towns like little kingdoms. In the worst cases, the companies controlled everything, with no debate. Miners were expected to vote as the company desired; they paid high prices at monopolist company-owned stores; they were treated by doctors paid by the company; they lived where they were told to live, in areas segregated by race or ethnic origin; they often suffered in silence if abuses arose. In short, their lives became socially, physically, and psychologically controlled by a corporate fiefdom.

Some coal areas, on the other hand, continued to be managed well. The companies still dominated in these places, but at least more benevolence was involved. Many families experienced prosperity for the first time; many children of miners now had the benefit of education and went on to success in other occupations. Still, when hard times hit the coalfields and when profits declined, even the best of the company towns suffered. The physical infrastructure could not be kept up, and unpainted houses gathered the ever-present coal dust hanging in the air and turned gray. Sanitation declined, as creeks filled with litter and garbage that remained uncollected. At those moments, the gulf separating the operators living on the hill from the miners in the valley suddenly seemed much broader. Over time, the miners and their families would not suffer in silence.

Protests and strikes would be an ever-present part of the reign of King Coal.

Those who entered the mines to dig coal risked much every day. Changes took place over the years, as the oil lamp on the hat became a carbide one, as the tracks of the car that took workers into the mines turned from wood to steel, as the power that moved those cars evolved from mule to motor, as the tools for digging the mineral converted from hand tools to cutting machines. But certain things varied little. The Kentucky Office of State Inspector of Mines was created in 1884, but it more often chronicled the problems rather than solved them. In the half century after that date, seventy-three dust and gas explosions occurred in the state's mines. Collapsing roofs remained a danger, and ventilation problems persisted. One miner remembered that he and others in the coal mining communities "not only knew the pain of broken bones, but also the pain of broken hearts." As more and more mines opened, and as larger numbers of workers ventured underground, deaths rose (see table 14.2). A 1903 report found most mines in a "deplorably bad condition," and it meant little to the forty-two people who died in Kentucky mines in 1912 that the number of deaths compared with the number employed in Kentucky was lower than the US average. There is little

Table 14.2. Kentucky Mine Deaths, 1890–2014

Period	Deaths
1890–1899	95
1900–1909	274
1910–1919	754
1920–1929	1,614
1930–1939	1,203
1940–1949	1,328
1950–1959	689
1960–1969	451
1970–1979	379
1980–1989	242
2006–2014	49

Source: Claude E. Pickard, "The Western Kentucky Coal Fields" (PhD diss., University of Nebraska, 1969), 97; Kentucky Department of Mines and Minerals, *Mines and Minerals Report* (1991); Kentucky Division of Mine Safety, 2015.

irony in the historical markers posted in Harlan County, which show that far more people have died in the mines there than in military actions. Going into the mines was sometimes like going to war.

But go the miners did, both with courage and fatalism, and their work resulted in the production of massive amounts of coal from both the western and eastern Kentucky fields. A million tons was produced in 1879, and that figure increased to more than 5 million two decades later. Between 1900 and 1907 production doubled, then nearly doubled again by 1914, and almost tripled between 1914 and 1929. By 1920 Pike County alone produced almost as much coal as the whole state had in 1900. High demand through World War I was followed by a slump in the early 1920s, and again during part of the 1930s. Then the industry experienced adequate demand in the 1940s, a bad market in the 1950s, and a large jump in prices per ton following the 1973 oil embargo. Kentucky coal prices, adjusted for inflation, increased 100 percent between 1973 and 1978—above the national average—and new fortunes were made before the 1978 peak year. The dominant pattern of coal production in Kentucky, however, continued to be one of boom and bust and increasingly the latter.

Three other trends have characterized the coal industry since 1950: the mechanization of the mines and overall loss of jobs; the increase in strip/mountaintop removal mining; and the changing pattern of consumption. Between 1885 and 1929, for example, the coal workforce increased from forty-five hundred to more than fifty thousand, then peaked in 1948 at sixty-six thousand. But changing factors soon affected demand. By 1956, all L&N trains, for example, had switched from coal to diesel power, and the percentage of homes in Louisville heated by coal had declined from 90 percent in 1940 to 10 percent twenty years later. Mechanization also began to replace men in the mines. In 1950, machines loaded almost 70 percent of the nation's coal. That fact, coupled with the depressed 1950s market, drastically reduced the numbers of min-

ers to twenty-seven thousand by 1972. Sizeable out-migrations followed, particularly from the eastern Kentucky coalfields, where, as one person remarked, "The three R's they teach in Kentucky schools are . . . readin' and writin' and Route 23 North." In the decade of the 1950s alone, over a third of the region's people had migrated elsewhere. During the oil embargo of the 1970s, employment rose with an increase in production, only to fall again from 1979 to 2002, under both Republican and Democratic presidential administrations, to a little over one-third the previous number. Then the higher costs to produce coal in Appalachia, the expanded coalfields of the western United States, with their "cleaner" coal and better shipping rates, the cheap price of natural gas, and the environmental concerns about burning coal all added to the woes, particularly in the eastern coalfields. The good-paying coal jobs grew scarcer. By 2015 only some ten thousand miners worked in the coal industry, and just five thousand in the eastern fields. The industry accounted for under 1 percent of the commonwealth's employment numbers. Coal increasingly was becoming a minor part of the state's economy.

A second major change in coal production took place. In the decades after 1940, more Kentucky coal was mined above ground. Although some surface mining occurred as early as 1919, by 1940 only 2 percent of the state's "black gold" was mined by that method. By 1960 a third of the state's coal came from the so-called strip-mining method, and in 1974 over half did. The state's courts in cases in 1921, 1956, and other times had basically supported the owners of such mineral rights as the "dominant" owners of the land. Only a constitutional amendment in 1988 changed that interpretation. Stronger standards governing reclamation of the land were also adopted after 1966, and the number of surface mines slowly declined in relation to underground mines. By 2012, some 36 percent of the total state coal production came from above-ground mining. Although a safer method—only two miners died in 2014—strip mining and mountaintop removal took a terrible toll on Kentucky's

Two miners work in an underground coal mine, 1920s. (Kentucky Historical Society Collections, Frankfort, KY)

natural landscape and environment. Various writers compared the state's coalfields to battlegrounds. Once-scenic lands, unreclaimed from the ravages of the strippers, soon featured deep gashes on the hills and soil erosion in the valleys. Then in 2000 in Martin County, one of the worst environmental disasters in the southern United States occurred when some 300 million gallons of coal slurry burst out of a waste impoundment and killed aquatic life and polluted rivers and streams for hundreds of miles. While bringing jobs, salaries, and some economic wealth to Kentucky, King Coal also brought scars to the countryside.

By the first decades of the twenty-first century almost all the state consumption of coal came from the use of utilities. As a result, coal's future seemed as dark as the mineral itself. The state had gone from being ranked ninth in coal production in 1910 to third by 1929 and still held that rank by the start of the twenty-

first century. But only 11 percent of US coal came from Kentucky by 2002. Although coal is a nonrenewable resource, large reserves still remained.

With all its benefits and all its debits, King Coal still lived in the psyche of the people, although it ruled on a nonexistent throne.

Other extractive industries in Kentucky took a secondary place to coal. In 1865 the legislature granted charters to some 140 oil or oil and mining companies, and the first of many postwar oil booms was on. In county after county at various times during the following century, a boom would bring "wildcatters" to a town, and some profits would be followed by a return to normalcy. Overall state production fluctuated greatly, with 63,000 barrels in 1900 being followed by 1.2 million six years later and 9.2 million in 1919. The peak was reached in 1959, at 27.3 million barrels, but another decline followed. At no time did the common-

Table 14.3. Kentucky Coal Production, 1870–2015

Year	Amount mined (thousands of tons)
1870	150
1879	1,000
1892	3,025
1900	5,329
1907	10,753
1914	20,383
1920	38,892
1929	60,705
1947	88,695
1954	58,600
1974	136,800
1987	165,192
1990	173,322
2015	61,414

Source: Willard Rouse Jillson, "A History of the Coal Industry in Kentucky," *Register of the Kentucky Historical Society* 20 (1922): 21–45; Commonwealth of Kentucky, *Report of the Inspector of Mines*, later the *Report of the Department of Mines and Minerals*; data from the US Energy Information Administration. Note: When figures from different sources disagree for certain years, what seems to be the most official source is cited.

wealth become a major oil producer, although one petroleum company, Ashland Oil, did attain significant status.

Beginning as a refining operation in 1924, what became Ashland Inc. grew under the leadership of Paul G. Blazer and others through emphasizing refining, road construction, coal production, and inland waterway networks. More recently the company sold its refining arm, its construction business, and other earlier areas of emphasis. It instead focused on its profitable Valvoline motor oil line (later split into a separate company), acquired other properties, diversified, and developed its position as one of the world's largest specialty chemical companies. The early involvement of Ashland in education, through corporate support, stressed the contrast often shown between Kentucky companies and those with headquarters elsewhere. The colonial-style economy affected the state in many ways.

Fluorspar from Kentucky made up over half of the US production of that mineral in the 1920s. On the eve of World War II the state still ranked first in its production. A half century later, however, foreign imports and a declining market had almost ended production of the mineral in the commonwealth. By then Kentucky ranked second in the production of ball clay (used in ceramics) and fourth in lime. Still, crushed stone, natural gas, and all the rest never threatened to topple the throne of King Coal.

Rivers, Rails, and Roads

Transportation was a key element of Kentucky's commercial and agricultural development. At the end of the Civil War, the state's rail system was damaged in some places and consisted of relatively few miles of track anyway. A boom would soon prompt municipal leaders in town after town to seek out iron rails, but rail expansion would take time. With the exception of a few roads of worth, the commonwealth's system for horses and carriages was either poor or virtually nonexistent. As had been the case for nearly half a century, then, the state's most extensive transportation network in 1865 remained its rivers.

With well over a thousand miles of commercially navigable waterways, Kentucky offered numerous possibilities for river travel. People on the rivers knew the horror of accidents like one in 1868, when the *America* and the *United States* collided and sank, with significant loss of life, near Warsaw. They also knew pride: in 1870, for example, the two captains in the famous steamboat race between the *Natchez* and the *Robert E. Lee* were both Kentuckians. Most important, however, was the economic benefit of river travel. Kentuckians could transport their goods to market easier and quicker, whether they were shipping timber on the Big Sandy, crops from the Upper Cumberland to Nashville, or various items on the Ohio. People located on or near a river had reasonably easy access to other places along the rivers, for visiting, travel, or amusement. Rivers also provided traveling entertainment at times, in the form of showboats, with their plays, music, comedy, and occasional bawdiness. Although scattered remnants would long remain, the showboats reached their peak around the turn of the century. Several generations of Kentuckians from Ashland to Paducah, however, had thrilled to the cry "Showboat's coming!"

River travel declined as other modes of transportation improved. By the 1870s and afterward, congressional and state appropriations resulted in more locks and dams on key rivers, improving access while "canalizing" the waters. The last lock on the Kentucky River was completed in 1917. But river forces were fighting a rearguard action in a technological battle they had already lost. By the 1930s most secondary rivers had lost their showboats and their riverboats. Barges on the Ohio and a few other waterways continued to provide an important service for the rest of the century, but the era of the rivers as the vital arteries in Kentucky's transportation network had long ended.

The new transportation god that Kentuckians worshiped came cloaked in steam and smoke. As it made its way into town, some saw it as a devil, while most proclaimed it as a savior to their communities. The advantages the railroads brought were many and obvious. A Glasgow paper in 1869 noted that the train would allow people to travel a hundred miles in four hours, rather than in days, as before. Markets would thus be brought closer, so fewer foods would spoil, and prices of goods available in the town would decline, since transportation costs would be less. People could visit friends and relatives easier; they could go to large towns, such as Louisville, and be back the same day; they could see a whole new world of possibilities opening before them, as they would have a mobility never before thought possible. Such advantages, and the perceived disadvantages of not being on the rail lines, encouraged towns across Kentucky to donate land or rights of way or to vote for taxes to pay off bonds whose funds would go to attract railroad companies. The Glasgow paper, in pleading for voters to approve such a tax in 1869, noted, "We heard a sensible gentleman living in the country remark a few days ago that the difference between the present price of eggs and butter in the market and the price when we get the Rail-

Table 14.4. Railroad Mileage in Kentucky, 1870–2010

Year	Mileage
1870	1,017
1880	1,530
1886	2,098
1890	3,000
1900	3,060
1929	4,062
1984	3,356
1994	2,929
2010	2,526

Source: Kentucky Railroad Commission, *Eleventh Report of the Railroad Commission* (1981), 6; J. J. Hornback, "Economic Development in Kentucky since 1860" (Ph.D. diss., University of Michigan, 1932), 145; Kentucky Department of Economic Development, *Kentucky's Locational Advantages for the Auto Parts Industry* (1984); *Worldmark Encyclopedia of the States* (1996).

road would more than pay the tax which it is proposed to vote on."

Counties that refused to provide adequate support for many human services eagerly went into debt for the railroads. In many cases, the decision proved a wise one, for some places not on the railroads withered away. But often the railroad companies had already made their choices, and the money that towns offered only made the financial deal better for the lines. Unfortunately, some places lost entirely, as residents voted for bonds and handed the funds to a new company, only to see it go into bankruptcy while they still had to pay off the bonds. In others, railroad mania controlled citizens' better judgment, and they made financial commitments beyond their capacity. By 1878 local governments began to experience debt problems, and nine counties and one city defaulted at least once on payments. Green County went without a sheriff from 1876 to 1920 because no one would accept the office, the duties of which included collecting tax payments to pay off a failed railroad bond.

Other disadvantages rode into Kentucky life with the railroads. As the first major businesses in the state, the rail companies raised issues that required new answers. Kentucky railroad mileage almost tripled between 1870 and 1890, and the L&N, headquartered in the state but with tracks all over the region, became the chief corporate citizen of the commonwealth. As various parts of the rail system came under attack, particularly from farm groups, the railroads reacted by using their power to influence politics generally and political decisions affecting transportation specifically.

In 1884 Milton Hannibal Smith became chief executive officer of the L&N, an office he would hold for more than thirty years. By the time he took over, people such as German immigrant Albert Fink, who had engineered what was at the time the world's largest truss bridge, over the Ohio River at Louisville, had made the line strong. In 1886 the L&N and other southern railroads, which ran on a different gauge than those elsewhere in the nation, all changed their rails to conform to the rest of the United States, further aiding in the movement of rail traffic across the country.

But the legislature had created the Railroad Commission of Kentucky in 1880, and though it was weak Smith feared the future. Attempts at influencing politics caused more resentment toward lines that already charged high or inconsistent rates in some areas. The issues coalesced in the Goebel race, and following the governor's assassination, the Railroad Commission in 1900 was given the power to fix rates. Court cases weakened the commission's actions for some fifteen years, however, and during that time Kentucky exercised less state control over the railroads than any other southern state. By 1930 the commonwealth's attorney general argued that Kentucky's economic growth had been limited by discriminatory rates by railroads, which "have taken the advantage of us." It cost more, for instance, to ship items from Louisville to Bowling Green, a distance of 114 miles, than to ship the same materials to St. Louis, some 280 miles away. Steel could be sent 138 miles from Ashland to Danville at the same cost required to ship it 430 miles north. The attorney general argued that agricultural and industrial rates were much lower north of the Ohio River. Others noted that in 1909, the major railroads in the state had twenty-two direc-

tors, but only two were from Kentucky. Outside control once again became an issue.

Railroad excesses, however, often blinded critics to the benefits the railroad had brought to the state. As a Lewisburg observer recalled, "We had trains, of course, which was the life's blood of all the small towns in Kentucky." Although early train riding was not always comfortable—cinders and soot could blow back through open windows, and closed ones left cars hot and stuffy—train travel improved over the years. Diesel began to replace coal as a fuel in 1939, and other improvements followed. At least through the 1940s, rail travel provided the core of the state's transportation system. But that core steadily eroded, as symbolized by the end of passenger service in the state. Most of that service was curtailed in the 1960s, but nearly all of it was gone by 1971. Mergers brought new names to Kentucky lines, and by the 1980s, nearly 90 percent of the state's railroads came under the control of three lines—the Chessie System (which represented the C&O), the Seaboard System (which included the L&N), and Illinois Central. In 1986 the first two merged and formed CSX, a holding company with headquarters in Virginia. The Norfolk Southern's lines also passed through Kentucky. Railroads in the state now chiefly handle freight, and the golden age of railroading has become only a misty memory.

At the same time that railroads became important across Kentucky, the state's cities began to replace mule-driven street railways and trolley cars with electric ones. By 1890 places such as Louisville, Henderson, and Lexington offered electric streetcars, and by the first decade of the twentieth century smaller communities, such as Somerset, offered commuters that luxury. The company in Frankfort was typical—it ran from six in the morning until eleven at night, required a nickel to ride, and placed blacks in the rear of the car. Overall, some seventeen street railroad systems operated in Kentucky.

Larger cars with service to outlying areas soon followed, and interurbans featured hourly runs at relatively high speeds. Such activity encouraged the growth of suburbs and of commuting, but a new form of transportation ended these services. The last interurban ran to Henderson in 1928, and the last to Louisville in 1935. The last streetcar made its way to the shops in Lexington in 1938, and the last in Louisville a decade later. A newer form of transportation had made them unprofitable and unused. The automobile age had arrived.

Many factors slowed the arrival and acceptance of automobiles in Kentucky. The expense of the early vehicles meant that fewer citizens in a poor state could afford them, but more important was the condition of roads in the commonwealth. Other than the toll roads, which had been outlawed or purchased after the Tollgate Wars in the 1890s, Kentucky had few serviceable roads as the twentieth century opened. One traveler in the eastern mountains found "not a single well-made wagon road." Future president Franklin D. Roosevelt echoed those remarks in 1908, when he wrote his wife about the "horrible" roads leading to Harlan. He went over "a so-called wagon road—positively the worst road I have ever seen or imagined and one which was not very easy to traverse on horseback." Across Kentucky, dusty roads in summer became quagmires of mud in the rain and frozen ponds in winter. In bad weather many people simply did not even try to travel. Nor did the system of maintenance in most locales help. Kentucky still used a legal system of forced labor, with origins back in England, whereby most males of a certain age had either to work on roads or to pay a fee to avoid doing so. Poor results usually followed.

In 1914 almost one of every six Kentucky counties was not served by a railroad. People in those areas received few of the benefits of modern transportation. Only poor roads were available for buggies, runabouts, carriages, and wagons, so many Kentuckians remained isolated. As late as 1928 Burkesville, the seat of Cumberland County, was connected to the "outside" world only by water. A year later a report remarked on the "pathetic" roads in other counties. Even if one were lucky enough to have an automobile, travel often remained difficult. For example, in 1928, it took one man

five days to drive his new Model T from Irvine to Booneville—a distance of some forty miles—because of poor roads.

As a result, automobiles became commonplace at far different times in different places in the commonwealth. Central Kentucky towns saw the first cars in 1900, and towns like Somerset, London, and Bowling Green had their first automobiles before 1910. Many mountain counties, however, had few cars before 1930.

In most parts of rural Kentucky, though, the automobile age came earlier. The number of cars rose from nearly 20,000 in 1915 to more than 127,000 six years later. Kentuckians had 272,000 passenger vehicles in 1928 and more than 1 million three decades later. Bus lines provided public transit for even more people. The new transportation not only offered more freedom and greater recreational opportunities but also promoted consolidated schools, the growth of suburbs, job mobility, and new factory locations. Vacation patterns changed for families, as did courtship rituals. No longer would male-female contacts be chiefly limited to parlors or porches in a home, for the automobile gave mobility to the young as well—with the attendant worries by parents about such liberation.

Such advantages brought increased demands on state government to take a role in promoting better highways. Candidates sought to outdo each other in support of highways, so much that Governor A. O. Stanley noted in 1915, "To say that you are in favor of good roads is like saying you are in favor of good health or good morals." In 1912 the fledgling Kentucky State Highway Commission was organized, and two years later a system was planned to connect county seats. In 1916 and 1921 federal acts provided more support. Using gasoline taxes and licensing fees, the state commission began to spend large amounts of money. Later a vehicle-usage and weight-distance tax further funded the commonwealth's roads. The last stagecoach line in the state had ended in 1911, when a coach made its final run from Monticello to Burnside. That cessation symbolized the start of the new age, one which by 1930 brought 4,400 miles of state-

UPS flights out of its hub in Louisville make Standiford Field a very busy airport. (NBC News)

maintained roads. That year Kentucky devoted 47.6 percent of its state funds to highways. The old macadamized, wood block, or brick streets in cities began to be replaced by asphalt, and real rural roads began to be constructed for the first time. Haphazard planning, however, often resulted in incomplete connections, and the commonwealth for a time earned the nickname "the Detour State." By World War II many parts of rural Kentucky still remained unserved by good roads.

Kentucky's answer to the question of poor roads in some areas was to build highways financed by state bonds, to be retired by toll receipts. In 1956 the first of those, the Kentucky Turnpike from Louisville to Elizabethtown, opened; nineteen years later all tolls were removed from that road, far ahead of schedule. That pattern, like the earlier pattern in bridge building, was repeated across the state. The toll roads, combined with the chiefly federally funded interstate highway system authorized in 1956 and with the state's continued devotion to road construction, meant that by the

late twentieth century Kentucky had a strong road network, one that aided commercial and agricultural interests while promoting more regional ties. By the mid-2010s, the commonwealth's over 78,000 miles of public roads included 27,000 miles of state-maintained roads with 762 miles of interstate highways and 648 miles of limited access parkways.

By that time the greatest twentieth-century innovation in transportation had finally become commonly used as a method of movement. Air travel had required Kentuckians to make greater leaps in acceptance than any other. No longer would they be earthbound, as people had been for eons. They could now fly at great speeds. For those who remembered horses and carriages, such things seemed almost impossible. But change did occur, albeit slowly. Louisville's first airport, Bowman Field, was initially used in 1919. A terminal was constructed there a decade later, and finally concrete runways were built nearly ten years after that. The construction of a new airport in Louisville, Standiford Field, and a major one in northern Kentucky, serving that area as well as Cincinnati, indicated the growing acceptance of passenger travel by air. After United Parcel Service made Louisville's airport a hub, it ranked as the nation's second and the world's seventh busiest in air cargo traffic. The sounds of planes overhead—once an occasion of wonder—had become commonplace.

Kentucky had changed a great deal since 1865 in regard to agriculture and commerce, but perhaps no change had been greater than the innovations in transportation. A people largely limited in a day to a trip that would take them no farther than their county seat could by the late twentieth century be continents away in the same amount of time. Such mobility made the late twentieth century seem, by comparison with the past, almost another world. In many ways it was.

15

Culture and Communications, 1865–2015

By the start of the twentieth century, writers usually considered Kentucky as part of the South and often described its cultural mores in negative ways, echoing the manner in which southern culture was frequently portrayed. The commonwealth's violence before and after the turn of the century only added to an emerging image of a culturally benighted Kentucky. At least into the first third of the 1900s, and perhaps beyond, such national views of the state persisted. Yet the state had made contributions in art, architecture, dance, motion pictures, photography, sculpture, and theater. Kentuckians also had real strengths in music, literature, and journalism, both on a regional and national scale. Only slowly, however, did the commonwealth begin to shake off its "barefoot and backward" cultural image.

The Press

By the end of the Civil War and the start of Kentucky's Readjustment, the newspaper was the choice reading material of most Kentuckians. In 1872 some ninety state papers had a circulation of nearly two hundred thousand. Many of those readers chiefly perused a local weekly. These county newspapers seldom told of matters beyond the nation's borders and usually focused on events very close to home. Syndicated stories on religion, health, morals, and style appeared after 1865, and standard patent medicine advertisements helped pay the bills for a time, but usually the editors filled their pages with local fare. The weather, farming, fashion, morbidity, lawlessness, race, religion, and, of course, politics dominated the columns. Since names make news, such sheets, according to one historian, seemingly tried "to

print the name of every . . . man and woman in the county at least once a year." Readers apparently sought such fare, for by 1930 the seventy-odd weeklies of 1872 had grown to two hundred. But modified markets, new media, and higher costs brought changes to presses that had often been run by a small staff, out of a few rooms, with little profit. From the 1960s on, local papers increasingly became part of newspaper chains. Often the local voice could still be heard, but "safe" editorial stands and less idiosyncratic views usually resulted. At the same time, however, various specialty presses continued to find a readership, albeit usually a small one. Through all those newspaper columns, an individual style of journalism still emerged on occasion, a fragile memory of an earlier era when Kentuckians chiefly read a local paper, edited by a person most of them knew personally.

Although many Kentuckians long received their news through the pages of a community weekly, more and more turned to larger-city dailies as the decades passed. Some people subscribed to both. In certain parts of the commonwealth, the newspaper of choice might be one published nearby, though outside Kentucky's borders. Some in western Kentucky read papers from St. Louis or Memphis; in south-central Kentucky, from Nashville; in the southeastern part of the state, from Knoxville; and in northern Kentucky, from Cincinnati. More readers, however, perused either a Kentucky paper from a nearby large city or the paper that for nearly a century was the state's single major newspaper.

On November 8, 1868, a significant event took place in Kentucky journalism, for on that day subscribers to the *Louisville Courier* and the

Louisville Journal found that those papers had merged. A new newspaper, the *Louisville Courier-Journal*, had been formed. With the inclusion of the *Louisville Democrat* soon afterward, the merger was complete. The paper's twenty-eight-year-old editor, Henry Watterson, would make the *Courier-Journal* the leading southern journal for a time, with the largest circulation in the region for some twenty years. He also would make the *Courier-Journal* the state's major paper, as he became a spokesman for Kentucky, the South, and the Democratic Party.

Henry Watterson was the leading Kentucky journalist for a half century after 1868. Son of a Tennessee congressman, Watterson briefly served in the Confederate army, but even before the end of the Civil War, he entered the newspaper business. As editor of the *Courier-Journal*, he proved to be moderate on many issues, conservative on some, progressive on others. His real strength, however, was not his philosophy but his ability to write—to turn a memorable phrase, to make a dull subject lively, to entertain. When discussing a possible Democratic president in 1892, for example, he said that renomination would lead the party "through a slaughterhouse into an open grave." Refusing to support another party candidate four years later, Watterson cried out, "No compromise with dishonor." When some criticized his opposition to candidates from his own Democratic Party, he responded, "Things have come to a hell of a pass/ When a man can't whip his own jackass." On another issue, woman suffrage, the editor took a very conservative stand, calling the women's rights leaders "blatant zealots" and "immoral" "he-women." In another editorial he termed them "Crazy Janes and Sillie Sallies" and said that if women got the vote, "the wench and the harlot will muster at the polls."

No matter what his editorial stances, Watterson took them with flair, gusto, and showmanship. Blind in one eye, nearsighted in the other, and missing part of one thumb, the editor wrote his column by hand with a pen, a practice that constantly created problems for typesetters who could not read his prose. Once his expression "forty miles of conflagration" be-

Henry Watterson, editor of the *Louisville Courier-Journal*, was the leading journalist in the South for half a century. (The Filson Historical Society, Louisville, KY)

came "forty mules of California." The prototype of the southern colonel, Marse Henry—as he became known once his hair and mustache turned white—also caused concern at times in the financial department. Generally, he left business matters to his capable publisher, Walter Haldeman, but on occasion Watterson would take petty funds from the cash drawer for some paper-related expenses. The accountants asked him to leave a record of what he took. Watterson's note the next time read simply, "Took it all." It was this man who likely had more influence nationally than any late nineteenth-century southern editor and who won a Pulitzer Prize in 1917.

As it turned out, the 1917 prize marked the beginning of the end for Watterson as editor. His wartime editorials angered some; his stances against Prohibition, woman suffrage, and the League of Nations contradicted those of a new owner. In 1919 he retired as editor, and in a sense the personal journalistic style began to leave the Kentucky scene as well. On

Watterson's death in 1921 the *New York Times* wrote about "that Wattersonian style, pungent, vivid, superlatively personal, those adhesive epithets, that storm of arrows, . . . the swift sarcasm, the free frolic of irresistible humor—it was as if the page was not written but spoke and acted before you."

The new owner of the *Courier-Journal* was Robert Worth Bingham. For the next sixty-plus years, the Bingham family would leave a mark on the paper as indelible as Watterson's. Over time, various papers challenging the *Courier-Journal*'s supremacy died out, ranging from the Republican *Louisville Commercial* to the merged *Louisville Herald-Post*. With the latter's demise in 1936, the *Courier-Journal* and its companion, the afternoon *Times* (begun in 1884), had the major newspaper field of the Falls City to themselves. Politically active in one faction of the Democratic Party, Robert Worth Bingham used the papers as a forum for his views. His ties to President Franklin D. Roosevelt brought him the ambassadorship to Great Britain in 1933, and thereafter his involvement with the papers lessened. Bingham's death in 1937 ushered to the forefront his son George Barry Bingham, who soon made the papers nationally known as leaders in reform causes. The morning *Courier-Journal* and the afternoon *Times* took stands generally more liberal than those of most Kentuckians, on issues of race, education, ethics, conservation, and other matters. In 1946 writer John Gunther called the *Courier-Journal* "one of the best newspapers in the country . . . a splendid liberal force," while *Time* magazine in 1952 listed it among the nation's four best newspapers. It continued to garner high rankings in later surveys. Publishers such as Mark F. Ethridge and Barry Bingham Jr. and talented columnists such as Allan Trout, Joe Creason, John Ed Pearce, and C. Ray Hall joined good reporters on both the state and national levels to give both papers a deservedly strong reputation that won them ten Pulitzer Prizes by 2005. Internal conflicts in the Bingham family, however, ended in the sale of the papers to the Gannett chain in 1986. The afternoon *Times* soon ceased production, in a cost-cutting measure, and the change from a Ken-

tucky-owned, family-dominated paper to one connected more to national ownership continued across the commonwealth.

By that time the *Courier-Journal*'s primary position in Kentucky was under challenge from the *Lexington Herald-Leader*. That paper traced its origins to different sources. In 1895 two Democratic papers—the *Lexington Daily Press*, started in 1870, and the *Morning Transcript*, founded in 1876—had merged to form one paper, which soon became the *Morning Herald*. With its editor Desha Breckinridge, it was perhaps the most reform-minded paper in the state in the first two decades of the twentieth century, taking strong Progressive Era stands on woman suffrage and racial matters. The subject of many of the Breckinridge editorials on politics was the afternoon *Kentucky Leader*, founded in Lexington in 1888 to thunder the Republican cause. Following the death of Breckinridge in 1935, the two papers merged in 1937 under the ownership of John G. Stoll, while keeping their separate political outlooks and separate names. The newspapers took more conservative stances, however, and refused, for example, to print stories about local civil rights activities in the late 1950s and early 1960s. In 1973 the Knight-Ridder national newspaper chain purchased the papers. The McClatchy Company, in turn, acquired Knight-Ridder in 2006. As the single edition *Herald-Leader*, the Lexington paper won a Pulitzer Prize and had the state's second-largest circulation. It was dominant in central and eastern Kentucky, while the *Courier-Journal* had wide circulation in south-central and western Kentucky, with some enclaves elsewhere, left over from the days when it was the unchallenged statewide newspaper. The old personal-style, often-vitriolic journalism in which Breckinridge crossed verbal swords with Watterson or Bingham had softened into calmer, more politically oriented differences in later decades, only to be replaced by competition directed by national chains.

While the *Courier-Journal* and the *Herald-Leader* increasingly dominated Kentucky journalism, many strong editors had long made their own contributions, sometimes from smaller towns. W. P. Walton of the *Stanford In-*

terior Journal, Harry A. Sommers of the *Elizabethtown News*, the Dyches of the *London Sentinel-Echo*, the Joplins of the Somerset papers, and Al Smith of the *Russellville News Democrat*, for example, had all contributed to the vitality of journalism in the commonwealth.

Others made their mark in somewhat larger-circulation markets. In Paducah, three newspapers—the *Sun*, the *Daily News*, and the *Democrat*—went through a series of mergers that produced the *Paducah Sun-Democrat* in 1929. Various members of the Paxton family led the paper. Similar actions took place in Owensboro, where Urey Woodson edited the *Messenger*, founded in 1877, while in 1909 former gubernatorial candidate Samuel W. Hager purchased the rival *Inquirer*, set up in 1884. In the late 1920s the two merged as the *Messenger and Inquirer*; members of the Hager family long operated the paper. In northern Kentucky, newspapers were identified more with Cincinnati parents than as independent sheets. In 1890 the *Kentucky Post* was founded as one of the Scripps's "penny papers" and began to build a solid base. It closed in 2007. In Frankfort, the Republican *Commonwealth*, edited by elderly Albert G. Hodges, shut down its presses in 1872 rather than support a party candidate the editor opposed. The Democratic *Yeoman* of S. I. M. Major, with editorials from the pens of Henry T. Stanton and J. Stoddard Johnston, never had such serious pangs of conscience and put out various editions—weekly, triweekly, or daily—depending in part on whether the Kentucky General Assembly was in session. But the *Yeoman* did not see the start of the twentieth century either, and by 1912 a series of mergers brought forth the *State Journal*, which became a politically influential paper in a very political city. Across Kentucky, newspapers started, prospered, folded, merged, and finally emerged as healthy papers.

Other presses sought to reach a more specialized audience. In Louisville, for example, the *Anzeiger* published news in a German-language edition until its demise on the eve of World War II. The *Kentucky Irish American* met the reading needs not only of the sons and daughters of Eire but also of the labor union forces initially and, later, of Catholics generally. With witty writers such as John Michael ("Mike") Barry, the *Irish American* continued until November 1968. Balancing that religious orientation was the controversial atheist sheet, *The Blue Grass Blade* (1884–1910), whose editorials got their editor placed in prison.

At one time, the black press counted some fifty newspapers, but few lived long lives. The *Lexington Standard* that ran for two decades after 1892, the *Louisville News* (established in 1912, closed in World War II), and the *Louisville Leader* (1917–1950) found some success, as did the religious newspaper the *American Baptist* (1879–present). Not until the founding of the *Louisville Defender* in 1933, however, did black Kentuckians have a strong and lasting editorial voice in the state. Under the guidance of Frank L. Stanley Sr. and his successors, the *Defender* spoke out for integration and racial equality. Away from the state, Kentucky-born Ted Poston of Christian County and Alice A. Dunnigan of Logan County both became major black journalists at the national level, while white writers Arthur Krock of Glasgow won four Pulitzers early, and Helen Thomas later served as White House bureau chief for United Press International.

Literature: The Rise to Prominence

In a book published in London, England, in 1870, an author who had visited Kentucky some years earlier remembered the state's citizens as urbane, polite, agreeable, and "remarkable for intellectual activity, but not for literary accomplishments." His analysis of the literary landscape at that time was correct. Low educational levels, a provincialism born out of rural isolation, and an orientation that led the talented to other fields all slowed the development of literature in the state. Yet that situation would change by the beginning of the twentieth century, and for most of the subsequent decades Kentucky played a significant role on the national literary scene. It is difficult to determine what caused greatness in Kentucky writers, what common factors existed in their lives, what brought them to achieve. A survey of the careers of Kentucky authors shows a wide variety of backgrounds: some grew up poor, others did not; many had unhappy childhoods, many did not; they came from all regions of the state. Perhaps the most common feature was that they felt comfortable creating in the loneliness that writing entails. But whatever the source of the fine writing, the Kentucky cultural patterns that both shaped authors and gave them subject matter for their books in the end helped produce strong literary achievements in the commonwealth.

By the late nineteenth century, writing that centered on a particular region, exploiting that landscape and place, had gained much favor among American reading audiences. The so-called local color school brought to the forefront two Kentucky authors, James Lane Allen and John Fox Jr., who would be among the most respected and best known of their generations. In a sense, their rise to prominence marked the emergence of Kentucky as a place of significant literary achievement.

In 1892 Lexington's James Lane Allen wrote that "Kentucky has little or no literature," but already he had begun to change that status. Tall and handsome yet distant, with aristocratic manners, few friends, and a vain personality—he once became angry when an acquaintance yelled for him to come on into a room, rather than opening the door for him—Allen first taught school, then turned totally to writing in the 1880s. In a series of articles and books, he portrayed the romance, gentility, and honor of earlier times. An excellent collection of short stories, *Flute and Violin* (1891), brought him some acclaim, and *A Kentucky Cardinal* (1894) and its sequel, *Aftermath* (1895), added to his reputation. But it was *The Choir Invisible* (1897) that made Allen nationally and internationally known. Set in frontier Kentucky, the novel deals with a man's love for a married woman. Duty and honor eventually conquer passion, and he leaves behind "a love that was forbidden." Appearing at a time when the United States seemed, to many, to be setting aside ethics and morality, the well-crafted work became immensely popular.

Angered by slights, real and imagined, and unhappy with the treatment he received

Novelist James Lane Allen of Lexington achieved international acclaim for his 1897 novel *The Choir Invisible*. (Kentucky Historical Society Collections, Frankfort, KY)

at times in his home state, Allen left Kentucky in the 1890s and came back only occasionally. Virtually all of his novels, however, continued to be set in the Bluegrass, for Allen could not leave behind that world of his imagination. Interestingly, at the peak of his popularity, he turned to other themes, as he sought to make a transition by combining romance with realism. His *Reign of Law* (1900) dealt with the controversy between religion and evolution, earned him considerable ministerial opposition, and again made the best-sellers' list. Three years later *The Mettle of the Pasture* won both popular and critical acclaim, as it dealt forthrightly with double moral standards for the sexes. Another Allen book would not emerge for six years, and like its many successors, *Bride of the Mistletoe* did not achieve much recognition. The reading taste of America had changed, and Allen's prose had as well. The man once called the nation's greatest novelist was almost forgotten by the literary world when he died in 1925.

Allen's Kentucky successor in the American mind was a former student of his, John Fox Jr. of Paris, Kentucky. In many ways, Fox represented the antithesis of Allen. Small and sinewy, he enjoyed the company of people, liked sports, and attracted friends. Whereas Allen wrote of the central Bluegrass, Fox chose Appalachia and became the first Kentucky writer of note to deal with the evolving character of that region. While Allen had been educated in Kentucky but left the state to write, Fox went to Harvard and took a job at a New York newspaper but returned to the region to achieve his fame. Short stories, such as "On Hell-fer-Sartain Creek" and "A Mountain Europa" (1892), were followed by novels set in Appalachia. Fox's first major best seller combined the eastern Kentucky region and the Bluegrass, as it told the story of a mountain orphan who comes to Lexington, becomes accepted in an aristocratic household, finds his new family and his new love torn apart by the Civil War, but returns from battle to see "the sundered threads, unraveled by the war . . . knitted together fast." *The Little Shepherd of Kingdom Come* (1903) would sell more than a million copies and would later be made into several motion pictures.

After some less successful works, Fox then wrote his best book, *The Trail of the Lone-some Pine* (1908). *Little Shepherd* had presented a somewhat sentimental and outdated picture of the Civil War, but Fox's new novel broke fresh literary ground. It portrayed the struggle taking place in the mountains, as the forces of change and modernization warred with the culture of tradition and stability. Through the love story of a young mountain woman and an "outsider" man, Fox presented a generally balanced and sympathetic picture of a region struggling to find a new identity. When Fox died of pneumonia in 1919, that struggle was still continuing.

Other authors of the era also used the Appalachian region as the setting for their prose, though none of them would be able to write as well or as understandingly as had Fox. Charles Neville Buck of Midway and Louisville, for instance, spent two decades, starting in 1910, writing numerous popular novels featuring standard plot formulas, stereotypical feud characters, and exaggerated mountain drama. During the same period Lucy Furman, in books such as *The Quare Women* (1923), wrote of events she experienced at Hindman Settlement School.

In another part of Kentucky, however, a very different kind of writing had been taking place, and it too proved popular to a national readership. Louisville and its environs at the turn of the century and after had attracted a large literary colony, which included patrons such as the Belknaps and the Speeds, journalists such as Henry Watterson, poets such as Cale Young Rice and Madison J. Cawein, geographers such as Ellen Churchill Semple, and novelists such as Charles Neville Buck. But the women of the Authors Club formed the core, and three of those writers dominated—Annie Fellows Johnston, Alice Hegan Rice, and George (Georgia) Madden Martin.

Annie Fellows Johnston had written little before the 1892 death of her husband, who left her with three stepchildren. While visiting Pewee Valley in Oldham County, she became enchanted with the lifestyle, which she perceived as very much like life in antebellum times. Using that setting, she wrote *The Little Colonel* (1895), the first of a dozen works in a popular series that usually sold a hundred thousand copies per book. A witty woman with "a kind of spiritual aristocracy" about her, Johnston wrote stories stressing Victorian, nineteenth-century values. In *The Little Colonel* a bright and innocent child, through her sweetness, brings together a family split by wartime memories and postwar actions. Such themes proved long popular, and a line of clothes and a series of motion pictures bore the Little Colonel name. Such sentimental writing was not great literature, but it was very popular.

Similar themes came from the pen of Alice Hegan Rice. Her inspiration for writing resulted from philanthropic work in a Louisville slum area, where she met an optimistic and cheerful woman. Using that model, Alice Hegan wrote *Mrs. Wiggs of the Cabbage Patch* (1901), a widely successful, sentimental book that eventually sold more than 650,000 copies in a hundred printings. It combined a developing national interest in the urban poor with a solution that focused on individual achievement in the face of adversity. The book ends with Mrs. Wiggs saying, "Looks like ever'thing in the world come right, if we jes wait long enough!" Hegan married Cale Young Rice the next year, and other best sellers with not dissimilar themes followed: *Lovey Mary* (1903), *Sandy* (1905), and *Mr. Opp* (1909) among them. An intelligent, caring woman, Rice in her books seldom took her interests to a higher level, and the books remained popular more for their charming optimism than their literary worth. Rice died in 1942, and her poet husband, "a lost soul" without her love, committed suicide the next year. In a sense the couple's deaths symbolized the death of innocence expressed in the works of writers like Annie Johnston and Alice Rice.

Two other women authors in the same Louisville milieu achieved some national recognition, though they focused their writing in different ways. George (Georgia) Madden Martin wrote the very popular Emmy Lou stories, which told of a young girl, but later books—*Selina* (1914) and *Children in the Mist* (1920)—looked more at women in the changing century. As the chair of the Association of Southern Women for the Prevention of Lynching, Martin worked actively in reform efforts as well. Eleanor Mercein Kelly came to the commonwealth in 1901 as a result of marriage and began to write first about Kentucky and then about the world. Her career would span enough years to link the Authors Club generation to a new group of Louisville-based authors.

Outside the Falls City, some scattered authors also published works of interest. In northern Kentucky John Uri Lloyd gained national fame for his studies of plants that had medicinal value and as a chemist He also achieved regional recognition as author of the local color novel *Stringtown on the Pike* (1900) and more than half a dozen other books, including the early science fiction novel *Etidorhpa* (1895). In Bowling Green, women's rights leader Eliza Calvert Obenchain, who wrote as Eliza Calvert

Hall, gained recognition for her short stories, the best of which appeared in her popular book *Aunt Jane of Kentucky* (1907). Farther to the west, Paducah produced Irvin S. Cobb, who moved successfully from newspaper reporter and editor to author of the popular Judge Priest stories, which were collected in book form and made into a motion picture. Cobb was also a humorist and raconteur, as well as a scriptwriter and actor. Friendly and sociable, Cobb continually stressed his state ties, calling himself the Duke of Paducah. Nationally known, he became a Kentucky version of his friend Will Rogers. In short, all across Kentucky, authors were writing prose that was being read by millions of Americans.

The Maturing of the Literary Craft

Of the ten books on the *Publishers Weekly* bestsellers list in 1903, five were written by Kentuckians. Two decades later, however, many of the authors who gave the state its literary strengths in the first years of the century had either died or had passed the peaks of their popularity. It seemed that the commonwealth might revert to the barren literary days of the nineteenth century. Within a few short years, though, a new generation of Kentucky-born or Kentucky-based authors would come to the forefront and would in many ways eclipse their popular predecessors.

The first of these new writers was Elizabeth Madox Roberts of Springfield. Having read widely in her youth and listened to "phantom books" in the oral stories of her father, Roberts taught school for a time, but the poor health that plagued her all her life interrupted that activity. The reserved, tall, slender woman became almost a rustic recluse, except that she went to the University of Chicago in 1917 and left there confident and inspired to write. Her first novel appeared when she was forty-five years old; her last came a dozen years later. In that time Roberts became one of the nation's most-praised writers. The initial review of her work in the *New York Times* concluded that "there has not been a finer first novel published in this country for many years." Critics

Springfield novelist Elizabeth Madox Roberts drew on the history of Kentucky for her novels, including *The Great Meadow* (1930). (Elizabeth Madox Roberts Society, http://emrsociety.com/)

compared her with Ernest Hemingway, Theodore Dreiser, and Sinclair Lewis, often suggesting that she eclipsed them all. One critic said that Roberts was America's greatest writer.

Her first novel, *The Time of Man* (1926), touched on most of the themes displayed in her important works. In flowing and slow-paced prose, Roberts tells the story of the voiceless rural people and portrays their strength and vitality and "the glory in the commonplace" of their lives. Her characters display a strong will, a "power of the spirit," that allows them to fight the larger external forces always threatening their emotional lives. *In My Heart and My Flesh* (1927), everything is taken from a woman of prominence, but she overcomes what one writer called her "descent into the living veins of her soul." Roberts's book *The Great Meadow* (1930) remains perhaps the best historical novel set on the Kentucky frontier. In it the heroine once more demonstrates the power to achieve from within. All three books have women as the chief characters, and Ellen Chesser, Theodosia Bell, and Diony Hall are strong examples "of hopes ever defeated and ever renewed."

Other books, some of short stories and poetry, came from Roberts's pen, but continued ill health brought the writer's life to an end in 1941, at the age of fifty-nine. Unfortunately for her literary reputation, she became less and less read and studied as time passed, only to be recognized again much later. In her time, she personified Kentucky literature. As one critic wrote, the state stood like "an immense territorial ghost" in her life: "Its past, still animated in her imagination, accompanied the present."

Roberts had led the way, but in the 1920s through the 1930s, a notable group of writers burst forth on the Kentucky landscape, including Robert Penn Warren, Allen Tate, Caroline Gordon, Jesse Stuart, James Still, and Harriette Arnow. Part of what has been called the Southern Literary Renascence, these writers brought to Kentucky its own distinguished literary rebirth as well. In contrast to Allen, the Authors Club of Louisville, and others before them, the members of the new generations, like Roberts, grew up in small-town and rural places and mainly wrote of agrarian themes. Their world of reference was the western Kentucky of Warren and Gordon or the Appalachia of Stuart, Still, and Arnow. More diversity, different outlooks, and fresh approaches resulted.

The most honored of this group of authors was Robert Penn Warren of Guthrie. Before his life ended, he became the only writer to win Pulitzer Prizes in both fiction and poetry, and in 1986 he was named the nation's first poet laureate. With Murray-born Cleanth Brooks, he coauthored the immensely influential *Understanding Poetry* (1938), which ushered in the New Criticism, with its emphasis on a close analysis of literary works.

Most of all, Warren wrote. Growing up in Todd County, the tall, thin boy saw around him a subculture of violence, exemplified in the Black Patch War of the region. His schooling at Vanderbilt University exposed him to the intellectual questioning of the Fugitives group there and resulted later in a contribution to their agrarian paean, *I'll Take My Stand* (1930). Spending much of the rest of his career as a college professor, "Red" Warren wrote short stories, poetry, and prose and excelled in

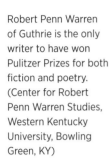

Robert Penn Warren of Guthrie is the only writer to have won Pulitzer Prizes for both fiction and poetry. (Center for Robert Penn Warren Studies, Western Kentucky University, Bowling Green, KY)

all three areas. His novels often used Kentucky settings and generally dealt with the themes of "the Ambiguity of Truth, . . . the power of the past, the painful path to self-knowledge." Warren's first novel, *Night Rider* (1939), was followed by a second work, then his Pulitzer Prize–winning *All the Kings Men* (1946), set in Louisiana with a Huey Long figure at the center. Four years later Warren returned to a Kentucky setting, retelling the story of Jereboam Beauchamp's tragic life in *World Enough and Time* (1950). One of his strongest works, written in a kind of narrative poetry, came next. It is a book that eludes easy clarification. In *Brother to Dragons* (1953) Warren revisited in his imagination the brutal murder of a slave that nephews of Thomas Jefferson carried out in antebellum Kentucky. Warren's long narrative poem gives voice to Jefferson, revealing how the murder affected him. (The historical story would be well told in 1976 by Boynton Merrill Jr. in his *Jefferson's Nephews*.) In Warren's novels *Band of Angels* (1955) and *The Cave* (1959), based on the Floyd Collins rescue, he used his home state once more as the basis for his stories.

In a sense, these works marked Warren's turn back to poetry, and he won his second Pulitzer for *Promises: Poems, 1954–1956* (1957). A plethora of books (on such matters as civil rights), essays, and poems (winning Warren

a third Pulitzer Prize) continued to flow from Warren's mind as he became arguably the most respected man of letters in the United States. Near the end of his life he once more returned to the Kentucky he had physically departed but that seldom left his writing consciousness, in his books *Jefferson Davis Gets His Citizenship Back* (1980) and *Portrait of a Father* (1988). Throughout his life of writing fiction, Warren had portrayed the conflict of evil and idealism within, and the agony of souls in search of self-salvation, of places where "In the turpitude of time / Hope dances on the razor edge." In 1989 the most renowned and honored author that Kentucky ever produced died. Yet unlike the situation in many of his books, at his death no ambiguity existed regarding his life and his contribution to literature: they had been monumental.

Three other Kentucky-born authors had careers in which Warren played an important role. Cleanth Brooks left Kentucky when young. He was at Vanderbilt at the same time as Warren, and later he coauthored three important textbooks with the man from Guthrie: *An Approach to Literature* (1936), *Understanding Poetry* (1938), and *Understanding Fiction* (1943). Together the two Kentuckians also founded the all too short-lived *Southern Review,* one of the strongest literary quarterlies ever prepared in the United States. Brooks would go on to write other important works as one of the nation's foremost critics.

Allen Tate, like Brooks, was born in Kentucky (near Winchester). He also went to Vanderbilt, where, like Warren, Brooks, and so many others, he fell under the influence of John Crowe Ransom and also was a classmate of Warren's. Like Warren, he wrote an essay in *I'll Take My Stand* and became a college professor. Unlike "Red," however, Tate seldom used Kentucky settings in his writings. Interestingly, however, his poem "The Swimmers," which was identified as taking place in the commonwealth, may have been his best poetic work. The man who later held the chair of poetry at the Library of Congress had a distinguished career as critic, teacher, and writer.

Caroline Gordon had connections to Robert Penn Warren in two ways. She too had been born in rural Todd County, almost a decade before Warren, and their families had known each other. It was through Warren that she met Allen Tate, and in 1924 Gordon and Tate were married. In places such as New York, various cities of Europe, and Clarksville, Tennessee, the two hosted many of America's leading literary figures and became known for their own work. (They divorced in 1946, remarried that same year, and divorced again in 1959. They "collaborated, supported, and destroyed each other.") Gordon stressed the role of agrarianism, of family, of place, of historical ruin in the South, as she wrote of the world of her youth, with books often set on the Kentucky-Tennessee border. Works such as *Penhally* (1931), *Aleck Maury, Sportsman* (1934), *None Shall Look Back* (1937), and *The Garden of Adonis* (1937) gained much critical praise, but Gordon's detachment from her characters left a popular readership unsatisfied. In later years she, like Elizabeth Madox Roberts, would be less honored than in her lifetime, but the fact that a 1987 book on fifty post-1900 southern writers included Gordon showed her importance in the literature of Kentucky, the South, and the United States.

All these authors—Warren, Brooks, Tate, and Gordon—had been born between 1895 and 1906, had come from an agrarian, western Kentucky background, and had written about a Kentucky and a South searching its history and its present for moral and personal answers. In eastern Kentucky another group of writers emerged from very different backgrounds, and their writing touched themes important to Appalachia.

First to burst on the scene—and burst he did—was Jesse Hilton Stuart of Greenup County. Son of a virtually illiterate father, Stuart grew to be a person who almost could not stop writing. In fact, his literary reputation would likely have been even stronger had he accepted editors' advice to tighten more of his work or even not to publish some of it. As it was, the physical act of writing gave him pleasure, and he wrote with uncontrolled zest and zeal. After education at present-day Lincoln Memorial University in Harrogate, Tennessee, Stuart went to Vanderbilt, where another of the Fugitives who had influenced Warren and the others became one of his mentors. Donald Davidson's advice—"Stick to your hills, Jesse, and write about the people you know"—proved valuable, and from his W-Hollow home, schoolteacher, principal, and author Jesse Stuart began to tell the myriad stories of his hill people.

In 1934, a large collection of poems, *Man with a Bull-Tongue Plow*, gave Stuart instant recognition. Two years later, what probably is his best collection of short stories, *Head o' W-Hollow*, appeared, followed by an autobiographical account and then his first novel, *Trees of Heaven* (1940). Next, *Taps for Private Tussie* (1943) sold more than a million copies, as it presented a satiric and broadly boisterous look at a mountain family. Some criticized it for perpetuating stereotypes; others praised it. The comic *Foretaste of Glory* (1946) and Stuart's excellent and poignant account of his years of teaching, *The Thread That Runs So True* (1949), added to his readership. A tall and powerfully built man, he survived a massive heart attack in 1954—he would die from the effects of it another three decades later—and he continued to write, lecture, and visit foreign lands. He always returned to W-Hollow, and his vigorous and raw energy and his powerful words made him the most popular Kentucky author in his native state. For all Stuart's weaknesses, Kentuckians still liked the man who wrote

I take with me Kentucky embedded in my brain and heart,
In my flesh and bone and blood
Since I am of Kentucky
And Kentucky is part of me.

Although he grew up in Alabama, James A. Still lived an early life somewhat similar to Jesse Stuart's. Like Stuart, he was born in 1906, went to Lincoln Memorial University and then to Vanderbilt, became associated with a Kentucky school (as librarian at Hindman Settlement School in Knott County), and lived in a log cabin, near Wolfpen. But there most similarities ended, except that both men wrote of the eastern mountains they knew. In one critic's view, "James Still is realistic where Stuart is melodramatic, poetic when Stuart is often sentimental." The reserved Still tried for perfection before sending his work out; the bombastic Stuart hated to rewrite and quickly moved on to another project. Still thus was also unlike Stuart in that his output was limited. For a long time, three slim volumes published within four years represented his book-length work: *Hounds on the Mountain* (1937), a collection of poems; his best-known book, *River of Earth* (1940), a novel whose simple, clear, and strong prose tells the story of a family in transition in the coalfields; and *On Troublesome Creek* (1941), a compilation of his short stories. Still wrote more short stories and poetry after that initial output, but he seemed almost forgotten until two collections of short stories appeared, *Pattern of a Man* (1976) and *The Run for the Elbertas* (1980). Well received by critics, as most of his work was, they sparked a kind of Still revival.

Stuart may have had more popular success and less critical praise than he deserved; Still, the reverse. But another of their generation tasted success from both the public and the critics and may have been the strongest novelist of the three. Born two years later than Stuart and Still, the diminutive Harriette L.

Simpson grew up in Wayne County, attended Berea College, taught school briefly, went back to graduate from the University of Louisville, then taught again. She published her first book in 1936, and married a newspaperman, subsequently writing as Harriette Simpson Arnow. In 1944 the couple moved to Michigan, and she lived there the remainder of her life. Like so many who left the commonwealth, though, Arnow built on her experiences, memory, and observations and used Kentucky characters or settings in most of her writing. In *Mountain Path* (1936) she portrayed Appalachian life of earlier times, while *Hunter's Horn* (1949) told a symbolic story of a fox hunter's obsession during a depression generation's decaying life. A *Saturday Review* poll placed *Hunter's Horn* first among the novels of that year, outdistancing George Orwell's *1984*, for instance. But Arnow's masterpiece, and one of the most powerful novels ever written by a Kentuckian, was *The Dollmaker* (1954), which won the National Book Award. In that work, Gertie Nevels's family moves from Kentucky to Detroit, and the life she once knew is taken away by the industrial North. In a grim and tragic portrayal, this strong woman fights a failing battle with a dehumanizing and impersonal foe. The small and slight Arnow was more than just a tough, realistic novelist, however, and in two social histories based on solid research, she portrayed the life of the frontier along the Cumberland River. *Seedtime on the Cumberland* (1960) and *Flowering of the Cumberland* (1963) join with a memoir of her early life, *Old Burnside* (1977), to give a more nostalgic view of a land in change. Arnow told the story of her people honestly and well.

Coming later to the state scene but touching on some of the same Appalachian themes was Arkansas-born Janice Holt Giles, who moved to Kentucky in 1939. After marriage, she settled first in Louisville and then in south-central Kentucky, and she told of the urban-rural conflict in a strong book, *The Enduring Hills* (1950). A year later, *Miss Willie* touched on similar topics, as an outsider to rural Kentucky finds that values of importance exist in her new world as well. Soon afterward, Giles turned to writing historical novels from her Adair County home and became well known for books set on the Kentucky frontier—*The Kentuckians* (1953), *Hannah Fowler* (1956), and *The Land beyond the Mountains* (1958). She also wrote of other times: *The Believers* (1957), for instance, deals with the Shaker experience in the state. Her husband, Henry Giles, wrote several strong volumes as well.

Another historical novelist of the same generation was A. B. ("Bud") Guthrie Jr. Like Janice Holt Giles, Guthrie was born outside the state, but he spent the years 1926 to 1953 in Lexington as a reporter. While there, he wrote the first two parts of his trilogy of the westward movement, *The Big Sky* (1947) and *The Way West* (1949), the latter of which won a Pulitzer Prize in 1950.

Numerous other writers of that generation left their mark on the state as well. Their work ranged widely, from the protest novels of Leane Zugsmith (*The Reckoning*) and Edith Summers Kelly (*Weeds*) to the supposed humor of Cordia Greer-Petrie (the Angeline series) and the historical fiction of Isabel McMeekin and Dorothy Park Clark (who collaborated in writing as Clark McMeekin), Ben Lucien Burman, Felix Holt (whose book *The Gabriel Horn* [1951] sold more than a million copies), Alfred Leland Cobb, and Gene Markey. But one of the most interesting of the group was Elizabeth Hardwick, born and educated in Lexington. Although her novels received mixed reviews (except for the much-praised *Sleepless Nights* [1979]) and her short stories varied in quality, Hardwick found her niche and made her impact as an essayist and critic, helping found the *New York Review of Books*. Immensely influential in New York and national literary circles, she said of her home state: "This was, is, truly home to me, not just a birthplace." Kentucky remained fertile literary ground.

Two very different kinds of writing came from unexpected sources in Kentucky. In 1936 salesman Duncan Hines of Bowling Green published his first guidebook to good eating in the United States. It became an instant success and there soon followed a guide to lodging, a cookbook, a series of signs indicating places were "Recommended by Duncan Hines," and then his own brands of food. His books alone sold over two million copies by the time of his death in 1959, and it all had made his name synonymous with quality and good taste.

At another level, a much more philosophical writing emerged. Three days after the attack on Pearl Harbor, on December 10, 1941, a strong, short, and stocky man, Thomas Merton, entered the Abbey of Our Lady of Gethsemani near Bardstown and began the process of prayer and austerity that would eventually make him a Trappist monk. This choice followed his birth in France, years of wandering, and a varied educational background. In those monastic halls of silence, however, Merton spoke out loudly through his prolific writings on matters theological and historical. During the next twenty-seven years he produced some fifty volumes of poetry and prose. His 1948 autobiographical account of his pilgrimage and conversion, *The Seven Storey Mountain,* sold a million copies and brought international acclaim to him and royalties to the monastery. Later books such as his reflective *The Sign of Jonas* (1953) and *Thoughts in Solitude* (1958) made him one of the nation's best-known and most widely read religious and philosophical writers. By the 1960s Merton's growing concern with social justice brought him to travel more, explore Far Eastern and Indian religions, and write about nuclear war, race relations, and religious rapprochement. On one overseas trip in 1968—on the anniversary of the day he entered Gethsemani—Merton died from electrocution, having apparently touched a fan with faulty wiring while bathing. Yet his influence still lives on.

New Generations of Writers

Over the years certain places had attracted writers connected with Kentucky like a magnet: the nineteenth-century Bluegrass, with Allen and Fox; turn-of-the-century Louisville, with its Authors Club of Johnston, Rice, Martin, and others; post–World War I Vanderbilt University, where Warren, Tate, Brooks, Stuart, and Still went; and, in the late 1950s, the University of Kentucky, in Lexington.

"The Conscience of Kentucky," author Wendell Berry of Henry County. (Courtesy of Guy Mendes)

Between 1956 and 1962 a half-dozen writers who would go on to win acclaim received degrees from the university: Walter Tevis, Wendell Berry, Ed McClanahan, James Baker Hall, Gurney Norman, and Bobbie Ann Mason. The university at that time was not a literary mecca. It was, however, a place where at that moment in history those talented people were touched by professors and events in a way that sparked and developed their interest in writing. Like other authors from Kentucky, many would leave the commonwealth; unlike earlier writers, however, most would come back. Yet none of these writers had ever left it in their prose.

Wendell E. Berry in some ways most evoked the Kentucky spirit in essays, poetry, and fiction that stressed agrarian concerns and the place of people and personal responsibility in this era and on this earth. His novels include *The Memory of Old Jack* (1974), *Jayber Crow* (2000), and *Hannah Coulter* (2004), all of which remain some of the best fictional works in a Kentucky setting. Berry's strongest

presentation of his themes, however, came in a series of essays, including *A Continuous Harmony* (1972) and *The Unsettling of America* (1977). In these works he criticized the impersonal corporate and governmental influence on traditional farming, which, together with societal changes, made it more a business than a way of life. With that shift, he feared, would come the death of important parts of an agrarian lifestyle that brought strengths to a rapidly changing world. A major spokesman for the new agrarianism, Berry tells his readers that bigger is not better; that home, neighbors, and community come first; that quality work, of whatever kind, is reward enough; that individuals must not worship a technology that sees the world as a machine, and instead must see the earth as "a living creature"; and that without history, learning, and a sense of place, "We are adrift in the present, in the wreckage of yesterday, in the nightmare of tomorrow." Living a simple life on a farm in rural Henry County, Berry remains the conscience of Kentucky and of the United States.

Walter Tevis came to Kentucky to live when he was ten years old, went to college in the state, and used experiences gathered while working in a poolroom near the university campus as the basis for his first successful book, *The Hustler* (1959), and its later sequel, *The Color of Money* (1984). Both were made into motion pictures, as was his science fiction novel, *The Man Who Fell to Earth* (1963). Bothered by personal problems that almost ended his career, Tevis left his professorship at Ohio University and again took up writing full-time, but he died of lung cancer at the age of fifty-six.

James Baker Hall of Lexington, Edward P. McClanahan of Bracken and Mason Counties, and Gurney Norman of Hazard had been friends at college. All received prestigious fellowships at Stanford University, and all taught in institutions of higher education outside Kentucky before returning to the commonwealth. As Hall noted, they needed "to escape provincialism," then to return to capitalize on the same trend: "Kentucky breeds an intense identification of oneself as a Kentuckian, which focuses you in on things local. That . . . is useful to fiction writers and poets [whose] . . . stories come most successfully from embodied lives, not ideas." Hall, through his combined interest in poetry, photography, and prose; Norman, through works such as the immensely popular *Divine Right's Trip* (1971), which sold two million copies, and his Appalachian-based *Kinfolks* (1977); and McClanahan, through his earthy and marvelously funny *The Natural Man* (1983), all demonstrated the creativity that resulted from physical and spiritual journeys to and from the state.

"People think my first name and my middle name are Mayfield Native. Everything I've ever read in the paper started out 'Mayfield native Bobbie Ann Mason.'" Mason did indeed grow up in western Kentucky and wrote of that area in most of her work. Literally not "one of the boys" in the group of budding writers at the university, she left Kentucky to write first for movie magazines, then earned a PhD in literature and began composing fiction. On her twentieth submission to the *New Yorker*, she was accepted, and as a late bloomer at age forty, she had arrived. *Shiloh and Other Stories* (1982), *In Country* (1985), which became a motion picture, *Spence + Lila* (1988), *Feather Crowns* (1993), which won the Southern Book Award, and her memoir, *Clear Springs* (1999), all stamped her as an important American writer.

Some authors with state connections even modified the writing genre. Louisville-born Hunter S. Thompson used first-person prose and controversial countercultural approaches to create what became known as "Gonzo Journalism" in works such as *Fear and Loathing in Las Vegas* (1971).

A whole host of writers with Kentucky ties remain on the contemporary scene, some with reputations already made, others making them still. While popular mystery writer Sue Grafton did not often show a conscious state influence in their work, other novelists do. Certain literary figures successfully create in the fields of poetry, fiction, and nonfiction, while others remain true to only one genre. Some authors, such as black novelists Gayl Jones and bell hooks (Gloria Jean Watkins) speak for an underrepresented group in Kentucky fiction,

while others write from a long-common background. Literary figures such as Barbara Kingsolver, in books such as *The Bean Trees* (1988) and *The Poisonwood Bible* (1998), plus novelists such as Fenton Johnson and so many others, all show the diversity that represents Kentucky literature.

Historical Writing

Two very different historians dominated the writing of Kentucky's history, Richard H. Collins and Thomas D. Clark. Collins was more a compiler and reviser than a historian, but his two-volume work, *A History of Kentucky* (1874), became the research bible for several later generations. Taking his father's earlier history, editor and attorney Collins got numerous people to contribute material, wrote part himself, and produced a book filled with facts, lists, and information. Over the next half century numerous authors added to the story produced by Collins or put the story in more narrative form. Many state histories basically started with Collins's *History*, including works by Nathaniel S. Shaler (1884), Zachariah F. Smith (1885), W. H. Perrin, J. H. Battle, and G. C. Kniffin (1887), Elizabeth S. Kinkead (1896), Robert M. McElroy (1909), E. Polk Johnson (1912), William E. Connelley and E. Merton Coulter (1922), and Temple Bodley and Samuel M. Wilson (1928). Most of those authors were not trained historians. Such a trend would continue later in the persons of authors such as Willard Rouse Jillson and Lexington's J. Winston ("Squire") Coleman Jr., whose prolific writings covered a wide range of topics.

Similarly, in a later era, attorney Harry M. Caudill of Letcher County became what might be best termed a historical essayist. Although his history was criticized by some, Caudill drafted powerful, advocacy-style prose that brought national attention to his native Appalachia. In books such as *Night Comes to the Cumberlands* (1963), *My Land Is Dying* (1971), and *The Mountain, the Miner, and the Lord* (1980), he wrote eloquently about the coal land and what he saw as the strengths and weaknesses of the people who inhabited it.

Historian Thomas D. Clark at the University of Kentucky, 1968. (Portrait Print Collection, University of Kentucky Special Collections and Research Center, Lexington, KY)

The era of writing from the pens of professionally trained historians can best be dated to September 14, 1928, when Mississippi's Thomas Dionysius Clark came to graduate school in the commonwealth. With a PhD from Duke University in hand by 1932, Clark would teach at the University of Kentucky from 1931 until 1968, serving as chair of the history department for many of those years. During that time and later, excellent historians, particularly in the field of southern studies, made the University of Kentucky one of the best history schools in the nation, with W. Clement Eaton, Holman Hamilton, Albert D. ("Ab") Kirwan, Charles P. Roland, and George Herring among the faculty.

Clark himself wrote books in numerous fields—southern history, western history, the frontier—and served as president of most of the professional organizations in each area. First and foremost, however, he wrote of the commonwealth. Perhaps his best-named book was *Kentucky: Land of Contrast* (1968). Throughout his career, Clark wrote of that place of contrast, and his *History of Kentucky* (1937) stood as the standard for six decades. He also worked to ensure that future historians would have better access to materials from which they could write their own revisions. He helped build up the University of Kentucky's Special Collections, pushed for the funding of the state archives, and, when he was over ninety years old, was among several who encouraged the formation of the Kentucky Historical Society's History Center. In 1990 Clark was named the state's historian laureate for life, a title he held until his death in 2005 at age 101.

By that time the landscape for writing state history had changed, and dozens of professional historians at historical societies or at private colleges and regional universities were presenting various facets of the state's past through increasingly well-written and well-researched works. Representing the most prolific of these was Lowell H. Harrison of Western Kentucky University, William E. Ellis of Eastern Kentucky University, and James C. Klotter of the Kentucky Historical Society and then Georgetown College. Various encyclopedias added to the state's knowledge base—a pathbreaking one on Kentucky, edited by John E. Kleber and published in 1992, was followed by excellent similar works on Louisville, Northern Kentucky, and African Americans in the commonwealth. At the same time, authors representing groups who had previously written little of the state's history began to present new interpretations of the commonwealth's past. Kentucky-born black historian George C. Wright told of racial violence and of African American life, then joined with Marion B. Lucas of Western Kentucky University to produce the much-needed two-volume *History of Blacks in Kentucky* (1992). Similarly, women historians began to issue fresh examinations of the female experience—"herstory"—in Kentucky history, as exemplified by the contributors to *Kentucky Women; Their Lives and Times* (2015). All in all, the writing about Kentucky's past had become more diverse and more professional, but much still remained undone. Clio, the muse of history, continued to cry out for more toilers in the field—and for more respect from the public.

Historians, both amateur and professional, found more publications available to them as the years passed. In 1903 the *Register of the Kentucky Historical Society* began, and then in 1926 *The Filson Club History Quarterly* (later *Ohio Valley History*) also started providing an outlet for scholarly articles and reviews. A growing public library movement, supplemented by bookmobiles, made books more easily available across Kentucky. In the 1940s the University of Kentucky Press began, offering Kentucky authors a state publisher to produce their books. A number of universities and colleges, plus two historical groups, formed a consortium in 1969, and as the renamed University Press of Kentucky the new institution achieved even greater regional respect as a publishing house. It showed the strengths of a cooperative approach and offered a seldom-copied example of the benefits of state collaboration instead

of competition. A special press in Louisville is the American Printing House for the Blind, the nation's oldest and the world's largest publishing house for the visually impaired. Like many parts of the Kentucky world, it remains better known outside the state than in it.

Poets, Artists, Architects, and More

Many of Kentucky's best poets had strengths in other areas as well, as the careers of Roberts, Warren, Stuart, Still, Merton, and Berry attest. When the lives of those who primarily owed their success to their output of poems are examined, a very mixed picture results. In contrast to the field of fiction, poetry in Kentucky did not become one of the state's cultural strengths. Of the late nineteenth- and early twentieth-century poets, some owed their fame chiefly to a single work, such as Henry T. Stanton's "The Moneyless Man" (1865) or James H. Mulligan's endlessly quoted "In Kentucky" (1902). Others voiced the otherwise silent thoughts forged in forgotten aspects of Kentucky life. Black poet Effie Waller Smith of Pike County wrote three volumes of verse by the time she was thirty, but she virtually disappeared from the state literary scene until being "rediscovered" near the end of the twentieth century. Louisville's Joseph S. Cotter is generally regarded as the state's first significant black poet. While serving as a teacher and administrator in the Falls City's black schools, he achieved some national recognition for his many volumes of lyric poetry. His son and namesake was a poet of much promise as well but died at the age of twenty-three in 1919. When *A Brief Anthology of Kentucky Poetry* appeared in 1936, neither Smith nor the Cotters were included among the ninety-three poets listed. Segregation separated races even in the arts. The anthology also discriminated based on religion, for it did not include Israel J. Schwartz, a man called the author of the first important Yiddish literature produced in America. The Lithuanian-born Schwartz came to Lexington in 1918 and wrote his book-length narrative epic poem *Kentucky* over the next four years. Published first in a journal, then in 1925 as a book, it told of an immigrant's experiences in this new world and his attempts to reconcile the past with the future.

More traditional sources of poetry included Robert Burns Wilson of Frankfort, James T. Cotton Noe of Washington County and Lexington, and Edwin C. Litsey of Lebanon, all of whom attracted some regional attention. But of all the poets who lived in the half century after the Civil War, however, one—a strange one—dominated and achieved an international reputation. Born into a Louisville family in which the mother was a spiritualist and the herbalist-farmer father spoke only German, Madison J. Cawein combined the influences of his parents in producing verses that both celebrated nature and filled it with dryads, demigods, nymphs, and fairies. He had to work in a poolroom and betting parlor to make a living and often did not return home until late at night. He rose early, before his job started, and wrote then. Beginning with his *Blooms of the Berry* (1887), the too-prolific Cawein averaged more than a volume of verse a year. Later, Joyce Kilmer called Cawein "the greatest nature poet of his time," and modest success brought an end to the Kentuckian's poolroom days. Later financial reverses, however, again brought him near poverty. In his poems, the shy and lonely Cawein could write:

This is the truth, as I see it, my dear,
Out in the wind and the rain:
They who have nothing have little to
        fear,—
Nothing to lose or to gain.

But he felt he had lost much, and he died of apoplexy at the age of forty-nine. The voice of "the Kentucky Keats" was stilled early.

Following Cawein, Elizabeth Madox Roberts and then a host of other writers began to produce excellent poetry that far departed from Cawein's traditionalism, including, more recently, Tony Crunk, Nikky Finney, Jonathan Greene, George Ella Lyon, David McCombs, Maurice Manning, Richard Taylor, Jane Gentry Vance, Crystal Wilkinson, and Jeff Worley, among many talented others. Representative of the fresh outlooks they brought was Frank X

Walker of Boyle County. He coined the term "Affrilachia" to highlight the African American contributions to Appalachia and Kentucky. As one of his poems noted,

indeed,
some of the bluegrass
is black.

In the field of visual art, Kentucky produced even fewer nationally recognized figures than it did in poetry. Before the Civil War, several artists had made a living chiefly by concentrating on portraits and by traveling to various states. With the increasing popularity of photography, some of the demand for portraiture declined, and Kentucky artists of the late nineteenth century became better known for their landscapes. Some of the more respected prewar artists saw careers end in the postwar period. The painter of horses, Edward Troye, moved to Alabama and died there in 1874. Samuel Woodson Price had become a Civil War general and returned to studios first in Lexington, then Louisville. His career in portraiture ended in 1881 with blindness brought on by a war wound. He lived on in darkness for thirty-seven more years and dictated two historical works.

German-born Carl C. Brenner came to prominence through his landscapes, particularly those featuring beech trees in the Louisville area. His father denied him attendance at an art academy in Munich. Brenner had worked first as a house and sign painter in Louisville after the family came to the United States in the 1850s. His career ended prematurely with his death before the age of fifty. Charles Harvey Joiner followed much the same path, working as a journeyman house and sign painter before opening a studio in Louisville in 1880. He too featured beech woods in his landscape views. During that same era poet Robert Burns Wilson settled in Kentucky, started painting in Frankfort after 1875, and produced portraits and landscapes in oil, watercolors, crayon, and charcoal. Works such as *Little Bo Peep: Mary Hendricks Swigert Moore* show the multiplicity of Wilson's talents. Louisville-born and -based

Paul Sawyier's painting *View of Wapping Street* depicts a Frankfort scene. (Kentucky Historical Society Collections, Frankfort, KY)

Patty Prather Thum studied under William Merritt Chase and Thomas Eakins, served as art critic of a Louisville newspaper, and painted landscapes and portraits that were widely exhibited. Dixie Selden of Covington studied under Frank Duveneck, used the same subjects as Thum, and displayed her more impressionist-style works across the United States. Hattie H. Hill went from Paris, Kentucky, to an art education in Paris, France, then returned to paint landscapes in the United States.

The most popular among the Kentucky landscape painters of the late nineteenth and early twentieth century was Paul Sawyier. Unfortunately for the Ohio-born Sawyier, much of his popularity came after his death, and his life was filled with constant struggles to make enough money to live. Studying under Chase

and painting his watercolors of river and city scenes around the Frankfort area, he appealed to a sense of nostalgia even in his own time, as he used his colorful, eclectic combination of tonalism and impressionism to portray Kentucky places. The withdrawn Sawyier resided for a time on a houseboat, but he finally left the state where he had lived for forty-three years and went to New York, seeking a better climate for his art. He found little respite there, but by the time of his death he had left a large body of works, such as *Scenes on Elkhorn Creek* and *Old Capitol Hotel*, which later gave him a strong reputation within the state.

All of these artists were minor masters, however, with only limited national reputations. Only one Kentucky artist of the first half century after the Civil War could be said to have achieved national prominence. That was Frank Duveneck of Covington. Leaving Kentucky to study at the Royal Academy in Munich in 1870, he spent much of the next twenty years in Europe. His 1875 showing at the Boston Art Club Exhibit brought him instant acclaim, as he bridged American and European realism through introduction of the Munich style. His broad brush strokes, his warm and dark tonality, and his powerful but delicate realism all showed the strengths displayed in *Whistling Boy* and *The Turkish Page*, as well as in cathedrals in his hometown. In 1888 his young American-born artist wife died, and a grief-stricken Duveneck returned to Covington to live and to the Cincinnati Art Academy to teach. There he became influential and popular as a warm and personable mentor, including among his students Kentucky artists Selden, Sawyier, John Bernard Alberts, and William Welsh.

Still, whatever sparked the creative genius of Kentucky authors touched state visual artists only seldom, and no lasting tradition influenced later artists. The vitality shown in the New Deal–commissioned public building murals did not endure. Only in the field of folk art did the state achieve much success, as exemplified in the simple but powerful figures of artists like Edgar Tolson of Wolfe County and in traditional textiles and pottery.

In other fields of artistic endeavor, individual Kentuckians achieved some national recognition, but widespread achievement remained elusive. Louisville cartoonists Paul Plascke and, later, Hugh Haynie and Lexington's Joel Pett enlivened journalism, while Fontaine Fox's "Toonerville Trolley" series at its peak appeared in more than 250 newspapers. Interest in photography in the state sparked the establishment, near the turn of the start of the twentieth century, of the Kentucky-Tennessee Photographers Association, one of the first such organizations in the South. Around the same time William G. Stuber left Louisville to direct the Eastman Kodak Company's sensitive-material laboratory; in 1924 he became president of the company. Later Ralph Eugene Meatyard (with his gothic symbolism), Robert May, Van Deren

Coke, and others in the Lexington Camera Club made their mark in the field. In 1969 Moneta J. Sleet Jr. of Owensboro became the first black American to win a Pulitzer Prize for feature photography.

The sculptures of two Louisvillians—Enid Yandell, as exemplified in the Daniel Boone statue in Cherokee Park, and, later, Ed Hamilton, who sculpted "The Spirit of Freedom" at the African American Civil War Memorial in Washington, DC—represented all too rare success for a Kentuckian in the field of formal sculpting.

James Lane Allen wrote in the 1880s that Kentucky's postwar architecture featured no "native characteristics" and had become like that of much of the rest of the United States. In a sense he was correct, for the new technology, with circular saws, machine-made nails, and easy transportation, helped standardize construction. Architectural journals spread national trends to regional locations, where they were soon adopted. The state's premier postwar architects, Henry Whitestone and Charles Julian Clarke, helped professionalize the field, and in 1890, the year the state's first skyscraper was built, the University of Kentucky also graduated its first engineering student. In 1900, 118 architects, 2 of them women, worked in the state. By then Kentucky had seen the influence of High Victorian Gothic Revival styles after 1860, Italianate, and the heavy solid stone construction of the Romanesque Revival introduced to the commonwealth by Mason Maury in 1886 and best exemplified in the old Fayette County Courthouse. From the 1890s to World War II the Colonial Revival style proved very popular, particularly in the architecture of horse farms. Post–World War II business and public buildings had a more functional, style-less form, one characterized by its critics as shapeless, dull, and utilitarian. For these observers, the distinctive postmodernist style of the Humana Building, constructed in Louisville in 1985, proved a welcome, if controversial, relief.

For individual families, the large, rambling two-story frame houses, with extensive porches, continued to be common in rural areas, while simple box houses dominated in coal camps. Increasingly, though, town and city dwellings took on a different face. The parlor of the early post–Civil War era had been the public buffer shielding the private places in the house; the front porch had been a place of meeting and relaxation; for some, servants and their quarters had been a part of the mix. By the 1920s much of that had changed. The cottage, then the bungalow (or California) style, featuring small, affordable one-story homes with low roofs, had become very popular. Another national form, the prairie style, did not become commonplace, and indeed, the Frank Lloyd Wright–designed Ziegler House in Frankfort represents perhaps the only example of that style in the South.

With the growth of the automobile suburb, particularly after World War II, the ranch style invaded Kentucky and found little resistance. Throughout, various revivals—Tudor, Italianate, Renaissance—appeared and found support as well. A late 1980s comparison of one Kentucky town with twenty others across the nation showed that it had more ranch-style homes (44 percent) than the norm, fewer two-story dwellings, fewer garages, about the same percentage of porches, and much more brick construction (43 percent versus an average of 25). In short, the fairly typical Kentucky town was characterized by a brick ranch-style home with a porch. But perhaps the major and most welcome post–World War II trend in Kentucky architecture was the restoration of old homes. Into the 1960s such actions proved sporadic, and many historic structures were lost to parking lots. Ironically, however, the slow growth of some Kentucky towns and cities left many older structures still intact when historic preservation began to become more commonplace. As a result, many parts of the commonwealth have been able to combine past and present through architecture.

The Sounds of Music

In the areas of poetry, drawing and painting, photography, sculpture, and architecture, Kentuckians had made only marginal marks on the national scene. But people of the commonwealth would make a significant impact in their music. A rich tradition of song had long existed in the state, particularly in the folk ballads. Those songs remained mostly unheard and uncollected until the twentieth century. Books such as *A Syllabus of Kentucky Folksongs* (1911) and *Lonesome Tunes* (1916) changed that, as did those who collected and sang the old tunes. Such a revival occurred in a more formal way with Louisville-born John Jacob Niles, who gathered songs across Appalachia and often transformed them. He then performed with his dulcimer all over the United States, operating as the "mountain minstrel" from a central Kentucky base. Even more authentically Appalachian in background was Jean R. Ritchie, who grew up in a "singing family" of fourteen children in Viper, became a Phi Beta Kappa graduate of the University of Kentucky, and then began recording traditional ballads in their original form in 1952 as part of a folk revival. That revival would later include Louisvillian Mary Travers of the popular Peter, Paul, and Mary trio. Sarah Gertrude Knott of Paducah started the National Folk Festival in 1934. It would be the first such group to feature multicultural and multiregional traditional culture.

Change was coming to the mountains and to all of Kentucky, even as the old tunes were being preserved and recorded. What one author has called "the music of the damned—not the elect" was becoming popular by the 1920s, and the availability of radio gave "hillbilly" music a way to reach almost everyone. What by the 1950s would be called country music gave the voiceless an outlet. It gave people a way to express their hopes, fears, frustrations, and life stories and gave comfort in time of need or just simple enjoyment at the end of a hard day. Kentucky became a major producer of the people and songs that made country music popular.

At first the music came through recordings. Philipine ("Fiddin' Doc") Roberts of Madison County became the most widely recorded fiddler, a tradition continued by "Blind Ed" Haly and then Clifford Gross. But the real boon came when Chicago's WLS radio station began its *National Barn Dance* program in the 1920s. There Garrard County's Bradley Kincaid became a star, and his songbooks sold hundreds of thousands of copies. John Lair of Rockcastle County brought the idea to the Bluegrass State and in 1937 started the *Renfro Valley Barn Dance*, which rivaled Nashville's *Grand Ole Opry* for a time. Louisville's WHAS radio broadcast live music into the 1930s as well. All those sources gave those who had migrated out of the state a way to reconnect through music with the folkways of back home. From those bases, individual bands like the Prairie Ramblers and the Coon Creek Girls, with Lily May Ledford, also began to be widely heard.

So too did a series of individual stars. While some singers like Aunt Molly Jackson expressed the anger of the working class, more mainstream efforts gained greater attention. Clyde J. ("Red") Foley grew up near Berea and by 1930 joined the WLS team. His "Peace in the Valley" would become the first million-seller gospel song, while "Chattanoogie Shoe Shine Boy" was the first country recording to go to the top of the popular music charts. Louis M. ("Grandpa") Jones, born to sharecroppers in Henderson County, toured with Bradley Kincaid and became a regular on the *Grand Ole Opry*. Four months after Jones's birth, the performer who became known as Pee Wee King was born in Wisconsin. He later moved to Louisville. While there he composed many of his most popular works, including "Tennessee Waltz." From Muhlenberg County, Merle Travis's "Sixteen Tons" added to his legacy. All four men would be inducted into the Country Music Hall of Fame. A second wave of performers followed, with Loretta Webb Lynn of Butcher Hollow in Johnson County being perhaps the best known. Singing of a life that saw her born a "coal miner's daughter," she married at age thirteen and was a mother of four by age eighteen and a grandmother by twenty-nine. In 1972 she was selected as the first female Country Music Association entertainer of the year, and eight years later she was named entertainer of the decade in her field. Others in that second generation included Mary Frances Pennick of Dry Ridge, who sang as Skeeter Davis;

Tom T. Hall of Olive Hill; and Diana ("Naomi") Judd of Ashland, who joined with her daughter to perform as the Judds. More recent lights on the music stage have included Dwight Yoakam, Matraca Berg, Billy Ray Cyrus, John Michael Montgomery, Sturgill Simpson, and Chris Stapleton.

Most of the Kentucky-born country music performers found success away from Kentucky, but a study of country music in the state saw that as only one characteristic. Most performers also took a strong sense of place and heritage with them and sang about their experiences, and virtually all used a popular style that made their music readily accessible. The state sent out more than just talented performers; Bluegrass music became, as one writer said, "Kentucky's most famous export." The acknowledged Father of Bluegrass was William S. ("Bill") Monroe of Rosine in Ohio County. Influenced by African American guitarist Arnold Shultz and by both Kentucky and Carolina ballads, he perfected the mandolin style and high-pitched rendition that brought success in "Blue Moon of Kentucky" and other tunes. His Blue Grass Boys band was the prototype for the performance of that type of music, and Monroe's twenty-five-million record sales attest to the popularity of the man who also joined the Country Music Hall of Fame. Out of that same tradition came such performers as the Osborne Brothers, J. D. Crowe, and Ricky Skaggs. Don and Phil Everly, as the Everly Brothers, found success in the crossover "rockabilly" style. By 1980 Kentucky had contributed more "stars" to country music than any other state except Texas. Moreover, the state has also been the setting for songs sung by non-Kentucky artists, such as John Prine's protest song "Paradise," set in Muhlenberg County.

Coming from a different background but born out of the same human needs were blues and jazz. The so-called Father of the Blues, Alabama-born W. C. Handy, lived in Henderson in the 1890s and wrote later that "there I learned to appreciate the music of my people. . . . The blues were born because from that day on, I started thinking about putting my own experiences down." In Louisville, whose Walnut

Street became a scaled-down version of Memphis's Beale Street, similar influences operated on guitarist Sylvester Weaver, trumpeter Jonah Jones, singer Sara Martin, vibraphonist Lionel Hampton, singer Helen Humes (who in 1938 replaced Billie Holiday in the Count Basie band), and a score of other important blues performers. Jazz guitarist Jimmy Raney proved to be an extraordinary innovator in his field. Yet as in country, many of the best blues and jazz musicians left the state and performed elsewhere.

While all these important new forms were influencing American music, more traditional music continued to be popular. William S. Hays, a Louisville native who wrote for the *Courier-Journal*, achieved fame as one of the nineteenth century's most popular songwriters. Following in the tradition of Stephen Collins Foster, he wrote gentle, sentimental lyrics, and his more than three hundred songs sold more than twenty million copies. Later, the Hill sisters in Louisville received credit for composing "Happy Birthday to You," while Haven Gillespie of Covington found success in the field as well, with his best-known tune being "Santa Claus Is Comin' to Town" (1934). Also in the twentieth century, Danville's Robert Todd Duncan broke many color barriers as his baritone voice was heard across America, with his first fame coming from his performance as Porgy in George Gershwin's "Porgy and Bess." (Ironically, the Civil Rights Movement in Louisville would accelerate in 1959 after African Americans were denied admittance to the Brown Theater to see the same play.)

Classical music remained popular through all eras, but not until 1937, when Robert S. Whitney became conductor of what would become the Louisville Orchestra, was there a strong, sustained classical presence in Kentucky. During Whitney's tenure, the orchestra commissioned new music, and the city gained some fame as a musical center. At various times, smaller symphony orchestras also found success in Lexington, Owensboro, Paducah, and elsewhere. In 1952, the Louisville Opera opened—the twelfth oldest in the nation. That city's Roland Hays became the first African American to have a successful career as a con-

cert singer, but his career represented a rarity for Kentuckians, black or white, in that arena.

A meeting place of northern and southern influences, Kentucky produced various kinds of music and musicians. Not all would be appreciated in their times, but the words of one Kentuckian rang true. He said that he would rather listen to Bluegrass than Beethoven, but that did not mean he was uncultured; it only meant that he had different tastes in music than other critics. Some in the state liked one style, some another. There were many musical Kentuckys, and in most of them citizens of the commonwealth made major contributions to the national scene.

Theater, Radio, and Film

Kentucky has attracted and presented solid plays, as well as stage actors and actresses and playwrights. Mary Anderson of Louisville became internationally known as an actress in the nineteenth century, but she was an early exception. Better known were the theaters at which Anderson debuted. Louisville's Macauley's Theatre had opened in 1873 and was one of the first great theaters west of the Appalachian Mountains; it would later present the initial American production of Ibsen's *A Doll's House*. The final play at Macauley's came in 1925, the year the original building was demolished; years afterward, the name would go to another Louisville theater. In some ways more successful was Actors Theatre of Louisville, begun in 1963. Under the direction of Jon Jory and others, and through the annual Humana Festival of New American Plays, it became perhaps the nation's best regional theater. Premieres of over a dozen Pulitzer Prize–winning plays cemented its reputation. In 1996 a *Time* magazine article concluded, "From now on, maybe Broadway should be called 'Off-Louisville.'" When combined with such institutions as the Louisville Ballet, one of the oldest such companies in the South, and strong local patronage of the arts, Actors Theatre gave the Falls City and Kentucky a strong cultural presence.

Individuals such as playwright Cleve Kinkead (*Common Play*) and drama critic John

The 1916 film *Intolerance* was a massive undertaking by the innovative and influential director D. W. Griffith of Oldham County.

Mason Brown, both from Louisville, made an early impression, but not until after 1950 did Kentucky playwrights make a significant impact on the national stage. Louisville's John Patrick (Goggan) won a Pulitzer Prize for drama in 1953 for *Teahouse of the August Moon* and wrote several successful screen adaptations as well. Thirty years later, another Louisvillian, Marsha Norman, won the same prize for her *'night Mother*, first presented at Actors Theatre. Fort Knox–born playwright Suzan Lori Parks became the first African American woman to win a Pulitzer Prize for drama for her 2001 play *Topdog/Underdog*. Frankfort's George C. Wolfe attended an all-black school but found more diversity in New York later when he created the award-winning musical *Jelly's Last Jam* and produced and directed other successful works.

While theater continued to be popular through the years, in the late nineteenth cen-

tury it had been dominant. Other forms of entertainment came with the twentieth century, radio among them. Louisville's WHAS, owned by the Bingham family, served as the state's major voice over the airwaves after its 1922 opening. In its first two decades WHAS produced much innovative and original programming, but financial demands finally made the station like others across the commonwealth, not dissimilar to those across the country. Other than musical personalities, few national radio figures came forth. Perhaps the best known were Harlan County's Cawood Ledford, who gained national acclaim for his sports broadcasts, and Bob Edwards of Louisville as host of "Morning Edition" on National Public Radio.

In the area of motion pictures, Kentucky made a much stronger impact, both as a subject and as an influence on individuals. No more important person appeared than the man called the Father of Film—David Wark Griffith of Oldham County. Coming from southern roots that included a slaveholding Confederate father, Griffith moved from acting in bit parts to become arguably the most influential director in film history. He changed moviemaking forever. First at the Biograph Company, where he worked with Mary Pickford and Lillian Gish, and then through his own efforts, he made the craft look at itself in new ways. Experiments in camera movement, film length, editing, fadeouts, close-ups, color, and lighting, among other innovations, made him a model for international filmmakers. Yet the brilliant Griffith was a paradox: a man whose most famous and successful film, *The Birth of a Nation* (1915), brought about racial tension and aided in the formation of a new Klan movement, yet who in *Broken Blossoms* (1919) gave a very sensitive and touching treatment of race; a person who made strong and powerful antiwar motion pictures but also a strong film supporting World War I; a Kentuckian who stressed artistic freedom and the evils of bigotry in his masterpiece, the film spectacular *Intolerance* (1916), yet contributed in other films to prejudice. Director of the first important feature-length film, called "the greatest creative genius that cinema has ever known," D. W. Griffith would have been given even larger later praise had he not reflected his southern, Kentucky racial roots so well. By the 1920s his era had ended, and his last years were spent in alcoholism and poverty, mostly back in the region of his birth. His director's mantle was worn, more imperfectly, by a student of his, Charles A. ("Tod") Browning of Louisville, who directed *Dracula* (1931) with Bela Lugosi, as well as the cult classic *Freaks* (1932). The emphasis on the horror genre would be taken up later by director John Carpenter of Bowling Green.

Numerous actors and actresses with Kentucky ties performed in films over the years, in all kinds of roles, and a listing of some names suggests the variety of talent: Una Merkel of Covington, Irene Dunne of Louisville, Tom Ewell of Owensboro, George Reeves of Ashland and Versailles, Victor Mature of Louisville, William Conrad of Louisville, Oscar-win-

ner Patricia Neal of Packard, Warren Oates of Depoy, Rosemary Clooney of Maysville, Florence Henderson of Owensboro, and Ned Beatty of St. Matthews. More recently, Lily Tomlin of Paducah; Lee Majors of Middlesborough; Harry Dean Stanton and Jim Varney, both of Lexington; Tom Cruise and Jennifer Lawrence, both of Louisville; Josh Hutcherson of Union; Ashley Judd of Lexington and other places in the commonwealth; Johnny Depp of Owensboro; and George Clooney of Augusta all continued the state's long involvement in film.

Yet in many ways, the most important aspect of all was the portrayal of the state in film, through a large number of motion pictures, particularly in the early years of the industry. From 1904 to 1938, the word *Kentucky* appeared in some twenty-eight film titles, and numerous other films featured the state in other ways. Four themes resulted from the depiction of the commonwealth on celluloid: Land of Plantations, as shown in a series of *Uncle Tom's Cabin* films; Land of Horse Racing, as exemplified in *Kentucky* (1938); Land of Feuds and Moonshine, as presented in dozens of silent movies, several done by D. W. Griffith; and Land of the Pioneer, as portrayed in *The Great Meadow* (1931). To those in the public whose views of the commonwealth were formed chiefly from the screen, Kentucky came across in stereotypical fashion as either a romantic place of mansions and racehorses or as a violent home for Indian fighters and feuding mountaineers. In fact, in the formative years of the industry, the Appalachian theme dominated, in the same way that Westerns would later. Almost nothing that showed twentieth-century Kentucky, except an occasional Derby, would appear in the films featuring the commonwealth, and in the public image the state remained mired in times past, suspended from modern America.

Nevertheless, Kentucky had cultural strengths not usually emphasized. The Kentucky stereotypes seldom included cultural Kentucky, which was a rich resource in many areas of the state. Benighted Kentucky would be the common image, not enlightened Kentucky. The commonwealth's cultural strength, interestingly, would be in areas involving words, in literature, music, and, to a lesser degree, film. The oral traditions, whether in the "phantom books" stories told to Elizabeth Madox Roberts, or the songs sung to Jean Ritchie, or the tales of southern heroism learned by D. W. Griffith, all heavily influenced talented Kentuckians to achieve in their respective areas. Often those people had to leave the state to put all the traditions into perspective, but the most successful built on that heritage and often used it in their work. Some returned with a different outlook and found they actually could go home again, with success. In short, while weak in some areas, Kentucky overall had a long history of solid cultural achievements. These have not been fully appreciated, but at the same time they have proved vitally important in shaping the lives not just of citizens of the commonwealth but also of the nation and, sometimes, of the world.

16

The Transitional Twenties

The 1920s were years of transition in Kentucky, not because the state and its people suddenly moved from one era to another, but because citizens of the commonwealth confronted change. In that decade modernism moved into Kentucky, though fundamentalism followed with its own counterattacks. While the forces of reform and reaction each won victories, in the end the state rejected extremes and took a course of conservative moderation. The twenties alerted Kentuckians to what might lie ahead, for modern America could not be totally rejected. The decade prepared them for the greater changes coming from the New Deal of the 1930s.

Mindsets, Morals, and Manners

To many Kentuckians, the world after the Great War seemed to be falling apart before their eyes. The rise of Lenin and communism (or Bolshevism, as it was also called) sparked drastic fears of revolt and revolution. In the commonwealth, the "Red scare" brought Desha Breckinridge of the *Lexington Herald* to declare that Russian agents in the United States were a greater threat to the nation than the recently defeated German armies had been. Nationally, bombings by anarchists, numerous race riots, the Boston police strike, and then, later, the scandals of the Warren Harding presidency all made chaos seem the norm. Coming after a searing war and the debilitating influenza epidemic, such events suggested little future hope, at least to some. Henry Watterson, now retired from the *Courier-Journal*, was troubled further by Prohibition and woman suffrage—both now in effect. He told a friend in 1920 that "the world is on the way to another col-

lapse. . . . Another Dark Age interlude and another civilization with its strange gods." He predicted that by the year 2013, with the Bolsheviks having dominated Europe, Asia, and Africa, Prohibition "having degenerated America," and the aftereffects of woman suffrage having allowed females to dominate males, "the flag will drop," and all would be lost.

Others saw the situation differently. While they did not approve of the violence or the manner in which change was coming, they did see a need to move on from one era to another. As one Kentucky youth wrote later, after the Great War "henceforth forever the door was closed to innocence." The thoughtful author Elizabeth Madox Roberts concluded in a later letter to a friend, "It was about that time the great change came to all places." Some of that change, such as electricity, was welcomed. Other aspects of change were debated, and elements of the population opposed certain alterations. When the twentieth century finally knocked on the doors of many Kentuckians, they hesitated to answer.

In 1910 Kentuckians had lived generally as had those of a half century earlier. Out of a population of 2,289,903 in 1910, 88 percent had been born in Kentucky; only 40,000 residents were foreign-born. Kentuckians had only begun to be touched by new currents of change sweeping the nation. By 1920, however, those waves were proving harder to resist, if resistance was even sought. Over the next century, change would come quicker and quicker, giving each generation less time to adapt. Kentuckians, like other Americans, had to try to keep the best of their past and reconcile tradition with change, while not slipping into a blind resistance to anything new or an equally

The "modern" woman and the "sinful" automobile both worried some Kentuckians in the 1920s. (Kentucky Historical Society Collections, Frankfort, KY)

sightless acceptance of all that was fashionable. Hard decisions lay ahead.

For much of Kentucky, the new era of the twenties affected the citizenry only little. Rural and some small-town populations remained similar in certain ways to their earlier counterparts. Even some people in larger urban areas changed little. Yet everyone saw or heard about the new ideas, the fresh outlooks, and the different lifestyles that were becoming the pattern for the United States. Many did not like what they saw.

All the old rules of conduct seemed to be modified, particularly for women. Now the national model appeared to be the youthful "flapper," with her short skirts, boyish figure, rouge-covered face, and bobbed hair. She smoked cigarettes, drank illegal whiskey and bathtub gin, and danced strange new dances to the sensuous tones of the saxophone. All these trends at least touched Kentucky. A girl at Bethel Woman's College in Hopkinsville was expelled for bobbing her hair. Another woman recalled that when her schoolteacher mother began wearing pants in the early 1920s, that action aroused much negative comment: "And, oh, it was bad when she started riding her horse astride instead of side-saddle!" The dance crazes that featured the bunny hop, turkey trot, fox trot, tango, and Charleston could earn admiration for agile participants, as one girl noted in

her diary: "Mills sure can knock off the Black Bottom." But they also brought censure from numerous places. A member of the Kentucky Purity League had earlier denounced the "sin-crazed age" with its dances "and all the other twists and squirms," and speakers in numerous church pulpits continued to echo those sentiments. As late as 1930 a Baptist congregation in Paducah split when members were suspended for dancing, card playing, and attending motion pictures. Conversely, three years later a Kentucky Birth Control League was organized in Louisville, with Jean Brandeis Tachau as its president.

Many critics of society blamed the automobile and the movie theater for what they saw as the problems of the state. Kentucky had 127,300 motor vehicles in 1921, and if the popular press was to be believed, every one of those conveyances was the scene of "petting parties." Almost as bad were the very popular motion picture shows, sparked by the innovations of D. W. Griffith and the beginning of the star system. Regular theater with its "scanty attire" had long been criticized, but the widespread availability of film and the 1920s subject matter added to the faultfinding. A judge declared that "the majority of delinquent boys are movie fiends," while a state senator tried (and failed) to set up a censorship board to control viewing. The films went on, and by

1925 moviegoers of the newly emancipated age were viewing, without restriction, such fare as *The Painted Flapper; Eve's Secret* ("Love in a Modern Eden and He Learned about Women from Her"), and *I Want My Man.*

The new mass-media culture propelled sports into the national spotlight as well. In Kentucky, the Derby became a national event, so that Irvin S. Cobb could proclaim, "Until you go to Kentucky and with your own eyes behold the Derby, you ain't never been nowheres and you ain't never seen nothin'!" Across the United States, boxing, tennis, golf, football, and, most of all, baseball amassed an avid following, and fans cheered their favorite heroes and teams. Kentuckians supported John D. ("Jughandle Johnny") Morrison of Owensboro, a pitcher who won more than a hundred games; Liberty's Carl Mays, a pitcher whose submarine delivery won him more than twenty games a year five times in the 1915–1929 period; outfielder Bobby Veach of McLean County, who played with Ty Cobb and from 1912 to 1925 had more than two thousand hits; Maysville's Don Hurst, who led the 1932 league in runs batted in; and outfielder Earle B. Combs of Owsley County, who batted over .300 nine times and led the league in numerous categories while in the Yankees' "Murderers' Row" lineup that included Babe Ruth. For his feats, Combs, called the Gray Fox, would become the state's first Hall of Famer in baseball.

The widespread interest in sports also affected colleges and high schools, where organized sports became a more important part of activities, although not always with unanimous approval. Big-time sports had invaded the commonwealth. As the years passed the focus on sports would bring positive and negative results, but in the 1920s few questioned the trend.

Mass communications also meant that what might formerly have remained isolated incidents now became international spectacles. One Kentucky case illustrated that phenomenon vividly. On January 30, 1925, an obscure thirty-seven-year-old explorer named Floyd Collins became stuck and partially buried in Sand Cave, not far from Mammoth Cave. Efforts to rescue him gained national attention, and a young *Courier-Journal* reporter, William B. ("Sheets") Miller, would win a Pulitzer Prize for crawling into the narrow shaft and talking to Collins. But the whole matter resembled a carnival, as cutthroat on-site radio reporters vied with sensational print journalists while a young Charles Lindbergh flew film from Kentucky to waiting urban centers. Ballads were composed in what students of the matter have called "one of the first truly *national* media events." In a rescue dig complicated by arguments over strategy and command responsibility, workers finally reached Collins some two weeks after he had been trapped. He had been dead three days. Later the body was removed and placed in a glass-covered coffin for tourists to view in another cavern. Robbers stole the corpse a few years afterward, but Collins's remains, minus a leg, were recovered, to go on display again. Only much later did the body find the solitude of a grave. Collins in his lone explorations had joined what in the 1920s was a "floodtime for heroes."

The Counterattack: Evolution and the Klan

Conservative religious beliefs, first and foremost, had dominated the commonwealth for most of the nineteenth century, despite its welcoming of different religions, such as the Shakers, in the aftermath of the Great Revival. The prominence of atheist C. C. Moore, who published the "freethinking" *Blue Grass Blade*, was an anomaly. His controversial views on birth control, thoroughbred gambling, tobacco use, religious texts, and women's rights eventually resulted in convictions for obscenity and blasphemy. He served five months in federal prison in 1899 before the president commuted his sentence. Orthodoxy ruled.

But by the early 1920s some Kentucky places of worship, chiefly in urban areas, had accepted a more liberal theology that sought to reconcile science and Darwinian theory with religious teachings. In other churches, however, observers found very different outlooks. Two studies of mountain religion, for instance, both stressed the supernatural and superstitious aspects of worship there, and across the state a strong conservative strain dominated, producing defenders of traditional theology. Out of this milieu a militant evangelicalism emerged, one that had tasted victory in the Prohibition fight. A Baptist association in 1921 voted to initiate a campaign against "moving pictures, dancing, immodest 'undress,' mixed bathing, divorce, Sunday baseball, card playing, horse racing, gambling, and violation of prohibition laws." And Protestant fundamentalists saw evolution as a key reason that American society had strayed so far from the righteous path, and they sought to correct the situation.

As early as 1900 the evolution issue had provoked controversy, for author James Lane Allen had defended his religious questioning in *Reign of Law* before attacks from a theology school president. By 1921 Baptist minister John W. Porter of Lexington led a fight to purge evolution from schools. His book *Evolution: A Menace* (1921) implored that Christ "shall not be crucified on the cross of a false philosophy, called evolution," while his church's state association declared that it would withhold funds from any school teaching the subject. In fact, denominational colleges were polled to see if their staff included any professors with such "soul- and life-destroying" beliefs. Several teachers refused to state their positions and resignations followed. At Methodist-supported Asbury College, five professors were fired over the issue.

Former presidential candidate William Jennings Bryan pledged his aid to the cause when he spoke in the state that year, and he returned the next January to address a joint legislative session. A day after Bryan's talk, bills were introduced in each house of the Kentucky General Assembly to prohibit the teaching of "Darwinism, atheism, agnosticism, or evolution." Kentucky had become the first state where fundamentalists had enough power to propose anti-evolution bills. The fight was on.

Later, in some other southern states, key leaders stood aside when the issue arose, doing little. In Kentucky, the governor and the state school superintendent did stay out of the fight,

but others in opposition did not. Their involvement, their willingness to take a chance, made a difference. Three men played the most important roles. Two religious leaders, Dr. E. L. Powell of Louisville's First Christian Church and Dr. E. Y. Mullins, president of the Southern Baptist Theological Seminary in Louisville, spoke before the general assembly in opposition to the anti-evolution bill, revealing the diversity of religious thought on the issue. Dr. Frank L. McVey, president of the University of Kentucky, said forthrightly in a public letter that evolution was taught at his school, for failure to do so would make the university a laughingstock in the scientific community. He did add, however, that "there is no conflict between the theory of evolution and the Christian view." Backed by leading state newspapers, all three men called for tolerance, freedom of speech, and the separation of church and state.

Proponents of the bill referred to those "who worship at the shrine of the ape," and argued that much of the philosophy regarding the subject came from Russia and Germany. In March 1922, the anti-evolution bill in the Kentucky House came up for a vote. A tie resulted, and each side rushed to find a representative willing to break the forty-one to forty-one deadlock. Breathitt County legislator Bryce Cundiff finally cast the deciding ballot that defeated the bill. The next year Kentucky Wesleyan College suspended a faculty member for his support of evolution. In 1925 Paducah-born and University of Kentucky–educated John T. Scopes became the center of attention as the defendant in the famous "Monkey Trial" in Dayton, Tennessee. His sister was fired from her teaching job in Paducah for her own stands on that issue in Kentucky. In 1926 and again in 1928, anti-evolution bills introduced in the Kentucky General Assembly went nowhere. With that the effort ended, at least for many decades. A religiously conservative state, Kentucky had been the first major battleground in the anti-evolution fight, but in the end it had beaten back the forces of anti-intellectualism, time after time. Ironically, about the same time, another Kentuckian, Dr. Thomas Hunt Morgan, was leading a Columbia Uni-

Thomas Hunt Morgan won a Nobel Prize in 1933 for his research in genetics. (J. Winston Coleman Photographic Collection, Transylvania University Library, Lexington, KY)

versity research team in fruit fly experiments that strengthened the genetic theory behind evolution. A great-grandson of Francis Scott Key and a nephew of Confederate general John Hunt Morgan, Thomas Morgan had grown up in Lexington and had received a master's degree from the present-day University of Kentucky, before leaving the state for further schooling and research elsewhere. His efforts culminated in a Nobel Prize in 1933. Sixty years later, Falmouth-born Phillip Sharp won another Noble Prize for his work in genetics as well. In 1976, that prize also went to Lexington-educated chemist William Lipscomb, and in 2002, Berea College–educated John B. Fenn won the prestigious award as well. Home of evolutionists and anti-evolutionists, Kentucky continued to be a place of contrasting views.

At the same time the anti-evolution forces were declining from their peak strength, another group began rising to oppose the forces of change in America. The so-called second Ku Klux Klan, in the words of a historian, "was re-born in the war-time, weaned during the immediate postwar unrest." Partially stimulated by Griffith's 1915 film *The Birth of a Nation*, the group represented a protest against modernism and gave voice to the belief that only white Protestant Anglo-Saxons should guide the nation's fortunes. While it included blacks on its list of enemies, as the earlier KKK did, the revived Klan focused even more on immigrants, Catholics, and Jews.

Given the composition of Kentucky's population, the state did not appear to be particularly fertile ground for the rapidly growing movement. In 1926 the commonwealth's religious census enumerated 126,000 Catholics and 15,000 Jews, and the two groups together comprised only about 8 percent of the adult population. Moreover, while prejudice against both groups had been periodically evident throughout Kentucky's history, so too had acceptance. For a decade beginning in 1871, Paducah's mayor had been Jewish, and when Somerset was incorporated as a city in 1888, its first mayor was of that faith as well. But other than in Louisville, the number of Jews in the state was minuscule. The same held true for the foreign-born, for immigrants made up less than 2 percent of the commonwealth's population.

African Americans constituted a somewhat more sizable bloc—9.5 percent of the population in 1920—but in recent decades they had experienced declining rights and increasing segregation rather than successful challenges to the emerging racial status quo. When Toledo player Moses Walker—considered the first African American major league player—took the field at a professional baseball game in Louisville in 1884, many considered that the first integrated game at that level. But such pathbreaking racial actions proved short-lived. More common was the 1892 act segregating railroad cars. It marked the beginning of a series of formal actions that made the black and white worlds even more separate. Such changes did not take place all at once, but gradually. Both races had used Henderson's city park for years, but in 1903 African Americans were restricted to one area only. In Lexington in 1916 and Louisville in 1924, parks for blacks only replaced the formerly integrated system of sharing pools, tennis courts, and baseball fields. In the Kentucky Derby, blacks had ridden fifteen of the first twenty-eight winners, but after 1911 the race became an all-white affair. Memories grew dim of three-time winner Isaac Murphy, who took his mount to victory in 44 percent of all his rides, or of Jimmy Winkfield, who won two straight Derbys in 1901 and 1902. Winkfield left America because of an increasingly hostile environment and then grew wealthy as a horseman in Europe. By the mid-1920s, then, Kentucky had segregated racing, transportation, parks, hotels, theaters, library systems, orphans' homes, restaurants, funeral parlors, and more. Louisville's police force, fire fighters, and jail employees had become segregated by 1890. In other areas, such as juries, blacks were excluded altogether. Black activists such as Albert Ernest Meyzeek and I. Willis Cole spoke out but to no avail. Segregation had planted deep roots in Kentucky soil, and African Americans reasonably wondered whether their rights would wither away further in the future.

In some places, increased segregation was not enough. Night Riders earlier had forced African Americans out of parts of western Kentucky, such as Birmingham in 1908, and by 1919 the actions had shifted eastward. In October an armed mob of some 150 whites in Corbin, angered by erroneous rumors of an attack by blacks on a white man, seized itinerant railroad workers in the dark of night, placed them in a barricaded area ("like cattle," one recalled), then forced them to board a train and leave town. Between two and three hundred black residents left; only a few elderly African Americans remained. Less spectacularly but just as effectively, through various means, other towns did the same over time and proudly boasted of their whiteness.

The victories won by blacks proved even more significant, given the climate in which they occurred. Weak attempts by whites to take away the vote all failed, for instance, although violence and gerrymandered districts sometimes gave the desired effect. In 1914 Louisville and other Kentucky cities passed segregation ordinances that forbade both blacks and whites from buying homes in areas where the other race predominated. A Kentuckian by birth, the wealthy William English Walling had, more than perhaps anyone, been responsible for founding the National Association for the Advancement of Colored People (NAACP) in 1910. Now a branch opened in Louisville, and C. H. Buchanan, a white man, and William Warley, a black man, tested the segregation ordinance. Eventually heard by the US Supreme Court as *Buchanan v. Warley* (1917), the case resulted in the rejection of the Louisville ordinance, in a rare national victory in that era for black rights. Warley's action cost him his job at the post office. Victories took their toll.

Such successes were few for African Americans, but despite that and despite the relatively small numbers of immigrants, Jews, and Catholics in Kentucky, the newly formed KKK spoke out about the supposed threat to the United States from such groups. But the Klan never found Kentucky a very comfortable home. Indiana to the north was a center of Ku Klux activity, and the Klavens were strong to the south, but the Klan philosophy never took hold in the Bluegrass State as strongly as in those areas. The KKK did have strength and influence: a contemporary estimate placed membership at fifty thousand to two hundred thousand, very likely an overestimate. More recently a historian suggested that thirty thousand Kentuckians joined the Klan's ranks. The Klan did gain support, as rallies drawing crowds of five thousand or more took place in communities as diverse as Paintsville in the east and Owensboro in the west. The message came through clearly in a document issued by the Warren County Klan: "We believe in the Protestant Christian Religion; White Supremacy; Separation of Church and State." It portrayed Jews and Catholics— "these representatives of the Pope"—as controlling Bowling Green's government and called for "pure blooded 100% American" rule.

As in the anti-evolution fight, however, Kentucky leaders spoke out against the Klan, often at some political risk. In Lexington, Owensboro, Louisville, Pulaski County, Hopkins County, Laurel County, and elsewhere, judges, mayors, and city council members either publicly attacked the KKK or refused to allow its members to meet on public property. A similar stance by Paducah mayor Wynn Tulley showed the dangers inherent in such a position: he alone on the Democratic ticket did not win reelection in 1923. Still, when the minister who had authored *The Kall of the Klan in Kentucky* (1924) spoke, he found little official sympathy. Owensboro arrested him on conspiracy charges (later dropped), and similar harassing activities dogged him as he spoke across the state, blaming the ills of the United States on blacks and aliens. By the last half of the 1920s, inept and corrupt national leadership, violent actions, and an unresponsive citizenry in Kentucky had brought the Invisible Empire to its knees. It would have lingering influence for a time in some places, but the Second Klan's effect on the state, though significant, had been brief.

As the world around them continued to change, some Kentuckians still worried about the ways all that was occurring. Longing for an aristocratic control as in days of old, W. G. Clugston wrote in 1923 in H. L. Mencken's *American Mercury* magazine about "the collapse of Kentucky." Arguing that "the manners, the customs and the ideals of the people are so completely altered that there is little left of the old stripes and patterns," he concluded that "every circle of society is changed." In reality, however, while certain old traditions had been modified or even lost, some had adjusted to the new era and had emerged even stronger. Others remained virtually untouched. Despite all the fears and concerns, Kentucky had not fallen apart when confronting modernism. In fact, some of the constant nature of the state showed very clearly—unfortunately—in the politics of the twenties.

Bosses, the Bipartisan Combine, and the Governors

In May 1919, A. O. Stanley had resigned the governorship to take a seat in the US Senate, thus making Lieutenant Governor James D. Black of Knox County the chief executive of the commonwealth. Governor Black immedi-

ately set about to win election to a full four-year term, but he had to face the popular, barely defeated 1915 candidate Edwin P. Morrow. Black ran a weak, careful campaign, defending Stanley's "wet" views and overall record and President Wilson's handling of a coal strike. He lost handily, receiving 214,114 votes to Morrow's 254,290. In December 1919 Morrow became the fourth Republican inaugurated as governor since 1895. In that same time, five Democrats had served in the office. The two-party system seemed strong in Kentucky.

Yet as Morrow and other governors elected during the next decade would discover, "party" was a fluid concept in the 1920s. The real power centers remained not the voting booths but the headquarters of the political bosses, who had their greatest influence in those years. Moreover, new players were joining the political game, and they would bring to the table more money and different agendas, further complicating elections. The two most visible of the fresh faces were James B. Brown and Robert Worth Bingham, both Louisville millionaires.

Bingham had grown up and been mostly educated in North Carolina. He had come to Kentucky following a marriage that would later end tragically in a train accident. He had served as county attorney, as an appointed short-term mayor of Louisville, and as an appointed judge, afterward operating for a time as a political independent, supporting one party or the other. The defining moment in his life came when his second wife died in 1917. One of the wealthiest women in the United States, she left Bingham $5 million, to the surprise of her family. He had married her only recently, in November 1916. The circumstances of her death brought rumors from Bingham's enemies, and while nothing criminal had occurred, the stories would haunt the Binghams for decades. Bingham used part of his inherited wealth to purchase the *Louisville Courier-Journal*. He allied with former governor Beckham and the political boss Percy Haly (who went on to the newspaper's payroll) and formed a faction in the Democratic Party. Aristocratic in bearing, with a stable of polo ponies and dozens of purebred hunting dogs, Bingham loved

A Lexington mob surges forward just before shots were fired in the Will Lockett riot, 1920. (J. Winston Coleman Photographic Collection, Transylvania University Library, Lexington, KY)

things British, used his wealth to aid friends and good causes and to oppose enemies, and represented a curious combination of reformer and conservative.

Bingham's one-time ally and later opponent, Jim Brown, had fewer paradoxes. Kentucky-born, he had worked his way up through the banking ranks, with the help of boss John Whallen, and had made millions. "Colorful, careless, and reckless," Brown would take friends to casinos at French Lick, Indiana, and cover their gambling losses. He once spent fifty-nine thousand dollars in one such outing. Working into the night, sleeping, vampire like, in the day, he too purchased newspapers—the *Louisville Herald* and the *Louisville Post*—and combined them to give him a voice to oppose Bingham. Brown led the largest financial institution south of the Ohio River, and the two very rich men soon became factional political enemies.

Meanwhile, all around them, the behind-the-scenes power brokers—Ben Johnson, J. Dan Talbott, Billy Klair, Allie Young, Mickey Brennan, Maurice Galvin, and Thomas Rhea, among others—still dominated, still made deals. That so-called invisible government offered the real key to electoral success.

Operating in such an atmosphere, Morrow had to tread carefully, but he did have some success. Unlike previous Republican governors, he had control of the Kentucky House, and he persuaded a Democratic senator to defect, creating a party balance in the upper house. A Republican lieutenant governor could break a tie in the Kentucky Senate. Still, Morrow faced a legislature torn by factionalism, regionalism, and bickering. By his second legislative session, he also had a Democratic-controlled general assembly—with the first woman legislator, Mary E. Flanery, in it—and had to deal with a hostile political party. Still, Morrow had a fairly productive term, despite his veto of much-needed additional appropriations for the University of Kentucky and his silence during the anti-evolution fight. His administration ratified the woman suffrage amendment and created the bipartisan Kentucky State Board of Charities and Corrections and two new teacher-training colleges for whites at Morehead and Murray. A one-cent per gallon gasoline tax (the fifth in the nation) helped finance road projects, while a racetrack levy supported an increase in teachers' salaries. Convict labor was prohibited in highway construction, and the Kentucky Child Welfare Commission was established. Other legislation passed during his administration aided the tobacco cooperative movement. Indicating the search for nostalgia in an era of change, the state purchased Federal Hill in Bardstown, known as My Old Kentucky Home, and authorized a monument to Jefferson Davis in Fairview.

Some of Morrow's finest moments as governor, however, concerned blacks in Kentucky and took place outside the halls of the capitol. The worst side of racial violence in Kentucky had taken place in Livermore in 1911 when a mob seized Will Porter, placed him on the stage of an opera house, turned on the footlights, and began emptying their pistols. An estimated two hundred rounds were fired. No convictions followed. An illustrated account of the episode appeared in a Paris, France, newspaper. In some ways, it represented the nadir of race relations in the commonwealth. A start on the road back to respect for the law had come in 1917, when Governor Stanley had rushed by train to Murray, in a successful attempt to keep a lynching from occurring. No racial egalitarian, Stanley did support the rule of law over lynch law: "That is the difference between savagery and civilization."

That attitude was tested in February 1920. African American Will Lockett had been arrested for the murder of a white woman, and rumors of an attempted lynching spread. Morrow provided a National Guard force to protect the prisoner, and Lockett stood trial in Lexington. A large crowd faced the soldiers as the court heard testimony. According to one account, a cameraman called on the some four thousand citizens to "shake your fists and yell" for his pictures. But as they did so, others took up the action, and the mob surged forward, intent on taking Lockett. The National Guard opened fire, killing at least six people and wounding perhaps fifty more. Army veterans from Camp Taylor soon joined the guard, and martial law was established. Meanwhile, Lockett was convicted, in a sham trial characterized chiefly by its brevity, and was later executed. The national press, however, praised the "Second Battle of Lexington" for showing that "Lynchers Don't Like Lead." Law had triumphed over the mob. The legislature passed an anti-lynching law, and during the next four years, four county officials in four different places were removed from office when they allowed mobs to take prison-

ers from their jails. Those prisoners had been killed, however, and the people responsible for their deaths had gone free. The state still had a long way to go to rid itself of lawlessness. The Lockett affair had sent a strong signal to the South, but even in Kentucky not everyone got the message.

Kentuckians did listen to the siren song of politics, as usual. The key issue in the early 1920s seemed to be whether Morrow's win had been a personal rather than a party triumph, or whether the Republican Party had become a consistent challenger to the Democrats. Election results gave a mixed response. In 1920 and 1922 Republicans won only three of eleven congressional seats but did capture Louisville's, showing that the party had become, in Walter Baker's later words, a "coalition of rich and poor, black and white, town and mountain." In the presidential race of 1920 Kentucky's electoral votes went to Democratic choice James M. Cox, who barely edged out fellow Ohioan and eventual winner Republican Warren G. Harding by 4,000 votes, 456,497–452,480. In the first election in which all Kentucky women could vote, the state had resisted the Republican presidential tide that swept over the other border states.

Kentucky also led the nation in voter turnout, when 71.2 percent of its citizens voted, including a large number of women. The votes of women may have been significant in the one other important race in 1920, that for US senator. Incumbent J. C. W. Beckham had not achieved an impressive record. He also had not voted on the suffrage issue and in a private letter had called the extension of the franchise to women "a serious mistake." Sensing Beckham's vulnerability, Republicans put forth a virtually untested wealthy corporation lawyer who worked in Cincinnati but lived in Covington. His workplace plus the fact that his mentor, boss Maurice Galvin, was brother to the Cincinnati mayor made critics argue that Richard P. Ernst sought to be Ohio's third senator. Attacking the League of Nations as "unjust and un-American," the Republican sought to capitalize on postwar discontent, Beckham's weakness on suffrage, and Democratic factionalism.

Aided by some questionable late returns from the mountains, Ernst won the race by 5,000 votes, 454,226–449,244.

The real test of Republican strength would come in the attempt to win the governor's race two times in a row with two different candidates. As it turned out, such a double victory did not occur over the next hundred years. Democrats appeared confident that 1923 would be their year, and each of the factions put forth a strong candidate. The acknowledged front-runner, J. Campbell Cantrill of Scott County, had long served in Congress, where he had opposed suffrage and Prohibition, and had been a leader in the central Kentucky tobacco cooperative fight. The old Stanley wing and most of the veteran politicians supported Cantrill.

The challenger also came from Congress but represented western Kentucky and the small farmers of the protest movements there. Paducah's Alben W. Barkley would become well known, but during the 1923 Democratic primary race he was a forty-five-year-old relative newcomer to the state scene. When Barkley, in an unusual move for Kentucky, actually took stances on controversial issues, he shaped the race. Chastising the labor and railroad lobbies, attacking the racing interests by promising to end pari-mutuel betting, and calling for a production tax on coal, Barkley brought the Bingham, Beckham, and Haly triumvirate to his side. But most of the other bosses stood behind the conservative Cantrill, and Barkley's definition of the issues united the eastern half of the state against him.

Born in a log cabin of tenant farm parents, Barkley would become the dominant state politician in the twentieth century. He was already showing the strengths that would win him election after election. A reporter in 1923 saw him as "the most vigorous personal campaigner and speech-maker ever seen in Kentucky." Barkley, called the Iron Man, gave ten to fourteen speeches a day. As a later writer noted, Barkley could turn a speech "delivered from the bed of a hay wagon into something resembling the Sermon on the Mount." But that was not enough in 1923, and Barkley lost the primary by nine thousand votes, the only defeat of his career.

In a regional outcome, he won almost all the counties west of a line running from Louisville to Middlesborough, while Cantrill carried almost all the counties east of there.

When Cantrill died of a ruptured appendix soon after the primary, however, a new nominee had to be selected by the Democratic state committee, under Jim Brown's control. It chose Congressman William J. Fields. Known as "Honest Bill from Olive Hill," the onetime traveling salesman had a good voting record and few enemies. His Republican opposition, Attorney General Charles I. Dawson of Bell County, had once been a Democrat, and Dawson's attempts to tar Fields with the appellation "Dodging Bill from Olive Hill, who answers no questions and never will" were matched by Fields, who labeled Dawson "Changing Charley." The race ended with an easy Democratic win: Fields garnered 356,035 votes to Dawson's 306,277.

Fields came to office without a great deal of respect, for he owed his selection to Cantrill's death and his election to a weak opposition. He did not help his situation by his actions. On the day of his inaugural, Fields, a simple man, prohibited any dancing in the executive mansion. Later his frugality caused him to keep dairy cows on the lawn of the governor's house. Both acts brought condescending sneers from urban critics. A wider group condemned Fields's nepotism. As the term wore on, Fields reacted to the *Courier-Journal's* attacks by responding in petty public letters that discredited their author. Finally, even though Fields was an honest man pursuing worthy goals, he could never disengage himself completely from the bosses who backed him.

From the very beginning of Fields's term, it seemed that the factions and parties were using the time to rehearse for the 1927 gubernatorial show. With Beckham early seen as a candidate, Bingham's paper and the allies of the onetime Boy Governor began to paint a picture of a corrupt force that transcended party and had to be stopped. They called their opposition the bipartisan combine. In truth, various groups were working to protect their own turf, whether that involved racing, coal, or other interests. But such activity rarely took place as a formal, concerted conspiracy. Rather, those with the common enemy of Beckham, Bingham, and Haly generally coalesced in an informal way. Thus, both Democratic factions actually had elements of reform and reaction within, and both sought the same end—power.

All that is not to say that the Jockey Club was not a formidable foe, for it was. The state's Racing Commission, formed in 1906, quickly outlawed the then-prevalent betting practice of bookmaking and replaced it with pari-mutuel wagering. In 1918 prominent men—including, initially, Bingham—had formed the state Jockey Club as a further aid to a thoroughbred industry under siege. By the 1920s only three states still had legal betting at racetracks. But as the attacks on racing increased, so too did the Jockey Club's response to them. Like the L&N lobby before, the monopolist Jockey Club grew more powerful. At one time the club reputedly had thirty legislators on its payroll.

Standing in opposition were forces that emerged from both the earlier crusades for Prohibition and the new moral concerns of the 1920s. Urban reformers joined religious fundamentalists and some Klansmen in support of a strong anti-pari-mutuel gambling movement. The supporters of this movement wished to end betting at tracks and to cleanse the body politic of what was seen as a corrupting influence. Lotteries had been abolished in the 1890s; perhaps now gambling at racetracks could follow.

All of the forces operating in the decade seemed to come together in 1924. In the legislature a bill to outlaw pari-mutuel betting passed the Kentucky House easily but lost by a fourteen to twenty-four split-party count in the Kentucky Senate. By that ten-vote margin the state retained racing. That controversial issue was matched by an attempt to change the composition of the State Board of Charities and Corrections from a bipartisan makeup to a partisan one, and to give the governor, not the board, the power to select those heading the various institutions.

The state supported a series of charitable institutions—the Eastern, Western, and Central State Asylums for the Insane, two Kentucky

Houses of Reform, a Home for Incurables, the Institution for the Education and Training of Feeble-Minded Children, the Kentucky Children's Home Society, the Kentucky Home Society for Colored Children, the Kentucky Institution for the Education of Deaf-Mutes, and the Kentucky Confederate Home. Segregated, always underfunded, usually overcrowded, these institutions faced continual problems. In 1901, for example, the Eastern Kentucky Asylum for the Insane noted that it had annually received $200 per patient up to 1880 but only $150 since 1895. Thirteen percent of the patients at the Central Kentucky Asylum died in one twelve-month period. In that same year of 1901, seventy-five of the pupils at the state school for the deaf in Danville had to sleep on mattresses placed in hallways. A 1901 report stated that at Frankfort, where the mentally challenged were housed, males came on the grounds to "enter into contacts unholy" with unsuspecting females there. The auditor's office also complained about the "costly and dangerous" practice of paying seventy-five dollars annually to individuals to take care of "pauper idiots" in their homes. By the mid-1920s most of those matters had improved only marginally.

Symbolic of attempts to reform, modernize, and professionalize the state's institutions was what was happening in the prisons. Since Governor Blackburn's time, some changes had occurred, but problems remained. One study reported in 1921 that 41 percent of the inmates at the Frankfort prison had syphilis, that sanitation continued to be poor, and that overcrowding in the "Black Hole of Kentucky" persisted. The whipping post had been abolished only in 1913. In 1920 Joseph P. Byers, a respected national authority, had been chosen as commissioner of public institutions to bring needed change. He hired expert non-Kentuckians for some key professional jobs, fired one warden, and generally tried to remove the prisons from the game of political patronage. Byers's activity angered political figures who used the prison spoils system to reward supporters and who assessed contributions from those employees. They almost gleefully used against Byers a 1923 riot at Eddyville, which left three officers dead.

More than twenty-five thousand rounds had been fired before military men found one prisoner dead and two others the victims of a suicide pact. In the 1924 legislature a bill sought to remove Byers, and despite opposition from all the state's major newspapers, it barely failed to pass, by a forty-four to forty-six count. Not pleased at the prospects for his future, Byers resigned the next year. Significant change in the prison system came slowly.

When Governor Fields proposed a $75 million-bond issue to build highways, provide additional money to education and the prisons, and eliminate the state debt, with funding coming from a road and gasoline tax, he expected support. Instead he got opposition, particularly from one faction of his own party. Seeing boss Billy Klair as a man active in road bonding, fearing "a lifetime burden of taxation," and distrusting the placement of so much money in Fields's hands, Bingham and the *Courier-Journal* faction strongly opposed the idea. The ensuing debate grew bitter. The governor called the editor a "carpet-bagger from North Carolina," while the *Lexington Herald* asked, "Can't we be pros for a little while instead of perpetual antis?" People in the mountains, with their poor roads, particularly spoke out for the bond issue, which in truth would have provided the state a needed influx of funding. The general assembly passed the decision to the voters, setting up a referendum in the fall elections.

Those 1924 elections would prove to be important ones for Kentucky. The Kentucky Senate race found incumbent A. O. Stanley opposed by the "dry" forces (who had a long memory) and the "dry" governor of his own party, by the Ku Klux Klan, and by a handsome, wealthy, and well-educated former New Englander who had never held elective office. Republican Frederic M. Sackett Jr. had married into the prominent Speed family of Louisville and had gained the support of the *Courier-Journal* and Stanley's old enemies, Beckham and Haly. No Kentucky senator had won reelection in some forty years, a writer declared. Would that situation change now? The presidential race did not help Stanley a great deal either. Democrat John W. Davis stirred little

enthusiasm, although his opponent, Calvin Coolidge, hardly proved a campaign dynamo either. Still, the presence of Progressive Party candidate Robert M. La Follette suggested that both parties would lose votes to him.

The results of the 1924 elections shocked some Kentuckians. For the second time ever, a Republican carried the state in the presidential race: Coolidge received 398,966 votes, and Davis got 374,855. La Follette gathered 38,465 votes, mostly among laborers in the cities and coal counties. With apathy prevalent, voter turnout fell greatly from the 1920 level. The results in the Senate race were similar to the presidential contest: Democrat Stanley lost to Sackett, 381,623–406,141. As the loser had said of Sackett, "His ten millions are a power." In March 1925 Kentucky would have two Republican US senators. The bond issue, garnering 275,863 votes for, 374,328 against, went down to defeat. Kentucky would have to "pay as you go," though it might not go very far as a result. Only in the congressional races, in which new House member Frederick M. Vinson won, did the faction-ridden Democrats hold fast. A Republican tide, aided by Democratic divisions, had swept the state.

If anything, the 1920s showed that political currents could change rapidly. The 1925 city elections in Louisville proved so corrupt that the winning Republicans were later swept from office by a court decision. A person who was present at the time commented that for $100,000 the bribable 1926 legislature would have "repealed the Ten Commandments." Then on January 11, 1926, Republican congressman John W. Langley of Pikeville formally resigned his seat after the US Supreme Court refused to review his conviction for violating the Prohibition laws. Paroled that same year, he published a book entitled *They Tried to Crucify Me* (1929). The evidence, however, suggested that "Pork Barrel John" had accepted a bribe in order to assist in the withdrawal and eventual illegal sale of more than a million gallons of bourbon whiskey. If his district's voters could not reelect John Langley, they could select his politically astute wife, Katherine G. Langley. In 1927 she became the state's first (and the nation's eighth) female member of Congress. She would get the president to commute her husband's sentence, win reelection by a large margin, and serve for four years in Congress. But when John Langley sought to regain his seat and she did not want to give it up, the ensuing family quarrel, coupled with the effects of the Depression, ended both careers. The electorate seemed to be more forgiving of political corruption than family disputes.

To the man challenging Republican incumbent senator Ernst in 1926, such developments proved fortuitous. Congressman Alben Barkley saw that "Coolidge prosperity" had not touched Kentucky as much as elsewhere and that his opponent had little popular appeal. Ernst's opposition to a bonus for veterans, his age (twenty years older than Barkley), and his lack of support for fellow party member Langley during his legal troubles all hurt. But the key factor was Democratic unity. Members of one faction wanted Barkley to win so they could be victorious. Supporters of the other faction wanted him to win so they could get him out of the state, out of the way in Washington. That combination brought victory to Barkley and the Democrats by a 20,000-vote margin, 286,997 to 266,657. But the party's "love feast" of 1926 was soon over.

Beckham and Betting

Now, finally, the curtain raised on the 1927 governor's race. As expected, Beckham's hat flew into the ring, and his faction backed that action wholeheartedly. In fact, A. O. Stanley, defeated by Sackett in 1924 and angry at Governor Fields for his role in the loss, even announced that he would support his old and bitter enemy Beckham. But powerful Democrats, including those allied with the racing and mining interests, as well as the governor, backed the Canadian-born former speaker of the Kentucky House, Robert T. Crowe of Oldham County. Nevertheless, the better-known Beckham, winning heavily in western Kentucky, took the primary by nearly twenty-four thousand votes.

On the Republican side stood Flem D.

Sampson of Knox County. A college roommate, then a law partner, of Goebel conspiracy figure Caleb Powers, Sampson had been chief justice of the state's highest court and had the full backing of mountain Republicans. He offered free textbooks, opposed the tonnage tax on coal, indicated that the pari-mutuel issue should be a legislative matter, and generally tried to avoid controversy: "I'm just plain old Flem. When I'm elected Governor of Kentucky, come into my office and sit down and say 'Howdy Flem!'" Beckham Democrats, in turn, said the Republican should be called "Flim-Flam Flem" instead, and their candidate made the differences between himself and Sampson clear as he again called for an end to racetrack betting. Ironically, the pari-mutuel bill had its origins in Beckham's own gubernatorial administration, and his opposition pointed out the reversals on the issue by both Beckham and Bingham. But the onetime Boy Governor countered with attacks on the Jockey Club lobby, suggesting that it was pouring large sums of money into Sampson's campaign coffers. Many of Beckham's fellow Democrats, including Governor Fields, Billy Klair, and Jim Brown, deserted their party's candidate as the issue became clear. Would it be Beckham or betting?

When the results came in, every Democrat was elected except one—J. C. W. Beckham. Sampson won easily, 399,698–367,567, as Democrats had split their tickets. But making certain that the rest of the Democratic field won may have taken much hard work manipulating the returns, since the margins in those races were microscopic. Lieutenant Governor James Breathitt Jr. won by 159 votes out of more than 700,000 cast, for example. There may not have been any formal agreements that anti-Beckham Democrats would vote for a Republican as governor in exchange for taking the rest of the offices, and there likewise may not have been a formal bipartisan combine. Nonetheless, the racing and coal interests and, indeed, the Republicans seemed pleased with the outcome. Beckham was beaten.

The new governor quickly discovered that any coalition that had existed during the race slowly vanished amid the reality of partisan politics. Initially, though, the situation looked strong for the Republicans. The national Democratic nomination of Al Smith of New York, with his "wet" views, ties to the Tammany Hall "machine," eastern accent, and, most of all, Catholic religion, made the 1928 presidential campaign a very difficult one for the state party. Sampson asked voters to select Herbert Hoover "if you want to preserve the churches." Senator Barkley, who seconded Smith's nomination, recalled later that the religious issue split Democrats "worse than an Oak Ridge atom." Rural, "dry" Protestant Democrats simply could not bring themselves to vote for the urban, "wet," Catholic candidate of their party, and Republican Herbert Hoover's 177,000-vote win in Kentucky gave his party the state's biggest majority to that time, as well as Kentucky's electoral votes. Democrats, who won only 41 percent of the ballots, also suffered a major setback in the congressional races, as nine of the eleven congressmen rode Hoover's coattails into office. The state Democratic Party was in tatters.

The next battleground also seemed to produce a Republican victory. Sampson had selected the Democrat "Boss Ben" Johnson to head the Kentucky Highway Commission, the price for Johnson's support. There Johnson and his commissioners ruled over a small fiefdom. As a later governor noted, "All politics, but especially rural politics, has long been the politics of roads." With few restrictions, the highway department spent nearly 45 percent of the state's total budget, employed some ten thousand people, and directly influenced fifty thousand more through contracts or family ties. Legislators wanting highways for their districts easily swapped votes for roads. People seeking steady jobs also commonly offered to pay a portion of their salaries if a position could be attained, and the party in power generally built thoroughfares to their supporters first. When elections grew near, more weed cutters and road workers went on the payroll, and their votes went to those who hired them. Legislative control, party financing, patronage—all this meant that the Highway Department had become "the most politically significant function of the state

government." The governor could not leave a post that powerful in the hands of someone he could not control, and in December 1929 he dismissed Johnson. Although Sampson seemed to have won, the power of the bosses showed that such victories were illusions.

The 1930 Kentucky General Assembly quickly rendered Governor Sampson politically powerless. First, two contested seats went to Democrats, and with a sizable majority, the party passed "ripper" bills, which ripped the power of appointment from the chief executive and placed it under Democratic control. The Highway Commission was reorganized, and to the surprise of few, Johnson soon regained his post of power.

The key fight, however, centered on one of the state's most scenic areas, Cumberland Falls. In 1927 a hydroelectric company had purchased the site, and Samuel Insull's powerful influence came into play as he sought to use the falls to generate electrical power. Sampson, citing the jobs to be gained, favored the Insull plan. Meanwhile, conservationists, led by journalist Tom Wallace and with the support of over 90 percent of the state's newspapers, favored acceptance of the offer of Louisville-born millionaire T. Coleman du Pont of Delaware. He indicated that he would buy the Falls and present it to Kentucky as a park. In a mostly party vote, both houses accepted the du Pont plan. Sampson immediately vetoed the bill, saying that it would hurt industrial development, but his veto was overridden. The Cumberland, at the Falls, remained undammed.

That autumn, in the 1930 elections, a relatively unknown Democrat, Kentucky Court of Appeals judge M. M. Logan of Bowling Green, defeated conservative Republican congressman John M. Robsion for the US Senate seat vacated when Sackett accepted appointment as ambassador to Germany. Democrats also won nine of the eleven congressional seats, and the delegation in Washington was strongly Democratic once more. Politically, the Republicans' once-bright prospects had dimmed so much as to be almost invisible. The party's dark period had begun, and it would largely last for many decades.

Governor Flem D. Sampson (*left*) visits Cumberland Falls, 1929. Sampson had supported a plan to dam the Cumberland River to generate electrical power. (University of Louisville Photographic Archives)

Kentucky's 1930 population of 2,614,589 —ranking the state sixteenth in the nation— represented only a 59 percent increase over the 1880 figure, while the United States had seen a 144 percent rise during the fifty-year period. The decade of the twenties had not been one of Kentucky's best eras. Bootlegged whiskey, from Golden Pond and elsewhere, together with gunfights between revenue agents and moonshiners, had added to the state's violent image. On the agrarian landscape, however, little had changed, in some ways. Despite advances, only 2.8 percent of farms had tractors (one-fifth of the American average); only 4.3 percent were lighted by electricity (one-third the national mean); and only one-fourth had telephones (versus one-third of US farm homes). A man returned to the Marshall County home he had left forty years earlier and first saw the changes—timber cleared, the old homestead abandoned, the trees grown large, the creek deeper. But then he went to a relative's home, ate, and talked to the people, and he concluded that "everything there seemed more like old times than anything I saw during the day." Like the physical changes that man saw, changes taking place in American society in the twenties had chipped away at Kentucky character and lifestyles, but beneath the surface much remained as before. Attempts to reverse the modernization process, in the form of Klan activity or in the anti-evolution bills, had failed. Efforts to rekindle the moral crusades against gambling, as in earlier times, had not succeeded. Yet it was not so much that Kentuckians had embraced the changes around them or that they even wanted most of these changes. Rather, they simply accepted the times and went on with the basics as before. In the upcoming years all that would change.

17

Old Problems and a New Deal

Economic Want

Economically, the 1930s would prove to be one of the most difficult decades in Kentucky's history. The 1920s, however, had well prepared the state's residents for hardship. Farmers suffered the most. Techniques that depleted and eroded the soils combined with a depressed market for agricultural products in the 1920s to produce agrarian distress. The tobacco economy collapsed soon after the end of World War I, while corn acreage decreased nearly one-fifth between 1920 and 1930. In the five-year period ending in 1928, Kentucky ranked forty-seventh among forty-eight states in farm income. Its 1930 per capita farm earnings average of $148 stood well behind the Southeast's $183 mean, which itself trailed the national norm. The state's farmers were in trouble.

Then came 1930 and an unprecedented drought. In some places it did not rain at all for a month and a half. In most, precipitation averaged less than half the normal summer levels. Ice factories stopped production, water rationing began, farm animals suffered, and the Bluegrass turned "so brown that there did not seem to be a vestige of life remaining." In Franklin County the agricultural agent reported that only 15 percent of the corn crop had survived. By August the value of state crop losses exceeded $100 million. Debt-ridden farmers could hear the voice of disaster growing louder.

Sadly, that cry echoed all across Kentucky, and not just in rural areas. The stock market crash of October 1929 marked the beginning of a national economic depression that would leave few untouched. To a state already hurt by the effect of Prohibition, a declining coal economy, and a decade-long agricultural depression, the new blow struck hard. Nor was the commonwealth prepared to deal with the staggering numbers of people in need. At the time, the prevailing system of "poor relief" dictated that the county court magistrates heard each request, each month, and then decided whether to grant relief through an order to pay or to reject the claim. One study indicated that counties could average as little as nine cents per capita in aid, and "money is given with no regard to the available resources of the applicant or the community. No attention is paid to the mental or social fitness of the recipients." Limited funds, favoritism, politics, and other factors, the report concluded, made local relief efforts an utter failure. If no other options were available, the needy would go to what was called an almshouse or poorhouse or pauper farm to live. Small and underfunded, such institutions could not adequately meet needs either.

It became increasingly clear that something different would have to be done, for the scope of the problem exceeded anything seen before. The Red Cross director for Kentucky reported in 1930 that "the picture of distress . . . in the eastern part of our state is almost unbelievable. . . . There is a growing army of itinerants traveling on foot." That same year a Danville newspaper proclaimed that the area was suffering "from the greatest depression as well as the greatest drought that this country has ever known." Whereas one in twenty of the city's population lived on local charity in 1927, by 1932 one in four did. In Louisville in 1932, 23.5 percent of white workers and 37.2 percent of black workers were unemployed. And even those still employed felt the effects—Universi-

WORLD'S HIGHEST STANDARD OF LIVING

There's no way like the American Way

As the depression took its toll on Kentucky, *Life* photographer Margaret Bourke-White captured this arresting scene in Louisville during the 1937 flood. (*Life Magazine*, Time, Inc.)

ty of Kentucky faculty went without pay for two months, while many miners worked only part time. The story was repeated across Kentucky. In 1930 a medical worker in the mountains predicted starvation if nothing was done; the next year she described "a state of acute famine." One of her Bluegrass relatives told an out-of-state friend that the commonwealth was facing "a damn bad situation." In 1932 an Inez attorney noted the lack of jobs and the hard times and concluded that "the people feel that there is something radically wrong." From Pikeville to Paducah, people wandered from place to place, walking, riding, seeking work, a job, some hope. Few found what they sought.

In some ways, state banks symbolized the despair. Over the decades a small number of banks had failed every year. In 1928, for instance, three near Hazard closed their doors in one week owing to the state of mining. In the Great Depression, however, those few failures now became many. In 1930 some 5 percent of the state's more than four hundred banks ceased doing business; the next year another 8 percent closed; in 1932 nearly 12 percent more followed. Deposits that had peaked at $385 million in June 1929 had fallen to under $230 million six years later and would not again reach the 1929 figure until 1943. The greatest bank failure was that of the state's—

and the South's—largest financial institution, the BancoKentucky Company. Poorly managed by Jim Brown, with his insider loans, unsecured notes, and misappropriated funds, the bank closed its doors on November 16, 1930. That action caused widespread panic and the closing of other banks, including two African American banks that had funds deposited at BancoKentucky. Brown, his financial empire, and his newspapers all went bankrupt. The city, the state, and the people of the commonwealth only slowly would take financial risks in the future, for the BancoKentucky example long haunted them. Unable to face even tomorrow, two bank presidents in Paducah, one in Mercer County, and the head of an insurance agency in Louisville all committed suicide.

Kentuckians had trusted banks and had placed their savings there. Some lost a lifetime of work. Gradually, many of the banks reopened, but usually they returned only part of the funds to those who had entrusted their money to the banks' care. In 1936, for instance, the sixteen banks that completed liquidation proceedings paid anywhere from 5 percent to 100 percent on earlier deposits, with a per-bank average of around 60 percent. For depositors who received the average return, 40 percent of their funds had vanished almost overnight, and all of their money had been unavailable, owing to legal proceedings, while the depression raged around them. They did not want that ever to happen again.

The depression held Kentucky firmly for many years. When federal aid became more available in 1933, almost whole counties went on relief. In Morgan County, over 85 percent of families accepted federal support; in Magoffin County, the December 1933 figure was 68 percent; in other places the needs were similar. Farm values dropped nearly 30 percent in the five years after 1930, and by 1940 they still remained below the 1930 average. As late as 1938 over one-third of Kentucky's counties appeared to be nearing default on their debts, while an additional one-fourth were overdue on payments. On top of all that, in the cold of January 1937 a flood submerged large parts of the state. On the Ohio River, two-thirds of Louisville's businesses were under water, and thousands of people had to be evacuated. Up and down the river, the same results occurred. In Paducah, where seven-eighths of the town was submerged, it was "three weeks of high water and Hell." Over the region, drowned animals filled the streets and rivers, and homeless people sought shelter. The devastated economy once more suffered. Two years later, in 1939, the Frozen Creek flash floods that swept through the hollows in eastern Kentucky left almost eighty dead in Breathitt, Rowan, and Lewis counties. Nature was not helping Kentucky recover.

Yet the commonwealth weathered the drought and the floods and survived the depression better than many places. The end of Prohibition and the continuation of tobacco smoking aided the state economy in those sectors; the general absence of industry meant relatively little damage there; the overall lack of wealth left people only a little way to fall; and the rural nature of the commonwealth allowed families to live off the land. In fact, people returned to Kentucky, and the decade of the 1930s saw the state's population increase faster than the national average for the first time since before the Civil War. From distant places, those who had migrated in search of jobs that had disappeared now came home to crowd in

with their families in hollows, hills, and other places throughout the state. By 1940 the state's 2,845,627 people lived less in urban areas than a decade before (30 percent of the population was urban in 1940). When trouble came, Kentuckians had returned to their rural roots.

Depression-Era Politics

The portly, balding, and cigar-smoking Ruby Laffoon of Madisonville looked like the stereotypical politician. Born in a log cabin, he had become an attorney, entered politics, lost more races than he won, then served as circuit court judge. It did not seem a strong background for a gubernatorial candidate, but supported by the bosses and his politically powerful cousin Polk Laffoon, he became the Democratic nominee in 1931, the choice of the only Democratic gubernatorial convention after 1903. His youthful opponent, Louisville's Republican mayor, William B. ("Billy") Harrison, gained the support of the *Courier-Journal*, attacked the supposed bipartisan combine, and benefited from opposition to the Catholic bosses backing Laffoon. But all Laffoon had to do was to mention Sampson's failed governorship, Hoover's problem-laden presidency, and the depression, and victory was his. He won by a huge margin, 446,301 to 374,239.

Laffoon spent most of his administration trying to deal with a depressed economy and searching for funds. State expenditures in 1931 had been $46 million; in Laffoon's first full year they fell to $34.3 million. The commonwealth went deeper into debt by issuing more and more promises to pay, in the form of interest-bearing warrants. Warrants as a percentage of total state receipts increased from 24 percent in 1931 to 40 percent in 1932. By the end of the governor's term, warrants exceeded $20 million. Faced with that fiscal disaster, having already made huge cuts in the budget (especially in education), and having to pledge more funds to match new federal relief programs, "the Terrible Turk from Madisonville" asked the legislature to enact a sales tax. Political disunity in the Democratic Party resulted, both from that action and as bosses who sought political spoils now found that few crumbs could be offered. Merchants opposed the tax proposal, as did money-poor citizens, and in March 1932 a mob of some one hundred stormed the Governor's Mansion, damaging some items inside. The tax failed to pass. The next year, after Lafoon called a special session to try to get the tax passed once more, he had angry demonstrators fed in a warehouse. Again the Kentucky General Assembly refused.

Convinced that the opposition sought his political ruin, Governor Laffoon lashed out at the *Courier-Journal* as "Public Enemy No. 1" and suggested that the attacks by businessmen were led by a "bunch of New York Jews." During Laffoon's term, the board of charities was made partisan, the highway commission was reorganized with the chief executive's supporters, and various powers were "ripped" from the lieutenant governor and auditor, who opposed Laffoon. Next, the governor allied with the Republicans in exchange for patronage and got a needed reorganization bill passed. He also more than doubled the whiskey levy and finally got his sales tax through in 1934, but inexplicably, he also reduced the real estate tax to one-sixth its previous level. Overall, though, the state finally had achieved some needed fiscal stability. That had come at a great cost, however, both politically and personally. A sad figure by term's end, Laffoon lived in the mansion under guard to keep another mob away, went into a sanatorium to be treated for exhaustion, and then had to have surgery for appendicitis. In 1935 Laffoon left an office that had overwhelmed him.

Laffoon had been crippled in a childhood accident, and ironically, another politician with a physical disability, Franklin D. Roosevelt, had entered the national political stage during Laffoon's term. Unlike the Kentuckian, who faltered before the heat of the spotlight, FDR gloried in it. He projected confidence and gave listeners the sense that things could be better. As the nominee for president on the Democratic ticket in 1932, he had the election in hand before he began, for all the reasons that had given Laffoon his victory a year earlier. One Kentucky political boss said of FDR that "I believe he could go home and

go to sleep and wake up elected. . . . Everybody broke and out of work." On election day, Roosevelt won by the largest margin ever recorded in Kentucky, as he defeated Hoover by 580,574 votes to 394,176. At the same time, something happened that had not occurred in the twentieth century—a sitting US senator from Kentucky, in this case Alben Barkley, won reelection. Even better for the majority party, an attempt at reapportionment had been voided by the courts, so the nine candidates with the greatest statewide vote totals would be selected to go to Congress. Districts that were normally Republican were swamped by the vote over the commonwealth, and Democrats won all nine seats. It was a massive sweep. With only a few exceptions, Democrats would dominate state elections in Kentucky for the next six decades.

At the time that Roosevelt came into office, many people, like the editor of one Kentucky newspaper, were "gravely apprehensive," for unrest was everywhere. Certain commentators feared that the entire system might be in jeopardy. But the president's immediate and active response, causing people to hope once more, helped change attitudes. The same editor in March 1933 wrote that "the spirit here really . . . is very much better." The state also had some hope of change because FDR included numerous Kentuckians in his administration. In 1937 Barkley would become majority leader of the US Senate, while Frederick M. Vinson later became important in several capacities. The president appointed Stanley Reed of Maysville to the Supreme Court, where he joined two other Kentucky-born justices, and made Bingham ambassador to Great Britain. Several other citizens of the state served in key positions.

With these appointments, plus the actions taken in the New Deal, Roosevelt became virtually unbeatable in the state. In 1936 he won 58.4 percent of the state vote; four years later, in his controversial third-term bid, he took 57.4 percent; in 1944, in the midst of war, Roosevelt garnered 54.5 percent. In all those elections the state outcome never stood in doubt, and he carried two-thirds of all Kentucky counties. Many saw FDR as one Ken-

tuckian did, "He was a father figure . . . an inspiration, a hero." At the same time, the New
Deal programs that aided labor unions and
blacks brought about a change in the makeup
of the Democratic Party in the commonwealth.
Before Roosevelt, virtually all African Americans registered and voted Republican, the party
of Lincoln. But the scant support given during
the Hoover term combined with the aid provided by the New Deal to bring about at least
a gradual shift. It would take nearly thirty years
for that change to become a constant, but by
1936 the Louisville black voting wards were already giving a majority to Roosevelt. Similarly,
the New Deal's pro-union actions brought the
Eastern Coalfield to turn from the Republicans
as well. Whereas the Democrats carried only
eight of thirty-two eastern counties in 1924, by
1936 they carried a majority of them. A new,
broader, and more powerful Democratic coalition was being forged.

The New Deal

Much of the Democratic success resulted directly from the effects of the New Deal. A generation that had known mostly economic distress in Kentucky now saw the possibility of
better days. As Robert Penn Warren noted,
many had thought that "things lay beyond any
individual effort to change them," but now the
crisis demanded action "because you had to
have action or die."

Almost immediately, the government repealed the Volstead Act, the enforcement arm
of Prohibition, and on "Foamy Friday" in April
1933, some places in the commonwealth began legally serving alcoholic beverages once
more. Many areas remained dry, however, even
after the adoption of the Twenty-first Amendment later that year. But many Kentuckians
now went back to work at distilleries across the
state.

Federal action addressed problem after
problem, in an often bewildering array of programs, most of which became known by their
acronyms. A need existed to provide security
for the young. The result was Aid to Families
with Dependent Children (AFDC), through

which in 1939 some forty-five thousand Kentucky families received an average of $8.73 per
month. The National Youth Administration
(NYA) gave part-time work or aid to young
people of high school and college age, allowing
them to remain in school. What about security for the elderly? The Social Security Act of
1935 provided that for the first time. And what
about financial security? A series of acts helped
Kentuckians refinance mortgages or, in the case
of the Federal Housing Administration (FHA),
get new low-interest loans. Bank deposits were
guaranteed to a certain level under the Federal
Deposit Insurance Corporation (FDIC).

The greatest efforts went to help those
without jobs. Immediate needs were met on
a short-term basis by direct payments under
the Federal Emergency Relief Administration
(FERA). Longer-range solutions focused on
providing relief funds in return for labor on
public projects. Professionals found an outlet, as out-of-work teachers provided instruction to illiterate citizens, artists painted murals
through the Federal Art Project, and various
people worked in the Federal Writers Project, which, among other activities, produced
archival guides and several histories. Other
Kentuckians worked in sewing rooms and the
like, but the largest group labored in the Public Works Administration (PWA), which built
sewers, post offices, and river facilities, and particularly in the Works Progress (Projects) Administration, or WPA.

A Henderson woman with diabetes was
"right down in despair" until her husband
started working on a WPA project: "First off
he bought us some groceries, things that would
last. . . . Then he had a chance to get that little heatin' stove for two dollars and . . . some
coal. . . . They got us some mattresses from the
relief to take the place of our straw and husk
ticks." For a family in Newport, "those were
mighty hard years. . . . Our savings were gone.
We had a hard time getting enough to eat."
Then the husband began working on a WPA
project, but poor health forced him to stop; the
wife received WPA relief employment at a sewing center, and that "started to get [us] on our
feet." For those two families and for the near-

The WPA created jobs for many Kentuckians. Here WPA workers build a sewer in Owensboro. (Goodman-Paxton Photographic Collection, University of Kentucky Special Collections and Research Center, Lexington, KY)

ly sixty thousand people employed by WPA by Christmas 1935, such work saved them. The WPA built or improved numerous buildings and greatly helped in the modernization of the state's infrastructure. Workers constructed schools, gymnasiums, recreation centers, parks, privies, roads, bridges, culverts, and more, and many of these projects served to break down isolation.

The land itself received attention as well. The Agricultural Adjustment Act had to be re-examined after the first version was declared unconstitutional, but in the end the Agricultural Adjustment Administration (AAA) controlled production in an attempt to raise prices. Some livestock was killed in order to do that, and restrictions were placed on tobacco production. Despite indifferent success among small farmers, especially in eastern Kentucky, the project succeeded in bringing more money, overall, to state farms. The commonwealth's forests benefited from the Civilian Conservation Corps (CCC). Eighty thousand young Kentucky CCC workers reforested the land; helped control soil erosion; built lodges, cabins, and trails in parks; and thereby helped awaken the people of Kentucky to environmental matters. The damming of rivers through the Tennessee Valley Authority (TVA) together with the Rural

Electrification Administration (REA) provided cheap and widespread electricity throughout the region, but especially in rural areas. TVA's construction of Kentucky Dam, completed in 1945, in a sense signaled the end of the New Deal. That massive dam, the federal narcotics hospital at Lexington, and the US Bullion Depository at Fort Knox, however, only symbolized all that had occurred.

The most significant change of the New Deal had been mental rather than physical. The roads and buildings all made a difference, but acceptance of the involvement of the federal government in the lives of Kentuckians was a greater change. Need overrode a philosophy centered in localism and individualism. Large portions of the population now accepted programs that provided security to farmers, laborers, the elderly, and the young. The individual was not solely responsible for his or her well-being; society had a role to play as well. Governmental involvement had given more stability to the economy and more protection to consumers. Not everyone accepted that, and some bitterly criticized Roosevelt's actions. Certain programs had not worked; some had benefited certain groups more than others. People recognized that important compromises had been made and some important things had been given up. Most, though, readily accepted what had taken place, for their lives and, most important, their future hopes had improved as a result of the New Deal.

Labor and the Coal Wars

Labor unions had existed in Kentucky since before the Civil War, but most had had only limited success because of hostile courts, unsympathetic government and governors, and plentiful strikebreakers. Only in 1935, with the passage of the federal Wagner Act and the creation of a National Labor Relations Board, did that situation change drastically. The new law provided that employees had the right to join unions and to bargain collectively, and it also gave governmental protection to those rights. Several fundamental issues were thus settled, but in some ways the law came a few years too late to spare the state from an episode that further damaged Kentucky's image.

In the years soon after the Civil War, various unions of skilled or semiskilled workers had been organized, mostly in Louisville and northern Kentucky. In 1877 some two thousand laborers marched in Louisville, bringing out a large militia force in answer; in 1893 a large strike against the L&N failed. The Knights of Labor had local assemblies in Kentucky by the late 1860s but had virtually disappeared by 1900, when the national convention of the American Federation of Labor (AFL) met in the Falls City. Soon afterward, the Kentucky State Federation of Labor, with James McGill as president, was established. By 1902 about 12 percent of Kentucky factories were unionized. Sporadic strikes, a few victories, and many defeats followed, with the Newport Rolling Mills Strike of 1921–1922 being one of the most bitter. In 1919 a steel strike left a half dozen people wounded in an exchange of shots, troops, and machine guns, and then in early 1922 tanks fired into strikers, trying to keep company workers from crossing picket lines. Injuries and arrests followed.

Of the 223 Kentucky strikes listed in one account for the 1880–1900 period, however, 81 occurred in the state's coalfields, both in the east and west. In 1873 a "miners' union" was established in Boyd and Carter Counties, and from that beginning the impulse spread. The issues of concern were not just job security and higher wages but also safety and fair practices. From 1876 to 1878 strikes in Rockcastle County sought to raise miners' wages from four to five cents per bushel of coal (a bushel of coal contains about eighty pounds). Other similar work stoppages took place elsewhere. In 1890 the United Mine Workers of America (UMW) formed. Kentucky workers joined nationwide strikes in 1894 (involving more than thirty-five hundred men), 1919 (involving twenty thousand Kentucky miners), 1922, and 1924. The depressed coal industry of the 1920s offered little hope for success, however, and UMW membership in the state fell from nineteen thousand in 1912 to fewer than one thousand by 1931. As one miner succinctly explained, "If you kicked too much, or complained too much about [working conditions] . . . you would soon be hunting for a job." Since coal companies often operated their own towns, strikers could be evicted from their homes as well.

In Webster County in the western Kentucky fields, mining tragedies had killed ten miners in 1910, sixty-two in 1917, six in 1925, and sixteen more in 1927. Such conditions, coupled with the depressed economy and its effect on wages, brought continued attempts to unionize and continued opposition from the operators. Several union men were beaten and injured. In 1930, frustrated strikers even flew a plane over one mine and dropped bombs, though no one was hurt. Finally, hungry miners returned to work. Nine years later, another mine disaster took the lives of twenty-eight more Webster County miners.

As the effects of the depression spread throughout the eastern Kentucky coalfields, conditions grew so bad that workers believed they too had no choice but to challenge the mine owners. In one Kentucky county, operators remained more intransigent than elsewhere, and abuses seemed more flagrant. Out of those conditions arose the image of "Bloody Harlan" and the Harlan County Coal Wars of the 1930s.

Harlan County had experienced a huge population increase in the years before 1930, and with that expansion came massive societal disorganization for those sixty-five thousand people. The once-proud coal towns had fallen on hard times in the 1920s as coal prices dropped, and the scant profits often went to stockholders, not toward making repairs. Tensions rose, violence increased, and class animosity intensified. Then came the additional problems of the national depression. By 1932 one-third of Harlan County's mines had closed, and four thousand miners had lost their jobs. Those who did work labored harder for less: Payment in the 1920s for digging a ton of coal was 81 cents; by 1931 it had fallen to 35 cents per ton. Relief from the New Deal lay in the future, so hungry, desperate, jobless people roamed the region, looking for work or just food. Company evictions left many homeless and hungry, and even more just angry. As one miner cried out, "We don't live; we just exist." And another stressed, "We don't want to get rich. We want to eat."

In May 1931, a coal company cut wages again and miners protested in a meeting. Following that gathering, management instituted mass firings and evictions from the camps of many of those involved. Soon after, what became known as the battle of Evarts took place: over a thousand shots were exchanged between miners and the coal company's paid deputies, sometimes called "gun thugs." In an ambush of company cars, at least one miner was killed, and three died on the operators' side. With the UMW virtually absent, the Communist-oriented National Miners' Union (NMU) came in to fill the void and to offer help, through soup kitchens. Although few Harlan County miners supported the NMU, its presence caused the conservative owners to fear the worst. The owner of the Creech Coal Company proclaimed, "They'll bring a union in here over my dead body." Each side armed itself, but the operators controlled the county and its legal machinery. As Aunt Molly Jackson sang,

What can we do about it
To those men of power and might?

Well, I'll tell you, Mister Capitalist
We are going to fight, fight, fight.

No one could be neutral, and a folk song asked, "Which side are you on?" People had to choose.

All attention seemed to focus on Harlan County. A group of national writers, which included Theodore Dreiser and John Dos Passos, visited the area, and one of their number called the situation "the most outstanding example of industrial despotism and official depravity in the history of coal mining." Soon a deputy killed an NMU organizer and some writers were beaten. Out-of-state student groups who came to investigate conditions were refused admission to the county. The NMU soon left, but other union organizers remained, and several were beaten. In September 1935, a car bomb killed the county attorney, and more murders followed. Yet the publicity in some ways exceeded the reality, for union conflicts in other places in the United States took a larger toll. But the very ferocity of the fight, the uncompromising nature of the operators, and the length of the struggle made Bloody Harlan nationally known.

In 1935 a state investigating committee reported that "coal mine operators in collusion with certain public officials" had created "a virtual reign of terror." Two years later, the LaFollette Civil Liberties Committee, a special committee of the US Senate, held national government hearings that focused more attention on the situation and reached similar conclusions. Finally, with the provisions of the Wagner Act in operation, the Harlan County Coal Operators' Association reluctantly capitulated and signed a contract with the union. UMW membership in Harlan County rose to fifteen thousand by 1940, and while the violence had ended only for a time, the legitimacy of unions seemed settled at last. Miners began to speak of their lives as divided into two parts—"Before the Union" and "After the Union"—for it made that much difference in their lives.

What turned out to be most damaging to the miners in the long run, however, was mechanization of the coalfields. Workers almost worshiped national UMW president John L. Lewis

Table 17.1. Kentucky Coal Production and Employment, 1950–2015

Year	Coal production (1,000 tons)	Employees
1950	80,988	74,457
1960	61,612	34,473
1970	125,308	27,689
1995	153,493	21,125
2015	61,414	9,557

Source: Jerry Napier, "Mechanization and the Central Kentucky Coal Fields" (unpublished manuscript); Kentucky Coal Facts (2016).

as he stood up to even the president in calling strikes. But following a crucial work stoppage, Lewis signed a 1950 wage agreement, which practically freed companies to mechanize.

Between 1950 and 1965 mechanization caused the number of employees in Kentucky's underground mines to fall by 70 percent. The average amount of coal mined per person per day had gone from 4.75 tons to 14 tons. Many young, displaced miners could find no other jobs in the area. Harlan County lost twenty thousand people during the 1950s, and across the coalfields massive migrations took place.

From the 1940s into the 1980s, unions, both in the coalfields and in other areas of Kentucky, played an important role, not just in economic matters but in political ones as well. Union endorsements meant votes, and labor lobbies had a major influence on legislatures. Despite a strong start—Kentucky ranked thirteenth nationally in union membership in 1939—the state soon settled into the middle ranks. It did have more strikes and more lost time than the American norm in the three decades after 1952 and had a relatively higher percentage of labor union members than did the rest of the South. Overall, however, Kentucky had only an average amount of union activity. By the early 1980s less than 20 percent of the manufacturing plants in the state were unionized. Reflecting national trends, the numbers continued to drop after that, to 11 percent in 2013. With less cohesion, influence, and control, unions became far less important in political races, and by the

early twenty-first century the golden age of unions appeared to be over.

Happy

The 1930s saw many transformations take place in Kentucky, as unions became powerful after years of weakness, as the New Deal brought an entirely new outlook on federal-state relations, and as the older political leadership began to pass from the scene, to be replaced by a fresh cadre. One of the newcomers, Albert Benjamin ("Happy") Chandler, burst onto the Kentucky scene almost overnight. State senator, lieutenant governor, and governor, all by the age of thirty-seven, he would go on to become one of the dominant Kentucky political figures of his era, serving later as US senator, again as governor, as baseball commissioner, and as a faction leader in the Democratic Party. A following that was more personal than political became the core from which he operated for more than thirty years. During that time Chandler would throw off the bosses who had orchestrated his rise and would be dominated by no one. He was Happy. That said it all.

Born near Henderson, Chandler saw his mother leave him when he was four. He worked hard, but he could also call on a strong speaking (and singing) voice, some athletic skills, and a will to achieve. Very early he came to believe he was destined to be president, and he moved steadily, and for a time successfully, toward that goal. Politically allied to the Beckham-Haly-Bingham faction, Chandler became a pariah in the Laffoon administration, and what powers he had as lieutenant governor were stripped from him. But a key constitutional strength remained: at the time, a Kentucky governor who traveled outside the state lost all powers to govern. The Laffoon forces planned to call a convention, which they could control, and thus they would select the person whom they wanted to be the party nominee. But when Laffoon went to Washington to address some relief matters, acting governor Chandler called a special session of the legislature for the purpose of enacting a primary election law. A furious Laffoon hurried back and canceled the call, but the courts ruled Laffoon's action illegal. When the session met, Laffoon forces, expecting elderly J. C. W. Beckham to be the nominee of the opposition, enacted a possible two-stage primary, which would wear down the old politician.

For personal reasons, however, Beckham did not run. The youthful Happy Chandler, backed by Bingham money, did. Political boss and Laffoon choice Thomas Rhea soon found himself facing an extremely tough campaigner. Wearing white suits, singing songs like "Sonny Boy," hugging voters, and kissing babies, Chandler dominated a gathering with his flamboyant personality. His speeches were short for the time, and he conducted assemblies like revival meetings, making asides to people in the crowd whom he would call by name. Beneath the exuberance and brassy enthusiasm, though, also lay a hard, determined soul, and Happy did not spare his opponents. Rhea he labeled "Sales Tax Tom," and he called on his audience to redeem the state from "Ruby, Rhea, and Ruin." A veteran reporter watched all this and concluded that Chandler was the best campaigner he had seen during the last thirty years: "By methods he probably doesn't understand himself he has become one of them," that is, one of the crowd itself. It was a show, a personal tour, and the charismatic Chandler was the star.

Known as the Sage of Russellville, or the Gray Fox, Thomas Rhea was a shrewd politician who knew that he had few strengths on the political stump. His forte had been behind-the-scenes organization, and he now had to depend on that for victory. The first primary ended with Rhea ahead and Chandler second by nineteen thousand votes, but Rhea did not get enough support to avoid a runoff. In a large turnout, Chandler won this time, 260,573 to 234,124. The two-primary strategy had cost the Laffoon-Rhea forces the election. Embittered, Laffoon and Rhea, together with most of the highway commissioners and others in the administration, refused to support the nominee, and many went with the Republican candidate, King Swope of Lexington. No real policy differences separated Swope and Chandler, though, and the legacy of Hoover versus the

New Deal doomed the Republicans. In the largest vote cast in the state up to that time, Chandler won by a 556,262 to 461,104 count.

Hardly hesitating, the new governor began to put his stamp on the state government. He received resignations from or fired thousands of employees, replacing them with loyal Chandlerites, but to his credit, he also brought to Frankfort numerous college professors, whose innovative ideas helped streamline the bureaucracy. A needed Government Reorganization Act in 1936 not coincidentally gave the governor more power, but it also made the government run more efficiently. A law calling for a single primary replaced the two-primary law that had won Chandler the governorship. Philosophically a follower of Virginia's Harry F. Byrd (a godfather to a Chandler child), Happy not only used Byrd's ideas about reorganization but also followed his fiscal conservatism. Bitterly opposed to a sales tax, Chandler got the Kentucky General Assembly to abolish that Laffoon legacy and replaced the revenues with liquor and cigarette taxes. With Prohibition ended, the alcoholic beverage industry brought new money into the state's coffers. Combined with federal dollars, the new taxes gave Chandler the opportunity to reduce the state's debt significantly. The fiscal windfall also allowed construction of a new penitentiary at LaGrange, since the 1937 flood had forced evacuation of the outdated prison in Frankfort. Finally, the influence of Louisville's Charles W. Anderson Jr., the first African American elected to a southern legislature in the twentieth century, combined with the availability of state money to allow passage of a law giving a total of five thousand dollars annually to fund attendance by black students at out-of-state graduate schools, since segregation denied them such opportunities in Kentucky. Overall, the flush fiscal times allowed Chandler's "pay-as-you-go" philosophy to work. In later years, under different circumstances, such a view would create problems.

In one way, Chandler had been lucky in financial matters. He also benefited and received some credit from the federal government's new programs aiding the elderly and

President Franklin D. Roosevelt, Governor A. B. ("Happy") Chandler, and Senator Alben W. Barkley in northern Kentucky during the 1938 US Senate race. (University of Kentucky Special Collections and Research Center, Lexington, KY)

others. The new Boy Governor further gained from political circumstances. As it turned out, Percy Haly and Robert Worth Bingham both died in 1937, and Beckham's demise followed three years later. With the leadership in that long-standing faction virtually gone, Chandler moved into the void and led the remnants of the group. All this was heady stuff for the new governor, and he now looked to take his success to the national stage, as US senator. In the 1936 primary, incumbent senator M. M. Logan had defeated Beckham and rising political newcomer John Y. Brown Sr. (in the first of Brown's seven unsuccessful attempts for that office) and had, like Barkley, won reelection over a Republican opponent. Logan's seat would not be open, it seemed, until 1942. That was too long for Happy to wait. Chandler thus decided to challenge Alben Barkley in the 1938 US Senate race. It would be a battle of giants.

Chandler went into the race supremely confident. He had never lost, had a generally popular administration, and had built a strong political organization. Like others before him, he did not hesitate to involve state government in the election, as employees were solicited for funds while new workers were hired in exchange for their and their families' votes. The "Old Bear," J. Dan Talbott, served as the governor's patronage czar and used his powers effectively. Most of all, though, Chandler's strength

was Happy Chandler the campaigner. He expected to overwhelm "Old Alben."

What Chandler did not expect was that Barkley could match him on the campaign trail and could draw support from the federal government to counter the state effort. Like his mentor Byrd, Happy did not philosophically support much of the New Deal, and its leader, Franklin D. Roosevelt, knew that. Roosevelt also called Chandler a "dangerous" person, of the populist, Huey Long type he disliked. Besides all that, FDR had handpicked Barkley for the post as Senate majority leader, and defeat would amount to a repudiation of the president. Roosevelt said some favorable things about Chandler as he made a series of whistle-stop talks across the state, but his clear choice was Barkley. As Edward F. Prichard Jr. remarked, the president's words about the governor seemed to say, "You're a good boy, but you won't do." Behind the scenes, the federal relief agencies, particularly the WPA, worked for Barkley's election in such a brazen way that Congress would soon make such action illegal. Each machine—federal and state—geared up for the vote.

Barkley might well have won without all that extra help, though, for he had always been a popular, if long-winded, campaigner in his own right. Although sixty years old (versus Chandler's forty years), the tireless Iron Man probably made more speeches each day than his opponent. It was hard to vote against Barkley because he had become nationally known for his strong keynote addresses at the 1932 and 1936 Democratic conventions and had acquired many allies by speaking as a party loyalist in other races. Backed by the *Courier-Journal* and by the labor unions—both of which had supported Chandler when he ran for governor in 1935—Barkley had a great many allies. He also could capitalize on opportunity. When Chandler fell ill from drinking some water, and when it was weakly suggested that the liquid had been poisoned to slow Chandler's bid, a laughing Barkley announced that he would put "an ice water guard" on his staff. When he spoke and started to drink from a glass, Barkley would purposely hesitate, shudder, and put the glass away, eliciting much laughter. Chandler had a dynamic personality and some state allies, but Barkley had more support, including the president's endorsement. The incumbent won easily, 294,391 to 223,149. While a good ally of his friends, Chandler was also a good hater, and he never forgave Barkley and Roosevelt. He spoke bitterly of them the rest of his life. After all, they had defeated destiny.

World War II

Ironically, fortune smiled once more on Happy Chandler. In 1939, when Senator Logan died, Chandler resigned as governor and was appointed to the vacant Senate seat by the new governor, Keen Johnson. Then Chandler won the seat in a special election. He joined his enemy Barkley in the Senate just as the nation began to face a challenge even greater than the depression. Across the face of the globe, militant governments threatened weaker nations, drawing the world closer to war. Kentuckians had seen the Italians take Ethiopia, the Germans seize Austria and Czechoslovakia, and the Japanese conquer part of China. During that time the state's congressmen had voted with the majority on legislation concerning neutrality acts and defense spending, except for the reactionary isolationist mountain Republican John M. Robsion, who, it seemed, opposed anything

and everything. But with the Japanese attack on Pearl Harbor on December 7, 1941, all the discussion regarding peace or war ended.

The start of World War II meant that lifestyles and the usual ways of doing things changed, often drastically. As in most wars, governmental intervention in the economy, and thus in everyday lives, increased, but the federal actions of the New Deal had set the stage, so such intervention did not seem so unusual. Still, governmental rationing of sugar, coffee, butter, cheese, and meat, together with gasoline (around three gallons a week for most people), tires, fuel oil, shoes, and even bubblegum all meant sacrifice on the homefront of at least a limited scope. But "victory gardens" on small plots—"you can hardly walk across a front yard without stepping on someone's Victory Garden," wrote a Lexingtonian—furnished up to 40 percent of the vegetables consumed nationally in 1943, and the overall good crops of the wartime years helped overcome shortages. The value of state crops and livestock more than doubled in the war years. Unlike people in many parts of the world, most Americans did not go hungry.

The war required raw materials, and scrap drives brought in junk iron and aluminum for the effort. Factories switched from making consumer goods to producing battlefield equipment. The maker of Louisville Slugger baseball bats, for example, converted to the building of rifle stocks, while the Ford plant in that city produced over 93,000 Jeeps instead. Meanwhile, state distilleries shifted to making industrial alcohol, in the end producing one-third of the national output. Not all went smoothly, however. When the huge Ken-Rad Company of Owensboro refused to sign a contract with a union in 1944, the government intervened and took over the plant. An agreement quickly followed. New factories also sprang up to fill new needs. Louisville, for instance, became the nation's largest maker of synthetic rubber, since most overseas rubber-producing areas were in enemy hands. Still, despite a booming economy, Kentucky did not offer as much as did places elsewhere and placed tenth among the southern states in the value of its wartime federal government contracts. As a result, the commonwealth would come out of the conflict in the same relative position as it entered it.

All across America, everyone was searching for workers. A mass exodus to better-paying jobs in the North and West resulted, with some 13 percent of the population leaving the state between 1940 and 1950. Knox County in Appalachia lost 30 percent of its people in wartime, for example. Occasional labor shortages in Kentucky showed that, in contrast to the depression decade, now anyone who wanted to work could do so. State per capita income rose from only 54 percent of the national average in 1940 to 65 percent within five years. For many, the wartime economy provided long-sought financial security—even if for some that meant departing Kentucky.

Those labor shortages brought, for the first time, large numbers of women into the workforce. Not only did they toil in factories, but they also entered what had once been solely male domains. In Lexington, women drove taxicabs and stood guard at the gates of the new Blue Grass Ordnance Depot, for example. Even the "Rosie the Riveter" icon had a Kentucky connection—when a film was produced, it featured Rose Monroe of Pulaski County as the real-life "Rosie." In job after job, women showed that they could do the same work as men. Once the war ended and soldiers returned, however, many women had to give up their jobs to the veterans and go back to more traditional "women's work." But a start had been made.

Away from factories, women helped the war effort in other ways. To conserve cloth, short sleeves were touted, and bathing suits became smaller. The scarcity of silk and then nylon hose induced more women to wear trousers, a break with tradition that brought forth much discussion in some circles. In whatever form of dress, women staffed USO canteens for soldiers, prepared surgical dressings, led neighborhood collection efforts, aided hospitals and the Red Cross, and conducted war bond drives. With a huge rise in income all across the economic spectrum, but with no new cars or durable consumer goods on which to spend that

Rose Monroe of Pulaski County would be the model for a film version of "Rosie the Riveter" but also represented the thousands of women who left their Kentucky home to aid the war effort. (Ypsilanti Historical Society, Ypsilanti, MI)

money, savings soared. By buying bonds, civilians financed the war effort. Cashing them in after the conflict ended would produce a postwar consumer buying spree.

Signs of the war stood all around Kentuckians. Military bases at Fort Knox and the newly formed Camp Campbell and Camp Breckinridge expanded greatly—with over 30,000 infantry receiving training at Breckinridge, while one-fourth of all US armor trainees went through Campbell. At the same time, the US Army Corps of Engineers built depots or ordnance works in Paducah, Viola, Henderson, Louisville, Lexington, and Richmond, plus Darnall General Hospital in Boyle County and Nichols General Hospital in Louisville to care for troops. The gold vault at Fort Knox became the temporary home of the Declaration of Independence and the US Constitution. The Army Air Force took over Bowman Field, and it served as the site of the nation's first glider pilot combat training. Meanwhile, beginning in 1943, some ten thousand German and Italian prisoners of war (POWs) were placed in fifteen camps across Kentucky. Many worked in agriculture to replace the American men fighting overseas. The most visible example of their presence remains the nearly two dozen large, wonderful murals painted by a German POW at Camp Breckinridge, to remind him of his distant home. He never saw that homeland again, however, dying of disease, one of some twenty other POWs buried in the state. Death affected all. Aircraft, soldiers, the wounded, POWs—all made the conflict visible to the people of the commonwealth.

Yet for all the changes, daily life remained remarkably stable. Although several colleges suspended sports, the Derby went on. Listening to radio programs or going to a motion picture became even more popular pastimes. Milk was still delivered daily to homes, and mail still came twice a day, as before. Even segregation continued, but it seemed ironic that in a war against fascism and for democracy, German POWs could eat in some Kentucky restaurants while their black guards could not. That struggle for equality would be fought after the current war was won.

For those serving in the military, fighting in forgotten places across the oceans, the relative calm, the prosperity, the peace of wartime America seemed a lifetime away. Whether in the Pacific theater, with its heat and rain and malaria, or in the European arena, with its cold and mud and frozen feet, stretches of utter boredom would be mixed with periods of utter terror and death.

Kentuckians' involvement began early, for it was a military chaplain from Murray who at Pearl Harbor cried out, in the middle of the attack, "Praise the Lord and pass the ammunition!" The unfortunate commander of the naval forces at the base was another Kentuckian, Admiral Husband E. Kimmel of Henderson. A seaman from Louisville who had been on the sinking USS *Arizona* later recalled his reaction: "The whole harbor was on fire. . . . I went into a state of shock." For those who had recently been in a tank company in the Kentucky National Guard but had been sent to the Philippines just days before, the hell lasted much longer than at Pearl. Of the sixty-six men who left Harrodsburg, twenty-nine died before war's end. After the group surrendered in the Philippines, they had to endure the Bataan Death March, where their captors bayoneted men, buried others alive, beheaded some, and left many prisoners dying from dysentery or malnutrition. Only years later did the survivors return from prison camps to tell their stories or to bury them in their memories.

A Lexingtonian recalled hearing the news of Pearl Harbor: "You knew the military was going to be part of your life. You just knew it." A college student in the same city would write later of his leaving: "From the train I gave a final salute to the years of youth that had died at Pearl Harbor. I never saw myself again." Before it all ended, 306,715 Kentuckians entered the armed forces, and they fought in virtually every theater. At the leadership level, Admiral Willis A. ("Ching") Lee of Owen County led battleships in the Pacific, while General Simon B. Buckner Jr. of Hart County commanded army forces at Okinawa, where he was killed, the highest ranking American officer who died in the conflict. Throughout all the ranks, though, men fought and died. They were symbolized in the person of Private Franklin R. Sousley of Fleming County, one of the marines in the famous picture of the raising of the American flag on Iwo Jima. Sousley was killed soon afterward, and he became one of the nearly eight thousand Kentuckians who never came back. In the case of William R. Buster of Mercer County (who did return), over 10 percent of his 1939 West Point class were killed in the war. Too many Gold Star Mothers wept across Kentucky and the nation.

War's end in 1945 returned to the commonwealth many people with changed attitudes. A Knox County man recalled that the fighting was so hard, "I even forgot how to cry. . . . We were hardened. Life didn't mean much." Yet he shook off part of that and became a long-time educator after the conflict. He joined others who had stayed and evolved as well. The lives of women and blacks would not be the same again, for brief glimpses of possibilities would not be forgotten in later years. As one wrote, "We couldn't possibly have been the same person after the war that we were before because of what we did and what we saw." Nor would Kentucky remain the same, for the mass migration had taken away many of the young, seldom to return. The greatest change, though, came among those who had left to fight. Some brought back wounds, others scarred memories. A Warren County captain had gone to a liberated German concentration camp, but it was too late for the hundreds of dead he saw, "stacked like cord-wood" ready to be burned before the Americans arrived: "The tragedy . . . hangs like a shadow over the place even now." He could not forget that, or the faces of combat and the dead young men. For others, however, the travel to distant places and the contact with people from other parts of the United States proved a maturing experience, which left them more sophisticated and broadminded. Still other soldiers simply came home, at least on the surface unchanged from the experience, as they took up the life they had left when they went to fight with others against a common enemy. In the end, the United States had faced massive military might, had beaten it, and had done so in a way that left the homeland unscathed and even prosperous. Americans now wanted to reap the benefits of their action in a postwar world.

Wartime Politics

When Happy Chandler resigned in October 1939 to become US senator, his lieutenant governor took the reins of office, less than a month before the general election for a full term. Keen Johnson, though, had already been campaigning for the post and had beaten John Y. Brown Sr. in the primary. The new governor was very unlike his predecessor, for Johnson was usually quiet and reserved. Moreover, he had represented the Laffoon-Rhea side in the 1935 election and thus initially had not been a Chandler ally. He had made peace with Chandler, however, and Happy backed Johnson as he faced the once-defeated Republican gubernatori-

al choice, King Swope. The Democratic candidate won easily, 460,834–354,704. Son of a preacher, and a World War I veteran, the journalist from Richmond became governor soon after war began raging in Europe. Before he left office, the conflict had encompassed the United States and the world.

Johnson presided over what he himself called a cautious, frugal, and conservative administration, but one with solid accomplishments. Despite lowered road receipts due to rationing, the state debt was paid in full, and a surplus accumulated. Various groups, particularly in education, argued that more funds should have been spent. Funding for the Teachers' Retirement Act, an enabling law that allowed the TVA to proceed, and a thorough legislative redistricting—the first in nearly fifty years—all passed. A constitutional amendment to allow the use of voting machines instead of paper ballots met with the voters' approval in 1941 as well. Other than the war and all the restrictions it brought, though, the key event in the Johnson administration was the rebirth of internecine factionalism in the Democratic Party.

When Chandler ran for a full Senate term in 1942, a now-bitter enemy faced him in the primary and accused the incumbent of using his office to receive favors—especially the construction of a swimming pool—during wartime restrictions. Namesake of a former governor but not related, John Y. Brown Sr. was the son of a tenant farmer and came from western Kentucky roots not unlike Chandler's. Brown believed that Happy had promised to support him for senator earlier and had reneged, and he now became almost a perennial candidate. Brown lost, and Chandler took the race handily, in both the primary and the general election. Two years later, in 1944, Senate majority leader Alben Barkley won reelection easily as well, although his break with the president on a veto that year angered FDR and may have cost the Kentuckian the vice presidency, which went to Harry Truman. The real party bitterness, however, came from within Johnson's administration, as an ambitious attorney general brought up various problems, real or imagined, while a muckraking *Courier-Journal* reporter unearthed more. When the Democratic primary for governor started in 1943, the usually gentle Johnson grew so angry at his own party's attacks on him that he called one candidate a Casanova and another a phony farmer and a "carpet bagger from North Carolina." In the end, Johnson's choice, J. Lyter Donaldson of Carrollton, won and faced a formidable Republican, for a change.

Simeon Willis appealed to voters as a political outsider. By 1943 he had not held office for a decade, having left a seat on the state's high court and returned to a law practice in Ashland. The tall, dignified-looking Ohioborn son of a Union veteran, Republican Willis echoed the corruption and bossism themes of the losing Democrats in their primary and presented himself as the reformer, above partisan bickering. He also advocated repeal of the income tax, a stance his opponent would not take. A capable man, but also one "whose personality sent shock waves of apathy through the state," Donaldson ran what observers termed "a very leisurely and indifferent campaign," one based on national issues of wartime unity. In a close race decided by fewer than 9,000 votes, Willis won, 279,144 to 270,525, and for the first time in a dozen years a Republican sat in the gubernatorial office. As it turned out, an even longer time would pass before that phenomenon occurred again. Willis's victory had been more personal than political.

Facing a Democratically controlled legislature and a wartime situation, Willis had many problems, party oriented and otherwise, but his scandal-free administration greatly increased aid to education and old-age assistance, funded a series of state tubercular sanatoriums, and provided some support for black rights. Wartime inflation, the relative prosperity owing to the economy, and additional federal dollars brought a budget increase from $31 million in 1943–1944 to more than $52 million by the end of Willis's administration. Leaders in neither party gave much support to a repeal of the income tax, and a huge budget surplus resulted. Who would spend it in the next administration, Democrats or Republicans?

In November 1945, Senator Chandler resigned his seat to become baseball commissioner. The race to fill the remainder of the term came down to Democrat John Y. Brown (again) versus a Republican newcomer, John Sherman Cooper. Born in Somerset and partly educated in Ivy League schools, Cooper had won election as county judge and, at first glance, seemed destined to go little higher. Not a good public speaker, habitually late, often forgetful, he seemed to do only one thing right on the campaign trail—win. Cooper, a liberal, could secure the vote of the conservative Republicans; he could appeal to factional Democrats, especially Chandler, who often supported him; and he could typically count on the endorsement of the now usually Democratic *Courier-Journal* with its urbane young editor, Barry Bingham Sr. Cooper's very weaknesses appeared to endear him to voters, and in 1946 he defeated Brown, 327,652 to 285,829. That victory seemed to bode well for Republicans in the governor's race the next year. But Chandler's absence lessened factionalism, and the generally united Democrats faced a Republican Party now itself infected with the virus of factionalism. As had occurred with Johnson four years earlier, Willis's own party candidate criticized his governorship. That stance won the primary in 1947 but doomed the Republican in the general election. Once more Democrats won.

By then a series of studies had emerged, focusing on what actions Kentucky should take in the new postwar world. They noted that the state had been through an agricultural depression in the 1920s, a massive drought in 1930, a nationwide general depression in the 1930s, a damaging flood in 1937, and a searing world war in 1941–1945. A whole generation had faced problem after problem. During that time parts of the face of Kentucky had changed through New Deal construction projects and through wartime building. In some ways even more important parts of the commonwealth's psyche had changed, as the long-standing localism and states' rights views had been severely tested by the effects of the Roosevelt revolution. Less clear, particularly given recent Republican success, was the change taking place in the electorate. Democrats had formed a new and stronger coalition that included labor, urbanites, and, increasingly, blacks. The effects of the depression under a Republican president plus a New Deal under a Democratic one severely damaged Kentucky Republicans, who had successfully competed for a quarter century. Only sporadically and slowly would the new Democratic dominance in state elections be threatened.

Yet for all the modifications taking place in Kentucky life, many of the old problems still remained, ranging from party divisiveness to a struggling economy, from sizable out-migrations to segregation and educational neglect. Kentucky had gone through a trying period, but in some ways the problems still to be faced would prove even more demanding and more difficult to solve.

18

Education and Equality, 1865–2015

When soldiers, black and white, and workers, men and women, returned from World War II, they found a chaotic educational system that stood near the bottom nationally in most categories. It featured bad facilities, underfunded districts, poorly paid teachers, racial segregation, and political meddling. It also included dedicated people and students who loved learning. Neither characterization represented recent, wartime developments, for behind each stood a long history.

Commentators on Kentucky had long recognized the importance of education to the commonwealth's development. A geologist-historian in 1884 concluded that "the educational problem is by far the most serious of all the difficulties before this state." More than six decades later a study said, "There is an amazingly high degree of correlation between what a state invests in education and the standard of living of its people." Some thirty years after that, a former governor declared that "you can't have a progressive state without an adequate educational system." Unfortunately, analysis and action did not always coincide.

Shaping the System, 1865–1908

In the first forty years after the Civil War, people who became teachers generally did so out of desperation or dedication. Young men seeking to rise up the economic ladder often started their professional careers as teachers, but they usually moved on. Young unmarried women in many locales had few other choices if they wanted an independent existence. In some of those same places, however, local custom dictated that if women married, they would leave schoolteaching behind. That outlook contin-

ued into the early part of the twentieth century. A few teachers, men and women, stayed in education because they had no further options. Others remained in the ranks because they enjoyed the work and could see that they made a difference in people's lives.

Dedication was often required, for teachers had to go through a great deal just to secure and keep their jobs. With no seniority or tenure system in existence until the mid-twentieth century, teachers as a rule found themselves underpaid, underprepared, and underappreciated. Yet some sought the job. The hiring process centered on the school district. Wherever up to one hundred school-age children lived, a district was formed. By 1907 Kentucky had some eighty-five hundred districts. Each served as a distinct and separate unit, with its own governing system, headed during most of the late nineteenth and early twentieth centuries by three elected trustees. This system meant that by 1907 nearly twenty-five thousand Kentuckians—almost one in ninety of the state's entire population—served as a school trustee. While such a scheme certainly ensured local control, three serious problems also arose. One was apathy. In some places no one sought the position of trustee, and those who did responded to the schools with the indifference they brought with them to office. That lack of interest contributed to the second problem, since a trustee's job requirements remained lax. By 1907 an estimated five thousand trustees—one-fifth of the total—could not read or write. Illiterates led some school systems. The third problem reversed the first; that is, sometimes there was too much trustee involvement.

Trustees had almost total local power because they set school taxes, hired teachers, and fixed salaries. As a result, local trustee elections often brought out more voters and inspired hotter debates than presidential contests. A dispute in one such 1933 race at Prather Creek in Floyd County ended in thirty gunshots and three wounded people, plus five dead ones. In many districts, teachers applying for positions had to pay trustees in order to be hired and had to pledge to support the trustees in political races. When the state instituted examinations for applicants for teaching positions, to restrict entrance of the uneducated into the system and to classify those in it, what were termed "unscrupulous" trustees skirted that process. They installed their favorites by selling exam questions to applicants or to "question peddlers," who did the selling for them. The local examination system continued until 1920. Even after an elective county superintendent's position was established in 1884, the trustee system continued, in one form or another, for another half century. But the trustees' local interjection of politics into education would live on, and in some places at least, the county superintendents later became virtual political bosses. They might supervise the biggest payroll in the county in small places, and through bus drivers, cooks, janitors, and teachers they could command a significant voting group. The ability to decide who received contracts to provide the necessities for the schools gave superintendents even more power. As a result, learning sometimes was not the chief goal of a county's educational system.

Once a teacher was hired, he or she—and in 1907, 58 percent of Kentucky educators were women—was assigned to a school. In most cases it was a one-room school, for even in 1920, half of all Kentucky children and three-fourths of all rural students went to one-teacher schools. As late as the 1940s, 65 percent of the commonwealth's nearly six thousand schools remained under the control of just one teacher.

In the late nineteenth and early twentieth centuries, the school day started at 8:00 or 8:30 a.m., featured a recess in the morning and another in the afternoon, included an hour for the consumption of a lunch brought from home, and ended at 4:00 p.m. Months of attendance varied, often depending on whether the school was in a rural area, where schools operated around farm needs, or in an urban setting. Legally the minimum term ran five months (increased to six in 1904 and to seven a decade later). By the 1910s pupils usually began in July and finished in January or went to school from September to March.

New teachers faced an assortment of students, for the one-room school included various grades and many ages. One Logan County teacher began work as soon as she finished high school and found that nine of her forty-nine students were older than she. Overall, the number of pupils per teacher varied a great deal, not only from one place to another but also during the year. Average attendance in 1882 stood at 33 percent of the eligible school-age population. According to the state superintendent of public instruction, this poor figure was due in large part to indifferent parents. Finally, in 1896 the state passed a weak compulsory education law, the first one in the South. Still, daily attendance in 1900 stood at only 36 percent. Even then, calls for farm labor in growing or harvesting seasons—the so-called "tobacco vacations"—further decimated the school ranks in rural areas.

In fact, significant differences existed between rural and urban education. One early study found that the average rural school term lasted only two-thirds as long as the city terms and that students in rural schools tested about two and a half years behind those in urban districts as a result. Schools in large cities also offered greater options. In 1891, for example, kindergarten became part of the public system in Lexington, apparently the first city in the South to make this opportunity available to young children.

While many of the differences between rural and urban schools resulted from local attitudes, more significant was money. Studies showed that the taxable wealth per teacher was twenty times higher in Louisville than in the poorest Appalachian county in 1921, and property assessments in the state's wealthiest areas stood over thirty times higher than those in the poorest areas in 1943. Thus, poverty-ridden places found it practically impossible to secure anywhere near the funds available to the richer places. In 1901 the state's fifteen largest cities raised $600,000 from local taxation, while all the rest of the state together produced only $250,000. Not all of the disparity resulted from inequalities in wealth, however, for rural districts had a well-deserved reputation of not supporting education through local taxes. An 1895 educator acknowledged that "local taxation by districts, subject to the will of the people, is a failure." Aside from the differences in wealth among districts, the greatest problem in Kentucky educational funding was (and would long remain) the apathy, indifference, or even opposition to local taxation to support adequate schools. As one historian argued, "Unable to see a larger world and a different future, public education and its costs did not seem necessary. The state . . . was not a land of great expectations."

In 1882 a superintendent lamented that "the people generally are opposed to voting a tax to pay the teachers better." It showed. Salaries in the 1880s ranged from $9.33 to $28.00 per month, and by 1900 the average across the state stood at $215.00 per year, about the wage of a general laborer. Author Elizabeth Madox Roberts taught in Washington County in 1907 for a total salary of $198.03. It was little wonder that one-sixth of the state's teachers left the profession each year.

Students entering the one-room schoolhouse to face their new teacher knew little about such issues. They did know, though, that the building itself did not promote learning. The worst type was described by Kentucky governor Preston Leslie in 1874:

A little square, squatty, unhewed log building, blazing in the sun, standing upon the dusty highway or some bleak and barren spot . . . without yard, fence, or other surroundings suggestive of comfort to abate its bare, cold, hard, and hateful look, is the fit representative of the district schoolhouse of the Commonwealth. . . . The benches—slabs with legs in them so long

as to lift the little fellows' feet from the floor. . . . The desks—slabs at angles, cut, hacked, scratched. Full of foul air and feculent odors. These are the places in which a cruel parsimony condemns childhood to pass its bright young days. . . . The schoolhouse . . . seems to have been built simply for a pen for prisoners, at the smallest possible outlay. . . . It stands [as] an offense to justice, kindness, taste. . . . It invites no one to its interior, and sends a shudder through the frame of the pupil, daily, who approaches it.

A Rockcastle County educator echoed that analysis in 1881, calling the log schools in his district "places of punishment rather than learning." The cruelest cut came in the superintendent of public instruction's 1905 report, which declared that "hundreds of farmers in Kentucky have more comfortable barns in which to shelter their stock than they have school-houses in which to train the minds and mould the characters of their children."

The log buildings declined rapidly, though, and of the 8,115 schools in 1917, only 123 were log; 87 percent were still one-room, though. Generally, those white frame buildings sat on stone pillars, with the wind whipping beneath the floors, and in the worst cases they featured a leaky roof, broken windows, and a dusty floor. More often they were tight little buildings with an insufficient potbellied stove but little else. Water would be hauled from a well or stream—sometimes far distant—and would be made available in a common drinking bucket, with a community dipper. Fortunate students had frame outdoor toilets; others went into the woods, or as one remembered, "the boys went up the creek . . . while the girls went down the creek."

Inside, teaching tools remained limited or nonexistent. An eighteen-year-old Jessamine County teacher in the early twentieth century received her year's supply from the superintendent: a box of chalk, some erasers, a coal bucket, a mop, and floor oil. A chalkboard or perhaps a globe might offer the only aid to students, who typically used either the

McGuffey books (whose author once taught in Kentucky) or publications from the Louisville firm of Morton and Griswold, featuring the Goodrich reader. One survey of nearly six hundred school libraries in Kentucky found that they each contained only forty-three books on average. Teachers had little support available.

Yet teachers persevered, endured, and, in some cases, succeeded. Despite all the problems—the poor physical facilities, the political overtones, the underpaid teachers, the unequal funding, the local apathy—learning still took place. In the mostly one-room schools, students often helped other students, and the good teachers did well and left a lasting impression on many of their pupils. Overall, the situation was in dire need of change if the state's educational promise was to be fulfilled. Nevertheless, some individuals overcame all the obstacles and educated generations of students.

Separate and Unequal

The effect of the Civil War on Kentucky's schools had been nearly disastrous. During the conflict, one state superintendent wrote that the lack of funds, the fighting, and the general disruption had "thrown backward" the system: "Entire counties have been utterly prevented from keeping up a single school." In 1862 only 159,000 students attended classes, compared with 286,000 two years earlier, in a more peaceful time.

Recovering from that situation was hard enough in the postwar world, but Kentucky also had new challenges to face. Thousands upon thousands of freed slaves now desperately sought education for their children, and emancipation alone would bring large numbers of new students into the system. But most whites did not support inclusion of blacks in the public schools because some wanted the former slaves educated only as workers, through a limited, second-class approach. In 1866 the state did pass a law that dealt with black education, but significantly it mandated an entirely separate system. For almost a century, then, Kentucky would fund a costly dual system, with two sets of schools, two sets of administrators, two sets of teachers and supplies. This system stretched the state's few resources thin.

The problem with the 1866 law was that only taxes collected from blacks could be used in the schools for black children; funds from whites would support white education only. Then two years later the general assembly further limited the "Colored School Fund" by ordering that any money from taxes collected from black residents would go to paupers first, before being spent on education. Given the fact that most African Americans came out of slavery without money or property, their property taxes yielded a very small total, only $2,232 as late as 1871. After funds from that source went to the poor, no money was left for education. Black public schools remained virtually nonexistent. The Freedmen's Bureau sought to fill the void, and by 1869, its 267 schools provided education to thirteen thousand blacks. Yet like most Freedmen's Bureau activities, the schools attracted strong—and violent—opposition. School after school was burned, and teacher after teacher was whipped or driven away. Yet for some three years soon after the close of the war, those schools and teachers gave black Kentuckians their chief opportunity for learning.

In an 1869 election, white voters agreed to raise school finances through a fourfold increase in taxes, and overall funds jumped in one year from $283,000 to $968,000. That same year, the Colored Education Convention met to lobby for further funds. Most black schools, however, continued to languish under the separate system, because of the small amount of taxable property owned by African Americans. Finally, in 1874 the federal government dangled the lure of $60,000 before the state if Kentucky would establish a uniform system of black schools. Superintendent of Public Instruction H. A. M. Henderson, a former Confederate general who opposed "mixing" whites with "ignorant Africans," could not resist the bait. The change took place, but the inequality of the segregated system still showed in 1880, when annual expenditures per student totaled $.48 for black students versus $1.45 for whites.

That disparity brought African Americans,

led by John H. Jackson, the first president of the Colored Teachers State Association, and by Mary E. Britton, to call for a law combining the two school funds, so that equal monies could be appropriated to the two separate systems. When the proposal failed to receive legislative support, the scene shifted to the federal courts. In April 1882, in the case of *Kentucky v. Jesse Ellis,* the existing state funding plan was ruled unconstitutional. Members of the general assembly responded with a plan to establish a combined funding system with the same per capita rate for black and white schools, to raise the tax rate, and to abolish the poll tax, paid only by blacks. Put before the voters in an August 1882 referendum, the plan was adopted by nearly a seventeen-thousand-vote margin. The plan applied only to state funding, though; local systems still discriminated. In August 1883 Judge John W. Barr, in the case of *Claybrook v. Owensboro*, ruled such discrimination "void," since it violated the Fourteenth Amendment to the US Constitution. The two systems could remain separate, but in regard to calendar, curriculum, and funding, they must—on the surface at least—be equal. The state's superintendent of public instruction, like his predecessor a former Confederate officer (although he was a chaplain), agreed that "all the pupil-children of the commonwealth should enjoy equal privilege for preparing for intelligent citizenship."

The dual system of segregated schools could not do that, though, for the separation in itself suggested inequality. Moreover, in practice, school buildings for black pupils generally did not match those for whites, and only the support from various outside funding agencies, such as the Rosenwald Fund, allowed the construction of some schools. African Americans also often received as their textbooks the worn-out leftovers from white classrooms.

Nonetheless, despite all the handicaps, black schools still remained a highly prized part of community life. The state's 714 black public high school students and 93 graduates in 1900 led the segregated South, for example, and in 1907 a higher percentage of black youths attended school daily than did whites. Since the teachers in the black schools had often found their choice of occupation limited by segregation, some of the best and the brightest went into education, a highly honored profession among African Americans. With fewer blacks than whites using teaching as a springboard to other jobs, more stability and a better-educated teaching corps characterized many schools. In 1921, for instance, only 23 percent of white teachers had had a year or more of college, but 46 percent of black educators did. Pay discrimination did exist—Fulton County in 1904 paid white teachers $43.50 per month and black teachers $25.71—but the overall picture was more mixed. Because of their higher educational levels and classifications, African American teachers in nineteen Kentucky counties earned a higher average salary than their white counterparts in 1904. In fifty-eight counties, though, the reverse held true. By 1916 the overall average salary for a white teacher stood at $322.76, for a black teacher at $310.05. While discrimination could in some cases be overcome, it remained an ever-present reminder to blacks of the badge of inferiority assigned them by white society.

One Kentucky school practiced a different philosophy, one that honored racial equality. Berea College had been founded by abolitionist John G. Fee and almost from its earliest times had offered equal access to education, regardless of gender or race. Black students outnumbered whites every year but one between 1866 and 1894, and individuals from both races held leadership positions in various campus organizations. For twenty years interracial dating was permitted. Such a policy of equality never found widespread acceptance among the state's whites, though, and the *Lexington Observer and Reporter* in 1870 called Berea "a miscegenation school," one "of the meanest Yankee type." But some five years later the president of Berea College told of the goals sought by the school: "The great work of Berea looks to a vast and fundamental change in the views, tastes, feelings, and customs of society. White and colored people must be perfectly equal before the law." For nearly four decades the school held firm to that commitment, although it emphasized education for Appalachian students more heavily near the end of that period.

As increasing segregation took place in Kentucky life in the late nineteenth and early twentieth centuries, however, Berea's policy of racial integration found more and more critics. Finally, in January 1904 legislator (and nephew of feud leader James Hargis) Carl Day of Frozen Creek in Breathitt County called for an end to the "contamination" of white students at the college and introduced a bill "to prohibit white and colored persons from attending the same school." Since privately funded Berea College was the only integrated college in the South, Day's target was clear and his aim good. Supported by the superintendent of public instruction and not opposed by Governor J. C. W. Beckham, the Day Law became reality. Berea's president, though more racially conservative than his predecessors, led an appeal through the courts. In 1906, however, the commonwealth's highest judicial body ruled the key parts of the law constitutional. Meanwhile, black graduates of Berea, led by minister James Bond, began a fundraising drive to establish a separate school should a final appeal fail. In 1912 Lincoln Institute opened its doors in Shelby County as a high school and teacher training school, but the orphan never realized its founders' hopes of becoming a new black Berea. The school gained status in the black community when its first black principal, Whitney M. Young Sr., took over in 1935, but by then other institutions had seized much of the leadership role in black education.

In November 1908, the US Supreme Court ruled in the case of *Berea College v. Kentucky.* Justice John Marshall Harlan, a Kentuckian, dissenting from the majority opinion, asked, "Have we become so inoculated with prejudice of race that [Kentucky] . . . can make distinctions between such citizens in the matter of . . . meeting for innocent purposes simply because of their respective races?" His fellow justices in essence answered yes, as they turned down Berea's appeal. The Day Law remained in force, and biracial education in Kentucky and the South legally ended for nearly a half century.

Whirlwinds and Doldrums, 1908–1954

Like sinners who knew the errors of their past ways and were ready to repent, Kentucky leaders by the early 1900s saw an educational revival sweeping the South and decided that they too wanted to join the crusade. Such an attitude had been so foreign previously that a superintendent of public instruction in the 1860s had complained about a legislature "almost uniformly unfriendly, indifferent, and evasive" to educational support. Historians in the 1880s proclaimed the typical legislator of their era "lamentably indifferent" to school improvements. The evil of the local trustee system, the parsimonious allocations, the expensive segregated system, and so much more cried out in support of such assertions. Yet even during those years Kentucky had stood reasonably well compared with other southern states. Now state after state began devoting more attention—and funds—to education. Virginia in 1905 and 1906 took major steps in that direction and in the succeeding decade saw school revenue triple and per capita expenditures double. Kentucky had to act or fall behind.

The 1906 Kentucky General Assembly first looked at the vexing issue of teacher training. It was then handled by summer county institutes lasting only a few days or by the normal (teacher training) departments of some private schools and the present-day University of Kentucky, which proved too far distant for many to attend. In response, the legislature created two regional normal schools, which became Eastern Kentucky University, at Richmond, and Western Kentucky University, at Bowling Green. (In 1922 two additional normal schools were authorized for Murray and Morehead.)

Major reforms earned the next Kentucky General Assembly, in 1908, the title of the Education Legislature. With the strong support of the Kentucky Federation of Women's Clubs and of Superintendent of Public Instruction John G. Crabbe of Ashland, a bill was passed that required public high schools to be established in each county and a minimum school tax to be enacted. It also abolished the small school districts and their trustees and made the county the fundamental unit. Subdistrict trustees remained, and members of the county boards of education were elected from those smaller areas, but a broader system still emerged. Higher education received more funding as well.

Unwilling to rest on their educational laurels, advocates of Kentucky's schools followed with what were called Whirlwind Campaigns. During a two-month period in late 1908, nearly three hundred talks were given to audiences totaling more than sixty thousand people; even more read the discourses in newspapers and pamphlets. The summer of 1909 saw more than a hundred speakers go forth on a second campaign in an effort to keep the reform spirit alive. Local funding increased fivefold in a year, and the 1910 census showed that over 57 percent of the school-age population attended school, nearly the national average and far above the 48 percent figure of 1900. Between 1911 and 1919 the number of high schools in the state increased from 157 to 400. The educational winds seemed to be blowing strong.

Illiteracy among adults still loomed as a significant problem, however. In 1900 the state's illiteracy rate had been 16.5 percent, which, though second best in the South, trailed the national figure of 10.7 percent. One in six Kentuckians over the age of ten could not read or write. A decade later more than two hundred thousand Kentuckians (12 percent of the adult population) remained illiterate. Of those Kentucky soldiers who went into the service, at least one-quarter could neither read nor write. Seeking to correct such situations, the charismatic and controversial Cora Wilson Stewart in 1911 organized classes to be held at night—thus their name, moonlight schools—and demonstrated that such methods could work in her native Rowan County and elsewhere. Three years later she received a legislative appropriation of five thousand dollars and set up the Kentucky Illiteracy Commission, which in its brief six-year existence did much good. Textbooks were published, literacy was made a condition of parole for prisoners, and many had the opportunity to learn to read. But Stewart's publicity efforts overstated her importance and

the results. By 1920 the state's literacy rate was over 8 percent. The decline since 1910 represented about the same drop as in the decade before the commission was formed. Continued effort was what was needed, though, and despite Stewart's continuing national efforts, the death of the state commission in 1920 hurt the commonwealth's efforts to combat illiteracy for generations.

Attacks on the state's educational problems came on several fronts. In addition to the focus on public school reform and the fights against illiteracy, some private citizens turned their attention to rural education in the isolated parts of the Kentucky mountains. Born out of the urban settlement schools of London, New York, and Chicago, the rural settlement school movement had several varied elements. While all the schools sought to change the population around them, most did so through an approach centering on industrial arts and vocational training, although a few, such as a school at Caney Creek, stressed a classical education. Many teachers came from New England or had been educated in the new women's colleges there, but others had their roots in Kentucky. All the teachers, however, approached their work as missionaries intent on doing good. While their fund-raising efforts required that they portray the area as a place of great needs, thus perpetuating stereotypes of the region, at the same time they did provide an education to children who had no other options.

In 1902, Katherine Pettit of Lexington and May Stone of Louisville founded Hindman Settlement School on Troublesome Creek in Knott County and thus started what has been called the first rural social settlement school in the nation. Eleven years later Pettit and Ethel de Long of New Jersey founded Pine Mountain Settlement School in Harlan County and started a similar program. In 1915, Alice Geddes Lloyd of Boston came to Knott County and set up her community center. With June Buchanan of New York, Lloyd established Caney Junior College (later Alice Lloyd College) in 1923, at Pippa Passes. The school required its students to conduct "no unauthorized meetings with the opposite sex" and to pledge to remain in Appalachia once their education was completed. The three schools joined with numerous others to give mountain youth a needed educational option into the 1940s, but most of the settlement schools would have to find alternative ways of operating once better transportation and public schools arrived.

The Education Legislature of 1908, the Whirlwind Campaigns, the Kentucky Illiteracy Commission, and the settlement schools all seemed to demonstrate that a true educational awakening was taking place in the Bluegrass State. The reform, however, was not as deep or as long-lasting as it appeared, for Kentuckians had not even kept up with the educational change taking place all around them. In 1900 Kentucky had stood fourth in the South in educational spending per student, and in the twenty years after that the state had increased expenditures per pupil by 238 percent. But the nation's and the South's figures had gone up even more in that period, and by 1920 the state ranked only eleventh in the South. Its per pupil spending, which had been only half the national average in 1900, had fallen to just one-third the norm by 1920. Kentuckians thought that they had accomplished a great deal in those decades, and they had, but it was not enough. The promise had not been realized, and not for many, many more decades would the will be present once again. Generations of Kentuckians were doomed to an educational system that soon stood near the bottom in most national categories.

The years between 1908–1909, when the Whirlwind Campaigns occurred, and the 1930s were not barren of action. In 1918 the legislature established a Division of Vocational Education. Two years later a law made the county school board popularly elected and gave the board the power to select a county superintendent and all employees. (Twelve years later, however, the county superintendent would again become an elected official.) The 1920 act also gave the state Department of Education responsibility for the teacher certification process, ending the problem-ridden teachers' examinations at the local level, and required a high school diploma for elementary teachers after 1936. By 1935 a bachelor's degree was required for high school teaching. The 1930s saw several major changes take place: in 1930 a stronger State Textbook Commission was formed; in 1934 a major new school code was funded, following the recommendations of a committee appointed by Governor Ruby Laffoon a year earlier; and in 1938 the first Teachers' Retirement Act was passed, with full financing to come much later.

Nevertheless, a series of studies, from the 1920s through the 1940s, showed that many of the actions taken had only a limited effect on a bad situation. Kentucky stood fortieth in the nation in expenditures per pupil in 1912, forty-fourth in 1920, and forty-first in 1930. A 1921 study noted that a third of rural teachers had only an elementary-level education. Twenty years later, in the year before Pearl Harbor, the commonwealth spent forty-eight dollars per student per year, while the US average was ninety-four dollars. The state's capital outlay for schools increased 214 percent between 1934 and 1952, but the South's shot up 667 percent during the same period.

The same trends existed concerning attendance and the length of the school term. By the 1920s, a third of rural schoolchildren had dropped out of school after the fifth grade. In 1943, Kentucky students spent sixteen fewer days in the classroom than the average American student, a statistic that ranked the state last nationally. For students ages ten to fourteen, the commonwealth in 1900 had ranked first in attendance in the South, both for white and black students; by 1940 it ranked last and next to last in the two categories. By 1940 some 95 percent of the children in the United States received an elementary school education, but only 63 percent of Kentucky children did. It was little wonder that by the end of World War II, the commonwealth ranked absolutely last in the nation in the percentage of the population over twenty-five who had a high school diploma. Five years later, the median education level in the state stood at 8.4 years. Given the dismal educational picture overall and the fact that only seven states in 1940 paid their teachers less than the $1,507 average salary that instructors in Kentucky received, one observer noted that Kentucky's greatest export was not bourbon or thoroughbreds but schoolteachers.

In 1954, however, one action gave some promise that the future might be better. The inequality between wealthy and poor districts had long plagued the system. In an attempt to change that situation, voters in 1941 approved a constitutional amendment that allowed 10 percent of school funds to be appropriated on some basis other than pupil population. A 1949 amendment increased this figure to 25 percent of funds. These actions gave poorer districts much-needed money. After the passage of another constitutional amendment four years later, the 1954 Kentucky General Assembly went one step further and established the Minimum Foundation Program, in an effort to provide greater balance in public school funding. There was thus some hope that the years ahead in Kentucky education would be brighter. That same year changes in the system of school segregation also heralded greater opportunities.

Before *Brown*

Change had been in the air for more than a decade before the critical year of 1954. The first major suggestion that the state's system might be modified came from outside education, when in 1938 the US Supreme Court in *Hale v. Kentucky* overturned a Paducah man's conviction because of "a systematic and arbitrary exclusion of Negroes from the jury list." For well over thirty years, no blacks had sat on a state jury deciding an interracial case. That practice, said the court, clearly violated the Fourteenth Amendment and must stop.

In education, some progress had occurred as well. In 1942 the city of Louisville equalized the salaries of black and white teachers, and that same year the two racially separate teachers' unions merged. A public study by one of the postwar planning groups, the Committee for Kentucky, obliquely suggested that the "waste and inefficiency" resulting from segregation should end. Problems still remained, however, as a 1940s survey of state educational facilities showed. It found that black school buildings had half the value of white ones; by

1954, in the western part of the state, only eighteen of forty-three school districts had a black high school, necessitating African Americans often going great distances to obtain education. The doctrine of "separate but equal" seldom addressed the second part as well as the first. More than that, the spiritual deprivation arising from segregation continued to be worse than any building inequities.

A new black leadership led by a Louisville cadre that included Charles W. Anderson Jr., the Reverend C. Ewbank Tucker, and *Louisville Defender* editor Frank Stanley Sr. began to probe for ways to desegregate the whole system. In 1941, black student Charles L. Eubanks applied for admission to the segregated engineering school at the University of Kentucky, on the grounds that no other such educational opportunity existed in the commonwealth. The school refused his application, and a legal challenge followed. After dragging on for years, the case was dismissed on technical grounds in 1945. That same year troops returning from World War II found that the black and white members of the armed forces, who had faced death together on foreign battlefields, could not be educated together in Kentucky's schools.

In 1948 the first legislative session during the administration of Governor Earle C. Clements made a dent in the formerly ironclad Day Law when it provided that black medical personnel could take postgraduate courses in white public hospitals. At the same time African American Lyman Johnson, a navy veteran and history teacher from Louisville, applied to take courses at the graduate school of the University of Kentucky. Once more the petition was denied, and attorneys began to prepare their cases. Hurried attempts were made to set up a makeshift program at the black college in Frankfort. That activity fooled no one, though, and in March 1949 Judge H. Church Ford of the US District Court ruled that Johnson was being denied equal access to education and must be admitted to the university. After a bitter meeting of the university's trustees, the school did not appeal. In the summer session of 1949 more than two dozen African American students joined Johnson on the campus. For the first time in forty-five years, integrated classes took place at a Kentucky school.

Such developments worried some citizens. A St. Matthews' woman asked the governor to strengthen the Day Law to prevent further black attendance at state schools. "I would hate to think that my sons would attend a school with a negro; eat in the same room; play on the same team and learn to accept them socially." Another Kentuckian asked a University of Kentucky dean, "Who gave you the right to compell our children to sin Against God, by compelling them to intermix with Negro's?" According to the courts, the US Constitution gave that right; according to other people of the commonwealth, simple justice did. In 1950 the Kentucky General Assembly further amended the Day Law to allow colleges to desegregate if they offered classes not available to blacks at segregated colleges. That year Berea College and several Catholic schools did just that. In fact, before 1954 nearly six hundred African Americans had enrolled at formerly white college campuses. Secondary and elementary education, however, still remained segregated.

Ironically, it appeared that the rapidly crumbling wall of constitutional segregation would be finally torn down at the national level by a Kentuckian. In 1946 President Harry Truman had named his close friend Frederick M. Vinson of Louisa as chief justice of the United States. The new appointee's already distinguished and varied career included stints as congressman, federal judge, wartime director of economic stabilization, and secretary of the Treasury. Known for his good memory, mathematical ability, poker and checker-playing prowess, political astuteness, and bushy eyebrows, Vinson was described in 1946 as a tall man with a mountain twang in his voice, a leader with "a sense of American continuity in time." Truman hoped that Vinson's fair, calm, sociable, and patient attitude could unite a divided court that included fellow Kentuckian Stanley Reed and, for a time, former Kentuckian Wiley Rutledge. The chief justice's attempts to compromise and forge a united court

Fred Vinson of Louisa was the first Kentuckian to be appointed Chief Justice of the United States. President Harry Truman sent Vinson to the Supreme Court in 1946. (Library of Congress Prints and Photographs Division)

often failed, however, and dissenting opinions continued to be commonplace. Still, his actions would set the stage for a predecessor who would be able to accomplish those goals.

Basically pragmatic, with a tendency to support the state over the individual, Vinson soon found his court confronting segregation and racial prejudice piece by piece. In *Sweatt v. Painter* (1950) Vinson spoke for a unanimous court in ordering a black student admitted to the previously all-white University of Texas Law School. The court also struck down aspects of segregation in *McLaurin v. Oklahoma State Regents* (1950) and *Henderson v. United States* (1950) and in so doing came very near to declaring that separate education could never be equal. By 1953 another key case drew near a decision, and it seemed only a matter of time before the Vinson Court would rule that the nation's system of segregated schools was unconstitutional and illegal. Whether its leader could get a unanimous decision or even induce Reed's support was uncertain, however.

On September 8, 1953, Chief Justice Vinson died at the age of sixty-three of a massive heart attack. The segregation case the US Supreme Court had been hearing would be decided by a group now headed by new Chief Justice Earl Warren. In a unanimous decision in 1954, it ruled segregation illegal, in *Brown v. Board of Education of Topeka, Kansas*. By declaring that "in the field of public education the doctrine of 'separate but equal' has no place," for such a policy is "inherently unequal," the US Supreme Court accelerated a long-developing civil rights movement.

What would be Kentucky's reaction to the decision? It quickly became clear that across the South massive resistance to integration was the common response. Such an attitude by Kentucky leaders would not be unpopular, for the commonwealth's racial mores differed chiefly only in degrees from those of the rest of the South. Yet at the same time, the state had been moving independently to dismantle the system of segregation bit by bit during the past few years. Acceptance of the decision or resistance to it both seemed possible.

Implementing Integration

Strong leadership came to the forefront and made Kentucky an early model of peaceful integration for the South and for the nation. That leadership came at three levels. The commonwealth's chief newspaper at the time, the *Courier-Journal* came out in favor of acceptance of the *Brown* decision and supported the actions of others who did so. In the political arena, both US senators spoke in favor of the decision, while Governor Lawrence W. Wetherby resisted southern efforts to oppose *Brown*. On March 1, 1955, the governor stated clearly that "Kentucky will meet the issue fairly and squarely for all." In the gubernatorial elections of 1955 and 1959, no candidate for either party took a prosegregation stance.

The victor in the 1955 race was Happy Chandler. His mailbag quickly filled with dire warnings of doom should integration occur. A Hopkinsville woman concluded, for example, that if such a step took place, "we might as well open the doors of Hell." From Lexington a woman warned that the races might next be swimming together in pools. A Madisonville paper criticized the court decision for breaking down "the character of the Anglo-Saxon race."

The governor's background provided clues that he could support either southern extremists or the US Supreme Court. As a US senator, Chandler had voted against anti-lynching and poll tax repeal bills. In 1948, he had headed the racially conservative Dixiecrat movement in the state, had entertained its candidate J. Strom Thurmond in his home, and had given little evidence that his racial views varied drastically from those of others of his generation. Yet at almost the same time, he had faced the question of integrating baseball in his position as commissioner of that sport. While Chandler would overstate his role later, it remains correct to say that had he opposed the move, integration of baseball would have been much more difficult. Instead, he supported the action.

The man who integrated baseball in the twentieth century was Jackie Robinson, who had had a less than ideal experience during his military service at Kentucky's Camp Breckinridge and who had been roundly booed when he appeared in a minor league game in 1946 in Louisville. Yet when Robinson entered the major leagues in 1947, his chief supporter and friend on his team, the Brooklyn Dodgers, was Louisville's Harold ("Pee Wee") Reese, later elected to baseball's Hall of Fame. In a sense, Robinson's varied experiences with Kentuckians represented the divisions existing within the society.

And the rules were different across the commonwealth. Mae Street Kidd grew up in Millersburg in Bourbon County and would later represent Louisville in the Kentucky General Assembly for some seventeen years. So light-skinned that, as she said, she had trouble "passing for black," she grew up in an integrated neighborhood and could try on clothes in Millersburg stores, in contrast to most African Americans in Kentucky. Her white father's family and his black family intermingled and attended funerals of family members together. But in most of the state that would not be the norm. Discrimination still dominated. What historian Gerald Smith has termed "the blurred lines of segregation in Kentucky" made it all even more complex.

But in 1956 Governor Chandler indicated publicly that the US Supreme Court's decision was the law of the land and he would enforce the law. Privately in letters he said he did not know whether he as an individual favored integration, but "I do not think it is Christian, and I know it is not lawful, to deny any of our fellow citizens equality of opportunity and protection under our laws." Already blacks were attending public institutions of higher education in Kentucky, and in 1955 the commonwealth's highest court finally ruled the Day Law unconstitutional. That summer a young black woman entered Lafayette High School in Lexington, and soon afterward several students integrated the Wayne County system during the regular school term. By fall, as historian William E. Ellis notes, 92 of the state's 160 districts had integrated peacefully.

A few resisted. On August 31, 1956, nine black children enrolled in the Union County school at Sturgis. Anger at the action resulted in the father of two of the children being fired from his job, the family's water being disconnected, and their being unable to buy goods in Sturgis stores. It took courage to challenge the status quo.

When classes began, a crowd of several hundred people opposed the attempt to integrate the school. While the situation seems to have been resolved locally, press reports spurred Governor Chandler to bring in police and troops, and that action intensified the dispute. On the night of September 6, a prosegregation white citizens' council held a meeting attended by a thousand people. Nevertheless, calm followed. Meanwhile, at the nearby town of Clay, similar events and reactions brought Kentucky National Guard forces there as well. The state's attorney general issued an interpretation of the *Brown* decision that allowed the local school

board to reject integration for the moment but to draw up a plan for it to take place in the near future. The some one thousand state troops and soldiers were withdrawn, a court case ordered full desegregation the next year, and in 1957 blacks and whites sat in the same classes at Sturgis High School. A boycott by some students ended quickly when they were given unexcused absences. In 1965 the once all-black high school closed, and integration was complete. Symbolically, however, the incidents at Sturgis and Clay showed Kentuckians that the state government would support the integration process, by force if necessary. No further incidents of that scope occurred, and school segregation began to end peacefully.

Leadership also came from school officials themselves. In Louisville, superintendent Dr. Omer Carmichael instituted a plan that rapidly integrated the city's major system and gave Louisville a national reputation as a model for the South. Under the plan, the entire system was redistricted without regard to race, and pupils were assigned to the nearest school. Voluntary transfers were allowed, however, which meant that in practice the plan was far less sweeping than it seemed on the surface. Future problems would result from that situation, but by the fall of 1956 fifty-five of the city's seventy-five schools, containing almost three quarters of the student population, had integrated without major opposition. A reporter for the *New York Times* watched classes open and announced: "Segregation died quietly here today."

In one sense, integration and the state's reaction to it showed how far Kentuckians had come in a little more than eight decades. During the immediate post–Civil War years, white people of the commonwealth had matched those elsewhere in resistance to black rights. Lynchings and segregation had continued well into the twentieth century. But in the 1950s white citizens were still far from racial egalitarians. That same year as the *Brown* decision, for example, activists Anne and Carl Braden purchased a home in a white neighborhood and then sold it to an African American couple in a deliberate attempt to integrate Louisville housing. The new owners, Charlotte and Andrew Wade, soon saw their windows broken, their loan and insurance revoked, shots fired into the house, and a cross burned nearby. Meanwhile, in the McCarthy era that saw a communist hysteria grip the nation, the Bradens were criticized for their actions on integration. Then on a Sunday morning, a bomb destroyed half of the Wade home. Soon after, in an attempt to silence them, Anne and Carl Braden were indicted for sedition and an attempt to disrupt race relations. Anne's brother severed all ties with her; Carl lost his job. He was found guilty and sentenced to fifteen years in prison. His conviction would be overturned by court rulings that invalidated the sedition laws. The Wades rebuilt their home and continued to live in it. But the episode showed that some citizens would not be deaf to racial appeals in later years. Nor was integration in the state quite so widespread as journalists pictured it. Yet the press, the politicians, and the school officials had set the standard and the examples at a crucial time. When confronted by racial questions in the 1950s, Kentucky reacted in a way that allowed it to be viewed as a leader in integration. A decade after the *Brown* decision, still only 62 percent of Kentucky's African Americans attended schools with whites, but that same year only 2 percent of those in the South did. It was a strange but welcome position for the state.

Civil Rights in the Sixties and Beyond

Kentuckians still had a long way to go on racial matters, however, and the state's leadership position would rise and fall over the next few decades. Education had been only the first fight on the integration front, and attention soon turned toward achieving equal rights in other areas.

In politics, African Americans in Kentucky had continued to vote, so the struggles taking place elsewhere in the South regarding voting rights were largely absent in the state. Gains did take place in other areas, however. In 1961 the first black woman, Amelia Tucker, was elected to the legislature; six years later Georgia Davis (later Georgia Davis Powers) be-

came the first black woman elected as state senator. In 1968 the city of Glasgow, where white voters outnumbered blacks by ten to one, made educator Luska J. Twyman Kentucky's first black mayor elected to a full term. Still, despite the individual gains, by 1970 African Americans comprised less than 1 percent of elected officials in the commonwealth.

Away from the political world, change was taking place in ways both small and large. In 1952, a federal judge had ruled that Louisville golf courses must be open to all. The next year, when the Mississippi Valley Historical Association held its national meeting in Lexington, one hotel in the city opened its doors to black guests for the first time. The next year the city directory there dropped the "c" (for "colored") designation after people's names. In 1955 the Kentucky Court of Appeals banned all segregated public recreational facilities in the state. Change occurred slowly and piecemeal, but it occurred.

The most significant victories, though, were won in the 1960s. At the beginning of that decade, stores, restaurants, theaters, pools, and other public places remained segregated in many areas of Kentucky. In Hopkinsville, for example, where 30 percent of the population was not white, housing, public toilets, theaters, restaurants, motels, and county fair competitions remained segregated. Two of the twelve councilmen and four of the thirty-five policemen were black, however, and the library, sporting events, and religious services had been integrated. Faced with such situations across Kentucky, blacks, and their white allies, began an eventually successful series of "sit-ins," "stand-ins," and boycotts of eating places and stores, particularly in Lexington, Frankfort, and Louisville. Perhaps the first sit-ins occurred in Louisville in 1942 at the Main Library, then in 1953 at a bus station, and then three years later at theaters, clothing stores, and lunch counters—well before the more publicized ones in North Carolina. In Lexington, the newly formed Congress of Racial Equality (CORE) held its first sit-in at a restaurant in 1959.

And when arrested, as some of the protest-

Martin Luther King Jr. (right center) led the 1964 March on Frankfort. (Calvert McCann Photographs, University of Kentucky Special Collections and Research Center, Lexington, KY)

ers were, they increasingly faced juries that included, at long last, members chosen from a more diverse pool. But change came slowly. A Mt. Sterling paper reported in 1964 how the circuit court jury had an African American juror for the first time ever and a woman for the only time in the last half century. Not until 2006 did an African American justice—William E. McAnulty—sit on the state's highest court.

In 1960, the Kentucky Commission on Human Rights was formed and began to issue reports on civil rights. It found in 1961 that state parks and bus terminals were open to all races, but that twenty-six of eighty-seven drive-in theaters surveyed were not. The next year it noted that six cities still had "whites only" pools but that thirty-five of forty Little League baseball programs had been integrated. In fact, sports became a key area for gains by blacks, and in 1967 University of Kentucky football player Nate Northington became the first African American athlete to play in the Southeastern Conference. Increasingly, whites who

had decried integration would find themselves cheering the sporting accomplishments of a black high school or college player on their favorite team.

Resistance to integration continued, though. When working as a janitor as a young man, Jesse Crenshaw confronted a white supervisor about the discrimination that still existed. The man told him some things could not change. Crenshaw, who became a lawyer and legislator, later noted, "At sixteen, I knew that was not true. I knew there were many things you could change." To him and others, it became clear that further action would be needed to bring about full change. At the national level, Kentuckian Whitney M. Young Jr. led the National Urban League through the decade and became a major spokesman for racial moderation: "We must learn to live together as brothers or we will all surely die together as fools." At the state level, Governor Bert T. Combs, in the last year of his term of office, issued a Fair Services Executive Order and a Code of Fair Practices, which affected those dealing in state

The fight being fought in 1964 for human rights and equality continues still. (Calvert McCann Photographs, University of Kentucky Special Collections and Research Center, Lexington, KY)

contracts. That same year, the city of Louisville passed a bill "to prohibit discrimination in public places"—probably the first in the South. The major achievements, however, came under governor Edward T. ("Ned") Breathitt Jr. Attempts to pass a statewide public accommodations bill in 1964 brought the Reverend Martin Luther King Jr., the Reverend Ralph Abernathy, and Jackie Robinson to a March rally attended by thousands at the state capitol. A sit-in and fast in the legislative gallery by supporters of civil rights followed. But neither the original Norbert Blume draft nor a compromise bill could secure the governor's strong support or enough votes to get out of committee before the session ended. Months later a national civil rights bill became law. The two US Kentucky senators and Representative Carl D. Perkins voted for it, and four other Kentucky congressmen opposed the bill. That national action, accomplished under a Democratic president, helped the situation in the state when a stronger anti-discrimination bill came before the Kentucky General Assembly in 1966.

This time the bill had the more forceful backing of Governor Breathitt. As a young attorney after World War II, Breathitt had found the double standard of justice for blacks and whites morally unacceptable. He stated that it "was against everything that I had been taught at the university and that I believed in." With the support of new legislative leaders, the resulting Kentucky Civil Rights Act passed easily and was signed into law at the base of the statue of Abraham Lincoln in the capitol rotunda. The first such act in the South, and broader than the national act, the law opened public accommodations to all races and prohibited discrimination in employment in firms with eight or more workers. That same year Bardstown took the lead in enacting a local open housing ordinance. In 1968 the commonwealth became the first state in the South to pass a comprehensive Fair Housing Act.

At that time Kentucky seemed to have avoided the racial tragedies that had ended in beatings and death elsewhere for those supporting civil rights. But the successes blinded too many to the still unsolved problems, issues smoldering beneath the surface tranquility. Following the murder of Dr. Martin Luther King Jr. in 1968, a May rally in the Parkland section of Louisville erupted in some minor disorders, the police moved in, and then, as one observer noted, "all hell broke loose." Before the rioting ended, many black businesses were destroyed, two black teenagers were killed, dozens of people, black and white, were injured, and nearly five hundred individuals were arrested. More than two thousand National Guard members joined city and county police in restoring order. Across Kentucky that summer several black churches and businesses were bombed, and a September exchange of shots between blacks and a white supremacy group meeting near Berea left two whites dead. The state had prided itself on its moderate stance on race, but the summer of 1968 left a scar, reminding Kentuckians that the fight for racial equality could not stop.

In the field of education, the promise of the 1950s seemed to be continuing. The number of schools with students of both races rose from 41 in 1955 to 685 a decade later, while the percentage of blacks in desegregated classrooms increased from 46 in 1962 to 68 in 1964. But by 1968—the year of the riot—the city once held up as a national model now saw headlines that read, "Schools Move Back Toward Segregation." Ten Louisville schools remained either all-black or all-white; in twenty-five others, over 95 percent of the students were of one race. The situation worsened between 1968 and 1974, as the growth of suburbs drew whites from the city. By then, the school system was more segregated than it had been two decades earlier. As a result, the federal judiciary became involved. A district court's decision favorable to the existing system was overturned at a higher level, which ordered the city and county school systems to merge "not only to eliminate the effects of the past but also to bar future discrimination." Court-ordered busing for racial balance brought forth a violent reaction by whites, especially in the southwestern parts of Jefferson County. Demonstrators damaged school buses, looted stores, and destroyed other property in September 1975 riots, which resulted in fifty people injured—including at least twenty law enforcement officers—and some two hundred arrests. State and local police, together with over eight hundred members of the National Guard, brought an uneasy peace.

Louisville's—and the state's—once-strong record on race appeared to be only a distant memory. Yet the integration taking place across the commonwealth was resulting in drastic change. In 1974 some 29 percent of Kentucky African Americans went to schools that were over 90 percent black; six years later none did.

National studies, based on 1986, 1991, and 2001 figures, proclaimed Kentucky schools the most integrated in the United States.

American Indians also found new opportunities to push for more equal treatment. Although Native peoples disappeared in the historic records of the nineteenth and twentieth centuries, often categorized as "colored" or "black" in legal and bureaucratic documents, they have always been in Kentucky, occasionally revealing their presence. In the 1930s, Cherokees established an "Indian village" outside Richmond as a tourist destination, taking advantage of Americans' fascination with the "Vanished Indian." In the 1980s, however, the American Indian Movement (AIM) became an important voice for the protection of native remains in Kentucky. For years, Native Americans had sought ways to protect the skeletal remains of their ancestors. Often, during construction projects, skeletons would be uncovered. If they were determined to be native remains, they were often sent to laboratories to be studied, instead of being reburied with dignity like the remains of black and white persons. In 1987, looters destroyed the Slack Farm burial mound near Uniontown, Kentucky. They tossed hundreds of native remains to the side as they stole the relics. The looters were arrested and charged with "desecrating a venerable object," but that was the only law that protected antiquities. The destruction and case made national news. Dennis Banks, former leader of the American Indian Movement, led the reburial ceremonies and a movement for Kentucky to pass strict legislation against grave desecrations. Protection of Native American graves became a national issue, and in 1990, the Native American Graves Protection and Repatriation Act (NAGPRA) became law.

Native Kentuckians began to make their presence known in Kentucky. In 1988, Cherokees who joined the labor force at the Toyota plant outside Georgetown created a culturally distinct community. In the mid-1990s, First Lady Judi Patton, whose family tree included Cherokee ancestors, worked to gain greater state recognition of Native American contributions and influence in Kentucky's history and culture. Her work resulted in the Kentucky Native American Heritage Commission in 1996. Other efforts, such as the Kentucky Native American Heritage Museum (1999), provided mobile outreach to schools, libraries, museums, festivals, and powwows in Kentucky. Today, dozens of powwows are held in Kentucky annually, including one in Hopkinsville that commemorates the Cherokees' Trail of Tears in 1838–1839.

Although civil rights movements shaped by race and gender achieved much success in the late twentieth century, the gay rights movement challenged other types of discrimination. Lesbian, gay, bisexual, and transgender (LGBT) peoples historically have migrated and congregated in cities for anonymity, collective security, and the creation of "families" where they can find emotional support and fellowship. In Kentucky, Louisville and Lexington have historically been the centers of LGBT life, with Covington (outside Cincinnati) also providing safe spaces. Not surprisingly, Lexington, Louisville, and Covington have ordinances banning workplace discrimination based on sexual orientation, but so too do Danville, Frankfort, Morehead, Midway, and Vicco—the smallest town in the nation with workplace protections for LGBT peoples. Lexington voters elected an openly gay state senator in 1996 and a mayor in 2010, with little fanfare.

In some regards, Kentucky has proven more willing than many other states to recognize and eliminate LGBT discrimination. In 1992, eleven years before the US Supreme Court struck down sodomy laws nationally, Kentucky's Supreme Court had declared the state's sodomy statute unconstitutional in *Kentucky v. Wasson*. Similarly, although Kentucky was not among the first states to end employment discrimination based on sexual orientation or gender identity, it is one of only a few southern states to have done so. Ending such discrimination happened through executive orders by governors Paul Patton in 2003 and Steve Beshear in 2008.

On other issues, however, Kentucky has proven less willing to extend equal rights to its LGBT citizens. In 1970, a Louisville lesbian couple tried to gain a marriage license, giving rise to *Jones v. Hallahan*, the nation's second court case to challenge state law against the marriage of same-sex couples. Although they lost the case, their effort empowered the Louisville Gay Liberation Front, an organization that had struggled to gain purpose. Despite LGBT activism over the next few decades, in 2004, voters adopted an amendment to the state constitution that denied same-sex marriage. Eleven years later, the US Supreme Court ruled all such laws as unconstitutional. Still, many Kentuckians disapproved of same-sex marriage on religious grounds. A Rowan County clerk, for example, made national headlines when she ignored the Supreme Court ruling and refused to issue a legal license to a gay couple. As with other equal rights initiatives, addressing LGBT rights creates tensions and animosities as societies work through the challenges of breaking down historical barriers and recognizing equal opportunities for and treatment of all citizens.

Kentucky Education Reform Act

The educational history of the commonwealth in the decades after the 1954 *Brown* decision was marked by historic peaks and valleys. For example, higher requirements for educators caused the percentage of teachers with college degrees to grow from 51 percent in 1950 to 94 percent fifteen years later. In the 1960s, the end of segregated systems and funds from the new sales tax provided state schools with an influx of money. State aid to education more than quadrupled in the decade after 1964, more than the national average in that expansive time. The commonwealth's expenditures on higher education rose nearly 400 percent from 1960 to 1968. In that same decade Kentucky Educational Television began its successful operation under the guidance of Leonard Press with programming such as "Comment on Kentucky," hosted for thirty-three years by Al Smith. In expenditures per pupil in average attendance, the state's figure increased from 65 percent of the national figure in 1963 to 79 percent in just six years.

Constant, consistent support did not

characterize later years, though, and educational valleys proved more prevalent. Various chief executives of the commonwealth might periodically infuse more budgeted funds, and the physical facilities might grow adequately, but more often whatever occurred simply kept Kentucky at its previous level. It really had no place to fall. Despite being number one in the nation in the percentage of salary increases for teachers in the 1960s, the state still ranked forty-second in teachers' pay in 1968, and fortieth a decade later.

By the 1980s, Kentucky ranked fiftieth in adults with a high school education, forty-ninth in college graduates, forty-second in expenditures per student, and forty-first in teacher-pupil ratio. The state cowered at or near the bottom in almost all educational categories. Because of the commonwealth's poorly educated workforce, one economist compared Kentucky to a Third World country. Given the increasing need for a better-educated population, state leaders feared for the future.

Governor Martha Layne Collins, a former schoolteacher herself, got some significant reforms passed in the 1985 and 1986 sessions. But an action was under way that would soon transform the entire system. In a court case led by former governor Bert Combs, some sixty-six underfunded school districts sued the state, and in 1988 circuit judge Ray Corns supported their position regarding the lack of equity in distribution of funds. Appealed to the state's highest court, the case of *Rose v. Council for Better Schools* (1989) brought an even more far-reaching decision by the Kentucky Supreme Court, led by Chief Justice Robert Stephens. The court ruled that "Kentucky's entire system of common schools is unconstitutional" and ordered the Kentucky General Assembly, in essence, to start over and "re-create" an efficient and fair system. Beginning with a clean slate, the legislature crafted an entirely new approach, financed by an increase in the sales tax. House Speaker Don Blandford, Senate president pro tempore John ("Eck") Rose, and budget leaders Joe Clarke and Mike Moloney joined in an uneasy and not altogether smooth partnership with Governor Wallace G. Wilkin-

son to enact what became known as the Kentucky Education Reform Act of 1990 (KERA).

KERA combined elements of strong local control with strong central powers. An anti-nepotism section and passages that restricted more blatant forms of local patronage could be enforced by the state Department of Education, which could (and did) take over some local systems that did not operate as required under the new guidelines. A statewide testing system was established to determine progress and accountability, with financial rewards accruing to districts that met established goals. Yet in other areas, more control flowed away from Frankfort to schools. Local councils of teachers, parents, and administrators had greater powers to determine curriculum and other such matters than before. The reforms stressed hands-on activities, individual progress, and an ungraded primary system with teams of teachers. Finally, KERA raised school district revenues by an average of 30 percent in four years, greatly increased teachers' salaries in the poorer school districts, and funded computer technology for each classroom and for the state. But much remained to be done for the state's over 1,200 public schools. KERA represented an almost unprecedented modification of an entire school system, however, and other states began looking to Kentucky as a model.

Not everyone agreed with the changes, and alterations soon followed. The key point, however, may not have been the form or the details of KERA, but rather its spirit. The act placed education in Kentucky at center stage and declared that the state considered learning crucial to the future. But the support and the spirit for continued educational progress remained sporadic over the next two and a half decades. Advances occurred—by the 2010s, the commonwealth had one of the best high school graduation rates in the nation. In 1995, Kentucky school spending per pupil had risen to thirty-second in the nation, but nearly two decades later, that ranking had declined slightly. For the some 44,000 teachers, their average salaries did rise to twenty-sixth nationally in 2015. A Harvard study also placed the state eighth in student improvement over the last two decades; in roughly that same period, the commonwealth's overall educational ranking went from forty-third to thirty-second. But also in 2013, Kentucky ranked first in the nation in the percentage of students in its schools who were homeless and in the bottom fifth of the states in high school graduates. And after ranking first in the nation in 1998 in eighth graders who had a computer in every classroom, the spending per student on technology fell from $112 that year to $8 four years later.

So, the questions remain for the future: Can the state produce both the leadership and the grassroots support to make education a priority? Will the determination be there to provide the needed resources? Will Kentucky understand that education is a priority and not an afterthought? Or will it, as in the early 1900s, again let the opportunities slip away?

Higher Education

Emerging from the Civil War, the state's system of higher education stood in disarray if not in shambles. What had once been the best of the prewar schools, Transylvania University, had barely survived, and other struggling institutions had seen enrollments drop drastically. Numerous institutions had the name "college" attached to them but offered no more than a secondary level of education. Most of such schools had a teacher or two, taught students of one sex, and struggled annually for existence. Private colleges generally started that way, or as a normal (teacher training) school, often connected to a particular religious group. They then usually transformed into colleges offering a two-year program, in the process changing locations at least once. Kentucky Wesleyan College, for example, opened in 1866 as a Methodist school at Millersburg, moved to Winchester in 1890, then to Owensboro sixty years later. What became Spalding University started as Nazareth College, for women, in 1920, changed its name in 1963, merged with Nazareth College in Nelson County in 1971, and became coeducational two years later. Alice Lloyd, Campbellsville, Cumberland, Lindsey Wilson, and Pikeville were all junior colleges

by the 1920s and began offering baccalaureate degrees between 1957 and 1986.

On the other hand, some institutions that had existed before the Civil War functioned fairly steadily as four-year colleges soon after the conflict ended. Georgetown College, which had closed for a few months at the beginning of the Civil War and had only 35 students in 1863, by 1870 numbered 145 in its preparatory and college departments. When the separate female seminary merged with the men's college in 1892, enrollment jumped to 397, and growth continued after that. Berea College, which had opened briefly as a secondary school before the Civil War, welcomed its first college-level students in 1869, but as late as 1890, of its total enrollment of 355, only 28 students were taking college courses. Under President William G. Frost, that number rose to 215 by 1920. Berea's emphasis on student work and tuition-free education gave it a special status as the decades passed. In Danville, Centre College became the strongest of the state's private colleges in the late nineteenth and early twentieth centuries. Although it had only seven graduates during the war year of 1863, the school grew to include a law department, then merged in 1901 with another Presbyterian institution, Central University in Richmond. Soon after the Centre College football team won what was called the greatest upset in that sport's first half century in a 1921 game with Harvard, the Danville school grew to enroll 315 students; by 1926 it became coeducational, although women students did not move onto the campus until the 1957–1981 presidency of Dr. Thomas A. Spragens, who also doubled the student body and greatly expanded the physical facilities and endowment. The school had developed a strong academic tradition as well.

Not all colleges succeeded, however, and the 1868 closing of Shelby College in Shelbyville marked an equally common trend. The names of Logan Female College in Russellville (founded in 1846, closed in 1931), Gethsemani College near Bardstown (1851–1912), and Eminence College in Eminence (1857–1895) stand as testimony that some tried and failed.

Table 18.1. Selected Private Four-Year Colleges and Seminaries, 2015

College	Location	Founded
Alice Lloyd College	Pippa Passes	1923
Asbury University	Wilmore	1890
Bellarmine University	Louisville	1950
Berea College	Berea	1869
Brescia University	Owensboro	1950 (1925)
Campbellsville University	Campbellsville	1924
Centre College	Danville	1819
Georgetown College	Georgetown	1829
Kentucky Christian University	Grayson	1919
Kentucky Wesleyan College	Owensboro	1866
Lindsey Wilson College	Columbia	1903 (1923)
Midway University	Midway	1847
Spalding University	Louisville	1920
Thomas More College	Fort Mitchell	1921
Transylvania University	Lexington	1780
Union College	Barbourville	1879
University of the Cumberlands	Williamsburg	1889 (1913)
University of Pikeville	Pikeville	1889 (1918)
Major Seminaries	**Location**	**Founded**
Asbury Theological Seminary	Wilmore	1923
Louisville Presbyterian Seminary	Louisville	1901
Southern Baptist Theological Seminary	Louisville	1859

Notes: Brescia, so named in 1950, was preceded by Mount S. Joseph College, established in 1925. Founded in 1903, the Lindsey Wilson Training School expanded its curriculum and became Lindsey Wilson College in 1923. Founded in 1889, Williamsburg Institute was renamed Cumberland College in 1913. Established as an elementary and secondary school in 1889, Pikeville College began offering college courses in 1918.
Source: John E. Kleber, editor in chief, *The Kentucky Encyclopedia* (1992).

Even then, they failed in only one sense, for the schools had educated generations of students.

Most of the nineteenth-century discussion of higher education in the commonwealth, however, focused on the state's role in what was occurring in Lexington. After the main building of Kentucky University in Harrodsburg (formerly Bacon College) burned in 1864, the energetic John B. Bowman engineered a move that he hoped would result in a great "university for the people." In 1865 the legislature agreed that Transylvania University would merge with and take the name of Kentucky University. At the same time, the commonwealth established the Agricultural and Mechanical (A&M) College, to be financed through the proceeds of the sale of some public land, under the national Morrill Land Grant Act. A&M would be an independent college but, together with a law department and a College of the Bible, would be part of the new Kentucky University. Funded by public and private funds and operated by both church and state, the hybrid school had problems from the start. Financial concerns growing out of the Panic of 1873 and debate over denominational control added to the difficulties. Finally, in 1878 the A&M College had only sixty students on its campus on Henry Clay's old estate of Ashland, and the general assembly separated it totally from Kentucky University. That private school retook the name Transylvania College some three decades later, and its law school closed, reopened, then closed for good in 1912. After struggles and successes common to most private colleges in Kentucky, Transylvania University emerged as a small and strong liberal arts college with a good academic reputation.

Meanwhile, across town, the A&M College, under its "insightful as well as spiteful" president James K. Patterson, was trying to find success in its role as the commonwealth's chief public institution of higher learning. Leaving its old Ashland campus, the school started life anew on some city parkland. Additional acres were added for a developing agricultural experiment station, started in 1885. The state established a property tax to give the institution a financial base, required the college to offer free tuition to two students from each county, and created a teacher training department (which admitted the first women students on campus in 1880). In 1908 the school's name was changed to State University, and a college of law was authorized; eight years later it became the University of Kentucky.

In higher education, however, as at other levels, a dual system existed. With the exception of Berea College until 1904, blacks found their options restricted to segregated colleges. In medical education, for instance, Louisville National Medical College, under the leadership of Dr. Henry Fitzbutler, opened in the fall of 1888. The next year it conferred the first MD degree to a black person in the state's history and in 1891 graduated the first woman doctor educated in the state, of any race. But the first institution of comprehensive higher learning for blacks, and for many decades the strongest, was the Kentucky Normal and Theological Institute, established in Louisville in 1879. Five years later the name was changed to State Colored Baptist University, and under the presidency of former slave and Civil War veteran William J. Simmons, it grew to include law and medical schools. After President Simmons left to found Eckstein Norton Institute at Cane Springs in Bullitt County, Charles H. Parrish Sr. succeeded him. The institution's name was eventually changed to Simmons University, and it gave African Americans their best col-

lege instruction in the state. By 1930, however, problems with debt caused the University of Louisville to purchase Simmons's property. The school was renamed Louisville Municipal College and opened in 1931 as a physically separated and segregated branch of the then-private University of Louisville. Twenty years later, as the walls of integration were falling, the institution's students, and one of its faculty members, merged into the University of Louisville system. Louisville Municipal College was no more.

Within a decade after emancipation, blacks in Kentucky had called out for a state-supported school for their race, since they could not, by law, attend A&M College (later the University of Kentucky). Accordingly, in 1886 the general assembly established in Frankfort what was then called the State Normal School for Colored Persons, later known as Kentucky State University. Underfunded, used for political patronage by whites to reward black supporters, and devoted to a philosophy of industrial education as advocated by Booker T. Washington, the institution grew slowly, functioning chiefly as a teacher training school with only elementary and secondary level classes. A 1917 national study criticized its factional leadership, "unsatisfactory" discipline, lax accounting methods, and unhappy students. Finally, under the thirty-three-year presidency of Rufus B. Atwood, the school became a strong four-year college, moving away from the emphasis on industrial education. Enrollment increased from 200 in 1929 to 590 eight years later, and a strong faculty was recruited. Like many conservative black college presidents whose appropriations depended on white votes in the state legislature, Atwood had to walk a fine line. He had to be the spokesman for blacks in Kentucky, yet he could not alienate white allies or his funding would be cut and black education would suffer, and he could even be out of a job. He had to push for integration as a leader of African Americans, but achieving that goal would diminish his school's role in the black community. It was a dilemma he and others could never fully solve.

The state supported one other black college during the early twentieth century, for in 1918 David H. Anderson's industrial school in Paducah received legislative funding. As West Kentucky Industrial College, it fought to rival Kentucky State but never did. With Atwood's urging, the general assembly ceased state funding for the Paducah school in 1938 and merged its collegiate functions with the Frankfort college. By that time Kentucky blacks had two basic higher education choices—Kentucky State or Louisville Municipal College.

By contrast, white students were seeing a proliferation of state-supported schools in the twentieth century. Teacher training schools established at Richmond and Bowling Green in 1906 and at Morehead and Murray in 1922 began to grow, and their exact roles in the overall system would be long debated. Over time they evolved into multifaceted universities. At what sometimes would be proclaimed the state's flagship university, the University of Kentucky, appropriations—and perhaps will—kept it from attaining status for a long time as anything other than just another school for Kentuckians. Its president noted in 1904 that the commonwealth gave the school some $36,000 to operate, while Wisconsin supported its state university with $471,000, and other places did even more. By World War I the school had only fifty-four out-of-state students. New president Frank L. McVey served from 1917 to 1940 and built a stronger academic base, so the goal of developing a strong, major university had come nearer. The growth of the school's athletic programs created controversy but also aided its visibility in the 1940s and 1950s. In 1956 the state's second medical school was authorized for the University of Kentucky's campus, and in 1962 the legislature approved a community college system of two-year colleges, to be administered by the university. Often set up in locations chosen as political rewards, the community colleges proliferated to fourteen by 1995 and educated a quarter of the state's college students. The 1997 fight over governance of the community colleges under the Patton administration resulted in their independence from the UK system and merger with the technical schools. As the Kentucky Communi-

ty and Technical College System (KCTCS), it currently covers sixteen schools and seventy campuses, with over one hundred thousand students in 2010. About two-fifths of those students attending public higher education in the state attend a KCTCS school.

Other actions, though, increasingly confused the picture of how the state-funded system of higher education should operate and spread the available resources even thinner. The Council on Postsecondary Education helped planning somewhat, but its lack of strong central authority restricted its power. The four regional colleges developed strong political constituencies and grew rapidly (see table 18.2), particularly when soldiers returned home after World War II and in the general growth associated with the "baby boomers" of the 1960s. Then in 1968 the state created what became Northern Kentucky University, merged a community college into the newly built campus at Highland Heights, and later agreed to support an Ohio law school that affiliated with the university. At about the same time, in 1970, the previously private and municipally funded University of Louisville, with its medical and law schools, entered the state system as well. Located in large metropolitan areas, both of the new state schools expanded their student populations and physical plants very quickly. That came at a cost to other schools in the syatem. State appropriations to the University of Kentucky, for example, fell from 54 percent of its total funding in 1970 to 41 percent in 1979 to some 20 percent by 2010. In the dozen years after 2002, state funding for all universities as a percentage of total postsecondary education went from 30 percent to 14 percent. The result was a kind of hidden tax increase in the form of higher and higher tuition. All that fought the ideal of affordable higher education for Kentucky's children and made the long-existing rivalry for the commonwealth's increasingly scant educational money grow even stronger. Matters such as "mission creep" and legislative protectionism caused one educational leader to cry out that many simply were "playing at reform."

Yet for all the changes, many elements of

Table 18.2. Enrollment at State-Supported Colleges and Universities, 1930–2015

Institution	1930	1950	1970	1990	2015
Eastern Kentucky Univ.	1,179	1,861	8,872	15,371	16,844
Kentucky State Univ.	138	716	1,279	2,512	1,586
Morehead State Univ.	846	824	5,315	8,622	10,875
Murray State Univ.	902	1,665	6,320	8,097	10,988
Northern Kentucky Univ.	—	—	1,328	11,260	14,720
Univ. of Kentucky	3,245	8,476	16,251	23,081	30,720
Univ. of Louisville	—	—	7,193	23,610	22,367
Western Kentucky Univ.	2,739	1,833	9,760	15,240	20,068
Community College System	—	—	5,835	40,758	80,071

Source: Kentucky Legislative Research Commission, *Report*, no. 14, n.s., 66; *Kentucky College and University Enrollments, 1970* (1970); *Kentucky College and University Enrollments, Fall 1990* (1991), 6–7; Kentucky Post-secondary Education Data System, 2016. Note that the merger with the technical college system affected the community college totals. Dashes indicate entities not in existence or not part of the state system at the time.

the universities varied only in degree. At the leadership level, boards and governing bodies, or even governors, often forced furious fights with college presidents. Politics brought about the removal of several Kentucky State University presidents early in the century, while the actions of the state's chief executives in the 1940s caused Morehead State University to lose its accreditation briefly. In the midst of the student unrest in the late 1960s, Governor Louie B. Nunn complained about the "filth and smut" coming from the University of Kentucky, while his ally on the university's board, former governor Happy Chandler, wrote of the Communist infiltrations of the school. Such hostile attitudes hastened the resignation of the university president. In 1970 the burning of a building on campus during another protest brought Nunn to call out the National Guard and impose a curfew. Overall, however, student protests in the state remained generally peaceful. Other governors, in the 1980s and 2010s, removed all members of the Murray State University and University of Louisville Board of Regents, so they could control controversies involving the schools' presidents. In the 1980s, a different state chief executive took actions that hastened the departure of another University of Kentucky president.

More changes took place in student life. Immediately after the Civil War, colleges and universities operated under strict rules. At Ken-

tucky University (Transylvania), for example, students were required to attend chapel daily and on Sunday, and they had to abstain from drinking, smoking, profanity, card playing, or criticizing the university. These rules were apparently broken with abandon. Moreover, scholars were forbidden from attending "exhibitions of immoral tendency; no race-field, theatre, circus, billiard-saloon, bar room or tippling house," although they went anyway. By 1922 the student paper criticized first-year students for not wearing their mandatory caps and, when they did wear them, for not tipping them to professors. Four decades later, the turbulent 1960s brought an end to most such rules, including semiformal dress for candle-light suppers each evening.

Schools across the commonwealth went through similar transitions. Before fraternities and sororities became more prevalent in the first decades of the twentieth century, literary societies added to the cultural life of both colleges and communities. Oratorical contests and theatrical groups attracted as much public interest as sports would later do. Rules changed too. In the late nineteenth century, the A&M College (University of Kentucky) operated much like a military school, with some two hundred published rules and a 5:30 a.m. wake up, daily room inspection, compulsory chapel, afternoon military drill, and a scheduled seven hours of required study each day before the

An early dormitory room at the University of Kentucky. (Glass Plate Negative Collection, University of Kentucky Special Collections and Research Center, Lexington, KY)

sound of taps at 10:00 p.m. As late as the 1960s, women students had to be in their dormitories by a specified time or face sanctions. At nearby Georgetown College in the 1890s, students had to attend chapel every school day, had to be in their rooms by 7:00 p.m., and had to refrain from attending "any exhibitions of an immoral tendency" or frequenting "any barroom or tippling house." In 1968 a decision by the governing board to allow student dancing on campus—which had been banned until then—brought much criticism from the Kentucky Baptist Convention, which voted that it "strongly opposed" the action. Meanwhile, Berea College prohibited radios for students into the 1930s. Alice Lloyd Junior College had always prohibited contact—in conversation or in classrooms—between the sexes and required uniforms for women and coats and ties for men, but in the 1960s those rules were relaxed as well.

Throughout the decades, however, much remained the same in students' lives. Across the years, they complained about tuition and difficult professors, rebelled against certain rules, and wrote letters home asking parents for more money. Student pranks seemed ever present: in the nineteenth century a University of Kentucky president once found a horse in a second-

floor chapel room, and in the next century April Fool editions of campus newspapers proliferated. College authorities continued to deal with student transgressions, whether panty raids of one era, or nude streaking of another, or demonstrations in several. Some students attended college during periods of activism regarding social issues, while others did so in times of apathy. No matter what the time frame, students at campuses across the state most of all learned, thought, dated, and graduated.

For all the problems education in Kentucky faced at all levels, success stories numbered thousands upon thousands. Billy Duvall grew up poor and had to drop out of school to help earn money for his family. Virtually illiterate for most of his life, and facing racial prejudice as well, he only much later learned to read and write. But his son went to college and then graduate school. In the same era, William N. Lipscomb Jr. received his elementary, secondary, and undergraduate college education in the state; in 1976 he won the Nobel Prize in chemistry. The illiterate man who raised a college graduate and the Nobel laureate both demonstrated that Kentucky education, with all its weaknesses and variety, still had many successes in virtually every classroom, every year.

19

A Half Century of Kentucky Politics, 1945–1995

In 1947 Republican governor Simeon Willis turned the reins of office over to his Democratic successor. That event would mark the beginning of twenty uninterrupted years of governorship by Democrats, coupled with similar control of the state legislature. But that all masked the fact that, as a journalist wrote, "Kentucky was more a three-faction than a two-party state." Or as political activist Ed Prichard also noted, "Happy Chandler is the leader of the Republican wing of the Democratic party." Those divisions meant that in the presidential and US senatorial contests, however, the Republicans won the important races in the state more often than did their opposition. By the time Republicans took the governorship again in 1967, when Louie B. Nunn began his term, it seemed that a new majority party might be forming in Kentucky. That was not to be, though, and after Nunn left office in 1971, Democrats again ruled supreme at the state level for the next two and a half decades, while dividing national presidential and senatorial races with Republicans. Only in the last decade of the century did the state's longtime minority party begin to make serious inroads into the electoral process, ones that eventually made it the de facto majority. That change came amid several other significant shifts in party politics.

Democratic Ascendancy

Taking the oath of office as governor in 1947 was a man who would quickly become the state's most powerful politician over the next decade and a half and who would form and lead one of the state Democratic Party's two factions. Earle C. Clements had made his way

up through the ranks from his west Kentucky, Union County base, serving as sheriff, county clerk, county judge, state senate majority leader, and two-term congressman. Allied to the Thomas Rhea faction and to Alben Barkley, Clements almost naturally became a Chandler foe. He soon led those opposed to Happy. Such a split, though, might have occurred no matter what, for Clements sought power in his own right and usually found it.

Governor Clements would be most often described as a consummate politician, in the positive sense of that term. Not a particularly good speaker, not a man the press trusted, not a person who could hide a strong temper, he won few of his victories in open forums. To him politics was a game, a serious one, and the former football player and coach played it outside the glare of public lights. Intelligent, detail-oriented, methodical, secretive, sometimes cold and tough, "Cautious Clements" could also be personable one-on-one, and he skillfully formed behind-the-scenes alliances to achieve his goals. Once he decided on a course of action, his word and his commitment were good. More than anything, he simply had the best organizational skills of anyone of his generation in Kentucky politics.

Clements's 1947 victory also symbolized the ascendancy of western Kentucky in the Democratic Party. Barkley was already powerful, and four of the first seven post–World War II Democratic governors would emerge from the western part of the state. Moreover, with Chandler strong in the central Bluegrass but an anathema in Louisville, Clements quickly formed a powerful alliance with the "Fourth Street" political leaders in the Falls City. The well-organized Clements faction sought to counter the personality-oriented Chandler faction in the fight for dominance in the state.

As governor, Clements did not offer the Kentucky General Assembly a gentle hand. The unfriendly *Kentucky Times-Star* of Covington referred to "the Clements steamroller" in the 1948 session, while the not overly supportive *Courier-Journal* called the 1950 gathering "the most ruthlessly operated in anybody's memory." With a three-to-one Democratic margin in both houses, the governor saw his major programs all passed in the first session, and overall, he got a great deal accomplished. Without much fanfare, the legislature lowered racial barriers by twice amending the Day Law. It increased the gas tax to help fund rural roads, raised the distilled spirits tax, and instituted the first tax on pari-mutuel betting, then used those new funds to raise teachers' salaries and lower the inheritance tax. Clements also created a state police force to supersede the sometimes inefficient and partisan highway patrol, and he funded what became the Legislative Research Commission. He stressed economic development and the state parks as well.

Clements also took a keen interest in the 1948 presidential and senatorial races, for Republican John Sherman Cooper held a Senate seat, and Republicans fully expected to capitalize on problems of housing, prices, strikes, and more to win the presidency from Harry Truman. The nomination of Alben Barkley as Truman's vice-presidential choice made the Democratic task in Kentucky easier, for the Iron Man remained immensely popular. Kentucky delegates to the party's convention, however, opposed Truman's civil rights policy, and some southern politicos had expressed their own disapproval by forming the States' Rights Party, or Dixiecrats, led by J. Strom Thurmond of South Carolina. In the end, though, Kentucky Democrats remained loyal to their favorite son. The Truman-Barkley ticket won a massive victory in the state, with 466,756 votes to Thomas Dewey's 341,210; the Dixiecrats, who carried four southern states, took only 1.3 percent of the ballots in the commonwealth. President Truman's razor-close national victory ensured a continued Democratic presence, and Kentucky

influence, in Washington. In January 1949, Chief Justice Fred Vinson of Kentucky swore in Truman—whose grandparents had come from Kentucky—as president, while Associate Justice Stanley Reed of Kentucky administered the oath of office to "the veep," Barkley.

The year 1949 also marked the beginning of a series of complex actions regarding Kentucky's two Senate seats. Between January 1949 and January 1955 eight men served as senator. For one seat, the longtime Democratic congressman Virgil M. Chapman of Bourbon County, "Mr. Tobacco," challenged incumbent Republican Cooper in 1948. Not sympathetic to civil rights or labor unions and rumored to have a drinking problem, Chapman would not normally have seemed a serious challenger. In fact, Cooper did receive 100,000 more votes than his party's presidential candidate that year. Barkley's presence on the ticket, though, brought out a huge Democratic majority, and Chapman rode those coattails to defeat Cooper by almost 125,000 votes. Ironically, Senator Chapman would die in an automobile accident in March 1951, and Cooper would win the election to fill the rest of the term.

The other Senate seat had been Barkley's, but when he left it in 1949 for the vice presidency, Clements appointed an ally to serve for a year and a half, then ran for the full term himself in 1950. Easily defeating the very conservative Republican and earlier gubernatorial candidate Charles I. Dawson, Clements resigned as governor and took his seat in the US Senate. Within a very short time the newcomer gained the attention of Senator Lyndon B. Johnson, became his close confidant, and was selected assistant floor leader. To add to the Democratic success, after the end of Alben Barkley's vice-presidential term in 1953, the seventy-six-year-old and sight-impaired Barkley challenged Senator Cooper in 1954 for that seat. Indirectly, Barkley had cost Cooper the 1948 race by his presence on the national ticket; now he directly caused his defeat by more than 70,000 votes. In January 1955 Kentucky had two major Democratic leaders in the Senate.

Clements's resignation as governor, effective in November 1950, meant that his lieutenant governor was now chief executive, a year before the general election. New governor Lawrence W. Wetherby had been a fairly minor juvenile court trial commissioner before his selection, but Clements had wanted a Louisville–Jefferson County person, and Wetherby had been chosen. Although he would stress that he came from Middletown rather than nearby Louisville, Wetherby was only the second person from the state's most populous county to serve as governor in the twentieth century.

A gregarious person and an avid sportsman, Wetherby had to overcome a popular press presentation of him as a less-than-serious chief executive. (One photograph shows him driving a sulky pulled by an ostrich.) In truth, he had a good administration, with a good record. He did have the disadvantage of serving as governor during the unpopular Korean War (1950–1953).

Forrest Pogue of Crittenden County had been the first historian of D-Day and had presciently written from Europe in 1944, "Too many people expect the war to settle everything. . . . The winning of a war . . . does not mean that we have peace automatically." Now, only six years later, over 88,000 Kentuckians once more would go off to fight in a foreign land. Of those, over a thousand never returned from combat. Wars of various sizes and forms would continue to be a part of Kentucky life.

Wetherby, like others of his era, also had to operate under the considerable political shadow of his mentor, Clements. Wetherby, however, achieved on his own. Facing a 1951 election for a full term, he called a special session in March of that year and used a fiscal surplus to provide more funds to teachers (who represented a substantial voting bloc). In the election itself, Wetherby faced an old guard Republican judge, Eugene Siler of Williamsburg. Stressing his fundamentalist, anti-Catholic, and anti-liquor views, Siler made inroads in rural areas but virtually forfeited the growing urban vote. Wetherby won, 346,345–288,014.

The genial governor worked well with his general assembly. In education, a Minimum Foundation Program began, the school term was lengthened, and teacher tenure was strengthened. The legislature also took Kentucky State College out from under the control of the all-white State Board of Education and allowed it to set up its own board, giving the school at last the same system of governance as all the other state institutions of higher learning. While Wetherby in 1951 had ordered each state tuberculosis sanatorium to be open to all, the next year, the general assembly integrated all state-licensed hospitals. Wetherby also spoke out forthrightly for the US Supreme Court's decision in *Brown v. Board of Education*.

The Kentucky Highway Authority, with the power to issue bonds to raise revenue for construction, began the first of what would be a series of toll turnpikes constructed over the next decades (ones usually connected to a sitting governor's home region). The Wetherby legislatures also created the Kentucky Department of Mental Health and the Kentucky Youth Authority, issued initial but weak strip mining regulations, increased the so-called sin taxes, and passed a state constitutional amendment that gave eighteen-year-olds the vote (approved by the state's voters in 1955). As the Wetherby administration ended in 1955, then, the Clements faction could point to two constructive gubernatorial terms. No Democratic faction in the century, though, had elected three straight candidates. Everyone knew that the factional opposition in the 1955 governor's race would be formidable indeed.

Happy Days Again?

Happy was back. Denied a second term as baseball commissioner by unhappy major league owners, A. B. Chandler had returned to his Versailles law practice in the summer of 1951. He had been too late to influence the governor's race that year but had used the four years since to rebuild his political base and to renew old contacts. Now he sought a second gubernatorial term in 1955.

The selection of a candidate to oppose Chandler in the Democratic primary presented a problem for the Clements-Wetherby forces. Kingmakers such as William H. May of Brighton Engineering recognized that their most politically astute and available candidate was the colorful Lieutenant Governor Emerson ("Doc") Beauchamp, but his unimposing appearance, gravelly voice, and connections to boss-dominated Logan County all were deemed liabilities. To the surprise of almost everyone, Earle Clements virtually handpicked a long-shot candidate, Bert T. Combs. An eastern Kentuckian who spoke with a mountain twang, Combs sat as judge on the state's highest court, but that experience was virtually the extent of his political background. Untested and relatively unknown, he did have a reputation for integrity and intelligence. But would that be enough against the veteran campaigner Chandler?

Since Combs really had no record for Happy to attack, Chandler focused his attention instead on the factional leaders and went for their political jugular. Referring to "Clementine and Wetherbine," he cried out that "Old Earle" called up "that little Hitler" Wetherby and told him exactly what to do. Not only that, roared Chandler, but Wetherby had frivolously spent the state's funds to air-condition the capitol: "We could raise the windows; there are shade trees around." The governor, said Happy, had also wasted the people's money by buying a new twenty-thousand-dollar rug. An invoice showing that the cost was twenty-seven hundred dollars did not slow the salvos. Then Happy turned to the new toll road from Louisville to Elizabethtown: "It doesn't start anywhere, it doesn't go anywhere," it should never have been built. Likewise, he said, the new state fairgrounds and Freedom Hall, both in his favorite target of Louisville, should not have been constructed either. As soon as Clements, Wetherby, or Combs started to defend against one attack, Chandler would shift to another, all presented in his entertaining style. A British observer called him "a rare natural spokesman. . . . His sentences were short and they balanced like a chant." His loudspeakers blared out: "Be like your pappy and vote for Happy."

Judge Combs helped Chandler, for in his low-key campaign-opening address, he honestly admitted that a sales tax might be needed to solve the state's fiscal concerns. With Chan-

dler's anti-tax reputation, such a stance represented a form of political hara-kiri in Kentucky. Not only that, but the candidate read his dry speech poorly. The saying immediately went up: "Combs opened and closed on the same night." Doc Beauchamp, who had been rejected in part because of his poor speaking ability, reportedly told Clements, "And you said I couldn't give a speech!" The results surprised few: Chandler won the primary by some 18,000 votes. In the general election, Republicans put forth still another lackluster candidate, Edwin R. Denney, a reserved US attorney from Rockcastle County. Chandler dominated the race. His meetings seemed like evangelical gatherings, while his opponent's, said a *New York Times* reporter, took on "some of the chilling qualities of a wake." A 129,000-vote margin—the biggest in a governor's race to that time—and 58 percent support showed Chandler's continuing appeal.

Chandler's presence in the governor's mansion would play a key role in three elections scheduled for 1956—the presidential contest, the regular US Senate race, and a special election to fill the other Senate seat. The special election had been called as a result of what had happened on April 30, 1956. That day Senator Barkley gave an address to students at Washington and Lee University in Virginia, and in the midst of the talk he collapsed and died of a heart attack. A politician could have asked for no better final remarks than the last words he spoke to the audience: "I would rather be a servant in the house of the Lord than to sit in the seats of the mighty."

Barkley's death not only meant that the most powerful political player from Kentucky in the century was gone, but it also meant that the state would elect two senators the same year, which also happened to be a presidential election year. For president, Republicans renominated popular incumbent Dwight D. Eisenhower, who had almost carried Kentucky four years earlier. On the Democratic side, Chandler set his eyes on the prize and went to the national convention as a "favorite son" choice. His acrid enemy, Mike Barry of the *Kentucky Irish American*, wrote, "Any time Chandler is referred to in Chicago as 'Kentucky's favorite son,' it should be made unmistakably clear that the sentence is incomplete." As it turned out, Happy got virtually no votes outside Kentucky, Adlai Stevenson was renominated to run again, and an unhappy governor returned to Kentucky and gave the national Democratic ticket little support.

In the senatorial races, Clements was up for reelection, and the lateness of Barkley's death had left the selection of the other Democratic nominee in the hands of the State Central Committee, still dominated by people loyal to Clements. They chose Wetherby as the second nominee. The party knew that the hard task would be electing Wetherby, but they expected Clements to win. After all, in one term he had already been named in a *New York Times* story as one of the four top Democratic leaders. When Lyndon Johnson suffered a heart attack, Clements became the acting Senate majority leader. Unfortunately for the state party, this task kept him away from the campaign trail quite a bit in 1956. Had Clements been able to focus more on Kentucky, the eventual outcome could have been very different. What time he did have he often devoted to Wetherby's campaign, in an effort to help him achieve victory.

An additional obstacle for Clements and Wetherby was their party's own governor. Of Chandler, a reporter wrote to Clements: "The fellow on the first floor, I am convinced, means nothing but ill for both you and Lawrence [Wetherby]. He may publicly say he is for you, but he's not going to urge anyone else to be in your camp." The administration used few of its resources to work for a ticket that the governor did not like at all. In essence, Chandler supported the Republican nominees.

For that reason and others—the African American vote was almost evenly divided in registration still yet—Republicans felt they had an excellent opportunity not only to carry the state for "Ike" but also to elect one senator. Eisenhower had lured away from his diplomatic post in India the party's veteran campaigner John Sherman Cooper, to run against Wetherby. Former senator Cooper was well known, and he did not have to contend with

the Barkley factor any longer. Still, it surprised seasoned observers every time Cooper won, for he seemed to do so much wrong. Journalist John Ed Pearce wrote: "Watching him in action, it is easy to sense but hard to explain why John Cooper is a formidable campaigner. He is not a dramatic speaker. His delivery is halting, low. He violates all the rules. . . . Yet to all of this there is agonizing sincerity—in the sad, soft smile and the slow, soft speech—that entraps audiences and infuriates his opponents." Despite being divorced, despite an earlier nervous breakdown (which no one mentioned during his races), despite his halting manner, he had appeal. Later, a Paducah attorney noted that "so many Kentuckians . . . feel Cooper is a good Democrat [who] just gets registered wrong." Backed by an infusion of funds from the Taft family of Ohio, John Sherman Cooper had an excellent chance for victory.

Not so his Republican running mate for the second Senate seat. Thruston Ballard Morton came from the wealthy "River Road Crowd" in Louisville, and his grandfather had been lieutenant governor under Edwin P. Morrow. A fresh postwar face, the handsome and hardworking Morton had been elected to Congress, then had served as an assistant secretary of state in Washington, but in 1956 he had had little statewide experience. Moreover, his campaign style was not typical for Kentucky. His shy and quiet manner coupled with his Louisville, millionaire background made him appear almost aloof at times. But he could also be very pleasing on television and did well in smaller crowds, where he felt more at ease. Morton, as one reporter recalled later, also had another side: "He's a very earthy guy. He's a gut fighter. He's a nice guy, gut fighter." That side he kept hidden, but he would need it to defeat Clements.

Actually, the two Republicans were not so different as their south-central Kentucky and Louisville backgrounds suggested. Both had graduated from Yale, both moved easily in eastern and upper-class circles, both had good relationships most of the time with Barry Bingham Sr. and the *Courier-Journal*, both had a World War II military background, and both seemed to dislike formal campaigning. Yet both could fight hard (and not always on the high road), and both could be effective vote getters in their own special ways.

And get the votes they did. With eighteen-year-olds voting for the first time in a general election in the state in 1956, Eisenhower won big, and his victory helped the Republican Senate races in Kentucky. Chandler's opposition to Clements and Wetherby, and Clements's absence from the state, contributed to the outcome. Cooper defeated Wetherby by 65,000 votes, and Clements found himself in a surprisingly close contest as well. As a key Republican insider recalled later, "We began to call eastern Kentucky . . . and tell them to slow down their count . . . and hold back 'til we got the votes in from western Kentucky, so that we'd know what we needed instead of them knowing what they needed." By whatever methods, Republicans (and Chandlerites) got enough votes so that Clements lost by some 7,000 votes out of more than 1 million cast. "Landslide Morton" joined Cooper as a US senator. As it turned out, not for sixteen years would Democrats elect another senator.

The defeat shocked Clements, who had not lost an election in his thirty years of public office, and it hurt his considerable ego greatly. Given his ties to later president Johnson, he very likely would have become Senate majority leader in the future, as had his mentor Barkley, and Kentucky would have had a major influence in the nation's capital. Instead, Clements—a man of pride—never ran for political office again, and he focused his immediate efforts on defeating the Chandler faction that was partially responsible for his loss. Not only Republican victory but Democratic bitterness were the legacies of 1956.

Politics dominated Chandler's legislative sessions, and the accomplishments of his second term as governor were much more limited than those of his first term. Opposition by the "rebels," a group of Democratic legislators who were friendly to the Clements faction, meant that Chandler had to ally openly with the Republicans, giving them patronage in exchange for general assembly votes. The result, said one

newspaper, "was less of a legislative session and more of a political convention." Trying to balance campaign promises on taxes with the state's financial needs (as pointed out by Combs), the Chandler coalition first lowered racetrack taxes and later raised them, broadened the income tax base and then reduced it, and finally expanded the truck, corporate, and liquor levies. Given that Kentucky had a serious need for more physicians—Kentucky by mid-century had only one doctor per 1,240 people, with rural areas much worse—the governor got approval, but limited funding, for a new medical center in the commonwealth. The Kentucky State Health Department's headquarters was moved from Chandler's bête noire of Louisville to the capital city, and a bill passed that authorized the highway department to use its own workforce rather than award contracts, a move the opposition saw as an attempt to build a stronger political machine for the administration.

Several other actions strengthened that perception. Chandler abolished the merit system coverage of the children's bureau that protected employees from political interference. According to a National Civil Service League publication, he then replaced the employees with those of less training—and more loyalty to the administration. In the Kentucky Department of Corrections Division of Probation and Parole, which had once been heavily influenced by politics, a new law required competitive exams and strong qualifications. But as the director of that division noted in February 1956, "We have now had seven new officers employed in the last 60 days. At no time have I talked with any of these officers before they were employed and have known nothing concerning their qualifications prior to their employment." He soon resigned. A year later, scandals in the highway department brought the resignation of its commissioner. And when a vacancy occurred in the position of clerk of the Kentucky Court of Appeals, it appointed one person and Chandler another. The governor ordered the Kentucky Finance Commission not to pay the court's choice; the judges and attorney general told the state treasurer to issue the checks. Finally both sides agreed to a constitutional test of the situation, and eventually the interpretation of the court of appeals was upheld.

Still, despite all the controversy, the political positioning by both factions, and the building of political armies for the next governor's race, Chandler had, above all, taken the high ground on the explosive question of racial integration. Possibly with gritted teeth, a journalist for his old enemy, the *Courier-Journal*, wrote in May 1958: "No governor south of the Mason and Dixon line has been so forthright and as consistent as he in upholding . . . the concept of law and order." Bingham even penned a personal letter, saying that Happy "acted with commendable dignity and determination." Demagogue and democrat, political alley fighter and statesman, Chandler at the end of his second term still defied easy definition, except that he was Happy, sui generis. That was all that need be said.

The Sixties

In the 1959 gubernatorial primary, the Chandler faction gave its full support to Lieutenant Governor Harry Lee Waterfield. The western Kentuckian was a strong candidate in his own right, but having the administration behind him gave even more advantages, as a series of letters showed.

The campaign's organizational chairman wrote the Kentucky Department of Revenue: "I am told that . . . [two men] of your Department are not helping our cause. . . . Please check into this." The same man wrote the department of public safety: "We have several complaints that the State Police are recommending wrecker service in Pulaski, Laurel, Knox, and Nelson Counties to garages that are our opponents. . . . Please look into this matter and straighten it out." The department of highways received a letter from Waterfield: "It is desired that you set up the following [seventeen] temporary maintenance jobs in the counties indicated below." The organizational chairman wrote a Bardstown man: "I hear the rumor that the Henry and Oldham

County Highway Garages have stopped paying their 2% [of salaries into campaign coffers]." The Department of Economic Security heard from the same individual: "Our good political friends at the Shelbyville Coca-Cola plant are anxious to put a coke machine in your Economic Security Building across the river. How about it?" A field report from Owsley County indicated that "one State Highway employee has at this time succeeded in getting 33 Republicans to re-register as Democrats with the promise of building a large concrete-pipe culvert." The writer of a field report for the Department of Industrial Relations said: "I attach special significance to Mr. Nickell's request [for a road] as he has expressed a willingness . . . to cooperate in naming Republican election officers who are in sympathy to our cause." From Johnson County, a field report commented: "Laurel Creek Road. Mullins wants this down the south or Paintsville side of the creek. . . . Mullins says the north side is Republican while the south side is much more Democratic. He says don't consider contracting down the north side until after the election."

The anti-Chandler forces faced two significant problems. An obvious one was the support the current state administration could give Waterfield. Even more serious, however, was the fact that those who opposed Chandler were not united. Clements, who faced some tax questions, declined to run. That left two others to oppose the Chandlerites. Former Louisville reform mayor Wilson W. Wyatt had managed Adlai Stevenson's presidential bid in 1952 and brought to the race a good record, a good mind, and a good initial base of support. The question remained, however, whether Wyatt, with his "patrician air," could extend his support statewide and overcome perceptions such as that of a local attorney who "considered him an egghead and not his kind of folk or people, and that he would probably not do anything helpful for his section." The other anti-Chandler faction candidate was Bert Combs, back for a second run. Divided, the faction could not defeat Waterfield and the Chandler group, as the polls showed. The old professional Earle Clements brokered a January 1959 meeting at the

Former governors of Kentucky. From left to right: Julian Carroll, Wendell Ford, Louie Nunn, Bert Combs, Lawrence Wetherby, and A. B. "Happy" Chandler, 1979. (University of Kentucky General Photographic Prints, University of Kentucky Special Collections and Research Center, Lexington, KY)

Standiford Airport Motel in Louisville, showed Wyatt that he trailed the field, and in an all-night session, worked out an arrangement whereby the two camps could merge, with Wyatt running for lieutenant governor and gaining promises of support for later races.

The race was now Combs versus Waterfield, the Clements faction versus the Chandler one, the former judge against the former journalist, eastern Kentucky opposite western Kentucky. Both men had lost earlier primaries, and both had learned from those experiences. But again, the best target was the sitting administration, and Combs turned the political tables on Chandler, whose actions now came under fire. One example was the so-called crippled goose incident. Happy had been accused of shooting at some geese a few minutes before the allotted legal time began and had been fined. His refusal to pay first brought forth duck and geese calls at Waterfield rallies, and then later the Combs forces paraded ducks with signs around their necks that read: "Happy Killed My Pappy." Similarly, it had been rumored that Chandler forces had placed their 2 percent assessments from state employees in a Cuban bank, where the funds could not be traced. But when Fidel Castro seized the Cuban government, those

funds had been taken as well, so the story went. Combs pictured Chandler looking out over the water, crying out, "Castro! Castro! Send back my 2 percent!"

Chandler countered, calling Combs a "Bertie of Paradise," and a "Clements parrot," while Waterfield pointed to his opponent's legal effort on behalf of coal operators. The election had been decided at the Standiford Airport Motel, though, and even earlier, when Combs learned from his 1955 defeat. He garnered 292,462 votes to Waterfield's 259,461, with the difference coming in Wyatt's home county. In the general election, against another weak Republican candidate, Combs defeated John M. Robsion Jr. by 180,000 votes, 516,549–336,456. Combs was in, and Clements was back.

Fortune smiled on the new governor, and he backed that up with some shrewd political moves. Military veterans had been pushing for a bonus, and Chandler forces, confident that the proposal would lose, had agreed to allow a popular vote on a sales tax to fund such a bonus. But the measure had been approved by some 38,000 votes, and Combs's legislature had to shape the details. It was generally agreed that a tax of one-half of 1 percent could fund the bonus, and most expected a 1 percent tax. But the Combs camp knew the state needed money, particularly for education, and boldly advocated—and got—a 3 percent tax. As a journalist said later: "It was a fraud, but it was the greatest fraud of this century." By 1963 some four hundred thousand veterans and their beneficiaries had received more than $126 million as a bonus, but the real winners were those who benefited from the many millions more that went into the state budget, year after year. Unlike many chief executives who faced tight budgets, Combs had money to spend.

One of the most progressive gubernatorial administrations of the century resulted. For the first time, an extensive state merit system was established by law (which also meant that Combs's allies would not be ousted by a future unfriendly administration), and an executive decree desegregated public accommodations. A Human Rights Commission was created, and assessing political campaign funds from state employees became a felony. A new requirement for the statewide use of voting machines brought political boss and vote counter "Doc" Beauchamp to proclaim that "instead of precinct workers, what we need these days is good mechanics." Meanwhile, the administration aided local officials in their largely successful efforts to "clean up" Newport, the "Sin City of the South"—a place where, it was said, the population was "30,000 by day and 100,000 at night."

The state's first billion-dollar budget increased school funds 50 percent, formed a community college system, and fully funded—ironically—the Albert B. Chandler Medical Center at the University of Kentucky. A $100 million bond issue provided even more money for a system of toll highways and for state park construction. One study showed that by 1962 Kentucky had increased its appropriations faster than any state over the last five years, with per capita expenditures doubling in that period. Even the courts helped, for a 1962 ruling decreed that the state's (amended) constitutional limitation on salaries could be interpreted to mean salaries as adjusted for inflation. The so-called rubber dollar ruling helped government attract more professionals.

The one major negative of Combs's administration was chiefly a media creation. This was ironic, since Combs as a rule had excellent publicity both at the state and national levels. (One state journalist, for instance, wrote certain Combs speeches, then praised them editorially the next day.) But Earle Clements had wanted to be named as head of the powerful Kentucky Highway Commission, and Combs had done so. Then a news story broke that suggested that the state was getting ready to purchase some poor-condition trucks at a very favorable rate from a firm controlled by Combs's former finance chairman. Some argued that "the truck deal" problem would have been caught and corrected through the review process. Others said that it was a political payoff and that Clements had been simply trying to carry it out for others. Yet another faction indicated it was a Clements deal, pure and simple. Combs canceled the proposed lease, contradicted his highway commissioner's testimony, and he and Wyatt made Clements the scapegoat. Clements took these actions as a personal and public rebuke. "Very bitter," Clements resigned his post. When asked at a news conference if he would have fired Clements had he not resigned, Combs answered, "No comment." To Clements, that response was an insult and a betrayal of trust. Thereafter he took every opportunity to oppose his former ally and his supporters. Yet it also marked the beginning of the end of the Clements domination of that Democratic faction.

All this activity proved crucial in the 1962 US Senate race, which pitted incumbent Republican Thruston Morton against Lieutenant Governor Wyatt. Democratic prospects, at one level, did not seem good, for in 1960 Republican senator Cooper had easily defeated former governor Keen Johnson in his bid for reelection to the Senate. That same year Republican Richard Nixon had carried Kentucky by a sizable margin—80,000 votes—as well. The results of the 1960 presidential race, however, had been skewed by the Catholicism of Democrat John F. Kennedy. *The Western Recorder*, the voice of Baptists in Kentucky, came out against the Democrat, and considerable anti-Catholic political literature was spread over the state, often from Protestant pulpits on Sunday mornings. As a rule, Republicans did not speak out openly against the anti-Catholic attacks, and religion permeated all parts of the race. Catholic Al Smith had gotten 41 percent of the state's votes in 1928; Catholic Kennedy received 46 percent thirty-two years later. The increase was not enough. The *Courier-Journal* concluded: "Kennedy lost Kentucky because of his religious faith." But Democrats could argue that religion was not an issue in the 1962 Senate race and that they had a popular administration behind Wyatt.

They also had a split party. Old former foes Chandler and Clements now combined to oppose the Combs-Wyatt alliance. Morton did not depend on Democratic factionalism alone, however, and his campaign became what one observer called one "of misrepresentation, smear, and confusion." Wyatt's early advocacy of Americans for Democratic Action was presented as support for socialism; his call for what later became Medicare was used against him among members of the health care profession; his opposition to a loyalty oath was seized upon to brand him "soft on communism." Wyatt had a campaign brochure printed, for distribution on election day in African American wards in Louisville, which showed a black hand grasping a white one in unity. Republican strategists got a copy early, reproduced it by the thousands, spread it among whites in western Kentucky, where the integration question was particularly volatile, and gained votes as a result. What even the incumbent's son termed a "nasty" race ended in a Morton victory by almost 50,000 votes, but the senator had lost friends, including the Binghams, in winning as he did. Disturbed by that, Morton, the former chairman of the Republican National Committee and the first Republican to win two full consecutive terms as senator, would not seek reelection six years hence. Wyatt never sought public office again either. In effect, the 1962 race ended the careers of two key party leaders.

National and even international issues continued to be more and more dominant in state political races in the 1960s. Civil rights,

the cold war and communism, and the Vietnam War all entered into state campaigns. So too did another issue that affected only parts of the United States, but certainly had an impact in Kentucky. That was the so-called War on Poverty. In 1963 Harry M. Caudill's *Night Comes to the Cumberlands* appeared. Not particularly strong in its history, it was forceful and passionate in its call for action and attacks on the pillaging and pollution of a place and its people. The story Caudill and authors of other studies told was not a pleasant one.

The mountain region was not poor, but as one author noted, its people were. By 1960 the coal mines had been in a period of general stagnation for nearly four decades. Mechanization had produced unemployed miners who received little aid from the operators. For some the only salvation had been out-migration to places like Chicago's Uptown or Dayton's East End, where the former Kentuckians became "O-tucks" (Ohio-Kentuckians). Between 1940 and 1950 nearly a quarter million people left the state's Appalachian counties; the next decade saw a net migration of 340,000 people, 32 percent of the area's population. It was an exodus akin to the great overseas migration from Europe in the nineteenth century.

Worse for Kentucky, those who departed Appalachia were the young and those, on average, who were better educated. They left behind a region of great promise and much natural beauty, but one plagued by pollution, illiteracy, poor medical care, bad roads, few colleges, substandard housing, and absentee ownership. (As late as 1980, 42 percent of the surface land in the region was corporate owned.) Whereas in 1950 some 63 percent of US homes had hot water, a bath, and an indoor toilet, only 2 percent of the houses in Wolfe County, Kentucky, did. That county—the second poorest in the United States in 1960—had a median income of $1,455, compared to the national average of $5,660, and no one in the county reported making annually more than $10,000. The educational level of the people stood at under eight years of schooling, versus the American median of almost eleven. Such conditions existed across many parts of Kentucky, and as a result, counties such as Leslie, Harlan, and Letcher lost half their populations between 1940 and 1970. By 1960 two of every five households in Appalachian Kentucky had incomes below the poverty line, and in 1970, some 65 percent of Clay County's population lived in poverty. US congressman Carl D. Perkins testified that one-third of the workers in his congressional district were unemployed in 1961. Poverty was a Kentucky problem and a national one.

President Kennedy had seen Appalachian poverty during his election campaign and had later initiated actions to deal with the issue. Following his death, those actions reached maturity under President Lyndon B. Johnson, who visited the region in April 1964. The approach taken was both pragmatic and idealistic and had both successes and failures. The Volunteers in Service to America (VISTA), the Appalachian Volunteers (AVs), Head Start, the Appalachian Regional Commission (ARC) —all were attempted solutions. While the ARC focused on infrastructure, other groups sought to educate or empower local citizens. As one historian noted, "Resembling more a conflagration of scattered assaults . . . than a well-orchestrated battle, the war to end poverty in the mountains was waged on multiple levels." Some of those efforts had the desired effect, but others fragmented and failed. Certain ventures challenged long-established local elites, who struck back. Two civil rights activists, Anne and Carl Braden, again became the focus of legal action, while Alan and Margaret McSurely came to Kentucky from Washington, DC, angered Pike County officials, and were arrested for criminal syndicalism. The "radical" books confiscated ranged from works by Karl Marx to the writings of Barry Goldwater. After a federal court ruled the statute under which they were charged as unconstitutional, the couple eventually went free, only to see their home bombed. All that brought more negative national publicity for the region.

Poverty was not eradicated, but the war against it weakened its hold on eastern Kentucky. Some recognized, as did Robert F. Kennedy in 1968, that "Despite all the riches un-derground, the most important riches of the area are above ground: they are the people." Out-migration slowed drastically in the 1960s, and the region's per capita income as a percentage of the national average rose from 45 percent in 1965 to 66 percent in 1979. The infant mortality rate by 1990 was one-fourth what it had been three decades earlier.

However, by the second decade of the twenty-first century, one-fifth of the nation's one hundred lowest-income counties were still in Kentucky, and over a fourth of the state's counties—almost all in Appalachia—had over a quarter of their people living below the federal poverty line. By 2012, 19.4 percent of all Kentuckians lived in poverty—the fifth highest rate in the nation. Also, the number of children living in poverty in the commonwealth increased from one in five in 1979 to one in four thirty-five years later. And the problem is not simply a rural one, for some 40 percent of the overall numbers of people in poverty came from urban areas. In the 1960s, amid much debate, some anger, and considerable political infighting, a start had been made to combat poverty, and some successes had resulted. But the War on Poverty had been but a skirmish; the main battle had not been won. Hunger and want remained a fact of life to many Kentuckians.

Political fights loomed on the horizon as well, and they soon erupted in another contentious Democratic Party primary in 1963. Happy Chandler sought an unprecedented third term and began his familiar attacks on the sales tax and on his opposition's expenditures. Targeting the floral clock that Combs had built near the capitol, for example, he would say that in Frankfort, the time must be "two petunias past the Jimson weed." Opposing the old campaigner was a surprise choice. As Clements had done with him, Combs unexpectedly selected Edward T. ("Ned") Breathitt Jr. of Hopkinsville, and Combs's administration put all its support behind the thirty-eight-year-old former legislator. Nephew of a Democratic lieutenant governor, grandson of a Republican attorney general, and related to the nineteenth-century governor who shared his surname,

Table 19.1. Personal Income per Capita, 1930–2016

Year	Kentucky	US	Kentucky as % of US	State rank
1930	$321	$611	52.5	40
1940	$315	$585	53.8	43
1950	$988	$1,497	66.0	46
1960	$1,623	$2,258	71.8	43
1970	$3,138	$4,047	77.5	43
1980	$8,051	$9,940	80.9	43
1990	$14,747	$18,666	79.0	44
2016	$39,499	$49,571	79.7	43

Breathitt came across on the increasingly important television screen as a fresh and enthusiastic young man. Chandler never quite adapted to the new campaign methods, and his attacks fell flat. When young, he had represented the new approach to campaigning; now his opponent did, and the circle was complete. Chandler went down to defeat by more than sixty thousand votes, losing all but one congressional district. Shocked by his first personal defeat in a quarter century, he would later charge that "it was stolen." The large margin of victory and a lack of evidence, however, give that argument little force. Happy found it hard to see that political time—as measured on the floral clock or elsewhere—had passed him by. He would win no other races. The Chandler era had ended, though "Happy" did not know it.

For a change, victory was not automatically assured for the Democrats, however. To his credit, Chandler had not really incited racial tensions in his primary bid. The general election would not follow the same pattern. That factor, combined with recent Republican victories and the now-familiar support by Happy for the Republicans, gave the GOP optimism. The Republican candidate was the capable Louie B. Nunn of Glasgow, and he, with the aid of his brother Lee, would seek out the opposition's weakest link and then hammer at that over and over. In this instance, Nunn capitalized on Combs's executive order concerning open housing in his attempt to get votes, particularly in western Kentucky. Appearing on television with the flag, a Bible, and Kentucky statutes around him, Nunn pointed to the civil rights order and said, "My first act will be to abolish this." The unfriendly *New Republic* ac-cused him of conducting "the first outright seg-regationist campaign in Kentucky," but Nunn knew that he had no chance of victory through the standard Republican arguments of the past twenty years. He wanted to win, and he came very close to doing so, losing to Breathitt by 13,000 votes, 436,496–449,331. The *New York Times* commented sadly on the "marked reversal for the forces of racial moderation in this border state whose whites had heretofore supported moderate to liberal candidates."

Yet the liberal candidate had won, and Ned Breathitt proceeded to forge a good record, despite having to overcome budgetary disadvantages Combs never faced. Hindered in his first session by the death of longtime legislative leader Richard P. Moloney, the new governor had only mixed success. In what is usually the weaker, lame-duck second session, however, he dominated. Sometime Chandler ally Lieutenant Governor Waterfield was stripped of his powers, former governor Wetherby—now in the state senate—was selected president pro tempore, and the control was so complete that the budget introduced on January 4, 1966, passed in virtually the same form ten days later, garnering margins of ninety-nine to zero and thirty-one to five.

Overall, the Breathitt administration could point to a major statewide Civil Rights Act, a stronger strip mining law, a new Corrupt Practices Act, more funds for rural roads and education, and initial funding for Kentucky Educational Television. It, however, missed an opportunity after the state's highest court ruled in 1965 that property must be assessed at its full value for tax purposes. At the time, tax assessors set the median assessment rate at 27

University of Kentucky students protest the Vietnam War. (University of Kentucky General Photographic Prints, University of Kentucky Special Collections and Research Center, Lexington, KY).

percent. A large tax increase and much greater funding would follow, if no action was taken. But Breathitt called a special session that established that the revenue raised could be no greater than 10 percent from the previous year. The administration's chief defeat came when a proposed new constitution, based on national models, was submitted to the voters. The 1891 document was more a code of laws than a flexible, living constitution, and had already been heavily amended (and by the twenty-first century would be amended some fifty times). Opposed by county leaders, the proposed constitution lost by a huge margin, 510,099–140,210.

At the same time, the expanding Vietnam War sparked increasing demonstrations and unrest. The first Kentuckian died in Vietnam in 1962. Eventually about 125,000 Kentuckians served in Southeast Asia; more than 1,000 died, and others returned with wounds physical and mental. In all wars, for those who go off to fight, "war sometimes never ends." Back home, anger between those who opposed the conflict and the larger group of those who supported the government's prosecution of it divided generations, communities, and whole families and left its own scars on those involved. Muhammad Ali's declaration that "I don't have no personal quarrel with those Vietcong" and refusal

to be induced via the draft because of his religious beliefs cost him his heavyweight boxing crown and represented only the most vocal example of the opposition to the war.

Other young Kentuckians went off to fight—"I felt the typical invincibility of a teenager," one recalled—and had to bear what another termed "the haunting cross of combat." The hardest burden came later, in June 1969, when elements of an activated National Guard unit were attacked at a forgotten place called Fire Support Base Tomahawk. In one night five men from Bardstown were killed. That small town suffered perhaps the greatest loss per capita of any community in the country.

Easily victorious in his 1966 bid for reelection over John Y. Brown Sr., Senator Cooper had been among the first political leaders to question the war, and his sponsorship of the Cooper-Church Amendment to cut off funds to expand the conflict in Indochina reflected his desire to forge a peace. By 1967 two other World War II veterans, Republican senator Morton and Congressman Tim Lee Carter of south central Kentucky, both broke with the administration and became critics of American policy. Strong feelings remained prevalent in the state, however, and Vietnam and the civil rights movement would be important issues as the commonwealth moved toward still another governor's race, in 1967.

Republican Resurgence and Retreat

With factionalism fading, Chandler's and Waterfield's separate 1967 attempts to defeat the Combs-Breathitt candidate in the Democratic primary failed badly, and the party's nomination went to a well-qualified and well-prepared former journalist, legislator, and public official, Henry Ward of Paducah. Hopeful Republicans experienced one of their hardest-fought and bitterest primaries, with possible gubernatorial victory as the great lure. A moderate, Marlow W. Cook had been elected Jefferson County judge in 1961 and reelected four years later. Louie Nunn, the defeated candidate of four years earlier, opposed him. Facing an attractive and strong candidate, Nunn attacked the "liberal, former New Yorker" from the urban area, then struck out at what he saw as Cook's weakest point, his Catholic religion. Some Nunn allies also criticized what they termed Cook's "Jewish backers." Such anti-Semitic overtones brought Senator Cooper and Representative Carter to speak out against such tactics and to support Cook, while Louisvillian Morton—aided by Nunn in his earlier Senate race—remained silent. Rural votes and religious influences helped Nunn beat Cook in the primary by a small margin.

Using racially oriented tactics four years earlier, Nunn had barely lost to Breathitt, an attractive candidate backed by a strong administration. Now, in 1967, Ward proved much weaker on the campaign trail and generated little enthusiasm. As usual, Chandler supported the Republicans. Nunn in turn capitalized on the race issue and the uneasy mood of the nation, since riots, demonstrations, and general unrest appeared in the news seemingly daily. A *Hazard Herald* writer, who was "tired of beatniks, hippies, and civil fighters," and a conservative Kentucky Republican congressman speaking for Nunn, who blamed the societal "degeneration" on bearded protesters and the promises of LBJ's "Great Society," expressed that anger. The result was the first Republican

victory in a Kentucky governor's race in twenty-four years: Nunn won by a count of 454,123 to 425,674. Even then, the victory represented something of a personal triumph for Nunn, for half of the other elected offices, including lieutenant governor (Wendell H. Ford), went to Democrats, and that party continued to control both legislative chambers. Still, Republicans held the governorship, both US Senate seats, and three of the seven House posts.

The next year Kentuckians would give Richard Nixon their presidential electoral votes, as they did every time he ran. Faced with the choice for US senator of Catholic Marlow Cook on the Republican side or a Democratic woman, Katherine Peden, Kentucky voters collapsed the religious barrier first. Cook took Morton's vacated Senate seat in 1968. Predictions became commonplace that Kentucky—like many southern states—was turning Republican.

In that heady atmosphere, Governor Nunn came to Frankfort, bringing with him a group of young and fresh "whiz kids," reminiscent of Chandler's first term. Working with the Democratic legislature, Nunn presided over an administration characterized by much accomplishment and much controversy. Even though party cohesion is not usually strong in the Kentucky General Assembly, the specter of a Republican governor, a Democratic lieutenant governor, and a Democratic legislature haunted the sessions, and Nunn successfully vetoed 25 percent of the bills passed in 1968 and 14 percent two years later. The general assembly also enacted the first statewide open housing law south of the Ohio River, a bill drafted by black legislators Georgia Davis (Powers), Mae Street Kidd, and Hughes McGill. Governor Nunn, who had campaigned on a platform of restricting such actions, let the bill become law without his signature.

But the key issue concerned money. Faced with a budget deficit, Nunn squarely proposed and the legislature passed an increase in the sales tax to five cents per dollar. That tax hike allowed large amounts of money to go into the new Kentucky Educational Television system that started in 1968, and general education, and permitted the University of Louisville and Northern Kentucky University to be brought into the state system.

At the same time, events outside the capital occupied much of the governor's attention. He sent troops to Louisville during the May 1968 race riots that left two dead, and to the University of Kentucky in May 1970, following the destruction by arson of a building on campus in what was likely an antiwar-related action. Saying that the campus was in "clear and present danger," Nunn ordered armed soldiers to enforce a curfew that also affected the week of final examinations. Conflict and constructive actions marked the Nunn years. Yet despite the accomplishments and despite the prediction of a wave of Republican wins in the future, the Nunn administration from 1967 to 1971 marked the gubernatorial high-water mark for the party for the next quarter century. Why did the Republican resurgence die at that time, while in other southern states it persisted?

First of all, as riots ended, as the racial question faded, and as integration became basically accepted, race declined as a divisive issue in elections. Since the state did not have a sizable black population, the later concern of white voters did not reach the same level as elsewhere. Second, the sales tax increase hurt the Republicans a great deal, even though it passed with Democratic votes. When the state retail sales tax had first been approved in 1959, the people had voted on it, and if the amount did turn out to be larger than expected, many had been paid hundreds of dollars in a veterans' bonus and could not really repudiate their votes. But no such mitigating factors affected Nunn, and like most candidates he had spoken out against more taxes. Then came the increase to five cents per dollar, called "Nunn's Nickel." Finally, the Watergate episode that ended in Nixon's resignation in 1974 and also a string of gubernatorial candidates that presented little challenge to a Democratic opposition injured the Republican Party itself. Not until generational replacement shifted allegiances much later would Republicans win sizable numbers of victories. Until then, a Democratic tide swept the state once more.

The 1971 Democratic primary for governor ended the political career of one leader and started the rise of another. Lieutenant Governor Wendell H. Ford of Daviess County had been Bert Combs's executive assistant, but now he hoped to win the nomination from his old boss. Combs sought to leave his federal judgeship for the governor's office. Ford, however, ran a better-organized campaign, which focused on the 1960 sales tax, Combs's age, and the former governor's desire to leave the better-paying federal post. In a relatively quiet race, Ford confounded the experts and defeated overconfident Combs followers by over 40,000 votes. "This is the end of the road for me politically," said Combs. He was right, although he would continue to be active in public affairs, including educational reform. Republicans put forth young attorney Tom Emberton, who had grown up in south-central Kentucky, and he ran a solid race. But the former Nunn aide had to try to defend the sales tax increase and never could generate voter excitement for his cause. The seventy-three-year-old Happy Chandler, running as an independent, third-party candidate, added to the mix, but in the end he only received 39,493 votes. Emberton garnered 412,653 votes, and Ford won with 470,720.

Democratic factionalism was dead for just about the only time in the century. Combs, Clements, Chandler—all had gone from center stage, and a basically united party resulted. The first beneficiary of that situation was Wendell Ford. The son of a state senator, he had been in the insurance business and then had climbed the political ladder. Legislation passed during Ford's gubernatorial administration removed the sales tax from food products and extensively reorganized state government. The commonwealth's first significant severance tax on coal was authorized, and considerable funding was given to education, environmental protection, and the infrastructure. Moreover, when John Sherman Cooper announced that he would not seek reelection as US senator in 1972, Ford's campaign manager, forty-six-year-old Walter D. ("Dee") Huddleston, defeated Nunn for that seat by nearly 34,000 votes. (Cooper, who had been ambassador to

India and Nepal and had served on the Warren Commission investigating President Kennedy's assassination, later was appointed ambassador to East Germany.) Two years later, in 1974, during the Watergate scandal, Ford ran against incumbent US senator Cook and defeated him easily. Kentucky had two Democratic senators for the first time since 1956. Ford would go on to win reelection after reelection to the Senate, at one time serving as majority whip. Freed of factional attacks, the quieter Ford rivaled Barkley in his ability to win.

What factionalism existed in the Kentucky Democratic Party resulted from the rivalry of the supporters of Ford and of his lieutenant governor, Julian M. Carroll of Paducah. Yet that contention was muted. The Carroll forces supported Ford for senator because his election and resignation as governor would make their man the state's chief executive. On December 28, 1974, Carroll became governor. Eleven months later, after a lackluster race, he won election to a full term, carrying every congressional district and defeating coal company owner Republican Robert E. Gable by the record margin of 470,159–277,998.

The first governor from the Jackson Purchase, Carroll entered his full term with a mandate, an ample treasury, and perhaps as much experience as any of his twentieth-century predecessors. An attorney and excellent stump speaker, he had served ten years in the legislature (four as speaker of the house), three in the lieutenant governor's office, then one as governor. He brought an extensive knowledge of the details of government to the job and so controlled his first legislative session that an observer said, "A cockroach couldn't crawl across the Senate floor without an OK from the governor stamped on his back." During his term, Carroll pumped considerable money into the secondary and elementary schools, expanded the state park system, provided aid to the poor to help pay fuel bills, and abolished the bail bonding system. Moreover, the governor implemented a constitutional amendment that voters quietly approved in 1975, which drastically reorganized the state's legal system and made it a model for the nation. Under this amendment the position

of county judge became totally administrative. A district court system formed the core of the revamped judicial plan. The amendment also renamed the state's highest court the Kentucky Supreme Court and created a new Kentucky Court of Appeals to hear cases from the circuit courts.

Yet Carroll experienced little good fortune outside state government. A few months before he took office, over two dozen tornadoes had ripped through the state, leaving behind seventy-seven deaths and much devastation. Now, floods, severe winters, the Scotia mining disaster that cost 26 lives in Letcher County in 1976, and the Beverly Hills Supper Club fire in Campbell County that left 165 dead in 1977 brought more grief and eventually some regulatory reforms. Carroll's problems compounded when he briefly left the commonwealth in 1978. Acting governor Thelma Stovall—the state's first woman lieutenant governor—used her powers to call a special session of the legislature, as her onetime ally Chandler had done before his first gubernatorial election. A candidate for governor in 1979, Stovall likely hoped to help her chances, and the Kentucky General Assembly obliged by passing House Bill 44, a measure that limited annual property tax increases. Nor did Carroll help himself by certain actions. Sensitive to criticism, he reacted to attacks—some from his politically ambitious auditor—with an attitude that induced enemies to call him Emperor Julian. Charges that his administration had favored its friends through leases and preferential personal service contracts gained credence when Carroll's choice as party chairman resigned in the wake of an FBI investigation and eventually was sentenced to two years in prison. A scandal involving the state's insurance policies netted two further convictions—one of a cabinet secretary—but those were overturned on appeal. While Carroll left office in 1979 under a cloud, the sound and fury exceeded the eventual results. Still, it was a warning of what was to come later.

New Politics or No Politics?

The 1979 election proved to be something of a watershed, dividing the past form of political campaigning and candidates from what would be the immediate future form. At first the Democratic primary seemed to be rather traditional, with Terry McBrayer, backed by the Carroll administration, fighting off challenges from western Kentucky congressman Carroll Hubbard Jr., state auditor George Atkins, and the Bingham-backed millionaire and former Louisville mayor Dr. Harvey Sloane. The initial front-runner, Lieutenant Governor Stovall, faltered badly owing to health problems.

Then forty-five-year-old John Y. Brown Jr. unexpectedly entered the race, and everything changed. Son of a politician father who had run often and won little, Brown had married a former Miss America, Phyllis George, ten days before his announcement. Now he interrupted his honeymoon for his first political race ever. Wealthy through his involvement in Kentucky Fried Chicken, Brown—like so many before him—promised to run government like a business. The difference this time was that his self-funded campaign sold that image well in carefully crafted television events and advertisements, and the handsome candidate and his attractive wife appeared, as Governor Carroll noted later, "as sort of a fresh breath of air in a stale campaign." The "John and Phyllis Show" worked: Brown surprised everyone by winning the primary with 165,158 votes, receiving 25,000 more than Sloane, his nearest competitor. He had received less than 30 percent of the total vote, but in a crowded field that proportion was enough by far. Brown's victory upset the Republican plans, for they believed the other candidates all had major liabilities on which their hard-hitting candidate, former governor Nunn, could capitalize. About the only thing Nunn could attack now was his opponent's flashy lifestyle, and that approach went nowhere. Continuing what was called his showbiz campaign, with its emphasis on the 3Ms—millions, media, and Miss America—Brown won by more than 176,000 votes, 558,088–381,278. The former salesman had successfully sold himself to Kentuckians.

Brown's race and his subsequent term as governor showed four trends that would continue for some time. First of all, television be-

came the all-important medium, as film editing increasingly replaced local organizations as a key. Political scientist Jasper Shannon wrote that "policy and philosophy yielded to personality and images," and voters became spectators watching from their living rooms, rather than organizers and participants. This situation brought about a second trend, the emergence of the self-funded, wealthy candidate. If any twentieth-century Kentucky governor had been a millionaire before Brown, he had only been marginally so at best. At least four of the five governors elected between 1979 and 1999 would be in that category, however. With no real limits on campaign spending, they would have a great advantage in the battle for television time.

The new governor had called his style the New Politics; veteran party leaders worried that it might be no politics. All patronage came from the Brown camp, not from Democratic Party headquarters, and the chief executive virtually ignored local party organizations. Instead, the future would be based not on party or factional allegiance but on shifting personal alliances, a third trend. Finally, Brown—who rode a motorcycle to his office on occasion—displayed a very casual attitude toward governing. He did not influence the selection of party leaders, which meant the winners had less allegiance to him and his programs. His hands-off attitude also took him on vacation during one of his two legislative sessions, and his lieutenant governor, Martha Layne Collins, served as chief executive for the more than five hundred days Brown was out of state during his four-year term. That fourth trend allowed the Kentucky General Assembly to become very independent, perhaps for the first time.

Well-liked by the press, Brown received the *Courier-Journal's* praise at the end of his gubernatorial term for his "unparalleled" record. The newspaper cited his reduction of state government personnel, strong increases in the compensation to remaining employees, the use of competitive bidding, and passage of a weight-distance tax on trucks. But on examination, Brown's overall cupboard of accomplishments was actually fairly bare. Seeking a con-

stitutional amendment that would allow him a second term, Brown saw that proposal fail by a large margin. The state jobless rate went from 5.6 percent the year he became governor to 11.7 by the time he left, the highest figure in more than a decade. In 1983—the last year of the Brown administration—the state's per capita income was lower in relation to the nation's than it had been five years before. Despite claims about cuts in spending, overall expenditures increased 33 percent during Brown's term, although very little of those new funds went into the financially strapped educational system. Bad publicity resulted when the governor admitted withdrawing $1.3 million in cash from a Florida bank, ⸻ to cover his gambling debts. His off⸻ seri-
ous health problem⸻
for a time and on⸻
lapsed when he un⸻ ⸻cted governor of Ken-
ation. Recovering⸻
could look back⸻
tion, at least wit⸻ ⸻0-vote win (561,674–
take pride in sc⸻ ⸻he state would have a
had occurred.⸻ ⸻e first time.
of much left ⸻ ⸻r-old Collins had grown
   As usual⸻ ⸻graduated from the Uni-
come govern⸻ ⸻and then taught school.
office. Back⸻ ⸻level politics in her new
ic primary⸻ ⸻ County, she gained Ford's
administr⸻ ⸻75 won election to the office
Stumbo f⸻ ⸻ntucky Court of Appeals. In
Governo⸻ ⸻d out a surprising 4,500-vote
close pr⸻ ⸻ocratic primary and went on
than 6⸻ ⸻ongressman Hal Rogers to be-
votes,⸻ ⸻t governor during Brown's ad-
199,7⸻ His frequent absences and will-
P. ("J⸻ ⸻ her represent him at statewide
mer⸻ ⸻mensely aided her bid to become
Bur⸻ ⸻ne study noted that typically some
ca⸻ ⸻ of the primary voters in Kentucky
ag⸻ ⸻lly seen a candidate in the year be-
d⸻ ⸻ection; some 36 percent saw Collins,
l⸻ ⸻apparently made a good impression.
⸻victory puzzled some observers, for
⸻ky—in their view a conservative state—
⸻ected one of the first half dozen wom-
⸻ernors in the nation. Perhaps they forgot
⸻he state had been a leader in the women's

rights struggle early in the century. More than that, the commonwealth's vaunted individualism may have caused voters—some of whom were perhaps hesitant to support women candidates in theory—to judge Collins on her merits, based on their personal contacts with her. For whatever reason, as she noted on election night, "We made history, Kentucky."

Collins's first full year as state leader in 1984 was not a memorable one, however. The general assembly rejected her proposals and program, and her husband's financial activities were already starting to attract the attention that would eventually land him in prison and limit her later political prospects. That same year the state lost its most influential member in Congress, when the quiet and unassuming but politically astute Carl D. Perkins died. Congressman for more than a quarter century, fourth in seniority in the House, the honest, shrewd, and tenacious man from Hindman had long aided the poor and supported education. He would be missed. Democrats also lost another important player when the results of the 1984 Senate race came in. Senator Huddleston had forged a good record, had won reelection rather easily in 1978, and had enough strength to cause former Governor Brown to drop out of the race before the primary vote occurred. As a result, Huddleston had been expected to win again over the relatively unknown Republican judge executive A. M. ("Mitch") McConnell of Louisville. Alabama-born, a man who had overcome childhood polio, an attorney, an intern for John Sherman Cooper, and a former legislative assistant for Senator Cook (who now supported Huddleston in the canvass), McConnell proved to be a tough campaigner. He used what became known as the effective "hound dog" commercials and simply ran a better race than the incumbent. The surprising results gave Republicans and McConnell a five-thousand-vote win, 645,530–639,721. The victor would be the only Republican to win major statewide elections between 1968 and 1998. Then, two days before Christmas of 1984, a key Democratic party adviser died.

In the 1940s Edward F. Prichard Jr. had been viewed by many as the most politically

Ed Prichard (*front, left*) of Bourbon County rose rapidly to positions of power, fell even more quickly, but came back to become a respected leader. (University of Kentucky Special Collections and Research Center, Lexington, KY)

talented and intellectually gifted Kentuckian of his era. Law clerk to US Supreme Court justice Felix Frankfurter and then with an office in the White House before the age of thirty, Prichard numbered among his friends Katherine Graham, publisher of the *Washington Post*, who called him "the most impressive man of our generation." But if he had received seemingly endless gifts of talent from the gods, they had also given him a fatal flaw, what he later called "a moral blind spot." In 1948, he helped "fix" a meaningless election and in a politically charged atmosphere was convicted. His appeal could not be heard by the US Supreme Court, for too many justices had to disqualify themselves since they knew him. In 1950 President Truman pardoned him, five months into his federal prison term, but "Prich" lived in his own private prison of humiliation for years more.

Slowly he made his way back, behind the scenes, to be a key adviser to the Clements-Combs camp, and "the Philosopher" helped fashion their wins and programs. Opponent Chandler once sought to make Prichard an issue and labeled him a "jailbird." Prich replied: "It is true that I have served time in the federal reformatory. I have associated with murderers, robbers, rapists, and forgers, criminals of all kinds, and let me say, my friends, that every one of them was the moral superior of A. B. 'Happy' Chandler." Finally, near the end of his life, a blind Prichard helped initiate the educational reform movement that would bear legislative fruit after his death. Like a figure from a Greek tragedy, Prichard had been shown the highest laurels, only a fingertip away, but then had been driven to the lowest depths. At last he had rebuilt his shattered life, and he died a highly honored Kentuckian. But now he too was gone.

Despite the 1984 setbacks for Collins and for her party, by the time she left office in 1987, she would receive wide praise for what had taken place on her watch. Called by a veteran politician, "of all the governors I have known, she was by far the hardest worker," Collins grew in office. The only female governor in the country, she was considered for the vice presidency in 1984, chaired the Democratic National Convention that year, and then had two successful legislative sessions. A 1985 special called session resulted in an additional $300 million for education, to reduce class size, increase teachers' salaries, and construct more classrooms. The former schoolteacher had made educational reform fashionable. She also had success in economic development, with the capstone coming in December 1985, when Toyota announced the construction of a billion-dollar automotive plant near Georgetown. A sizable incentive package tied to the Toyota plant brought Collins some criticism, but the growth of allied industries connected to the plant, as well as its later expansion, muted that censure quickly. Finally, Collins had a good working re-

lationship with the legislature by the time she left office, something that would not be said of a Kentucky governor over the ensuing decade.

The Democratic primary still effectively decided who the next governor would be, and the 1987 primary seemed a repeat of eight years earlier. John Y. Brown Jr. was back, as was 1983 candidate Grady Stumbo, former governor Julian Carroll, plus administration-backed Lieutenant Governor Steve Beshear. This time, however, the fresh face with the seemingly unlimited bankroll was another political newcomer who—like Brown—had never held political office and who had generally rose outside the party structure, forty-five-year-old Wallace G. Wilkinson. After growing up in Casey County, Wilkinson had made several fortunes, through bookstores, real estate, and other ventures (and after his term ended would lose his fortune, declaring bankruptcy with over $400 million in debts). But in 1987, he advocated a state lottery as a way to distance himself from the other candidates. That tactic worked, as his 35 percent of the total gave him nearly 58,000 votes more than his nearest competitor, Brown. Wilkinson's success spilled over to the general election, particularly since a strong Republican candidate unexpectedly withdrew from the race. Aided by political operative James Carville, Wilkinson carried 115 counties and won over Republican state legislator John Harper of Shepherdsville by a record vote of 504,674–273,141.

Unlike fellow millionaire Brown, who almost avoided legislative involvement, Wilkinson took a hands-on and sometimes confrontational approach, which produced what the governor termed "open political warfare" between the executive and legislative branches. With Wilkinson's election seen as a mandate for a lottery, the Kentucky General Assembly passed an amendment that, when approved by the voters, allowed a state lottery after a hiatus of nearly a century. In that same election citizens endorsed another important constitutional amendment, which required landowners' approval before surface (strip) mining could occur, thus negating much of the old broad form deed. When the state supreme court ruled

Kentucky's entire educational system unconstitutional, action also had to be taken on that issue by the governor and legislature in the 1990 session. After many disputes, where the governor later noted that he "wanted to create the greatest amount of tension possible," the publicly charming but privately stubborn Wilkinson reluctantly agreed to modify his funding package and to support instead an increase in the sales tax to six cents per dollar, to finance educational reform. He and the legislative leadership also used a healthy number of promises of roads and projects in exchange for votes to pass the Kentucky Education Reform Act (KERA). A compromise, for which no individual nor any branch of government could claim sole credit, the educational reform package was the key action taken during the Wilkinson years. With a good record on prisons and the environment, with a weaker one regarding appointments, state leases, and bond sales, the governor had focused attention on rural areas and illiteracy. But his style almost overcame his actions, and many found it hard to forget the first as they evaluated the second.

BOPTROT and Beyond

In 1951 a losing candidate for governor had attacked the political immorality and corruption in the state capital, "our Ninevah on the Kentucky River." That was nothing new, for criticism had long existed regarding the influence of lobbies, the way votes were secured, and, on occasion, the general quality of the elected officials themselves. Journalists in the 1950s and later noted that the liquor lobby kept a twenty-four-hour open house, with free drinks, for any member, "a temptation that proved fatal to many a lawmaker away from home and the cold eye of the Baptist Church." One member was known for drinking out of a milk carton on the chamber floor; it was less well known that the carton contained a mixture of half milk, half vodka. And antics could be very open. When a bill passed as a result of some political dealings, or even a monetary payoff, it was labeled a turkey bill, and members would yell out, "Gobble, Gobble, Gobble," as the vote was taken.

In 1972 a live turkey was released on the house floor, with the name of a bill on a sign around its neck. Capers such as that brought a versifier to conclude:

> Our ancestors settled the country
> when it was wild and dense,
> then politicians took over
> and it's been unsettled since.

In the three decades after the end of World War I, the pattern for the Kentucky legislature had been rather settled, however. The typical legislator was a white, middle-aged male who attended a Baptist church, practiced law, voted Democratic, and during the successful sessions usually followed the governor's wishes on key votes and in the selection of leadership. While turnover in the Kentucky Senate generally matched national trends, Kentucky House members changed at a much more rapid rate, owing in part to the practice of rotating the nomination among the counties constituting a district. At a time when a rate exceeding 50 percent was deemed "excessive turnover," in the decades of the 1940s and 1950s nearly 62 percent of the legislators in the house changed in each ten-year period. Slowly, though, those rates decreased. A strong committee system developed, members were better informed, and professionalism grew. The Kentucky General Assembly attracted more members oriented to their legislative careers and, not coincidentally, less likely to accept gubernatorial guidance. The general characteristics did not change, except that the typical legislator had an average of three years of experience in 1970 but over ten years in 2011. (See table 19.2.) The state continued to be very near the bottom nationally in the percentage of women legislators and did not rank high in minority representation either. One change in the composition of the general assembly had taken place, however. In 1960 Catholic members made up less than 13 percent of the total, but thirty years later Catholic members represented 29 percent of state legislators. One longtime barrier to elective office in the state had been broken down, but others remained.

Table 19.2. Characteristics of the Kentucky Legislature, 1970–2011

Year	Democrats	Republicans	Average Age	Average year experience	Men	Women	Minorities
1970	95	43	47	3.0	133	5	4
1980	104	34	46	5.7	130	8	4
1990	100	37	50	8.8	130	7	3
2011	73	61	56	10.5	112	26	8

While the state legislature was undergoing change, most of it positive, one other element of Kentucky politics—corruption at the local level—seemed to resist modification. In the two years after 1976, for instance, sheriffs or deputies in five eastern Kentucky counties were convicted of extorting funds from bootleggers. The 1980s began with the Fayette County sheriff resigning after pleading guilty to mail fraud, and the county judge executive of another locale had the same experience the following year. In 1992 the Muhlenberg County judge executive pleaded guilty to spending county funds for personal use, and the next year the county attorney in Lexington and the sheriff in Jefferson County both went to jail. Political corruption at the local level may not have been any worse than in earlier times, but law enforcement agencies now vigorously prosecuted such fraud, and the media publicized it. The local level, though, was only part of the story.

Members of the Kentucky General Assembly came out of that local political environment, and in Frankfort, they continued some long-traditional practices, despite a changing situation. Moreover, by 1979 and afterward, the legislature had become increasingly independent and was in a state of transition as a result. Whereas deals before had been made in the governor's office with one person in charge, now deals had to be made with many. The once-considerable power of the chief executive to influence legislative outcomes decreased, and the vote of each legislator took on more importance. When the decline of party allegiance was added to the mix, suddenly lobbyists found themselves playing by a whole new set of rules. The result was a long and major political scandal that drew national attention to

Kentucky and hurt the image of the evolving independent legislature.

Federal investigators named their operation BOPTROT, for the Business Organizations and Professions Committee (BOP) and for the trotting track involvement (TROT). By the end of their probe in 1995, twenty people and one organization—the Jockey Guild—had been convicted or had pled guilty to a variety of crimes. Sixteen of the twenty individuals were legislators or former legislators, from both parties, and they included the Kentucky speaker of the house. Another was Governor Wilkinson's nephew and appointments secretary; yet another was a former state auditor and gubernatorial primary candidate. A few were guilty only of lying to the FBI. Most were involved in bribery, extortion, mail fraud, racketeering, or a combination thereof, and crimes were usually captured on camera or videotape. Generally, a racing lobbyist had given those who were convicted small bribes, while the vice president of a health care concern had given a more sizable amount, to vote for bills of importance to them, particularly in the 1990 session. Although Kentuckians traditionally have displayed a high degree of tolerance for political corruption, what seemed to disturb them most about BOPTROT was the smallness of most of the bribes (a few hundred dollars). As one historian noted: "It's embarrassing that our legislators were bought off so cheap—almost for a mess of pottage."

But even that was not all. In 1993 the husband of former governor Collins was convicted of extortion and tax fraud involving forced investments in his businesses and kickbacks from firms doing business with the state. A state legislator was convicted in the same year of extorting money from a woman in order to help her win leniency for her husband on a federal charge. In 1994 former nine-term congressman Carroll Hubbard pleaded guilty to felony charges of using campaign funds and congressional workers for his personal benefit, while former congressman Chris Perkins also pleaded guilty to bank fraud and misuse of campaign funds. In 1996, a former state Revenue Cabinet supervisor admitted to funneling $4.2 million in state funds to a shell corporation he had set up. For a time, citizens wondered whether anyone would be left untouched by what the *Economist* called "one of the worst political scandals in Kentucky's history." BOPTROT cast a long shadow over the state's subsequent actions.

Kentuckians went to the polls to elect a governor in 1991 knowing almost nothing of all that. Instead, they could see new trends. The shift of dominance from western Kentucky to the central part of the state was clear in the primary. Six of the seven candidates in the two parties came from Lexington or an adjacent county. The three previous governors—Brown, Collins, and Wilkinson—all fit that pattern as well. That area had boomed in the 1970s and beyond and had attracted the young and the ambitious. Soon a fourth straight governor from the area would be elected.

For Democrats, the field of serious candidates narrowed as Martha Wilkinson, the governor's wife, dropped out because of a lack of support, while a long-shot candidate running on a platform of legalizing marijuana saw his chances go up in smoke. The eventual victor was Lieutenant Governor Brereton C. Jones, who had grown up in West Virginia, had served as Republican minority leader in the legislature there, and had then moved to Kentucky, changed his registration to Democratic, and operated a thoroughbred farm in the Bluegrass. In the Republican primary, congressman Larry Hopkins barely overcame a late challenge from Lexington attorney Larry Forgy. But in the general election, Hopkins's negative advertisements, mistakes about his record, and his involvement in the US House scandal involving "bounced" checks all hurt him, for

Jones carried all but thirteen counties and won by almost a quarter million votes, 540,468–294,452, representing the largest gubernatorial margin in the state's history.

Widely perceived as a reformer, Jones came to office with much support from opinion makers and legislators, as well as a voter mandate. All that brought high expectations. Early on, however, the state's two largest newspapers became critical of the governor and remained so. Moreover, a good working relationship between the executive and legislative branches never really developed, and some harsh language worsened divisions. Yet beyond the rhetoric, the Jones administration and the Kentucky General Assembly actually fashioned a good record. It did not come easily. One regular session ended without a budget, and one of the many special sessions accomplished almost nothing. Still, the legislature passed one of the strongest ethics laws in the United States. Heavy restrictions were placed on lobbyists, and, though modified over the years, by 2015 Kentucky's ethics laws remained some of the most stringent in the nation. Campaign finance reforms also limited the advantages that wealthy candidates once had. A runoff primary was enacted, whereby a second primary would be held—as when Chandler had won the governorship in 1935—if no candidate received 40 percent of the vote. (Had that rule been in effect earlier, all three governors before Jones would have had to run in a second primary race.)

The voters also approved a constitutional amendment, which did not apply to the sitting governor. It permitted future chief executives to serve a second consecutive term, ended the remission of the governor's powers when leaving the state, and caused the governor and lieutenant governor to run as a slate instead of separately. Other actions taken during Jones's term included a mandatory seatbelt law, the establishment of a new health care system, additional funds for a revitalized park system, a four-year phaseout of the inheritance tax, and provision for the largest budget reserve trust fund (or surplus) in the state's history—coming from the core taxes that bring monies into the state, including sales, income, corporate, coal severance, and property taxes. The governor also appointed the first woman, Sara Combs, to sit on the Kentucky Supreme Court.

During the Jones administration, Democrats also carried the state for successful presidential candidate Bill Clinton, who won 665,104 votes in Kentucky, compared with Republican George Bush's 617,178 and independent candidate Ross Perot's 203,944. But in the ten elections for president stretching from 1956 to 1992, Democrats had won Kentucky's vote only when southerners—Lyndon Johnson, Jimmy Carter, and Bill Clinton—were the party candidate. In all the other races, Republicans won, usually by a sizable margin. In a state in which Democratic voter registration remained constant, at almost 68 percent of the electorate between 1975 and 1987, a lot of "closet Republicans" hid behind Democratic labels. By 1994 they appeared to be emerging from the closet in larger numbers. Republicans won four of six congressional seats, controlling that delegation for only the second time. One of those winning Republican candidates filled the seat of the powerful Democrat William H. Natcher, who died that year, after casting a record 18,401 consecutive votes in Congress.

Such trends caused Democratic concern as the 1995 governor's race began, and early prognosticators predicted a pathbreaking victory by Republican Larry Forgy as he faced Lieutenant Governor Paul E. Patton of Pike County. Yet when the results came in on election day, Democrats found themselves in the unfamiliar position of having won as one-time underdogs in the race, by a margin of more than 21,000 votes, 500,787–479,227. What had happened? Simply stated, Forgy lost, and Patton won. Forgy lost, in part, owing to three factors. First of

all, he became identified with the Christian right, and while he gained some votes from that, his action also caused some in his own party to desert him, particularly in Louisville, and made him less of an option to moderate Democrats, especially in his home base of Lexington. Second, his attacks on KERA seemed another move away from the center to the right, and some Republican supporters of educational reform looked elsewhere. A bipartisan pro-KERA response also followed. In both cases, Forgy's actions seemed, on the surface at least, unnecessary, for votes from both the Christian right and the anti-KERA forces were likely his already. Finally, he was also unlucky, for the budgetary actions of the Republican majority in the US Congress on issues affecting the elderly were used against him, taking some of the focus away from the unpopularity of the Clinton administration in Kentucky.

Forgy did not only lose, however. Patton also won the election. One voter spoke of "sleeping Democrats. With the campaign so close . . . it prompted us to get active." For the first time in a long while, the once-traditional Democratic voting blocs—labor, education, blacks—came out in force and made a difference in Louisville in particular, which gave Patton his winning margin. Running well in his native region and recapturing much of western Kentucky for the Democrats, Patton won in the closest race in thirty-two years and became the first eastern Kentuckian chosen governor since 1959. He also became the fifth of the past seven governors who had used the office of lieutenant governor as a stepping-stone to the governor's mansion. All those people had been Democrats. In the fifty-year period since the end of World War II, Republicans had won only one gubernatorial election in Kentucky. That would change.

20

A Political Metamorphosis, 1995–2015

Looking at one level of government, it seemed little had changed in regard to Kentucky politics in the two decades after 1995. Democrats held the governor's office sixteen of those twenty years and remained in control of the state House of Representatives all of that time. Yet, looking at other levels of the commonwealth's political system showed an entirely different pattern. For the times, they were a-changin'.

In the South, a political metamorphosis had mostly occurred by 1995. The Republican party grew increasingly conservative and focused on states' rights—positions previously held by conservative southern Democrats. The Democratic party's support for racial change and other social movements in the 1960s and beyond had broken the back of the "Solid South"—including Kentucky—that had been the bulwark of the Democratic party for almost a century after Appomattox. But that trend came late to the Bluegrass State. In Kentucky, the Democracy remained largely more conservative than the national party, and race appeared less pervasive as an issue. Democratic leaders also displayed a populist bent, while the Republican party continued to make missteps at the state level. All these factors delayed the transformation of the commonwealth from a Democratic bastion into a Republican one, but all that only postponed the moment. By 2015, Kentucky had followed the South fully into the Republican camp.

In 1996, southerner Bill Clinton became the last Democratic presidential candidate to carry Kentucky. During that same time, the party of Lincoln controlled at least four of the six congressional seats. After 1999, the GOP became the majority party in the state senate. Moreover, after Democratic senator Wendell

Ford's retirement that same year, Republicans held both senate seats. By 2015, Mitch McConnell became the majority leader of the US Senate. Yet the Democratic party did not go quietly into the political night and continued to win significant victories, particularly in Louisville and Lexington, where it elected mayors and members of Congress; in state legislative districts; and in governor's races. If balanced in a different way than before, the two-party system continued to be a factor in Kentucky politics.

But the composition of the parties did change, as old coalitions disappeared and new political strengths depended on different groups and issues. The Democratic coalition forged out of the fires of the New Deal became the dominant party for three decades afterward and included the old southern Democrats, plus the newer constituencies of labor unions, African Americans, and urban Catholics. That took away two Kentucky groups that had previously voted consistently Republican—coal miners who cast ballots as the owners asked and African Americans. During the 1960s, moderate Republicans like Louisvillians Marlow Cook and William Cowger made inroads into the increasing black Democratic vote. However, Louie Nunn's racially charged campaigns for governor in 1963 and 1967 negated those gains, making Kentucky African Americans dependable Democratic voters into the twenty-first century.

But that New Deal Democratic coalition began to fragment. By the 1980s, the Republican party's opposition to cultural matters such as abortion, affirmative action, feminism, and gay rights brought the self-described "Moral Majority" or Religious Right to vote increasingly Republican. Kentuckians now placed more emphasis on such social issues than on the economic issues long emphasized by Democrats. Catholics too began to peel from the old coalition. Meanwhile, unions declined in numbers and influence, to only 11 percent of the state workforce. (And union members no longer voted as a bloc anyway.) A coalition of evangelical religious groups, white males, and states' rights conservatives now rose to power. Or perhaps the "new" Republican party was simply the post-Confederate Democratic party operating under a different label. But as Republicans evolved, Democrats changed as well, adding different constituencies, including minority groups such as Hispanics, suburban "Soccer Moms," and younger voters. Increasingly, a rural-urban political divide occurred in Kentucky.

Two eastern Kentucky leaders who had much influence on the region and state—Republican congressman Harold "Hal" Rogers and Democratic governor Paul Patton. (University of Kentucky General Photographic Prints, University of Kentucky Special Collections and Research Center, Lexington, KY)

The Patton Years

Paul Patton, the first governor since 1800 who could run for a full second term as the state's chief executive, had no difficulty achieving that aim. Following a very successful first term, he found the opposition fielded no real threat to his reelection. Josephine Ellen "Peppy" Martin of Hart County emerged as the Republican nominee. A virtual unknown, she made mistake after mistake, and received no party backing. Patton had angered some of his labor allies because he supported limiting workers compensation payments, but few alternatives existed for them. To some, the only question seemed to be whether the colorful Reform Party nominee Gatewood Galbraith of Lexington would outpoll the Republican. In the end, he did not, but did receive 15 percent of the vote, the best ever for a third-party gubernatorial candidate in the commonwealth. Patton won easily, with 62 percent to Martin's meager 22 percent, and he carried all state constitutional offices into the Democratic column as well. Those two consecutive terms thus gave Patton an unprecedented opportunity to implement his agenda. But, as it turned out, the governor would experience both tremendous highs and devastating lows before he left the governor's mansion.

The fifty-eight-year-old Patton came to office well prepared. After gaining personal wealth through coal mining interests, he became active in the Democratic party, served as Pike County judge executive, finished third in the lieutenant governor primary in 1987 to Brereton Jones, then four years later had taken that office. An underdog in his 1995 race for governor, he had won, with the aid of advisor Andrew "Skipper" Martin. Reflecting on past strengths of the state, he had stressed early in his first term that "We can learn from history." In his second inaugural, the governor emphasized that only leadership can bring all people together for a common purpose and that Kentuckians must seize the moment: "We cannot afford the status quo." He reminded citizens that in times past, the state featured "resources squandered, talents wasted, opportunity lost." Patton took those words to heart and fashioned a strong administration with significant achievements, but he also created other lost opportunities.

Patton's most controversial action in his first term involved educational reform and especially who would control the community college system in the commonwealth. The governor argued that the system would expand if the numerous two-year colleges, under the administration of the University of Kentucky, were merged with the state's many technical schools into a new, independent educational entity. That proposal sparked intense and powerful opposition, including that of former Governor Ned Breathitt, chair of the university's board of trustees. But Patton stressed, "I will stake my entire governorship on this effort." Very skillful in working with the general assembly—early in his administration, he had the best working relationship with the legislature of any governor in over two decades—Patton saw the education reform bill pass by seventy-three to twenty-five and twenty-five to thirteen margins in a 1997 special session. The act increased support for research at both the University of Kentucky and the University of Louisville, set up funds to promote excellence at all state universities, established a new board to control community colleges and technical schools, and formed the Kentucky Council on Postsecondary Education to coordinate higher education activities. Reforms continued over the next two regular legislative sessions with seed money for endowed chairs at universities—the so-called "Bucks for Brains" program—and the establishment of Kentucky Educational Excellence Scholarships (KEES). By 2002, some 56,000 students had become a part of the KEES program. And at the secondary and elementary school level, Kentucky revised its school testing, funded a whole series of technological advances, including computers in every classroom, increased aid to early childhood education, and placed increased emphasis on adult education. Patton wanted to be an education governor, and a good case can be made that he succeeded.

Bolstered by a good economic climate early in his governorship, Patton recommended and the Kentucky General Assembly gleefully approved many local projects, with both parties benefiting, as well as a pay raise for the legislators. But more controversial blips began to appear on the Patton radar along the way, some emanating from his office, some from

the legislature. The general assembly diluted the campaign finance and ethics laws, passed laws that produced fewer awards for black-lung benefits to miners, placed more restrictions on abortions, and allowed guns in churches and government buildings. Moreover, several Patton staff members were indicted for evading funding limits in the 1995 race, and the governor eventually pardoned them at the end of his term. Still, by the start of his second term, most observers ranked Patton high on the list of good governors.

In 2000, by a 52 to 48 percent margin, the voters approved a constitutional amendment that finally allowed annual legislative sessions, rather than every two years as before. This afforded governors the opportunity to do more. But Patton's legislative ambitions did not go entirely as planned. In 1999 Republicans had gained control of the state senate when two "lame-duck" Democrats switched parties after the election. Before then, Patton had been able to get his key legislative packages passed. But now he faced a more difficult task, and it grew harder due to personality conflicts between Patton and senate leader David Williams. One cause of the divisions came when Patton indicated that Williams had given him assurances that he could secure enough votes in the senate to pass a tax bill Patton desired. In return, the governor would not back candidates seeking to unseat Republican incumbents. But when the votes did not materialize in the senate, Patton made the agreement known. Williams denied a deal had been struck and then called the governor "a mouthy drunk." Patton, in turn, produced a document by Williams, listing the expected votes. After that exchange, civility all but disappeared for the rest of the term, and less legislation resulted.

Still, actions occurred. Another constitutional amendment abolished the outdated railroad commission. Louisville's merged government option was placed on the ballot. Other measures strengthened coal mine regulations, reapportioned voting districts, and restricted telemarketing. But the party feuding produced deadlock as well. In the 2002 budget negotiations, Republicans sought to remove funding for the 1992 campaign laws that provided public financing for races, and Democrats sought to keep the system in place. No compromise meant no budget, and a special session of the legislature failed to resolve the issue after a week of debate. Patton then initiated a spending plan, in lieu of a budget. That plan would last until the next regular session finally passed a budget. But, for the governor, the budget impasse soon paled in comparison to a personal scandal that ended any hopes that he would run for the US Senate after his term ended (a race he likely would have won) and also greatly weakened his ability to accomplish much during the rest of his term as governor.

It involved a woman. After first denying every charge and rumor, a tearful Patton in September 2002 admitted on statewide television that he had carried on an affair with Tina Conner of Clinton. She had indicated that the married governor had begun their relationship five years before, and they had subsequently met in hotels rooms in Louisville and Lexington. Conner claimed that he had used his office to help her nursing home and new construction company receive favorable treatment. She went on to allege that after the governor broke off the sexual liaison after two years, he had retaliated against her. She sued him for sexual harassment, among other charges. While acknowledging the relationship, the embattled governor rejected all her other accusations. Conner's lawsuits would be later dismissed in the courts, and Patton only received a reprimand from the Kentucky Ethics Commission. But the damage to his career went much deeper. A man with many solid accomplishments and a hard-working chief executive, he had forfeited his political future. But, like Ed Prichard earlier, Patton would rise again and still play an important role in his region, as chancellor and president of a college. But it could have been so much more.

A New Era for Republicans?

As the 2003 gubernatorial election approached, Republicans had been wandering in the political wilderness, lost from the governor's mansion for over three decades. But the Promised Land now seemed not only in sight but almost a given. With both US senators and five of six members of Congress belonging to the party and with Governor Patton's problems, confident Republicans expected a victory at last. In the subsequent party primary, McConnell-backed Ernest L. "Ernie" Fletcher won, with 57 percent of the votes over Louisville's Rebecca Jackson's 28 percent and Glasgow's Steve Nunn's 13 percent. Fletcher's chief problem in that race had involved his running mate, Hunter Bates, who had recently been Mitch McConnell's chief of staff in Washington. Nunn's campaign brought suit against Bates, on the grounds that he did not meet the constitutional requirements regarding residency. The court ruled him ineligible, and, in the midst of the race, Fletcher had to switch to Steve Pence of Louisville. But that had little effect on the end result—an easy victory. Republicans now had a candidate who appeared ready-made for Kentucky politics. Fifty-year-old Ernie Fletcher was a "born-again" Christian lay minister, a physician with a degree from the University of Kentucky, a pilot in the Air Force Reserves, a former state legislator, and a two-term member of Congress from Lexington.

His opponent was another central Kentuckian and the heir to a long-familiar name in state politics. Grandson of "Happy" Chandler, the forty-three-year-old A. B. "Ben" Chandler had won races as much on his merit as his name. Moderate and with an independent streak, as state auditor, then as attorney general since 1996, Chandler had angered some in his party by getting indictments of some of Patton's top advisors and for pursuing the case against a Legislative Research Commission aide for prostitution and gambling in connection with social gatherings he organized. Opposing Chandler in the Democratic primary had been Bruce Lunsford, a wealthy former CEO of a healthcare company in Louisville, and Jody Richards, speaker of the Kentucky House and bookstore owner from Bowling Green. Initially seen primarily as a Lunsford-Chandler contest, the race saw millionaire Lunsford spend $8 million of his own funds against Chandler. After a hard-hitting campaign with negative

Republican governor Ernie Fletcher. (Kentucky Department for Libraries and Archives, Frankfort, KY)

fort, and with voters seeking a change, Fletcher became the first Republican governor in thirty-two years—ending the longest streak in the nation at that time. He won by over 109,000 votes, a record for his party. Democrats did take three constitutional offices, which, as events unfolded, would prove important.

In his inaugural talk, the new governor spoke about the poverty of the spirit and said, "We will restore hope." But almost all Kentucky governors face an immediate disadvantage in that their first legislative session begins about a month after their inaugural, and they are expected to produce a proposed budget soon after that. Starting a new administration, filling key positions, finding out the financial condition of the government, setting the tone for the coming years—all those responsibilities simultaneously vie for the attention of a governor. And a change in party leadership magnifies those challenges as many new administrators must be brought on board quickly. Fletcher faced that situation early and had issues with the legislature as a result.

In his first session, little occurred and no budget emerged—the second straight time that had happened. Like Patton, Fletcher operated the state under his own spending plan. But the next year, the state supreme court limited that option more when it ruled that a governor could spend funds without a budget but only on items specifically mentioned in the constitution and in statutes. Problems also arose when state workers and teachers threatened to strike over a proposed significant increase in employee health insurance. A special legislative session in October addressed the issue and averted a strike. And then in the 2005 session, a nasty fight erupted over a contested election. A Republican state senate candidate in Louisville had won the general election, but courts had ruled her ineligible to serve because she lived in Indiana and did not meet residency requirements. The opposition candidate was thus certified as the winner. But the Republican majority in the senate seated their party candidate anyway, despite two court rulings, causing Democrats to leave the chamber in protest. The dispute even triggered the move of a for-

ads by both candidates, with polls not in his favor, Lunsford dropped out of the race just four days before election day and announced his support of Richards. That made the race closer, but Chandler still prevailed by ten thousand votes, with 50 percent to Richards's 46.5. No huge policy differences had existed between the two except that Chandler endorsed passage of a constitutional amendment to put slot machines at race tracks to increase the state's education fund. (After the primary, a bitter Lunsford then endorsed Fletcher near the end of the general election. Later, Fletcher would appoint him to head a commission to cut waste in state government. Some observers, pointing to the presence of McConnell's wife on Lunsford's board, argued that Lunsford was primarily in the race to exhaust Chandler's war chest. Whether mere speculation or not, Lunsford's race did drain Chandler's campaign funds. But Chandler faced an uphill struggle anyway.)

With better funding—Fletcher outspent Chandler two-to-one, including much outside money—with the Patton scandal hanging over Democratic heads, with Fletcher running on the long-used slogan of cleaning up Frank-

mer Democrat-turned-Republican from the GOP to Independent status instead. Later, in December, the state supreme court ruled that one candidate was ineligible to serve and the other had not received a majority of votes cast, and so declared the seat vacant.

Despite those problems, and his cool relationship with David Williams, Fletcher did have some success in getting several proposals enacted. The legislature passed and the voters then approved a constitutional amendment to prohibit same-sex marriages (which would later be voided by a US Supreme Court decision). The governor also did not veto a law providing state funding to start a pharmacy school at a private university. The state courts, too, later would declare that act invalid. More lasting action followed the governor's proposal to modify the revenue system. The Republican senate and Democratic house followed up by raising the tax on cigarettes from three to thirty cents, lowering taxes on those with incomes below the poverty line, and reducing corporate taxes by some 30 percent. The timing of all that, coupled with an improving national economy, gave Fletcher needed funds to do things. Also, during the governor's term, a seat-belt law, stronger mine-safety regulations, an increase in mine inspectors, a 20 percent increase in funding for higher education, better teacher pay, funds for new school computers, an increase in the state minimum wage above the federal level, cost-effective changes in Medicaid, the largest bond issuance to that time, and incentives for alternative fuel and renewable energy plants to locate in the commonwealth all became law. Moreover, in 2006, the budget passed on time, the first time that had occurred since 2000, and Fletcher appointed the first African American to sit on the state's highest court. All in all, a solid record had been achieved. But another matter pushed all that aside in the minds of many voters and would dominate his administration for months.

The Hiring Scandal

The controversy, and the governor's actions regarding it, eventually caused Lieutenant Governor Steve Pence—who had prosecuted BOP-TROT—to say he would not run with Fletcher again and prompted senate Republican leader Williams to insist that Fletcher could not win reelection and should not run.

What had happened was that under pressure to give party friends jobs, especially after being out of power for so long, key Republicans circumvented the merit system. By law, for positions under the merit system, politics cannot be a factor in filling the posts. Of course it can be a factor subtly, but where Fletcher forces made mistakes involved the systematic and overt nature of the actions—with a "Hit List" and more—and they thus took illegal actions. Moreover, by using emails and text messaging, they had left a clear electronic trail. Had the governor trusted his instincts when the story first broke during his trip to Asia, he would have been better served. In his initial response, Fletcher had indicated that if mistakes had been made, he would penalize those responsible. Had he stuck to that course, it would have cost him some political capital temporarily, but overall he likely could have moved on. But on his return to Kentucky, he decided to fight it fully, which drew attention to the issue over many months, and brought new charges.

In November 2004, the Kentucky Executive Branch Ethics Commission staff first learned of allegations of merit system violations; by the March 2005 meeting the board heard specific charges. Attorney General Greg Stumbo, a Democrat, then opened an investigation. By June and July, indictments began appearing. In August, the governor issued blanket pardons to nine administration employees, including the head of the Republican party, the governor's deputy chief of staff, and the head of the Transportation cabinet. Overall, pardons eventually covered a total of fifteen named individuals (and fourteen others in sealed indictments). The day after issuing the pardons, the state's governor invoked his Fifth Amendment rights and refused to testify before the grand jury, both damning political moves. He would be later indicted as well, on three misdemeanor counts regarding what the grand jury called "widespread" official misconduct for placing people in merit jobs for political reasons. Fletcher thus became the third governor to be indicted—joining William S. Taylor, implicated in the Goebel assassination, and Flem Sampson, accused of benefiting from textbook sales.

Soon after the indictments, Lieutenant Governor Pence announced that he would not run for reelection with Fletcher. Later the governor asked his lieutenant governor to resign, but Pence refused. Then in mid-September, Fletcher fired nine state officials, saying they had used "poor judgment" and had made "mistakes" regarding the merit system, and also called for the resignation of the Republican state chairman, an action the party resisted. Fletcher's removals and actions angered many in his own party. As a paper noted, "Fletcher is the captain of a sinking ship." Finally, in August 2006, a judge ruled that the governor could not be prosecuted unless he was first impeached, a finding that seemed to go against existing legal precedent and would likely have been overturned on appeal. Soon after, Fletcher signed an agreement denying he broke any laws but admitting wrongdoing in his administration, in exchange for the attorney general dropping the charges against him. As part of the agreement, the governor would accept resignations of Fletcher-appointed members from the Kentucky Personnel Board, and Stumbo would offer a list from which to choose replacements. After a seventeen-month investigation, the grand jury issued its final report in November, concluding that the violation of state merit laws "was formulated at the highest levels of state government and approved by Governor Fletcher." Poor decisions had turned what should have been a minor embarrassment into a full-blown scandal involving pardons, the Fifth Amendment, firings, hurt party feelings, backroom deals, and more—none of which helped the reelection chances of the man who had pledged to clean up Frankfort.

Still, despite opposition from some party leaders, some serious health issues, and the scandal, Fletcher remained determined to run for a second term. In truth, he had grown in office and could boast a reasonable record of accomplishments, the hiring mess notwithstand-

ing. But he faced significant opposition, even within his own party. In the primary, Anne Northup, former congresswoman from Louisville, and Paducah businessman Billy Harper, who used over $5 million of his own funds, both challenged the sitting governor. But the major contender to Fletcher's job, Northup, had several strikes against her as she faced rural, evangelical voters—she was from Louisville, was a woman, and was Catholic. Moreover, Harper's presence in the race split the anti-Fletcher vote. In the subsequent contest, Northup did carry the area around her hometown, but she had expected more support from party leaders, many of whom, like McConnell, remained openly neutral. Fletcher turned away his rivals, garnering 50 percent to Northup's 37 and Harper's 13.

Meanwhile, in a reversal of four years earlier, when Patton's problems had been a liability to party success, now Democrats saw that Fletcher's political issues offered them similar good prospects for victory. That situation brought out many candidates. In early May—two weeks before the primary—one of those challengers, state treasurer Jonathan Miller, dropped out of the race and endorsed Steve Beshear, who favored expanded gambling. At that stage, the race had become Beshear versus Louisville businessman Bruce Lunsford, house speaker Jody Richards, and former lieutenant governor Steve Henry of Louisville. But angry Chandler allies opposed Lunsford while other Democrats bitterly recalled his aid to Republicans. Henry enjoyed name recognition, but an accusation that he had overbilled patients in his medical practice hurt him. Richards got into the race late and was hindered by having to stay in Frankfort for a special session. To the surprise of many (and perhaps because of the Miller support), Beshear won by a large enough margin to avoid a run-off election, receiving 41 percent of the vote, to Lunsford's 21 percent and Henry's 18 percent, with Jody Richards at 13 percent and perennial outsider Gatewood Galbraith at 6 percent.

Long shot Steve Beshear had seemed an unlikely winner when he entered the race. After serving as Martha Layne Collins's lieutenant governor, he had finished third to Wallace Wilkinson in the 1987 Democratic primary for governor, had lost handily in a 1996 US Senate race to McConnell, and had been largely out of the political spotlight since then. But he looked gubernatorial, sounded like rural Kentucky, had the support of both major newspapers in the state, and carried none of the electoral baggage of a Lunsford or Henry. Now he faced an unpopular incumbent and won easily, with 59 percent of the votes cast. Most experts had considered the Fletcher election the start of Republican domination of the governor's office; that had not occurred. Also, continuing a trend of lower turnout and greater apathy among the electorate, voter turnout declined from the 40 percent of four years earlier to 37 percent in 2007—a troubling trend that would persist. But no matter the circumstances, the sixty-three-year-old Beshear had made a remarkable comeback, winning the post he had sought twenty years earlier.

Democratic governor Steve Beshear. (Kentucky Governor's Office, Official Photo)

Beshear and the Budget

From Dawson Springs in west Kentucky, Steve Beshear had attended the University of Kentucky Law School, had been elected to the legislature, had won the post of attorney general, had served as lieutenant governor, had suffered two political defeats, and had continued his Lexington legal practice. His victory now meant that a central Kentuckian eventually would be governor for twenty-eight of the past thirty-six years, a pattern interrupted only by the Patton terms.

When governors take office, few know what to expect in regard to the economy and the resulting budget with which they will have to work. Some are fortunate—as was Bert Combs—in that they have a sudden influx of funds from a new source of income—in his case, a voter-approved sales tax. Others create additional funding through some often unpopular but needed taxes—as with Governor Louie Nunn's "Nunn's Nickel." But a few chief executives face difficult financial times and find few options available, as was the case in the depression with Ruby Laffoon. Unfortunately for

Steve Beshear, his administration mirrored the last category.

When sworn in as governor, the new chief executive asked citizens' help in making Kentucky "America's Next Frontier"—one of new technologies, new entrepreneurs, new environmental protections, new imaginative solutions. But almost as soon as the new governor took office, a devastating recession struck the nation, and its effects would largely last for the entire Beshear administration. The commonwealth's chief executive thus had few opportunities to advance new initiatives or expand existing ones. Instead, he spent much of his efforts trying to balance a declining budget in imaginative ways. In 2008, for instance, he had to address a "grim" $1 billion shortfall, and other than eliminating the run-off primary, the legislature did little. His campaign platform had advocated expanding gambling at racetracks in order to raise needed funds, but while the Democratic house finally passed a measure that could allow that, the Republican senate did not bring the measure to a vote. So with no ma-

417

jor new revenue streams, the budget, as Beshear aptly stated, became "austere to the point of pain."

Surprisingly, all that did not seem to damage the governor much when he sought reelection in 2011. In fact, his budget-balancing cuts seemed to have been carried out in a responsible manner. His choice of Jerry Abramson, the popular mayor of Louisville, as his lieutenant governor represented a good political move as well. (In 2014, then-Lieutenant Governor Abramson resigned to take a federal post, and the governor appointed the highly respected Crit Luallen to replace him.) On the other hand, however, Democratic president Barack Obama was unpopular in Kentucky, the economy had not recovered much, and Beshear faced a tough, knowledgeable Republican opponent in the person of senate leader David Williams. Both candidates had well-funded war chests—the governor through four years of fundraising, and Williams reportedly through millions donated by his father-in-law. Both men knew state government well. And both understood the political game. The stage seemed set for high political drama.

Yet, in the end, the election of 2011 proved to be a rather lackluster affair. The governor managed to distance himself from the president, stressed his prudent budget cutting and safeguarding of vital services like education, and emphasized his plans for the commonwealth once better times returned. But the key factor seemed to be a widespread dislike for the man one paper termed "the Bully from Burkesville." While a smart, politically astute, and often moderate leader at times, Williams had also angered many on both sides of the aisle by his blunt words and sometimes arbitrary actions. To some, it seemed he dictated often and compromised seldom. That image may have been unfair, but it was widespread, and on the campaign trail, Williams did little to change minds. Moreover, his opposition to Beshear's call for expanded gambling seemed hypocritical to some when the senator reported gambling losses (and gains) on his own tax returns. And, finally, to avoid a major primary challenge, Williams had named that possible

opponent as his lieutenant governor running mate. Richie Farmer of Clay County seemed an ideal choice in that he had been an idolized University of Kentucky basketball player before his election as agriculture commissioner. But he turned out to be a public relations disaster. First, a messy divorce made news, and then stories arose about financial and ethics irregularities in his department—later, the resulting felony convictions would send him to federal prison. With another dismal voter turnout, the incumbent won easily by a 170,000 margin and with 56 percent of the ballots. His party also carried most of the other statewide elected offices. Williams gained only 35 percent while now-third-party candidate Gatewood Galbraith received 9 percent.

A two-term governor, but one with the opposition in control of the state senate and with a recession still around, Beshear worked with new leadership in the legislature—with the house now led by Greg Stumbo by 2009 and the senate by Robert Stivers by 2013—to produce some changes in government. Bills dealing with drug abuse, deregulation of telephones, dating violence, tighter ethics laws, criminal code reform, and increasing compulsory education to age eighteen all passed. Both houses approved redistricting bills following the 2010 census figures, but the state's highest court voided the initial attempt, and the process had to be redone. And across all administrations in the two decades, nature took its toll. A major flood in 1997, the worst drought of the century in 1999, crippling ice storms in 2003 and six years later, then violent tornadoes in 2012 that killed twenty people, and record snowfalls in 2015 all challenged citizens and governments as well.

On budget matters, courts ruled that video instant gambling at racetracks was legal, while an increased cigarette tax and the addition of the sales tax on package sales of alcoholic beverages balanced some new tax breaks. But financial issues persisted, and in 2010 the general assembly once more failed to pass a budget in its regular session. During a May special session legislators finally crafted a state spending plan. Medicaid and pension-fund shortfalls plagued the budget as well. By 2014, the state budget had been reduced by $1.6 billion over the last seven years, with some state agencies experiencing cuts of over 40 percent. Universities had made up adjusted-for-inflation cuts of 27 percent chiefly by raising tuition—a not-so-hidden form of tax increase.

But the chief accomplishment of the Beshear years concerned health care. Kentucky had one of the unhealthiest populations and one of the highest rates of uninsured citizens of any state in the nation. Passage of the Affordable Care Act on the federal level gave the commonwealth the opportunity to set up its own network—called Kynect—one that cut the number of uninsured in half and gave over 400,000 Kentuckians access to quality health care. Kentucky's seamless success made the state a model for the nation. That action, however, represented one of the few major initiatives undertaken by the administration. More often, budget woes forced Beshear to operate more as "a caretaker governor." But in the last two years of his term, the administration did gain some economic momentum and led the nation in new economic development investment per capita. Given the political realities he faced, Steve Beshear had done reasonably well.

The Federal Scene

As opposed to the governors' races and the local contests, Republicans largely dominated elections involving the federal offices of president, senator, and representative. In the presidential races, for example, in 1996, Democrat Bill Clinton won big in Jefferson County and carried the state with 46 percent over Bob Dole's 45 percent and Ross Perot's 9 percent (with women increasingly voting Democratic and men Republican). At the same time, the Perot ballots were strong in the same antiestablishment, anti-government areas that had given a sizeable vote to George Wallace years earlier. Those feelings would grow into a potent Tea Party movement later.

The year 1996 represented the last time a Democrat would win the state in the presidential sweepstakes over the next two decades. And the races were not even close—in 2000 George W. Bush won Kentucky by some 15 percent over Al Gore and four years later easily took the state's electoral count again by a 60–40 percent margin over John Kerry. Because of the expected outcome, presidential candidates seldom even campaigned in the commonwealth. Despite Democrat Barack Obama's sizeable national win in 2008, he lost the commonwealth to John McCain by a 41–57 percent margin; in his successful bid for a second term, Obama did even worse, carrying only four counties and losing the state by 400,000 votes.

The same picture emerged in regard to one US Senate seat as well. Mitch McConnell won election after election, in the process becoming the longest-serving senator from Kentucky and eventually the majority leader of the US Senate. In that regard, he also became the most powerful Kentuckian in Washington since the days of Barkley, Clements, Cooper, and Ford, and certainly the most influential in the early twenty-first century. Moreover, Taiwan-born Elaine Chao, wife of the once-divorced McConnell, was chosen as the US Secretary of Labor in 2001, adding to the family's national influence. And throughout the years, McConnell won his races easily: defeating later governor Beshear in 1996 by a 55–43 percent margin; winning by a record margin for a Republican with 65 percent of the vote over Lois Combs Weinberg of Knott County in 2002; defeating Bruce Lunsford by a closer 53–47 percent six years later; and carrying his race by an unexpectedly large margin in 2014. In that contest, McConnell, at age seventy-two, faced a primary challenge, a rarity for the incumbent. Then-political newcomer Matt Bevin took well-funded Tea Party stands against McConnell, who struck back with strong attacks and easily carried the day by a 60–35 percent margin. Despite not being endorsed by his primary opponent, McConnell won a record sixth term surprisingly easily in the general election. Stressing his congressional seniority and tying his opponent to the unpopular-in-Kentucky President Obama, McConnell defeated Secretary of State Alison Lundergan Grimes of Lexington by a 56–41 percent vote. Together, the two spent almost $80 mil-

The longest-serving US senator from Kentucky, Mitch McConnell of Louisville. (US Senate Majority Leader's Office)

lion—with about three-fourths of it coming from out-of-state sources. Not charismatic, like his hero Henry Clay, Mitch McConnell more often operated behind the scenes as a focused "Insider" and skilled dealmaker who always ran strong campaigns and usually kept his end goal clearly in his sights. Those attributes won him numerous victories in Kentucky and in Washington.

But Republican success in the other US senator seat did not come as easily. After Wendell Ford's retirement in 1998, the vacant seat beckoned to both parties. On the GOP side, Jim Bunning won the primary easily. After he had been badly defeated for governor in 1983 by Martha Layne Collins, he had won election to the US House and had served in that post for some dozen years before winning the US Senate primary. One of the most conservative members of Congress, Bunning matched well his district in that regard. But he could also be aloof on the campaign trail and gained few votes on the hustings. In short, he had both strengths and weaknesses.

So too did his Democratic opponent. Like Bunning, "Scotty" Baesler owed some of his success to name recognition based on sports—in his case as a starting guard for an Adolph Rupp basketball team. In a contest of basketball versus baseball heroes in Kentucky, the round-

ball candidate would usually win the affections of the electorate. But the changing political makeup of the state made that less certain in 1998. After basketball, Baesler had graduated from the University of Kentucky Law School, had been a judge then mayor in Lexington, and in 1992 had won election to Congress. In the party's primary, his 34 percent of the vote had narrowly beaten Louisville businessman and former head of the state crime commission Charlie Owen (29 percent) and Lieutenant Governor Steve Henry (28 percent). In the subsequent general election, Bunning ran very well in his home congressional district and Baesler did not in his, and that proved the difference in a close race. The northern Kentuckian won by under 7,000 votes out of 1.1 million cast, and with that, for the first time in twenty-six years, both Kentucky US senators were Republican.

They barely stayed that way six years later, when Bunning sought reelection in 2004. Termed the "Underperformer" in Congress by *Time*, the incumbent—according to one observer—"seemed to blunder almost every time he opened his mouth." He faced a little-known opponent in state senator Dr. Daniel Mongiardo of Hazard. The incumbent's seat initially seemed safe. But "Bumbling Bunning" committed numerous errors that made the race competitive. He described his opponent as someone who looked like the son of Iraqi dictator Saddam Hussein and got the date wrong for the 9–11 attacks. He declared (without any support) that Democratic "thugs" had injured his wife, angered some in Louisville with comments about a bridge issue there, did not show up in person for a joint debate but instead used a teleprompter from a Washington, DC, studio, and on and on. National Democrats sensed a possible upset and poured funds into the race; Republicans brought in McConnell to bolster their cause. In the end, three things saved Bunning's seat. First, the presence on the ballot of the state constitutional amendment that would ban same-sex marriages brought out sizeable numbers of conservative evangelical groups; so too did the presidential election-year vote. Together that gave the state a high turnout of 64 percent. And, finally, in a race where the vote was expected to be close, the difference may have come after David Williams suggested that the unmarried Democrat was "limp-wristed" and a "switch hitter." (Mongiardo would later marry in 2008.) When the results came in, Democrats won Louisville and Lexington by huge margins, but Republicans did just well enough in northern Kentucky and in rural areas to give Bunning a 22,000 vote margin. By comparison, President George W. Bush had carried the commonwealth by over 350,000 votes, and his coattails proved just long enough to bring the incumbent senator victory as well.

In 2010, with Bunning begrudgingly stepping down, that open seat once more beckoned to both parties. The race, particularly on the Republican side of the primary, drew national attention. With the conservative, libertarian, antiestablishment, so-called Tea Party movement defeating incumbents and challenging others across the nation, the state provided another testing ground for the faction. In Kentucky, before the Tea Party's involvement, the early front-runner and expected victor in the Republican primary had been the tall, Harvard-educated, Secretary of State Trey Grayson from northern Kentucky. A McConnell protégé, he also enjoyed the backing of popular eastern Kentucky congressman Hal Rog-

ers. With the support of the state's two most powerful political leaders, Grayson seemed a shoo-in. But the dynamics changed when Tea Party choice Randal "Rand" Paul entered the race. A political neophyte in that he had never held any political office, he had, however, observed his Texas congressman father's Libertarian races for president at the national level. Utilizing those well-established paternal networks, Rand Paul raised funds quickly and used those monies in an extensive advertising campaign that gained him quick recognition in the race. Not happy with McConnell's and the party's non-support of his early fundraising, which had hastened his decision not to run for reelection, Bunning now endorsed Paul, the Bowling Green ophthalmologist and the outsider. The party split. Grayson, more "laid-back" and not particularly good in crowds, faced an unexpected challenge. Moreover, Paul proved an invisible target, in that he said little, had no record to attack, and took few specific stands—except for a general appeal to those dissatisfied with government and cultural change. That strategy proved enticing to Republican voters, and Paul shocked the establishment with an easy 58–35 percent win over Grayson.

The Democratic primary proved to be much closer, almost a dead heat. Attorney General John "Jack" Conway of Louisville opposed Lieutenant Governor Daniel Mongiardo, who had the support of Governor Beshear. Conway had served in the Patton administration, had lost a close race against Anne Northup for Congress, and now had the endorsement of the state's two Democratic congressmen, plus Luallen and Louisville mayor Abramson. Few real issues separated the two well-funded candidates, and it came down to a classic urban-rural split in the vote. The young and photogenic Conway received a large vote from Louisville and central Kentucky. With name recognition from his earlier, surprising race with Bunning, Mongiardo carried the rural areas in the East and West. With a late push, Conway won a very close race by some four thousand votes—44–43 percent.

In the general election, a libertarian with no political experience faced a moderately liberal Democrat with a good background in government. But Conway did little to persuade voters to abandon their previous patterns and cast their ballots for him. Even after drawing national attention for saying that he thought civil rights legislation had overreached, Paul easily defeated Conway by a 56–44 percent margin. And an unusual victor became senator. Forty-seven-year-old Rand Paul had few Kentucky connections the first thirty years of his life. Born in Pennsylvania, raised in Texas, interning in Washington in his father's congressional office, and graduating from Duke Medical School, he had then moved to Bowling Green to start his practice. Working in several of his father's campaigns over the years, the younger Paul had learned his political lessons well. When the Tea Party movement took root in Kentucky, he became its face and had won. As a libertarian, Paul basically opposed the government's involvement in most federal activities and supported massive cuts in defense spending, energy, education, foreign aid, housing, and more. In his first speech in Congress, he had criticized Henry Clay for his compromises and vowed that would not be his course. He usually followed that dictum. Seen as a true believer by some and an obstructionist by others, he and fellow senator McConnell differed greatly in their view of politics, but, in some ways, both represented part of the Kentucky political mind. In 2015, Paul sought to win the Republican nomination for president, but after gaining little support, dropped out of the race to focus on his reelection bid in 2016.

Congressional Races

As recently as 1992, Democrats held four of the commonwealth's six congressional seats. But within four years that trend had reversed, and Republicans thereafter consistently carried either four or five of the six districts.

In 1996, victor Clinton had failed to sweep into office others of his party. In Louisville, Republican Anne Northup became the second woman elected to Congress from Kentucky when she defeated the Democratic incumbent by some seven hundred votes. She

would hold that post for a decade until the Democrats reclaimed it in 2006, when Democrat John Yarmuth, a former Marlow Cook Republican staffer, defeated her 51 to 48 percent. At times, he would be the only Democratic congressman from the state.

The other Democratic seat came from one of two districts. One was a surprise, since Patton fraternity brother and former county judge executive Ken Lucas of Boone County won in usually staunchly Republican northern Kentucky and served from 1999 until 2005. But his election represented more a personal success than a party one, and that seat soon became safely Republican again. More contested was the district centered around Lexington. When Democrat Scotty Baesler gave up his seat to run for the Senate, Republican Ernie Fletcher won the post. Then, after Fletcher's election as governor in 2003, he stepped down, and in a kind of musical chairs, his defeated Democratic opponent Ben Chandler replaced him and won the district easily. For two years, Chandler was the only Kentucky Democrat in Washington, until Yarmuth's election. But that twosome lasted only briefly, for in 2012, that Sixth District saw Tea Party follower G. H. "Andy" Barr IV defeat Chandler by a 51–47 margin, by tying him to the unpopular president in an election year.

The story for the other three congressional districts followed a much more consistent story line. Over two decades, in none of those districts was the Republican candidate tested, with only a few exceptions. In eastern Kentucky Hal Rogers of Somerset won very easily and by 2015 had served some thirty-four years in Congress, part of it as the chair of the powerful Committee on Appropriations. He represented what one historian has termed the Kentucky oxymoron overall—voting for "more federal money and less government."

The two western Kentucky districts showed similar results for the party, though those holding those seats made less of an impact in the nation's capital. In the oddly shaped First District, one-time Democrat Ed Whitfield won as a Republican in 1994, ousting an incumbent Democrat, and held the seat until he stepped down over two decades later. After Democrat Bill Natcher died in 1994, two different Republican representatives—Ron Lewis and then Brett Guthrie—served the Second District in that same time frame. They were the first of that party to win the district since the Civil War.

The Governor's Race, 2015

Both parties had high expectations for victory in 2015. On the Republican side, the front-runner was former legislator and current Commissioner of Agriculture James "Jamie" Comer Jr. of Monroe County, the highest-ranking Republican in state government. He was in turn challenged by former state supreme court justice Will Scott, Louisville businessman and recently defeated mayoral candidate Hal Heiner, and financial planner and Tea Party advocate Matt Bevin, also of Louisville. With Heiner and Bevin dividing the Louisville vote, and with Scott expected to carry a few eastern Kentucky counties, that left the main battlegrounds to be the rest of rural Kentucky and urban areas of northern Kentucky. Bevin used his self-funded treasury to fend off various attacks on him and then, near the end of the race, Heiner's campaign was accused of being behind damaging accusations about Comer and a former girlfriend. All that infighting hurt both men and aided the Bevin candidacy. As it turned out, the contest would be decided by less than a single vote in each county. Bevin won by 83 votes over Comer, out of 214,000 cast. After a recanvass, due to the closeness of the count, the results were Bevin 70,479 (33 percent), Comer 70,396 (33 percent), Heiner 57,946 (27 percent), and Scott 15,364 (7 percent). Comer did well in rural areas, but the victor owed the win to a sizeable urban northern Kentucky vote on his behalf. And so a man born in Colorado, raised in New Hampshire, educated in Virginia, and who had worked in Pennsylvania and Massachusetts before coming to Kentucky just sixteen years earlier, now carried Republican hopes into the general election.

Once the primaries ended, the general campaign geared up quickly. Bevin, after a bit-

ter primary and in the wake of an equally bitter primary race against McConnell for the US Senate seat the year before, did not have a united party, but did have a well-funded campaign and the state's increasingly Republican voting patterns—aside from gubernatorial races—in his favor. Unpopular with many mainline party members, unendorsed by a single major paper in the commonwealth, Bevin emphasized his anti-party, anti-government, and anti-president stands. Meanwhile the Democrat did not campaign well and—as had McConnell a year before against Bevin—used mostly negative ads. Conway, perhaps mistakenly, hoped for a small turnout overall and a large Louisville vote to help his chances. Preelection polls indicated Conway would win. But the presence of Jenean Hampton, the first African American candidate for lieutenant governor, on Bevin's ticket may have reduced the black Democratic vote in the Falls City. Moreover, a controversial and illegal stand by a Rowan County clerk who refused to follow the US Supreme Court rulings regarding issuance of marriage licenses to gay and lesbian couples energized the state's evangelical religious voters. While the overall turnout was small, the more conservative elements did cast their ballots. All that, and Conway's failure to persuade voters on key issues, brought Bevin an unexpectedly easy 53–44 percent victory. Whether a businessman with no previous experience would have a stronger administration than other chief executives with such backgrounds—Brown and Wilkinson—remained to be seen. Whether the third Republican governor since World War II would fare better than the previous two—Nunn with an unpopular tax, Fletcher with the hiring scandal and its aftermath—remained to be seen. Whether Kentucky would continue down the red road of Republicanism or forge a different path also remained to be seen.

Kentucky politics thus remains confused, complex, and convoluted. Yet amid all that, a trend has emerged. As an observer noted of one southern state: "Mississippi believes in the two-party system; it just believes in having them one at a time." So too some thought of Kentucky, as it changed from a state where Democrats usually won, to a place where both parties consistently contested for most major offices, to a commonwealth where Republicans generally proved more successful. Yet its political landscape still is different in some ways than places south and north, and its politics often still are "the damnedest."

Politics Present and Future

While some commentators, and citizens generally, criticize the governors, others find fault with legislators and disparage the lobbyists (who spent $8.7 million in the 2014 legislative session). But, in truth, all areas of government have come under increasing scrutiny. Good candidates may not run because of the searching media inquiries into their careers and the political attacks on their personal lives. Others may find offensive the fund-raising activities needed to win office. Still more may feel they will be criticized if they compromise and equally censured if they do not. Yet, at the same time, those in political life can also effect real good for their constituents, their state, and their nation. They can also leave a record of accomplishment and achievement. They can also leave a legacy to future generations.

Still, to some observers, the issues under discussion sometimes seem the wrong ones. A journalist who had covered the Kentucky General Assembly for thirty years summarized his impressions in a valedictory column: "I've watched far too many state legislators waste too much time obsessing over the Five G's—guns, God, gays, gynecology, and G-strings—while spending far too little time focusing on the Five E's that could actually . . . move the state forward—education, economic development, . . . equitable taxation, environmental protection, and . . . ethics."

All that creates some degree of cynicism among voters. That, in turn, produces indifference or a sense of powerlessness. As a result, even with all the close races, voter turnout plummeted. By 1976 Kentucky had fallen to forty-first in the nation in that category. In the key 1994 congressional races, fewer than 28 percent of those who could cast ballots in the commonwealth did so—the next to lowest turnout in the nation. In the state in which the 1900 turnout of 83 percent almost led the nation and where the 1920 figure did lead, in the commonwealth where politics is "the damnedest," in a place where a newspaper editor once complained about the "manic pre-occupation" of the people with the subject, voters now seemed apathetic, angry, even bored. Except for presidential races, they stayed away from the polls in droves. In the 2015 party primaries only one in eight eligible voters participated; in the governor's race that year, only 30 percent turned out, and only 11 percent of those under the age of twenty-four. More than two-thirds of the state's registered voters seemingly did not care. Could some candidate or some cause reignite their interest?

Politics of the twenty-first century differ in some ways from the campaigns of decades and centuries before, but some important traditions live on, not all of them positive. But will the colorful stories of the Stanley-Morrow race ever be matched? Will the oratory of individuals like Henry Clay, John C. Breckinridge, "Billy O'B." Bradley, Alben Barkley, or Happy Chandler ever again be an important part of political success? Will a well-crafted media image be more important than local organizational ability, such as exhibited by Earle Clements? Will the results of political polls be more crucial than a candidate's ability? Will image trump reality? New generations will answer those questions.

21

New Challenges, Old Traditions

In the years after World War II, Kentuckians experienced the greatest changes in their recorded history. The atomic age arrived. Men walked on the moon. Women's rights expanded. Segregation ended. Television, air conditioning, automobile ownership, and computers became commonplace. Almost instant communications resulted from the presence in virtually every home first of radios, telephones, and televisions, then "smart" phones and computers. The world grew smaller, and opportunities to visit foreign areas grew wider through easily available airplane travel. Trips that took months a century before now took a day. Information that would formerly have taken days or weeks to assemble and transmit now issued in minutes or hours. The state moved from an agricultural and coal economy to a more diversified base, and for the first time statistics showed that the state was more urban than rural.

Yet at the same moment, many elements of Kentucky life continued. Some individuals fought hard to resist change, seeking to carry forth worthy parts of the past into the new millennium. The commonwealth struggled to find and keep its identity in a rapidly changing world.

Images

Some of the conceptions Americans held of Kentucky disappeared over the years, such as the gambling and vice associated with Newport, just across the Ohio River from Cincinnati. Other perceptions proved much harder to eradicate and, in fact, sometimes grew more enduring. Paducah-born author Irvin S. Cobb wrote that "ghosts walk Churchill Downs on Derby Day. . . . The whole place . . . is crowd-

ed with memories." Through the efforts of promoter Matt Winn and others, the Kentucky Derby, held on the first Saturday in May, became the nation's greatest horse race, and the commonwealth's identification with the thoroughbred grew stronger, aided also by the attention given Kentucky-raised jockeys like Eddie Arcaro and Steve Cauthen. Nor was that image a false one. In presenting a special subscription offer in 1965, Mike Barry of the *Kentucky Irish American* added a proviso: "This offer may be withdrawn at any time. Any time we have that Real Good Day at the track." The day after the Derby the same Mike Barry would be given time at Sunday mass to explain to the congregation exactly what had taken place on Derby day. Such interest, together with the presence of other major tracks, such as Keeneland, made Kentucky the home for horses.

Allied to this view of Kentucky was the image of the Colonel. In the nineteenth century cartoonists had made newspaperman Henry Watterson almost the personification of the South. Kentuckian D. W. Griffith had perpetuated that stereotype in film, as did other filmmakers. Annie Fellows Johnston's book *The Little Colonel* and similar publications included the same representation, and governors furthered the myth by issuing thousands of Kentucky Colonelcies. Then came Harland D. Sanders. Not particularly successful in the first decades of his life, the Indiana-born Sanders made a modest start at a Corbin restaurant, began to franchise Kentucky Fried Chicken in 1953, and by the end of the decade had more than two hundred fast-food outlets. The image of Colonel Sanders spread across the country. Although Sanders sold his interest in the domestic part of the company's operations for

$2 million in the early 1960s, he became an even greater part of the corporation's advertising strategy. Continued publicity made him an internationally known figure—a 1976 poll ranked him the second most recognizable celebrity in the world. He became a part of the mythology of Kentucky.

Add to all that the long-time identification of the state with bourbon, and the archetypical Kentucky Colonel was complete. He sat on the veranda of his white-columned mansion, drinking a mint julep or bourbon and water, watching his thoroughbreds run in the fields of bluegrass, with a Stephen Collins Foster melody playing softly in the background. The fact that almost no Kentuckians lived that life did not make the image any less real as a representation of the state and its people.

A very different alternative image existed as well. In this scenario the Kentuckian sat propped up against a log cabin instead of on the porch of a mansion, drank moonshine rather than bourbon, and enjoyed the sport of feuding over racing. The long-suffering hillbilly lived on. One author counted more than three hundred silent films—"mountain melodramas"—that focused on moonshining and feuding between 1910 and 1916 alone. A stereotyped media presentation of Appalachia continued after that. Some representations were specific to Kentucky, and some were more general, but all contributed to the image of a region and its people. In 1934 comic-strip characters Li'l Abner and Snuffy Smith appeared, and Li'l Abner eventually appeared on stage and in a motion picture. Television programs such as *The Real McCoys*, *The Beverly Hillbillies*, *Green Acres*, and *The Dukes of Hazzard*, while often showing the lead characters in positive ways, all fed the image. In 1992 the Pulitzer Prize–winning play *The Kentucky Cycle* presented a sordid picture of the region, in what one journalist termed "the literary equivalent of a drive-by shooting."

Attention resulting from Lyndon Johnson's War on Poverty produced books, articles, and television stories, rarely focusing on the positive aspects of the places or people under study. Some citizens in the Appalachian re-

Two icons of Kentucky—Rosine's Bill Monroe, the father of Bluegrass music, and Corbin's Colonel Harland Sanders, the founder of Kentucky Fried Chicken restaurants. (International Bluegrass Music Museum, Owensboro, KY)

gion, not surprisingly, grew defensive; others saw themselves almost as a minority group, assailed by prejudices from without. And the image of eastern Kentucky was often expanded to describe the entire state. A citizen could answer the inquiry "Where are you from?" with the response "Kentucky" and be greeted with "Oh, a hillbilly." That image ignored much reality, but it lived on nationally for generation after generation.

Not as persistent, or perhaps not as prevalent, were three other images, which can be classified as beauty, boxing, and basketball. When George Gallup polled Americans in 1956, Kentucky was cited as one of the "most beautiful" states. That strength became the basis of a strong state park system focused on lakes, scenic areas, and historic sites. According to one accounting, by 2015 tourism had become the commonwealth's third largest revenue-producing industry, generating some $13.7 billion annually. Yet paradoxically, all places of beauty were not always treated well. In 1972 author Wendell Berry flew over the mountain region and cried out about the strip mining: "This industrial vandalism can be compared only with the desert badlands of the west. The damage

University of Kentucky basketball coach Adolph F. Rupp (*center*) with members of the undefeated 1953–1954 team and longtime assistant coach Harry Lancaster. (Mack Hughes Negatives, University of Kentucky Special Collections and Research Center, Lexington, KY)

has no human scale. . . . It is a domestic Vietnam." The environmentalist concluded of his native state: "We have despised our greatest gift, the inheritance of a fruitful land." By the 1990s more than one-third of the public lakes in Kentucky had pollution problems, eight of the state's counties experienced ozone pollution, and almost half of the commonwealth's private wells—20 percent of the population relied on such sources—tested positively for bacterial contamination. More time would be needed to determine whether Kentuckians would fully protect a strength of the state—its natural beauty and historic resources—for generations yet unborn.

The motion picture *2010* was set in that future, in outer space. In the film, the main character, an American, gives his Russian counterpart some bourbon from Kentucky. She asks him what else they have in this place, Kentucky, and he answers that they play good basketball there. The image of Kentucky as a basketball-playing state remains in the minds of many Americans. In the *Encyclopedia of Southern Culture*, under the entry "Basketball," the writer concluded that "if there is one team and one region of the South that is most noted for its basketball it is Kentucky."

He traced that situation to a man from Kansas, Adolph F. Rupp.

Coming to the University of Kentucky in 1930, Rupp coached there for forty-two years, winning a then-record 875 games and four national championships. Despite a gambling scandal involving players that caused the cancellation of the 1952–1953 schedule, Rupp's Wildcat teams dominated the college game in the decade after 1945, including a record 129-game home winning streak. A driven, forceful, colorful man, "the Baron" in his trademark brown suit reluctantly retired in 1972, to be succeeded by Joe B. Hall of Harrison County, who coached the UK team to a fifth national championship. By that time, as one reporter noted, one of the few things uniting the state was a love for Wildcat basketball. A recent poll revealed that outside Louisville, 70 percent of the people who followed sports were University of Kentucky fans, 9 percent were University of Louisville fans, and smaller percentages followed other schools or favored none at all. With no major professional teams in the state, college basketball had become the only game around, the sport of choice, part of the state's culture. Rupp and other coaches had brought a rich tradition of success to a state often ranked at or near the bottom in other national categories. A love affair was born, and every loss was like a death in the family. In 1996, 1998, and 2012, under three different coaches, the Wildcats won national championships, placing the school second in overall titles won. In 2015, it also ranked first among colleges and universities in games won.

Basketball in Kentucky went beyond the activity at one university, however. Along with Rupp in the national Basketball Hall of Fame are four of his players, Cliff Hagan, Frank Ramsey Jr., Louie Dampier, and Dan Issel, but also at least ten other Kentuckians: former Western Kentucky University coach Edgar A. Diddle of Adair County, whose 759 victories ranked fourth on the major-college list at the time of his induction; Paducah native Clarence ("Big House") Gaines, who won more than 800 games at North Carolina's Winston-Salem State; University of Louisville coach Denny Crum, who brought two national championships to his school; Coach Rick Pitino, who took Kentucky to a national championship; Coach John Calipari, who won a national title at the University of Kentucky; Kentucky high school players and later professional stars Arnie Risen and Dave Cowens; University of Louisville players Wes Unseld and Darrell Griffith; and Murray State University player "Jumping Joe" Fulks, who led the professional league in scoring in one year. Kentucky, Louisville, and Western combined to make the commonwealth the first state to win one hundred tournament games, while at various categories of the small-college level, Kentucky Wesleyan won eight titles, Kentucky State University four (one in women's basketball), Georgetown College two, Thomas More College two (in women's), the University of Pikeville one, and Northern Kentucky University one (women's). Even the cheerleaders won titles—the University of Kentucky squad took home twenty-one national trophies by 2016.

Indicative of the commonwealth's priorities, one minister recalled a Louisville wedding at which he officiated in the 1980s. It was time to begin, but the groom and his friends were watching a tightly played contest involving their favorite team. After some discussion with her intended, the bride came to the preacher and said, "Why don't we just delay the wedding until after the game?" Forty minutes late, the marriage took place. It is not recorded whether it endured, but devotion to the college game certainly does.

That interest expanded when women's basketball began again in the 1970s. Actually, women had played the sport at the University of Kentucky a year before the men had—in 1903—but changing views had caused the school to cancel intercollegiate women's teams just two decades later. Other schools had as well, deeming it "too strenuous." In 1932 the state governing body also canceled the high school women's tournament, thus effectively limiting most women's basketball until the hoops' teams started again in earnest forty years later, following the federal Title IX requirement for equal opportunity in athletics.

By then, high school games had long sparked intense interest. Howard ("Howie") Crittenden of Pilot Oak in Graves County was the last of ten children, and he lived in a house without electricity or indoor plumbing. On December 25, 1947, at the age of fourteen, he received the first Christmas gift he had ever gotten, and the first item he ever owned that was new. It was a basketball. Five years later, as a member of the 1952 Cuba Cubs, Crittenden was a starter on the state championship team. He later became a school principal. Such stories of success through sports fed the dreams of many Kentuckians, although not until the 1958 state tournament did black and white players compete together. The absence of divisions in high school basketball also meant that every school had the chance to win the state tournament, the Sweet Sixteen, no matter what the enrollment. While urban institutions generally dominated these tournaments, victories by rural teams such as the undefeated Brewers of Marshall County in 1948, or teams from Edmonson County in 1976 and Breckinridge County in 1965 and 1995, became part of the lore that kept interest strong. Still, attendance at most high school games decreased; different interests and the presence of top games on tele-

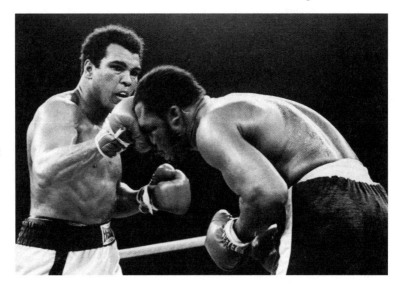

Muhammad Ali lands a right to the head of Joe Frazier during their famous 1975 fight in Manila. (AP/Wide World Photos)

vision took precedence. High school basketball may never again achieve the popular support it enjoyed between 1920 and 1970.

Numerous other sports have attracted Kentuckians over the years. Football at the high school level may attract more fans per game now than the more storied basketball. Danny Sullivan and Darrell Waltrip drove to victories in auto racing, while the opening of Kentucky Speedway near Sparta exemplified the interest in NASCAR racing. Gay Brewer Jr., Frank Beard, Bobby Nichols, Kenny Perry, Steve Flesch, Jodie Mudd, Justin Thomas, and J. B. Holmes all won multiple professional golf tournaments. Success at the Olympics ranged from Willis A. Lee of Owen County, who won seven medals—five of them gold—for marksmanship in shooting in 1920 to Mary T. Meagher, of Louisville, who brought home three gold medals for swimming from the 1984 Olympics. The variety of sports included the Birchfields of Stamping Ground in Scott County, father and son, who captured the US Croquet Association national doubles championship in 1982. In 1999, Louisville resident Tori Murden became the first woman to row across the Atlantic Ocean.

Older sports, such as hunting and fishing, continued to be popular, and conservation measures increased the available wildlife. The state's deer population, for instance, grew from a meager 2,000 in the 1940s to more than 750,000 in the 2010s, while elk were also successfully reintroduced in the commonwealth. Bloodier contests, including organized dog fights with pit bulls and cockfights with roosters, still occasionally occurred. And much newer sports for the state, such as soccer and lacrosse, have experienced steady increases in popularity.

Yet despite all the interest in basketball and the growth of other sports, the most recognizable person from the commonwealth in the last half of the twentieth century and early part of the twenty-first was likely the man who grew up in Louisville as Cassius M. Clay Jr. He later changed his name to Muhammad Ali. Descended from slave great-grandparents of Logan County, Ali rose to become world heavyweight boxing champion in 1964, but he later had his title stripped because he refused induction into military service. His conviction was overturned years later, and he won the title a second time (1974–1978), lost it briefly, then regained the championship from 1978 to 1979. Colorful—"Float like a butterfly, sting like a bee"—and controversial, Ali joined earlier boxer Marvin Hart and later ones Jimmy Ellis and Greg Page in wearing that crown, but none wore it with the flair or excitement that he did. As a result, in the 1976 poll that ranked Colonel Sanders the second most recognizable celebrity in the world, Ali ranked number one. To many he was, as he proclaimed himself, "The Greatest."

Thus, when the word "Kentucky" is spoken, the images in the American and world mind are many and varied: bourbon and basketball, natural beauty and strip mines, Muhammad Ali and Colonel Sanders, the goateed colonel and the white mansion, the bearded mountaineer and the log cabin, the Derby and more. Such images perhaps ignore more than they include and, in some ways, hinder a full understanding of the state as it is. Yet these stereotypes shape the view of the commonwealth held by many people, and they are the things some see as distinctively Kentuckian. Influenced and shaped by such stereotypes, Kentucky cannot avoid them. The question for the future is how the state will deal with those images and whether it can build on the positive parts of its past, for its future.

Trends I

A college professor noted that "'Kentucky' does evoke, if one subtracts the glamor of the Derby and UK basketball, the image of a rural, backwoods state to too many people. Yet, the state is largely urban. . . . It is a state with a sophisticated transportation system, distinguished public parks, important universities, and industries with worldwide ties and markets." While parts of that analysis could be debated, the underlying theme is sound: changes over recent decades have transformed many aspects of people's lives and, indeed, the face of the commonwealth. Long-established images—some reflecting reality, some not—often overshadow significant trends that are, in many ways, more important to understanding this place called Kentucky.

The decades after World War II brought forth change with increasing speed. The 1950s saw an affluent society, a consumer economy, affordable homes, flashy large cars, and suburbia. It also featured drive-in theaters, the growth of television, Communist "witch hunts," discount stores, game shows, "cruising," crew cuts, Elvis and rock and roll, Marilyn Monroe, *Play-*

boy, Civil Defense shelters and worries of nuclear war, polio vaccines, Sputnik, and the U-2 spy plane incident (whose pilot had Kentucky ties). By the end of the 1960s, 94 percent of the state's households had a television set, and during that decade Kentuckians watched protests concerning civil rights and Vietnam and learned about the Cuban missile crisis, the Beatles, JFK and Camelot, urban renewal, interstates, the Pill, bra burning, and the murders of John and Robert Kennedy, Martin Luther King Jr., and Malcolm X. Later decades included Watergate, shopping malls, streaking, the Moral Majority, AIDS, space shuttles, the fall of the Berlin Wall, more wars and conflicts, a computer revolution, the 9–11 bombing and other terrorist attacks, and a major recession, among various matters. Changes occurring during the second half of the twentieth century and the first decades of the twenty-first were more sudden and, in some ways, greater than any experienced by Kentuckians ever.

One of the major changes taking place during those decades concerned women. Achieving the right to vote in 1920 had only represented one step toward equality, and in the years before World War II, only halting progress had occurred. The depression of the 1930s actually reversed several trends. Women lost some of the ground they had earlier won. Wartime demands of the 1940s opened new doors of opportunity, but in many cases the return of soldiers closed some of those again. By 1950 men and women were marrying younger than they had since the government began keeping such statistics. As one historian noted, "If there was a women's movement in the fifties, it led directly to the wedding chapel."

Change had been taking place over time, however, that made the 1950s only the dark before the dawn. The freedoms unleashed by the war were remembered, new appliances made tasks in the home easier to perform and allowed time for other pursuits, the declining number of children per family meant fewer years spent in child-rearing and more time available to work once that phase of life had ended, and the need for an additional income in families still below the poverty level remained high. All these factors brought increasing numbers of women into the public working world in Kentucky. In 1940, just before America's involvement in World War II, 17.6 percent of the women in the commonwealth were in the workforce; by 1960, some 27 percent were—one-fourth of them married. On the eve of the women's movement of the 1960s, the state's female workforce had increased in median age from thirty-two in 1940 to forty, and women were employed chiefly in clerical, technical, and service jobs. Women comprised 96 percent of the private household workers in Kentucky, 80 percent of the food servers, 79 percent of the laundry operators, 75 percent of the cooks, and 67 percent of the clerical force. The earlier prohibitions against married teachers had fallen, and most professional women were educators. Otherwise, women workers generally remained in low-paying jobs. Considerable changes took place during the next two decades, however. The percentage of working-age women in the labor force climbed from 27 percent in 1960 to 50 percent in 1980 and then to almost 60 percent in 2000. In the decades after 1960, women began to make inroads into selected professions as well. By 2002, for example, women comprised one-fourth of the attorneys in the commonwealth, and that figure has continued to grow.

Meanwhile, major modifications took place in societal mores. Later poet and children's book author George Ella Lyon recalled that when she entered Centre College in 1967, women could not wear slacks on Danville's Main Street. Across Kentucky, schoolgirls were often not permitted to don pants unless the temperature dropped to low levels. That soon ended. But as historian Margaret Ripley Wolfe notes, the greatest change during the 1960s may have been the new availability of birth-control devices: "This may have done more for southern women . . . than all the laws ever written and enacted."

What did all these transformations mean for women in public life? Dating from the late nineteenth century, when women first served as county superintendents of public instruction, women in Kentucky began to make slow advances into holding public office. Frankfort elected women to its city council in 1923, soon after the passage of the Nineteenth Amendment to the US Constitution. Louisville selected its first woman alderman six years later. At the state level, the first woman member of the House, Mary E. Flanery of Catlettsburg, took her seat in 1922; the first woman senator, Carolyn Conn Moore of Franklin, came to office twenty-eight years later. Emma Guy Cromwell was the first woman to hold a constitutional office in the executive branch when she won election as secretary of state in 1923. Thelma Stovall took the oath as the commonwealth's first female lieutenant governor in 1975, and Martha Layne Collins became governor eight years later. In the judiciary, the first woman to preside over a court was Kathleen Mulligan of Lexington, who served as a municipal judge in 1928. A greater problem, though, was simply getting women on juries. The first woman to sit on a case in Johnson County did so only in 1926. The first time people of both sexes served together on a jury in Garrard County came two decades after that. When voters in 1993 elected Janet Stumbo to the Kentucky Supreme Court, to succeed the first woman to serve there, Sara Combs, the election marked the culmination of a long struggle in the legal realm.

Yet despite the advances, step by step, year by year, and despite some actions—such as the election of Governor Collins—far in advance of the nation, Kentucky continued to lag behind in achieving gender equality. For example, the state ranked low nationally in the percentage of women legislators (18 percent) and stood thirty-seventh out of the fifty states in female elected officials. Yet Kentucky was a state that had led in the southern women's rights movement and had ratified the Nineteenth Amendment. It was one of a minority of states in the South to support the unsuccessful Equal Rights Amendment of the 1970s, and when the legislature later reversed that decision, Lieutenant Governor Stovall, as acting governor, vetoed the action. Kentucky remains a place of paradox. The commonwealth's women do a disproportionate amount of the housework and provide for the care of both young and old, but

Table 21.1. Women and Careers, 1960 and 1980

Occupation	Women as % of total, 1960		Women as % of total, 1980	
	KY	US	KY	US
Lawyer, judge	2	3	9	14
Physician	5	7	13	13
Engineer	1	1	4	5
Banking manager	13	13	28	34

Source: Catherine O'Shea, "Success and the Southern Belle," *Southern Magazine* 2 (August 1988): 42.

they have more personal independence than ever. Although they have greater economic possibilities than ever before, they increasingly suffer from the feminization of poverty—the fifth highest rate in the United States. They win public office as individuals, but not as a group. They eschew most aspects of what critics call a radical feminism but strongly advocate equality under the law. They support those who choose to work in the home but stress the importance of having the freedom to make a choice.

Relationships between the sexes cannot be fully understood either, for behavior within the home often remains hidden, except for an occasional glimpse. A minister in eastern Kentucky, for instance, told in his memoir about the first wedding he performed, decades earlier. The young bride brought all her earthly possessions with her, in two pillowcases. The groom seemed to be of a patriarchal spirit, and at the conclusion of the quiet service, his wife meekly walked behind him, lugging her belongings. But once the young husband thought he was out of sight of the minister, he took her burden and put his arm around her. The two walked down the road to their new home, beside each other, as partners. While women in Kentucky may not all yet be walking in full step as complete partners, their road to equality is much smoother than before.

For Kentucky women, and men as well, another postwar trend concerned violence in the commonwealth. In 1882 the *Nation* reported that Kentucky, with 1.6 million people, recently had more homicides than eight other states combined, with an aggregate population of more than 10 million. At the turn of the century a Chicago paper compiled statistics from the previous decades and found that

Kentucky's average of 398 reported murders per year ranked it sixth among the states. In the middle of the depression, in 1933, Kentucky's homicide rate of 14.5 per 100,000 people placed it eighth highest in the country. Two years later 530 murders took place in the state. The commonwealth was a violent place.

Slowly and gradually, however, Kentucky's place on murder row was taken by other states, and the commonwealth became comparatively safer. By 1976 its murder rate stood fourteenth in the nation; almost a half-century after that, it ranked twenty-eighth.

However, while a well-founded image of violent Kentucky still existed in some stereotypes, and while better communication resulted in citizens' having greater knowledge about violence statewide, in truth, a larger population experienced many fewer murders than Kentuckians of a half century earlier. Kentucky, compared with the nation at least, was a safe place to live.

It was also a place of much greater mobility than ever before. While the end of most passenger train service—in Glasgow in 1955, Owensboro in 1958, and Lexington in 1971, for example—hurt transportation in the state, the widespread road-building program helped assuage the loss. Toll roads, most of which had become free of tolls by the 1990s, added to the existing interstates and a strong rural roads system to give Kentucky a well-connected network. People could commute greater distances for jobs, and they had easier access to shopping, cultural events, and entertainment than before. In the 1970s, attorney Tom Waller of Morganfield and Paducah recalled what all that meant in his lifetime, beginning in the 1920s:

Table 21.2. Homicide in Kentucky, 1930–2015

Year	Homicide rate (per 100,000 residents)
1933	14.5
1940	14.1
1950	8.9
1960	6.0
1970	10.3
1983	7.4
1989	7.9
1993	7.0
2015	4.7

Year	Number of Homicides
1930	487
1935	530
1940	400
1950	262
1963	200
1970	331
1976	344
1989	293
2015	209

Source: Bulletin of the State Board of Health of Kentucky; Kentucky Vital Statistics Reports; FBI Uniform Crime Reports.

water hardly anywhere because of the danger of dysentery. And you dare not drink milk at all because it'd give you all kinds of maladies. You slept where you could get to. You sometimes encountered bedbugs. That was just the risk you had to take. You . . . had a public bathroom at the hotel [and] in a small town you had no bathing facilities at all. An outdoor privy. Flies were very prevalent. We had no pesticides. Mosquitos were bad.

Then came an era when we got roads from county seat to county seat. They were all-weather roads. . . . We used tax money. We employed health people. We cleaned up the hotels. Today I can leave my home at 5 o'clock in the morning and be in Frankfort . . . for a session of the court. I don't have to have a bath. There's no dust, no flies, no mosquitos. You can drink water. You can drink milk whenever you want to. . . . I can be home for dinner. While that seems to have changed us, it hasn't changed us a particle. We are just able to do things we couldn't do before. Just as now we are unable to do things we will be able to do later on.

Whether or not the people changed, their options certainly did as a result of transportation trends.

Better roads transformed communities and counties, in both positive and negative ways—highway fatalities numbered over 760 in 2015. Isolation had caused some locales to develop a variety of individual businesses, and roads would dry up the need for those services. Health care, professional requirements, and economic wants now could be satisfied by driving to a larger town, in less time than it took an ancestor to get to the county seat. Other places saw what was called the Walmart invasion, as larger, all-purpose stores built on the edge of town took away downtown trade and hurt small businesses in the area.

By the 2010s, then, urban and semi-urban places in Kentucky had developed into at least three general categories: crossroad towns, county seats, and cities. The crossroad towns

To go from my home to Frankfort, then, I could either go by mud roads or dust roads or the railroad. To go by rail meant that I'd leave Morganfield at 9:00 o'clock in the morning, go to Henderson, . . . then at 2 get a train to Louisville, then at Louisville . . . next morning take a slow train [to Frankfort]. . . . By the time you got home you'd lost at least three days.

As soon as automobiles became prevalent we began making that trip by automobile. In the winter the roads made it generally impossible to get there. In the summer the dust was unbelievable. I'd leave Morganfield at noon and spend the night in the vicinity of Leitchfield or Elizabethtown. . . . The next day . . . [I'd] get into Frankfort by 10 o'clock. . . . We had lots of blowouts, lots of bearing failures. The roads were bad. You couldn't drink the

had perhaps developed from a country store where roads met or had grown because of specific local circumstances—a situation near a railroad or river stop, proximity to timber or coal, or a central location offering services to scattered farmers. These places might be characterized by a flashing traffic light, a church, a small post office, a branch of a bank, a grocery, a service station, and an eclectic collection of homes. Houses ranged from one or two large-columned ones, either new or old, to older frame ones and newer brick domiciles, seldom connected by sidewalks or lit by a public system of streetlights.

Of Kentucky's 120 counties, almost a third had a county seat whose population did not exceed two thousand people in 2010. In those county seats, downtown activity usually revolved around a courthouse, where attorneys' offices mixed with scattered stores, sometimes featuring antique shops. Other professionals—a few doctors, employees at the federal and state government offices—operated in a variety of places. But in some of those locales the downtown still lived, and surrounding it were eating places, banks, churches, auto dealerships, a post office, and a library. An area slightly more removed from the center integrated businesses with aged houses, a few old and impressive, a few old and decaying. Then in the next circle of activity might be the former edge of town, with small groceries, some eating establishments, agricultural-oriented stores, and a scattering of economic enterprises. Finally, the new business section—too small to be called suburbia—featured small stores, convenience-type groceries, fast-food places, and, in larger towns, a shopping center and larger chain stores. Newer homes surrounded all that.

Finally, the larger towns, usually themselves county seats, grew to become regional centers or almost extended suburbs of sizable cities. By 2010, Kentucky had only forty or so places of ten thousand to sixty thousand people. Those cities presented more contrasts. Some of their downtowns became stagnant, as new and extensive suburban shopping areas developed in ways that made them little distinguishable from other such places across the

United States. Near the courthouse area, several noble mansions remained as reminders of a pre-automobile age when people walked or rode a trolley to the town's core. But poorer homes usually characterized the courthouse fringe. In the suburbs, new schools, parks, and playgrounds dominated. Many residents found that making trips to the shopping fringes or to malls in nearby cities seemed more convenient than waiting through downtown traffic lights and locating suitable parking. Towns more removed from the larger metropolitan areas became regional centers themselves and built their own malls, motion-picture theaters, and the like, in turn creating satellite communities.

Despite the urbanization of the state by 1970, however, statistics showed that Kentucky changed little in that regard after that. In 2010, the commonwealth remained only 58 percent urban, leaving it as the eighth most rural state in the nation. The old ideal of agrarian living, now coupled with the availability of city pleasures, remains strong in Kentucky. Increasing mobility through better roads and growth of a communications infrastructure has liberated rural dwellers and made their goals attainable once more. Many Kentuckians still prefer to see before them a rural landscape rather than an urban one. The city still has not won the hidden heart of the state.

Trends II

Better transportation and increased mobility, lower crime rates, the opening of opportunities to women—most Kentuckians welcomed such trends. The results of other developments in the state, however, left a more mixed legacy.

Kentucky continued to face problems in pollution, for example. From 1963 to 1977, the commonwealth licensed private operators to dispose of low-level radioactive waste. Many of the nearly five million cubic feet of such material ended up in the Maxey Flats site in Fleming County. Contaminated soil and water resulted, and in 1986 the area was listed as one of the nation's worst hazardous waste sites; remedial work over the years concluded in 2015 when a soil layer capped the waste. That same

One of the nation's worst environmental hazards was at Maxey Flats in Fleming County. (*Lexington Herald-Leader*, February 4, 1975)

for nearly a third of ninth grade students used the "filthy weed." As a result, critics noted, the commonwealth stood second in the United States in deaths from coronary heart disease, sixth in chronic respiratory disease, and first for men and sixth for women in deaths from lung cancer. By the bicentennial of its statehood, Kentucky had the third highest overall rate of death in the nation. By 2015, citizens' average life expectancy of seventy-six years—three years less than the national average—ranked the state forty-fifth on the mortality scale.

Many medical advances had occurred in Kentucky and in the nation during the twentieth and twenty-first centuries, however. Women like Linda Neville, who helped reduce trachoma, and Mary Breckinridge, whose Frontier Nursing Service provided nurse-midwives and health care to the mountains, aided greatly in the medical field. Individuals of both sexes worked so that deaths from tuberculosis in the state dropped from 1,748 in 1943 to 77 three decades later and to almost none after that. Polio virtually vanished, as did several other once-dreaded diseases. Kentucky surgeons in 1999 performed the nation's first hand transplant. All that had an effect: The adjusted death rate declined by 37 percent between 1930 and 1960, and people lived longer. In 1900 only 77,000 Kentuckians (4 percent of the total population) were over the age of sixty-five; by 2014, 875,000 (20 percent) were older than sixty. By that time citizens of the commonwealth enjoyed the best health care ever. Still, the presence of illegal methamphetamine labs and the ready availability of OxyContin (called by some "hillbilly heroin") and other drugs remained a problem for Kentucky. In 2015, it ranked fifth worst in the nation for drug overdose deaths. Ironically, for forty years, starting in 1935, one of the nation's two federal narcotic hospitals had operated near Lexington. But by 1975, that facility had ceased such treatment. For the commonwealth, however, the drug ghosts still ride.

year, another study focused on air pollution and placed Jefferson (Louisville) and Muhlenberg as two of the fifty most polluted counties in the nation. Fortunately, that situation significantly improved. In 2011, an environmental group had ranked Kentucky the fourth worst state for coal and oil-fired plant air pollution.

Some of those issues added to the commonwealth's long-standing health concerns. The state's citizens used traditional products of the commonwealth in sizable amounts; for example, a 1987 study showed that despite being one of the two "driest" states, with places forbidding the legal sale of liquor, Kentucky still led the nation in the consumption of bourbon—one case per year per seven people. Statistics from 2013 indicated that the state also ranked first nationally in the percentage of the adult population who smoked—30 percent. And the future did not seem promising,

For twenty-first-century Kentucky, the problem of the distribution of physicians remained acute, as Fayette County had among the highest numbers of doctors for the population in the United States, while some rural counties had among the lowest. Problems of poverty added to the concerns, and some 17 percent of the state's people had no health insurance in 2010. But federal insurance had reduced that figure to under 6 percent within five years. For a few, the option of being an apostle of clairvoyant Edgar Cayce of Hopkinsville, who gave trance-induced health readings and had a national following long after his death in 1945, seemed the only alternative.

Another statistic, troubling to some Kentuckians, concerned the aging of the people. Statistics showed that the commonwealth's 13.7 percent population increase during 1970–1980 was higher than the national average, for only the second time since 1810–1820. But in the decades since then, the commonwealth has again grown slower than the nation, so by 2010 its population of over 4.3 million ranked it twenty-sixth in size nationally. The lack of real growth resulted from two key factors, the familiar one of out-migration and the newer one of a very low birthrate. In fact, by the late 1980s Kentucky's birthrate was the sixth lowest in the nation. But within thirty years, the rate had increased to slightly more than the national average, and the state ranked thirtieth. Still, fewer children lived in the state in 1990 than had in 1900. Average household size—which had once been very high—declined from 4.1 in 1940 to 3.1 in 1970 and to 2.5 in 2014, while the median age of the state's residents jumped from twenty-one years in 1900 to twenty-nine years in 1980 and to well over thirty-eight by 2013—significantly more than the US average. Kentucky grew older.

By the 2010s several other demographic trends had become clear. First of all, Kentucky remained very homogeneous. The state's population—51 percent of whom were women—stood high nationally in the percentage of those born in the state who remain there—seven of ten. Moreover, it was also among the "whitest" of states, with that group comprising over 88 percent of the population. African Americans made up 8 percent, with comparatively few Asians and Native Americans (under 2 percent of the total). In 96 of the commonwealth's 120 counties, blacks comprised less than 1 percent of the population. Of the African Americans who lived in Kentucky in 2014, over half lived in Lexington and Louisville. The Hispanic population in Kentucky has increased rapidly in the last decade, but, compared to the United States overall, remains small—under 4 percent in 2014 versus a US average of nearly 18 percent. Similarly, the commonwealth has a very low percentage of foreign-born in its population—about one in thirty versus the nation's one in eight. One author surveyed such statistics and concluded that the state had little population diversity and one of the highest percentages of English-speaking people in the United States. That also means that as the nation becomes more diverse, Kentucky may still be viewed more as outside mainstream America, a place less changed by ideas from beyond its borders.

Men and women of all races attended church. In a 2008 national survey, Kentucky ranked in the top ten among the states in the percentage of people who indicated religion formed an important part of their lives, who worshipped regularly, who believed in the literal interpretation of scripture, and who prayed daily. Overall, by 2011, almost half of those who considered themselves religious belonged to an Evangelical Protestant group (vs. the US average of one-fourth). Mainline Protestants comprised 17 percent (about the American mean) while Catholics made up 14 percent (about half the national figure). Historically Black Baptists formed one in twenty Kentuckians while unaffiliated Christians were one in eight of the commonwealth's faithful. Under 1 percent each were members of the Church of Jesus Christ of Latter-Day Saints (Mormon), the Jewish faith, Jehovah's Witnesses, Muslims, Buddhists, Hindus, and other faiths. The largest number of specific adherents were Baptists ("who don't drink or chew or go with girls who do") followed by Roman Catholics. Overall, Kentucky remains part of the "Bible Belt" in its religious makeup.

As a group, Kentuckians did not rank high in worldly wealth. Fairly consistently, the commonwealth stood somewhere in the forties among the states in per capita income (forty-fourth in 2012). At the same time, almost one in five of the state's residents received federal aid in the form of the Supplemental Nutrition Assistance Program (eighth highest in the nation). Of the one hundred poorest counties in America, sixteen are in Appalachian Kentucky. In one of those, over half the children live below the poverty level; in the entire state, 27 percent fell in that category. And, overall, the state's 2015 falling unemployment rate of 5.7 percent still remained higher than the national figure of 5 percent and ranked the state thirteenth in the United States.

Those who worked and those who did not were all part of a poorly educated population, compared with the United States generally. Kentucky ranked in the lower tier in the proportion of the population that had graduated from college. In 2012, only 21 percent of the population over age twenty-five had finished a college undergraduate degree (compared with a national figure of over 28). Yet at the same time, the merged Lexington–Fayette County city population stood ninth highest in the United States in the percentage of college graduates. Despite such success stories, those who wished to upgrade the state's educational level had much to overcome in the race for a well-educated citizenry.

In 1992 the general assembly created the Kentucky Long-Term Policy Research Center and charged it with drawing conclusions about the decades ahead. Three years later the members of that group pointed out several dozen trends affecting the state's future. They noted the homogeneity of the people and their rural character and predicted only moderate population growth. The Center pointed to the commonwealth's sharply declining birthrate and concluded that "the aging of our population is perhaps the most striking population trend affecting Kentucky." Regarding the economy, the authors stressed the danger signs for coal and tobacco, emphasized the tourist potential of historic attractions, recounted the dramatic gains made by the state in manufacturing, and accented the importance of small businesses to future growth. The Center recited concerns

over income inequality, child poverty, health care, and environmental integrity and called for action on each issue. It noted the state's prominence and progress in educational reform but made it clear that at present, "By virtually every measure, Kentuckians are undereducated and ill prepared to meet the challenges the future will bring." Finally, the Long-Term Policy Research Center affirmed that the most successful and prosperous communities in the state featured high levels of civic involvement. People, they concluded, could make a difference. A quarter of a century later, in 2010, the state ended its funding to the Center, but the issues still generally remain.

As journalist Al Smith noted in 2007, Kentucky had several strengths—its central location in America, its good transportation options, its medical centers, its colleges, its farmland, its abundant waterways, its automotive industry, and its cheap electricity. But, he noted, it also carried with it significant weaknesses—its low educational attainment, its undereducated workforce, its health problems, its poverty, its increasing costs for higher education, and more.

So, by the early years of the twenty-first century, then, questions still remain: Will Kentucky stress unbridled individualism, or a spirit of caring for others and for community? Will it let the rich get richer and the poor poorer, as has occurred over the last four decades, or will it devise ways to help the less fortunate more? Will the commonwealth continue to underfund its schools and teachers, or will it support them and feed the minds of the future? Will the state accept short-term profits, or will it protect those things that made it unique, including its natural beauty? Will Kentucky disregard the health concerns of its citizens, or will it concentrate efforts and improve the life of its people? Will it see a one lifestyle, one religious tradition, and one way of doing things as the only way, or will it be accepting of diversity in all those areas? Will the commonwealth waste its resources and despoil its environment, or will it use its natural assets wisely and well? Will state politicians ask, "How does this help my party?" or will they ask, "How does this help my commonwealth?" Will Kentucky officials follow their own selfish ends, or will they do the people's business? Will its citizens vote casually and infrequently, or will they work to understand issues and participate in the system? Will the commonwealth be complacent, satisfied, and content, or will it be questioning, searching, and inquiring in its outlook? Will it follow, or will it lead? Will it repeat the past, or will it learn from history?

How Kentuckians answer these and other questions will determine the state's future. The commonwealth has the option. If it goes for a positive, future-oriented option, that means it and its leaders will have to make hard choices, display strong will, and show real courage. In the past, it has done all those things on occasion. But such moments have been far too rare, and the benefits all too brief. The past is all about learning from it, to help us as we move forward. If Kentuckians accept the words of a futurist—"We must love our grandchildren more than we love ourselves"—they will move forward. If they act only for the moment, for the present, and ignore the past and the future, then they will not. The choice is Kentucky's, all of its people, together.

But there is another part of Kentucky life that is harder to define and articulate, but one equally crucial to the future. This aspect might be called the soul of Kentucky.

Change and Nostalgia

Over the years, observers, both foreign and domestic, praised what they saw as special qualities of Kentucky. The British observer and member of Parliament James Bryce wrote in 1898 that among the southern states, Kentucky was one of the two that he found had the most individuality, with its dignity, polish, and strong leaders. He found it "a sort of nation within the great nation." Less than a decade later, in 1906, the *London Daily Mail* published the observations of "an English litterateur of much repute" who had lived in the United States more than eleven years. He called Kentuckians "undoubtedly the finest people in the states," pointing to their manners, hospi-

tality, courage, and confidence. "With all their freeness and easiness," he noted, "they are still self-poised and self-contained." The writer ended with perhaps his greatest praise: "I will even go so far as to say that even their lawyers look less dishonest than [other] lawyers."

The perceptive novelist Elizabeth Madox Roberts looked at her native state and concluded, in much the same tone, that "Kentucky has form and design and outline both in time and space, in history and geography. Perhaps the strongly marked natural bounds which make it a country within itself are the real causes which gave it history and a pride in something which might be called personality." Another chronicler of the state, in the 1942 book "*Weep No More My Lady*," approvingly repeated the quote given him by "a gentleman of the old school": "Kentucky is not so much a political unit as a soul; an achievement in character."

Various commentators over time did not completely agree on the aspects of the Kentucky character that made the place special to them, but they—and others—understood that the people shared a common memory and a common heritage that gave the state some degree of distinctiveness. As author Wendell Berry noted of his Kentucky birth: "It is a complex inheritance, and I have been both enriched and bewildered by it." But other American places had a special quality as well. The question was not whether the state was distinctive—for all places have at least some degree of that—but how it was special, and what such uniqueness meant to the people in their own era and to the future.

Perhaps the only real constant in Kentucky's history had been change. Robert Penn Warren, born in 1905, noted, "My father's was a different world." A *Courier-Journal* reporter in 1940 looked at a part of the state and concluded, "The pattern of life as our grandfathers knew it is broken and we don't know what to put in its place." Two decades later an editorial in the *Cumberland Tri-City News* reminisced, "Often now, we talk of the time when prices were low, days were not so rush, rush, and there was time to spend with friends, without a feeling of pressure with many things to do and no time to do it in. We all recognize that those days are gone forever." He then quoted the president of the 1890 constitutional convention—"Times change and we change"—and summarized, "We know that the good old days were wonderful ones but few, if any of us want to travel a backward path."

Life had changed in the lifetimes of Warren and his father, as well as the journalists. In an earlier era, events revolved around home and church, and perhaps school and the country store. But generations saw the decline of the family farm and the abandonment of once-prosperous villages. Time brought with it longer lives, fewer diseases, better sanitation, improved educational levels for the general populace, increased mobility, easier communication, convenient labor-saving devices, and more. At the same time, new technology made former luxuries almost necessities. Mechanization permitted people to do more but at the same time produced less need for community-oriented, cooperative efforts.

The fate of the front porch symbolized all that change. American homes in the nineteenth century and much of the twentieth were places "to get out of." They were hot in the summer, and screening was not introduced generally until the 1880s. Insects swarmed through open windows, or else closed ones left no ventilation. People moved to front porches, where they greeted promenading friends, did chores such as "breaking beans," and even courted members of the opposite sex. The ideal house had a front porch shaded from the afternoon sun. By the late twentieth century, however, home buyers paid better prices for homes whose cookout-site backyards were in the shade of the early evening. Porches often disappeared completely. People traveled by automobile instead of by foot and did not wait for others to come to them. Larger homes and smaller families gave individual members of the household more privacy and separateness; air conditioning and entertainment via television or social media devices left families and individuals closed away behind shut doors. Barry Bingham Sr. looked at such trends and asked, "Does that same child ever look out of the real window . . .

any more? Does he open it to hear the sounds of ordinary people living around him?"

John Egerton, who grew up and was educated in Kentucky, looked at the evolving landscape of his home area and of the nation and penned a book he called *The Americanization of Dixie: The Southernization of America.* He and other observers noted a national sameness: similar newspapers or social media to read, food to eat, stores to visit, television programs to watch, and clothes to wear. All that helped give a sense of national unity, but it warred with regional distinctiveness. A person could get on an airplane in one part of the country, arrive in another region at an airport like all others, go down streets lined with fast-food places just like those left behind, and then stay in a hotel or motel whose name and rooms matched exactly those in many other locales. Venturing into the suburbs, the same visitor might see homes whose architectural styles looked like those he or she had left. At a shopping mall, few of the store names would be unfamiliar. Many places in many Kentucky towns and cities looked like hundreds of others across the country.

Some Kentuckians welcomed such change with open arms; others accepted it and adapted to it; some resisted bitterly. As a reporter said of one Kentucky town in 1991: "Mayfield will take its changes in little doses, sometimes even going ahead to the past." At the other end of the state, an observer noted that same year, "I think there was a feeling for a long time that Maysville didn't want to change. It was happy the way it was. It didn't want to be bothered by the outside world. That's changed." A historian looked at the process of change over time and affirmed: "It is indicated from their history again and again that important segments of the American people, though driven like tumbleweed before the buffeting winds of change and upheaval, attempted to do nothing more than remain where they stood, to keep old ways familiar, even to flee the present and the future into a nostalgically golden yesteryear secluded somewhere far off among remembrances of things past." He defined that sense of nostalgia as a preference for things "as they are believed to have been."

Throughout the decades, citizens of Kentucky had sometimes retreated into nostalgia. Now, in an even more rapidly changing world, Kentuckians had to be careful to honor their past but not to be chained to history. They had to be positive that they went into the future with a sense of perspective and not as prisoners of presentism. They had to preserve worthy traditions and strengths but avoid uncritical nostalgia and insular complacency, and they had to face change armed with a sense of their history and what was important to them, while realizing that change was important and part of history too. As writer Bobbie Ann Mason wrote of her youth and sense of place, "We've been free to roam, because we've always known where home is." It remains a difficult balancing act. Such hopes were perhaps best expressed when Bingham told what Louisville sought, which in a sense was what Kentucky sought as well: "What we want is a modern city that still remembers the past, as old bricks remember the sun of many summers and the soft rains of a hundred autumns. That is what gives them character and beauty." Kentucky sought to build its future from those same solid foundations.

Continuity

The Americanization of Kentucky was real, but it also had a false front. Behind that, another Kentucky still lurked, one with traditions and a culture that proclaimed that a distinctiveness lived on. Living lives tied loosely to the past, recreating parts of a world left behind, helped Kentuckians deal with the great changes occurring all around them.

Amid the modifications taking place, certain aspects of earlier times continued to endure, including those focusing on the human character. Historian David Kennedy explained that there are

> timeless contrasts in the life of persons and societies about which historical study speaks eloquently: sorrow and happiness; success and defeat; effort and reward; effort and failure; love and hatred; birth,

guilt, shame, pride, compassion, cruelty, justice, injustice, death. These in one form or another are the great fixed elements in the lives of all people, everywhere and at all times. History provides us with a means of vicariously sharing in their travails and triumphs . . . even as our own experiences themselves become a part of the story. In this way we are all . . . bonded to our fellow mortals, living, dead, and yet to be born.

For Kentuckians that common heritage was part of a collective memory that many citizens sought to preserve.

What that meant to individuals was personified by Addie King Ledford and Curtis Burnam Ledford. Born on Coon Branch in Harlan County in 1876, Burnam Ledford spent his early years milking cows and bringing in wood for the open fireplace where his mother cooked. Their log home had in it a Bible, a dictionary, and regular issues of the *New York Tribune*. In 1889, however, feud violence drove the family to Garrard County, where Ledford lived the rest of his life. He briefly returned to Harlan County to marry Addie King, who had been born there in 1885. They had thirteen children—three of whom died young—before she ceased childbearing at age forty-three. As their chronicler, John Egerton, notes, "Like the vast majority of Americans past and present, they had been relatively anonymous people, just ordinary folks; they had not 'made history,' in the customary usage of the term. But they had seen history and lived it."

Burnam Ledford had spoken to his great-grandmother, who remembered when George Washington was president; he recalled church services at which Republican Unionists sat on one side, Confederate Democrats on the other, and blacks in the balcony. He heard Goebel speak, voted in his first election against him, and recounted learning of Goebel's murder. He, in fact, remembered the assassinations of all presidents killed except Lincoln. Addie Ledford grew up amid the Howard-Turner feud. She voted for the first time in 1920. "I wasn't very proud of it," she commented. "I got used to it though, and I've never failed to vote since then." She saw her thirty-two grandchildren and thirty-nine great-grandchildren growing to maturity by 1978. When those younger family members visited, they found that all people have stories that make history more than a lifeless abstraction. By February 1983 Burnam was 106 old, and Addie was 98. "In their reconstruction of it, history was a concrete and personal thing, a continuous story in which they and their forebears and their descendants were directly involved. In their eyes, it bound the past to the present, the distant to the near-at-hand; it made unknown people important, ordinary places extraordinary, common things significant. History gave meaning and continuity to their lives" and to the lives of those around them.

Family reunions that reinforce generational ties and memories, searches of the genealogical landscape that bind groups together, preservation of historical places that keep alive the meaning of the activities of those who went before, construction of aspects of a folk culture that carries forward past traditions—all these indicate that the hand of tradition still lies heavily on the commonwealth. Singer Rosemary Clooney told of her favorite memory of her home state: "The memory keeps coming back, and I review it every summer. On the drive from Augusta to Maysville, there's a kind of meadow that drops down to the river. On summer nights, that meadow has fireflies that almost light up the earth. I've driven my grandchildren there to show them this, and they're filled with as much wonder as I was when I was a child. It's the most beautiful thing I've ever seen." Her transference of experiences to a new generation meant that through the children those memories would live on. In that sense, the future of the state as a place of some special distinctiveness lies less in the physical aspects of Kentucky—the fast-food outlets, the sameness of places—than in the people themselves. A Shepherdsville man recounted, "My favorite thing about the town is the people. . . . We've got people that if you need something, there are people here you can turn to."

University of Kentucky president Otis A. Singletary Jr., who came to the commonwealth later in life as the school's chief executive officer, noted in 1979, "I have always divided the world into two camps, places I can live and places I can't. I can live in Kentucky because it has ghosts. Your past is not all that remote to you. You are not alienated from it. . . . Your folk characters . . . keep our folklore, our customs, our history alive. That's why Kentucky is so charming and different. I think that while that may change, it will change slowly."

Those ghosts of the past have appeal to many Kentuckians and, as Singletary noted, give the state strengths. Yet at the same time, slavish adherence to that history can be as bad as too little, and the results can haunt Kentucky. Various commentators have complained over the years about the resistance of the state's citizens to positive change. On the other hand, others have criticized those who bring about change by destroying distinctiveness and the things that make the state special to some who live in it. The task of future generations will be to be future-oriented *and* history-minded, to honor their ancestors *and* to prepare their world for their grandchildren to look globally and locally. It can be done. Whether it will be done right is the question.

One of the state's several history-minded governors was Bert Combs. In his last speech as chief executive, he said, "These have been years of great change in the world and in our state. . . . Yet . . . it is the spirit that survives, and the spirit of Kentucky is strong. We may change . . . but the spirit of Kentucky endures." That spirit was present in December 1991, when Combs was buried in a cemetery overlooking his Clay County birthplace. After the graveside service concluded, with those present joining hands to sing "Amazing Grace," the procession of the famous and the friends went back to a church, where a large assortment of food was waiting for those who had made their way over long distances. Journalist John Ed Pearce was one of those affected by the neighborliness, by the warmth, by the caring people: "How long it had been since I had felt that wave of loving care lap around me." Those people holding hands, singing that favorite song, told him what community meant. He knew why Combs had returned there, to his home, once more.

Such a sense of community and of place could be in rural Kentucky or urban Kentucky, or it could be absent in either place. It could be taken too far and result in parochial, restricted visions, or it could give needed stability in a sea of change.

Frontiers

Change came with increasing speed as the decades passed, and adjustments had to take place faster, if they were made at all. But much of what seemed unique to an era often was not. Virtually every generation complained about the young, saying things were "not like that" when they were that age. People of almost every era criticized new fashions in clothes, or new dances, or strange, different musical tastes. The scandals might involve dresses showing ankles in the early 1900s, or a flapper's outfit of the 1920s, or a miniskirt of the 1960s, or cross-dressing in the 2000s. They might focus on shocking actions, such as women wearing slacks, or both genders wearing shorts in public. To a later generation, each debate might seem tame and the outcry surprising. But to those at the time it seemed to signify dangerous trends. Yet in fact, those who decried the indecent pictures, or the state of morality, or the high taxes, or the violence, or the corrupt officials, existed in every period from frontier times to the present. That in itself was part of the continuity of Kentucky.

Through the eras, the commonality of the human experience at least matched the great changes taking place, as attorney Tom Waller argued: "Folks are folks. . . . People are born, reach maturity, old age, and die. . . . Human emotions never change. They were the same 200 years ago as they are now, and will be 200 years from now. . . . [But] we are always heading toward a better day for more people. And it's all right. It's all right." In 1971, state attorney general John B. Breckinridge made the same point about the problems faced by each era: "They may change from generation to generation. But basically they're the same problems arising out of ignorance and prejudice and bias and selfishness and avariciousness. And every generation . . . will have in it that vanguard that will contain within it the seed of progress."

Yet too much should not be made of that universality, for differences did—and do—exist from generation to generation, and distinct new influences in each era to some degree created new reactions. Still, worlds that seem far apart—frontier Kentucky and the twenty-first-century commonwealth—are not so far distant from each other. After all, a coauthor of this book talked to a man who was alive during the Civil War, and Burnam Ledford of the 1980s had spoken to a person who was alive during the 1790s.

People of the frontier settlements admired nature but also abused it, as did their modern-day descendants. They lived in solitary homes sometimes without close ties to neighbors, but they did occasionally become involved in group activities such as church meetings, weddings, and other frolics, not unlike Kentuckians of the twentieth-first century. They sought economic well-being, better lives for their children, and security, as did those who came after. Even in the variety, similarities lived on. The frontier had its heroes, usually men who could shoot and kill, or women who could nurse a wound or raise a strong family. By the twenty-first century, the new hero might be a sports figure, or an entrepreneur, or a humanitarian. The frontier was made up primarily of people with little formal education, yet settler colonials were learned in other ways, more intimate with the environment and reading the rhythms of nature better. While modern-day citizens point to the wonders of technology, is their awe any greater than that of those who first saw airplanes fly or, earlier, those who looked before them and experienced the wonders of western land they believed beckoned to them?

Boone and others looked over a physical frontier and sought to meet its challenges. In the present day, some frontiers are more distant in miles, such as those in space, but others are the same frontiers challenging the human mind, from settlement times on. Strengths grow out of Kentuckians' history and their de-cades of living on the land. But problems per-sist, as they have for centuries. Much remains undone. Each generation has had to meet the challenges of new frontiers.

That the spirit present in each era lives on becomes clear when thousands of Kentuckians gather to watch a sporting event. The strains of the national anthem may be followed by the antebellum verses of the state song, "My Old Kentucky Home." More people sing the state song than the national one. The emotions felt and expressed show that this place of once-artificial boundaries, this place called Ken-tucky, still is important to them and still means something to those who call it home.

Appendix A

Some Facts and Figures

When the boundaries of Kentucky were finally fixed, the state lay approximately within 36°30' and 39°9' North latitude and 81°58' and 89°34' West longitude. It contains 40,395 square miles, of which 745 are water surface and 39,650 are land. The area in square miles translates into 25,376,000 land acres and 476,800 acres of water. The commonwealth ranks thirty-seventh in geographic size among the fifty states. The greatest distance east-west is about 458 miles and 171 miles at its widest north-south point. Seven other states touch Kentucky's boundaries. At 4,145 feet, Big Black Mountain in Harlan County is the state's highest point; the lowest elevation is 257 feet at a site in Fulton County along the Mississippi River. The average elevation is about 750 feet.

Prehistoric Kentuckians may have told each other, "If you don't like the weather, wait until the sun moves a hand's width." The state's weather can and does change quickly. The mean annual temperature for the state is 55° Fahrenheit, but the averages for the state's regions vary between 40° and 60°. Temperatures are judged to be extreme in Kentucky if they exceed 100° or fall below -10°. The normal mean precipitation varies from about 50 inches in the southern part of the state to about 38 inches in the mountains. The state average is close to 46 inches. In most years, little precipitation falls in the form of snow, although heavy snows do occur. The growing season ranges from 190 to 210 days.

Kentucky's motto is "United We Stand, Divided We Fall." The official state bird is the cardinal, the flower is the goldenrod, the tree is now the tulip poplar (it was formerly the Kentucky coffeetree), and the song is "My Old Kentucky Home" by Stephen Collins Foster.

Appendix B

Kentucky's Governors

Isaac Shelby (1750–1826), 1792–1796 and 1812–1816; of Lincoln County; native of Maryland; active in American Revolution and frontier campaigns against the Indians; counties in nine states named in his honor. Democratic Republican.

James Garrard (1749–1822), 1796–1800 and 1800–1804; of Bourbon County; born in Virginia; Revolutionary War soldier; first to live in first governor's mansion; first Kentucky governor to serve two full successive terms. Democratic Republican.

Christopher Greenup (1750?–1818), 1804–1808; of Mercer and Fayette Counties; born in Virginia; soldier; one of the first two Kentucky representatives in Congress after Kentucky entered the Union; elected governor in 1804 without opposition. Democratic Republican.

Charles Scott (1739–1813), 1808–1812; of Woodford County; born in Virginia; soldier; officer in Braddock expedition (1755) and general in Revolutionary War; represented Woodford County in Virginia Assembly. Democratic Republican.

George Madison (1763–1816), 1816; of Franklin County; born in Virginia; Revolutionary War soldier; Indian fighter; hero of War of 1812; captured at River Raisin; elected governor in 1816 but died the same year. Democratic Republican.

Gabriel Slaughter (1767–1830), 1816–1820; of Mercer County; born in Virginia; farmer; regimental commander at the battle of New Orleans; twice lieutenant governor; became

governor upon Madison's death. Democratic Republican.

John Adair (1757–1840), 1820–1824; of Mercer County; born in South Carolina; Revolutionary War soldier; fought in Indian wars; aide to Governor Isaac Shelby in 1813 battle of the Thames; elected to US House of Representatives for one term, 1831–1833. Democratic Republican.

Joseph Desha (1768–1842), 1824–1828; of Mason County; born in Pennsylvania; soldier in Indian campaigns; fought in battle of the Thames (1813); state legislator; served in US House of Representatives, 1807–1819. Democratic Republican.

Thomas Metcalfe (1780–1855), 1828–1832; of Nicholas County; born in Virginia; stonemason; nicknamed Old Stonehammer; soldier in the War of 1812; served ten years as US congressman and senator; died during cholera epidemic of 1855. National Republican.

John Breathitt (1786–1834), 1832–1834; of Logan County; born in Virginia; lawyer; served in Kentucky legislature and as lieutenant governor; died in office. Jackson Democrat.

James Turner Morehead (1797–1854), 1834–1836; of Logan County; as lieutenant governor succeeded to the governorship upon death of John Breathitt; US senator, 1841–1847; political ally of Henry Clay. Whig.

James Clark (1779–1839), 1836–1839; of Clark County; born in Virginia; served in Kentucky legislature; as state circuit court judge, rendered decision that started Old and New Court fight; died in office. Whig.

Charles Anderson Wickliffe (1788–1869), 1839–1840; of Nelson County; lawyer; six-term US representative; became governor upon death of Clark; postmaster general for President John Tyler, 1841–1845; grandfather of Governor J. C. W. Beckham. Whig.

Robert Perkins Letcher (1788–1861), 1840–1844; of Mercer (later Garrard) County; born in Virginia; lawyer; served in state legislature and US Congress; American minister to Mexico, 1850–1852. Whig.

William Owsley (1782–1862), 1844–1848; of Lincoln County; born in Virginia; lawyer; served in state legislature; long service as justice of Kentucky Court of Appeals. Whig.

John Jordan Crittenden (1786–1863), 1848–1850; of Woodford County; lawyer; aide to Isaac Shelby and was present at the 1813 battle of the Thames; resigned governorship to become US attorney general; served a total of twenty years in US Senate. Whig.

John Larue Helm (1802–1867), 1850–1851 and 1867; of Hardin County; as lieutenant governor succeeded to the governorship after Crittenden resigned in 1850; elected in his own right in 1867; state legislator; openly sympathetic to Confederate cause. Whig, then Democrat.

Lazarus Whitehead Powell (1812–1867), 1851–1855; of Henderson County; lawyer; state legislator; US senator; favored Kentucky neutrality during Civil War. Democrat.

Charles Slaughter Morehead (1802–1868), 1855–1859; of Nelson County; lawyer; two-term Whig member of Congress; elected governor on American (Know-Nothing) Party ticket.

Beriah Magoffin (1815–1885), 1859–1862; of Mercer County; lawyer; after being permitted to name his successor as governor, resigned because of his Confederate sympathies. Democrat.

James Fisher Robinson (1800–1882), 1862–1863; of Scott County; lawyer; Whig state senator. Became governor on Magoffin's resignation since the lieutenant governor had died. Union Democrat.

Thomas Elliott Bramlette (1817–1875), 1863–1867; of Cumberland (now Clinton) County; lawyer and circuit judge; commissioned in Union army. Union Democrat.

John White Stevenson (1812–1886), 1867–1871; of Kenton County; born in Virginia; as lieutenant governor succeeded to the governorship upon death of John L. Helm; US senator, 1871–1877. President of American Bar Association. Democrat.

Preston Hopkins Leslie (1819–1907), 1871–1875; of Clinton County; lawyer and state legislator; accepted appointment in 1887 as governor of Montana Territory; died in Montana. Democrat.

James Bennett McCreary (1838–1918), 1875–1879 and 1911–1915; of Madison County; lawyer; soldier with Generals John Hunt Morgan and John C. Breckinridge in Confederate service; served eighteen years in US House and Senate; first to occupy new governor's mansion (1914). Democrat.

Luke Pryor Blackburn (1816–1887), 1879–1883; of Woodford County; first physician to serve as Kentucky governor; volunteer in cholera and yellow fever epidemics in Kentucky and throughout the South; prison reformer. Democrat.

James Proctor Knott (1830–1911); 1883–1887; of Marion County; lawyer, congressman, and noted orator; attorney general of Missouri before returning to Kentucky in 1862; one of the framers of the present Kentucky constitution. Democrat.

Simon Bolivar Buckner (1823–1914), 1887–1891; of Hart County; West Point instructor; served in Mexican War and later with Confederacy; editor of *Louisville Courier*. Pallbearer in U. S. Grant's funeral. Democrat.

John Young Brown (1835–1904), 1891–1895; of Hardin County; lawyer and congressman; his "three-year legislature" adjusted laws to the new constitution. Democrat.

William O'Connell Bradley (1847–1914), 1895–1899; of Garrard County; lawyer; US senator, 1909–1914; uncle of Governor Edwin P. Morrow. First Republican governor.

William Sylvester Taylor (1853–1928), 1899–1900; of Butler County; lawyer; Kentucky attorney general; lost the governorship to William Goebel in a contest decided by the legislature. Republican.

William Goebel (1856–1900), 1900; of Kenton County; born in Pennsylvania; lawyer; state senator; declared governor after being shot by assassin on the grounds of the Old Capitol; only governor in US history to die in office as result of assassination. Democrat.

John Crepps Wickliffe Beckham (1869–1940), 1900–1903, 1903–1907; of Nelson County; lawyer and state legislator; speaker of Kentucky House; elected lieutenant governor on Goebel ticket and succeeded to governorship upon Goebel's death; US senator, 1915–1921; grandson of Governor Charles Anderson Wickliffe. Democrat.

Augustus Everett Willson (1846–1931), 1907–1911; of Jefferson County; born in Mason County; law partner of John Marshall Harlan; lost bids for US House or Senate five times. Republican.

Augustus Owsley Stanley (1867–1958), 1915–1919; of Henderson County; born in Shelby County; lawyer; served six terms in US House; elected to US Senate in 1918; resigned as governor in 1919; later chaired International Joint Commission to mediate disputes arising along the US-Canadian border. Democrat.

James Dixon Black (1849–1938), 1919; of Knox County; lawyer; state legislator; first assistant attorney general of Kentucky; as lieutenant governor succeeded to governorship upon Stanley's resignation; defeated for election in his own right. Democrat.

Edwin Porch Morrow (1877–1935), 1919–1923; of Pulaski County; lawyer; served in Spanish-American War; US district attorney; nephew of Governor William O. Bradley. Republican.

William Jason Fields (1874–1954), 1923–1927; of Carter County; resigned after almost thirteen years in US Congress to become governor; called Honest Bill from Olive Hill. Democrat.

Flem D. Sampson (1875–1967), 1927–1931; of Knox County; born in Laurel County; lawyer; circuit judge; chief justice of Kentucky Court of Appeals. Republican.

Ruby Laffoon (1869–1941), 1931–1935; of Hopkins County; lawyer; chaired first Insurance Rating Board in Kentucky; Hopkins County judge. Democrat.

Albert Benjamin Chandler (1898–1991), 1935–1939 and 1955–1959; of Woodford County; born in Henderson County; lawyer; state senator; lieutenant governor; US senator; commissioner of baseball; nicknamed Happy. Democrat.

Keen Johnson (1896–1970), 1939–1943; of Madison County; born in Lyon County; publisher of *Richmond Daily Register*; as lieutenant governor succeeded to governorship upon resignation of Albert Benjamin Chandler, who went to US Senate; elected in his own right that same year. Democrat.

Simeon Willis (1879–1965), 1943–1947; of Boyd County; born in Ohio; lawyer; appointed to Kentucky Court of Appeals; member of Republican National Committee. Republican.

Earle Chester Clements (1896–1985), 1947–1950; of Union County; served in US Army during World War I; sheriff; county clerk; county judge; state senator; US representative; resigned governorship to assume seat in US Senate. Democrat.

Lawrence Winchester Wetherby (1908–1994), 1950–1951, 1951–1955; of Jefferson County; lawyer; judge of Jefferson County Juvenile Court; lieutenant governor on Clements ticket; became governor upon Clements's resignation; elected in his own right in 1951. Democrat.

Bert T. Combs (1911–1991), 1959–1963; of Floyd County; born in Clay County; lawyer; judge on Kentucky Court of Appeals, 1951–1955; judge of US Court of Appeals, Sixth Circuit, 1967–1970. Democrat.

Edward Thompson Breathitt Jr. (1924–2003), 1963–1967; of Christian County; lawyer; served in state legislature, 1952–1958; personnel commissioner; later a railroad executive. Democrat.

Louie Broady Nunn (1924–2004), 1967–1971; of Barren County; lawyer; elected county judge of Barren County; city attorney of Glasgow. Republican.

Wendell Hampton Ford (1924–2015), 1971–1974; of Daviess County; state senator; lieutenant governor; resigned governorship to assume seat in US Senate, where he served as Minority Whip. Democrat.

Julian Morton Carroll (b. 1931), 1974–1975, 1975–1979; of McCracken County; member of Kentucky House of Representatives, 1962–1971; speaker of Kentucky House, 1968–1971; state senator, 2005–; as lieutenant governor succeeded to governorship upon resignation of Ford; elected to the office in his own right in 1975. Democrat.

John Young Brown Jr. (b. 1933), 1979–1983; of Fayette County; attorney; successful business executive with Kentucky Fried Chicken; involved in the ownership of professional sports teams. Democrat.

Martha Layne (Hall) Collins (b. 1936), 1983–1987; of Shelby and Woodford Counties; public school teacher and home economist; elected clerk of Kentucky Court of Appeals in 1975 and lieutenant governor four years later; only woman to be elected governor of Kentucky; president of St. Catherine College, 1990–1996; active in other colleges and universities. Democrat.

Wallace Glenn Wilkinson (1941–2002), 1987–1991; of Casey and Fayette Counties; business leader and real estate developer; author of *You Can't Do That, Governor!*. Democrat.

Brereton C. Jones (b. 1939), 1991–1995; born in Ohio; served in West Virginia legislature as Republican; horse farm owner in Woodford County; Democratic lieutenant governor. Democrat.

Paul E. Patton (b. 1937), 1995–2003; born in Lawrence County; active in many aspects of the coal business; judge executive of Pike County; chair of Kentucky Democratic Party, 1981–1982; secretary of Cabinet for Economic Development; lieutenant governor. Democrat.

Ernest Lee Fletcher (b. 1952), 2003–2007; from Lexington; born in Mt. Sterling; US Air Force; University of Kentucky College of Medicine; Baptist lay minister; Kentucky House of Representatives and US House; later CEO of Ohio health care company. Republican.

Steven Lynn Beshear (b. 1944), 2007–2015; born in Hopkins County, from Fayette and Clark Counties; University of Kentucky College of Law; served as legislator, as attorney general, and as lieutenant governor under Martha Layne Collins. Democrat.

Matthew Griswold Bevin (b. 1967), 2015–; from Louisville; born in Colorado and raised in New Hampshire; US Army; worked in manufacturing and financial sector. Republican.

Governors of Confederate Kentucky

George W. Johnson (1811–1862), 1861–1862; of Scott County; wealthy planter and slaveholder; Democratic state legislator; member of two 1861 Russellville conventions that formed the Confederate state of Kentucky; elected governor by second convention; killed at Shiloh.

Richard Hawes (1797–1877), 1862–1865; born in Virginia; Clark County then moved to Bourbon County; Whig member of state legislature and US Congress; became Democrat; major in Confederate army; upon Johnson's death, appointed to succeed to the governorship; postwar lawyer and judge.

Appendix C

Kentucky's Counties

County	Date Established	County Seat
Adair	1801	Columbia
Allen	1815	Scottsville
Anderson	1827	Lawrenceburg
Ballard	1842	Wickliffe
Barren	1798	Glasgow
Bath	1811	Owingsville
Bell	1867	Pineville
Boone	1798	Burlington
Bourbon	1785	Paris
Boyd	1860	Catlettsburg
Boyle	1842	Danville
Bracken	1796	Brooksville
Breathitt	1839	Jackson
Breckinridge	1799	Hardinsburg
Bullitt	1796	Shepherdsville
Butler	1810	Morgantown
Caldwell	1809	Princeton
Calloway	1822	Murray
Campbell	1794	Alexandria
Carlisle	1886	Bardwell
Carroll	1838	Carrollton
Carter	1838	Grayson
Casey	1806	Liberty
Christian	1796	Hopkinsville
Clark	1792	Winchester
Clay	1806	Manchester
Clinton	1836	Albany
Crittenden	1842	Marion
Cumberland	1798	Burkesville
Daviess	1815	Owensboro
Edmonson	1825	Brownsville
Elliott	1869	Sandy Hook
Estill	1808	Irvine
Fayette	1780	Lexington
Fleming	1798	Flemingsburg
Floyd	1799	Prestonsburg
Franklin	1794	Frankfort
Fulton	1845	Hickman

Appendix C

County	Date Established	County Seat
Gallatin	1798	Warsaw
Garrard	1796	Lancaster
Grant	1820	Williamstown
Graves	1823	Mayfield
Grayson	1810	Leitchfield
Green	1792	Greensburg
Greenup	1803	Greenup
Hancock	1829	Hawesville
Hardin	1792	Elizabethtown
Harlan	1819	Harlan
Harrison	1793	Cynthiana
Hart	1819	Munfordville
Henderson	1798	Henderson
Henry	1798	New Castle
Hickman	1821	Clinton
Hopkins	1806	Madisonville
Jackson	1858	McKee
Jefferson	1780	Louisville
Jessamine	1798	Nicholasville
Johnson	1843	Paintsville
Kenton	1840	Independence
Knott	1884	Hindman
Knox	1799	Barbourville
Larue	1843	Hodgenville
Laurel	1825	London
Lawrence	1821	Louisa
Lee	1870	Beattyville
Leslie	1878	Hyden
Letcher	1842	Whitesburg
Lewis	1806	Vanceburg
Lincoln	1780	Stanford
Livingston	1798	Smithland
Logan	1792	Russellville
Lyon	1854	Eddyville
Madison	1785	Richmond
Magoffin	1860	Salyersville
Marion	1834	Lebanon
Marshall	1842	Benton
Martin	1870	Inez
Mason	1788	Maysville
McCracken	1824	Paducah
McCreary	1912	Whitley City
McLean	1854	Calhoun
Meade	1823	Brandenburg
Menifee	1869	Frenchburg
Mercer	1785	Harrodsburg
Metcalfe	1860	Edmonton

County	Date Established	County Seat
Monroe	1820	Tompkinsville
Montgomery	1796	Mount Sterling
Morgan	1822	West Liberty
Muhlenberg	1798	Greenville
Nelson	1784	Bardstown
Nicholas	1799	Carlisle
Ohio	1798	Hartford
Oldham	1823	La Grange
Owen	1819	Owenton
Owsley	1843	Booneville
Pendleton	1798	Falmouth
Perry	1820	Hazard
Pike	1821	Pikeville
Powell	1852	Stanton
Pulaski	1798	Somerset
Robertson	1867	Mount Olivet
Rockcastle	1810	Mount Vernon
Rowan	1856	Morehead
Russell	1825	Jamestown
Scott	1792	Georgetown
Shelby	1792	Shelbyville
Simpson	1819	Franklin
Spencer	1824	Taylorsville
Taylor	1848	Campbellsville
Todd	1819	Elkton
Trigg	1820	Cadiz
Trimble	1837	Bedford
Union	1811	Morganfield
Warren	1796	Bowling Green
Washington	1792	Springfield
Wayne	1800	Monticello
Webster	1860	Dixon
Whitley	1818	Williamsburg
Wolfe	1860	Campton
Woodford	1788	Versailles

Source: Kentucky County Data Book, Kentucky Historical Society Research Contribution, no. 8 (n.d.).

Note: Each date given is the year in which the county was established by statute. Some counties were formed in the year following their legal approval.

Selected Bibliography

Abbreviations

Antiques	The Magazine Antiques	JSH	Journal of Southern History
CWH	Civil War History	MVHR	Mississippi Valley Historical Review
FCHQ	The Filson Club History Quarterly	OVH	Ohio Valley History
JAH	Journal of American History	Register	Register of the Kentucky Historical Society
JNH	Journal of Negro History		

Sources for Kentucky history are voluminous. Out of necessity, only a small number of them are listed here. J. Winston Coleman Jr., *A Bibliography of Kentucky History* (1949), is quite complete for books and pamphlets published before 1948 but does not include articles. Some of the works published between 1949 and 1981, including nonbook materials, are discussed in Ron D. Bryant, comp., *Kentucky History: An Annotated Bibliography* (2000); James C. Klotter, "Clio in the Commonwealth: The Status of Kentucky History," *Register* 80 (1982): 65–88; idem, "Moving Kentucky History into the Twenty-first Century: Where Should We Go from Here?" *Register* 97 (1999): 83–112; and idem, "Charting the Path of Twentieth-Century Kentucky: Current Courses and Future Directions," *Register* 113 (2015): 171–99. See also the bibliography of Klotter, ed., *Our Kentucky*, rev. ed. (2000).

Both for their information and guides to additional sources, encyclopedias are indispensable. John E. Kleber, editor in chief, *The Kentucky Encyclopedia* (1992), is foremost among Kentucky's historical encyclopedias. Others of note are Gerald L. Smith, Karen Cotton McDaniel, and John A. Hardin, eds., *The Kentucky African American Encyclopedia* (2015); Paul A. Tenkotte and James C. Claypool, eds., *The Encyclopedia of Northern Kentucky* (2009); and John E. Kleber, ed., *The Encyclopedia of Louisville* (2001). Considered alongside the *Atlas of Kentucky* (1998), edited by Richard Ulack, Karl Raitz, and Gyula Pauer, these encyclopedias give the commonwealth perhaps the best set of reference books in the nation. Martin F. Schmidt, *Kentucky Illustrated: The First Hundred Years* (1992), depicts many aspects of state history before the advent of good photography.

The *Register of the Kentucky Historical Society* (1903–), *The Filson Club History Quarterly* (1926–2002), and its successor, *Ohio Valley History* (2001–), contain articles on most aspects of the state's history. Each has an annual index, and the summer 1989 issue of the *Register* has a general guide to its articles through 1988. Indices are available online. The *Mississippi Valley Historical Review* (1914–1964) and its continuation as the *Journal of American History* (1964–), as well as the *Journal of Southern History* (1935–), have published numerous articles on Kentucky history. Many other journals and magazines have carried occasional pieces. With the exception of *The Filson Club History Quarterly*, full text of articles in these journals is available online through either JStor or Project MUSE.

Thomas D. Clark, *A History of Kentucky* (1937; revised in 1950 and 1960), was the standard history of the state for six decades throughout the twentieth century. Steven A. Channing, *Kentucky: A Bicentennial History* (1977), was limited by the format of the series in which it was published. A more recent overview is James C. Klotter and Freda C. Klotter, *A Concise History of Kentucky* (2008). Of the pre–Civil War histories, John Filson, *The Discovery, Settlement, and Present State of Kentucke* (1784), is more of a travel account than a history, but it also contains the "autobiography" of Daniel Boone, which Filson wrote. Humphrey Marshall's partisan *History of Kentucky* (1812), revised and enlarged to two volumes in 1824, is still useful, but Mann Butler, *A History of the Commonwealth of Kentucky* (1834), is a better account. Lewis Collins, *Historical Sketches of Kentucky* (1847), was revised and expanded by Collins's son, Richard H. Collins, into *History of Kentucky*, 2 vols. (1874). The Collinses' works contain a great deal of information but little analysis. That assessment is also true of Mrs. William Breckinridge Ardery and Harry V. McChesney, eds., *Kentucky in Retrospect: Noteworthy Personalities and Events, 1792–1967* (1942; reprinted and updated, 1967). Three one-volume histories appeared in the 1880s: Nathaniel S. Shaler, *Kentucky: A Pioneer Commonwealth* (1884); W. H. Perrin, J. H. Battle, and G. C. Kniffin, *Kentucky: A History of the State* (1887); and Zachariah F. Smith, *The History of Kentucky* (1885). All were published in later editions. Shaler's account is the most readable; Perrin, Battle, and Kniffin's contains the most information.

Several multivolume works were published during the first half of the twentieth century. Each devoted half or more of its contents to uncritical genealogical and biographical sketches of Kentuckians, most of them men. The best of these histories are E. Polk Johnson, *A History of Kentucky and Kentuckians*, 3 vols. (1912); William E. Connelley and E. Merton Coulter, *History of Kentucky*, edited by Charles Kerr, 5 vols. (1922); Temple Bodley and Samuel M. Wilson, *History of Kentucky*, 4 vols. (1928); and Frederick A. Wallis and Hambleton Tapp, *A Sesqui-Centennial History of Kentucky*, 4 vols. (1945). Additional biographical references can be found in *Biographical Encyclopedia of Kentucky* (1878); *Biographical Cyclopedia of the Commonwealth of Kentucky* (1896; reprinted in 1980); H. Levin, *Lawyers and Lawmakers of Kentucky* (1897; reprinted in 1982); and J. Winston Coleman Jr., *Kentucky's Bicentennial Family Register* (1977). Also useful are such specialized sources as Lowell H. Harrison, ed., *Kentucky's Governors*, rev. ed. (2004); *Biographical Directory of the United States Congress, 1774–1989* (1989); Francis B. Heitman, comp., *Historical Register and Directory of the United States Army*, 2 vols. (1903); and David Porter, *Biographical Dictionary of American Sports: Basketball and Other Indoor Sports* (1989).

Much of the study of Kentucky has focused on manuscripts and on state and local records. Many of the government records are found in the original or in microform at the Kentucky Historical Society and the Kentucky Department for Libraries and Archives, both in Frankfort, or online. While the Kentucky *Senate Journal* (1792–) and *House Journal* (1792–) do not report debates or discussions in the respective bodies, they contain material such as messages of the governors. The *Acts of the General Assembly* (1792–) indicate which bills survived the legislative process and the scrutiny of the governors. Most major organs of the Kentucky state government have issued reports and documents from time to time, and most of these have been published. Among the most important are the *Reports* of the superintendent of public instruction, the *Reports* of the Kentucky Court of Appeals, and the *Reports* of the Kentucky Bureau of Agriculture, Horticulture, and Statistics. Such reports became more frequent after the Civil War with the formation of new divisions of the state government. Also important is Adelaide R. Hasse, comp., *Index of Economic Material in Documents of the States of the United States: Kentucky, 1792–1904* (1910). Vital for the pre-statehood years are William W. Hening, comp., *The Statutes at Large: Being a Collection of All the Laws of Virginia, 1619–1792*, 13 vols. (1809–1823); James R. Robertson, *Petitions of the Early Inhabitants of Kentucky* (1914); and *The Calendar of Virginia State Papers and Other Manuscripts*, 11 vols. (1875–1893).

The state's universities, as well as the Kentucky Historical Society and the Filson Historical Society, all hold special collections of manuscripts, books, photographs, oral interviews, and microform copies of research materials. Some can be accessed online. The largest university collections are at the University of Kentucky, the University of Louisville, Western Kentucky University, and Eastern Kentucky University, but smaller collections offer excellent coverage of certain subject areas. Berea College, for example, has an outstanding collection of slavery and antislavery materials. Many important collections are located out of state in such depositories as the Library of Congress, the National Archives, the University of Chicago, Duke University, and the University of North Carolina. The Draper Collection at the State Historical Society of Wisconsin contains a wealth of information on Kentucky and Kentuckians, most of it for the period before 1850. Major guides to state collections are *A Place Where Historical Research May Be Pursued: An Introduction to Primary Research Sources in the University of Louisville Archives, William F. Ekstrom Library* (1981); Jeanne Slater Trimble, comp., *Guide to Selected Manuscripts Housed in the Division of Special Collections and Archives, Margaret I. King Library, University of Kentucky* (1987); Mary Margaret Bell, comp., *Manuscripts of the Kentucky Historical Society* (1991); and James J. Holmberg, James T. Kirkwood, and Mary Jean Kinsman, comps., *Guide to Selected Manuscript and Photograph Collections of The Filson Club Historical Society* (1996). Cary C. Wilkins, comp., *The Guide to Kentucky Oral History Collections* (1991), is valuable for the twentieth century. The ten-year Kentucky Guide Project, under the auspices of the Department for Libraries and Archives, produced a comprehensive survey of the state's 285 repositories. A general overview, *Guide to Kentucky Archival and Manuscript Collections*, was published in 1988.

Doctoral dissertations on aspects of Kentucky history reflect a great deal of research and often contain information not found elsewhere. Searches can be done online. Research libraries often have copies of at least some of the Kentucky studies, and individual copies of most of them can be purchased from University Microfilm International, Ann Arbor, Michigan. Many of these dissertations were later published, wholly or in part, in book and article form. There is no comprehensive listing of MA theses. Many of the state's counties and towns have histories that are helpful for various phases of Kentucky's history.

1. A Place Called Kentucke

The peoples who inhabited what later became Kentucky have undergone serious reevaluation since Bennett H. Young, *The Prehistoric Men of Kentucky* (1910); W. D. Funkhouser and W. S. Webb, *Ancient Life in Kentucky* (1928); Lucien Beckner, "Kentucky before Boone: The Siouan People," *Register* 46 (1948): 384–96; and Douglas W. Schwartz, *Conceptions of Kentucky Prehistory* (1967). Anthropologists have led the way. Among the better of the more recent evaluations are David Pollack, Charles Hockensmith, and Thomas Sanders, *Late Prehistoric Research in Kentucky* (1984); A. Gwynn Henderson, *Kentuckians before Boone* (1992); idem, "Dispelling the Myth: Seventeenth-and-Eighteenth Century Indian Life in Kentucky," *Register* 90 (Bicentennial issue, 1992): 1–25; and the early essays in R. Berry Lewis, ed., *Kentucky Archaeology* (1996): Richard W. Jeffries, "Hunters and Gatherers after the Ice Age," 39–78; Jimmy A. Riley, "Woodland Cultivators," 79–126; R. Barry Lewis, "Mississippian Farmers," 127–60; and William E. Sharp, "Fort Ancient Farmers," 161–82. Lucien Beckner, "Eskippakithiki: The Last Indian Town in Kentucky," *FCHQ* 6 (1932): 355–82, describes the Indian town that had been abandoned before European colonization of Kentucky. John R. Swanton, *The Indians of the Southeastern United States* (1987); Charles Hudson, *The Southeastern Indians* (1989); Francis Jennings, *The Founders of America: From the Earliest Migrations to the Present* (1993); and the articles in Robbie Ethridge and Charles Hudson, eds., *The Transformation of the Southeastern Indians, 1540–1760* (2002) provide good contexts for study of native peoples active in Kentucky. Two especially significant native populations are studied in Jerry E. Clark, *The Shawnee* (1977); and Theda Perdue, *The Cherokee* (1989).

The Shawnees' forced departure from the Ohio River valley and eventual return occurred within larger patterns of eighteenth-century Native American cultural conflict and migrations. Among useful sources are Randolph C. Downes, *Council Fires on the Upper Ohio: A Narrative of Indian Affairs in the Upper Ohio Valley until 1795* (1940); Francis Jennings, *The Ambiguous Iroquois Empire: The Covenant Chain Confederation of Indian Tribes with English Colonies from its Beginnings to the Lancaster Treaty of 1744* (1984); Michael N. McConnell, *A Country Between: The Upper Ohio Valley and Its Peoples, 1724–1774* (1992); and A. Gwynn

Henderson, "The Lower Shawnee Town: Sustaining Native Autonomy in an Indian 'Republic,'" in *The Buzzel about Kentuck: Settling the Promised Land,* ed. Craig Thompson Friend (1999), 26–55.

There is very little scholarship on women in pre-colonial Kentucky. William E. Connelley and E. Merton Coulter, *History of Kentucky,* edited by Charles Kerr, 5 vols. (1922), 1: 75–93, has the best account of Mary Draper Ingles's ordeal; also Winfred Partin, "Mary Draper Ingles: The First White Woman in Kentucky," *Kentucky Images Magazine* 4 (1985): 9–12. In comparison, Nonhelema Hokolesqua has been grossly understudied: see Craig Thompson Friend, "Nonhelema Hokolesqua, Jemima Boone Callaway, and Matilda Lewis Threlkeld: Searching for Kentucky's Female Frontier," in *Kentucky Women: Their Lives and Times,* ed. Melissa A. McEuen and Thomas H. Appleton Jr. (2015), 8–32. On Shawnee women, see C. F. and E. W. Voeglin, "The Shawnee Female Deity in Historical Perspective," *American Anthropologist* 46 (1944): 370–75; and Colin Calloway, *The Shawnees and the War for America* (2007).

Frederick Jackson Turner's "frontier thesis" remains a powerful analytical model in early Kentucky historiography; see Turner, "The Significance of the Frontier in American History," in *The Frontier in American History* (1921), 1–38. For critiques, see Stephen Aron, "The Significance of the Kentucky Frontier," *Register* 91 (1993): 298–32; Michael A. Flannery, "The Significance of the Frontier Thesis in Kentucky Culture: A Study in Historical Practice and Perception," *Register* 92 (1994): 239–66; and John Mack Faragher, *Rereading Frederick Jackson Turner: "The Significance of the Frontier in American History" and Other Essays* (1998).

2. The Invasion of Kentucky

Willard Rouse Jillson, "The Discovery of Kentucky," *Register* 20 (1922): 117–29, discusses the first European explorations into Kentucky. The journals of Dr. Thomas Walker and Christopher Gist are included in J. Stoddard Johnston, *First Explorations of Kentucky* (1898). Kenneth P. Bailey, *Christopher Gist: Colonial Frontiersman, Explorer, and Indian Agent* (1976), is a full biography; as is Allen Powell, *Christopher Gist, Frontier Scout* (1992). On Walker, see David M. Burns, *Gateway: Dr. Thomas Walker and the Opening of Kentucky* (2000). Lucien Beckner perhaps gave too much credit to Findley in "John Findley: The First Pathfinder of Kentucky," *FCHQ* 43 (1969): 206–15. A popular account of the early explorations is Dale Van Every, *Forth to the Wilderness: The First American Frontier, 1754–1774* (1961). George M. Chinn, *Kentucky: Settlement and Statehood, 1750–1800* (1975), covers the explorations in considerable detail.

Two surveys of European colonization of trans-Appalachia are Thomas D. Clark, *Frontier America: The Story of the Westward Movement* (1939); and Ray Allen Billington, *Westward Expansion: A History of the American Frontier* (1974). Thomas Perkins Abernethy's *Three Virginia Frontiers* (1940) is a good introduction to the exploration of Kentucky, and Otis K. Rice, *Frontier Kentucky* (1975), is an excellent summary.

Lord Dunmore's War is treated in Randolph C. Downes, "Dunmore's War: An Interpretation," *MVHR* 21 (1934): 311–30; and Virgil A. Lewis, *History of the Battle of Point Pleasant* (1908).

Daniel Boone's earliest excursions into Kentucky have been recounted many times. Among the best are John Mack Faragher, *Daniel Boone: The Life and Legend of an American Pioneer* (1992); and Michael A. Lofaro, *The Life and Adventures of Daniel Boone* (1978), both of which examine the legend as well as the life. See also Meredith Mason Brown, *Frontiersman: Daniel Boone and the Making of America* (2008). Other Long Hunters have warranted less study, although Ted Franklin Belue, *The Hunters of Kentucky: A Narrative History of America's First Far West, 1750–1792* (2003), is a solid introduction. Charles G. Talbert's fine biography, *Benjamin Logan: Kentucky Frontiersman* (1962), is the best. Kathryn H. Mason, *James Harrod of Kentucky* (1931), offers a standard biography, but see also Neal O. Hammon, "Captain Harrod's Company: A Reappraisal,"

Register 72 (1974): 243–61. Edna Kenton, *Simon Kenton: His Life and Period, 1750–1836* (1930), is the best account of a great woodsman. A fascinating pioneer is recalled in Anna M. Cartlidge, "Colonel John Floyd: Reluctant Adventurer," *Register* 66 (1968): 317–66. Brent Altsheler, "The Long Hunters and James Knox, Their Leader," *FCHQ* 5 (1931): 169–85, recalls the exploits of another less well-known Kentucky explorer.

The role of land companies in colonizing Kentucky is underappreciated. Malcolm J. Rohrbough's *Trans-Appalachian Frontier: Peoples, Societies, and Institutions, 1775–1850* (1978; reprint 2007) is excellent for providing national contexts. Thomas Perkins Abernethy, *Western Lands and the American Revolution* (1937), is a good introduction to land acquisition in the West, as is Samuel M. Wilson's *Kentucky Land Warrants, for the French, Indian, and Revolutionary Wars* (1917; reprint, 1994). The Ohio Company is examined in Kenneth P. Bailey, *The Ohio Company of Virginia and the Westward Movement, 1748–1792* (1939); and Alfred P. James, *The Ohio Company: Its Inner History* (1959). On the Indiana Company, see George E. Lewis, *The Indiana Company, 1763–1798* (1941). Archibald Henderson, *Dr. Thomas Walker and the Loyal Land Company of Virginia* (1931), reprinted from *American Antiquarian Society Proceedings* 41 (1931), is a good survey of the Loyal Company. On the tension between companies' objectives and colonists' expectations, see Stephen A. Aron, "Pioneers and Profiteers: Land Speculation and the Homestead Ethic in Frontier Kentucky," *Western Historical Quarterly* 23 (1992): 179–98.

In "Pioneers in Kentucky, 1773–1775," *FCHQ* 55 (1981): 268–83, Neal O. Hammon tries to ascertain who came to Kentucky during 1773–1775. Hammon has been tireless in exploring land laws, surveying, and claims; see "Fincastle Surveyors in the Bluegrass, 1774," *Register* 70 (1972): 277–95; "The Fincastle Surveyors at the Falls of the Ohio, 1774," *FCHQ* 47 (1973): 268–83; "Settlers, Land Jobbers, and Outlyers: A Quantitative Analysis of Land Acquisition on the Kentucky Frontier," *Register* 84 (1986): 241–62; *Early Kentucky Land Records, 1773–1780* (1992); and "Pioneer Routes in Central Kentucky," *FCHQ* 74 (2000): 125–43. An excellent description of the region's early routes is Karl Raitz, Nancy O'Malley, Dick Gilbreath, and Jeff Levy, *Kentucky's Frontier Trails: Warrior's Path, Boone's Trace, and Wilderness Road* (2008).

3. Colonial Kentucky, 1774–1792

Thomas D. Clark traced the establishment of Kentucky's boundaries in both *Historic Maps of Kentucky* (1979) and "The Jackson Purchase: A Dramatic Chapter in Southern Indian Policy and Relations," *FCHQ* 50 (1975): 302–20. But see also P. P. Karan and Cotton Mather, eds., *Atlas of Kentucky* (1977; rev. ed., 1998); and William Withington, *Kentucky in Maps* (1980). An example of the continuing boundary disputes is related in Eugene Oliver Porter, "The Kentucky-Ohio Boundary," *FCHQ* 17 (1943): 39–45. Kentucky's geography is described in P. P. Karan, *Kentucky: A Regional Geography* (1973); Wilfrid Bladen, *A Geography of Kentucky* (1984); and Kentucky Geographic Alliance, *Kentucky: Geographic and Historical Perspective* (1989). Robert M. Rennick, *Kentucky Place Names* (1984), explains the origins of the names of many places in the state. Thomas P. Field found few Indian-derived names in his study, "The Indian Place Names of Kentucky," *FCHQ* 34 (1960): 237–47.

George W. Ranck, *Boonesborough, Its Founding, Pioneer Struggles, Indian Experiences* (1901), is still a good account of the settlement of Boonesborough. On the personalities in Boonesborough, the reader should note Charles W. Bryan Jr., "Richard Callaway, Kentucky Pioneer," *FCHQ* 9 (1935): 35–50; and R. Alexander Bate, "Colonel Richard Callaway, 1722–1780," *FCHQ* 19 (1955): 3–20, 166–78. Daniel's brother is credited with his own accomplishments in Willard Rouse Jillson, "Squire Boone," *FCHQ* 16 (1942): 141–71; and Ted Igleheart, "Squire Boone, the Forgotten Man," *FCHQ* 44 (1970): 356–66. The first journey to the site of Boonesborough is described in Neal O. Hammon, "The First Trip to Boonesborough," *FCHQ* 45 (1971): 249–

63; and "The Journal of William Calk, Kentucky Pioneer," *MVHR* 7 (1921): 363–77. An interesting account of early settlement as it appeared to Elizabeth Thomas is Louise Phelps Kellogg, ed., "A Kentucky Pioneer Tells Her Story of Early Boonesborough and Harrodsburg," *FCHQ* 3 (1929): 223–36. The roles of Richard Henderson and the Transylvania Company are described in Archibald Henderson, "Richard Henderson and the Occupation of Kentucky, 1775," *MVHR* 1 (1914): 341–63.

Accounts of some other early settlements include Charles R. Staples, *The History of Pioneer Lexington* (1939); Neal O. Hammon, "Early Louisville and the Beargrass Stations," *FCHQ* 52 (1978): 147–65; and Ellen Eslinger, "Migration and Kinship on the Trans-Appalachian Frontier: Strode's Station, Kentucky," *FCHQ* 62 (1988): 52–66. Thomas Froncek, ed., *Voices from the Wilderness: The Frontiersman's Own Story* (1974), includes some Kentucky voices, as does Darren R. Reid, ed., *Daniel Boone and Others on the Kentucky Frontier: Autobiographies and Narratives, 1769–1795* (2009). Willard Rouse Jillson, *Pioneer Kentucky* (1934), locates most of the early stations and forts, but better contextualization of stations and forts is found in Nancy O'Malley's *"Stockading Up": A Study of Pioneer Stations in the Inner Bluegrass Region of Kentucky* (1987); and idem, *Searching for Boonesborough* (1990). Thomas D. Clark, ed., *The Voice of the Frontier: John Bradford's Notes on Kentucky* (1993), contains several articles on the early settlements and their Indian problems. Timothy Flint, *Indian Wars of the West* (1833); and John A. McClung, *Sketches of Western Adventures* (1847), are two of the many accounts of Indian warfare written from the perspective of the European pioneers.

Among the many interesting accounts of early pioneer life are Roseann R. Hogan, ed., "Buffaloes in the Corn: James Wade's Account of Pioneer Kentucky," *Register* 89 (1991): 1–31; Lucien Beckner, ed., "Reverend John D. Shane's Interview with Pioneer William Clinkenbeard," *FCHQ* 2 (1928): 95–128; Robert B. McAfee, "The Life and Times of Robert B. McAfee and His Family and Connections," *Register* 25 (1927): 5–37, 111–43, 215–37; Charles G. Talbert, "William Whitley, 1749–1813," *FCHQ* 25 (1951): 101–21, 210–16, 300–316; Chester R. Young, ed., *Westward into Kentucky: The Narrative of Daniel Trabue* (1981); and Ellen Eslinger, ed., *Running Mad for Kentucky: Frontier Travel Accounts* (2004). The Draper Collection at the State Historical Society of Wisconsin is rich in such personal accounts. Elizabeth A. Perkins, *Border Life: Experience and Memory in the Revolutionary Ohio Valley* (1998), is superb analysis of these first accounts.

The important opposition of George Rogers Clark to Richard Henderson's attempts to establish a government is traced in James Alton James, *The Life of George Rogers Clark* (1928); Temple Bodley, *George Rogers Clark, His Life and Public Service* (1926); John Bakeless, *Background to Glory* (1957); and Wilbur H. Siebert, "Kentucky's Struggle with Its Loyalist Proprietors," *MVHR* 7 (1920): 113–26. Robert Spencer Cotterill, *History of Pioneer Kentucky* (1917), is hostile toward Clark; William S. Lester, *The Transylvania Colony* (1935), is somewhat anti-Henderson.

Importantly, the last three decades of eighteenth-century Kentucky have undergone significant reevaluation over the past twenty years. The most notable revisions are Stephen A. Aron, *How the West Was Lost: The Transformation of Kentucky from Daniel Boone to Henry Clay* (1996); Perkins, *Border Life*; Ellen Eslinger, *Citizens of Zion: The Social Origins of Camp Meeting Revivalism* (1999); Craig Thompson Friend, *Along the Maysville Road: The Early American Republic in the Trans-Appalachian West* (2005); and idem, *Kentucke's Frontiers* (2010). Among dissertations related to this era that never became books are Fredrika Johanna Teute, "Land, Liberty, and Labor in the Post-Revolutionary Era: Kentucky as the Promised Land" (PhD diss., Johns Hopkins University, 1988); Gail S. Terry, "Family Empires: A Frontier Elite in Virginia and Kentucky, 1740–1815" (PhD diss., College of William and Mary, 1992); Todd Harold Barnett, "The Evolution of 'North' and 'South': Settlement and Slavery on America's Sectional

Border, 1650–1810" (PhD diss., University of Pennsylvania, 1993); Patrick Lee Lucas, "Realized Ideals: Grecian-Style Building as Metaphor for Democracy on the Trans-Appalachian Frontier" (PhD diss., Michigan State University, 2002); John H. Wigger, "Born of Water and Spirit: Popular Religion and Early American Baptists in Kentucky, 1776–1860" (PhD diss., University of Missouri-Columbia, 2003); Marion C. Nelson, "Power in Motion: Western Success Stories of the Jeffersonian Republic" (PhD diss., University of Pennsylvania, 2006).

Two good general but older accounts of the American Revolution are John R. Alden, *The South in the American Revolution, 1763–1789* (1957); and Don Higginbotham, *The War of American Independence* (1971). George Roger Clark's role is examined in Lowell H. Harrison, *George Rogers Clark and the War in the West* (1976); and John D. Barnhart, *Henry Hamilton and George Rogers Clark in the American Revolution* (1951). William Dodd Brown's "Dangerous Situation, Delayed Response: Col. John Bowman and the Kentucky Expedition of 1777," *Register* 97 (1999): 137–58, is an excellent account of why Kentuckians invaded native villages. Charles G. Talbert has written a series of articles on other Revolutionary-era military expeditions: "Kentucky Invades Ohio—1779," *Register* 51 (1953): 228–35; "Kentucky Invades Ohio—1780," *Register* 52 (1954): 291–300; "Kentucky Invades Ohio—1782," *Register* 53 (1955): 288–97; and "Kentucky Invades Ohio—1786," *Register* 54 (1956): 203–13. On the Native American contexts for war in colonial Kentucky, one should read Colin Callaway, *The American Revolution in Indian Country: Crisis and Diversity in Native American Communities* (1995); and idem, "The Continuing Revolution in Indian Country," in *Native Americans and the Early Republic,* ed. Frederick E. Hoxie, Ronald Hoffman, and Peter J. Albert (1999), 3–36. Thomas Boyd, *Simon Girty: The White Savage* (1928), is a biography of the man perhaps most feared by the Kentucky settler colonials.

Among the many interesting accounts of specific battles are Samuel M. Wilson, "Shawnee Warriors at the Blue Licks," *Register* 32 (1934): 160–68; Neal Hammon, *Daniel Boone and the Defeat at Blue Licks* (2005); Richard H. Collins, "The Siege of Bryan's Station," edited by Willard Rouse Jillson, *Register* 36 (1938): 15–25; Maude Ward Lafferty, "Destruction of Ruddle's and Martin's Forts in the Revolutionary War," *Register* 54 (1956): 297–338; Bessie Taul Conkright, "Estill's Defeat; or, The Battle of Little Mountain," *Register* 22 (1924): 311–22; and Neal O. Hammon and James Russell Harris, "'In a Dangerous Situation': Letters of Col. John Floyd, 1774–1783," *Register* 83 (1985): 202–36. See also Neal Hammon and Richard Taylor, *Virginia's Western War, 1775–1786* (2002). The Treaty of Paris is discussed in detail in Samuel F. Bemis, *The Diplomacy of the American Revolution* (1935).

The early roots of enslavement in Kentucky and the lives of the enslaved are grossly understudied. The best sources are J. Winston Coleman, *Slavery Times in Kentucky* (1940); Marion B. Lucas, *A History of Blacks in Kentucky*: vol. 1: *From Slavery to Segregation, 1769–1891* (1992); idem, "African Americans on the Kentucky Frontier," *Register* 95 (1997): 121–34; Gail S. Terry, "Sustaining the Bonds of Kinship in a Trans-Appalachian Migration: 1790–1811," *Virginia Magazine of History and Biography* 102 (1994): 55–76; Ellen Eslinger, "The Shape of Slavery on the Kentucky Frontier, 1775–1800," *Register* 92 (1994): 1–23; and Lyndon Comstock, *Before Abolition: African-Americans in Early Clark County, Kentucky* (2017). For the historical contexts for Kentucky slavery, see Ira Berlin, *Many Thousands Gone: The First Two Centuries of Slavery in North America* (1998); idem, *Generations of Captivity: A History of African American Slaves* (2003); and Philip Morgan, *Slave Counterpoint: Black Culture in the Eighteenth-Century Chesapeake and Lowcountry* (1998).

Women and family life have also been underappreciated in Kentucky's historiography. Suggestive introductions may be found in Margaret Ripley Wolfe, "Fallen Leaves and Missing Pages: Women in Kentucky History," *Register* 90 (1992): 64–89; and Randolph Hollingsworth, "'Mrs. Boone, I Presume? In Search of the Idea of Womanhood in Kentucky's Early

Years," in *Bluegrass Renaissance: The History and Culture of Central Kentucky 1792–1852*, ed. James C. Klotter and Daniel Rowland (2012), 93–130. Some useful studies are Kenneth C. Carstens, *Women on Kentucky's Western Colonial Frontier* (1996); and Honor Sachs, *Home Rule: Households, Manhood, and National Expansion on the Eighteenth-Century Kentucky Frontier* (2015). Useful as well are the early essays and introduction in Melissa A. McEuen and Thomas H. Appleton Jr., eds., *Kentucky Women: Their Lives and Times* (2015).

The rush to acquire land is addressed in almost every study of colonial Kentucky. Two works compiled by Willard Rouse Jillson, *The Kentucky Land Grants* (1925) and *Old Kentucky Entries and Deeds* (1926), provide an index to these transactions, but also Hammon, *Early Kentucky Land Records*. Marcia Brawner Smith, in "'To Embrace the Value of the Land': Land Survey Legislation in the Jackson Purchase, 1820," *Register* 91 (1993): 386–402, discusses land problems in the state's best-surveyed region. For information on specific land surveys and warrants, see the Kentucky Land Office website.

The most thorough study of Kentucky's separation from Virginia is Lowell H. Harrison, *Kentucky's Road to Statehood* (1992). Patricia Watlington's *The Partisan Spirit: Kentucky Politics, 1779–1792* (1972) is a meticulous study, although her assertion that political parties existed in Kentucky before the 1790s has been challenged. Joan Wells Coward, *Kentucky in the New Republic: The Process of Constitution Making* (1979), concentrates on the 1790s and is especially good on the 1799 constitution. *The Calendar of Virginia State Papers and Other Manuscripts,* 11 vols. (1873–1893); and James R. Robertson, *Petitions of the Early Inhabitants of Kentucky* (1914), are indispensable for a study of the statehood movement. The extant journals of the conventions are in the Manuscript Division, Kentucky Historical Society. The first convention journal was published in Thomas Perkins Abernethy, ed., "Journal of the First Kentucky Convention, December 27, 1784–January 5, 1785," *JSH* 1 (1935): 67–78. The *Kentucky Gazette* also printed some extracts from the convention journals, some of which are reprinted in Clark, ed., *The Voice of the Frontier.*

For several years Danville was the political capital of Kentucky. The best histories of the town are Richard C. Brown, *A History of Danville and Boyle County, Kentucky, 1774–1992* (1992); and Calvin Morgan Fackler, *Early Days in Danville* (1941). Thomas Speed, *The Political Club, Danville, Kentucky, 1786–1790* (1894), should be supplemented by Ann Price Combs, "Notes on the Political Club of Danville and Its Members," *FCHQ* 35 (1961): 333–52.

The Spanish Conspiracy has received much attention, a great deal of it highly partisan. William Littell was employed by some gentlemen accused of being participants to prove their innocence. His effort is best used in Temple Bodley, ed., *Littell's Political Transactions in and concerning Kentucky and Letter of George Nicholas, also General Wilkinson's Memorial* (1926). Humphrey Marshall, in *A History of Kentucky* (1812), was convinced of the guilt of the accused; Mann Butler, in *A History of the Commonwealth of Kentucky* (1834), defended them. John Mason Brown, *The Political Beginnings of Kentucky* (1889), is a defense of the author's grandfather and his associates; Brown was answered by another partisan grandson in Thomas Marshall Green, *The Spanish Conspiracy* (1891). Among the many articles dealing with this alleged conspiracy are Lowell H. Harrison, "James Wilkinson: A Leader for Kentucky?" *FCHQ* 66 (1992): 334–68; W. A. Shepherd, "Wilkinson and the Beginnings of the Spanish Conspiracy," *American Historical Review* 9 (1904): 490–506; and Arthur P. Whitaker, "Harry Innes and the Spanish Intrigue, 1794–1795," *MVHR* 15 (1928): 236–48. Elizabeth Warren wrote three articles on this topic: "John Brown and His Influence on Kentucky Politics, 1784–1795," *Register* 36 (1938): 61–65; "Benjamin Sebastian and the Spanish Conspiracy in Kentucky," *FCHQ* 20 (1946): 107–30; and "Senator John Brown's Role in the Kentucky Spanish Conspiracy," *FCHQ* 36 (1962): 158–76. Warren found Sebastian guilty and Brown innocent. Patricia Watlington, in "John Brown and the Spanish

Conspiracy," *Virginia Magazine of History and Biography* 75 (1967): 52–68, declared Brown guilty. Among the best studies of Wilkinson's devious career are Royal Ornan Shreve, *The Finished Scoundrel* (1933); James Ripley Jacobs, *Tarnished Warrior* (1938); Thomas R. Hay and M. R. Werner, *The Admirable Trumpeter* (1941); and Andro Linklater, *An Artist in Treason* (2009). A judicious evaluation is Thomas R. Hay, "Some Reflections on the Career of General James Wilkinson," *MVHR* 21 (1935): 471–94.

4. Kentucky in the New Nation

The best study of the 1792 constitution is Joan Wells Coward, *Kentucky in the New Republic: The Process of Constitution Making* (1979), and when combined with John D. Barnhart, "Frontiersmen and Planters in the Formation of Kentucky," *JSH* 7 (1941): 19–36; E. Merton Coulter, "Early Frontier Democracy in the First Kentucky Constitution," *Political Science Quarterly* 39 (1924): 665–77; and George L. Willis Sr., "History of Kentucky Constitutions and Constitutional Conventions," *Register* 28 (1930): 305–29, offers a thorough picture of the 1792 convention. The constitution is reprinted in Bennett H. Young, *History and Texts of the Three Constitutions of Kentucky* (1890). Further analysis may be found in Robert M. Ireland, *The Kentucky State Constitution: A Reference Guide* (2007).

Huntley Dupre, in "The Political Ideas of George Nicholas," *Register* 39 (1941): 201–23, discusses the most important member of the 1792 constitutional convention, and Vernon P. Martin, in "Father Rice, the Preacher Who Followed the Frontier," *FCHQ* 29 (1955): 324–30, describes the Presbyterian who led the antislavery fight in the convention. Sylvia Wrobel and George Grider, *Isaac Shelby: Kentucky's First Governor and Hero of Three Wars* (1974), is the best biography of a man who deserves a full study. The best sketch of Harry Innes is in Mary K. Bonsteel Tachau, *Federal Courts in the Early Republic: Kentucky, 1789–1816* (1978). Pratt Byrd, "The Kentucky Frontier in 1792," *FCHQ* 25 (1951): 181–203, 286–

94; and John D. Barnhart, *Valley of Democracy: The Frontier Versus the Plantation in the Ohio Valley, 1775–1818* (1953), place the statehood movement in social and economic contexts. On the legal ordering of the commonwealth, see Ethelbert D. Warfield, "The Constitutional Aspect of Kentucky's Struggle for Autonomy—1784–92," *Papers of the American Historical Association* 4 (1889): 23–30; and the works of Robert M. Ireland: "The Place of the Justices of the Peace in the Legislative and Party System in Kentucky, 1792–1850," *American Journal of Legal History* 13 (1969): 202–22; "Aristocrats All: The Politics of County Government in Antebellum Kentucky," *Review of Politics* 32 (1970): 365–83; *The County Courts in Antebellum Kentucky* (1972); and *The County in Kentucky History* (1976).

Mabel Weaks has edited some of Isaac Shelby's official papers and published them in *FCHQ* 30 (1956): 203–31; and *Register* 27 (1929): 587–94 and 28 (1930): 1–24, 139–50, 203–13. Rhea A. Taylor, "The Selection of Kentucky's Permanent Capital Site," *FCHQ* 23 (1949): 267–77; and Carl E. Kramer, *Capital on the Kentucky: A Two Hundred Year History of Frankfort and Franklin County* (1986), explain Frankfort's selection. Wrobel and Grider, *Isaac Shelby*, and Lowell H. Harrison, *Kentucky's Road to Statehood* (1992), describe the start of Shelby's first administration. H. E. Everman, *Governor James Garrard* (1981), carries the second governor through his two terms. A major political figure from his arrival in Kentucky in 1793 until his death in 1806 is studied in Lowell H. Harrison, *John Breckinridge, Jeffersonian Republican* (1969). An excellent study of the advantages given such men is Marion Nelson Winship, "Kentucky *in* the New Republic: A Study of Distance and Connection," in Friend, *The Buzzel about Kentuck*, 101–24.

The continued problems with Native Americans are recounted in Paul David Nelson, "'Mad' Anthony Wayne and the Kentuckians of the 1790s," *Register* 84 (1986): 1–17; idem, "General Charles Scott, the Kentucky Mounted Volunteers, and the Northwest Indian Wars, 1784–1794," *Journal of the Early Republic* 6 (1986): 219–51; G. Glenn Clift, *The*

"Corn Stalk" Militia of Kentucky, 1792–1811 (1977); and Harry S. Laver, *Citizens More Than Soldiers: The Kentucky Militia and Society in the Early American Republic* (2007). The often-neglected role of Scott is described in Harry M. Ward, *Charles Scott and the "Spirit of '76"* (1988). Milo M. Quaife, ed., "General Wilkinson's Narrative of the Northwestern Campaign of 1794," *MVHR* 16 (1929): 81–90; and William Clark, "William Clark's Journal of General Wayne's Campaign," *MVHR* 1 (1914): 418–44, are contemporary accounts of the decisive campaign.

Most Kentucky Democratic Republicans were pro-French, and the activities of Citizen Edmond-Charles Genêt have attracted several historians. Archibald Henderson, "Isaac Shelby and the Genêt Mission," *MVHR* 6 (1920): 451–69; Richard Lowitt, "Activities of Citizen Genêt in Kentucky, 1793–1794," *FCHQ* 22 (1948): 252–67; J. W. Cooke, "Governor Shelby and Genêt's Agents," *FCHQ* 37 (1963): 162–70; and Harry Ammon, "The Genêt Mission and the Development of American Political Parties," *JAH* 52 (1966): 725–41, discuss aspects of the affair. E. Merton Coulter, "The Efforts of the Democratic Societies of the West to Open the Navigation of the Mississippi," *MVHR* 11 (1924): 376–89; Thomas J. Farnham, "Kentucky and Washington's Mississippi Policy of Patience and Persuasion," *Register* 64 (1966): 14–28; and Matthew Schoenbachler, "Republicanism in the Age of Democratic Revolution: The Democratic-Republican Societies of the 1790s," *Journal of the Early Republic* 18 (1998): 237–61, examine the societies in the state. Eugene P. Link, *Democratic-Republican Societies* (1942); and Philip S. Foner, ed., *The Democratic-Republican Societies, 1790–1800: A Documentary Sourcebook of Constitutions, Declarations, Addresses, Resolutions, and Toasts* (1976), provide primary documents about the societies. Mary K. Bonsteel Tachau, "The Whiskey Rebellion in Kentucky: A Forgotten Episode of Civil Disobedience," *Journal of the Early Republic* 2 (1982): 239–60; and John W. Kuehl, "Southern Reaction to the XYZ Affair: An Incident in the Emergence of American Nationalism," *Register* 70 (1972): 21–49,

deal with two issues that created considerable excitement in the commonwealth.

The importance of villages to Kentucky's development is evident in George W. Ranck, *History of Lexington, Kentucky, Its Early Annals and Recent Progress* (1872); Alexander D. Finley, *The History of Russellville and Logan County, Ky., which is to some extent a history of Western Kentucky* (1878); R. S. Cotterill, "The Old Limestone Road: Pioneer Trade and Settlements along a Celebrated Kentucky Highway," *Kentucky Magazine* 1 (1916): 616–20; H. Mc'Murtrie, *Sketches of Louisville and Its Environs* (1819; reprint, 1969); G. Glenn Clift, *History of Maysville and Mason County* (1936); Charles R. Staples, *The History of Pioneer Lexington* (1939); William A. Leavy, "A Memoir of Lexington and Its Vicinity," *Register* 40 (1942): 107–31, 233–67, 353–75; 41 (1943): 44–62, 107–37, 250–60, 310–46; and 42 (1944): 26–53; Richard C. Wade, *The Urban Frontier: Pioneer Life in Early Pittsburgh, Cincinnati, Lexington, Louisville, and St. Louis* (1964); Clay Lancaster, *Vestiges of the Venerable City: A Chronicle of Lexington, Kentucky, Its Architectural Development and Survey of Its Early Streets and Antiquities* (1978); Allen J. Share, *Cities in the Commonwealth* (1982); George H. Yater, *Two Hundred Years at the Falls of the Ohio: A History of Louisville and Jefferson County* (1987); Nancy O'Malley, *A New Village Called Washington* (1987); Richard C. Brown, *A History of Danville and Boyle County, Kentucky, 1774–1992* (1992); and Kim M. Gruenwald, *River of Enterprise: The Commercial Origins of Regional Identity in the Ohio Valley, 1790–1850* (2002). On the failure of some urban dreams, see Mariam S. Houchens, "Three Kentucky Towns That Never Were," *FCHQ* 40 (1966): 17–21.

Herndon J. Evans, *The Newspaper Press in Kentucky* (1976); Donald B. Towels, *The Press of Kentucky, 1787–1994* (1994); and W. H. Perrin, *The Pioneer Press of Kentucky* (1888), are the best general surveys on the roles of newspapers in the commonwealth. George D. Prentice has been the subject of several studies, including Betty C. Congleton, "George D. Prentice: Nineteenth Century Southern Editor," *Regis-*

ter 65 (1967): 94–119; and idem, "The *Louisville Journal*: Its Origin and Early Years," *Register* 62 (1964): 87–103. J. Winston Coleman Jr., "John Bradford and the *Kentucky Gazette*," *FCHQ* 34 (1960): 24–34; and Thomas D. Clark, introduction to *The Voice of the Frontier: John Bradford's Notes on Kentucky*, edited by Thomas D. Clark (1993), provide sketches of Bradford. His role as a printer brought on a debate in the 1930s: see Willard Rouse Jillson, "A Sketch of Thomas Parvin—First Printer of Kentucky," *Register* 34 (1936): 395–99; and Samuel M. Wilson, "John Bradford, Not Thomas Parvin, First Printer in Kentucky," *FCHQ* 11 (1937): 145–51. Mary Verhoeff, "Louisville's First Newspaper—*The Farmers Library*," *FCHQ* 21 (1947): 275–300; and Martin F. Schmidt, "The Early Printers of Louisville, 1800–1860," *FCHQ* 40 (1966): 307–34, discuss early journalism in the Falls City. Other newspapers and editors are discussed in Paul C. Pappas, "Stewart's *Kentucky Herald*, 1795–1803," *Register* 67 (1969): 335–49; James D. Daniels, "Amos Kendall: Kentucky Journalist, 1815–1829," *FCHQ* 52 (1978): 46–65; Donald B. Cole, *A Jackson Man: Amos Kendall and the Rise of American Democracy* (2004); and Ronald Rayman, "Frontier Journalism in Kentucky: Joseph Montfort Street and the Western World, 1806–1809," *Register* 76 (1978): 98–111. Cherry Cartwright Parker, "*The Medley*: First Magazine of the New West," *FCHQ* 46 (1966): 167–78, discusses the start of magazines in Kentucky.

The movement for the second constitution is admirably traced in Joan Wells Coward, *Kentucky in the New Republic: The Process of Constitution Making* (1979). The case of an opponent of the movement is presented in Lowell H. Harrison, "John Breckinridge and the Kentucky Constitution of 1799," *Register* 57 (1959): 209–33. The text of the new constitution is in Bennett H. Young, *History and Texts of the Three Constitutions of Kentucky* (1890). George L. Willis Sr., *Kentucky Constitutions and Constitutional Conventions, 1784–1932* (1930), should also be consulted.

Kentucky's political orientation is examined in Thomas D. Matijasic, "Antifederalism in Kentucky," *FCHQ* 66 (1992): 36–59. The state's most persistent Federalist has been inadequately studied. A. C. Quisenberry, *The Life and Times of Hon. Humphrey Marshall* (1892), is the best effort. James Morton Smith, "The Grass Roots Origins of the Kentucky Resolutions," *William and Mary Quarterly*, 3d ser., 27 (1970): 221–45; and Adrienne Koch and Harry Ammon, "The Virginia and Kentucky Resolutions: An Episode in Jefferson's and Madison's Defense of Civil Liberties," *William and Mary Quarterly*, 3d ser., 5 (1948): 145–76, provide background on the Kentucky Resolutions. The controversial legislation is discussed in John C. Miller, *Crisis in Freedom: The Alien and Sedition Acts* (1951); and James Morton Smith, *Freedoms Fetters: The Alien and Sedition Laws and American Civil Liberties* (1956). Ethelbert D. Warfield, *The Kentucky Resolutions of 1798* (1887), overemphasizes the role of John Breckinridge. Paul Knepper, "Thomas Jefferson, Criminal Code Reform, and the Founding of the Kentucky Penitentiary at Frankfort," *Register* 91 (1993): 129–49; and idem, "The Kentucky Penitentiary at Frankfort and the Origins of America's First Convict Lease System, 1798–1843," *FCHQ* 69 (1995): 41–66, are excellent descriptions of a state institution that Kentucky provided at an early date. For a look at one aspect of the legal system, see Yvonne Pitts, *Family, Law, and Inheritance in America: A Social and Legal History of Nineteenth-Century Kentucky* (2013)

5. The First Generation of Kentuckians

Kentucky's populations at the turn of the nineteenth century are explored in Thomas L. Purvis, "The Ethnic Descent of Kentucky's Early Population: A Statistical Investigation of American and European Sources of Emigration, 1790–1820," *Register* 80 (1982): 253–66; Lee Shai-Weissbach, "The Peopling of Lexington, Kentucky: Growth and Mobility in a Frontier Town," *Register* 81 (1983): 115–33. Samuel M. Wilson, "Pioneer Kentucky in Its Ethnological Aspect," *Register* 31 (1933): 283–95, is an early survey; Mellie Scott Hortin, "A History of the Scotch-Irish and Their Influence in Kentucky," *FCHQ* 34 (1960): 248–55, examines one important group. Henry P. Scalf, *Kentucky's Last Frontier* (1966); and Carol Crowe-Carraco, *The Big Sandy* (1979), describe the settlement of eastern Kentucky. South-central Kentuckians are studied in James A. Ramage, "The Green River Pioneers: Squatters, Soldiers, and Speculators," *Register* 75 (1977): 171–90; Cecil E. Goode, *Southern Kentuckians: Historical Sketches of Barren and Surrounding Counties in Kentucky* (1989); and idem, *Heart of the Barrens* (1986). A countertrend to the state's immigration patterns is observed in John D. Barnhart, "The Migration of Kentuckians across the Ohio River," *FCHQ* 25 (1951): 24–32. For the effects of demographic shifts on enslavement, see Emil Pocock, "Slavery and Freedom in the Early Republic: Robert Patterson's Slaves in Kentucky and Ohio, 1804–1819," *Ohio Valley History* 6 (2006): 3–26.

The most influential general survey of the economic evolution of the United States is Charles S. Sellers, *The Market Revolution: Jacksonian America, 1815–1848* (1991). The economic developments that inspired immigration into Kentucky are covered in W. F. Axton, *Tobacco and Kentucky* (1975); John Solomon Otto, *The Southern Frontiers, 1670–1860: The Agricultural Evolution of the Colonial and Antebellum South* (1989); David Hackett Fischer, *Bound Away: Virginia and the Westward Movement* (2000); and Joan Cashin, *A Family Venture: Men and Women on the Southern Frontier* (1991). An excellent generational study is Joyce Appleby, *Inheriting the Revolution: The First Generation of Americans* (2000).

The purchase of Louisiana is discussed in all the general state histories and in such surveys of the westward movement as Ray Allen Billington, *Westward Expansion: A History of the American Frontier* (1974); and Thomas D. Clark, *Frontier America: The Story of the Westward Movement* (1959). Biographies of Thomas Jefferson, such as Dumas Malone, *Jefferson and His Time: Jefferson the President, First Term, 1801–1805* (1970), emphasize the transaction. Arthur P. Whitaker, *The Mississippi Question* (1934), is a good overall treatment of the issue. The Kentucky newspapers paid a great deal of attention to the question.

The Burr Conspiracy is discussed in all the standard state histories and in the biographies of Jefferson and comprehensive studies of his administration. Full-scale studies include Thomas Perkins Abernethy, *The Burr Conspiracy* (1954); Francis F. Beirne, *Shout Treason: The Trial of Aaron Burr* (1959); and Walter F. McCaleb, *The Aaron Burr Conspiracy* (1936). See also Milton Lomask, *The Conspiracy and Years of Exile, 1805–1836* (1982); and Samuel M. Wilson, "The Court Proceedings of 1806 in Kentucky against Aaron Burr and John Adair," *FCHQ* 10 (1936): 31–40. On the judicial context for the Burr trial, see Mary K. Bonsteel Tauchau, *Federal Courts in the Early Republic: Kentucky, 1789–1816* (1978). Henry Clay's involvement in the affair is discussed in Robert V. Remini, *Henry Clay: Statesman for the Union* (1991), and David S. Heidler and Jeanne T. Heidler, *Henry Clay* (2010), as well as the older biographies: Bernard Mayo, *Henry Clay* (1937); and Glyndon G. Van Deusen, *The Life of Henry Clay* (1937). Also helpful are *The Papers of Henry Clay*, 11 vols. (1959–1992). The first volume, which covers the Burr Conspiracy, was edited by James F. Hopkins; the associate editor was Mary W. M. Hargreaves.

Bradford Perkins, *Prologue to War* (1961); and Reginald Horsman, *The Causes of the War of 1812* (1962), are good on the background to the early nineteenth-century conflict. Robert B. McAfee, *History of the Late War in the Western Country* (1816), is an interesting contemporary account of Kentucky's part in the war. General accounts include John K. Mahon, *The War of 1812* (1972); and Francis F. Beirne, *The War of 1812* (1949). James Wallace Hammack Jr., *Kentucky and the Second American Revolution: The War of 1812* (1976); and Alec R. Gilpin, *The War of 1812 in the Old Northwest* (1958); G. Glenn Clift, *Remember the Raisin! Kentucky and Kentuckians in the Battles and Massacres at Frenchtown, Michigan Territory, in the War of 1812* (1961), concentrate on Kentucky's participation. Richard G. Stone Jr., *A Brittle Sword: The Kentucky Militia, 1776–1912* (1977), discusses the role of the state militia. A. C. Quisenberry wrote a series of articles on the war for the *Register* in 1912–1915; they form the basis for his book *Kentucky in the War of 1812* (1915). Federal Writers Project, *Military History of Kentucky* (1939), is dull but occasionally helpful. Samuel M. Wilson summarized the state's role in "Kentucky's Part in the War of 1812," *Register* 60 (1962): 1–8; James Russell Harris has added useful information in "Kentuckians in the War of 1812: A Note on Numbers, Losses, and Sources," *Register* 82 (1984): 277–86. The controversy over the Kentucky troops at New Orleans is covered in Robert V. Remini, *Andrew Jackson and the Course of American Empire, 1767–1821* (1977); Joseph G. Tregle Jr., "Andrew Jackson and the Continuing Battle of New Orleans," *Journal of the Early Republic* 1 (1981): 373–94; and John S. Gillig, "In the Pursuit of Truth and Honor: The Controversy between Andrew Jackson and John Adair in 1817," *FCHQ* 58 (1984): 177–201. See also Quinton Scott King, *Henry Clay and the War of 1812* (2014).

The nation's postwar surge of nationalism has been described in two books by George Dangerfield: *The Era of Good Feelings* (1952); and *The Awakening of American Nationalism, 1815–1828* (1965). As the Missouri Controversy indicated, bad feelings also existed. M. N. Rothbard, *The Panic of 1819* (1962), is a good account of the severe depression. Glover Moore, *The Missouri Controversy, 1819–1821* (1953), is a comprehensive account of the crisis. More recent studies are Robert Pierce Forbes, *The Missouri Compromise and Its Aftermath* (2007); and John R. Van Atta, *Wolf by the Ears: The Missouri Crisis, 1819–1821* (2015).

Arndt M. Stickles, *The Critical Court Struggle in Kentucky, 1819–1829* (1929), is a good early study of the New Court–Old Court Controversy. It should be supplemented with Arndt M. Stickles, ed., "Joseph R. Underwood's Fragmentary Journal of the New and Old Court Contest in Kentucky," *FCHQ* 13 (1939): 202–10; Edward H. Hilliard, "When Kentucky Had Two Courts of Appeal," *FCHQ* 34 (1960): 228–36; Frank F. Mathias, "The Relief and Court Struggle: Half-way House to Populism," *Register* 71 (1973): 154–76; Matthew G. Schoenbachler, "The Origins of Jacksonian Politics: Central Kentucky, 1790–1840"

(PhD diss., University of Kentucky, 1996); Tom Barton, "Politics and Banking in Republican Kentucky, 1805–1824" (PhD diss., University of Wisconsin, 1968); and especially Sandra Van Burkleo, "'That Our Pure Republican Principles Might Not Wither': Kentucky's Relief Crisis and the Pursuit of Moral Justice, 1818–1826" (PhD diss., University of Minnesota, 1988). The key elections in the struggle are discussed in Paul E. Doutrich III, "A Pivotal Decision: The 1824 Gubernatorial Election in Kentucky," *FCHQ* 56 (1982): 14–29; Billie J. Hardin, "Amos Kendall and the 1824 Relief Controversy," *Register* 64 (1966): 196–208; and Leonard P. Curry, "Election Year—Kentucky, 1828," *Register* 53 (1957): 196–212.

6. The World They Made

Transportation has been a vital concern for Kentuckians since the first years of settlement. Charles Henry Ambler, *A History of Transportation in the Ohio Valley* (1932), is a good introduction to the subject. Leland D. Baldwin, "Shipbuilding on the Western Waters, 1793–1817," *MVHR* 20 (1933): 29–44; and Stuart Seely Sprague, "Kentucky and the Navigation of the Mississippi: The Climatic Years, 1793–1795," *Register* 71 (1973): 364–92, indicate the importance of the steamboats. C. W. Hackensmith, "John Fitch: A Pioneer in the Development of the Steamboat," *Register* 65 (1967): 187–211, tells the story of an unlucky inventor. Navigation on the Kentucky River is described in Thomas D. Clark, *The Kentucky* (1942), revised in 1992; Mary Verhoeff, *The Kentucky River Navigation* (1917); William E. Ellis, *The Kentucky River* (2000); and J. Winston Coleman Jr., "Kentucky River Steamboats," *Register* 63 (1965): 299–322. The Green River has been studied by Helen Bartter Crocker in several works: *The Green River of Kentucky* (1976); "Steamboats on Kentucky's Green River," *Antiques* 105 (1974): 570–75; and "Steamboats for Bowling Green: The River Politics of James Rumsey Skiles," *FCHQ* 46 (1972): 9–23. Agnes S. Harralson captured the flavor of riverboating in *Steamboats on the Green and the Colorful Men Who Operated Them* (1981). Arthur

E. Hopkins, "Steamboats at Louisville and on the Ohio and Mississippi Rivers," *FCHQ* 17 (1943): 143–62, can be supplemented by Ben Cassedy, *History of Louisville* (1852), for an account of early steamboats at Louisville.

The Wilderness Road has received a great deal of attention. The famed Wilderness Road is best studied in William Allen Pusey, *The Wilderness Road to Kentucky* (1921); Robert L. Kincaid, *The Wilderness Road* (1947); and Thomas L. Connelly, "Gateway to Kentucky: The Wilderness Road, 1748–1792," *Register* 59 (1961): 109–32. Turner W. Allen, "The Turnpike System of Kentucky: A Review of State Road Policy in the Nineteenth Century," *FCHQ* 28 (1954): 239–59, is an excellent summary of the commonwealth's early roads. S. G. Boyd, "The Louisville and Nashville Turnpike," *Register* 24 (1926): 163–74, tells the story of a major road. J. Winston Coleman Jr., *Stage-Coach Days in the Bluegrass* (1935; reprinted in 1995), tells much about the roads and their use in addition to the stagecoach operations.

The best introduction to state railroads is Robert Spencer Cotterill, "Early Railroading in Kentucky," *Register* 17 (1919): 55–62. Studies of individual lines include Thomas D. Clark, "The Lexington and Ohio Railroad—A Pioneer Venture," *Register* 31 (1933): 9–28; Stuart Seely Sprague, "Kentucky and the Cincinnati-Charleston Railroad, 1835–1839," *Register* 73 (1975): 122–35; Thomas D. Clark, *The Beginning of the L&N* (1933); Kincaid A. Herr, *The Louisville and Nashville Railroad, 1850–1942* (1943); and Maury Klein, *History of the Louisville and Nashville Railroad* (1972). Carl B. Boyd Jr., "Local Aid to Railroads in Central Kentucky, 1850–1891," *Register* 62 (1964): 4–23, 112–33, shows the importance of local aid in early construction. John E. Tilford Jr., "The Delicate Track: The L&N's Role in the Civil War," *FCHQ* 36 (1962): 209–21, explains how vital the railroad was to the Union armies.

Much writing has been produced about agriculture, the basic economic activity in the state. Lewis C. Gray, *History of Agriculture in the Southern United States to 1860*, 2 vols. (1933), devotes considerable attention to Ken-

tucky. Richard L. Troutman, "Aspects of Agriculture in the Antebellum Bluegrass," *FCHQ* 45 (1971): 163–73, is an introduction to the Bluegrass region, while Thomas D. Clark, *Agrarian Kentucky* (1977); and James E. Wallace, "Let's Talk about the Weather: A Historiography of Antebellum Kentucky Agriculture," *Register* 89 (1991): 179–99, provide overviews for the state. Wallace's article is the best guide to the literature on agriculture. Richard L. Troutman, "Social and Economic Structure of Kentucky Agriculture, 1850–1860" (PhD diss., University of Kentucky, 1958), is an important study of the decade of the 1850s. Thomas D. Clark, *Footloose in Jacksonian America: Robert W. Scott and His Agrarian World* (1989), describes Scott's association with agrarian reform. William E. Axton, *Tobacco and Kentucky* (1975), is the most complete study of tobacco in the state, but see also the Tobacco Institute, *Kentucky's Tobacco Heritage* (n.d.). Corn, the vital pioneer crop, is discussed in Allan Bogue, *From Prairie to Corn Belt* (1963); and John C. Hudson, *Making the Corn Belt: A Geographical History of Middle-Western Agriculture* (1994). James E Hopkins, *A History of the Hemp Industry in Kentucky* (1951), describes all aspects of the production, manufacturing, and sale of hemp; Nadra O. Hashim, *Hemp and the Global Economy: The Rise of Labor, Innovation, and Trade* (2017), situates Kentucky in larger contexts; Ann I. Ottesen, "A Reconstruction of the Activities and Outbuildings at Farmington, an Early Nineteenth Century Hemp Farm," *FCHQ* 59 (1985): 395–425, examines one farm. An unsuccessful experiment is examined in Spalding Trafton, "Silk Culture in Henderson County, Kentucky," *FCHQ* 4 (1930): 184–89.

Horse and cattle breeding have drawn historians' attentions as well. Kent Hollingsworth, *The Kentucky Thoroughbred* (1976); Sara S. Brown, "The Kentucky Thoroughbred," *FCHQ* 25 (1951): 3–23; and Ken McCarr, *The Kentucky Harness Horse* (1978), discuss the horse, which has been so important in the state's history. Kentucky has a prominent place in Paul C. Henlein, *The Cattle Kingdom in the Ohio Valley, 1783–1860* (1951). The North Kentucky Cattle Importing Company, "Introduction of Imported Cattle in Kentucky," *Register* 29 (1931): 400–15; 30 (1932): 37–60, relates the role of that company. Richard L. Troutman, "Stock Raising in the Antebellum Bluegrass," *Register* 55 (1957): 15–28, shows the progress made by 1860. See also Lucien Beckner, "Kentucky's Glamorous Shorthorn Age," *FCHQ* 26 (1952): 37–53; and Worth Estes, "Henry Clay as a Livestock Breeder," *FCHQ* 32 (1958): 350–55.

Isaac Lippincott, *History of Manufacturing in the Ohio Valley to the Year 1860* (1914), is a comprehensive survey; J. B. DeBow, *Industrial Resources of the Southern and Western States,* 3 vols. (1852–1853), contains many references to Kentucky's industry. David L. Smiley, "Cassius M. Clay and Southern Industrialism," *FCHQ* 28 (1954): 315–27, examines Clay's advocacy of manufacturing. Julia Neal, "Shaker Industries in Kentucky," *Antiques* 105 (1974): 603–11, describes the manufacture and distribution of products at the two Shaker communities in the state. Iron manufacturing is examined in J. Winston Coleman Jr., "Old Kentucky Iron Furnaces," *FCHQ* 31 (1957): 227–42; Donald E. Rist, *Kentucky Iron Furnaces of the Hanging Rock Iron Region* (1974); and O. M. Mather, "Aetna Furnace, Hart County, Kentucky (1816–5[?])," *Register* 39 (1941): 95–105. The story of bourbon is told in Henry G. Crowgey, *Kentucky Bourbon: The Early Years of Whiskey Making* (1971); and Gerald Carson, *The Social History of Bourbon* (1963). Davis W. Maurer, *Kentucky Moonshine* (1974), reports on a persistent industry in the state. Saltpeter mining and the manufacture of gunpowder have attracted considerable attention. Some representative articles are Angelo I. George, "Saltpeter and Gunpowder Manufacturing in Kentucky," *FCHQ* 60 (1986): 189–217; Carol Hill and Duane DePaepe, "Saltpeter Mining in Kentucky Caves," *Register* 77 (1979): 247–62; and Gary A. O'Dell, "Bluegrass Powdermen: A Sketch of the Industry," *Register* 87 (1989): 99–117. Mammoth Cave has received attention in Burton Faust, "The History of Saltpetre Mining in Mammoth Cave, Kentucky," *FCHQ* 41 (1967): 5–20, 127–40, 227–62, 323–32.

A family enterprise is examined in Gary A. O'Dell, "The Trotter Family, Gunpowder, and Early Kentucky Entrepreneurship, 1784–1833," *Register* 88 (1990): 394–430. William Allen Pusey, "Grahamton and the Early Textile Mills of Kentucky," *FCHQ* 5 (1931): 123–35, describes another early state industry. Tyrel G. Moore, "Economic Development in Appalachian Kentucky, 1800–1860," in *Appalachian Frontiers: Settlement, Society, and Development in the Pre-Industrial Era,* edited by Robert D. Mitchell (1991), discusses the limited industry in eastern Kentucky.

Thomas D. Clark, "Salt, a Factor in the Settlement of Kentucky," *FCHQ* 12 (1938): 42–52, explains the importance of that commodity. Two salt operations are described in William M. Talley, "Salt Lick Creek and Its Salt Works," *Register* 64 (1966): 85–109; and Robert E. McDowell, "Bullitt's Lick, the Related Saltworks and Settlements," *FCHQ* 30 (1956): 241–69. The early coal industry is discussed in Roy Carson, "Coal Industry in Kentucky," *FCHQ* 40 (1966): 29–42; and Willard Rouse Jillson, "A History of the Coal Industry in Kentucky," *Register* 20 (1922): 21–45. Jillson also wrote "Kentucky Petroleum: Its History and Present Status," *Register* 17 (1919): 47–49, but also see Mrs. C. M. McGee, "The Great American Oil Well, Burkesville, Kentucky," *FCHQ* 33 (1959): 318–26.

Aspects of Kentucky's commerce have been studied in several articles: see Elizabeth Parr, "Kentucky's Overland Trade with the Antebellum South," *FCHQ* 2 (1928): 71–81; Thomas D. Clark, "Live Stock Trade between Kentucky and the South, 1840–1860," *Register* 27 (1929): 569–81; idem, "The Ante-bellum Hemp Trade of Kentucky with the Cotton Belt," *Register* 27 (1929): 538–44; and Martha Kreipke, "The Falls of the Ohio and the Development of the Ohio River Trade, 1810–1860," *FCHQ* 54 (1980): 196–217. An important person in the state's commercial development is presented in James A. Ramage, *John Wesley Hunt: Pioneer Merchant, Manufacturer, and Financier* (1974). Robert Spencer Cotterill, "James Guthrie—Kentuckian, 1792–1869," *Register* 20 (1922): 290–96, is a brief account of a man who was active in many phases of the state's economic and political life.

Basil W. Duke, best known for Civil War exploits, wrote *A History of the Bank of Kentucky* (1895), but also see Dale Royalty, "Banking and the Commonwealth Ideal in Kentucky, 1806–1822," *Register* 17 (1979): 91–107; idem, "James Prentiss and the Failure of the Kentucky Insurance Company, 1813–1818," *Register* 73 (1975): 1–16; and William C. Mallalieu and Sabri M. Akural, "Kentucky Banks in the Crisis Decade: 1834–1844," *Register* 65 (1967): 294–303. Nollie Olin Taff, *History of State Revenue and Taxation in Kentucky* (1931), is a valuable study of an often-neglected function of state government. James C. Klotter, "Two Centuries of the Lottery in Kentucky," *Register* 87 (1989): 403–23, relates the use of a nontax source of income. Paul Salstrom, *Appalachia's Path to Dependency: Rethinking a Region's Economic History, 1730–1940* (1994), discusses the origins of the economic problems in one of the state's most depressed areas.

Although the study of slavery has been more fruitful in recent years, it could use more research and analysis. Marion B. Lucas, *A History of Blacks in Kentucky: From Slavery to Segregation, 1760–1891* (1992), is now the standard study of black Kentuckians before 1891, complemented by Alice Allison Dunnigan, *The Fascinating Story of Black Kentuckians: Their Heritage and Traditions* (1982); and Kentucky Commission on Human Rights, *Kentucky's Black Heritage* (1971). *Kentucky Slave Narratives: Slave Narratives of the Federal Writers' Project, 1936–1938* (2006) is an excellent survey of the oral interviews of former enslaved persons, but they should be used cautiously with consideration of the passage of time and memories. Despite what some might consider racist undertones, still useful are J. Winston Coleman Jr., *Slavery Times in Kentucky* (1940), and Ivan E. McDougle, *Slavery in Kentucky, 1792–1865* (1918). Lowell H. Harrison, "Memories of Slavery Days in Kentucky," *FCHQ* 47 (1973): 242–57, is based on the WPA slave narratives for the state. Wallace B. Turner, "Kentucky Slavery in the Last Ante Bellum Decade," *Register* 58 (1960): 291–307; and Frank F. Math-

ias, "Slavery, the Solvent of Kentucky Politics," *Register* 70 (1972): 1–16, examine the "peculiar institution" just before the Civil War.

Due to its proximity to Ohio and Indiana, Kentucky saw more runaways than most southern states. Matthew Salafia's *Slavery's Borderland: Freedom and Bondage along the Ohio River* (2013) situates Kentucky in the regional contest between slavery and freedom. J. Blaine Hudson's *Fugitive Slaves and the Underground Railroad in the Kentucky Borderland* (2011) is a solid survey of the runaway process. A brief look is Keith P. Griffler, *Front Line of Freedom: African Americans and the Forging of the Underground Railroad in the Ohio Valley* (2004). The most famous fugitive episode was that of Margaret Garner: see Steven Weisenburger, *Modern Medea: A Family Story of Slavery and Child-Murder from the Old South* (1998), and Nikki M. Taylor, *Driven toward Madness: The Fugitive Slave Margaret Garner and Tragedy on the Ohio* (2016).

Harold D. Tallant, *Evil Necessity: Slavery and Political Culture in Antebellum Kentucky* (2003) is the best book on the intellectual justifications for enslavement. Jeffrey Brooke Allen, "The Origins of Proslavery Thought in Kentucky, 1792–1799," *Register* 77 (1979): 75–90; Edward M. Post, "Kentucky Law concerning Emancipation or Freedom of Slaves," *FCHQ* 59 (1985): 344–67; and Juliet E. K. Walker, "The Legal Status of Free Blacks in Early Kentucky, 1792–1825," *FCHQ* 57 (1983): 382–95, examine some interesting aspects of the lives of blacks during the era of slavery. Richard Sears, "Working Like a Slave: Views of Slavery and the Status of Women in Antebellum Kentucky," *Register* 87 (1989): 1–19, makes an unusual comparison. Boynton Merrill Jr., *Jefferson's Nephews: A Frontier Tragedy* (1976), recalls one of the state's most grisly crimes against a slave. W. B. Hartgrove, "The Story of Josiah Henson," *JNH* 3 (1918): 1–21; and Juliet E. K. Walker, *Free Frank: A Black Pioneer on the Antebellum Frontier* (1983), tell the stories of two exceptional men. Kentucky's controversial slave trade with the Lower South has been examined in J. Winston Coleman Jr., "Lexington's Slave Dealers and Their Southern Trade," *FCHQ* 12

(1938): 1–23; Thomas D. Clark, "The Slave Trade between Kentucky and the Cotton Kingdom," *MVHR* 21 (1934): 331–42; and William Calderhead, "How Extensive Was the Border Slave Trade?" *CWH* 18 (1972): 42–55.

On patterns of material refinement, Genevieve Baird Lacer and Libby Turner Howard, *Collecting Kentucky, 1790–1860* (2013) is without peer. To understand the economic circumstances that permitted Kentuckians to increase their standards of living, see Martin L. Primack, "Land Clearing under Nineteenth Century Techniques," *Journal of Economic History* 22 (1962): 484–97; Lee Soltow, "Horse Owners in Kentucky in 1800," *Register* 79 (1981): 203–10; idem, "Kentucky Wealth at the End of the Eighteenth Century," *Journal of Economic History* 43 (1983): 617–33; Elizabeth A. Perkins, "The Consumer Frontier: Household Consumption in Early Kentucky," *Journal of American History* 78 (1991): 486–510; Gary A. O'Dell, "The Trotter Family, Gunpowder, and Early Kentucky Entrepreneurship, 1784–1833," *Register* 88 (1990): 394–430; and Craig Thompson Friend, "Trotter and Sons: Merchants of the Early West," in *Human Tradition in Antebellum America,* ed. Michael A. Morrison (2000), 35–52. Also Louis B. Wright, *Culture on the Moving Frontier* (1955); and Arthur K. Moore, *The Frontier Mind* (1957), contain many references to Kentucky, some controversial. Michael A. Flannery, "Arthur K. Moore and Kentucky Culture," *FCHQ* 69 (1995): 25–40, is a needed critique of Moore's conclusions. For examples of articles dealing with specific aspects of Kentucky life, see Emmet V. Mittlebeeler, "The Decline of Imprisonment for Debt in Kentucky," *FCHQ* 49 (1975): 169–89; James I. Robertson Jr., "Revelry and Religion in Frontier Kentucky," *Register* 79 (1981): 354–68; Zachariah F. Smith, "Dueling and Some Noted Duels in Kentucky," *Register* 8 (1910): 77–87; and Robert M. Ireland, "The Problem of Concealed Weapons in Nineteenth-Century Kentucky," *Register* 91 (1993): 370–85.

Silversmiths have received the most attention among the state's artisans. Good starting points for a study of their work are Marquis Boultinghouse, *Silversmiths, Jewelers, Clock and Watch Makers of Kentucky, 1785–1900* (1980); Noble W. Hiatt and Lucy F. Hiatt, *The Silversmiths of Kentucky, 1785–1850* (1954); Margaret M. Bridwell, "Kentucky's Silversmiths before 1850," *FCHQ* 16 (1942): 111–26; and idem, "Edward West: Silversmith and Inventor," *FCHQ* 21 (1947): 301–8. State glassmakers have been studied in Jane Keller Caldwell, "Early Kentucky Glass," *Antiques* 52 (1947): 368–69; and Henry Charles Edelen, "Nineteenth-Century Kentucky Glass," *Antiques* 105 (1974): 825–29. Mary Washington Clarke, *Kentucky Quilts and Their Makers* (1976, reprinted in 1993); and Lou Tate, "Kentucky's Coverlets," *Antiques* 105 (1974): 901–5, describe activities that have attracted many Kentucky women since pioneer days. Linda Otto Lipsett's *Elizabeth Roseberry Mitchell's Graveyard Quilt: An American Pioneer Saga* (1995) is an interesting story of one particular quilt. Riflemakers have been considered in Thomas A. Strohfeldt, "The Kentucky Long Rifle," *Antiques* 105 (1974): 840–43; idem, "Jacob Rizer: A Bardstown Riflemaker," *FCHQ* 48 (1974): 5–15; and Shelby W. Gallien, "David Weller, an Early Kentucky Gunsmith," *FCHQ* 60 (1986): 5–36. For information on furniture makers, consult Mrs. Wade Hampton Whitley, *A Checklist of Kentucky Cabinetmakers from 1775–1859* (1970); and Lois L. Olcott, "Kentucky Federal Furniture," *Antiques* 105 (1974): 870–82. Kenneth Clarke and Ira Kohn, *Kentucky's Age of Wood* (1976), is an interesting discussion of woodworking during the nineteenth century. Frances L. S. Dugan and Jacqueline P. Bull, *Bluegrass Craftsman: Being the Reminiscences of Ebenezer Hiram Stedman, Papermaker, 1808–1885* (1959), tells a great deal about an interesting craftsman.

Much has been written about the day-to-day changes that occurred in the first half of the nineteenth century. Three good general accounts are Jack Larkin, *The Reshaping of Everyday Life, 1790–1840* (1988); William E. Collins Sr., *Ways, Means, and Customs of Our Forefathers* (1976); and Thomas D. Clark, *The Rampaging Frontier* (1939), but see also William E. Collins Sr., *Folkways and Customs of*

Old Kentucky (1971). Two of the best accounts of life in Kentucky after the early pioneer days are Daniel Drake, *Pioneer Life in Kentucky, 1785–1800,* edited by Emmet F. Horine (1948), which was first published in 1870; and Mann Butler, "Details of Frontier Life," *Register* 62 (1964): 206–29. Butler's incomplete book *The Valley of the Ohio* was edited by G. Glenn Clift and published in 1971. The work of Nancy Disher Baird and Carol Crowe-Carraco, *Pioneer Life in South Central Kentucky* (1988), prepared as a teacher's guide, merits wider circulation.

John H. Ellis, *Medicine in Kentucky* (1977), is a useful introduction to the subject. Emmet F. Horine, "A History of the Louisville Medical Institute and of the Establishment of the University of Louisville and Its School of Medicine, 1833–1846," *FCHQ* 7 (1933): 133–47, has been augmented by Dwayne Cox, "The Louisville Medical Institute: A Case History in American Medical Education," *FCHQ* 62 (1988): 197–219; and idem, "From Competition to Consolidation: Medical Education in Louisville, 1850–1889," *FCHQ* 66 (1992): 562–77. Among the articles dealing with aspects of Kentucky's medical history are Philip D. Jordan, "Milksickness in Kentucky and the Western Country," *FCHQ* 19 (1945): 29–40; Nancy Disher Baird, "Asiatic Cholera's First Visit to Kentucky: A Study in Panic and Fear," *FCHQ* 48 (1974): 228–40; idem, "Asiatic Cholera: Kentucky's First Public Health Instructor," *FCHQ* 48 (1974): 327–41; Lucien Beckner, "Groping for Health in the Mammoth Cave," *FCHQ* 20 (1946): 302–7; Aloma Williams Dew, "From Cramps to Consumption: Women's Health in Owensboro, Ky., during the Civil War," *Register* 74 (1976): 85–98; and Ronald F. White, "John Rowan Allen, M.D., and the Early Years of the Psychiatric Profession in Kentucky, 1844–1854," *FCHQ* 63 (1989): 5–23. The state's most famous operation has been studied in August Schachner, *Ephraim McDowell: "Father of Ovariotomy" and Founder of Abdominal Surgery* (1921); and Laman A. Gray, "Ephraim McDowell: Father of Abdominal Surgery, Biographical Data," *FCHQ* 43 (1969): 216–29. The patient has received attention in Mrs. Arthur Thomas McCormack, "Our Pioneer Heroine of Surgery—Mrs. Jane Todd Crawford," *FCHQ* 6 (1932): 109–23. Other physicians have received biographical attention: see J. Christian Bay, "Dr. Daniel Drake, 1785–1852," *FCHQ* 7 (1933): 1–17; P. Albert Davies, "Charles Wilkins Short, 1794–1863," *FCHQ* 19 (1945): 131–55, 208–49; Nancy Disher Baird, *David Wendel Yandell: Physician of Old Louisville* (1978); and idem, *Luke Pryor Blackburn: Physician, Governor, Reformer* (1979).

Travelers who wrote accounts of their experiences often commented on Kentucky culture. Eugene L. Schwaab, ed., *Travels in the Old South*, 2 vols. (1973); and Raymond E. Betts, "'Sweet Meditation through This Pleasant Country': Foreign Appraisals of the Landscape of Kentucky in the Early Years of the Commonwealth," *Register* 90 (1992): 26–44, are good starting points. Among the many publications that attempt to characterize Kentucky and Kentuckians, the following have particular interest: Harry Toulmin, *A Description of Kentucky in North America to Which Are Prefixed Miscellaneous Observations Respecting the United States* (1792); idem, "Comments on America and Kentucky, 1793–1802," *Register* 47 (1949): 3–20, 97–115; Gilbert Imlay, *A Topographical Description of the Western Territory of North America* (1793); Thomas Ashe, *Travels in America Performed in 1806* (1808); James Walker, "Diary of the Wilderness Road in the Year 1816," *Register* 39 (1941): 224–29; Earl Gregg Swem, ed., *Letters on the Condition of Kentucky in 1825* (1916); Frances Trollope, *Domestic Manners of the Americans* (1832); and Harriet Martineau, *Retrospect of Western Travel*, 3 vols. (1838). George Robertson, *Scrap Book on Law and Politics, Men and Times* (1855), offers some pertinent observations.

John B. Boles, *Religion in Antebellum Kentucky* (1976), is an excellent introduction to a topic about which much has been written. Boles's *The Great Revival, 1787–1805: The Origins of the Southern Evangelical Mind* (1972), is also a fine introduction to the rise of revivalism, but has since been surpassed by Christine Leigh Heyrman, *Southern Cross: The Beginnings of the Bible Belt* (1997). Also see Ellen Eslinger, *Citizens of Zion: The Social Origins of Camp Meeting Revivalism* (1999). Shorter studies include William L. Hiemstra, "Early Frontier Revivalism in Kentucky," *Register* 59 (1961): 133–49; Mariam S. Houchens, "The Great Revival of 1800," *Register* 69 (1971): 216–34; and Paul K. Conkin, *Cane Ridge: America's Pentecost* (1990).

Some of the most interesting articles on religion are Charles R. Staples, "Pioneer Kentucky Preachers and Pulpits," *FCHQ* 9 (1935): 135–57; Walter B. Posey, "Baptist Watch-Care in Early Kentucky," *Register* 34 (1936): 311–17; Howard Elmo Short, "Some Early Church Experiences," *Register* 49 (1951): 269–79; and George W. Ranck, "'The Travelling Church': An Account of the Baptist Exodus from Virginia to Kentucky in 1781," *Register* 79 (1981): 240–65. Lee Shai Weissbach, *The Synagogues of Kentucky: Architecture and History* (1995), makes important contributions to both religious and architectural history. Some of the most interesting religious writing deals with ministers: W. P. Strickland, ed., *Autobiography of Peter Cartwright, the Backwoods Preacher* (1856); David R. Driscoll Jr., "Stephen Theodore Badin, Priest of Frontier Kentucky," *FCHQ* 31 (1957): 243–66; the Reverend Monsignor Charles C. Boldrick, "Martin John Spalding, 1810–1872: Second Bishop of Louisville, 1848–1864," *FCHQ* 33 (1959): 3–25; John R. Finger, "Witness to Expansion: Bishop Francis Asbury on the Trans-Appalachian Frontier," *Register* 82 (1984): 334–57; Elder John Sparks, *Raccoon John Smith: Frontier Kentucky's Most Famous Preacher* (2005); and Richard L. Troutman, ed., *"The Heavens Are Weeping": The Diaries of George Richard Browder, 1852–1886* (1987).

The Shakers have attracted more attention than any group of comparable size. A fine general study is Stephen J. Stein, *The Shaker Experience in America: A History of the United Society of Believers* (1992). Both Kentucky communities are studied in Julia Neal, *The Kentucky Shakers* (1982). Julia Neal, *By Their Fruits: The Story of Shakerism in South Union* (1947); and Julia Neal, ed., *The Journal of Eldress Nancy* (1963), tell the South Union story. On textile manufacturing by the South Union Shakers, see Jonathan Jeffrey and Donna Parker, "A Thread of Evidence: Shaker Textiles at South Union, Kentucky," *Register* 94 (1996): 33–58. Thomas D. Clark and Gerald F. Ham, *Pleasant Hill and Its Shakers* (1968); and Samuel W. Thomas and James C. Thomas, *The Simple Spirit: A Pictorial History of Pleasant Hill* (1973), relate the story of the community at Pleasant Hill.

7. The Age of the Whigs

James A. Ramage and Andrea S. Watkins, *Kentucky Rising: Democracy, Slavery, and Culture from the Early Republic to the Civil War* (2011) is a solid survey of the social, cultural, political, and economic changes that the state witnessed during the first half of the nineteenth century. More focused on Lexington are the essays in James C. Klotter and Daniel Rowland, eds., *Bluegrass Renaissance: The History and Culture of Central Kentucky, 1792–1852* (2012).

Richard P. McCormick, *The Second American Party System: Party Formation in the Jacksonian Era* (1966); Frank F. Mathias, "The Turbulent Years of Kentucky Politics, 1820–1850" (PhD diss., University of Kentucky, 1966); and Wallace B. Turner, "Kentucky in a Decade of Change, 1850–1860" (PhD diss., University of Kentucky, 1954), are detailed studies of politics during the Jacksonian era. The two dissertations have been summarized in Frank F. Mathias, "The Turbulent Years of Kentucky Politics, 1820–1850," *Register* 72 (1974): 309–18; and Wallace B. Turner, "Kentucky State Politics in the Early 1850s," *Register* 56 (1958): 123–42. For the most influential general studies of the era, see Daniel Walker Howe, *What Hath God Wrought: The Transformation of America, 1815–1848* (2007), and Sean Wilentz, *The Rise of American Democracy: Jefferson to Lincoln* (New York: W. W. Norton, 2009). Among the best political studies of this period are Ralph A. Wooster, *Politicians, Planters, and Plain Folk: Courthouse and Statehouse in the Upper South, 1850–1860* (1975); Jasper B. Shannon and Ruth McQuown, comps., *Presidential Poli-*

tics in Kentucky, 1824–1948 (1950); Frank F. Mathias and Jasper B. Shannon, "Gubernatorial Politics in Kentucky, 1820–1851," *Register* 88 (1990): 245–77; William C. Richardson, *An Administrative History of Kentucky Courts to 1850* (1983); Robert M. Ireland, "Aristocrats All: The Politics of County Government in Antebellum Kentucky," *Review of Politics* 32 (1970): 365–83; and James W. Gordon, *Lawyers in Politics: Mid-Nineteenth Century Kentucky As a Case Study* (1990).

In addition to such well-known politicians as Henry Clay and John J. Crittenden, a number of other antebellum politicians have attracted scholarly attention. Such works include George Baber, "Joseph Rogers Underwood: Jurist, Orator, and Statesman," *Register* 10 (1912): 49–54; Lucius P. Little, *Ben Hardin: His Times and Contemporaries* (1887); Leland Winfield Meyer, *The Life and Times of Richard M. Johnson of Kentucky* (1932); Jonathan Jones, "The Making of a Vice President: The National Political Career of Richard M. Johnson of Kentucky" (PhD diss., University of Memphis, 1998); Orval W. Baylor, *John Pope, Kentuckian: His Life and Times, 1770–1845* (1953); William Stickney, ed., *Autobiography of Amos Kendall* (1872); Holman Hamilton, "Kentucky's Linn Boyd, and the Dramatic Days of 1850," *Register* 55 (1957): 185–95; John R. Dorman, "Gabriel Slaughter, 1767–1830," *FCHQ* 40 (1966): 338–56; Will D. Gilliam Jr., "Robert Perkins Letcher, Whig Governor of Kentucky," *FCHQ* 24 (1950): 6–27; George Baber, "James Guthrie: Lawyer, Financier, and Statesman," *Register* 10 (1912): 9–13; Robert Spencer Cotterill, "James Guthrie—Kentuckian, 1792–1869," *Register* 20 (1922): 290–96; John Wilson Townsend, *Richard Hickman Menefee* (1907); and Stephen W. Fackler, "John Rowan and the Demise of Jeffersonian Republicanism in Kentucky, 1819–1831," *Register* 78 (1980): 1–26.

Politicking in the antebellum years depended a great deal upon public speaking, and Kentucky had some masters of oratorical art. For a sampling, try Gifford Blyton and Randall Capps, *Speaking Out: Two Centuries of Kentucky Orators* (1977); and William C. Davis,

"Taking the Stump: Campaigns in Old-Time Kentucky," *Register* 80 (1982): 367–91.

The Mexican War created great excitement in the state. A. H. Bill, *Rehearsal for Conflict: The War with Mexico, 1846–1848* (1947); and Jack Bauer, *The Mexican-American War, 1846–1848* (1974), provide good overviews. Aspects of Kentucky's participation are discussed in Damon R. Eubank, "A Time of Enthusiasm: The Response of Kentucky to the Call for Troops in the Mexican War," *Register* 90 (1992): 323–44; James A. Ramage, "John Hunt Morgan and the Kentucky Cavalry Volunteers in the Mexican War," *Register* 81 (1983): 343–65; and Richard V. Salisbury, "Kentuckians at the Battle of Buena Vista," *FCHQ* 61 (1987): 34–53. See also Holman Hamilton, *Zachary Taylor: Soldier of the Republic* (1946); and K. Jack Bauer, *Zachary Taylor* (1985).

Frank F. Mathias, "The Turbulent Years of Kentucky Politics, 1820–1850," *Register* 72 (1974): 309–18; George L. Willis Sr., "History of Kentucky Constitutions and Constitutional Conventions," *Register* 28 (1930): 305–29; and Carl R. Fields, "Making Kentucky's Third Constitution" (PhD diss., University of Kentucky, 1951), provide overviews of constitution-making at midcentury. Frank F. Mathias describes a conservative trend in "Kentucky's Third Constitution: A Restriction of Majority Rule," *Register* 75 (1977): 1–19. Unlike its predecessors, the third constitutional convention kept a detailed record of its proceedings: see the 1,129-page *Report of the Debates and Proceedings of the Convention for the Revision of the Constitution of the State of Kentucky, 1849* (1849).

Henry Clay was the state's favorite son for half a century and one of the nation's leading statesmen. Robert V. Remini, *Henry Clay: Statesman for the Union* (1991); and David S. Heidler and Jeanne T. Heidler, *Henry Clay* (2010) are the best biographies, but Glyndon G. Van Deusen, *The Life of Henry Clay* (1937) and Bernard Mayo, *Henry Clay* (1937), are still useful. Mayo's work examines Clay only to 1812. For a full study that emphasizes Clay's presidential races, see James C. Klotter, *Henry Clay: The Man Who Would be President* (2018). Clay's role as a party leader is explored in George R. Poage, *Henry Clay and the Whig Party* (1936); and Clement Eaton, *Henry Clay and the Art of American Politics* (1957). The charge that haunted Clay after 1824 is studied in William G. Morgan, "The 'Corrupt Bargain' Charge against Clay and Adams: An Historiographical Analysis," *FCHQ* 42 (1968): 132–49; and idem, "Henry Clay's Biographers and the 'Corrupt Bargain' Charge," *Register* 66 (1968): 242–58. Frank F. Mathias, "Henry Clay and His Kentucky Power Base," *Register* 78 (1980): 123–39; and Everett William Kindig, "Western Opposition to Jackson's 'Democracy': The Ohio Valley as a Case Study, 1827–1836" (PhD diss., Stanford University, 1974), help explain why Clay was able to remain in the political foreground so long. Some of the facets of Clay's long political career are discussed in Thomas B. Jones, "Henry Clay and Continental Expansion, 1820–1844," *Register* 73 (1973): 241–62; Robert Seager II, "Henry Clay and the Politics of Compromise and Noncompromise," *Register* 85 (1987): 1–28; and Peter B. Knupfer, "Henry Clay's Constitutional Unionism," *Register* 89 (1991): 32–60. Clay's last great effort at compromise is admirably described in Holman Hamilton, *Prologue to Conflict: The Crisis and Compromise of 1850* (1964), as well as three other studies—Robert V. Remini, *Henry Clay: Statesman for the Union* (1992); John C. Waugh, *On the Brink of Civil War: The Compromise of 1850 and How It Changed the Course of American History* (2003); and Fergus M. Borderwich, *America's Great Debate: Henry Clay, Stephen A. Douglas, and the Compromise that Preserved the Union* (2012). The challenge of rising to Clay's example fell heavily on his children, as described in Lindsey Apple, *The Family Legacy of Henry Clay: In the Shadow of a Kentucky Patriarch* (2011).

Wallace B. Turner, "Kentucky in a Decade of Change, 1850–1860" (PhD diss., University of Kentucky, 1954), summarizes the political developments of the 1850s. David M. Potter, *The Impending Crisis, 1848–1861* (1976), presents an overview of the national problems; Michael E. Holt, *The Political Crisis of the 1850s* (1978), concentrates on the politics of the 1850s. Arthur C. Cole, *The Whig Party in the South* (1913), is still a sound study. Christopher R. Waldrep, "Who Were Kentucky's Whig Voters? A Note on Voting in Eddyville Precinct in August 1850," *Register* 79 (1981): 326–32; and E. Merton Coulter, "The Downfall of the Whig Party in Kentucky," *Register* 23 (1925): 162–74, attempt to answer two questions about the Whigs.

The Whigs were strong advocates for education. William E. Ellis, *A History of Education in Kentucky* (2011) offers the best overview on the subject. Ellis Hartford, *The Little White Schoolhouse* (1977); and Edwin A. Doyle, Ruby Layson, and Anne Armstrong Thompson, eds., *From the Fort to the Future: Educating the Children of Kentucky* (1987), are two good general studies of the state's public schools. Others include Moses E. Ligon, *A History of Public Education in Kentucky* (1942); Frank L. McVey, *The Gates Open Slowly: A History of Education in Kentucky* (1949); and C. W. Hackensmith, *Out of Time and Tide: The Evolution of Education in Kentucky* (1970). A perceptive overview is Thomas D. Clark, "Kentucky Education through Two Centuries of Political and Social Change," *Register* 83 (1985): 173–201. Edsel T. Godby, "The Governors of Kentucky and Education, 1780–1852," *Bulletin of the Bureau of School Services* 52 (1960): 1–122; Frank F. Mathias, "Kentucky's Struggle for Common Schools, 1820–1850," *Register* 82 (1984): 214–34; and William Hutchinson Vaughan, *Robert Jefferson Breckinridge as an Educational Administrator* (1937), all address the antebellum years. Marion B. Lucas, *A History of Blacks in Kentucky: From Slavery to Segregation, 1760–1891* (1992); and Clarence L. Timberlake, "The Early Struggle for Education of the Blacks in the Commonwealth of Kentucky," *Register* 71 (1973): 225–52, show what little was achieved in education for blacks before the Civil War. Ella Wells Drake, "Choctaw Academy: Richard M. Johnson and the Business of Indian Education," *Register* 91 (1993): 260–97, served as the only useful study of Choctaw Academy until Christina Snyder, *Great Crossings: Indians, Settlers, and Slaves in the Age of Jackson* (2017), which is an excellent study of the Choctaw Academy.

Higher education fared better in antebellum Kentucky than did the public schools. Alvin E. Lewis, *A History of Higher Education in Kentucky* (1899), is still useful although dated. Earl Gregg Swem, "Kentuckians at William and Mary College before 1861 with a Sketch of the College before That Date," *FCHQ* 23 (1949): 173–98, describes one alternative to attending a college in the state. Most of the accounts of higher education focus on a particular school. John D. Wright Jr., *Transylvania: Tutor to the West* (1973), can be supplemented by James L. Miller Jr., "Transylvania University as the Nation Saw It, 1818–1828," *FCHQ* 34 (1960): 305–18; William J. McGlothin, "Rev. Horace Holley: Transylvania's Unitarian President, 1818–1827," *FCHQ* 51 (1977): 234–48; James P. Cousins, *Horace Holley: Transylvania University and the Making of Liberal Education in the Early American Republic* (2016); Leonard Warren, *Constantine Samuel Rafinesque: A Voice in the American Wilderness* (2004); and Huntley Dupre, "Transylvania University and Rafinesque, 1819–1826," *FCHQ* 35 (1961): 110–21. James F. Hopkins, *The University of Kentucky: Origins and Early Years* (1951), clarifies the start of the University of Kentucky, while Dwayne Cox, "A History of the University of Louisville" (PhD diss., University of Kentucky, 1984), does the same for the University of Louisville. Elisabeth S. Peck and Emily Ann Smith, *Berea's First 125 Years, 1855–1980* (1955), revised in 1982; Walter H. Rankins, *Augusta College* (1957); Hardin Craig, *Centre College of Kentucky: A Tradition and an Opportunity* (1967); Robert Snyder, *A History of Georgetown College* (1979); and Felix Newton Pitt, "Two Early Catholic Colleges in Kentucky: St. Thomas and Gethsemani," *FCHQ* 38 (1964): 133–48, tell the stories of other early colleges.

The nativist movement led to the formation of the American Party, or the Know-Nothings, which flourished briefly in the 1850s. The best accounts of the party in Kentucky are Agnes Geraldine McGann, *Nativism in Kentucky to 1860* (1944); and Wallace B. Turner, "The Know-Nothing Movement in Kentucky," *FCHQ* 28 (1954): 266–83. Louisville's violent riot has been described in Charles E. Deusner, "The Know Nothing Riots in Louisville," *Register* 61 (1962): 122–47; and Wallace S. Hutcheon Jr., "The Louisville Riots of August, 1850," *Register* 69 (1971): 150–72. On the disputed role played by the *Louisville Journal*, see Betty C. Congleton, "George D. Prentice and Bloody Monday: A Reappraisal," *Register* 63 (1965): 218–39; and William C. Mallalieu, "George D. Prentice: A Re-appraisal Reappraised," *Register* 64 (1966): 44–50. Another view of the affair is offered in Philip Wayne Kennedy, "The Know-Nothing Movement in Kentucky: Role of M. J. Spalding, Catholic Bishop of Louisville," *FCHQ* 38 (1964): 17–35.

Romanticism heavily influenced Kentucky's culture and politics. Among the novels that appropriated the typology of the Kentucky pioneer are James Kirke Paulding, *Westward Ho! A Tale*, 2 vols. (1832), and James Fenimore Cooper's Leatherstocking Tales—*The Pioneers* (1823), *The Last of the Mohicans* (1826), *The Prairie* (1827), *The Pathfinder* (1840), and *The Deerslayer* (1841). On literary styles and their employment of frontier themes, see E. Douglas Branch, *The Sentimental Years, 1836–1860* (1934); Richard Slotkin, *Regeneration through Violence: The Mythology of the American Frontier, 1600–1860* (1973); Michael Allen, *Western Rivermen, 1763–1861: Ohio and Mississippi Boatmen and the Myth of the Alligator Horse* (1990); Daniel J. Herman, "The Other Daniel Boone: The Nascence of a Middle-Class Hunter Hero, 1784–1860," *Journal of the Early Republic* 18 (1998): 429–58; and Richard Taylor, "Daniel Boone as American Icon: A Literary View," *Register* 102 (2004): 513–33. The limited antebellum literature that was produced in Kentucky is discussed in William Smith Ward, *A Literary History of Kentucky* (1988); and John Wilson Townsend, *Kentucky in American Letters*, 2 vols. (1913). Dorothy Townsend added a third volume of *Kentucky in American Letters* in 1976.

The Beauchamp-Sharp affair is probably Kentucky's most dramatically Romantic story: the best study is Matthew G. Schoenbachler, *Murder & Madness: The Myth of the Kentucky Tragedy* (2009); also see Dickson D. Bruce Jr.,

The Kentucky Tragedy: A Story of Conflict and Change in Antebellum America (2006), and Willard Rouse Jillson, "The Beauchamp-Sharp Tragedy in American Literature," *Register* 36 (1938): 54–60.

Useful overviews of Kentucky's architecture are provided in Clay Lancaster, *Antebellum Architecture of Kentucky* (1991); idem, "Kentucky's Architectural Firsts," *Antiques* 52 (1947): 331–43; Rexford Newcomb, *Old Kentucky Architecture* (1940); and idem, "Kentucky Architecture: Your Heritage—Its Meaning Today," *FCHQ* 26 (1952): 209–22. Among the best specialized studies are Julian C. Oberwarth and William B. Scott Jr., *A History of the Profession of Architecture in Kentucky* (1987); Lois L. Olcott, "Public Architecture of Kentucky before 1870," *Antiques* 105 (1974): 830–39; J. Winston Coleman Jr., "Early Lexington Architects and Their Work," *FCHQ* 42 (1968): 222–34; James C. Thomas, "Shaker Architecture in Kentucky," *FCHQ* 53 (1979): 26–36; Rexford Newcomb, "Gideon Shryock—Pioneer Greek Revivalist of the Middle West," *Register* 26 (1928): 221–35; and Alfred J. Andrews, "Gideon Shryock, Kentucky Architect, and Greek Revival Architecture in Kentucky," *FCHQ* 18 (1944): 67–77. Richard S. DeCamp, *The Bluegrass of Kentucky: A Glimpse of the Charm of Central Kentucky Architecture* (1985), focuses on the Bluegrass region. William Lynwood Montell and Michael Lynn Morse, *Kentucky Folk Architecture* (1976), describes the most common architecture during the early days.

Kentucky artists of the antebellum years were most successful as portrait painters, before photography began to offer cheaper likenesses. A good starting place is Estill Curtis Pennington, *Lessons in Likeness: Portrait Painters in Kentucky and the Ohio River Valley, 1802–1920* (2011). J. Winston Coleman Jr., *Three Kentucky Artists: Hart, Price, Troye* (1974), can be supplemented with Gayle R. Carver, "Joel Tanner Hart: Kentucky's Poet-Sculptor," *Register* 38 (1940): 49–53; David B. Dearinger, "The Diary of Joel Tanner Hart, Kentucky Sculptor," *FCHQ* 64 (1990): 5–31; and William Barrow Floyd, "Edward Troye, Sporting Artist," *Antiques* 105 (1974): 799–817. The state's best-known portraitist is the subject of E. A. Jonas, *Matthew Harris Jouett: Kentucky Portrait Painter (1787–1827)* (1938). Two lesser-known artists are presented in Edna Talbott Whitley, "George Beck, an Eighteenth-Century Painter," *Register* 67 (1969): 20–36; and Martin F. Schmidt, "The Artist and the Artisan: Two Men of Early Louisville," *FCHQ* 62 (1988): 32–51. Artist Thomas Campbell and artisan Colin R. Milne started lithographic printing in the Falls City. The most recent biography of John J. Audubon is Gregory Nobles's *John James Audubon: The Nature of the American Woodsman* (2017). Another useful biography is Shirley Streshinsky, *Audubon: Life and Art in the American Wilderness* (1993). Clark Keating, *Audubon: The Kentucky Years* (1976); and J. David Book, "Audubon in Louisville, 1807–1810," *FCHQ* 45 (1971): 186–98, focus on the artist's time in Kentucky.

The theater provided entertainment for many Kentuckians from an early day. West T. Hill Jr., *The Theatre in Early Kentucky, 1790–1820* (1971), is a fine survey. John J. Weisert has written extensively on the Kentucky theater in such articles as "Beginnings of German Theatricals in Louisville," *FCHQ* 26 (1952): 347–59; "Beginnings of the Kentucky Theatre Circuit," *FCHQ* 34 (1960): 264–85; "The First Decade at Sam Drake's Louisville Theatre," *FCHQ* 39 (1965): 287–310; "Golden Days at Drake's City Theatre, 1830–1833," *FCHQ* 43 (1969): 255–70; and "An End and Several Beginnings: The Passing of Daniel Drake's City Theatre," *FCHQ* 50 (1976): 5–28. Music was also performed early in the state's history, as Joy Carden shows in *Music in Lexington before 1840* (1980). Burt Feintuck, *Kentucky Folkmusic* (1985); and Charles K. Wolfe, *Kentucky Country: Folk and Country Music of Kentucky* (1982), discuss the music most widely played in the state.

A favorite amusement for those who could afford it was a visit to one of the springs, described by J. Winston Coleman Jr. in *The Springs of Kentucky* (1955) and "Old Kentucky Watering Places," *FCHQ* 16 (1942): 1–26. Three of the best-known springs have received particular attention in Mai Flournoy van Deren Van Arsdall, "The Springs at Harrodsburg," *Register* 61 (1963): 300–328; Martha Stephenson, "Old Graham Springs," *Register* 12 (1914): 27–35; and Audrea McDowell, "The Pursuit of Health and Happiness at the Paroquet Springs in Kentucky, 1838 to 1888," *FCHQ* 69 (1995): 390–420.

The best study of the conflict over abolition, contextualizing Kentucky in a larger national narrative, is Stanley Harrold, *Border War: Fighting over Slavery before the Civil War* (2010). Lowell H. Harrison, *The Antislavery Movement in Kentucky* (1978), carries the issue to legal freedom in 1865; Asa E. Martin, *The Antislavery Movement in Kentucky prior to 1850* (1918), stopped with the third constitutional convention. Kentucky's early antislavery efforts are placed in context in Gordon E. Finnie, "The Antislavery Movement in the Upper South before 1840," *JSH* 35 (1969): 317–42. On the colonization effort, see J. Winston Coleman Jr., "The Kentucky Colonization Society," *Register* 39 (1941): 1–9; Jean Keith, "Joseph Rogers Underwood, Friend of African Colonization," *FCHQ* 22 (1948): 117–32; and Jeffrey Brooke Allen, "Did Southern Colonizationists Oppose Slavery? Kentucky, 1816–1830, As a Test Case," *Register* 75 (1977): 92–111. In "A Rising Social Consciousness in Kentucky during the 1850s," *FCHQ* 36 (1962): 18–31, Wallace B. Turner found the development of abolitionist thought; see Turner, "Abolitionism in Kentucky," *Register* 69 (1971): 319–38. Also helpful are Jeffrey Brooke Allen, "Means and Ends in Kentucky Abolitionism, 1792–1823," *FCHQ* 57 (1983): 365–81; and idem, "Were Southern White Critics of Slavery Racists? Kentucky and the Upper South, 1791–1824," *JSH* 44 (1978): 169–90. Stanley Harrold, in "Violence and Nonviolence in Kentucky Abolitionism," *JSH* (1991): 15–38, examines a difference of opinion that hurt the state's antislavery movement. Hambleton Tapp, in "The Slavery Controversy between Robert Wickliffe and Robert J. Breckinridge prior to the Civil War," *FCHQ* 19 (1945): 156–70, recalls an extensive pamphlet battle in Kentucky history.

Hambleton Tapp, "Robert J. Breckinridge and the Year 1849," *FCHQ* 12 (1938): 125–50; James P. Gregory Jr., "The Question of Slavery in the Kentucky Constitutional Convention of 1849," *FCHQ* 23 (1949): 89–110; and Victor B. Howard, "Robert J. Breckinridge and the Slavery Controversy in Kentucky in 1849," FCHQ 53 (1979): 328–43, deal with slavery and constitutional revision.

Cassius Marcellus Clay's violent encounters obscured the mildness of his antislavery views but have attracted numerous writers to study his career. The best biographies are David L. Smiley, *Lion of White Hall: The Life of Cassius M. Clay* (1962); and H. Edward Richardson, *Cassius Marcellus Clay: Firebrand of Freedom* (1976). Clay's own *Life of Cassius Marcellus Clay: Memoirs, Writings, Speeches* (1886), is often inaccurate and exaggerated in his favor. Among the many articles dealing with his antislavery stance are David L. Smiley, "Cassius M. Clay and Southern Abolitionism," *Register* 49 (1951): 331–36; idem, "Cassius M. Clay and John G. Fee: A Study in Southern Antislavery Thought," *JNH* 42 (1957): 201–13; Stanley Harrold, "The Intersectional Relationship between Cassius M. Clay and the Garrisonian Abolitionists," *CWH* 35 (1989): 101–19; and Lowell H. Harrison, "Cassius Marcellus Clay and the *True American*," *FCHQ* 22 (1948): 30–49. The unusual Clay-Fee relationship is examined in Richard Sears, *The Kentucky Abolitionists in the Midst of Slavery, 1854–1864: Exiles for Freedom* (1993).

8. Antebellum Kentucky

The rise of abolitionism is detailed in Randolph Paul Runyon, *Delia Webster and the Underground Railroad* (1996); J. Winston Coleman Jr., "Delia Webster and Calvin Fairbank—Underground Railroad Agents," *FCHQ* 17 (1943): 129–42; and Will Frank Steely, "William Shreve Bailey: Kentucky Abolitionist," *FCHQ* 31 (1957): 274–81. Larry Ceplair, "Mattie Griffith Browne: A Kentucky Abolitionist," *FCHQ* 68 (1994): 219–31, tells the story of a woman who freed her slaves, then moved to the North to write against slavery.

Victor B. Howard, *Black Liberation in Kentucky: Emancipation and Freedom, 1862–1884* (1983), is a detailed account that goes beyond the final legal action. See also Lucas, *A History of Blacks in Kentucky*. President Lincoln's concerns regarding slavery are treated in Robert W. Johannsen, *Lincoln, the South, and Slavery: The Political Dimension* (1991); William H. Townsend, *Lincoln and the Bluegrass: Slavery and the Civil War in Kentucky* (1955); and Lowell H. Harrison, "Lincoln and Compensated Emancipation in Kentucky," *Lincoln Heralds* (1982): 11–17.

Good overviews of the sectional controversies of the 1850s are David M. Potter, *The Impending Crisis, 1848–1861* (1976); Michael F. Holt, *The Political Crisis of the 1850s* (1978); Allan Nevins, *The Ordeal of the Union*, 2 vols. (1947); and idem, *The Emergence of Lincoln*, 2 vols. (1950). David M. Potter, *Lincoln and His Party in the Secession Crisis* (1942); and Kenneth Stampp, *And the War Came: The North and the Secession Crisis, 1860–1861* (1950; revised, 1970), focus on the 1860 election and the subsequent secession movement.

E. Merton Coulter, *The Civil War and Readjustment in Kentucky* (1926), is still the most complete study of developments in the state during the secession crisis. James R. Robertson, "Sectionalism in Kentucky from 1855 to 1865," *MVHR* 4 (1917): 49–63; and Harry August Volz III, "Party, State, and Nation: Kentucky and the Coming of the American Civil War" (PhD diss., University of Virginia, 1982), are good accounts of Kentucky's place in the sectional disputes and the secession movement. David L. Porter, "The Kentucky Press and the Election of 1860," *FCHQ* 46 (1972): 49–52, describes sharp differences within the state.

John J. Crittenden was a national leader in the futile efforts to find an acceptable compromise. Albert D. Kirwan, *John J. Crittenden: The Struggle for the Union* (1962), is a fine biography, but see also Donald W. Zacharias, "John J. Crittenden Crusades for the Union and Neutrality in Kentucky," *FCHQ* 38 (1964): 193–205; Jack Kelly, "John J. Crittenden and the Constitutional Union Party," *FCHQ* 48 (1974): 265–76; and Patsy S. Ledbetter, "John

J. Crittenden and the Compromise Debacle," *FCHQ* 51 (1977): 125–42. Damon R. Eubank explores Crittenden's legacy among his descendants in *In the Shadow of the Patriarch: The John Crittenden Family in War and Peace* (2009). Peter B. Knupfer, in *The Union as It Is: Constitutional Unionism and Sectional Compromise, 1787–1861* (1991), sees the 1860–1861 efforts as part of an American political tradition. Christopher R. Waldrep, "Rank-and-File Voters and the Coming of the Civil War: Caldwell County, Kentucky, as a Test Case," *CWH* 35 (1989): 59–72, is an interesting study that needs to be repeated for a number of counties.

On secessionists' effort to sway the commonwealth toward the Confederacy, see Berry Craig, *Kentucky's Rebel Press: Pro-Confederate Media and the Secession Crisis* (2018); also, Michael D. Robinson, *A Union Indivisible: Secession and the Politics of Slavery in the Border South* (2017); and Gary Matthews, *More American than Southern: Kentucky, Slavery, and the War for an American Ideology, 1828–1861* (2014). William T. McKinney, "The Defeat of the Secessionists in Kentucky in 1861," *JNH* 1 (1916): 377–91; Wallace B. Turner, "The Secession Movement in Kentucky," *Register* 66 (1968): 259–78; James E. Copeland, "Where Were the Kentucky Unionists and Secessionists?" *Register* 71 (1973): 344–63; and Lowell H. Harrison, "Governor Magoffin and the Secession Crisis," *Register* 72 (1974): 91–110, all examine the failure of the secession movement in the state. See also Lowell H. Harrison, *The Civil War in Kentucky* (1975), reprinted in 1988; and idem, "The Civil War in Kentucky: Some Persistent Questions," *Register* 76 (1978): 1–21. Kentucky's unusual neutrality is discussed in A. C. Quisenberry, "Kentucky's 'Neutrality' in 1861," *Register* 15 (1917): 9–21; Wilson Porter Shortridge, "Kentucky's Neutrality in 1861," *MVHR* 9 (1923): 283–301; and Steven E. Woodworth, "'The Indeterminate Quantities': Jefferson Davis, Leonidas Polk, and the End of Kentucky's Neutrality, September 1861," *CWH* 38 (1992): 289–97.

Much of the story of these troubled years can be found in the biographies of those who participated actively in the events. In addition to the biographies cited above for John J. Crittenden and Cassius M. Clay, the following sources are useful: Patrick Sowle, "Cassius Clay and the Crisis of the Union, 1860–1861," *Register* 65 (1967): 144–49; William C. Davis, *Breckinridge: Statesman, Soldier, Symbol* (1974); Frank H. Heck, *Proud Kentuckian: John C. Breckinridge* (1976); and Lowell H. Harrison, "John C. Breckinridge: Nationalist, Confederate, Kentuckian," *FCHQ* 47 (1973): 125–44. James C. Klotter, *The Breckinridges of Kentucky, 1760–1981* (1986), describes the roles of both Unionist Robert J. Breckinridge and his Confederate nephew, John C. Breckinridge, as well as some of the less well-known members of this family.

The Provisional Government of Confederate Kentucky is described in several articles by Lowell H. Harrison: "George W. Johnson and Richard Hawes: The Governors of Confederate Kentucky," *Register* 79 (1981): 3–39; "Letters of George W. Johnson," *Register* 40 (1942): 337–32; and "Confederate Kentucky: The State That Almost Was," *Civil War Times Illustrated* 12 (1973): 12–21. *The War of the Rebellion: A Compilation of the Official Records of the Union and Confederate Armies*, 128 vols. (1880–1901), usually cited as *Official Records*, is an incomparable collection of source materials for the Civil War period. Some thirty volumes contain information relating to Kentucky, including a number of documents dealing with the state's neutrality.

Too little has been written about women in antebellum Kentucky, in large part because they were so restricted by law and custom that they had little opportunity to demonstrate their talents. Margaret Ripley Wolfe, *Daughters of Canaan: A Saga of Southern Women* (1995), provides an excellent overview. Helen Deiss Irvin, *Women in Kentucky* (1979); and Margaret Ripley Wolfe, "Fallen Leaves and Missing Pages: Women in Kentucky History," *Register* 90 (1992): 64–89, are the best guides to the status of women in the commonwealth. Nancy Disher Baird and Carol Crowe-Carraco, "A 'True Woman's Sphere': Motherhood in Late Antebellum Kentucky," *FCHQ* 66 (1992): 369–94, describes a woman's "proper" role. In "Wom-

en in Louisville: Moving toward Equal Rights," *FCHQ* 55 (1981): 151–78, Carol Guethlein found that most progress came after the Civil War.

A few studies of individual women have been done. The essays in McEuen and Appleton, eds., *Kentucky Women,* provide the most recent biographies. Mary Todd Lincoln receives a thorough analysis in Catherine Clinton, *Mrs. Lincoln: A Life* (2009). Miriam Corcoran, "Catherine Spalding—Sister and Servant," *FCHQ* 62 (1988): 260–67; Sister Mary Michael Creamer, "Mother Catherine Spalding—St. Catherine Street, Louisville, Kentucky," *FCHQ* 65 (1989): 191–223; and Mary Ellen Doyle, *Pioneer Spirit: Catherine Spalding, Sister of Charity of Nazareth* (2006), tell of a woman who achieved a great deal on her own. Anna Cook Beauchamp gained fame because of her part in the Beauchamp-Sharp affair: J. W. Cooke, "Portrait of a Murderess: Anna Cook(e) Beauchamp," *FCHQ* 65 (1991): 209–30. Carol DeLatte, *Lucy Audubon: A Biography* (1982), tells the story of the life of the wife of a famous man. Still, too few studies exist of individuals; see Willard Rouse Jillson, "A Sketch of the Life and Times of Rebecca Witten Graham, of Floyd County, Kentucky, 1775–1843," *Register* 37 (1939): 116–26.

9. The Civil War in a Border State

Kentucky's role in the Civil War has received substantial coverage in the past two decades as the 150th anniversary of the war brought renewed attention. The most recent work is Dieter C. Ulrich and Berry Craig, *General E. A. Paine in Western Kentucky: Assessing the "Reign of Terror" of the Summer of 1864* (2017); Matthew E. Stanley, *The Loyal West: Civil War and Reunion in Middle America* (2017); Christopher Phillips, *The Rivers Ran Backward: The Civil War and the Remaking of the American Middle Border* (2016); John Philip Cashon, *Paducah and the Civil War* (2016); Bridget Ford, *Bonds of Union: Religion, Race, and Politics in a Civil War Borderland* (2016); Patrick A. Lewis, *For Slavery and Union: Benjamin Buckner and Kentucky Loyalties in the Civil War* (2015);

Kent T. Dollar, et al., eds. *Border Wars: The Civil War in Tennessee and Kentucky* (2015); Luke E. Harlow, *Religion, Race, and the Making of Confederate Kentucky, 1830–1880* (2014); Berry Craig, *Kentucky Confederates: Secession, Civil War, and the Jackson Purchase* (2014); Bryan D. McKnight, *Contested Borderland: The Civil War in Appalachian Kentucky and Virginia* (2012); Aaron Astor, *Rebels on the Border: Civil War, Emancipation, and the Reconstruction of Kentucky and Missouri* (2012); Stuart W. Sanders, *Perryville under Fire: The Aftermath of Kentucky's Largest Civil War Battle* (2012); and the "New Perspectives on Civil War–Era Kentucky" special issue of the *Register* 110 (2012).

In addition to the *Official Records*, other publications contain much information about Kentucky's part in the Civil War, including *Official Records of the Union and Confederate Navies in the War of the Rebellion*, 30 vols. (1894–1922); and Robert Underwood Johnson and Clarence Clough Buel, eds., *Battles and Leaders of the Civil War*, 4 vols. (1887–1888). E. Merton Coulter, *The Civil War and Readjustment in Kentucky* (1926), is excellent on economic and political developments; it pays little attention to the military situation. Lowell H. Harrison, *The Civil War in Kentucky* (1973), reprinted in 1988, is limited by the format of the series of which it is a part, but it does devote more attention to military affairs in the state. The rosters and brief histories of the Kentucky units in both armies are found in *Report of the Adjutant General of the State of Kentucky: Union Troops, 1861–1866*, 2 vols. (1867); and *Report of the Adjutant General of the State of Kentucky: Confederate Kentucky Volunteers*, 2 vols. (1918). Thomas Speed, *The Union Cause in Kentucky, 1860–1865* (1907); and idem, *The Union Regiments of Kentucky* (1897), should be balanced by the equally partisan J. Stoddard Johnston, *Kentucky*, vol. 9 of *Confederate Military History*, edited by Clement A. Evans, 10 vols. (1899). Hambleton Tapp, ed., "The Civil War Annals of Kentucky," *FCHQ* 35 (1961): 205–322, is a reprint of the annals originally published in Collins and Collins, *History of Kentucky*. Richard G. Stone Jr., in *Kentucky Fighting Men, 1861–1945* (1982), looks at the

Kentuckians who fought on each side in the Civil War.

The most famous Confederate unit from Kentucky has been well studied in Ed Porter Thompson, *History of the Orphan Brigade* (1898); William C. Davis, *The Orphan Brigade: The Kentucky Confederates Who Couldn't Go Home* (1980); and in two excellent diaries from members of the brigade: William C. Davis, ed., *Diary of a Confederate Soldier: John S. Jackman of the Orphan Brigade* (1990); and Albert D. Kirwan, ed., *Johnny Green of the Orphan Brigade* (1956). Kentucky's most famous Federal unit has been studied in Sergeant E. Tarrent, *The Wild Riders of the First Kentucky Cavalry: A History of the Regiment, in the Great War of the Rebellion, 1861–1865* (1894); and Hambleton Tapp, "Incidents in the Life of Frank Wolford, Colonel of the First Kentucky Union Cavalry," *FCHQ* 10 (1936): 82–99.

John Hunt Morgan has received more attention than any other state participant in the war. James A. Ramage, *Rebel Raider: The Life of General John Hunt Morgan* (1986), is a superior scholarly biography. Excellent accounts of Duke's command are Basil W. Duke, *History of Morgan's Cavalry* (1867); and idem, *Reminiscences of General Basil W. Duke, C. S. A.* (1911), but see also Lowell H. Harrison, "General Basil W. Duke, C. S. A.," *FCHQ* 54 (1980): 5–36; and Gary Robert Matthews, *Basil Wilson Duke* (2005). Edison H. Thomas, *John Hunt Morgan and His Raiders* (1975), is another modern study. Edwin C. Bearss did an intensive study of the Christmas Raid in "Morgan's Second Kentucky Raid, December, 1862," *Register* 70 (1972): 200–218; 71 (1973): 177–88, 426–38; 72 (1974): 20–37. Brief biographies of Kentucky's numerous generals can be found in Ezra J. Warner, *Generals in Blue* (1964); and Bruce S. Allardice and Lawrence Lee Hewitt, eds., *Kentuckians in Gray: Confederate Generals and Field Officers of the Bluegrass State* (2008). The role of Kentucky cavalrymen is well described in Kenneth A. Hafendorfer, *They Died by Twos and Threes* (1996).

The Battle of Mill Springs has been studied in Stuart W. Sanders, *The Battle of Mill Springs, Kentucky* (2013), and Raymond E.

Myers, *The Zollie Tree* (1964); R. Gerald Mc-Murtry, "Zollicoffer and the Battle of Mill Springs," *FCHQ* 29 (1955): 303–19; and C. David Dalton, "Zollicoffer, Crittenden, and the Mill Springs Campaign: Some Persistent Questions," *FCHQ* 60 (1986): 463–71. The disastrous Donelson campaign is considered in great detail in Benjamin Franklin Cooling, *Forts Henry and Donelson: The Key to the Confederate Heartland* (1987). The Confederate efforts to hold southern Kentucky are examined in Charles P. Roland, *Albert Sidney Johnston: Soldier of Three Republics* (1964); and William Preston Johnston, *The Life of General Albert Sidney Johnston* (1878). Steven E. Woodworth, *Jefferson Davis and His Generals: The Failure of Confederate Command in the West* (1990), is an excellent discussion of Confederate military leadership in the western theater. Thomas L. Connelly, *Army of the Heartland: The Army of Tennessee, 1861–1862* (1967); and Stanley F. Horn, *Army of Tennessee* (1933), provide good coverage of the periods when Confederates were in much of the commonwealth. The many specialized studies of aspects of the Civil War in eastern Kentucky include Henry P. Scalf, "The Battle of Ivy Mountain," *Register* 56 (1958): 11–26; Joseph D. Carr, "Garfield and Marshall in the Big Sandy Valley, 1861–1862," *FCHQ* 64 (1990): 247–63; and John David Preston, *The Civil War in the Big Sandy Valley of Kentucky* (1984).

The 1862 invasion of the state by Kirby Smith and Braxton Bragg is considered at length in Connelly's and Horn's histories of the Army of Tennessee and in James Lee McDonough, *War in Kentucky: From Shiloh to Perryville* (1994); Joseph H. Parks, *General E. Kirby Smith, C.S.A.* (1954); and Grady C. McWhiney, *Braxton Bragg and Confederate Defeat* (1969). Among the special studies of aspects of the campaign are Gary Donaldson, "'Into Africa': Kirby Smith and Braxton Bragg's Invasion of Kentucky," *FCHQ* 61 (1987): 444–65; Grady C. McWhiney, "Controversy in Kentucky: Braxton Bragg's Campaign of 1862," *CWH* 6 (1960): 5–42; Lowell H. Harrison, "Should I Surrender?—A Civil War Incident," *FCHQ* 40 (1966): 297–306; A. C. Quisen-berry, "The Battles of Big Hill and Richmond, Kentucky, September 1862," *Register* 16 (1918): 9–25; and Roger C. Adams, "Panic on the Ohio: The Defense of Cincinnati, Covington, and Newport, September, 1862," *Journal of Kentucky Studies* 9 (1992): 80–90.

The major engagement at Perryville has also attracted a number of writers. The most complete study is Kenneth A. Hafendorfer, *Perryville: Battle for Kentucky* (1991); its maps are especially good. It can be supplemented with Kenneth W. Noe's excellent *Perryville: This Grand Havoc of Battle* (2010); Robert P. Broadwater, *The Battle of Perryville, 1862: Culmination of the Failed Kentucky Campaign* (2010); Hambleton Tapp, "The Battle of Perryville, 1862," *FCHQ* 9 (1935): 158–81; Ralph A. Wooster, "Confederate Success at Perryville," *Register* 59 (1961): 318–23; and Christen Ashby Cheek, ed., "Memoirs of Mrs. E. B. Patterson: A Perspective on Danville during the Civil War," *Register* 92 (1994): 347–99. Edwin C. Bearss has examined an important decision in "General Bragg Abandons Kentucky," *Register* 59 (1961): 217–44.

Aided by the legend of the Lost Cause, Kentucky Confederates have received more attention than Unionists. These works help to balance the narrative: Elizabeth D. Leonard, *Lincoln's Forgotten Ally: Judge Advocate General Joseph Holt of Kentucky* (2015); Hambleton Tapp and James C. Klotter, eds., *The Union, the Civil War, and John W. Tuttle: A Kentucky Captain's Account* (1980); David G. Farrelly, "John Marshall Harlan and the Union Cause in Kentucky, 1861," *FCHQ* 37 (1963): 5–23; Roger J. Bartman, "Joseph Holt and Kentucky in the Civil War," *FCHQ* 40 (1966): 105–22; Robert L. Kincaid, "Joshua Fry Speed: Lincoln's Confidential Agent in Kentucky," *Register* 52 (1954): 99–110; A. M. Ellis, "Major General William Nelson," *Register* 4 (1906): 56–64; and Will D. Gilliam Jr., "Robert J. Breckinridge: Kentucky Unionist," *Register* 69 (1971): 362–85.

Many studies exist for specialized aspects of the war and Kentucky's role in them. John David Smith has written two interesting articles about the Union recruits in the state: "The Recruitment of Negro Soldiers in Kentucky, 1863–1865," *Register* 72 (1974): 364–90; and "Kentucky Civil War Recruits: A Medical Profile," *Medical History* 24 (1980): 185–96. The plight of the pacifist Shakers is recorded in Thomas D. Clark, *Pleasant Hill in the Civil War* (1972); and Julia Neal, "South Union Shakers during the War Years," *FCHQ* 39 (1965): 147–50. Richard L. Troutman, ed., "*The Heavens Are Weeping': The Diaries of George Richard Browder, 1852–1886* (1987), shows how the war affected a Methodist minister in south-central Kentucky. Paul G. Ashdown, "Samuel Ringgold: An Episcopal Clergyman in Kentucky and Tennessee during the Civil War," *FCHQ* 53 (1979): 231–38; and Frances L. S. Dugan, ed., "Journal of Mattie Wheeler: A Blue Grass Belle Reports on the Civil War," *FCHQ* 29 (1955): 118–44, show the war's effect on two other civilians. Palmer H. Boeger, "The Great Kentucky Hog Swindle of 1864," *JSH* 28 (1962): 59–70, describes the state's worst economic scandal of the war. Lon Carter Barton, "The Reign of Terror in Graves County," *Register* 46 (1948): 484–95; J. T. Dorris, "President Lincoln's Treatment of Kentuckians," *FCHQ* 28 (1954): 3–20; and Louis DeFalaise, "General Stephen Gano Burbridge's Command in Kentucky," *Register* 69 (1971): 101–27; and Bryan S. Bush, *Butcher Burbridge: Union General Stephen Burbridge and His Reign of Terror over Kentucky* (2008) help explain why most Kentuckians disliked the Lincoln administration despite its growing influence in the state. James Larry Hood explains this influence in "For the Union: Kentucky's Unconditional Unionist Congressmen and the Development of the Republican Party in Kentucky, 1863–1865," *Register* 76 (1978): 197–215.

James B. Martin, "Black Flag over the Bluegrass: Guerrilla Warfare in Kentucky, 1863–1865," *Register* 86 (1988): 352–75, is an excellent survey of a troublesome problem. Martin's article can be supplemented with Adam ("Stovepipe") Johnson, *The Partisan Rangers of the Confederate States Army* (1904); Albert Castel, "Quantrill's Missouri Bushwhackers in Kentucky," *FCHQ* 38 (1964): 125–32; Young E. Allison, "Sue Mundy: An Account of the Terrible Kentucky Guerrilla

of Civil War Times," *Register* 57 (1959): 295–316; and L. L. Valentine, "Sue Mundy of Kentucky," *Register* 62 (1964): 175–205, 278–306.

Several authors have studied the impact of the war on a particular locality. The Louisville story has been told in Robert E. McDowell, *City of Conflict: Louisville in the Civil War, 1861–1865* (1962); Charles Messmer, "Louisville on the Eve of the Civil War," *FCHQ* 56 (1976): 249–89; idem, "Louisville and the Confederate Invasion of 1862," *Register* 55 (1957): 299–324; idem, "Louisville during the Civil War," *FCHQ* 52 (1978): 206–33; and William G. Eidson, "Louisville, Kentucky, during the First Year of the Civil War," *FCHQ* 38 (1964): 224–38. Other localities have received special study in James Barnett, "Munfordville in the Civil War," *Register* 69 (1971): 339–61; Aloma Williams Dew, "'Between the Hawk and the Buzzard': Owensboro during the Civil War," *Register* 77 (1979): 1–14; Eliza Calvert Hall, "Bowling Green and the Civil War," *FCHQ* 11 (1937): 241–51, which was written in 1894; Helen Bartter Crocker, "A War Divides Green River Country," *Register* 70 (1972): 295–311; Glenn Hodges, *Fearful Times: A History of the Civil War Years in Hancock County, Kentucky* (1986); and *Kentucky Rebel Town: The Civil War Battles of Cynthiana and Harrison County* (2016).

Some of the best primary sources on the home front come from women's diaries like John David Smith and William Cooper Jr., eds., *A Union Woman in Civil War Kentucky: The Diary of Frances Peter* (2000); Nancy Disher Baird, *Josie Underwood's Civil War Diary* (2009); and Elizabeth Pendleton Hardin, *The Private War of Lizzie Hardin: A Kentucky Confederate Girl's Diary of the Civil War in Kentucky, Tennessee, Alabama, and Georgia* (1963).

African Americans' participation in the war has been largely neglected. Edwin Reiter's *The Road to Freedom: A History of the 108th Infantry Regiment* (2017) relates the story of how black Kentuckians had to fight for their freedom because the Emancipation Proclamation did not extend to the commonwealth. The plight of blacks at Camp Nelson during the Civil War has been studied in Richard D. Sears,

"A Practical Recognition of the Brotherhood of Man": John G. Fee and the Camp Nelson Experience (1986); and Marion B. Lucas, "Camp Nelson, Kentucky, during the Civil War: Cradle of Liberty or Refugee Death Camp?" *FCHQ* 63 (1989): 439–52.

On Kentucky's evolution from a moderately Union-leaning state to one that identified with the defeated Confederacy, see Anne E. Marshall, *Creating a Confederate Kentucky: The Lost Cause and Civil War Memory in a Border State* (2013), and Luke E. Harlow, *Religion, Race, and the Making of Confederate Kentucky, 1830–1880* (2014). For national context, see Gaines M. Foster, *Ghosts of the Confederacy: Defeat, the Lost Cause, and the Emergence of the New South, 1865 to 1913* (1987).

10. 1865 and After

The best sources for social history are various contemporary newspapers, the numerous county histories, the many personal printed recollections, the revealing letters and diaries, and, for later periods, the large body of collected interviews available in many repositories. Estate inventories and tax and census records are among the many other records that help recreate the life of a people. Still more work needs to be done on this aspect of Kentucky history.

There are many good masters' level graduate theses available, but those have not been cited, for reasons of space. For the same reason, more general, regional studies are not included as well. Readers should examine the earlier version of this work as well as historiographic articles by James C. Klotter in the 1982 and 1999 *Register* for some citations to key works.

Among the printed sources, John E. Kleber, editor in chief, *The Kentucky Encyclopedia* (1992), offers a wealth of information as do three other excellent works: Kleber, ed. *The Encyclopedia of Louisville* (2001); Paul A. Tenkotte and James C. Claypool, eds., *The Encyclopedia of Northern Kentucky* (2009); and Gerald L. Smith, Karen Cotton McDaniel, and John A. Hardin, eds., *The Kentucky African American Encyclopedia* (2015). Richard Ulack, Karl Raitz, and Gyula Pauer, eds., *Atlas of Kentucky* (1998), is a very helpful supplement. Shorter surveys include James Larry Hood, *Restless Heart: Kentucky's Search for Individual Liberty and Community* (2008), and James C. Klotter and Freda C. Klotter, *A Concise History of Kentucky* (2008).

On the fifty years after the end of the Civil War, several works provide the Kentucky setting: E. Merton Coulter, *The Civil War and Readjustment in Kentucky* (1926); Ross A. Webb, *Kentucky in the Reconstruction Era* (1979); Thomas D. Clark, *Kentucky: Land of Contrast* (1968); Hambleton Tapp and James C. Klotter, *Kentucky: Decades of Discord, 1865–1900* (1977); and James C. Klotter, *Kentucky: Portrait in Paradox, 1900–1950* (1996). The general histories mentioned at the beginning of this bibliography offer overviews as well.

On specific Kentucky matters, Thomas D. Clark's *Pills, Petticoats, and Plows: The Southern Country Store* (1944), is one of his best works, while J. Winston Coleman Jr.'s evocative *Springs of Kentucky* (1955) recreates a bygone era, and Shelia E. Brown Heflin, "Owensboro's Chautauqua Years, 1902–1932," *Daviess County Historical Quarterly* 1 (1983): 3–14, highlights one aspect of state culture. On the early urban setting, see Allen J. Share, *Cities in the Commonwealth* (1982). On Louisville specifically, see Gary P. Kocolowski, "Louisville at Large: Industrial-Urban Organization, Inter-City Migration, and Occupational Mobility . . . 1865–1906" (PhD diss., University of Cincinnati, 1978); and George H. Yater, *Two Hundred Years at the Falls of the Ohio: A History of Louisville and Jefferson County* (1987). On northern Kentucky, see Paul A. Tenkotte, "Rival Cities to Suburbs: Covington and Newport, Kentucky, 1790–1890" (PhD diss., University of Cincinnati, 1989).

There are many good city and county histories, too numerous to mention, and most provide the details needed to form wider generalizations. Among the best are John D. Wright Jr., *Lexington: Heart of the Bluegrass* (1982); Randolph Hollingsworth, *Lexington: Queen of the Bluegrass* (2004); Carl E. Kramer, *Capital on the Kentucky: A Two Hundred Year His-*

tory of Frankfort and Franklin County (1986); Lee A. Dew and Aloma Williams Dew, *Owensboro* (1988); John E. L. Robertson, *Paducah, 1830–1980* (1980); Carl B. Boyd Jr. and Hazel M. Boyd, *A History of Mt. Sterling, Kentucky, 1792–1918* (1984); Ann Dudley Matheny, *The Magic City: . . . Middlesborough . . .* (2003); Richard C. Brown, *A History of Danville and Boyle County, Kentucky, 1774–1992* (1992); William David Deskins, *Pike County* (1994); Lindsey Apple, Frederick A. Johnston, and Ann Bolton Bevins, eds., *Scott County, Kentucky: A History* (1993); and William E. Ellis, H. E. Everman, and Richard D. Sears, *Madison County* (1985). William Lynwood Montell has examined the Upper Cumberland region in a series of books that focus on race, religion, violence, and folklife.

11. Reconstruction, Readjustment, and Race, 1865–1875

The national and regional literature on the Reconstruction era is extensive. For Kentucky, county histories, newspapers, manuscript sources, and the various encyclopedias all are important.

Studies that focus on the process of freedom and the lives of those experiencing it for the first time include Victor B. Howard, *Black Liberation in Kentucky: Emancipation and Freedom, 1862–1884* (1983); Marion B. Lucas, "Kentucky Blacks: The Transition from Slavery to Freedom," *Register* 91 (1993): 403–19; Paul J. Lammermeier, "The Urban Black Family of the Nineteenth Century: A Study of Black Family Structure in the Ohio Valley, 1850–1880," *Journal of Marriage and the Family* 35 (1973): 440–56; Theodore H. H. Harris, "Creating Windows of Opportunity: Isaac E. Clark and the African American Experience in Kentucky, 1845–1914," *Register* 98 (2000): 155–78; Darrel E. Bigham, *On Jordan's Banks: Emancipation and Its Aftermath in the Ohio River Valley* (2006); and Marion B. Lucas, *A History of Blacks in Kentucky: From Slavery to Segregation, 1760–1891* (1992).

On the urban experience, see George C. Wright, *Life behind a Veil: Blacks in Louisville,* *Kentucky, 1865–1930* (1985), as well as three good articles on central Kentucky: Herbert A. Thomas, "Victims of Circumstance: Negroes in a Southern Town [Lexington], 1865–1880," *Register 71* (1973): 233–71; John Kellogg, "Negro Urban Clusters in the Postbellum South," *Geographical Review* 67 (1977): 310–21; and Kellogg, "The Formation of Black Residential Areas in Lexington, Kentucky, 1865–1887," *JSH* 48 (1982): 21–32. More studies are needed of other areas of the commonwealth as exemplified in Christopher Beckham, "The Paradox of Religious Segregation: White and Black Baptists in Western Kentucky, 1855–1900," *Register* 97 (1999): 305–22; and Charles L. Davis, "Racial Politics in Central Kentucky during the Post–Reconstruction Era: Bourbon County, 1877–1899," *Register* 108 (2010): 347–82.

On postwar killings, see J. Michael Rhyne, "A 'Murderous Affair in Lincoln County': Politics, Violence, and Memory in a Civil War Kentucky Community [1867]," *American Nineteenth Century History* 7 (2006); 337–59; and Rhyne, "'We Are Mobbed & Beat': Regulator Violence against Free Black Households in Kentucky's Bluegrass Region, 1865–1867," *OVH* 2 (2002): 30–42. Violence and the Freedmen's Bureau are examined in George C. Wright, *Racial Violence in Kentucky, 1865–1940* (1990); W. A. Low, "The Freedmen's Bureau in the Border States," in *Radicalism, Racism, and Party Alignment: The Border States during Reconstruction,* ed. Richard O. Curry (1969), 245–64; and Philip C. Kimball, "Freedom's Harvest: Freedmen's Schools in Kentucky after the Civil War," *FCHQ* 54 (1980): 272–88. Individuals leading the fight for black rights are highlighted in Kentucky Commission on Human Rights, *Kentucky's Black Heritage* (1971); Alice Allison Dunnigan, *The Fascinating Story of Black Kentuckians: Their Heritage and Traditions* (1982); W. D. Johnson, *Biographical Sketches of Prominent Negro Men and Women of Kentucky* (1897); and the *Kentucky African American Encyclopedia* (2015).

The changing political world of the decade after the Civil War can be partially reconstructed from the Kentucky *Acts of the General Assembly,* as well as the Kentucky *House Jour-*

nal and *Senate Journal.* General overviews include, for the Republicans, E. A. Jonas, *A History of the Republican Party in Kentucky* (1929); and Thomas L. Owen, "The Formative Years of the Kentucky Republican Party, 1864–1871" (PhD diss., University of Kentucky, 1981); for the opposition, see George L. Willis Jr., *Kentucky Democracy*, 3 vols. (1935). A good comparative study of select communities in Kentucky and Missouri is Aaron Astor, *Rebels on the Border* (2012). Presidential election statistics, with analysis, can be found in Jasper B. Shannon and Ruth McQuown, comps., *Presidential Politics in Kentucky, 1824–1948* (1950).

In-depth examinations of the era come from several sources and various viewpoints. The older but still useful E. Merton Coulter, *The Civil War and Readjustment in Kentucky* (1926), set the standard for four decades, with its analysis that Kentucky turned pro-Confederate by war's end. Thomas L. Connelly, "Neo-Confederatism or Power Vacuum: Post-war Kentucky Politics Reappraised," *Register* 64 (1966): 257–69, challenged that view, stressing instead the growth of regionalism and of various power blocs. In three studies, Ross A. Webb emphasized the commonwealth's anti-administration aspects rather than pro-Confederate elements: "Kentucky: 'Pariah among the Elect,'" in *Radicalism, Racism, and Party Alignment: The Border States during Reconstruction*, ed. Richard O. Curry (1969); *Kentucky in the Reconstruction Era* (1979); and "'The Past Is Never Dead, It's Not Even Past': Benjamin P. Runkle and the Freedmen's Bureau in Kentucky, 1866–1870," *Register* 84 (1986): 343–60. Taking a middle ground among the various views is Hambleton Tapp and James C. Klotter, *Kentucky: Decades of Discord, 1865–1900* (1977). More recently, Anne Marshall has presented a full analysis of how Kentucky turned to the pro-Confederate camp and the role of memory in that change. See her *Creating a Confederate Kentucky: The Lost Cause and Civil War Memory in a Border State* (2010).

The connection between politics and economics is developed in Metta M. Sublett, "The Role of the Confederate Veteran in the Industrial Development of Kentucky" (MPhil diss., University of Wisconsin, 1945); James P. Sullivan, "Louisville and Her Southern Alliance, 1865–1890" (PhD diss., University of Kentucky, 1965); and Leonard P. Curry, *Rail Routes South: Louisville's Fight for the Southern Market, 1865–1872* (1969). A good nineteenth-century source for brief treatments of year-by-year events is the *Annual Cyclopedia.*

Numerous biographical works exist. Among those dealing with Democratic leaders are Joseph F. Wall, *Henry Watterson* (1956); and for W. C. P. Breckinridge, James C. Klotter, *The Breckinridges of Kentucky, 1760–1981* (1986). A good case study of the postwar mindset of one individual is Patrick A. Lewis, *For Slavery and Union: Benjamin Buckner and Kentucky Loyalties in the Civil War* (2015). On the Republican leadership, see Ross A. Webb, *Benjamin Helm Bristow* (1969); on Harlan, see David G. Farrelly, "Harlan's Formative Period," *Kentucky Law Journal* 46 (1958): 367–406; Tinsley E. Yarbrough, *Judicial Enigma: The First Justice Harlan* (1975); Loren P. Beth, *John Marshall Harlan: The Last Whig Justice* (1992); and Linda Przybszewski, *The Republic According to John Marshall Harlan* (1999). Sketches of the governors appear in Lowell H. Harrison, ed., *Kentucky's Governors*, rev. ed. (2004), and of their abodes in Thomas D. Clark and Margaret A. Lane, *The People's House: Governor's Mansions of Kentucky* (2002)

12. Decades of Discord, 1875–1900

Robert M. Ireland has studied the question of violence in depth. His two articles "Homicide in Nineteenth-Century Kentucky," *Register* 81 (1983): 134–53, and "Law and Disorder in Nineteenth-Century Kentucky," *Vanderbilt Law Review* 32 (1979): 281–99, provide a good introduction. On individual instances of violence, see Ireland's "The Thompson-Davis Case and the Unwritten Law," *FCHQ* 62 (1988): 417–41; Ireland, "The Buford-Elliott Tragedy and the Tradition of Kentucky Criminal Justice," *FCHQ* 66 (1992): 395–419; James C. Klotter, *Kentucky Justice, Southern Honor, and American Manhood* (2003), on Richard Reid; and L. F. Johnson, *Famous Kentucky Tragedies* and Trials (1916, reprinted in 1972). See also William Lynwood Montell, Killings: Folk Justice in the Upper South (1986).

Feud violence attracted much attention to Kentucky, but some of the "troubles" have not received in-depth scholarly attention. An underappreciated early general examination is Charles G. Mutzenberg's Kentucky's Famous Feuds and Tragedies (1897, revised in 1917); other surveys are James C. Klotter, "Feuds in Appalachia: An Overview," FCHQ 56 (1982): 290–317; and John Ed Pearce, Days of Darkness: The Feuds of Eastern Kentucky (1994). On specific feuds, see the lengthy Majority and Minority Reports and Testimony Taken by the Rowan County Investigating Committee . . . March 16th, 1888 (1888); Fred Brown Jr. and Juanita Blair, Days of Anger, Days of Tears: The History of the Rowan County War (2007); T. R. C. Hutton, Bloody Breathitt: Politics and Violence in the Appalachian South (2013), which stresses the political connections; and a well-rounded work on Clay County, Dwight B. Billings and Kathleen M. Blee, The Road to Poverty: The Making of Wealth and Hardship in Appalachia (2000). The various Hatfield-McCoy studies include Virgil C. Jones, The Hatfields and the McCoys (1948); Otis K. Rice, The Hatfields and the McCoys (1978); Thomas Dotson, The Missing McCoys (2015); Lisa Alther, Blood Feud (2012); and, the most scholarly, Altina L. Waller's Feud: Hatfields, McCoys, and Social Change in Appalachia, 1860–1900 (1988).

Such violence attracted more attention to Appalachia and helped fashion an image of the region. On that developing stereotype, see, for example: James C. Klotter, "The Black South and White Appalachia," JAH 66 (1980): 832–49; Tommy R. Thompson, "The Image of Appalachian Kentucky in American Popular Magazines," Register 91 (1993): 176–202; and Cratis D. Williams, "The Southern Mountaineer in Fact and Fiction," Appalachian Journals (1975–76): 8–61, 100–162, 186–261, 334–92. Many late nineteenth- and early twentieth-century accounts of the region appeared, but two of the most influential were William G. Frost, "Our Contemporary Ancestors in the Southern Mountains," Atlantic Quarterly 83 (1899): 311–19; and Horace Kephart, Our Southern Highlanders (1913). A whole scholarly subfield has developed in Appalachian studies, and the analysis of the area is extensive. Studies include Richard B. Drake, A History of Appalachia (2001); John Alexander Williams, Appalachia: A History (2002); Ronald D Eller, Miners, Millhands, and Mountaineers: Industrialization of the Appalachian South, 1880–1930 (1982); Randall G. Lawrence, "Appalachian Metamorphosis: Industrializing Society on the Central Appalachian Plateau, 1860–1913" (PhD diss., Duke University, 1983); Paul Salstrom, Appalachia's Path to Dependency: Rethinking a Region's Economic History, 1730–1940 (1994); Mary Beth Pudup, Dwight B. Billings, and Altina L. Waller, eds., Appalachia in the Making: The Mountain South in the Nineteenth Century (1995); Mark Andrew Huddle, "Soul Winner: Edward O. Guerrant, the Kentucky Home Missions, and the 'Discovery' of Appalachia," OVH 5 (2005); 47–64; and Thomas A. Arcury and Julia D. Porter, "Household Composition in Appalachian Kentucky in 1900," Journal of Family History 10 (1985): 183–95.

The literature on late nineteenth-century politics and issues is quite sizable. Surveys of the political climate appear in Hambleton Tapp and James C. Klotter, Kentucky: Decades of Discord, 1865–1900 (1977); Gordon B. McKinney, Southern Mountain Republicans, 1865–1900 (1978); and Robert M. Ireland, Little Kingdoms: The Counties of Kentucky, 1850–1891 (1977). Individual leaders are studied in Nancy Disher Baird, Luke Pryor Blackburn: Physician, Governor, Reformer (1979); Arndt M. Stickles, Simon Bolivar Buckner (1940); Stephen Russell, Simon Bolivar Buckner: Beyond the Southern Storm (2005); James A. Barnes, John G. Carlisle (1931); Maurice H. Thatcher, Stories and Sketches of William O. Bradley (1916); Lowell H. Harrison, ed., Kentucky's Governors, rev. ed. (2004); John E. Kleber, editor in chief, The Kentucky Encyclopedia (1992); and the other state-based encyclopedias. William Goebel's life and death have fostered many works, including the good, near-contemporary R. E. Hughes, E. W. Schaefer, and E. L. Williams, That Kentucky Cam-

paign (1900). Also useful are Urey Woodson, *The First New Dealer* (1939); Thomas D. Clark, "The People, William Goebel, and the Kentucky Railroads," *JSH* 5 (1939): 34–48; and James C. Klotter, *William Goebel: The Politics of Wrath* (1977). Goebel's bitter enemies come alive in Mary K. Bonsteel Tachau, "The Making of a Railroad President: Milton Hannibal Smith and the L&N," *FCHQ* 37 (1963): 117–36; Edison H. Thomas, "Milton H. Smith Talks about the Goebel Affair," *Register* 78 (1980): 322–42; and Jim Short, *Caleb Powers and the Mountain Army* (1997)

The political unrest of the late nineteenth century is well covered in Edward E. Prichard Jr.'s sizable senior thesis at Princeton, "Popular Political Movements in Kentucky, 1875–1900" (1935), as well as a series of theses, dissertations, and articles, including Donald Schaefer, "Yeoman Farmers and Economic Democracy: A Study of Wealth and Economic Mobility in the Western Tobacco Region, 1850 to 1860," *Explorations in Economic History* 15 (1977): 421–37; Franklin T. Lambert, "Free Silver and the Kentucky Democracy, 1891–1895," *FCHQ* 53 (1977): 145–77; Thomas J. Brown, "The Roots of Bluegrass Insurgency: An Analysis of the Populist Movement in Kentucky," *Register* 78 (1980): 219–42; and Gaye Keller Bland, "Populism in Kentucky, 1887–1896" (PhD diss., University of Kentucky, 1979).

The fourth state constitution, reflecting some voter anger, has been analyzed in George L. Willis Sr., "History of Kentucky Constitutions and Constitutional Conventions," *Register* 29 (1931): 52–81; Rhea A. Taylor, "Conflicts in Kentucky As Shown in the Constitutional Convention of 1890–1891" (PhD diss., University of Chicago, 1948); and Kentucky Legislative Research Commission, *A Citizens' Guide to the Kentucky Constitution*, rev. ed. (2005). The long-winded and tedious debates are printed in full in the four-volume *Official Report of the Proceedings and Debates in the Convention . . . to . . . Change the Constitution of the State of Kentucky* (1890). For a study of earlier court cases, see Yvonne Pitts, *Family, Law, and Inheritance in America: A Social and Legal History of Nineteenth-Century Kentucky* (2013);

and for a good overview see Kurt X. Metzmeier, "History of the Courts of Kentucky," in *United at Last: The Judicial Article and the Struggle to Reform Kentucky's Courts* (2006): 15–26.

The Tate affair is carefully covered in Emmet V. Mittlebeeler, "The Great Kentucky Absconsion," *FCHQ* 27 (1953): 335–52; the segregation of railroads in Anne E. Marshall, "Kentucky's Separate Coach Law and African American Response," *Register* 98 (2000): 241–60; the Tollgate Wars, in a part of J. Winston Coleman Jr., *Stage-Coach Days in the Bluegrass* (1935, reprinted in 1995); the railroad lobby, in the Joint Committee Report, in Kentucky *Senate Journal* (1887–1888); and the 1895 election, in two articles by John Wiltz: "APA-ism in Kentucky," *Register* 56 (1958): 143–55; and "The 1895 Election," *FCHQ* 37 (1963): 117–36. The military (in feuds and the Spanish-American War) is addressed in Federal Writers Project, *Military History of Kentucky* (1939); Richard G. Stone Jr., *A Brittle Sword: The Kentucky Militia, 1776–1912* (1977); Stone, *Kentucky Fighting Men, 1861–1945* (1982); and the brief Kentucky Historical Society, *"A Splendid Little War": The Spanish-American War and Kentucky* (1998). For a violent wartime controversy, see Thomas E. Stephens, "Congressman David Grant Colson and the Tragedy of the Fourth Kentucky Volunteer Infantry," *Register* 98 (2000): 43–102. See also *Report of the Adjutant General of the State of Kentucky: Kentucky Volunteers, War with Spain, 1898–99* (1908). On state prisons, Robert G. Crawford's "A History of the Kentucky Penitentiary System, 1865–1937" (PhD diss., University of Kentucky, 1955) is excellent and can be supplemented with Kyle Ellison, "Changing Faces, Common Walls: History of Corrections in Kentucky," typescript, 10th ed. (1985); and the various warden reports in *Kentucky Documents* (1839–1943). Medical care in the commonwealth is surveyed in John H. Ellis's *Medicine in Kentucky* (1977); Gregory K. Culver, "The Impact of the 1878 Yellow Fever Epidemic on the Jackson Purchase . . .," *FCHQ* 71 (1997): 285–300; and in the reports of the Board of Health. Reform in the system is presented in *Report of the Kentucky Agricultural*

Experiment Station on the Enforcement of the Pure Food Laws (1904); and in Margaret Ripley Wolfe, "The Agricultural Experiment Station and Food and Drug Control: Another Look at Kentucky Progressivism, 1898–1916," *FCHQ* 49 (1975). Manuscript and newspaper sources are rich for this period as well.

13. Progressivism, Prohibition, and Politics, 1900–1920

No in-depth study examines the overall role of political bosses in Kentucky politics, and few works look at the individuals in much detail. James C. Klotter, *Kentucky: Portrait in Paradox, 1900–1950* (1996), provides an overview for the first half of the twentieth century, while Klotter and John W. Muir focus on one leader in "Boss Ben Johnson, the Highway Commission, and Kentucky Politics, 1927–1937," *Register* 84 (1986): 18–50. Johnson's son-in-law is perhaps overstudied in Orval W. Baylor, *J. Dan Talbott* (1942), while Johnson's important enemy Percy Haly unfortunately has not been the subject of much specific scholarly work. James Duane Bolin, in *Bossism and Reform in a Southern City: Lexington, Kentucky, 1880–1940* (2000), looks at one city's situation. John Erie Davis, "When the Whallens Were Kings," *Louisville* 30 (1979): 18–21, focuses on the Falls City, while J. Larry Hood, *Visions of Zion: Christianity, Modernization, and the American Pursuit of Liberty: Progressivism in Rural Nelson and Washington Counties, Kentucky* (2005); and George B. Ellenberg, "'May the club work go on forever': Home Demonstration and Rural Progressivism in 1920s Ballard County," *Register* 96 (1998): 137–66, give good local case studies. A fine presentation of one aspect of progressivism is Thomas H. Appleton Jr., "'Like Banquo's Ghost': The Emergence of the Prohibition Issue in Kentucky Politics" (PhD diss., University of Kentucky, 1981). See also Melanie Beals Goan, "The End of Kentucky's Winning Season?: A Fresh Look at Early Twentieth-Century Kentucky Decision-Making," *Register* 113 (2015): 201–32.

The Tobacco Wars, particularly in the Black Patch, have become one of the most studied, and best examined, aspects of Kentucky history. The field attracted much early study, starting with contemporary accounts, such as John L. Mathews, "The Farmers' Union and the Tobacco Pool," *Atlantic Monthly* 102 (1908): 482–91; John G. Miller, *The Black Patch War* (1936); and James O. Nall, *The Tobacco Night Riders of Kentucky and Tennessee, 1905–1909* (1939). After almost a scholarly hiatus for decades, four good dissertations all appeared at nearly the same moment. Three came out as books in 1993 and 1994. See Rick S. Gregory, "Desperate Farmers: The Dark Tobacco District Planters' Protective Association of Kentucky and Tennessee, 1904–1914" (PhD diss., Vanderbilt University, 1989); Tracy Campbell, *The Politics of Despair: Power and Resistance in the Tobacco Wars* (1993), particularly good on economics and the burley area; Christopher R. Waldrep, *Night Riders: Defending Community in the Black Patch, 1890–1915* (1993), which emphasizes community mores and legal issues; and Suzanne Marshall, *Violence in the Black Patch of Kentucky and Tennessee* (1994), which is strong on social matters. See also Bill Cunningham, *On Bended Knees: The Night Rider Story* (1983); and for the general context, William F. Axton, *Tobacco and Kentucky* (1975).

Kentucky politics in the first two decades of the twentieth century has been covered in some depth by several studies, including James C. Klotter, *Kentucky: Portrait in Paradox, 1900–1950* (1996) and Nicholas C. Burckel, "Progressive Governors in the Border States: Reform Governors of Missouri, Kentucky, West Virginia, and Maryland, 1900–1918" (PhD diss., University of Wisconsin, 1971). Parts of Burckel's dissertation appeared in two articles: "From Beckham to McCreary: The Progressive Record of Kentucky Governors," *Register* 76 (1978): 285–306; and "A. O. Stanley and Progressive Reform, 1902–1919," *Register* 79 (1981): 136–61. For lingering pro-Confederatism, see a good study of a place for veterans: Rusty Williams, *My Old Confederate Home* (2010). On other specific elections, see Jasper B. Shannon and Ruth McQuown, comps., *Presidential Politics in Kentucky, 1824–*

1948 (1950); Lowell H. Harrison, "Kentucky and the Presidential Elections, 1912–1948," *FCHQ* 26 (1952): 320–32; Glenn Finch, "The Election of United States Senators in Kentucky: The Beckham Period," *FCHQ* 44 (1970): 38–50; Percy N. Booth, "The Louisville Contested Election Cases," *Green Bag* 20 (1908): 81–90; Tracy A. Campbell, "Machine Politics, Police Corruption, and the Persistence of Vote Fraud: The Case of the Louisville, Kentucky, Election of 1905," *Journal of Policy History* 15 (2003): 260–300; and Thomas H. Appleton Jr., "Prohibition and Politics in Kentucky: The Gubernatorial Campaign and Election of 1915," *Register* 75 (1977): 28–54.

On individual political leaders, see the indispensable John E. Kleber, editor in chief, *The Kentucky Encyclopedia* (1992); Kleber, ed. *The Encyclopedia of Louisville* (2001); Paul A. Tenkotte and James C. Claypool, eds., *The Encyclopedia of Northern Kentucky* (2009); Gerald L. Smith, Karen Cotton McDaniel, and John A. Hardin, eds., *The Kentucky African American Encyclopedia* (2015); and Lowell H. Harrison, ed., *Kentucky's Governors*, rev. ed. (2004). See also Joseph F. Wall, *Henry Watterson* (1956); Harry M. Caudill, "The Strange Career of John C. C. Mayo," *FCHQ* 56 (1982): 258–89; C. C. Turner and C. H. Traum, *John C. C. Mayo* (1983); Thomas W. Ramage, "Augustus Owsley Stanley" (PhD diss., University of Kentucky, 1968); Ramage, "Augustus Owsley Stanley," in *Kentucky Profiles*, ed. James C. Klotter and Peter J. Sehlinger (1982); Mark Davis, *Solicitor General Bullitt* (2011); and Willard Rouse Jillson, *Edwin P. Morrow—Kentuckian* (1921). Ollie James has been the subject of several unpublished works, but deserves a full biography. The Kentucky *House Journal*, the *Senate Journal*, the *Acts of the General Assembly*, the newspapers of the period, and general Kentucky histories all provide needed general information on the era.

A definitive study of the women's rights movement in Kentucky has not appeared in print, but some strong works have set the stage for that event. Margaret Ripley Wolfe, "Fallen Leaves and Missing Pages: Women in Kentucky History," *Register* 90 (1992): 64–89, is a well-crafted starting place for studying women in Kentucky. Helen Deiss Irvin, *Women in Kentucky* (1979), provides a concise overview, and both Elizabeth Cady Stanton et al., eds., *The History of Woman Suffrage*, 6 vols. (1881–1922); and James C. Klotter, *Kentucky: Portrait in Paradox, 1900–1950* (1996), contain useful sections. A fuller study on suffrage is Claudia Knott, "The Woman Suffrage Movement in Kentucky, 1879–1920" (PhD diss., University of Kentucky, 1989); a more specific look appears in Carol Guethlein, "Women in Louisville: Moving toward Equal Rights," *FCHQ* 55 (1981): 151–78; and an overview in Dana M. Caldemeyer, "Yoked to Tradition: Kentucky Women and Their Histories, 1900–1945," *Register* 113 (2015): 453–76.

The two key leaders of the women's movement in the commonwealth have received excellent historical scrutiny. Paul E. Fuller, in his *Laura Clay and the Woman's Rights Movement* (1975), and in his "Suffragist Vanquished: Laura Clay and the Nineteenth Amendment," *Register* 93 (1995): 4–24, gives his subject her due. A more recent look at Clay appears in Mary Jean Smith, "Laura Clay . . .: States Rights and Southern Suffrage Reform," in Melissa A. McEuen and Thomas H. Appleton Jr., eds., *Kentucky Women* (2015). "Madge" Breckinridge received early attention by her talented sister-in-law, Sophonisba Breckinridge, in *Madeline McDowell Breckinridge* (1921), and more recently in Lindsey Apple, "Madeline McDowell Breckinridge . . .: A Sense of Mission," in McEuen and Appleton, eds., *Kentucky Women*. Madge Breckinridge finally found her biographer in Melba Porter Hay, *Madeline McDowell Breckinridge and the Battle for a New South* (2009). Her influential in-law is studied in Anya Jabour, "Sophonisba Preston Breckinridge . . .: Homegrown Hero," in McEuen and Appleton, eds., *Kentucky Women*. Melanie Beals Goan in her "Establishing Their Place in the Dynasty: Sophonisba and Mary Breckinridge's Paths to Public Service," *Register* 101 (2003): 45–74, compares two of the family leaders, while Goan's excellent *Mary Breckinridge, the Frontier Nursing Service, and Rural Health in Appalachia* (2008) focuses on one. James C. Klotter, in his *Breckinridges of Kentucky, 1760–1981* (1986), studies Mary, Sophonisba, and "Madge" Breckinridge plus progressive leader Desha Breckinridge, among others. Briefer overviews of various leaders appear in Eugenia K. Potter, ed., *Kentucky Women* (1997) and Mimi O'Malley, *Remarkable Kentucky Women* (2012), but other leaders deserve further study, such as given in Lynn E. Niedermeier, *Eliza Calvert Hall: Kentucky Author and Suffragist* (2007). On the child labor question, see Edward N. Clopper, *Child Welfare in Kentucky* (1919), and for a good case study of aid to working women, see Keith Harper, "'An Assurance that Someone Cares': The Baptist Home for Business Women, Louisville, Kentucky, 1905–1925," *Register* 98 (2000): 23–40.

On World War I, see Federal Writers Project, *Military History of Kentucky* (1939); and Richard G. Stone Jr., *Kentucky Fighting Men, 1861–1945* (1982), which cover the military side. See also Larry L. Arnett, *Call to Arms: A Collection of Fascinating Stories, Events, Personalities, and Facts about Kentucky's Military History* (1995) and David J. Bettez, *Kentucky Marine: Major General Logan Feland and the Making of the Modern USMC* (2014). The best work on the homefront in the commonwealth in World War I is the excellent, very comprehensive study by David J. Bettez, *Kentucky and the Great War* (2016). On vice in the commonwealth, see Thomas C. Mackey, "'Learning, Deducting, and Reporting': Louisville, Kentucky's Vice Report of 1915," *FCHQ* 74 (2000): 13–30, 85–108; Buddy Thompson, *Madam Belle Brezing* (1983); Maryjean Wall, *Madam Belle: Sex, Money, and Influence in a Southern Brothel* (2014); and, later, the memoir of a madam, Pauline Tabor, *Pauline's* (1971). Other aspects of the homefront come alive in Ronald Alexander, "To Hell with the Hapsburgs and Hohenzollerns: Henry Watterson Looks at World War I," *Journal of the West Virginia Historical Association* 1 (1977): 15–25; and Scott A. Meriman, "'An Intensive School of Disloyalty': The C. B. Schoberg Case under the Espionage and Sedition Acts in Kentucky during World War I," *Register* 98 (2000): 179–204. For the impact of the conflict on one immigrant group, see John

E. Kleber, "Anti-German Sentiment during the World Wars," in the broader study, C. Robert Ulrich and Victoria A. Ullrich, eds., *Germans in Louisville: A History* (2015). The *Report of the Activities of the Kentucky Council of Defense to January 1, 1919* (1919) is the official summary, and a vast amount of information lies in Fred Caldwell, *Kentucky in the World War, 1917–1918: Civilian Records*, 144 vols. (n.d.). The influenza epidemic is covered well in Nancy Disher Baird, "The 'Spanish Lady' in Kentucky, 1918–1919," *FCHQ* 50 (1976): 290–301; Bettez, *Kentucky and the Great War*; and Gregory K. Culver, "The Impact of the 1918 Spanish Influenza Epidemic on the Jackson Purchase," *FCHQ* 65 (1991): 487–504.

14. Bourbon Barons, Tobacco Tycoons, and King Coal

There is no comprehensive history of agriculture and its impact on Kentucky, though such a work is much needed. Thomas D. Clark's *Agrarian Kentucky* (1977) is a start, while other studies that provide some overviews are Hambleton Tapp and James C. Klotter, *Kentucky: Decades of Discord, 1865–1900* (1977); James C. Klotter, *Kentucky: Portrait in Paradox, 1900–1950* (1996); Judge Watson, "The Economic and Cultural Development of Eastern Kentucky from 1900 to the Present" (PhD diss., Indiana University, 1963); *Kentucky's Historic Farms* (1993); and Mark V. Wetherington, "'Buried in Original Records, Government Reports, Statistical Tables, and Obscure Essays'?: Kentucky's Twentieth-Century Agricultural History," *Register* 113 (2015): 271–306. Particularly rich are the early reports, with county breakdowns, of what was once called the Kentucky Bureau of Agriculture, Labor, and Statistics. For more recent periods, Kentucky Farm Bureau, *Kentucky Agricultural Facts*, 2nd. ed. (2015) provides figures, as does the US Census.

Various crops have spawned historical studies. A classic one is James F. Hopkins, *A History of the Hemp Industry in Kentucky* (1951). On tobacco, its culture, and its changes, see William F. Axton, *Tobacco and Kentucky* (1975); Michael T. Childress, *The Fu-*

ture of Burley Tobacco (1994); Jeffrey A. Duvall, "'Save Our Tobacco': The End of the Federal Tobacco Program in the Central Ohio River Valley, 1980–2005," *Register* 114 (2016): 189–222; John Van Willigen and Anne Van Willigen, *Food and Everyday Life on Kentucky Family Farms, 1920–1950* (2006); Ann K. Ferrell, *Burley: Kentucky Tobacco in a New Century* (2013); and John Van Willigen and Susan C. Eastwood, *Tobacco Culture* (1998). On the whiskey industry, see Gerald Carson, *The Social History of Bourbon* (1963; reprinted, 2010); Michael R. Veach, *Kentucky Bourbon Whiskey* (2013); and Chester Zoeller, *Bourbon in Kentucky: A History of Distilleries . . .* (2009).

A large literature exists on the thoroughbred industry, but few studies treat other aspects of livestock raising. Introductions to the horse include Kent Hollingsworth, *The Kentucky Thoroughbred* (1976); Bruce Denbo, ed., *The Horse World of the Bluegrass* (1980); and R. Gerald Alvey, *Kentucky Bluegrass Country* (1992). Ken McCarr, *The Kentucky Harness Horse* (1997) presents the standardbred story. More recent excellent examinations are Maryjean Wall, *How Kentucky Became Southern* (2010) and James C. Nicholson, *The Kentucky Derby* (2012). Henry Clay Simpson Jr. looks at a rare woman in the early industry in *Josephine Clay: Pioneer Horsewoman* (2005) while Pellom McDaniels III gives a life and times approach to the career of the most famous black horseman in *The Prince of Jockeys: The Life of Isaac Burns Murphy* (2013). *The Blood-Horse* (1916–) and the *Thoroughbred Record* (1877–) provide year-by-year accounts of the industry, while www.kentuckyderby.com offers good information on that part of the racing scene.

On the commercial side of Kentucky life, Charles B. Roberts, "The Building of Middlesborough," *FCHQ* 7 (1933): 18–33, tells a small part of the saga well, while the longer story is covered in Ann Dudley Matheny, *The Magic City* (2003).The early lumber industry and the independent loggers who made it are treated in Burdine Webb, "Old Times in Eastern Kentucky," *Southern Lumberman* (Dec. 13, 1936), and Thomas D. Clark, "Kentucky Logmen," *Journal of Forest History* 25 (1981): 144–

57. A more general, older economic overview is J. J. Hornback, "Economic Development in Kentucky since 1860" (PhD diss., University of Michigan, 1932); a good picture of the conditions at a particular year emerges from Kentucky Bureau of Agriculture, *Kentucky: Natural Resources, Industrial Statistics, Industrial Directory, Description by Counties* (1930). The more recent situation has to be reconstructed from a series of sources, including the Kentucky Department of Economic Development, *Kentucky Locational Advantages for the Auto Parts Industry* (1984); the *1996 Kentucky Desk Book of Economic Statistics* (1996); and various periodicals, including *Reviews and Perspectives; Kentucky's Global Connections;* University of Kentucky, *Kentucky Annual Economic Report;* Kentucky Cabinet for Economic Development information (online); and the *Lane Report.* For a look at the economy in 2000, see Paul Coomes, "Economy," in James C. Klotter, ed., *Our Kentucky: A Study of the Bluegrass State,* rev. ed. (2000).

While the one comprehensive history of the coalfields and those who worked there has yet to be written, many more specific studies exist. On the camps where workers lived, a good general overview (though thin on Kentucky) is Crandall A. Shifflett, *Coal Towns: Life, Work, and Culture in Company Towns of Southern Appalachia, 1880–1960* (1991). A fine case study is Thomas A. Keleman, "A History of Lynch, Kentucky, 1917–1930," *FCHQ* 48 (1974): 156–76. On the miners, see Bruce Crawford, "The Coal Miner," in *Culture in the South,* ed. W. T. Couch (1934); on children, women, and immigrants in the camps, see Mabel B. Ellis, "Children of the Kentucky Coal Fields," *American Child* 1 (1920): 285–405; Glenna H. Graves, "'In the Morning We Had Bulldog Gravy': Women in the Coal Camps of the Appalachian South, 1900–1940" (PhD diss., University of Kentucky, 1993); and Doug Cantrell, "Immigrants and Community in Harlan County, 1910–1930," *Register* 86 (1988): 119–41. Oral histories of importance are available as well.

On coal mining itself, brief introductions come from Willard Rouse Jillson, "A History of the Coal Industry in Kentucky," *Regis-*

ter 20 (1922): 21–45; Jillson, *The Coal Industry in Kentucky* (1924); and Henry C. Mayer, "A Brief History of the Kentucky Coal Industry," in *The Kentucky Underground Coal Mine Guidebook*, ed. Forrest Cameron (1985). On the often-ignored western Kentucky area, see Claude E. Pickard, "The Western Kentucky Coal Fields" (PhD diss., University of Nebraska, 1969), and a memoir, Michael D. Guillerman, *Face Boss: The Memoirs of a Western Kentucky Miner* (2009). On one system of coal extraction, see an early survey, the Kentucky Legislative Research Commission, *Strip Mining in Kentucky*, Research Publication no. 5, o.s. (1949). For the securing of mineral rights, see two excellent studies: Robert S. Weise, *Grasping at Independence: Debt, Male Authority, and Mineral Rights in Appalachian Kentucky, 1850–1915* (2001); and Stephanie M. Lang, "Selling the Mountains: The Broad Form Deed and the Economic, Legal, Social, and Political Transformation of Eastern Kentucky, 1880–1930" (PhD diss., University of Kentucky, 2009). On problems within the industry, see Jerry W. Napier, "Mines, Miners, and Mechanization: Coal Mine Mechanization and the Eastern Kentucky Coal Fields, 1890–1990" (PhD diss., University of Kentucky, 1997); Legislative Research Commission, *The Competitiveness of Kentucky's Coal Industry, Research Report No. 318* (2004); Silas House and Jason Howard, *Something Rising: Appalachians Fighting Mountaintop Removal* (2009); and Charles C. Mann, "Black Magic: Coal . . .," *Wired* 22 (2014): 72–81, 114–16. Indispensable are such primary sources as the *Report of the Inspector of Mines*, which began in 1884 and later evolved into the *Report of the Department of Mines and Minerals*, as well as the online information from the Kentucky Office of Mine Safety and Licensing. See also Curtis Seltzer, *Fire in the Hole: Miners and Managers in the American Coal Industry* (1985), and the numerous transcripts of congressional hearings through the years.

On the state's early oil industry, see the following works by Willard Rouse Jillson: "Kentucky Petroleum: Its History and Present Status," *Register* 17 (1919): 47–49; "The Re-born Oil Fields of Kentucky," *Register* 18 (1920): 35–

43; and *New Oil Horizons in Kentucky* (1948). The development of one of the state's largest corporations is detailed in Joseph L. Massie, *Blazer and Ashland Oil* (1960); and Otto J. Scott, *The Exception: The Story of Ashland Oil* (1968). Kentucky Department of Economic Development, *Energy and Natural Resources in Kentucky* (1984) covers other minerals.

The state's transportation history for the period since the Civil War has been examined well for certain areas, imperfectly for others. On the rivers, see Thomas D. Clark, *The Kentucky* (1942, revised in 1992); William E. Ellis, *The Kentucky River* (2000); Leland R. Johnson and Charles E. Parrish, *Kentucky River Development: The Commonwealth's Waterway* (1999); Helen Bartter Crocker, *The Green River of Kentucky* (1976); Carol Crowe-Carraco, *The Big Sandy* (1979); Richard E. Banta, *The Ohio* (1949); and Leland R. Johnson, *The Falls City Engineers: A History of the Louisville District, Corps of Engineers* (1975).

Railroads seem to have left a strong impression on those who rode them, and many have hastened to write on aspects of railroading history. Most scholars base part of their research on the *Report of the Railroad Commission of Kentucky*, which began in 1880. On early railroad mania, see Carl B. Boyd Jr., "Local Aid to Railroads in Central Kentucky, 1850–1891," *Register* 62 (1964): 4–23, 112–33; and Daniel W. Lynch, "The Development of State and Local Debt in Kentucky, 1890–1962" (PhD diss., University of Kentucky, 1965); Kincaid A. Herr, *The Louisville and Nashville Railroad, 1850–1942* (1943); John L. Kerr, *The Story of a Southern Carrier: The Louisville & Nashville* (1933); and Maury Klein, *History of the Louisville & Nashville Railroad* (1972), study one important line in depth. A more local study is Lee A. Dew, "Henderson, Kentucky, and the Fight for Equitable Freight Rates, 1906–1918," *Register* 76 (1978): 34–44. Most county histories look at railroads in the local area as well.

On highways, see the *Report of the Department of Public Roads*, which began in 1912 (and was later renamed). On early Kentucky-made automobiles, see Louis S. Schafer, "Early Engines," *Kentucky Living* 47 (1993): 14–

15. For a study based on one region, see Eve J. Weinbaum, *To Move a Mountain: The Global Economy in Appalachia* (2004).

15. Culture and Communications, 1865–2015

In addition to the sources cited in this chapter, briefer comments on Kentucky's cultural scene and those who operate in it can be found in *Kentucky Monthly, Kentucky Living, Kentucky Humanities*, and the Kentucky Arts Council website. A full history of journalism in the commonwealth has not yet appeared. Overviews include Herndon J. Evans, *The Newspaper Press in Kentucky* (1976); and Donald B. Towles, *The Press of Kentucky, 1787–1994* (1994). State newspapers deserve more individual scholarly study than they have received. Perhaps the best presented is the specialized press. See, for example, John Sparks, *Kentucky's Most Hated Man: Charles Chilton Moore and the Bluegrass Blade* (2009); Stanley Ousley, "The Kentucky Irish American," *FCHQ* 53 (1979): 178–95; and Clyde F. Crews, ed., *Mike Barry and the Kentucky Irish American: An Anthology* (1995).

Among the editors, Desha Breckinridge is covered in James C. Klotter, *The Breckinridges of Kentucky, 1760–1981* (1986). One giant, however, dominates that literature—Henry Watterson. The best full biography remains Joseph F. Wall, *Henry Watterson* (1956), but a more recent and more focused work is Daniel S. Margolies, *Henry Watterson and the New South* (2006). Other studies include Leonard N. Plummer, "The Political Leadership of Henry Watterson" (PhD diss., University of Wisconsin, 1940); Lena C. Logan, "Henry Watterson, Border Nationalist, 1840–1877" (PhD diss., Indiana University, 1942); and Robert K. Thorp, "'Marse Henry' and the Negro: A New Perspective," *Journalism Quarterly* 46 (1969): 467–74. From the pens of those who knew Watterson came Isaac F. Marcosson, *"Marse Henry": A Biography of Henry Watterson* (1951); and Arthur Krock, ed., *The Editorials of Henry Watterson* (1923). The editor wrote his recollections under the title *"Marse Henry,"* 2 vols.

(1919), and published some lectures in *The Compromises of Life* (1903). See also a section on Watterson in Carl R. Osthaus, *Partisans of the Southern Press* (1994). On Watterson's successor, Robert W. Bingham, see chapter 16. On the next editor, Barry Bingham Sr., see Samuel W. Thomas, ed., *Barry Bingham: A Man of His Word* (1993); *Remembering Barry Bingham* (1990); and Susan E. Tifft and Alex S. Jones, *The Patriarch* (1991). For memoirs of those involved in journalism, radio, and television, see John Ed Pearce, *Memoirs* (1997); Al Smith, *Wordsmith: My Life in Journalism* (2011); Smith, *Kentucky Cured: Fifty Years in Kentucky Journalism* (2012); Bob Edwards, *A Voice in the Box: My Life in Radio* (2011); O. Leonard Press, *The KET Story: A Personal Account* (2008).

Writing on Kentucky authors and Kentucky literature is appropriately large. Numerous general overviews exist, almost all focusing on the lives of individuals. One of the earliest was John Wilson Townsend, *Kentucky in American Letters*, 2 vols. (1913); a third volume came much later (1976) from the pen of Dorothy Townsend. Similar in approach are Ish Ritchey, *Kentucky Literature, 1784–1963* (1963); and Mary C. Browning, *Kentucky Authors* (1968). On the story lines of various books, see Lawrence S. Thompson and Algernon Thompson, *The Kentucky Novel* (1953). For briefer overviews, see James C. Klotter, "Little Shepherds, Little Colonels, and Little Kingdoms: A Selective Review of Kentucky Writing, 1784–1950," *Journal of Kentucky Studies* 3 (1986): 61–72; and Klotter, *Kentucky: Portrait in Paradox, 1900–1950* (1996). But by far the best study is William Smith Ward, *A Literary History of Kentucky* (1988).

Individual authors have generally attracted a good amount of attention. Among the most useful studies on the 1865–1915 period are William K. Bottorff, *James Lane Allen* (1964); Grant C. Knight, *James Lane Allen and the Genteel Tradition* (1935); Elizabeth Fox Moore, *John Fox, Jr., Personal and Family Letters and Papers* (1955); Warren I. Titus, *John Fox, Jr.* (1971); Thomas Nelson Page, "John Fox," *Scribners Magazine* 66 (1919): 674–83;

Sue Lynn McGuire, "The Little Colonel," *Register* 89 (1991): 121–46; and Abby M. Roach, "The Authors Club of Louisville," *FCHQ* 31 (1957): 28–37. In the later period, two Kentucky authors in particular—Elizabeth Madox Roberts and Robert Penn Warren—have generated considerable study. Among the works on Roberts are E. Lamar Janney, "Elizabeth Madox Roberts," *Sewanee Review* 45 (1937): 389–410; Woodridge Spears, "Elizabeth Madox Roberts" (PhD diss., University of Kentucky, 1953); Harry M. Campbell and Ruel E. Foster, *Elizabeth Madox Roberts* (1956); Earl H. Rovit, *Herald to Chaos: The Novels of Elizabeth Madox Roberts* (1960); and N. R. Stoneback and Steven Florczyk, *Elizabeth Madox Roberts: Essays of Reassessment and Reclamation* (2008). The Warren literature includes Leonard Casper, *Robert Penn Warren* (1960); Victor H. Standberg, *The Poetic Vision of Robert Penn Warren* (1977); James H. Justus, *The Achievement of Robert Penn Warren* (1981); Randolph P. Runyan, *The Braided Dream: Robert Penn Warren's Late Poetry* (1990); William B. Clark, *The American Vision of Robert Penn Warren* (1991); and James A. Grimshaw Jr., *Understanding Robert Penn Warren* (2001). Both Roberts and Warren, as well as Jesse Stuart and Caroline Gordon, are covered in Joseph M. Flora and Robert Bain, eds., *Fifty Southern Writers after 1900* (1987).

Various other Kentucky authors have been examined in some depth. See, for example, Michael A. Flannery, *John Uri Lloyd: The Great American Eclectic* (1998); Anita Lawson, *Irvin S. Cobb* (1984); William E. Ellis, *Irvin S. Cobb* (2017); Ruel E. Foster, *Jesse Stuart* (1968); J. R. Lemaster, *Jesse Stuart* (1980); H. Edward Richardson, *Jesse: The Biography of an American Writer, Jesse Hilton Stuart* (1984); James M. Gifford and Erin R. Kazee, *Jesse Stuart* (2010); Ted Olsen, ed., *James Still in Interviews, Oral Histories, and Memories* (2009); Dean Cadle, "Man on Troublesome," *Yale Review* 87 (1968): 236–55; Wilton Eckley, *Harriette Arnow* (1973); Glenda K. Hobbs, "Harriette Arnow's Literary journey" (PhD diss., Harvard University, 1975); Martha Billips, "Harriette Simpson Arnow . . .: A Writer's Life," in Melissa A. McEuen and Thomas H. Appleton Jr., eds., *Kentucky Women* (2015); William E. Ellis, "Walter Tevis," *Journal of Kentucky Studies* 12 (1995): 73–77; Louis Hatcher, *Duncan Hines* (2014); and Kay Johnson, "They had to get away to come home . . .," *Kentucky Alumnus* (1986): 7–11. Some of the best sources on more recent authors are the interviews with them in L. Elizabeth Beattie, ed., *Conversations with Kentucky Writers*, 2 vols. (1996, 2000). For more recent writers, see Jason Peters, ed., *Wendell Berry: Life and Work* (2007); Morris A. Grubbs, ed., *Conversations with Wendell Berry* (2007); Joanna Price, *Understanding Bobbie Ann Mason* (2000); William McKeen, *Outlaw Journalist: The Life and Times of Hunter S. Thompson* (2008); Lawrence S. Cunningham, *Thomas Merton and the Monastic Vision* (1999); entries in *The Dictionary of Literary Biography*; the several encyclopedias covering the commonwealth; and the appropriate sections in the textbooks cited above.

On Kentucky poetry, see the individual biographies mentioned above, as well as the general overviews cited earlier. In addition, see R. W. Thompson, "Negroes Who Are 'Doing Things,'" *Alexander's Magazine* 1 (Aug. 15, 1905): 25–26 (on Joseph S. Cotter); Otto A. Rothert, *The Story of a Poet: Madison Cawein* (1921); Lindsey Apple, *Cautious Rebel: A Biography of Susan Clay Sawitzky* (1997), offering more than just an examination of her literary life; David Deskins, "Effie Waller Smith," *Kentucky Review* 8 (1988): 26–46; and "An Interview with Frank X. Walker," *The Thread* 1 (2004): 1.

Kentucky historians have probably not examined their profession or its leaders enough. The works on Richard Collins include James P. Gregory Jr., "Lewis and Richard H. Collins," *FCHQ* 21 (1947): 309–26; and Stuart Seely Sprague, "Richard H. Collins and His History of Kentucky," *Register* 70 (1972): 17–20. A great deal has been written about the state's best known historian. See Bill Cunningham, *Kentucky's Clark* (1987); "Thomas D. Clark Memorial Issue," *Register* 103 (2005): 1–460; John E. Kleber, ed., *Thomas D. Clark of Kentucky* (2003); and Clark's autobiography, *My Century in History* (2006). More needs to be done regarding other followers of Clio in the commonwealth. For institutional history, see Jacob Lee, "Whether It Really Be Truth or Fiction: Colonel Reuben T. Durrett, the Filson Club, and Historical Memory in Postbellum Kentucky," *OVH* 9 (2009): 27–47; Thomas E. Stephens, "'A Glorious Birthright to Guard': A History of the Kentucky Historical Society," *Register* 101 (2003): 7–44; and a study of one of the executive directors of a historical society, Carlton Jackson's *Kentucky Maverick: The Life and Adventures of Colonel George M. Chinn* (2015).

Nancy Disher Baird's "Enid Yandell," *FCHQ* 62 (1988): 5–32, and Juilee Decker, "Enid Yandell . . .: Kentucky's Frontier Sculptor and 'Bachelor Maid,'" in Melissa A. McEuen and Thomas H. Appleton Jr., eds., *Kentucky Women* (2015), are the best studies of a Kentucky sculptor, and Robert C. May's *The Lexington Camera Club, 1936–1972* (1989) is the strongest work on photography. Other artists have been studied in more depth: see J. Winston Coleman Jr., *Three Kentucky Artists: Hart, Price, Troye* (1974); Coleman, *Robert Burns Wilson* (1956); Estill Curtis Pennington, *Lessons in Likeness: Portrait Painters in Kentucky and the Ohio River Valley, 1802–1920* (2010); Willard Rouse Jillson, *Paul Sawyier, American Artist* (1961); Arthur F. Jones, *The Art of Paul Sawyier* (1976); Justus Bier, "Carl C. Brenner," *American-German Review* 17 (1951): 20–29, 33; Royal Cortissoz, "The Field of Art—Frank Duveneck and His Munich Tradition," *Scribner's Magazine* 81 (1927): 216–20; and Walter S. Siple, *Frank Duveneck* (1936).

On architecture in the commonwealth, see Theodore M. Brown, *Introduction to Louisville Architecture* (1960); William Lynwood Montell and Michael Lynn Morse, *Kentucky Folk Architecture* (1976); Clay Lancaster, *Vestiges of the Venerable City: A Chronicle of Lexington, Kentucky, Its Architectural Development and Survey of Its Early Streets and Antiquities* (1978); and Julian C. Oberwarth and William B. Scott Jr., *A History of the Profession of Architecture in Kentucky.* County histories are also useful. John A. Jakle, Robert W. Bastian, and Douglas K. Meyer, *Common Houses in America's Small Towns* (1989), compares a Kentucky example

with national trends. See also Michael E. Birdwell and W. Calvin Dickinson, eds., *Rural Life in the Upper Cumberland* (2009) and various surveys of historic sites, often funded by the Kentucky Heritage Council. On the decorative arts, see Erick Doss, Jerrold Hirsh, and Jean M. Burks, *Kentucky by Design* (2015).

The richness of the state's musical traditions is well presented in several studies: Charles K. Wolfe, *Kentucky Country: Folk and Country Music of Kentucky* (1982); Bill C. Malone, *Southern Music, American Music* (1979); Malone, "William S. Hays: The Bard of Kentucky," *Register* 93 (1995): 286–306; and William Lynwood Montell, *Singing the Glory Down: Amateur Gospel Music in South Central Kentucky, 1900–1990* (1991). On the growth of country and folk music, see Ron Pen, *I Wonder as I Wander: The Life of John Jacob Niles* (2010); Michael Ann Williams, *Singing Tradition: John Lair and Sarah Gertrude Knott* (2006); Pete Stamper, *It All Happened in Renfro Valley* (1999); Jason Howard, *A Few Honest Words: The Kentucky Roots of Popular Music* (2012); James C. Claypool, *Kentucky's Bluegrass Music* (2010); and Nathan McGee, "If You Can't Go Home, Take Some of It with You: Twentieth-Century Appalachian Migration and the Music of Renfro Valley," *Register* 112 (2014): 589–612. A different kind of musical presentation in one city is covered in C. Pen Bogert, "Louisville Blues in the 1950s," *Blues News* (Dec. 1993): 1–2, (Jan. 1994): 1–2.

J. Winston Coleman Jr. wrote of an early pioneer of radio in Kentucky in *Nathan B. Stubblefield: The Father of Radio* (1982), while Terry L. Birdwhistell broke new historiographical ground with his "WHAS Radio and the Development of Broadcasting in Kentucky, 1922–1942," *Register* 79 (1981): 333–53. See also Francis M. Nash, *Towers over Kentucky: A History of Radio and Television in the Bluegrass State* (1995); and Dwight B. Billings, Gurney Norman, and Kathleen Ledford, eds., *Confronting Appalachian Stereotypes* (1999), where various authors examine such topics as images, labor and coal, and the play *The Kentucky Cycle*, among other things.

Early film history in one locale—Lexington—is covered in Gregory B. Waller, *Main Street Amusements: Movies and Commercial Entertainment in a Southern City, 1896–1930* (1995), while Marilyn Casto, in *Actors, Audiences, and Historic Theaters of Kentucky* (2000), looks at different aspects over a broader time period. The placement of films on Kentucky in a regional context occurs in J. W. Williamson, *Southern Mountaineers in Silent Films: Plot Synopses of Movies about Moonshining, Feuding and Other Mountain Topics, 1904–1929* (1994). See also Jerry P. Perry, "Kentucky Educational Television Network" (PhD diss., Syracuse University, 1977).

The literature on D. W. Griffith is vast. Examples are Robert M. Henderson, *D. W. Griffith: His Life and Work* (1972); Iris Barry, *D. W. Griffith: American Film Master* (1940); Raymond A. Cook, "The Man behind *The Birth of a Nation*," *North Carolina Historical Review* 39 (1962): 519–41; and Richard Schickel, *D. W. Griffith: An American Life*. The various stars of the Silver Screen from Kentucky are covered in a variety of works, ranging from good biographies to weak snippets in magazines.

16. The Transitional Twenties

Kentucky's specific demographics can be garnered from census reports, George A. Hillery Jr., "Population Growth in Kentucky, 1820–1960," *University of Kentucky Agricultural Experiment Station Bulletin* 705 (1966), and Thomas R. Ford, *Health and Demography in Kentucky* (1964). See Judith Gay Myers, "A Socio-Historical Analysis of the Kentucky Birth Control Movement, 1933–1943" (PhD diss., University of Kentucky, 2005). James C. Klotter, *Kentucky: Portrait in Paradox, 1900–1950* (1996), gives an overview of the first half of the twentieth century, while one specific incident and its surroundings are colorfully captured in Robert K. Murray and Roger W. Brucker, *Trapped! The Story of the Struggle to Rescue Floyd Collins* (1979). The state's sporting contribution can be briefly garnered from Mike Embry, "Kentuckians in the Halls of Fame," *Kentucky Living* 46 (1992): 12–16; and Henry C. Mayer, "Kentucky's All-Time All Stars," *Rural Kentuckian* 42 (1988): 28–30.

The anti-evolution fight generated considerable historical material, as well as contemporary passion. An early outcry was Alonzo W. Fortune, "The Kentucky Campaign against the Teaching of Evolution," *Journal of Religion* 2 (1922): 225–35. Later studies, generally all critical of the anti-evolution effort, include R. Halliburton Jr., "Kentucky's Anti-evolution Controversy," *Register* 66 (1968): 97–107; Milo M. Meadows Jr., "Fundamentalist Thought and Its Impact in Kentucky, 1900–1928" (PhD diss., Syracuse University, 1972); and three works by William E. Ellis: "Frank LeRond McVey—His Defense of Academic Freedom," *Register* 67 (1969): 37–54; "The Fundamentalist-Moderate Schism over Evolution in the 1920s," *Register* 74 (1976): 112–23; and *"A Man of Books and A Man of the People": E. Y. Mullins and the Crisis of Moderate Southern Baptist Leadership* (1987). On Thomas Hunt Morgan, see Ian Shine and Sylvia Wrobel, *Thomas Hunt Morgan: Pioneer of Genetics* (1976); and James A. Ramage, "Thomas Hunt Morgan," *FCHQ* 53 (1979): 5–25.

On the general background to the life of African Americans during the era, see George C. Wright, *Life behind a Veil: Blacks in Louisville, Kentucky, 1865–1930* (1985); and Marion B. Lucas and George C. Wright, *A History of Blacks in Kentucky*, 2 vols. (1991). For forgotten leaders, see: Berry Craig, "William English Walling: Kentucky's Unknown Civil Rights Hero," *Register* 96 (1998): 351–76; Karen Cotton McDaniel, "Elizabeth 'Lizzie' Frost . . .: Challenging Stereotypes and Building Community," in Melissa A. McEuen and Thomas H. Appleton Jr., eds., *Kentucky Women* (2015); Russell Wigginton, "'But He Did What He Could': William Warley Leads Louisville's Fight for Justice, 1902–1946," *FCHQ* 76 (2002): 429–50. Also helpful are contemporary magazines, such as the *Crisis*, as well as newspapers. The expulsion of African Americans from one city is well covered in Kristy Owens Griggs, "The Removal of Blacks from Corbin in 1919: Memory, Perspective, and the Legacy of Racism," *Register* 100 (2002): 293–310. The Will

Lockett riot spawned three good studies: Joe Jordan, "Lynchers Don't Like Lead," *Atlantic Monthly* 177 (1946): 103–8; J. Winston Coleman Jr., *Death at the Court-House* (1952); and John D. Wright Jr., "Lexington's Suppression of the 1920 Will Lockett Lynch Mob," *Register* 84 (1986): 263–79. For a needed corrective and model study that shows how reality and image often diverge (in this case, in Frankfort), see Douglas A. Boyd, *Crawfish Bottom: Recovering a Lost Kentucky Community* (2011). Klan activities in Kentucky are covered in general terms in David M. Chalmers, *Hooded Americanism: The History of the Ku Klux Klan* (1963), and more specifically to the state in Thomas D. Matijasic, "The Ku Klux Klan in the Big Sandy Valley of Kentucky," *Journal of Kentucky Studies* 10 (1993): 75–80. E. H. Lougher's *The Kall of the Klan in Kentucky* (1924) is a contemporary presentation.

The chaotic politics of the era have generated a full spectrum of studies, ranging from older overviews, such as E. A. Jonas, *A History of the Republican Party in Kentucky* (1929); and George L. Willis Jr., *Kentucky Democracy*, 3 vols. (1935), to specific election accounts, including Malcolm E. Jewell, *Kentucky Votes*, 3 vols. (1963). On the pari-mutuel issue, see M. P. Hunt, *The Story of My Life* (1941); and Robert F. Sexton, "The Crusade against Parimutuel Gambling in Kentucky: A Study of Southern Progressivism in the 1920s," *FCHQ* 50 (1976): 47–57. Sexton's dissertation, "Kentucky Politics and Society, 1919–1932" (University of Washington, 1970), gives a good analysis of the era's political character.

For information on the government of the commonwealth, see Nollie Olin Taff, *History of State Revenue and Taxation in Kentucky* (1931); Vance Armentrout, *An Inventory of Kentucky* (1922); and *The Government of Kentucky: Report of the Efficiency Commission of Kentucky*, 2 vols. (1924). An annual series called *The Kentucky Directory* offered details about legislators and government departments.

Individual studies of political leaders of the period range from full and extensive to sketchy and thin. On the Republican side, see Willard Rouse Jillson, *Edwin P. Morrow—Kentuckian*

(1921); Bernard V. Burke, "Senator and Diplomat: The Public Career of Frederic M. Sackett," *FCHQ* 61 (1987): 185–216; and the defensive autobiography of John W. Langley, *They Tried to Crucify Me* (1929). On the Democratic side, see George W. Robinson, "The Making of a Kentucky Senator: Alben W. Barkley and the Gubernatorial Primary of 1923," *FCHQ* 40 (1966): 123–35; James K. Libbey, *Alben Barkley* (2016); and Barkley's autobiography, *That Reminds Me* (1954). Behind-the-scenes Democratic operative Jim Brown is discussed in George R. Leighton, *Five Cities* (1939). The various encyclopedias and Lowell H. Harrison, ed., *Kentucky's Governors*, rev. ed. (2004), give sketches of politicians of both parties.

Books and articles on the Bingham family have appeared with regularity, but the historical profession would have been better served had several of the studies never made it into print. A good scholarly account of Robert Worth Bingham's life appears in William E. Ellis, *Robert Worth Bingham and the Southern Mystique* (1996). Family accounts usually focus on R. W. Bingham in some form, and they range from the solid—Marie Brenner, *House of Dreams* (1988)—to the angry—Sallie Bingham, *Passion and Prejudice* (1989)—to the weak—David L. Chandler and Mary V. Chandler, *The Binghams of Louisville* (1987).

Two controversial issues of the era were prisons and water use. On the latter, see Tom Wallace, "Caught in the Power Net," *Survey* 62 (1929): 389–94; and the good study by George W. Robinson, "Conservation in Kentucky: The Fight to Save Cumberland Falls, 1926–1931," *Register* 81 (1983): 23–38. On the penitentiary question, the *Report of the Board of Prison Commissioners* (from the agency that was later called the Department of Corrections) and various investigating committee reports in the Kentucky *House Journal* and *Senate Journal* are starting places. Joseph P. Byers, in "Parole in Kentucky," *Journal of Social Forces* 1 (1923): 135–36, presented the situation at the time, while later surveys usually have focused more on events than on the politics of prisons. See Robert G. Crawford, "A History of the Kentucky Penitentiary System, 1865–1937" (PhD diss., University of Kentucky, 1955); Kyle Ellison, "Changing Faces, Common Walls: History of Corrections in Kentucky," typescript, 10th ed. (1985); and Bill Cunningham, *Castle: The Story of a Kentucky Prison* (1994).

17. Old Problems and a New Deal

On conditions during the Great Depression and in wartime, important sources include newspapers, interviews, and county histories. On the hardship of the 1930s, see John E. L. Robertson, "The 1937 Flood in Paducah," *FCHQ* 71 (1997): 330–46; Pat Taylor, *Rivergees: Paducah's '37 Flood* (2010); and Rick Bell, *The Great Flood of 1937* (2007). The state reply to economic want is presented in Arthur H. Estabrook, "Poor Relief in Kentucky," *Social Science Review* 3 (1929): 224–42. Further discussion of the people's needs and the early situation can be found in James C. Klotter, *Kentucky: Portrait in Paradox, 1900–1950* (1996); and Donald W. Whisenhunt, "The Great Depression in Kentucky: The Early Years," *Register* 67 (1969): 37–54.

The effect on the banking industry can be observed through the annual *Report of the Banking Commissioner of the State of Kentucky* and in several specific bank histories, such as Thomas D. Clark, *A Century of Banking History in the Bluegrass* (1983); James C. Klotter and Henry C. Mayer, *A Century of Banking . . . in Owsley County, 1890–1990* (1989); Klotter, *A 100-Year Partnership, Hyden Citizens Bank and Leslie County, 1904–2004* (2005); and John E. L. Robertson, *The History of Citizens Bank and Trust Company of Paducah, Kentucky* (1988). The failure of the South's largest bank is well presented in Robert Fugate, "The Banco Kentucky Story," *FCHQ* 50 (1976): 29–46.

The story of the "Roosevelt revolution" in the commonwealth fortunately has been told well in George T. Blakey's *Hard Times and New Deal in Kentucky, 1929–1939* (1986); David Dick, *Let There Be Light: The Story of Rural Electrification in Kentucky* (2008); James Duane Bolin, "The Human Side: Politics, the Great Depression, and the New Deal in Lexington, Kentucky, 1929–35," *Register* 90 (1992): 256–

83; and Joseph E. Brent, "The Civil Works Administration in Western Kentucky," *FCHQ* 67 (1993): 259–76.

The struggle over labor rights during the New Deal erupted in violence in eastern Kentucky. For the general background on labor before 1930, see such varied sources as Herbert Finch, "Organized Labor in Louisville, Kentucky, 1880–1914" (PhD diss., University of Kentucky, 1965); James Duane Bolin, "'An Air of Tenseness': Labor Strife and Tragedy in Kentucky's Western Coal Fields, 1888–1939," *FCHQ* 73 (1999): 3–33; and *Labor History in Kentucky: A Teaching Supplement* (1986). See also John Hennen, "Toil, Trouble, Transformation: Workers and Unions in Modern Kentucky," *Register* 113 (2015): 233–70. On mining specifically, see Henry C. Mayer, "Glimpses of Union Activity among Coal Miners in Nineteenth-Century Eastern Kentucky," *Register* 86 (1988): 216–29, as well as the *Reports* of the Labor Inspector and the Adjutant General. Two good case studies—all too rare, unfortunately—are Bill L. Weaver, "Louisville's Labor Disturbances, July, 1877," *FCHQ* 48 (1974): 177–86; and Nancy S. Dye, "The Louisville Woolen Mills Strike of 1887," *Register* 82 (1984): 236–50. A full history of the labor movement would be welcome.

The background to the Harlan County Coal Wars is covered in: Margaret Ripley Wolfe, "The Towns of King Coal," *Register* 97 (1999): 189–201; Doug Cantrill, "Immigrants and Community in Harlan County, 1910–1930," *Register* 86 (1988): 119–41; and Paul F. Cressey, "Social Disorganization and Reorganization in Harlan County, Kentucky," *American Sociological Review* 14 (1949): 389–94. Several good studies examine the conflicts in some depth. These range from article-length accounts, such as Stuart Seely Sprague, "Hard Times in Bell and Harlan," *Mountain Review* 2 (1976): 19–22, 42–48, to book-length treatments, such as Paul F. Taylor, *Bloody Harlan: The United Mine Workers of America in Harlan County, Kentucky, 1931–1941* (1990); and the fine John W. Hevener, *Which Side Are You On* (1978). Federal hearings on the issue appeared in print: US Senate, *Violation of Free Speech and Rights of Labor Hearing,* 75th Cong., 1st sess. (1937). Considerably more material, often reflecting the viewpoint of one side or the other, also exists.

Politics permeated most issues of the 1930s and 1940s, whether relief economics or labor questions were in dispute. For the general and statistical background, see: Jasper B. Shannon and Ruth McQuown, comps., *Presidential Politics in Kentucky, 1824–1948* (1950); Lowell H. Harrison, "Kentucky and the Presidential Election, 1912–1948," *FCHQ* 26 (1952): 320–32; Malcolm E. Jewell, *Kentucky Votes,* 3 vols. (1963); Ernest Collins, "The Political Behavior of the Negroes in Cincinnati, Ohio, and Louisville, Kentucky" (PhD diss., University of Kentucky, 1950); John H. Fenton, *Politics in the Border States* (1957); James C. Klotter, *Kentucky: Portrait in Paradox, 1900–1950* (1996); and John Ed Pearce, *Divide and Dissent: Kentucky Politics, 1930–1963* (1987).

Political leaders have been studied in varying degrees of depth. On Alben Barkley, see the citations under chapter 21, as well as John Henry Hatcher, "Alben Barkley, Politics in Relief and the Hatch Act," *FCHQ* 40 (1966): 249–64; Walter L. Hixson, "The 1938 Kentucky Senate Election," *Register* 80 (1982): 309–29; and Donald A. Ritchie, "Alben W. Barkley: The President's Man," in *First among Equals: Outstanding Senate Leaders of the Twentieth Century,* ed. Richard A. Baker and Roger H. Davidson (1991). Similarly well examined is A. B. Chandler, though a comprehensive biography is lacking. See Happy's autobiography, *Heroes, Plain Folks, and Skunks: The Life and Times of Happy Chandler* (1989), which should be used with care, as well as Charles P. Roland, "Happy Chandler," *Register* 85 (1987): 138–61; Stephen D. Boyd, "The Campaign Speaking of A. B. Chandler," *Register* 79 (1977): 227–39; and Terry L. Birdwhistell, "A. B. 'Happy' Chandler," in *Kentucky: Its History and Heritage,* ed. Fred J. Hood (1978). Numerous contemporary works are also useful, such as Jasper A. Shannon, "Happy Chandler: A Kentucky Epic," in *The American Politician,* ed. J. T. Salter (1938); and Walter Davenport, "Happy Couldn't Wait," *Colliers* (July 16, 1938): 12–13, 49–51.

The governors before and after Chandler have been covered in Vernon Gipson, *Ruby Laffoon* (1978); Frederic D. Ogden, ed., *The Public Papers of Keen Johnson, 1939–1943* (1982); and James C. Klotter, ed., *The Public Papers of Simeon Willis, 1943–1947* (1988); as well as Lowell H. Harrison, ed., *Kentucky's Governors,* rev. ed. (2004); and the state-based encyclopedias. On specific elections, see Robert J. Leupold, "The Kentucky WPA: Relief and Politics, May–November, 1935," *FCHQ* 49 (1975): 152–68; and Glenn Finch, "The Election of United States Senators in Kentucky: The Barkley Period," *FCHQ* 45 (1971): 286–304. Peter Wallenstein, "Pioneer Black Legislators from Kentucky, 1860s–1960s," *Register* 110 (2012) 533–57, provides a good starting point for African American legislator Anderson.

On World War II, a very short overview is Kentucky Historical Society, *"Praise the Lord and Pass the Ammunition!": Kentuckians in World War II* (1994). On the military side, see Richard G. Stone Jr., *Kentucky Fighting Men, 1861–1945* (1982), for broad coverage, and Arthur L. Kelly, *Battlefire! Combat Stories from World War II* (1997), for specific accounts of Kentuckians who fought. For an excellent and poignant case study, see James Russell Harris, "The Harrodsburg Tankers: Bataan, Prison, and the Bonds of Community," *Register* 86 (1988): 230–77. Among the several memoirs and collected letters, good sources include Nancy Disher Baird, "'To Lend You My Eyes': The World War II Letters of Special Services Officer Harry Jackson," *Register* 88 (1990): 287–317; Philip Ardery, *Bomber Pilot* (1978); and Frank F. Mathias, *G. I. Jive: An Army Bandsman in World War II* (1977). The costs of conflict can be found in *World War II Honor Dead and Missing: State of Kentucky* (1946).

A good, full study of the commonwealth's wartime role appears in Richard E. Holl, *Committed to Victory: The Kentucky Home Front during World War II* (2015). A briefer overview is Mary Jean Kinsman, "The Kentucky Home Front: World War II," *FCHQ* 68 (1994): 363–78, while more specific topics are treated in Michella M. Marino, "Children, Conflict, and Community: Madison, Indiana, and Louisville, Kentucky, during World War II," *OVH* 12 (2012): 7–26; Aaron D. Purcell, "Bourbon to Bullets: Louisville's Distilling Industry during World War II, 1941–1945," *Register* 96 (1998): 61–87; James D. Cockrum, "Owensboro Goes to War," *Daviess County Historical Quarterly* 2 (1984): 2–9; Rhonda Mawhood Lee, "'Admit Guilt—And Tell the Truth': The Louisville Fellowship of Reconciliation's Struggle with Pacifism and Racial Justice, 1941–1945," *JSH* 76 (2010): 315–42; Antonio S. Thompson, *German Jackboots in Kentucky Bluegrass: Housing German Prisoners of War in Kentucky, 1942–1946* (2008); and Richard E. Holl, "Swastikas in the Bluegrass State: Axis Prisoners of War in Kentucky, 1942–46," *Register* 100 (2002): 139–66. The outmigration process is examined well in Olaf E. Larson, "Wartime Migration and the Manpower Reserve on Farms in Eastern Kentucky," *Rural Sociology* 8 (1943): 148–60; and Wayne T. Gray, "Population Movements in the Kentucky Mountains," *Rural Sociology* 10 (1945): 380–86.

18. Education and Equality, 1865–2015

The starting places for any history of education in Kentucky are the *Reports* of the superintendent of public instruction, the Legislative Research Commission's annual *Kentucky District Data Profiles,* and the Kentucky Department of Education, *Kentucky Education Facts* (online), all of which contain a wealth of primary material. Using those as the core, several general studies have been written, and in contrast to many areas of the commonwealth's history, the field boasts a good secondary literature. Barksdale Hamlett, in *History of Education in Kentucky* (1914), summarized those reports, while the Kentucky Education Commission's *Public Education in Kentucky* (1921) and the chapter on schools in the National Child Labor Committee's *Child Welfare in Kentucky* (1919) gave good summaries of the situation at the time they were published. The Kentucky Department of Education updated Hamlett's work under the title *History of Education in Kentucky, 1915–1940* (1940). Then two more descriptive and analytic works followed in the 1940s: Moses E. Ligon, *A*

History of Public Education in Kentucky (1942); and Frank L. McVey, *The Gates Open Slowly: A History of Education in Kentucky* (1949). A. W. Hackensmith's *Out of Time and Tide: The Evolution of Education in Kentucky,* followed in 1970. The best study is that of William E. Ellis, *A History of Education in Kentucky* (2011). For current statistics, see Legislative Research Commission, *Compendium of State Rankings,* 2015, Research Report No. 413 (2015). On the dynamics of the schoolroom, see Ellis Hartford, *The Little White Schoolhouse* (1977); and Constance Elam, "That's Just the Way It Was: Teacher Experiences in Appalachian Kentucky, 1930–1960" (PhD diss. University of Texas, 2003). A good brief introduction to the whole issue is Thomas D. Clark's "Kentucky Education through Two Centuries of Political and Social Change," *Register* 83 (1985): 173–201.

More narrowly based studies, both by chronology and by subject, include chapters in Hambleton Tapp and James C. Klotter, *Kentucky: Decades of Discord, 1865–1900* (1977), and Klotter, *Kentucky: Portrait in Paradox, 1900–1950* (1996). Also helpful are Fred A. Engle Jr., "The Superintendents and the Issues: A Study of the Superintendents of Public Instruction in Kentucky, 1890–1943" (EdD diss., University of Kentucky, 1965); and Terry L. Birdwhistell, "Divided We Fall: State College and the Normal School Movement in Kentucky, 1880–1910," *Register* 88 (1990): 431–56. On the early reforms, see Valerie R. Summers, "A New Rural Life: Kentucky Education Reform and the Country Life Movement, 1905–1920" (PhD diss., University of Kentucky, 2001); on the 1990 Education Reform Act specifically, see the Kentucky Legislative Research Commission, *A Guide to the Kentucky Reform Act of 1990* (1990); Paul D. Blanchard, "Education Reform and Executive-Legislative Relations in Kentucky," *Journal of Kentucky Studies* 10 (1993): 66–74; Richard E. Day, "Bert Combs and the Council for Better Education: Catalysts for School Reform," *Register* 109 (2011): 27–62; and Debra H. Dawahare, "Public School Reform: Kentucky's Solution," *University of Arkansas at Little Rock Law Review* 27 (2004): 27–54.

The moonlight schools of Cora Wilson Stewart have attracted much scholarly interest. Examinations of Stewart's work include a good biography by Yvonne Honeycutt Baldwin, *Cora Wilson Stewart and Kentucky's Moonlight Schools* (2006), as well as Willie E. Nelms Jr., "Cora Wilson Stewart and the Crusade against Illiteracy in Kentucky," *Register* 74 (1976): 10–29, 82 (1984): 151–69; and Florence Estes, "Cora Wilson Stewart and the Moonlight Schools of Kentucky, 1911–1920 . . ." (EdD diss., University of Kentucky, 1988). Another form of education, the settlement schools—particularly in eastern Kentucky—has generated some scholarly debate as well as a fair amount of study. An urban example is covered in Ann Taylor Allen and James F. Osborne, "Neighborhood House of Louisville: The Early Years, 1896–1903," *OVH* 10 (2010): 46–78. One early examination came in Ellen C. Semple, "A New Departure in Social Settlements," *Annals of the American Academy of Political and Social Science* 15 (1900): 157–60. Various limited works followed over the years. The arguments took new form with the critical focus on Hindman in David E. Whisnant, *All That Is Native and Fine: The Politics of Culture in an American Region* (1983). Several writers took issue with Whisnant's generalizations and challenged him: see Nancy K. Forderhase, "Eve Returns to the Garden: Women Reformers in Appalachian Kentucky in the Early Twentieth Century," *Register* 85 (1987): 237–61; P. David Searles, *A College for Appalachia: Alice Lloyd on Caney Creek* (1995); and Jess Stoddard, *Challenge and Change in Appalachia: The Story of Hindman Settlement School* (2002). See also Sarah Case, "Katherine Pettit . . . and May Stone . . .: The Cultural Politics of Mountain Reform," in Melissa A. McEuen and Thomas H. Appleton Jr., eds., *Kentucky Women* (2015). It would be welcome for such debate to occur in the study of education of women in the state, but the literature on that subject is briefer. A start on the kind of studies needed is Terry L. Birdwhistell, "An Educated Difference: Women at the University of Kentucky through the Second World War" (EdD diss., University of Kentucky, 1994).

African Americans often appeared almost as an afterthought in the early histories of Kentucky education, but slowly studies began to look at the so-called separate but equal system. The US Department of the Interior's *Negro Education*, 2 vols. (1917), gave a county-by-county breakdown, but more analysis came in Myrtle R. Phillips, "The Origin, Development, and Present Status of Public Secondary Education for Negroes in Kentucky," *Journal of Negro Education* 1 (1932): 414–23; Leonard E. Meece, "Negro Education in Kentucky," *Bulletin of the Bureau of School Service* (University of Kentucky) 10 (1938): 1–180; Howard W. Beers and Catherine P. Heflin, "The Negro Population of Kentucky," *Kentucky Agricultural Experiment Station Bulletin* 481 (1946); and Thomas C. Venable, "A History of Negro Education in Kentucky" (PhD diss., George Peabody College, 1953). An overview by black educator Clarence L. Timberlake—"The Early Struggle for Education of the Blacks of the Commonwealth of Kentucky," *Register* 71 (1973): 225–52—set the stage for the fine in-depth study presented in Marion B. Lucas and George C. Wright, *A History of Blacks in Kentucky*, 2 vols. (1992). A sizeable literature exists on the Day Law and its background, and includes Paul David Nelson, "Experiment in Interracial Education at Berea College, 1858–1908," *JNH* 59 (1974): 18–37; Marion B. Lucas, "Berea College in the 1870s and 1880s: Student Life at a Racially Integrated Kentucky College," *Register* 98 (2000): 1–22; and Scott Blakeman, "Night Comes to Berea College: The Day Law and the African-American Reaction," *FCHQ* 70 (1996): 3–26. Good studies of more limited focus include Lee A. Dew, "*Claybrook v. Owensboro*: An Early Victory for Equal Education in Kentucky," *Daviess County Historical Quarterly* 8 (1990): 3–15; George C. Wright, "The Founding of Lincoln Institute," *FCHQ* 49 (1975): 57–70; J. Morgan Kousser, "Making Separate Equal: The Integration of Black and White School Funds in Kentucky, 1882," *Journal of Interdisciplinary History* 20 (1980): 399–428; Alicestyne Turley-Adams, *Rosenwald Schools in Kentucky* (1997); and James Blaine Hudson III, "The History of Louisville

Municipal College" (EdD diss., University of Kentucky, 1981). A good overview is John A. Hardin, *Fifty Years of Segregation: Black Higher Education in Kentucky, 1904–1954* (1997).

Integration came to most Kentucky schools again in the 1950s, but the struggle for equal rights had been going on for many decades before that. Successful efforts were noted, for instance, in Marjorie Norris, "An Early Instance of Nonviolence: The Louisville Demonstrations of 1870–71," *JSH* 32 (1966): 487–504; George C. Wright, "The NAACP and Residential Segregation in Louisville, Kentucky, 1914–1917," *Register* 78 (1980): 39–54; and Wright, "Desegregation of Public Accommodations in Louisville," in *Southern Businessmen and Desegregation*, ed. Elizabeth Jacoway and David R. Colburn (1982), as well as John A. Hardin, "'Kentucky Is More Or Less Civilized': Alfred Carroll, Charles Eubanks, Lyman Johnson, and the Desegregation of Kentucky Higher Education, 1939–1949," *Register* 109 (2011): 327–50; Joshua D. Farrington, "'Even I voted Republican': African American Voters and Public Accommodations in Louisville, Kentucky, 1960–1961," *Register* 109 (2011): 395–422; and Gerald L. Smith, "Direct-Action Protests in the Upper South: Kentucky Chapters of the Congress of Racial Equality," *Register* 109 (2011): 351–94. The story of Kentuckians' roles in the integration of baseball can be followed in William J. Marshall, *Baseball's Pivotal Era, 1945–1951* (1999).

Integration took different forms across the commonwealth. The situation regarding integration can be followed, for example, in Louisville in Myrtle B. Crawford, "Some Aspects of Preparation for Desegregation in the Public Schools of Louisville," *Negro History Bulletin* 20 (1957): 79–82; Omer Carmichael, *The Louisville Story* (1957); Luther Adams, *Way Up North in Louisville: African American Migration in the Urban South, 1930–1970* (2010); Tracy E. K'Meyer, *Civil Rights in the Gateway to the South: Louisville, Kentucky, 1945–1980* (2009); K'Meyer, *From Brown to Meredith: The Long Struggle for School Desegregation in Louisville, Kentucky, 1954–2007* (2013); Jonathan Free, "'What is the Use of Parks?': The

Debate Over Parks and the Response of Louisville's African American Community to Racial Segregation, 1895–1930," *OVH* 9 (2009): 21–39; Sarah Hardin Blum, "Race, Housing, and the Making of Twentieth-Century Louisville, Kentucky" (PhD diss., University of Kentucky, 2006); Samuel Abramson, "Disorder at the Derby: Race, Reputation, and Louisville's 1967 Housing Crisis," *OVH* 15 (2015): 28–48; and Russell T. Wigginton, "Both Sides of the Track: Louisville and Nashville Railroad's African-American Workers in Louisville, Kentucky, 1915–1945" (PhD diss., University of Illinois, 2001). For more specific areas, on western Kentucky integration, see David L. Wolfford, "Resistance on the Border: School Desegregation in Western Kentucky, 1954–1964," *OVH* 4 (2004): 41–62; Lisa Bell, "Achieving Equality: Desegregation of the Owensboro Schools, 1955–1969," *Daviess County Historical Quarterly* 7 (1989): 26–33; David Lai, "'On the Frontier . . . of Integration and Desegregation': White Ministers and the 1956 School Desegregation Crisis in Henderson, Kentucky," *Register* 113 (2015): 675–702; and Jack Glazier, *Been Coming through Some Hard Times: Race, History, and Memory in Western Kentucky* (2012) (on Hopkinsville). On central Kentucky, see Patricia R. Bacon, "White Town/Black Gown: The Role of Kentucky State College in the Desegregation of Frankfort, Kentucky, 1940–1962" (PhD diss., University of Kentucky, 2004); and David L. Wolfford, "The Fayette County School Integration Controversy, 1971–72: Removing the Vestiges of Segregation," *Register* 101 (2003): 243–74. The University of Kentucky's integration of southern sports is covered in Joan Paul, Richard V. McGree, and Helen Fant, "The Arrival and Ascendence of Black Athletes in the Southeastern Conference, 1966–1980," *Phylon* 45 (1984): 284–90; and in Nate Northington's autobiography, *Still Running*. The later racial problems in Louisville are studied in John M. Thompson, "School Desegregation in Jefferson County, Kentucky, 1954–1975" (EdD diss., University of Kentucky, 1976); Scott Cummings and Michael Price, "Race Relations and Public Policy in Louisville," *Journal of Black Stud-*

ies 27 (1997): 615–49; Robert A. Sedler, "The Louisville-Jefferson County School Desegregation Case: A Lawyer's Perspective," *Register* 105 (2007): 3–22; and Kenneth H. Williams, "'Oh Baby . . . It's Really Happening': The Louisville Races Riot of 1968," *Kentucky History Journal* 3 (1988): 48–64. An excellent study that allows those involved to tell their story is Catherine Fosl and Tracy E. K'Meyer, *Freedom on the Border: An Oral History of the Civil Rights Movement in Kentucky* (2009). Advances and continuing problems were presented every year after 1961 in the very useful *Report of the Kentucky Commission on Human Rights*. See also Luther Adams, "My Old Kentucky Home: Black History in the Bluegrass State," *Register* 113 (2015): 385–420.

Individuals played key roles in bringing about civil rights. For an activist operating outside the establishment, see Catherine Fosl, *Subversive Southerner: Anne Braden and the Struggle for Racial Justice in the Cold War South* (2002). Within the system was Justice Frederick Vinson, who has been studied in some detail, although more work on his non-Court career would be welcome. See John Henry Hatcher, "Fred Vinson, Congressman from Kentucky: A Political Biography, 1890–1938" (PhD diss., University of Cincinnati, 1967); John P. Frank, "Fred Vinson and the Chief Justiceship," *University of Chicago Law Review* 21 (1954): 212–46; James Bolner, "Mr. Chief Justice Fred M. Vinson and Racial Discrimination," *Register* 64 (1966): 29–43; W. B. Johnson, "The Vinson Court and Racial Segregation, 1946–1953," *JNH* 63 (1978): 220–30; and Richard Kirkendall, "Fred M. Vinson," in *The Justices of the United States Supreme Court, 1789–1969*, ed. Leon Friedman and Fred L. Israel, 4 vols. (1969). A full biography is James E. St. Clair and Linda C. Gugin, *Chief Justice Fred M. Vinson of Kentucky* (2002).

On the black leadership, see such autobiographical-style works as Wade Hall, *The Rest of the Dream: The Black Odyssey of Lyman Johnson* (1988); Hall, *Passing for Black: The Life and Careers of Mae Street Kidd* (1997); *Alone Atop the Hill: The Autobiography of Alice Dunnigan*, ed. Carol McCabe Booker (2015); Georgia Davis Powers, *I Shared the Dream* (1995); as well as biographical studies such as Nancy J. Weiss, *Whitney M. Young, Jr., and the Struggle for Civil Rights* (1990); Dennis C. Dickerson, *Militant Mediator: Whitney M. Young Jr.* (1998); Carolyn R. Dupont, "Georgia Montgomery Davis Powers . . .: Purpose in Politics," in Melissa A. McEuen and Thomas H. Appleton Jr., eds., *Kentucky Women* (2015); Gerald L. Smith, *A Black Educator in the Segregated South: Kentucky's Rufus B. Atwood* (1994); and broader works such as Alice Allison Dunnigan, *The Fascinating Story of Black Kentuckians: Their Heritage and Traditions* (1982); and Kentucky Commission on Human Rights, *Kentucky's Black Heritage* (1971).

Little exists on Kentucky's gay and lesbian communities. See Catherine Fosl, "'It Could Be Dangerous!': Gay Liberation and Gay Marriage in Louisville, Kentucky, 1970," *OVH* 12 (2012): 45–64; Jeffrey Alan Jones, "Hidden Histories, Proud Communities: Multiple Narratives in the Queer Geographies of Lexington, Kentucky, 1930–1999" (PhD diss., University of Kentucky, 2001); and Charles House, *The Outrageous Life of Henry Faulkner* (1986).

For a full history of higher education in the commonwealth and the institutions that constitute it, see William E. Ellis, *A History of Education in Kentucky* (2011); a brief interpretation can be found in James C. Klotter, "Promise, Pessimism, and Perseverance: An Overview of Higher Education History in Kentucky," *OVH* 6 (2006): 45–60. Many more specific, fine college and university histories have been written. See, for example, James F. Hopkins, *The University of Kentucky: Origins and Early Years* (1951); Charles G. Talbert, *The University of Kentucky: The Maturing Years* (1965); Eric A. Moyer, *Frank L. McVey and the University of Kentucky* (2011); Kolan Thomas Morelock, *Taking the Town: Collegiate and Community Culture in the Bluegrass, 1880–1917* (2008); Dwayne Cox and William J. Morison, *The University of Louisville* (2000); Lowell H. Harrison, *Western Kentucky University* (1987); John A. Hardin, *Onward and Upward: A Centennial History of Kentucky State University, 1886–1986* (1987); Jennifer Williams, "Ties that Bind: James H. Richmond and Murray Teachers College during World War II," *OVH* 4 (2004): 49–66; Donald F. Flatt, *A Light in the Mountains: Morehead State University, 1887–1997* (1997); Nelda K. Wyatt, "Into the Promised Land: The Transformation of Eastern and Western Kentucky Normal Schools into Teacher Colleges, 1906–1922" (EdD diss., University of Kentucky, 1999); Lisa P. Collins, "Venturing Out: Students at Eastern Kentucky State Normal School, 1910–1924" (PhD diss., University of Kentucky, 2008); and William E. Ellis, *A History of Eastern Kentucky University* (2005).

There are also many good studies of private schools as well, including but not limited to the following: Elisabeth S. Peck and Emily Ann Smith, *Berea's First 125 Years, 1855–1980*, rev. ed. (1982); John D. Wright Jr., *Transylvania: Tutor to the West* (1975); Lee A. Dew and Richard A. Weiss, *In Pursuit of the Dream: A History of Kentucky Wesleyan College* (1992); Robert Snyder, *A History of Georgetown College* (1979); P. David Searles, *A College for Appalachia: Alice Lloyd on Caney Creek* (1995); Hardin Craig, *Centre College of Kentucky: A Tradition and an Opportunity* (1967); Kenneth C. Kinghorn, *The Story of Asbury Theological Seminary* (2010); and Lynn E. Niedermeier, *"That Mighty Band of Maidens": A History of Potter College for Young Ladies . . ., 1889–1909* (2001). See also individual entries in the various state encyclopedias. For an early survey of the state's schools, see Alvin F. Lewis, *A History of Higher Education in Kentucky* (1899), and for the status at the mid-twentieth century, see Kentucky Legislative Research Commission, *Public Higher Education in Kentucky*, Research Publication no. 25, o.s. (1951).

19. A Half Century of Kentucky Politics, 1945–1995

A comprehensive study of the Kentucky political world of the half century after World War II has not yet been written. As a result, often the best sources remain the state newspapers, the national magazines, collected interviews, and the *Kentucky Acts of the General Assembly*. Most of the studies covering the 1940s and 1950s focus on individuals, with some broader scope provided by John Ed Pearce, *Divide and Dissent: Kentucky Politics, 1930–1963* (1986); and Lowell H. Harrison, ed., *Kentucky's Governors*, rev. ed. (2004).

On the individual administrations, see Thomas H. Syvertsen, "Earle Chester Clements and the Democratic Party, 1920–1950" (PhD diss., University of Kentucky, 1982); John E. Kleber, ed., *The Papers of Governor Lawrence W. Wetherby, 1950–1955* (1983); John E. Kleber, "As Luck Would Have It: An Overview of Lawrence W. Wetherby As Governor, 1950–1955," *Register* 80 (1982): 397–421; George W. Robinson, ed., *The Public Papers of Governor Bert Combs, 1959–1963* (1977); and Robinson, ed., *Bert Combs, the Politician: An Oral History* (1991). One controversy in the Combs years has generated much study, including: Jason G. Shearer, "Urban Reform in Sin City: The George Ratterman Trial and the Election of 1961 in Northern Kentucky," *Register* 98 (2000): 343–65; Robert Gioielli, "Suburbs vs. Slot Machines: The Committee of 500 and the Battle over Gambling in Northern Kentucky," *OVH* 5 (2005): 61–84; Thomas Barker, Gary W. Potter, and Jenna Meglen, *Wicked Newport: Kentucky's Sin City* (2008); Robin Caraway, *Newport: The Sin City Years* (2009); and Jennifer B. Royer, "The Dark Side of Dixie: Illegal Gambling in Northern Kentucky, 1790–2000" (PhD diss., Texas Christian University, 2009). One election is covered in Philip A. Grant Jr., "The Presidential Election of 1948 in Kentucky," *Journal of Kentucky Studies* 6 (1989): 86–91. Jasper B. Shannon analyzes the situation four years later in *Presidential Politics in Kentucky, 1952* (1954), and examines the overall picture in "The Political Process in Kentucky," *Kentucky Law Journal* 45 (1957): 395–447. On another election, see John Paul Hill, "The Forgotten Campaign: The 1955 Kentucky Gubernatorial General Election," *FCHQ* 75 (2001): 85–108.

Wilson W. Wyatt Sr. told his story in his autobiography, *Whistle Stops: Adventures in Public Life* (1985). On Chandler, see the sources cited under chapter 17, plus Robert L. Riggs, "Happy Chandler Rides Again," *Satur-*

day Evening Post (Oct. 15, 1955): 19–21, 155–58; and Gladys M. Kammerer, "Kentucky's All Pervasive Spoils Politics," *Good Government* 75 (1958): 32–37. Louis C. Kesselman's "Negro Voting in a Border Community: Louisville, Kentucky," *JNH* (1957): 273–80, is one of the few studies of changing voter patterns in the era.

On the Republican side, an overview of senate races is provided in Glenn Finch, "The Election of United States Senators in Kentucky: The Cooper Period," *FCHQ* 46 (1972): 161–78. The two leaders of the party's successes have been studied in some depth, but more work is still needed. An excellent introduction to one of those key leaders is Bill Cooper, "John Sherman Cooper: A Senator and His Constituents," *Register* 84 (1986): 192–210. Other good works include Robert Schulman, *John Sherman Cooper: The Global Kentuckian* (1976); Richard C. Smoot, "John Sherman Cooper: The Paradox of a Liberal Republican in Kentucky Politics" (PhD diss., University of Kentucky, 1988); and Smoot, "John Sherman Cooper: The Early Years, 1900–27," *Register* 93 (1995): 133–58. On Cooper's fellow senator, see Sara J. Smiley, "The Political Career of Thruston B. Morton" (PhD diss., University of Kentucky, 1975); and Byron Hulsey, "Partisanship and the National Interest: Thruston Morton, Lyndon Johnson, and the Vietnam War," *Woodberry Forest Magazine and Journal* 34 (1994): 28–30.

The 1960s saw the War on Poverty and the Vietnam War both break out in full force. The state's role in the overseas conflict has not been examined in depth, but a fine case study of tragedy is Anthony B. McIntire, "The Kentucky National Guard in Vietnam: The Story of Bardstown's Battery C at War," *Register* 90 (1992): 140–64. See also Kentucky's *Report of the Adjutant General*; and Jim Wilson, *The Sons of Bardstown: 25 Years of Vietnam in an American Town* (1994). For the antiwar activities in the state, see John Ernst and Yvonne Baldwin, "The Not So Silent Minority: Louisville's Antiwar Movement, 1966–1975," *JSH* 73 (2007): 105–42.

For an overview of an advocate for change,

see Margaret Ripley Wolfe, "Lifting up His Eyes Unto the Hills: Harry M. Caudill and His Appalachia," *FCHQ* 76 (2002): 1–36; and Ronald D Eller, "Harry Caudill and the Burden of Mountain Liberalism," in *Critical Essays in Appalachian Life and Culture*, ed. Rick Simon (1982). On the migration patterns resulting from the problems of poverty, see Harry K. Schwarzweller, James S. Brown, and J. J. Mangalam, *Mountain Families in Transition* (1971); William W. Philliber and Clyde A. McCoy, eds., *The Invisible Minority: Urban Appalachians* (1981); and Stephen E. White, "America's Soweto: Population Distribution in Appalachian Kentucky, 1940–1986," *Appalachian Journal* 16 (1986): 350–60. The situation in the region itself is discussed in John C. Wells Jr., "Poverty amidst Riches: Why People Are Poor in Appalachia" (PhD diss., Rutgers University, 1977); "Appalachia As a Developing Nation," *Business Week* (July 18, 1970): 46–54; and Appalachian Land Ownership Task Force, *Who Owns Appalachia?* (1983). Federal efforts to address the situation are well surveyed in John M. Glen, "The War on Poverty in Appalachia," *Register* 87 (1989): 40–57. See also David E. Whisnant, *Modernizing the Mountaineer: People, Power, and Planning in Appalachia* (1980); Ronald D Eller, *Uneven Ground: Appalachia since 1945* (2008); Betty P. Duff, "Class and Gender Roles in the Company Towns of Millinocket and East Millinocket, Maine, and Benham and Lynch, Kentucky, 1901–2004 . . ." (PhD diss., University of Maine, 2004); Shaunna L. Scott, *Two Sides to Everything: The Cultural Construction of Class Consciousness in Harlan County, Kentucky* (1995); John R. Burch, *Owsley County, Kentucky, and the Persistence of Poverty* (2008); Thomas J. Kiffmeyer, *Reformers to Radicals: The Appalachian Volunteers and the War on Poverty* (2008); Margaret Ripley Wolfe, "Eastern Kentucky and the War on Poverty: Grass Roots Activism, Regional Politics, and Creative Federalism in the Appalachian South," *OVH* 3 (2003): 31–44; Anthony Harkin, *Hillbilly* (2004); Glen E. Taul, "Poverty, Development, and Government in Appalachia: Origins of the Appalachian Regional Commission, 1954–1965" (PhD diss.,

University of Kentucky, 2001); John R. Burch Jr., "The Turner Family of Breathitt County, Kentucky, and the War on Poverty," *Register* 107 (2009): 401–18. For the voices of those involved, see Alessandro Portelli, *They Say in Harlan County: An Oral History* (2011).

Not a great deal of historical analysis has appeared in books and articles on Kentucky politics covering the period since the mid-1960s. For a good historical overview, see George G. Humphreys, "Western Kentucky in the Twentieth Century: From the End of Isolation to the Collapse of the 'Gibraltar of Democracy,'" *Register* 113 (2015): 357–84. Most work has come from political scientists, and their efforts provide a good framework for further study: Malcolm E. Jewell and E. W. Cunningham, *Kentucky Politics* (1968); Joel Goldstein, ed., *Kentucky Government and Politics* (1984); Paul D. Blanchard, *Kentucky State and Local Government* (1987); Penny M. Miller and Malcolm E. Jewell, *Political Parties and Primaries in Kentucky* (1990); and the broad-based study Penny M. Miller, *Kentucky Politics and Government* (1994). See also the survey of a journalist: Neal R. Pierce, *The Border South States* (1975).

On specific administrations, good starting points are Kenneth E. Harrell, ed., *The Public Papers of Edward T. Breathitt, Jr., 1963–1967* (1984); Betsy Brinson and Kenneth H. Williams, "An Interview with Governor Ned Breathitt on Civil Rights . . .," *Register* 99 (2001): 5–52; Robert F. Sexton, ed., *The Public Papers of Louie B. Nunn, 1967–1971* (1975); W. Landis Jones, ed., *The Public Papers of Wendell H. Ford, 1971–1974* (1978); Elizabeth Fraas, ed., "'All Issues Are Women's Issues': An Interview with Governor Martha Layne Collins on Women in Politics," *Register* 99 (2001): 213–48; John Paul Hill, "Martha Layne Collins . . .: Textbooks, Toyota, and Tenacity," in Melissa A. McEuen and Thomas H. Appleton Jr., eds., *Kentucky Women* (2015); and Wallace G. Wilkinson's autobiographical *You Can't Do That, Governor!* (1995). For accounts of the bus tragedies, see John M. Trowbridge, Jason M. LeMay, and Jackie B. Hall, comp., *Kentucky National Guard: The Prestonsburg School Bus Disa*ster (2008); and James S. Kunen, *Reckless Disregard: Corporate Greed, Government Indifference, and the Kentucky School Bus Crash* (1994). On factors leading to Martha Layne Collins's win, see Liz Demoran, "We Made History, Kentucky," *Kentucky Alumnus* 53 (1983–84): 7. On Carl Perkins, see Robert S. Weise, "A New Deal in the Cold War: Carl D. Perkins, Coal, and the Political Economy of Poverty in Eastern Kentucky, 1948–1964," *Register* 107 (2009): 307–38. On operative/activist Ed Prichard, see Tracy Campbell's excellent, *Short of the Glory: The Fall and Redemption of Edward H. Prichard Jr.* (1998); and Kenneth H. Williams, "'I'm sure there are some that thought I was too smart for my own good': The Ed Prichard Oral History Interviews," *Register* 104 (2006): 395–608. On the state legislature, see Kwang S. Shin and John S. Jackson III, "Membership Turnover in the U.S. State Legislatures: 1931–1976," *Legislative Studies Quarterly* 4 (1979) 95–104; Malcolm E. Jewell and Penny M. Miller, *The Kentucky Legislature: Two Decades of Change* (1986); and A Kentucky Legislator, "How an Election Was Bought and Sold," *Harper's Magazine* (1960): 33–38. Also consult the *Legislative Record* and the Kentucky *House Journal* and *Senate Journal*.

A study of the state judiciary remains much needed. Starting places are John S. Palmore, *An Opinionated Career: Memoirs of a Kentucky Judge* (2003); Mac Swinford, *Kentucky Lawyer* (2008); Donald C. Wintersheimer, *Secrets of the Kentucky Supreme Court: A Memoir* (2010); Gerald R. Toner and Leslie W. Abramson, eds., *Kentucky Lawyers Speak* (2009); and *United at Last: The Judicial Article and the Struggle to Reform Kentucky's Courts* (2006).

20. A Political Metamorphosis, 1995-2015

Most of the history of politics in Kentucky over the past two decades remains to be written. Newspapers, a few oral histories, and even fewer memoirs can be supplemented by official records, but the accounts mostly lie still buried. Statistics can be accessed at the Secretary of State's Office (online), session outcomes in the various Legislative Research Commission's lengthy *Informational Bulletins* on each legislature's accomplishments, and lobbying activities from the Legislative Ethics Commission, *Ethics Reporter* (online). During part of the time frame, the *Kentucky Journal* and the *Kentucky Roll Call* (online) offered insights. For political scientists' take on the era, see James C. Clinger and Michael W. Hail, eds., *Kentucky Government, Politics, and Public Policy* (2013).

On various governors, see Paul Blanchard, "Governor Paul Patton," *Register* 102 (2004): 69–83; Fran Ellers, *Progress and Paradox: The Patton Years, 1995–2003* (2003); "Governor Ernie Fletcher," *Register* 102 (2004): 3–12; and Joshua D. Farrington, "The Republican Party and Modern Conservatism in Postwar Kentucky," *Register* 113 (2015): 307–20. For Mitch McConnell, a friendly biography is John David Dyche, *Republican Leader: A Political Biography of Senator Mitch McConnell* (2009); for McConnell's take, see *The Long Game: A Memoir* (2016). On weather-oriented problems, see the good work by Jerry Hill, *Kentucky Weather* (2005)

21. New Challenges, Old Traditions

A variety of sources were used in preparing this chapter, including newspapers, collected interviews, printed recollections, manuscript collections, and a wide range of official reports. Feature writers and columnists of the *Louisville Courier-Journal,* particularly when it published its own *Sunday Magazine,* provided key items, as did writers in the *Lexington Herald-Leader.* Other, smaller papers have been useful as well.

Two of the most recognizable Kentuckians were two of the most different: Harland Sanders and Muhammad Ali. On Sanders, see John Ed Pearce, *The Colonel* (1982); on Ali, see, for example, his autobiography, *The Greatest* (1975); Robert Hoskins, *Muhammad Ali* (1980); and John Egerton, "Heritage of a Heavyweight: The Ancestry of Muhammad Ali," in *Shades of Gray: Dispatches from the Modern South* (1991). For looks at how people outside the state view it, see Sarah O. Hardin, "The Image of Kentucky in Films: Images Versus Reality," *Register* 98 (2000): 367–84; and Anthony Harkins, "Colonels, Hillbillies, and Fightin': Twentieth-Century Kentucky in the National Imagination," *Register* 113 (2015): 421–52. On another of the state's images—basketball—the literature is voluminous and ranges from the truly awful to the awfully good. Catching the flavor of the high school sport is Dave Kindred, *Basketball: The Dream Game in Kentucky* (1976), while Mike Embry, in "Kentuckians in the Halls of Fame," *Kentucky Living* 46 (1992): 12–16, looks at those who gained national acclaim. A good study of one high school team is Marianne Walker, *The Graves County Boys* (2013). On women's basketball, the expert is Sallie L. Powell. See, for example, her "'Playing Fairly and Fiercely': Paradigms of the Early Years of Kentucky White Girls' Basketball, 1891–1919," *Register* 109 (2011): 153–86; and "Constructing the Modern Girl, Kentucky Style: An Examination of Gender and Race through the Lens of Kentucky Girls' High School Basketball Prior to Title IX" (PhD diss., University of Kentucky, 2012). Almost every year another work appears on University of Kentucky basketball, but three good introductions to the pre-1980 era are Bert Nelli, *The Winning Tradition* (1984); Harry Lancaster, *Adolph Rupp As I Knew Him* (1979); and Russell Rice, *Adolph Rupp* (1994). On Diddle, see C. Harvey Gardiner, *Coach Diddle, Mister Diddle: Motivator of Men* (1984).

On demographics, see Thomas R. Ford, *Health and Demography in Kentucky* (1964); Robert L. Ludke and Phillip J. Obermiller, eds., *Appalachian Health and Well-Being* (2012); plus the long-term studies noted below. A look at the process of urbanization is Carl E. Kramer, "The Evolution of the Residential Land Subdivision Process in Louisville, 1772–2008," *Register* 107 (2009): 33–82. Much more needs to be written about recent immigration to the commonwealth. For a start, see Nora Rose Moosnick, *Arab and Jewish Women in Kentucky* (2012); Legislative Research Commission, *Immigration to Kentucky; A Preliminary Description,* Report #305 (Frankfort, 2002).

For Kentucky's religious life, much exists. For samples showing the variety, see Clyde

F. Crews, *An American Holy Land* (1987) [on Catholics]; James Duane Bolin, *Kentucky Baptists, 1925–2000* (2000); Louis B. Meeks, *Kentucky Presbyterians* (1983); Carolyn DuPont, "White Protestants and the Civil Rights Movement in Kentucky," *Register* 113 (2015): 543–74; Rhonda Mawhood Lee, "God Alone is Lord of the Conscience: Fellowship of Reconciliation Activists Confront Church and State in Louisville, Kentucky, 1975–1995," *OVH* 7 (2007): 49–67; Richard J. Callahan Jr., *Work and Faith in the Kentucky Coal Fields* (2008); and Chad Berry, "The Great White Migration, Alcohol, and the Transplanting of Southern Protestant Churches," *Register* 94 (1996): 265–96.

On the role of women, see "The Legal Status of Women in the United States of America, January 1, 1938, Report for Kentucky," *Bulletin of the Women's Bureau* (1938); US Department of Labor, *Women Workers in Kentucky, 1960* (1960); Annie Harrison, comp., *Women in Kentucky State Government, 1940–1980* (1981); Nancy E. Baker, "Integrating Women into Modern Kentucky History: The Equal Rights Amendment Debate (1972–1978) as a Case Study," *Register* 113 (2015): 477–508; Margaret Ripley Wolfe, "Fallen Leaves and Missing Pages: Women in Kentucky History," *Register* 90 (1992): 64–89; Rebecca S. Hanley, "Emma Guy Cromwell and Mary Elliott Flannery: Pioneers for Women in Kentucky Politics," *Register* 99 (2001): 287–301; and Penny Jones, "The Slow and Unsure Progress of Women in Kentucky Politics," *Register* 99 (2001): 249–86. See also, Michal Smith-Mello, et al., eds., *The Future Well-Being of Women in Kentucky* (1999); and the Commission on Women's periodic *Fact Sheet* (online). The statistics on violence given in the text come from the FBI *Uniform Crime Reports* and the *Bulletin of the State Board of Health in Kentucky* (later *Kentucky Vital Statistics Report*), and a good discussion of the issue appears in Raymond A. Gastil, "Homicide and a Regional Culture of Violence," *American Sociological Review* 36 (1971): 412–26. For studies of the continuing fight to prohibit various substances, see William M. Ambrose, *Bluegrass Prohibition: Prohibition in Lexington, Fayette County, Kentucky, 1920–1934* (2009); Stanley D. Brunn and Thomas H. Appleton Jr., "Wet-Dry Referenda and the Persistence of Prohibition Forces," *Southeastern Geographer* 39 (1999): 172–89; and James Higdon, *The Cornbread Mafia* (2012). The environmental situation is outlined in Sarah Lynn Cunningham, "From Smoke-Filled Skies to Smoke-Filled Rooms: Louisville's Political Battles over the 'Smoke Evil,'" *OVH* 8 (2008): 43–71; Gerald Markowitz and David Rosner, "Uncovering a Deadly Cancer: The National Implications of Revelations of the B. F. Goodrich Plant in Louisville," *Register* 102 (2004), 157–81; Environmental Protection Agency, "Maxey Flats Nuclear Disposal" (online); Environmental Quality Commission, *State of Kentucky's Environment: 1994* (1995); and the Kentucky Department for Environmental Protection Annual Reports (online). On one reformer, see James Duane Bolin, "Linda Neville . . .: 'The Lady Who Helped Blind Children See,'" in Melissa A. McEuen and Thomas H. Appleton Jr., eds., *Kentucky Women* (2015); on polio, see Michael W. R. Davis, "Kentucky's 1944 Polio Epidemic," *FCHQ* 74 (2000); and on drug issues, see Nancy D. Campbell, J. P. Olsen, and Luke Walden, *The Narcotic Farm* (2008).

Studies of Kentucky's present status and future need have appeared periodically. Generally they have provided much information on current affairs, with more limited success as guideposts to development. Earlier works include *The Government of Kentucky: Report of the Efficiency Commission of Kentucky*, 2 vols. (1924); Howard W. Beers, ed., *Kentucky: Designs for Her Future* (1945); Postwar Planning Commission of Kentucky, *Final Report* (1945); Committee for Kentucky, *Reports* (1943–1950); and Harry W. Schecter, *Kentucky on the March* (1949). A more systematic recent approach came from the Kentucky Long-Term Policy Research Center, which, before its demise, published the newsletter *Foresight*, as well as book-length works, including the very useful *The Context of Change: Trends, Innovations, and Forces Affecting Kentucky's Future* (1994). Statistical information can be garnered online from the Appalachian Center at the University of Kentucky and the Kentucky Data Center at the University of Louisville

Continuity and a sense of place play roles as important in Kentucky as change; a fine case study is John Egerton, *Generations: An American Family* (1983). But more important are the voices of the people themselves, as presented in letters, memories, memoirs, and interviews. They best tell what Kentucky is and what it means to them.

Acknowledgments

All who should be thanked cannot be. Space, or even memory, does not allow that. The authors, for instance, owe a great debt to all those who have written earlier on the state's history, for they made our tasks—and our understanding—much easier. Inclusion of our predecessors' works in the Selected Bibliography constitutes only a partial recognition, and even then, much is omitted. While recognizing that those with whom we have worked all our lives have had an important influence on what is written herein, we wish to offer some particular thanks.

Both authors wish to note the special debt owed to Thomas D. Clark, for he did more to advance the cause of history in Kentucky than any other person. His work made the study of the state's past more accessible and much more enjoyable to all who wish to examine it. Our dedication of this book to him expresses only a part of our gratitude for all he did so well for so long.

We also have dedicated this work to Lowell H. Harrison. His contributions to the first edition of this book laid a solid foundation for any scholar who may have been asked to revise for a new edition. As the select bibliography undeniably indicates, Lowell's scholarship was fundamental to the ways in which we conceptualize Kentucky history, particularly its early years. We—scholars, citizens of Kentucky, history lovers—are all richer because of Lowell's vision of Kentucky's past.

We owe particular recognition to our spouses, Freda Campbell Klotter and Roderick Glenn Turner, for they are vitally involved in all we do. Without them this would be a poorer book, and we poorer people. To them and to all who were a part of this project we offer our heartfelt thanks, for everything.

Craig Thompson Friend, Chapters 1–9

Over the years, I have accumulated great debts to scholars who have contributed to how I think about Kentucky's and America's past. Some have read and commented on my scholarship. Others have been stalwart academic friends, willing to discuss ideas and offer thoughts. I am most grateful to Thomas H. Appleton Jr., who has been a superb proofreader. He is also a dear friend, and my life has been richer for his friendship. I am also appreciative of Joyce Appleby, Steven A. Aron, Andrew R. L. Cayton, Ellen Eslinger, Lorri Glover, Neal O. Hammon, Mary Wilma Hargraeves, A. Gwynn Henderson, Warren Hofstra, Judy Kertész, John Lauritz Larson, Melissa McEuen, Michael A. Morrison, Marion C. Nelson, Honor Sachs, Matthew Schoenbachler, Tim Silver, Daniel Blake Smith, and most significantly, Theda Perdue—all of whom have contributed to my thinking on Kentucky history in one way or another.

I also am indebted to historical organizations that have supported my research over the years. Acknowledgments have been made in previous publications, but I want to repeat my sincere thanks here. While the personnel have changed with the passage of time, the willingness and desire to help researchers have remained. My special thanks go to Mark V. Wetherington, James Holmberg, and the Filson Historical Society, which honored me with the first Filson Fellowship in 1993–1994 and has always welcomed me with open arms. Staffs at the Kentucky Historical Society, the Library of Congress, the Special Collections at the University of Kentucky, the National Archives, Transylvania University Special Collections, the Kentucky Library at Western Kentucky University, Mason County Historical Museum, and the Kentucky Department for Libraries and Archives also have been helpful over the years, often giving me the benefit of their extensive knowledge of Kentucky sources.

Finally, I thank James C. Klotter. Jim and I shared one year as faculty at Georgetown College, but I have been an admirer of Jim's scholarship for much, much longer. Jim embodies the ideal of the public scholar—one whose attention is on making history accessible beyond the academy. I was honored when he asked me to tackle the challenge of revising Lowell Harrison's part of this book. I hope that I have met his expectations.

James C. Klotter, Chapters 10–21

I wish to acknowledge the invaluable support provided over the years by the staff of various institutions. Many are no longer there, due to the passage of the years, but are recognized for their past connections. At the Kentucky Historical Society Library, Anne J. McDonnell, Ron D. Bryant, and Mary Winter, and Kim Lady Smith and the Kentucky Oral History Commission, gave important aid. Later support came from Georgetown College. Research aid was provided by Cheryl Conover, Dave Withers, Adam Branca, and Paul Newman. And, as always, help was provided in ways both large and small, by various toilers in the historical fields, including Lindsey Apple, Harold Tallant, Cliff Wargelin, Liyan Liu, Juilee Decker, John Kleber, Gerald Smith, Mike Hudson, Melissa McEuen, Richard Taylor, and others. At Special Collections, University of Kentucky Library, William C. Marshall's staff was especially supportive, as were, indeed, those working with the public at virtually all the research institutions across the state, notably those aiding William J. Morison at the University of Louisville, Mark Wetherington

at the Filson Historical Society, Charles C. Hay III at Eastern Kentucky University, Gerald F. Roberts at Berea College, Riley Handy at the Kentucky Library at Western Kentucky University, and Keith Heim at Murray State University. Aiding in the procurement of photographs were Mary Jean Kinsman of the Filson, B. J. Gooch of Transylvania University, Nancy Baird of Western Kentucky University, Bill Carner of the University of Louisville, Wade Hall of Bellarmine University, Pam Porter of the University of Kentucky, Holly Skaggs of the Louisville AAA Club, James Seacat of Actors Theatre of Louisville, Christopher Waldrep of Eastern Illinois University, and Nathan Pritchard of the Kentucky Historical Society. I am also grateful to the personnel at the Louisville Free Public Library, the Lexington Library, the Kenton County Public Library, the Owensboro Public Library, the Keeneland Library, as well as at the Library of Congress, the National Archives, the University of Virginia, the Virginia Historical Society, the University of North Carolina at Chapel Hill, Duke University, West Virginia University, the University of Chicago, and the State Historical Society of Wisconsin.

Those at the University Press of Kentucky (or formerly there) deserve not only thanks, but so much more. They include Leila Salisbury, Steve Wrinn, Anne Dean Dotson, Patrick O'Dowd, Tasha Huber, David Cobb, Mack McCormick, Teresa Collins, Craig Wilkie, Ashley Runyon, and Beth Van Allen.

Special recognition must be given to those who read parts or all of my early drafts and whose comments made the final version much better: Thomas H. Appleton Jr., Walter Baker, Terry Birdwhistell, Melba Porter Hay, Art Jester, Crit Luallen, and John David Smith. As one of the last authors who still write manuscripts by hand, I wish also to thank the courageous Glenda Harned for taking my prose and putting it into meaningful form.

Index

Page numbers in italics refer to figures, maps, and tables.